Three Worlds of Development

SECOND EDITION

Three Worlds of Development

The Theory and Practice of International Stratification

Irving Louis Horowitz

SECOND EDITION

New York
OXFORD UNIVERSITY PRESS *1972*

To the people of Bangla Desh:
may they learn from the past,
live in the present, and
instruct the future.

Preface to the First
Edition [1965]

This work is addressed to those who have felt the impact of a system of false alternatives with respect to the "East-West conflict"; and who are willing to forsake the security of both oversimplified ideologies and over-complicated models. The essential approach is a willingness on the part of the reader to avoid assumptions about the world being "naturally" divided into two irreconcilable antagonists. For this volume is designed as a qualitative study of three worlds of development.

It describes and explains the interaction and interpenetration of the three main sources of economic, political, and social power in the world today: the First World of the United States and its Western Allies, the Second World of the Soviet Union and its Eastern Bloc Allies, and the Third World of nonaligned, but variously committed nations of Latin America, Asia, and Africa. The book focuses on "overdeveloped" societies no less than problems of growth; and national forms of colonialism no less than classical international styles of colonialism.

To undertake an exploration of the developmental process is to be immediately confronted by perennial questions. Whether human relations in socio-economic form and content can actually progress, or whether history is a mere record of changes in such relations, clearly hinges upon how such terms as "progress" and "change" are defined. If by social change we mean large-scale behavioral revolutions which will transform human conduct, then there is, and will always be, much cause for pessimism. If, however, we are more modest, and assume development in human relations to be an ongoing process of human interaction and the relationships between such interaction to advance registered in the technological means they employ at any given historical point, then it is much more possible to be optimistic. If these processes, whether occurring in revolutionary lurches or by gradual evolution, are without particular appeal to the advocates of *human progress,* we must leave them with their dissatisfaction intact, and take our chances on a more problematic world of *human process.* One can sometimes approach perennial questions implicitly, rather than head-on in a heroic rush which is likely to produce great errors. If, by using heuristic measures for determining the needs and facts of development, one can deduce more significance, that is all to the good. But for our purpose, the issue of development is pressing, and we must make the best of our imperfect scientific condition for the sake of immediate clarification.

Three Worlds of Development offers a language for dealing with international stratification, and a style of handling social facts. For this reason, the book has as its subtitle *The Theory and Practice of International Stratification.* Economists of all persuasions have repeatedly insisted that problems of development are basically social and political, no less than economic and psychological. It is therefore hardly surprising that many younger sociologists and political scientists have entered the world arena to meet the issues directly and freshly. Cliches about "industrial man" or "mass man" will hardly do justice to the task of analyzing backward social relations in a universe of advanced technological achievements; elitism in an age of mass man; modern revolution in stagnant sectors of the economy; or, perhaps the ultimate anomaly, primitive jungle warfare in an age of thermonuclear weaponry.

The principles of stratification have frequently been applied at the national level and at lesser community levels. But in the main, they have desisted analysis at the international level, since industrialization or urbanization are less sophisticated indicators than levels of income or productivity. Yet it is evident that any study of the developmental process is bound to touch upon the main issues of stratification: superordinate and subordinate positions, the tendencies toward and away from egalitarianism, political and psychological as well as economic forms of stratification and differentiation.

I have increasingly been taken with the notion that certain key concepts in social psychology may be very serviceable for social stratification. A line of work extending from Georg Simmel to Anatol Rapoport on differences between dyadic and triadic relations needs to be linked to the more customary figures in the social science cosmos. Studies on the relative instability and the need for coalition characteristic of three-part relationships; on differences between consensus and conflict models for understanding interpersonal relations; on the effect of these models on theories of democracy and authoritarianism; finally on the picture of personality types and the types of reinforcements necessary to induce certain kinds of responses—all of these seemed clearly relevant to any serious examination of "three worlds" no less than "three persons." This reinforces for me the belief that we are living in the twilight of a sociological era in which the object of research can be neatly packaged into conventional lines.

Almost unfailingly, development is written about from the particularized standpoint of "the science of" politics, economics, sociology, anthropology, or psychology. The standpoint is derived from an author's professional commitments rather than from the developmental process as such. Clearly, a mastery of the entire literature on development from each of the disciplines would have been impossible. For studies of a global variety, the standpoint of any single social science is dubious as an intellectual tool and dreary as a bureaucratic reality. The standpoint of social science as a whole, of the collectivity of information, methods, and theories about the human condition, is another matter. An integrated approach allows the researcher and the experimenter to concentrate on problems of development in general, no less than its parts. The option to this open-ended approach is a further emphasis on disciplinary boundaries. This would yield formal elegance at the expense of the whole spectrum: economic development apart from political development, political development apart from social development, etc. To underscore who is "entitled" to study which part of the developmental tree still leaves unexamined the genesis, essential features, and types of environment of the development process as such.

The desperate attempt to define "urban sociology" and "rural sociology" in an age of economic affluence, rapid mobility and motility, and a communications network that shows no respect for neat sociological divisions is one symptom of this general impulse toward a reorientation of the social scientific imagination. The same situation obtains in other areas. It is becoming increasingly apparent that political sociology, social stratification, economic development, political socialization, complex cultures, among others, might be useful conventions for indexing and cataloguing purposes, but that such designations are nonetheless nowhere to be found in the real social world. What we do observe are men agreeing, men quarreling, men killing, men loving. And such "atomic" observations are the common property of all who care to look. Thus, social science can lend its distinctive focus and method that extend all the way from personality problems on one side to political problems on the other to help clarify the facts, truths, and meanings behind the dilemmas of the modern world.

Most literature on development is nation-centered. But the nation as an exclusive index of development presents grave difficulties. There is an absence of data on comparative rates of growth, or on unique historical aspects of area clusters which make for contrasting concepts of what is considered development. One purpose of this volume is to etch the elements of favorable or invidious contrast as we move from nation to nation, or even continent to continent. Developmental studies increasingly need analyses not only in depth but also in scope. Focusing on multi-national (no less than sub-national) characteristics of development permits studies along historical as well as analytical lines. The work already accomplished at the big research centers, and also by independent researchers, would indicate that the time is ripe for a general re-evaluation of the genesis of the problem of development.

This is a study in sociological meanings—a causal and an interpretative study. With few exceptions I have avoided the use of charts and diagrams. Even if it is true, as Galileo said, that nature writes its secrets in numbers, men still require an unraveling of these numbers in the form of words. At some points this qualitative emphasis made my chores more complex, but it also compelled me to think through the mass of data already compiled, without a mechanical reliance upon the mystique of data. In any event, the raw data add up to one thing: there exists a huge gap between rich and poor nations, and this gap shows no signs of narrowing. The current vast differences in living standards, estimated at anywhere from 30:1 to 50:1 between the countries at the top of the scale in contrast to those at the bottom, indicate the magnitude of the problem. The data contain few elements of surprise at this level.

The question of wealth and poverty, of superordination and subordination, of elites and masses, of the things which divide men so as to create advantages for some and disadvantages for others, are matters of public *interests* first, and of personal *values* a distant second. If there is a universal interest in survival, there is no such restraining consensus in how or in what style men are to survive. Coercion is not simply the opposite of persuasion, but a response to the limits of persuasion. War is not simply the antinomy of peace, but a response to situations which are unyielding to pacific strategies in the struggles of men for a better life.

This book is neither an appeal to the wealthy nations to spread their goods, nor is it an apocryphal statement of the dire consequences awaiting an absence of such sharing. I have enough confidence in the blind pursuits of self-interest to discount most evaluative claims of superiority. On the other hand, the book is written with a confidence that self-interest can be so defined as to make room for broader social interests. The men of the Enlightenment anticipated by some fifty years the French Revolution of social and economic development. And if their appeals to the benevolence of the monarchs and princes of the time fell on deaf ears, their parallel appeals to a revolution in economy and morality that would entail the maximum use of reason and passion became the common currency of the Revolution.

The same situation seems to be repeating itself today. For the last hundred years appeals to the wealthy nations have not produced the kinds of social changes that could bring poor nations and poor continents of the world into the modern epoch. But it is no less clear that these nations and continents, sometimes with more passion than reason, have taken it upon themselves to settle the question of the redistribution of the world's wealth, and the rearrangement of the centers of power. They certainly have not waited for the benevolence of the wealthy to catch up with the demands of the age.

It may well be that this book will have greater appeal to those who live and work in poor countries than to those who thrive off the limited affluence found in wealthy countries. *Nonetheless, in the belief that social science represents reason in society,* and in the further belief that reason can, at critical ages, replace narrow self-interest in the determination of what is true and useful, I feel justified in submitting my work to all those who share my convictions in the worth of social science as an applied science. And for those who do not share such convictions, perhaps the book will at least serve to sharpen the dialogue between reason and unreason—which by this time all who think must know is synonymous with the struggle between development and destruction.

I wish to thank first critics and colleagues of mine at Washington University: Richard D. Alexander, Roger Maconick, Martin Needleman, Juan Saxe-Fernandez, N. Aguiar Walker, Albert F. Wessen, and Patricia Woo. Their enthusiasm and encouragement were invaluable. Other friends and colleagues who read the manuscript at one stage or another, in whole or in part, are Herbert Blumer (University of California), Alex Fryer (Syracuse University,) Paul Honigsheim (late of Michigan State University), Rollin Posey (New College, Florida), and Roger B. Walker (Latin American Center for Research in the Social Sciences). Needless to say, none of the above-mentioned persons is in any way responsible for mistakes or miscalculations that may remain. Throughout the active period of preparing the manuscript for publication, I was fortunate to have Adeline Sneider as my secretary and typist. Her proficiency made additional technical aid superfluous.

Irving Louis Horowitz

Washington University
St. Louis, Missouri
September 1965

Preface to the Second Edition [1972]

I have prepared a second edition of *Three Worlds of Development* because I believe that the theoretical structure of the book remains as operational for diagnosing the development problems of the seventies as the first edition was for the sixties. Quite simply, the book hypothesizes that viewed from an economic, a political, a military, or a social perspective the world exists in a condition of unstable equilibrium, specifically, in a triadic relationship: the First World led by the United States, the Second World led by the Soviet Union, and the Third World comprising the Afro-Asian bloc and portions of Latin America. This Third World is as incapable of preserving its goals and its functions apart from either of the major power centers as it was five years ago. Meanwhile, the Cold War involves three players rather than two. Every calculation of the United States by the Soviet Union bears consequences for the structure of the Third World. Every evaluation of the Soviet Union by the United States requires that a similar evaluation be made of Third World elite and mass sentiment. But super-power accounting is not based upon parity but asymmetry; it is analogous to that made by fathers with respect to misguided and wayward sons.

One can analyze three worlds as one does three-person games. In fact, it must be acknowledged that our speculation about how the Soviet Union will act really means: How will Brezhnev and Kosygin act? For better or worse, the magnitude of analysis is not the sole source of difficulty in executing such analysis. *Three Worlds of Development* is effective as a conceptual tool, as well as an analytical or organizational arrangement of the world, precisely because the scale of analysis does not affect the predictabilities derived.

Indeed, one might even say that it is easier to predict the behavior of the Soviet Union or the behavior of India in any given situation than it is to predict the behavior of personal friends; many irrational and capricious acts characteristic of personal behavior do not have a parallel in the collective decision-making process of great world powers. A large number of three-nation, zero-sum games have unambiguous solutions—prescriptions that enable the participants to resolve conflict in a rational way.[1]

This historical vision of game theory is in my own judgment a valid conceptual framework for studying the development process. In this way the findings of social psychology concerning the nature and function of coalitions and groups can be linked with the research in social stratification concerning the aspirations and achievements of men at work. Having settled *ex cathedra* the utility of the schema employed in *Three Worlds of Development,* let me now proceed to the reconsideration.

A basic problem in the introductory chapter, "What Is the Third World?," is that the Third World has become, paradoxically, both more consolidated and less consolidated during the post-colonial period. One can now speak of Third World impulses within the very heartland of the American Empire: for example, in Canada and Guatemala; and one can also speak of Third World stances in Eastern European nations such as Czechoslovakia and Hungary. There can be little doubt that the movement of small nations against big nations is a new characteristic of the Third World. It is no longer simply the nature of their economic systems and political strategies that defines the Third World, but the antipathy of these small and dependent nations for large and imperial nations. This has become the hallmark of their political behavior.

We may be entering a period in which the polar centers of the First and Second Worlds will shift. Certainly, the challenge to Soviet suprem-

---

1. There is a growing interest in works in this area. The leads provided by John von Neumann and Oscar Morgenstern in their *Theory of Games and Economic Behavior* (Princeton: Princeton University Press, 1953) have mostly and unfortunately been channelized into "war game" theory. A notable and worthy exception is a study by Bernhardt Lieberman, "i-Trust: A Notion of Trust in Three-Person Games and International Affairs," *Journal of Conflict Resolution,* Vol. 7 (Sept. 1964), pp. 271–80; and more recently, the significant effort by Theodore Caplow, *Two Against One: Coalitions in Triads* (Englewood Cliffs, N.J.: Prentice-Hall, 1968).

acy in the Second World by the Chinese Maoist regime has been quite severe. China has no desire to be a member of the Third World. She does not see herself as small or neutralist or dependent. Rather, she sees herself as the vigorous heir to the Second World, to the leadership of the communist sphere.

Similarly, Western European nations which were subject to the overt influence of United States economic hegemony from the period of the Marshall Plan in the forties through the sixties found a natural and explosive leader in Charles de Gaulle, and his commitment to a French doctrine of continentalism. As an international posture, Gaullism constitutes a Western European challenge to United States supremacy. German or English counterparts of Gaullism also perceive themselves as part of the First World—the world of capitalist finance and democratic politics—and, as any Algerian can testify, not part of the Third World.

Though Gaullism (like Maoism) has certain nationalist, even idiosyncratic forms, its ideological substance is anything but capricious. It represents a last-ditch effort by the older European capitalist nations to recapture control of the First World—and by implication the overseas markets—from the United States, just as Maoism represents a similar internal economic struggle for control of the Second World. Within the larger triadic relationships extant in international monetary and political affairs, micro-units of tensions and polarization exist within each of the major power blocs. This internal conflict clearly has parallels in the behavior of individuals and small groups. A major new element in the trichotomy of international development, then, is extension of membership in the Third World to small satellite nations formerly under the orbit of one of the major powers. On the other hand, there has been genuine polarization within each of the First and Second Worlds where the object is to exercise decisive control over the destiny of each respective world.

The second chapter, "Sociological and Ideological Concepts of Development," should have placed greater emphasis on developing measurements for distinguishing underdevelopment from overdevelopment. The question of overdevelopment has troubled many commentators on the first edition, for they have felt that the concept of overdevelopment is ideological rather than sociological. While one can readily see how they might have reached such a conclusion on the basis of available information and on the basis of what was done with the concept, overdevelopment *can* be operationally defined as follows.

First, overdevelopment occurs when maximum levels of production are not achieved even though the plant capacity for full production is available.

Second, overdevelopment results when the disparity between wealth and poverty grows, despite a constant increase in the gross national product and in the over-all accumulation of wealth.

Third, overdevelopment occurs when conventional human skills available are outdistanced by technological advancements.

Fourth, overdevelopment is therefore an excess ratio of industrial capacity to social utility, while underdevelopment refers to an excess number of social demands in relation to the available production and consumer outlets.

It is extremely important not to identify or equate overdevelopment with any one social system or national economy. For example, there is a danger in overemphasizing the stagnation of the American economy during the 1950's, and of underemphasizing the dramatic growth of the economy during the 1960's. As for the distribution of income, here the United States exhibits a remarkable consistency. The income gap is not "narrowing" as liberal celebrationists declare, or "widening" as Marxist critics would have it. Further, one must be careful to distinguish the movement from an "industrial" age to a "cybernetic" age from the simple underutilization of conventional human skills. Certainly in the United States both phenomena are present. But in the area of advertisement and propaganda, the United States dramatically points up its peculiar problems of overdevelopment, since the very concept of social utility comes to be discarded in favor of an unwritten doctrine of infinite and immediate gratification. In any event, the existence of overdevelopment is certainly not something experienced exclusively by American capitalism.

Ideological postures are not to be dismissed or sneered at, for they often supply the impetus to social change. In this sense ideology may be considered a mechanism for achieving change. But with a purely ideological position, change is distorted—for instance, there are irrational demands for industrialization made by basically agrarian nations that is potentially profitable, or there are equally irrational demands for the manufacture of domestic goods that could more readily and more cheaply be purchased from foreign suppliers. But these ideological distortions cannot be resolved by a counter-ideology of modernization. Development implies a good deal more than satisfying consumer wants. It also entails political sovereignty and economic independence even thought the immediate costs may be heavy and unequally shared.

The chapter "The First World of United States Development" deals with an important new problem of overdevelopment: the swollen nature of political agencies that no longer have the capacity either to stir the energies of masses or to enlist the participation of influential elites. In part, and as a response to the bureaucratic and impersonal aspects of overdevelopment, new forms of politics have evolved. The drive for community control in education, the resistance to further taxation, disappointments with the war on poverty reflect a major crisis within the American system itself. The nature of United States political development is being questioned. The Left charges that the government is inefficient and elitist; the Right charges that the administration is too efficient and too beneficent. Whatever the final judgment about those who design federal programs, the discontent with the results of standard notions of engineered social change has been subject to searching inquiry from broad sectors of the American people.

The past five years have also seen the political isolation of the working class in the United States. This isolation is not so much imposed by the middle class, with which the working class shares common experiences and aspirations, as it is a consequence of separation of the middle class from the lower classes, particularly Negroes, ethnic minorities, and marginal sectors engaged in "deviant" life styles and career perspectives, such as students. Certainly, the newest and most dynamic factor in United States development during the sixties was the sharp cleavage, indeed the class war situation which developed between the organized working classes and the marginal lower classes. The combatants in this decade are not the historical enemies described by Marx but are more similar to enemies defined by fascist doctrines of the state. The working class has turned to the Leviathan with a vengeance. Not the liquidation of the state, but its celebration, has become of crucial importance. The working-class demands legitimacy, law, order, and a ruling class willing and capable of exercising full authority. Social radicalism in American life has become the province of the reviled *lumpenproletariat* and their intellectual underwriters. This development, shocking to classical ideologists, must rank as the most significant political event within the First World.

But Third World perceptions and attitudes toward the industrial

Goliaths remained essentially unchanged during the present epoch. The Third World is still not so much hostile to the United States as it is disenchanted with it. Its disenchantment is a result both of unfulfilled high expectations and of disillusionment with an inflexible American political process that seems far out of tune with the economic achievements and social policies which might be expected of what was, after all, the first new nation.

Third World perceptions of the United States have also been radically altered by the Vietnam War, which has generated the feeling that the first new nation is determined to remain the only new nation. Certainly the contrast between United States political goals outlined in general foreign-policy statements and United States political actions toward Vietnam reinforce a Third World predisposition to be correct and cordial, rather than intimate and friendly.

In evaluating "The Second World of Soviet Development," any defense or critique of the convergence theory must acknowledge that the Soviets are increasingly becoming the *Realpolitiker* of the European world. They now demand a sphere of influence doctrine no less binding and no less demanding than that announced by Metternich at the Congress of Vienna in 1814–15. Peaceful coexistence has been redefined. The slogan which began in the euphoric certitude of the rational supremacy of the socialist economy over the capitalist economy has not come to signify the informal division of spoils in the international dominion.

Although the Soviet Union has become sphere-of-influence-minded in the world at large, it is important to recognize that it has continued its internal transition from totalitarianism to authoritarianism. Though the screws have remained tight at the political level, they have been opened, if only as safety valves, at the cultural and economic levels. Here, too, the convergence hypothesis is borne out. It is the political behavior of the Soviet Union, rather than its economic or social gains, that most acutely separates the Third World from the Soviet Union, just as the political climate in the United States negates the possibility of Third World trust in her.

The economics of socialism has also come upon hard times. In Czechoslovakia, for example, ten years of socialist central planning resulted in a simulation of capitalist business cycles. Inventories of goods piled up, while total industrial output actually declined. With the sophistication of the Soviet economy, overinvestment in capital goods industries took place. Capital goods produced for the Soviet market by the East European satelites could no more be absorbed than could consumer items produced by Latin America be imported by the United States. Decentralization of economic units, competition within the economic sphere, methods for establishing profitability and efficiency and not just political utility, and means of creating personal and communal incentives have accelerated tremendously both within the Soviet Union and the Eastern European sphere. All of these developments have impressed upon the Third World the awareness that a decision to seek an economic "mix" is not simply a strategy for avoiding entrapment in the big power "camps," but more significantly, a matter of basic economic principles.

The relationship of the Third World to the United Nations ("The United Nations and the Third World: East-West —Conflict in Focus") has undergone manifest change in the past five years.[2] The United Nations has become a forum and organizational tool by which the small nations of the world—and that means almost all of the Third World nations—may express their sentiments and international desires. This polarization between the large nations and the larger United Nations membership was only dimly perceptible in 1963; then the struggle was limited to trade and tariff regulations, and the large nations still seriously considered the United Nations a legitimizing forum. With increased polarization of the world into large and small nations, however, the integrity of the United Nations has suffered. Its very impotence to function as an agency for world peace has tended to make the larger nations, East and West alike, China as well as the United States, tend to dismiss its importance. At the same time, its ineffectuality has made Third World nations even more convinced of the need for a mechanism for settlement of international disputes. The United Nations has become a far cry from what it was initially, and certainly from the League of Nations. Instead of providing a forum for big nations to express their sentiments and to show forbearance and toleration of the small nations, it functions quite the other way around, as a place of relative political impotence that constantly reminds the major powers that the Third World is a reality given its organizational coherence precisely by that structure by which they had hoped to guarantee their own hegemony.

The issues of mending and smashing ("Mending and Smashing: Eco-

2. I have dealt with this issue in some detail in a recent essay on "The Limited Effectiveness of the United Nations," *Stanford Journal of International Studies,* Vol. 3, No. 1 (June 1968), pp. 13–19, 38–45.

nomic Issues and Strategies") have become clouded with time. The choice between mending the social order and breaking it no longer seems as clear cut as it did a decade ago. All of the African nations, with the exception of South Africa, have undergone a smashing period and in the process have discovered that mending is something which has to follow, like healing, and is not merely an alternative strategy. Furthermore, smashing occupational colonialism is far simpler than smashing economic imperialism.

A major ideological assumption of many new nations of Africa and even some of the old nations of Latin America and Asia was that pronouncing an economy socialist was enough to usher in an age of economic development. Calamitous consequences in Indonesia, the Congo, Ghana, Egypt, Syria, and in Cuba and Chile in the Western Hemisphere demonstrate that mere political pronouncements are not to be equated with the actual smashing of social forms. For example, Nasser's announced socialism did not eliminate either the landholding aristocracy or the sheikdom. Similarly, the need for mending, for the healing and binding of wounds, is directly proportionate to the degree that a revolution has been complete.

To reconsider the chapter from a present vantage point would not be to minimize the importance of the problem of mending and smashing, but rather to emphasize that it is a matter of alternating currents rather than alternative choices. The issue is not simply a choice between taxation or expropriation but, more profoundly, a matter of destruction and reconstruction.

Perhaps the chapter containing the greatest degree of theoretical innovation was the one on Party charisma, in which the party apparatus of Third World nations rather than the leadership was presented as the basic repository of the charismatic dimension. The available evidence has largely upheld this conceptualization. The uni-party structure does seem to remain permanent despite a whole range of leadership turnovers. This is as true for the PRI in Mexico as it is for the Congress party in India. There is evidence that even in Algeria and Indochina the party apparatus has persisted after the deposition of Premier Ben Bella and President Sukarno respectively.

In the euphoria surrounding termination of colonial rule in Asia, Africa, and the Caribbean, the triumphant glow of nationalism shone most brightly on the new governments' optimistic plans for economic and social development. Particularly because the private sectors of these nations are backward or oriented toward export rather than domestic needs, their governments expected to play a dominant role in the development process. When the cheers of Independence Day or Revolution Day died away and the government addressed itself to translating ambitions into action, then the nation's critical dependence on the nation's bureaucracy became clear.

The public administration inherited from the colonial period is in many ways unsuited or unprepared for the demands now placed on it. To some extent it may suffer disorganization and demoralization as expatriate colonial officers return to their native country, even when their departure is a gradual phasing-out instead of a rout. Procedures are disrupted, projects are truncated, and traditional long and thorough training programs are interrupted. Despite rapid promotion of the lower ranks and crash training programs, filling all the vacancies with trained personnel often proves to be impossible. The salary scales and benefits appropriate to a developed nation's civil service tax the newly independent nation's economy sorely. Moreover, the structure and procedures of the bureaucracy, as well as the skills of native civil servants trained during the colonial period, are designed for the custodial tasks of colonial administration: preserving law and order, collecting taxes, maintaining transportation and communication systems. Little machinery or experience is available for the innovations the bureaucracy must now perform. Thus, after the mending or smashing issue is resolved, the greatest administrative challenge confronting the new governments is the problem of reaching an adjustment between politicians and civil servants whose relative power and status have just undergone an abrupt and drastic reversal.

In the difficult and often chaotic period immediately following independence, tremendous strains begin to appear between new nationalist politicians and inherited bureaucratic apparatus. In part, these frictions reflect the politicans' frustration with having to rely, in order to move toward their political goals, on an agency not of their making, outside of their single-party control, and whose loyalty to the new regime is questionable. The sources of tension and specific points of conflict between politicians and administrators in the newly independent nations, and the consequences of this conflict for government administration, have increased greatly during the past decade. Any future considerations of the Third World in the time to come must deal with this internal conflict.

Who is to make the revolution and who is to execute the revolution are decisive and divisive questions in the Third World. The maker of the revolution—the politican—is reluctant to admit to limits on his expertise. The executor of the revolution—the bureaucrat—is reluctant to admit the politican has a role in the post-revolutionary developmental process. These are the terms in which the whole question of conflict and consensus in the Third World must be reconsidered.

It is also clear that the theory of party charisma will have to reassess the consequences of the deposing of Sukarno in Indonesia, Nkrumah in Ghana, and a host of other African leaders who have been overthrown in internal coups d'état. The party structure has proven to be more brittle than I had foreseen. Direct and uncompromising military rule has replaced party charisma as a governing instrument. The result has not been the rise of multi-party nations in place of uni-party nations, nor the rise of democracy in place of charisma, but rather the institutionalization of bureaucracy in open military forms. Whether these forms are efficient and operational remains to be seen. The likelihood is that they will tend to suppress rather than to direct political life and that the party charisma will remain a viable instrument for the expression of pluralist sentiments in one-party states. Nonetheless, one cannot fail to be impressed by the movement toward militarism in the short decade since the national liberation period in Africa. Increasingly, it seems that Africa and Asia are being "latinized," that they are adopting patterns of military intervention and interference in civil life long characteristic of Latin America. This style may prove to be an uncomfortable identifying hallmark of the Third World.

The ninth chapter, "The Military Pivot," is as painfully applicable now as it was five years ago. The military continues to function internally as the symbol of national sovereignty as well as the basic option to civilian political rule. Although various forms of military rule do function to aid the developmental process, an account of the "hardware" costs clearly proves the armed forces are an expensive and efficient means of promoting economic change. Yet, while there may be some criticism of the costs of maintaining a military system as the leading vanguard of development, it seems to work better than corrupt civilian middle-class or landholding counterparts.

It is even more necessary than it was before to analyze the degree to which the military system of the Third World functions in liaison with forces in either the First or Second World to maintain a condition of semi-sovereignty rather than complete sovereignty. It often seems that military rule indicates an absence of political legitimacy in Third World nations. Certainly in Latin America the over-all drive toward military regimes is related to the increased power of the military missions maintained in Latin America by the United States. Similarly, military factionalism in the Middle East may be linked to the impact of the internal functioning of those regimes by Soviet military attachés. Increasingly the emphasis has shifted from external defense to internal security. The rise of civic action programs throughout the Third World indicates the extent to which the "enemy" has been located within the nation, rather than in foreign nations. And in this redefinition, the role of the First World can neither be dismissed or disguised.

The military cannot be simply perceived as a network which provides sovereignty for Third World nations, for it also functions to forestall the legitimacy of those self-same nations. The military of the Third World functions in a dual capacity: as the outward symbol of sovereignty and the inner substance of a failure to make that sovereignty respected by the masses of the subject population.

What in effect has happened in many new nations is that open military rule has become a means to adjudicate the problem of an inherited bureaucracy unresponsive to the need for revolution, and a modernizing political network unconcerned with the costs of revolution in developmental terms. When seen in such terms the actual role and function of the military can be viewed as an organic consequence of splits within the elite that must be resolved from the top, since the social sectors are poorly organized and the economic classes weakly developed. The military enforce the "socialism of the whole people"; while the political network continues to legitimate nationalism and the bureaucratic apparatus continues to urge a spirit of developmentalism. This crystallization of elites is certainly far more advanced now than it was a decade earlier.

The problem presented in "The Mental Set of Developing Man" remains polarized precisely in terms of where the blame ultimately rests. Do shortcomings originate within the person or within the society? What is responsible for the weakness in ourselves—the world that shapes us, or the inner world that motivates us? On this issue the developmental literature remains very much as it was several years ago; the works of psychologists such as McClelland and Hagan are unreconciled in intent and content with the work of Third World psychologists such as Franz Fanon and Albert Memmi.

Perhaps the problem can be made more explicit in methodological terms. We are confronted by a sociological counterpart to the Heisenberg effect. We have two divergent types of data. Aggregate data provide measures of gross national produce, electric energy output, and levels of production. On the other hand, behavioral and attitudinal measures deal with individual responses to social change, as experienced in jobs, family, and status position. The problem is that separating the data does not move us out of the methodological bind. If one focuses upon the structural data, society becomes the cause as well as the consequence of social underdevelopment and personal unrest. If attitude and opinion data are emphasized, the problem is formulated as one of low personal achievement and motivation.

Man is motivated to become developmental by either heroic or selfish visions of the self. The moral force of socialism rests on a belief in the heroic economy, while the morality of capitalism rests on a belief in the importance of self-serving economy. Logic leads those who emphasize attitudinal data to support the values and the canons of the capitalistic ethic, whereas those who seek support in structural arguments concerning underdevelopment usually advocate some form of socialism.

A new element in the methodological bind is the crisis of confidence in the heroic economy within the socialist empire. The struggle between the Soviet Union and China involves precisely the issues outlined in the mental set of developing man. To what does the political leader appeal? By which set of emotions is the social system finally governed?

Nor is this problem limited to the socialist world. If the Soviet Union has moved toward an economy of ego-gratification and personal aggrandizement, the American economy has suffered an unprecedented disaffection with material possessions among a portion of its citizenry. No longer moved to make sacrifices for commodity goods, they are increasingly motivated precisely by the values underlying the heroic economy. As a consequence, a phenomenon like Maoism can be taken seriously by a large segment of the affluent student population in the United States.

Developing man is on a constant intellectual treadmill in which a strategic choice has to be made either for self against society or for society against self. This choice bears implications not only for the character of economic systems but also for the psychic mixture that will be available to the Third World. The very concept of change may be at stake. For many of the younger generation, revolution must start with the regeneration and rejuvenation of the self; while for more traditional advocates of change, the society determines the solutions as well as dictates the problems.

The last section of *Three Worlds of Development*, "Toward a General Theory of Development and Revolution," can be considered as a whole, since it is here that the generalizations of the book are presented, and here that the over-all model of development outlined must ultimately stand or succumb to criticism.

The section deals with the various dilemmas confronted and decisions made in social development—such as necessary coercion versus internecine terrorism, achievement versus ascription in the developmental process, risk-taking and policy-making, imbalance between life styles and industrial styles and between industrial availabilities and educational achievements, and, finally, the imbalance between political and economic development. I add to this now a lengthier discussion of policy-making in the Third World.

A major consideration in development theory has become not only the kinds of policy advocated for the Third World but whether the promoters of such policies are to be the technological bureaucrats or the professional politicians. More profoundly, the choice lies between expertise and intuition, between the man of knowledge and the man of action.

There has been a conventional distinction between knowers and actors made in the literature of social science. But at the level of development, the differentiation has a special significance. The knower is often one who measures social change in long-range terms and sees development as a world-historic event over which individuals have limited control. The knower has the further advantage of being synthetic, organizing his tendency charts into systematic bodies of data. He evaluates development rather than participates in such processes. The actor is often one who measures social change in short-range terms; he sees development as a volitional set of decisions defined by the participants. The actor, while at a disadvantage in determining the historical role of any individual or agency in promoting change, has the distinct advantage of participation itself. In exchange for science he derives the payoffs of therapy; and in exchange for evaluation he has the joys (and the terrors) of decision-making.

It is clearer now than when *Three Worlds of Development* first appeared that the "development decade" has not fulfilled its tasks or its goals. According to all available statistics, the developed nations devel-

oped even more rapidly during the sixties, and the underdeveloped nations became even more dependent during these same years. In this
sense the question of what those publics and polities in the advanced
nations can do for the developed peoples in underdeveloped nations has
taken on greater urgency but less practical relevance. The age of international social welfare is being severely challenged by nationalism from
above and separatism from below. The Peace Corps idea and overseas
support programs have clearly been stop-gap measures, oftentimes providing more satisfaction for the helper than assistance for those being
helped.

My recommendation would be that developmentalists apply greater
pressure on their home nations and less pressure on the nations they
seek to assist. Political involvement, like technological innovation, begins at home. Social change and modernization of attitudes, if not of
artifacts, are not reserved for tribal Africans.

The main strength of science and scholarship no less than of policy
and pronouncement must be applied to wealthy and powerful nations,
the nations in which we live, the nations we serve and which in turn are
supposed to serve us. In order to help the underdeveloped nations we
must develop a foreign policy for our own nation consonant with the
free and unfettered aspirations of others. It also means that wealth-
producing capabilities must be reallocated on an international scale no
less than on a national scale. Overdevelopment must be partially conceptualized as the refusal to recognize that falling profits rather than
rising expectations are at the source of the economic existence and expansion of the Third World. This reexamination of *Three Worlds of
Development* may assist us, as thoughtful (and hence marginal) members of the First World, to recognize that solving the problems of our
social system is the basic mechanism for providing real foreign assistance for others.

Before all else, I wish to express my thanks to the many reviewers,
commentators, critics, and above all, users, of the first edition of *Three
Worlds of Development*. Usually, authors complain, often with justification, that their critics are less generous or capable in their evaluations
than they should be. For my part, I can say that for the most part I have
been dealt with fairly and fully. The public and personal criticisms received offered a basic catalyst for attempting a second edition of the
volume. In the process of answering my critics and commentators I came

to realize that greater clarity and simplicity was indeed called for. And in this very process, I hope that this edition will have far greater utility among the student population that has in fact become the mainstay readership of the book.

The warmest and most generous support I received in the process of rethinking *Three Worlds of Development* came from my former research assistant, now professor of economics at the University of Saskatchewan, John A. Richards. His warmth often took the form of heated discussion, and his generosity was usually expressed in meaningful criticism. This association taught me the fundamental importance of economic science in studying the Third World, and served to correct a growing tendency of mine toward an excessive reliance upon sociological and even ideational features in explaining events. Another significant intellectual input, one continued from the first edition, is that made by my dear friend of long standing, Leo S. Kaplan, of the Cooper Union in New York. His tremendous wealth of information on socio-economic conditions of both the First and Second Worlds underwrites a considerable amount of rethinking on my part of the nature of the political sociology of the Third World, particularly how it relates to the ongoing East-West conflict that has continued unabated for a quarter-century.

Two conferences were organized around issues and problems raised by and in *Three Worlds of Development*. The first, which took place in June 1968 at the University of California at Berkeley under the auspices of its International Studies Program, represented the sharpest and crispest dialogue that I encountered. It was a memorable experience, and one whose impact I hope is adequately reflected in the second edition. I want particularly to thank the sponsors of that event: Neil Smelser, Ivan Vallier, Ernest Haas, and Robert Bellah. A second conference held on the book took place a year later in September 1969 at Princeton University, under the auspices of Woodrow Wilson School of International Relations. This too was a worthwhile experience in which the sharpest sort of scholarly exchanges took place; and for which I had the great advantage of being confronted by a group of men from many disciplines working in the area of Third World Studies. I am particularly grateful to Paul Sigmund, C. E. Black, and Marion J. Levy, Jr., who were sharp rather than cross with me. These gentlemen, as well as the other participants, exuded a personal generosity that made the experience pleasurable as well as worthwhile.

The secretarial and technical assistance in the preparation of this edi-

xxviiiPREFACE TO THE SECOND EDITION (1972)

tion was at least equal to that of the first time around. My present secretaries, Lois McGarry and Mary Wilk, took the brunt of the workload—with a good naturedness that belied how difficult the task was. Often, and without fanfare, they made sure that the grammar and syntax of the author came off a trifle better in final text than initially in manuscript. Danielle Salti once again, as in the first edition, assumed the onerous tasks—the dirty work of preparing the index, checking the data for accuracy, making sure the right accents fell over the right letters, and generally performing the role of mother superior over all phases of production. No amount of thanks can equal the simple adumbration of deeds she performed.

But when all the appropriate bows in the direction of colleagues and cohorts are acknowledged, there remains the irreducible loneliness that comes from knowing that in the long run it is I alone who must accept responsibility for this work. And it is I alone who must confront the drastic imperfections of one man with the infinite perfections of the larger world.

Irving Louis Horowitz

Rutgers University
New Brunswick, N.J.
March, 1971

Contents

I

Foundations
of Development

1

Sociology of Three Worlds

I

In one of the most perceptive and imaginative sentences in *Das Kapital,* Marx wrote: "The country that is more developed industrially only shows to the less developed the image of its own future." [1] It is significant to note that what the mid-nineteenth century must have considered a wildly romantic thought is a commonplace today. Current events have become more complex than Marx could possibly have anticipated, more centered on facts than on images. The rise of the Third World, of a social universe in limbo and outside the power dyad of East and West, has generated new queries.

Assuming that the developed countries show to the underdeveloped the image of their own futures, the question arises, do these "expectant" nations accept this image? Are they prepared to accept modernism without qualifications? Does this include the exaggerated consequences of automated industrialism, of alienation and privatization? Will the antagonisms between the rich nations and the poor nations overwhelm potential commonalities of economy and culture? Do the less developed nations apply their energies to careful mending or to revolutionary smashing? Above all, does the developmental process change the terms of description and analysis, or provide them with a renewed urgency?

It is no exaggeration to say that the answers to these questions have been slow in coming. To some extent this is a consequence of the unevenness and lateness of development in some areas; cultural, ethnic, and

1. Karl Marx, *Das Kapital.* Chicago: Charles Kerr Publishers, 1905, Vol. 1, p. 13.

racial apartness of other areas; and the ways in which resistance to social change has inhibited these areas from emulating the economic systems of advanced nations. The emergence of a Third World; the transformation of world relations from a dyadic to a triadic balance; the
emergence on a mass scale of new nations, new economic systems, new
cultural products, new political forms—all bound up with national traditions, not infrequently synonymous with national myths—have created
a profusion of new issues for our times. Furthermore, the "image" of a
developed nation has been fragmented into "images" of developed nations. There is no question of rejecting development, except among those
people overwhelmed with nostalgia; the only question is what direction
such development is going to take. In the consciousness of a Third World
lives the example of a Second World no less than that of a First World
—of the socialist Soviet Union no less than the capitalist United States.
The *existence* of a development process is a social fact. The *recognition*
of a need for development is a social value. What binds the Third World
together is not just its being a geographic locale outside the main power
centers but a psychological unity built around a social value. The ideological accoutrements of these processes are responses and effects—
which in turn stimulate a desire for accelerated industrialization and
rapid modernization. But, above all, the ideology of the Third World is
a response to the pervasive problem of how to gain worldly preeminence.
It is always a matter of "catching up" and perhaps ultimately "surpass-
ing" those held to be most advanced. This in itself betrays the fact and
shame of backwardness.

Put another way, the developed nations are "causes," not just because
they are in the forefront of modernization and material wealth, but because they create the *conditions* for rebellion and revolution. The developed nations thus provide a chain of *effects*.[2] We might introduce the
three *effects* as follows: (1) Developing nations define themselves as
engaged in a protracted race with the most advanced sectors of the economic world. This is the *demonstration effect*. (2) Developing nations
define themselves as economically and socially experimental and lean
toward a "mix" rather than a "pure" system. The Third World believes
in neither socialism nor capitalism, but it also believes in them both.
This is the *fusion effect*. (3) Developing nations are those which have
the desire and the means to catch up to advanced forms of social and

2. See Gino Germani, "Stages of Modernization in Latin America," *Studies in
Comparative International Development*, Vol. 5, No. 8, 1969–70.

economic organization, and to do so in less time than it took the presently constituted advanced nations to reach their present levels. This is the *compression effect*.

At the outset we must undertake to sketch the features of the First and Second Worlds so that differentiation from the Third World is made operational. The removal of all ambiguity at such macroscopic levels of definition is clearly impossible, yet it is just as clear that such world historic divisions do exist and do have large-scale political and social consequences. The three worlds are contrasts in social structural evolution, contrasts too in their appearance in historical time.

II

What is meant by the First World is basically that cluster of nations which were "naturally" transformed from feudalism into some form where private ownership of instruments and means of production predominated. If these nations did not evolve out of feudalism, they at least grew out of the soil of Western Europe and started as capitalist states. Certain properties of this First World are clear: historically they had their initial "take-off" in the banking houses of sixteenth-century Italy, in the middle-sized industry of seventeenth-century France, and in the industrial mechanization of eighteenth-century England and nineteenth-century United States and Germany. Economically, they share an emphasis on industrialization and technology used for private enrichment and public welfare in uneven dosages.

First World nations have in common an internal generative power. Changes which took place in Western European nations and the United States have usually come about as a result not of invasion or of foreign conquest but through the internal breakdown of the older landed classes, a general disintegration of agricultural societies, or through the initiative and creation of new life styles. The basic characteristic of the First World is that economic development was a consequence of the internal machinery of each nation and not the result of international planned agreement. As a matter of fact, there was not even agreement between the nations on a nation-state system until very late in the development of capitalism—the late nineteenth century.

The First World has two geographical parts: Europe and North America. The break with traditionalism in the United States occurs differently as compared with that in Western Europe. For it gained its national independence only through a struggle with England; and only then could it adopt a central parliamentary system. But it is important to note that in both sectors of the First World the formation of the parliamentary state system followed the bourgeois dominance over the forms of economic production. While they were often supportive of each other, political styles and structures in the First World emerged from the class conflicts of an economic system based on laissez faire.

The rise of industrial capital was preceded by a profound expansion in commercial capital. In this, the United States repeated the "phasing in" process that capitalism had previously undergone in Europe.[3] The factory unit became the keystone of the industrial system and its by-products: hardened national boundaries, protectionist tariff arrangements, heavy migration from countryside to city. And when trade relations became socially expensive, that is, central to the life styles of ordinary people, technology stepped in to accelerate private capital investment. Industrial inventions yielded savings on labor costs and raw materials to the point that the factory itself, rather than any individual labor units, became the principal investment unit. It will be seen that this economic interpretation, however suited it may be for the study of classical capitalism, can hardly be applied to the Third World—since the relationship of politics to economics is reversed.

The system of competitive capitalism which developed in Western Europe was forced to go beyond its own domestic markets. The First World became colonialist as well as capitalist. It established overseas bases from which it drew raw materials or developed potential markets for the purchase of finished products; in so doing it created out of its own dilemmas the master dilemma of colonialism.

Even the most rabid believer in European preeminence would be hard put to deny that the United States of America is the best example extant of the First World—of the highly mobile, commodity-oriented, and ideologically egalitarian social system. It witnessed the development of capitalism not only unfettered by feudal structures but assisted by political legislation. There occurred a crystallization of the state and the economy at roughly the same time and by roughly the same socioeconomic groups; asynchronous and unstable elements were held in check during its development. And whatever interpretation of the origins of

3. See Maurice Dobb, *Studies in the Development of Capitalism*. London: Routledge & Kegan Paul, 1946, esp. pp. 123–76.

the United States is preferred, economist or revisionist, one ineluctable fact emerges—the United States is the best representative of parliamentary democracy and capitalist economics.[4]

The United States also benefited by the continuation, throughout the nineteenth century, of rifts and schisms within Europe. The European powers, especially Spain, Germany, France, and England, were in such keen competition with each other that they were unable to forge any détente against the first new nation. England attempted to capture by economic means what could not be accomplished through military means. During the War of 1812 it blockaded American ports; in the Civil War it played off Northern commercial against Southern agricultural interests; each attempt in turn failed.

France under both Napoleons attempted to impede the territorial expansion of the United States, but its own internal demands caused it, under Napoleon Bonaparte, to surrender all territorial claims from the Louisiana Purchase, while half a century later Louis Napoleon removed troops he had put in Mexico. Similarly, the Spanish conquests of America had generated aspirations for independence in all its territories. European colonialism served to stimulate United States expansive economic aspirations in the hemisphere. The United States was able to consolidate its national economy before it became caught in extensive European entanglements. Then, at the very point when further possibilities for United States internal geographical expansion were narrowing, the European community was finally riven in combat. World War I committed the United States to European affairs.

The United States should not be dismissed as a model of development for the Third World. The fact that the United States has performed a colonial role is a poor and inadequate explanation of why it does not serve as the perfect model. There are, after all, many cases of the oppressed adopting the methods and philosophies of their exploiters. What is more, the imperialism of the United States was until recently ambivalent and half-hearted. Economically self-sustaining and, unlike nineteenth-century England, totally independent of imperial holdings, it only

4. The argument between Charles A. Beard, *An Economic Interpretation of the Constitution of the United States.* New York: Macmillan Co., 1913; and his critics, especially Forrest McDonald in *We the People: The Economic Origins of the Constitution.* Chicago: University of Chicago Press, 1958, effects only a settlement of the type of unique "purity" of America—not the fact of such difference. Indeed, both Beard's "economism" and McDonald's "pluralism" can be embraced by a concept of parliamentary capitalism.

very recently made the effort to shape the world in its image, indeed only since the annexation of the Philippines and the domination of the Caribbean toward the end of the last century. Still, its anti-colonial sentiments, if not always its behavior, set definite limits to a pursuit of influence.

Then why has the United States, despite its enormous power and prestige, failed to capture the imagination of the Third World bloc? It is a failure not of propaganda but of structural inefficiencies. One could say, the failure of success.

First: The United States remains the classic case of national development without a national plan. This is a possibility denied to those nations now emerging as economic entities. Indeed, the United States wants the underdeveloped nations to provide a plan for non-planning: private enterprise, a stable price system, and fiscal responsibility. But the notion of national planning for individual capitalist expansion is precisely the contradiction that remains unresolved. Thus, the United States expects from other nations what was not a condition of its own growth. In this, the classic explanation of the mystic hand of the free and mysterious market looms as an apologia for capitalism, while powerful nations like the United States reject the possibility that other nations are entitled to the same sort of laissez-faire apologetics.

Second: Despite the enormous amount of earned income in the United States, income distribution continues to be very uneven. Distribution of wealth, in the form of monies and bonds, has remained virtually at the same level since 1929. The distribution of wages and salaries in the United States also indicates the gap between classes—the lowest income fifth receives only 2.5 per cent of the national wage and salary income as of 1960, while the highest fifth receives an extraordinary 47.0 per cent.[5] Thus, the United States has not resolved its problem of economic polarization, despite the existence of an incredibly high standard of living. Absolute rates of economic growth and even styles of life have grown evenly, but social divisions have remained fairly intact.[6] In most Third World nations, the problem is reversed. That is to say, absolute rates of growth for all classes remain minimal, while the relative growth of classes

5. See Bureau of the Census, *Statistical Abstract of the United States—1968.* Washington, D.C.: Government Printing Office, 1968, pp. 309–38. The percentages hardly vary over the last ten-year period, despite the enormous increase in business and manufacturing activities.
6. Compare on this issue Gabriel Kolko, *Wealth and Power in America: An Analysis of Social Class and Income Distribution.* New York: Frederick A. Praeger, 1962; and Herman P. Miller, *Income of the American People.* New York: Wiley Publishers, 1955.

with respect to each other displays considerable drawing together. For the United States to serve as a model, Third World nations would have to grant the possibility of increasing class polarization through the widening of the income gap—and it is precisely this risk such nations do not wish to run.

Third: Monopolistic and oligopolistic situations obtain in nearly every sector of the American society. This means that competition between private sectors and public sectors continues in the United States with an unabated fury. This can be seen with especial clarity in the "space-race"—where a multiplication of agencies and organizations have arisen, often in competition, for control of everything from property rights on the moon to domination of the earth satellites. But whatever the net benefits or deficits of this for the United States, it is clear that such competition prevents planning for the whole society and inhibits a full drive toward economic equity. The First World has become such an incredible plethora of money and material wealth that the Third World can no more meet the requirements of this system than it could the traditional, vigorous nineteenth-century capitalist model. It must purchase such fiscal and technical services at premium costs, with only an outside chance of breaking the underdevelopment barrier.

Fourth: Certain structural weaknesses in the Third World also serve to reduce the role of the United States as a model. The Third World presents a picture of multiplying nations and contrasting politics. Everything from tribalism to militarism tends to weaken ties between backward nations for their common ends. Uncritical emulation of the United States social system would mean reversing the current vast trend toward national separatism. Both the United States and the Soviet Union have adopted a cultural pluralism which enables them to absorb rather than to crush separatist claims without lessening the quality or the extent of development. The situation in the Third World remains such that ecumenicism on such a sophisticated level remains a dream for some, a nightmare for others—but a reality for few people.

III

The Second World is historically the Russian orbit, the Soviet Union and its bloc. The center of the Second World presents an ambiguous situation, for the old Russian world was colonized by Poles, Germans, and other Europeans, including the Swedes. Yet Russia also remained a colonial power. While Russian feudalism was accommodating capitalism, the emergence of revolutionary forces in the late nineteenth century inhibited this accommodation. Thus, instead of a movement from feudalism to capitalism, there took place a radical shift from feudalism to socialism. The period of capitalist expansion in Russia was extremely short-lived; no more than fifty years. Thus, one can speak neither of the failure nor success, obsolescence nor abortiveness, of capitalism in Russia.

The politics of old Russia was fatally centralized in official functions, residing in the divine royal person of the czar. Economic and political initiative lay in his hands. For this reason "modernizing" czars like Catherine or Peter the Great, no less than "backward" czars, left Russia a legacy of a stagnant agriculture on one hand and a fragmented industrial complex on the other. Commercial middle-class elements were considered traitors to Russia's aspirations because of their contacts with foreigners. These business transactions were in turn perceived as direct challenges to royal supremacy; they were thus despised by the traditional and nascent classes alike.

No social class could really carry forward industrialization without the aid of the throne. While Peter the Great's westernization policy fostered both industrialization and centralization of political authority, it remained for the bolsheviks to renovate the social structure so as to make possible the completion of industrialization. This combination of an autocratic-Byzantine heritage and of a modern industrialized self-conception arising from a revolutionary movement dedicated to removing this past makes the Soviet Union a world apart.

In its pre-revolutionary, semi-backward condition Russia resembles the Third World. In its post-revolutionary industrialized status, it resembles the First World. While this descriptive picture helps to explain the Soviet reality, the fact that the Soviet Union is also an ideological society further complicates matters. Marxism-Leninism, the ideological context within which Soviet self-reflection takes place, makes the U.S.S.R. a unique entity, differentiated from China, since the latter's entry in the modern world has compelled numerous doctrinal accommodations. By its past the Soviet Union is an Eastern culture forcibly westernized under the impact of European powers. Its revolutionary withdrawal from the capitalist sphere of influence gave it a new pride, and also a unique mark of sovereignty—that of being the first socialist state in the world.

That it *was* in fact first further enhances its uniqueness. The advantage of being first separates the Soviet Union from the Third World; while at the same time being first makes it a model for the Third World. The Soviet Union, unlike czarist Russia, is no longer a prostrate nation rent by foreign intervention and, even worse, by foreign debts. In its socialist orientation the Soviet Union stands as a model; but in its Russian traditions it stands apart.

The long and ambiguous historical genesis of the relations of Russia with the West, no less than the East, was well stated by Arnold Toynbee. He noted that an observer who is intimately acquainted with the history of Russia would have recalled that its technological competition with the West, which reached such a dramatic culmination in 1957 (the year of Sputnik), has had a long history. And Russian competition with the West, which we herein call the First World, started not with Lenin in 1917, but with Peter the Great in 1689.[7] Peter's adoption of the Western technology of his day had been so effective that it had enabled him to defeat decisively one of the great powers of the contemporary Western world—Sweden. Russia's historical victory over Charles XII at Poltava in 1709 had been won within twenty years of the initiation of Peter the Great's westernizing program and within twenty-six years of the Polish defeat of the Turks and Mohammedans under the ramparts of Vienna in 1683. Toynbee goes on to point out that Russia, alone of all the geographically non-Western countries, had succeeded in maintaining its political independence. (This is vital because it is a basic characteristic of the Third World that it was long dominated by colonial powers.) It was a central fact of Russian development, whatever its former feudal status, that it was never subjugated to a pure colonial status but remained politically independent.

The decisive contest between Russia and Sweden thus signalized Russian achievement near the start of the Industrial Revolution. This interpretation of Russia's role in modern history shows that it served to lead the East, not only in resistance to the modern West's bid for worldwide dominance, but, more important, it offered an alternative form of modernization. In effect, then, there was a long historic struggle between the Russian world (or the Byzantine world) and the Western capitalist world (or Protestant-Catholic world). As political loyalties intensified and as

7. Arnold J. Toynbee, "Russia's Place in History," *A Study of History* (*Reconsiderations*). London and New York: Oxford University Press, 1961, Vol. XII, pp. 537–38.

the gap between social classes within nations lost revolutionary dynamism, economic and social competition began to take a *national* form. The class struggle thus becomes subsumed and swallowed up by the struggle between world empires which symbolically, even romantically, clung to the language and metaphors of social class.

The problem of metaphor and definition now introduced, it remains a fact that Russian society is the first to take seriously problems of development in their modern, secular sense. Indeed, the Russian economists offered the first major dialogue on the relationship between economic backwardness and political modernization. Russian fin de siècle populists, such as Voronstov, Nikolayon, Bulgakov, and Tugan Baranovski, and their more orthodox Marxian critics, such as Plekhanov, Kautsky, and Lenin, raised the essential questions of the twentieth century: Can small nations ever escape from the clutches of big national imperialism? Can the real wants of masses be best satisfied by an agricultural mode of production or by a coercive system of factory labor? Can economic "stage-skipping" actually be brought about in a geo-political climate of hostile nations? Can capitalism promote an international division of labor which is rational and yet not harmful to both advanced and backward economies? Can social development ever really promote the needs of the great public, or must it initially promote the needs of selective social sectors? Can the development of a "self-contained" economy, such as that possessed by the United States, forestall the occurrence of violent anti-imperialist revolution? [8]

While the language of these discussions was strongly dominated by Marxian economics, and by the going rhetoric of Russian revolutionary groupings, the questions posed, no less than the answers given, made the late Russian and early Soviet period very special in the annals of economic development. Debates on the strategies of development in old Russia were directly connected to the practice of development in the new Soviet Russia. That there may have been dogmatic interpretations of these earlier discussions was itself not unanticipated. Such is the "inevitability" of the Russian temperament that it could not help but reinforce the infallibility of Marxian political economy.

8. For a brilliant examination of the historical aspects of development theory in Russia, particularly Marxian theory, see Rosa Luxemburg, *The Accumulation of Capital*. London: Routledge & Kegan Paul, 1951, esp. pp. 271–326. Also, for a superior political history of nineteenth-century Russia, one which considers economism and populism as expressions of developmental strategies, see Franco Venturi, *Il Populismo Russo*. Turin: Einaudi Editore, 1952 (two volumes).

The Socialist Revolution of 1917 was guaranteed by the competition between Russia and Germany for European preeminence. Perhaps no one in modern times has put the issue of Soviet development better than the once-revered, then reviled and finally recognized, *Tyrannus Rex,* Joseph Stalin. Speaking to the First Conference of Russian Industrial Managers held in 1931, he put the issue bluntly:

> It is sometimes asked whether it is not possible to slow down a bit in tempo, to retard the movement. No. This is impossible. It is impossible to reduce the tempo! On the contrary, it is necessary as far as possible to accelerate it. To slacken the tempo means to fall behind. And the backward are always beaten. But we do not want to be beaten. No, we do not want this! The history of old Russia is the history of defeats due to backwardness. She was beaten by the Mongol Khans. She was beaten by the Swedish feudal barons. She was beaten by the Polish-Lithuanian squires. She was beaten by the Anglo-French capitalists. She was beaten by the Japanese barons. All beat her for her backwardness—for military backwardness, for cultural backwardness, for governmental backwardness, for industrial backwardness, for agricultural backwardness. She was beaten because to beat her was profitable and could be done with impunity. . . . That is why we must no longer be backward. . . . We are fifty to a hundred years behind the advanced countries. We must cover this distance in *ten* years. Either we do this or they will crush us.[9]

It takes little historical acumen to recollect that ten years later, in 1941, Germany crossed the Russian frontier. And it takes only a moment to remember that Russia was not crushed. The Soviets were not beaten as their ancestors had been. If the bolsheviks have long labored under the cult of development, willing to sell short, if not entirely sell out, human liberties in the bargain with industrialization, it might be remembered that the Soviets have a historically minded ideology. History offers dramatic evidence that to be industrially advanced is to be victorious in the military sphere. And current Marxist ideology has continually asserted the same doctrine.[10]

9. Joseph Stalin, "We Do Not Want To Be Beaten" (from a speech delivered before the First Conference of Russian Industrial Managers, Moscow, Feb. 1931), in *Russian Literature Since the Revolution,* edited by Joshua Kunitz. New York: Boni & Gaer, 1948, pp. 455–56.
10. See, for example, V. I. Sokolovskii, *Soviet Military Strategy,* translated and annotated by H. S. Dinerstein, Leon Gouré, and Thomas W. Wolfe. Englewood Cliffs, N.J.: Prentice-Hall, 1963.

Why has the Soviet Union, despite the enormous impetus it has given to developmental theory and ideology at the political level, nonetheless had a relatively slender role in directly affecting economic institutions of the Third World? It will be noted that there seems to be a reversal— Third World nations seem to reproduce Soviet ideology (although this is in need of great qualification), while at the same time seeking to reproduce American technology. The first and most obvious reason is that American technical achievement is far greater than Soviet technical achievement. The emergence of socialism in one country, in Russia, has bred a rigid giganticism. Customarily, size is mistaken for efficiency, design has been isolated from function. Hence, in the Soviet developmental process, functions may be modern, but form remains baroque. At a heavy price, Soviet satellite nations of a more independent persuasion have had to repudiate this strain between social function and cultural norm. And such imbalance stands as a well-understood lesson to Third World nations.

The Soviets also resolved ethical and political decisions by administrative fiat and bureaucratic enlargement. It is this very institutionalization of a command society that the Third World is subjecting to skeptical scrutiny. Such problems as the dysfunctionality of large-scale organization units, techniques of increasing productivity (which are at the same time not disguised techniques of exploitation), and political tests of bureaucratic enterprise have not been seriously faced by the Soviets, precisely because of their rigid commitment to an ideology. But all of these are now under consideration in subtle ways within the Soviet Union, and even in bolder ways in the Third World nations. The classical nineteenth-century dialogue between capitalism and socialism has yielded to searches for options to both. Economic and political experimentation is nearly as intense with classic capitalist and socialist blocs as in the Third World itself. It is therefore dangerous to assume the usual bi-polar model, since it assumes a static rather than experimental attitude on the part of the peoples of Asia, Africa, and Latin America.

Many of the obstacles which prevent the United States from serving as an effective "model of models" also serve to obstruct, mutatis mutandis, the growth of Russia as the model of models.[11] Furthermore, the Soviet Union faces two additional handicaps in its struggle for universal recognition: its own ideological commitments to national self-determina-

11. See John Strachey, *The End of Empire*. New York: Random House, 1960, pp. 292–306.

tion, which, however much violated within its own borders, have been scrupulously observed in its relations to outside nations, and the hostility of the United States, a nation superior in power to itself and one quite ready to support any nationalist movements which adopt an anticommunist posture. Thus, it may be that "post-imperial" Europe will become the great balance wheel preserving harmonious growth in the Third World. There is increasing evidence that the Third World is turning to Western Europe as a way out from making any ultimate commitment to the American or Soviet model of development.

The phrase "Third World" itself indicates that a narrow choice between inherited industrial forms is no longer possible. The "natural dyad" which Soviet ideologists have long labored under has in fact been changed into a "natural triad." The Third World is a Third Force and a Third Position, irrespective of the canons of Marxism-Leninism which say that such a situation is impossible, except as a temporary aberration.

Russian development may be considered a pivot between the First and Third Worlds of development. Russia is both European and Asian. It has looked to the West for its economic ideology and turned to the East for its political domain. Russia is both liberator and exploiter, a nation which makes revolution in the name of all humanity, and yet imposes the strictest class and party dictatorship on a nation. Russia is both technologically advanced and artistically backward; jet design aircraft must compete with decadent Edwardian interior decorations. Russia is both a land of advanced workers and of backward peasantry. It represents an imperfect fusion of urban sophistication and industrial secularization. The Soviets too often substitute giganticism for miniaturization (refined perfecting), size for quality. Such a society cannot provide a "model of models" when it is still in the process of finding its own self-image and its own clear-cut directions.

IV

American political thinking generally focuses on choices between false alternatives. On one side we are deluged with propaganda informing us that peaceful coexistence is impossible between the United States and the Soviet Union. Even if coexistence were possible, it would be better for all concerned to be "dead than red" if coexistence were to lead to a

communist take-over. There are also melodramatic "contrasts" between a "God-fearing people" and a "God-less atheistic state," between
a two-party system and a one-party system, and between "free enterprise" and "state planning." [12] As a response to these oversimplified
versions of social systems, a new super-radicalism is emerging which
starts from the abstract notion that the architect of modern evil is the
industrial system. Since both the United States and the Soviet Union are
archetypes of this industrialization process, they are said to reveal a
common condition of dehumanization of labor, deprivation of historical
conscience, and emphasis on the values of material giganticism over any
other values.[13] Beneath this Sturm und Drang romanticism lies a nostalgic faith in the past. And this longing for paradise lost had led to drown-
ing concrete historicity, of specific differences between capitalism and
socialism, democracy and authoritarianism, development and stagnation,
poverty and wealth, market anarchy and social planning.

What the nations of the Third World are continually searching for
are specific ways in which some sort of "mixture" between the two giant
social structures can be brought about without destroying either the
vitality or integrity of their national development as such. Perhaps the
Third World cannot escape the problems of political eclecticism but it
has made a powerful and largely successful effort to define itself over
and against both the First and Second Worlds.[14] This it has been able
to do only by clearly separating the various reasons for the success offered by the United States and the Soviet Union—particularly those
reasons based on technological innovation from those based on rejecting
past colonial status.[15]

The Third World is characterized by the following set of conditions:
First, it tends to be politically independent of both power centers, the

---

12. Wladyslaw W. Kulski, *Peaceful Coexistence: An Analysis of Soviet Foreign
Policy*. Chicago: Henry Regnery Co., 1959. This is a good illustration of traditional Cold War scholarship based on the premise that the conflict between
East and West is basic and structural.
13. Herbert Marcuse, *One Dimensional Man*. Boston: Beacon Press, 1964. This
is a good example of the new-style romantic critique of industrialism.
14. See, for example, *United Nations Conference on Trade and Development
(Final Act)*. E/Conf. 46/L.28, 64–15050. 16 June 1964. Mimeograph.
15. This fact seems to be recognized more widely in the Soviet Union than in
the United States. The latter still insists on interpreting unfavorable events as
proof of the "immaturity" of the Third World, whereas Soviet theorists increasingly speak of "stages of maturation." See Thomas Perry Thornton (ed.), *The
Third World in Soviet Perspective*. Princeton: Princeton University Press, 1964.

United States-NATO complex and the Soviet Warsaw-Pact group. Second, the bulk of the Third World was in a colonial condition until World War II. Third, it draws its technology from the First World while drawing its ideology from the Second World. Thus, the Third World is non-American, ex-colonial, and thoroughly dedicated to becoming industrialized, whatever the economic costs.

The Third World is a self-defined and self-conscious association of nation-states. Definitions of the Third World position have been made at the Bandung Conference of Colored Peoples in 1955; the Belgrade Conference of Non-Aligned Powers in 1961; the Congress of African States in Addis Ababa in 1963; the Second Conference of Non-Aligned Nations held in 1964 at Cairo; and the Tri-Continental Conference at Havana in 1966. The leading nations involved in formulating the politics and ideologies of the Third World at this point are India, Ceylon, the United Arab Republic, Yugoslavia, Indonesia, Cuba, and Ghana. This informal web of association extends to every continent, with a nucleus of membership in Africa, Asia, and Latin America. Marginal membership must be accorded such nations as Canada (a new arrival on the scene of Third World politics), China (which prefers to consider itself "aligned" but "independent"), and Algeria (which although only recently independent is already a powerful voice in the formulation of policies for the Third World).

The rise and maturation of the Third World points up the instability and schismatic propensities of the coalition of nations. These "underdeveloped" nations have traditionally been the playground for wider international rifts. The Third World sometimes mirrors the ideological disputes between the Soviet Union and China on strategic matters concerning "peace offensives" or "revolutionary actions." At the same time, difficulties in offering an exact definition of the Third World become apparent. In terms of economic and organizational problems, for example, China ranks as a prime member of the Third World. Yet, in terms of its own explicit rejection of the concept of non-alignment, and its own interest in carrying nationalist revolutions to socialist revolutions, China must be considered as outside the Third World on political and ideological grounds.

Without wishing to minimize the grave importance of the Chinese socialist revolution, it is less important to determine where China "fits" than to consider the nations that define themselves as a part of the Third World. From this point of view, all nations not organically linked with the North Atlantic Treaty Organization or the Warsaw Pact are increasingly defining themselves as part of the Third World. The polarization of the world into a military stalelmate has made possible the redefinition of aims and functions of smaller powers within the NATO and Warsaw Pact Alliances. In the Soviet bloc, strong signs of independence are evident in Poland and Rumania. In the Western bloc the fissures are slower to appear because the control apparatus was weaker to begin with. Nonetheless, they can be found in the new attitudes of France and in the independent policies of the Scandinavian countries. Not only are former colonies caught in the crossfire of this organizational dissonance, but even some of the non-imperialist centers of Europe.

Within the bowels of capitalist Europe, Sweden anticipated the rise of a mixed economy. The Third Way of Sweden bears more than a superficial resemblance to the Third World of India. The *Force de frappe* of post-Gaullist France, however different in ambitions and traditions from the independent deterrent approach of a Maoist China, has a sympathetic relationship to the corresponding search for political and military independence in the "inscrutable East." The Third World, is, however amorphous and unwieldy, an expanding entity.

Before going into the special features of the Third World, we ought to point out that there is a Fourth World of undevelopment. That is to say, a world of tribal societies which for one or another reason are unconscious of alternatives to their own ways of life. The undeveloped society has no consciousness of being undeveloped. The Third World nations have a concept of emergence and characterize themselves as being developed socially and culturally, and of being *under*developed economically and technically. This gulf between *un*development and *under*development is thus central in relation to the definition of the Third World. We are dealing with mature peoples and backward economies.

Any definition of the Third World must account for the powerful psychological force of invidious comparison. To the degree to which a knowledge of differences in earnings and opportunities exists, to that degree there will be a competition in ideologies and orientations. The earning power of each citizen of the United States, measured by the gross national produce per capita, is ten times or more that of our "good neighbors" to the south in Brazil, Chile, Colombia, Mexico, Bolivia, and other nations in the hemisphere—outside of Argentina, Venezuela, Cuba, and Uruguay—and at least four times higher than these "exceptional" high income nations. This is in itself a brute fact making for "thirdness." [16]

This conscious awareness of difference is at its core an appreciation of invidious distinctions, what has euphemistically come to be called asynchronous forms of development. Ironically enough, this sense of difference is provoked by the competition of the First and Second Worlds. Through the inundation of propaganda in the form of films, books, periodicals, peoples of emergent nations are wooed for their political affections, and in this process they are made acutely aware of the riches of consumer affluence in the United States and the industrial-military complex built up over the past fifty years in the Soviet Union. The impulse for development is partly stimulated by these extrinsic features. It may be reinforced by women's magazines no less than political organs, by Hollywood films no less than by Soviet documentaries. However coated this passion for emulation is with slogans about folk identity and national culture, the economic and sociological demands for better living conditions and better credit terms are dictated by standards derived from the cosmopolitan centers. The consciousness of impoverishment stimulates an aura of frenzied immediacy to the process of social change. To catch up with "fully developed" societies becomes a definition of national purpose. To introduce doubt as to the value of this contest becomes a form of intolerable subversion. This is one primary reason why pluralistic and parliamentary politics have become increasingly scant in Third World nations. Controversy has itself come to be viewed as a luxury which only advanced nations can afford.

What are the character and scope of these asynchronous aspects in the developmental contest?

The developed regions grow rapidly because they are industrialized and sell finished commodities. The underdeveloped regions grow slowly because they are agriculturalized and sell primary products. The developed regions often determine conditions of production and also the price of primary goods.

The developed regions, in order to maintain their own privileged position, induce protective high-level tariffs, price-support programs,

16. See Gabriel A. Almond and James S. Coleman (eds.), *The Politics of the Developing Areas*. Princeton: Princeton University Press, 1960, pp. 455–63. See also George I. Blanksten, "The Aspiration for Economic Development," *The Annals of the American Academy of Political and Social Science*, 334 (Mar. 1961), pp. 10–19.

customs duties, etc., all of which create a sluggishness for the goods produced in the Third World. The underdeveloped world, for its part, cannot specify its own tariff arrangements without violating the terms of trade and financial loans.

The developed regions exhibit a relative evenness in their demographic patterns, production norms, and planning systems, which make scientific prediction of economic behavior possible. The underdeveloped nations exhibit extreme unevenness in these sociological factors of the economy and hence are disadvantaged in bargaining and negotiating.

These various abrasive features in the world system of invidious comparison are no longer in dispute. What remains open to question is what to do about them. Do these features represent "conflicts" or "contradictions"—items which can be removed without too much difficulty and without too much loss for either the developed or underdeveloped nations by mending, or only by revolution, by smashing? The selection between such alternatives rests on an article of faith, or rather, on contrasting strategies for stimulating social change. For some, contrasts between underdeveloped and fully developed nations can be removed through a concerted effort; that is to say, both "sides" can show long-range net gains by development. Former colonial powers make excellent contacts. The post-colonial status of England is often brought to bear in support of this argument. On the other side, there are those who insist that development and underdevelopment are defined in terms of each other; that underdeveloped nations can "emerge" only by the removal of imperialist economic relations and not simply colonial military occupations. They argue that former colonies make excellent economic partners instead of expensive status hobbies.

The Third World is often declared to be transitional: in a condition of movement from traditional to modern society by Western commentators, and in a condition of movement from capitalist to socialist society by communist authorities. Now while there is certainly a sense in which the precise form of Third World countries remains undefined, it is a mistake to adopt a teleological point of view which assumes a predetermined series of systemic outcomes. It is more important to realize the relative stability of socioeconomic forms in the Third World. Despite enormous pressures they remain relatively impervious to any tight fit with either First or Second World models of development.

The fact that the First and Second Worlds are always in competition within a relative balance of power makes possible the exercise of Third

World strategies in determining the role of foreign capital and aid, and not being determined by such capital.[17] To be a member of the Third World, in short, is not to make a choice in favor of one political bloc or another. As a matter of fact, it is to be very conscious and deliberate about not making this decision.

As might be expected, within the Third World there is a wide range of choices of economic methods. Thus it contains some very strange mixtures.

India and Brazil have more than 75 per cent of their productive industries in the capitalist sector, while Algeria and Egypt are more than 75 per cent nationalized. Yet all four nations belong to the emergent bloc. In other words, to be considered part of the Third World it is not necessary to limit the character of the national economic system. The political posture in relation to the main power blocs is thus central to defining conditions of "membership" in the Third World.

In addition to economic factors, there are politically compelling reasons why the Third World is likely to be expanded further. Nations such as Canada and Mexico in the Western Hemisphere are developing policies sharply independent of the United States. Similarly, Yugoslavia, Poland, and Rumania, which between 1945 and 1960 were designated, perhaps not improperly, as satellites of the Soviet Union, are now largely performing a role inside a Third World orbit and ideology. Nations which in the recent past were satellitic and even parasitic are now increasingly linking ideological arms inside an "integral" protective cover of Third World slogans. Paradoxically, at the very moment when the Third World is experiencing great difficulties in defining the scope and character of its economic mix, its political influence is becoming more sharply delineated. The political contraction of American and Soviet spheres of influence has proceeded so evenly that, although an equilibrium based upon a "delicate balance of terror" is maintained, a great deal is happening in the no man's land between the First and the Second Worlds. This is the widest possible definition of the Third World, but in the absence of clear political-economic guidelines it may turn out to be a definition which is operationally meaningful.

Many Third World nations have achieved their sovereignty in the present century, especially since World War II. The Latin American states are exceptions in that they had at least their formal sovereignty

17. See Albert O. Hirschman, *The Strategy of Economic Development.* New Haven: Yale University Press, 1958, pp. 202–8.

for a longer period of time. They represent old states, and not simply new states evolved out of old nations. This formal sovereignty is primarily political and not economic. Thus the initial phase of entering the Third World bloc is the establishment of national state sovereignty. The membership of the United Nations reflects this process. It has more than doubled its member states in its twenty-five years of existence. This tendency does not foreshadow the breakup of the nation-state for the sake of international government, but rather the development of the nation-state as a prelude to, and the organizing force in, the economic development process.

An essential factor about the international status of Third World nations is that they hold no dependencies. The First World drew political prestige and economic wealth from its colonial holdings. The Second World did likewise with its satellites. But the Third World cannot develop in terms of colonial holdings, since as ex-colonial nations they have neither such possessions nor do they have the possibility of developing colonial ambitions. The development of the Third World nation-state is not tied to foreign colonial expansionism, although it can stimulate what is called "internal colonialism." Third World nations do not compete for membership in the major power blocs. They generally form restricted regional organizations, such as the organization of Arab states, the organization of Pan-African unions, or the Latin American union. The policy of non-alignment militates against entry into such organizations as NATO or SEATO or the Warsaw Pact. Therefore treaty membership for Third World nations is considered undesirable and is avoided wherever possible.

In primary exchange economies, where raw materials are exported and finished commodities are imported, the gap between the Third World and the First and Second Worlds is widening, not narrowing. Therefore polarization between the Third World and the First and Second Worlds becomes increasingly keen. Preferential rates and prices between highly developed nations are established; and preferential prices for finished commodities over raw materials are set. As a consequence there is extreme unevenness in economic growth.[18]

Few Third World nations have fully mobilized their industrial po-

18. See Raúl Prebisch, *Nueva Política Comercial para el Desarrollo*. Mexico and Buenos Aires: Fondo de Cultura Económica, 1964; and more recently, *Development Problems in Latin America: An Analysis by the United Nations Economic Commission for Latin America*. Austin and London: The University of Texas Press, 1970, esp. pp. 32–60.

tential. As a general rule, when there is such a mobilization, it is of a sectoral nature, usually benefiting elite groups within the Third World nation-state, and it differs widely according to class interest. Thus the gap between classes keeps the level of development low and uneven. Judged by real income per person, 90 per cent of the Third World peoples earn less than one-tenth of the United States dollar level; while another 9 per cent earn less than one-fifth of the United States dollar level. Not more than 1 per cent of the world's population has comparable earning power. This lag increases as the gap between falling prices for agricultural products and finished commodities widens. Every major indicator reveals the same disparity. The United States, with 6 per cent of the world population, has or produces 25 per cent of the steel, 60 per cent of the automobiles, 40 per cent of the trucks, 33 per cent of the surfaced roads, 33 per cent of the electricity, 25 per cent of the railroad freight, and 50 per cent of the civil aviation mileage. The relationship between population distribution and gross national product is equally instructive. The First and Second Worlds combine to account for 80 per cent of the GNP, although they comprise roughly 28 per cent of the total population. The United States alone, with but 6 per cent of the world's population, accounts for 32 per cent of the GNP.[19] This sampling of data casts grave doubt that any "middle sector" will be the savior of the Third World, or save it from social revolution.

Often "uneven development" is considered erroneously as the antithesis of even development—or, as it is more conventionally called, "balanced growth." But this theory of equilibrium as the ideal condition for development, while perhaps of some value for Western European models, is inappropriate for Third World nations—where there is nearly a complete *inelasticity* of demand due to low income levels. What is really at stake is not balanced growth versus uneven development but the more modest and serious task of less uneven growth than what presently obtains. For example, in a nation such as Venezuela, petroleum accounts for approximately 90 per cent of the exports but employs only 2 per cent of the labor force. The bulk of Venezuelans continue to work in the unproductive agricultural sphere. And given the minimal number of skilled workers needed to produce high amounts of goods this condition of sectoral imbalance is likely to continue. The settlement is never going to be in terms of parity—90 per cent of the labor force in petro-

19. John McHale (ed.), *World Facts and Trends*. Binghamton, N.Y.: Center for Integrative Studies, State University of New York, 1970.

leum production—but an expansion of the domestic economy can serve to offset the degree of imbalance.

Unevenness of development is not a metaphysical curse. It reveals concrete components: money income and outlays above what is warranted by the capacity to produce for the purpose of satisfying consumer demands; imitation of patterns of industrial waste; high tariff restrictions for the purpose of taxing the foreign trade sector in place of a system of graded taxation; disinvestment in the domestic economy for the purpose of paying off purchases in foreign markets; low amounts received for raw materials and high costs for finished goods, etc. And while every economy in some profound sense is "uneven," the difference between developed and underdeveloped societies is the extent of imbalance.[20]

Any sound theory of social change must indicate what development excludes; that is, how it distinguishes itself from such cognate concepts as industrialization, externally induced transformation, growth of population and of the economy.

First, development differs from industrialization in that the latter implies a series of technological, mechanical, and engineering innovations in forms of social production. Social development for its part implies transformation in human relations, in the economic and political status in which men relate to each other, irrespective of the level of industrialization. Industrialization does produce stress and strain in human relationships which in turn has a large-scale effect on the over-all process of social development. But to identify industrialization with development is to run the grave risk of offering prescriptions for economic growth independent of social requisites.

Second, development differs from change in that the latter implies a continual adaptation through small steps and stages to an existent social condition. Development implies a genuine break with tradition—perceptible disruptions of the "static" equilibrium. Social development requires a new set of conceptual tools to explain "reality" whereas social change may leave intact old conceptual tools adapted to modified situations. Indeed, precisely what is modifiable is subject to change; while that which no longer contains the possibility of elasticity and plasticity is subject to development. That is why the notion of revolution is at least as important to development as the notion of evolution.

20. On this topic, see Ragnar Nurske, "Some International Aspects of the Problem of Economic Development," *American Economic Association Papers and Proceedings,* Vol. 42 (May 1952), pp. 571–83.

Third, development differs from externally induced transformation in that the latter implies a prime mover which is external to the developmental process. Thus, Caesarism, Stalinism, or simple old-fashioned imperialism may perform important functions with respect to the economic transformation of subject nations, but this is done for the prime, if not the exclusive, benefit of the mother country. Thus the building of a network of roads, communications systems, or the like is designed to expedite the shipment of raw materials to the home country. Similarly, the relationship of the urban complex to the rural regions may undergo transformations for the benefit of the city needs, of the needs of "internal colonialism," or of dominant minorities. Here too one cannot speak of development, despite the obvious stimulus such colonial contributions do make to long-run social development.[21]

Fourth, development differs from growth in population or national wealth since, like the simple process of quantitative change, these do not call forth any new process but are simply processes of adaptation. Furthermore, it should be noted that growth in "natural events" of a society may actually sap development—thus the rapid rise in population may in fact serve to lower the total financial reserves of a nation. In short, some types of growth may be dysfunctional with respect to the needs of a developing society.

Development implies a new technology which makes available consumer goods. New methods of production radically alter the position of labor with respect to management. New markets radically alter the position of old strata since they now must reckon with a new "technocratic" stratum in addition to their traditional rivals. It is precisely this revolutionary side of the developmental process that has come to characterize the Third World.[22]

In the main, the Third World is a low industrial, goods-producing area

21. On this matter of internal colonialism, see the following two brilliant studies: Pablo González Casanova, "Internal Colonialism and National Development," *Studies in Comparative International Development*, Vol. I, No. 4 (1965), pp. 27–37; and Rodolfo Stavenhagen, "Classes, Colonialism and Acculturation," *Studies in Comparative International Development*, Vol. I, No. 6 (1965), pp. 53–77.

22. For a serious theoretical appreciation of the developmental process, at the economic level at least, see Joseph A. Schumpeter, *The Theory of Economic Development*. Cambridge, Mass.: Harvard University Press, 1934. He was the first social scientist to develop a typology of development which distinguished development from change and from externally induced transformations. For criticisms of the developmental economists, see Chap. 12.

no less than a high commodity-cost area.[23] This affects the quality as well as the amount of foreign aid that they receive from the First and Second Worlds. Disregarding the question of whether this aid is harmful or beneficial, with or without strings, the fact is that the Third World *receives* economic assistance, some kinds of funds, while the First and Second Worlds represent funding agencies for it. Thus national independence does not in itself guarantee an end to foreign domination. This distinction between nations receiving aid and nations rendering aid is central to a definition of Third World economic sovereignty.

The Third World supplies world markets with primary commodities, primary agricultural supplies, nonferrous base metals, etc. The first and Second Worlds basically export primary commodities rather than manufactured goods. The Soviet Union has been more sensitive to the international imbalance between raw materials and finished products than has the United States. With the exception when wartime or famine conditions occur, export of primary commodities is never as financially lucrative as export of manufactured goods. While it is true that without these primary commodities there can be no manufacture of goods, still the source of primary supplies is wider than imagined. Therefore, the First World has tended to maintain the imbalance between the fully advanced and the underdeveloped nations. Contrary to the rhetoric of foreign aid, the extent of First and Second World assistance to Third World development is less a question of direct fiscal support than of prices paid for raw materials, costs of importing goods, and control of international trade and money markets.

The First and Second Worlds generally set market prices. For instance, the Soviet Union can set the price on wool; the United States, along with its Western European cotton manufacturers, can set the price on cotton. This ability to set the price is a characteristic of monopolies in general, and this ability to monopolize prices is a characteristic of the First World. Monopolization is therefore a form for preventing price and wage fluctuation in the metropolitan areas. At the same time, through controlling the flow of vital parts, this way prevents mass expropriation in the backward areas. Underdeveloped regions in the Third World suffer heavy price fluctuations and accentuated inflationary spirals, because they

23. The neglect of this correlation between low industrialization and high commodity costs in the Prebisch thesis has been called attention to by Ramón Ramirez Gómez. "ECLA, Prebisch, and the Problem of Latin America," *Studies in Comparative International Development,* Vol. II, No. 8, pp. 121–34.

cannot control world markets, set or regulate prices, or expropriate property or resources when this is nationally desirable or feasible.

V

In the Third World the *formal* political systems are nearly always and everywhere republican in character, while their *real* systems are nearly always authoritarian. They are neither monarchies nor total dictatorships. They are under the "rule of law"—that is, they have constitutions—but this lawfulness is deposited in the hands of the dynamic leader of the single party. They have a higher political directorate, often held in check only by even more conservative military elites. There is neither a developed parliamentary system nor the kind of relatively stable multi-party groupings found in Western Europe and the United States. Where parliamentary systems have been allowed to expand, they have been a conservative force which has served to fragment the political power of progressive social groups. Parliamentary rule is often present in older sectors of the Third World which already have achieved formal independence, as in Latin America. Here, for instance, the rural working masses have been systematically excluded from effective participation, either directly through disenfranchisement, or indirectly through electoral frauds of various sorts. In such circumstances the legislative branch becomes the legal front for property ownership. In Africa, nations have avoided this situation by abandoning the multi-party system.[24] Thus, in Syria, Algeria, Tunisia, Kenya, Egypt, and Guinea, there has been the gradual erosion of parliamentary norms in the name of mass participation. The Parliament has become an upper-class forum, while the President has become the hope of the masses. This struggle is simply another way of describing the differences between formal and real political systems in emerging nations.

Given the great importance of leadership, the revolutionary system is often identified in the minds of the mass with a particular party. Hence, the Congress Party, however amorphous its organization may be, retains a virtual monopoly of the political apparatus in India. The same is true

24. See Gwendolen M. Carter (ed.), *African One-Party States.* Ithaca, N.Y.: Cornell University Press, 1962. For a particular application of the one-party and one-nation approach, see Sékou Touré, "African Democracy and the Western Parliamentary System," in *African Politics and Society,* edited by Irving Leonard Markovitz. New York: The Free Press, 1970, pp. 218–25.

of the P.R.I. in Mexico. Thus, even in nations which are traditionally identified with Western values of democracy and libertarianism, parliamentary norms are more formal than real. To achieve even a minimum rate of growth, to enter the "take-off" period, Third World nations have had to recognize the need for central planning. And such high level planning is itself mainly a political act, necessarily under the aegis of the state system. The politics of this system, while often "benevolent" in character, cannot be said to be particularly concerned with the observance of parliamentary norms.

A parliament is a forum of conflicting and contrasting interests and opinions. As such, its ability to serve the "whole people" is subject to ridicule and, ultimately, to disrepute. In the cases of the Congo and Pakistan, parliamentary rifts prevented the normal functioning of society. And only with the passing of such nominally democratic forums was social order restored.

Parliamentary development can be afforded as a splendid luxury when time and history allow. This was the case for the United States in the nineteenth century. Whether there is a margin for parliamentary developments in the Third World depends on the role that parliaments perform in these nations. The case histories presently available are hardly encouraging. In Latin America they have tended to preserve the status quo and to retard the development of central planning.[25] It is hard to imagine the new African states following such a model. Therefore, there is within the Third World a development of radical political orientations without many basic constitutional safeguards. This absence of legitimacy is one reason why Western social democratic ideology has found it extremely difficult to champion the Third World cause.[26]

The authoritarian nature of the Third World has resulted from the rapid growth and consolidation of the one-party state. Yet, this rarely spills over into totalitarianism, into the control of the total social system. Technological advance and bureaucratic efficiency have not advanced to the point where this is possible. A verbal commitment to democratic values is retained. The democratic society remains a goal to be attained,

25. On this, see Irving Louis Horowitz, *Revolution in Brazil: Politics and Society in a Developing Nation.* New York: E. P. Dutton & Co., 1964, pp. 279–304; and for a more panoramic introduction, R. A. Gómez, *Government and Politics in Latin America* (revised edition). New York: Random House, 1963.
26. For a sound introduction to this subject, see Richard Harris, *Independence and After: Revolution in Underdeveloped Countries.* London: Oxford University Press, 1962.

while authoritarian solutions are considered temporary necessities. However, its governmental machinery is feared for its total control and the effect on the social system. Yet, almost every Third World nation has a written constitution and a formal legislative body. Oftentimes, these documents are tailored after those extant in the advanced Western democracies. But generally these documents serve to legitimize bodies which act as rubber stamps. Actual political structures bear a much closer resemblance to the Second World of the Soviet orbit than to the First World.

The Third World is subject to a unique set of political circumstances. Nearly every industrial, highly developed society has emerged in the wake of political, economic, or religious conflicts that have reached the point of open armed hostilities, and that have been resolved by the play of internal forces with a minimum of external intervention or interference. This is illustrated by the revolution of 1640–88 in England, the American Revolution of 1775–81, the French Revolution of 1789, the revolutions of 1905 and 1917 in Russia, and even the revolution of 1948–49 in China. At present, however, the costs of development under circumstances of international conflict have become prohibitive. Development must now, more than ever, be a response to both international and national pressures. Every one of these past revolutionary events resulted in part from the pressures exerted by a newly created working mass for participation in the political process. As much as anything else, these revolutions democratized politics by bringing about the participation of a vast, previously excluded public. These politically inspired revolutions were designed to transform the human species from masses into classes.

Third World nations, as presently constituted, have attempted to develop military alternatives to the First and Second Worlds—not just political options to military power, but genuine large-scale military force.[27] The most powerful Third World nations are nations that had popular revolutions, which means revolutions which have either crushed or eliminated the old elites rather than just reshuffling power among them. It is no accident that such nations as Algeria, Cuba, India, and Yugoslavia are leaders of the Third World; they represent the nations

27. On this, see Morris Janowitz, *The Military in the Political Development of New Nations.* Chicago: University of Chicago Press, 1964; and for corroborative data, *World Military Expenditures, 1969.* Washington, D.C.: United States Arms Control and Disarmament Agency, 1970.

which have had this fully developed "revolution from below." For this reason Mexico can probably be considered a more fully developed member of the Third World than Venezuela, because in the 1910–20 Mexican Revolution the old military caste was crushed. The old military caste was tied up with the feudal aristocracy and the landed nobility. The new military was at the outset a popular peasant militia.

In the Third World, where revolutions have been successful, the traditional military has either been crushed or fully absorbed into revolutionary actions. There has not always been an armed struggle between military groupings. Nevertheless, the national liberation front has been the major stimulus to successful popular reform and revolutionary movements in the Third World nations. In large measure the development of these nations is connected to the outcomes of these internal military conflicts.[28]

Third World nations also cannot really operate when they have foreign military bases on their soil. Dependent colonial states have in general granted extraterritorial rights to imperialist or colonialist powers. When a nation has a foreign military base, it is almost axiomatic that it is not fully accepted into the Third World. Therefore, one would have to say that East Germany is not a member of the Third World any more than South Vietnam is, for both these nations, irrespective of their radically different levels of development, are clear illustrations of regimes buttressed by the presence of foreign military bases, a presence which makes development as an act of sovereign states exceedingly difficult.

Ethnic and/or religious differences are exceedingly important in the Third World. With the exception of Latin America, religions of the Third World are neither Roman Catholic, Protestant, Jewish, or Greek Orthodox. They are, basically, Moslem, Shinto, Taoist, Confucian, Buddhist, Hindu, primitive. Even Latin American Catholicism has special dimensions, often infused, as in Haiti and Brazil, with non-Christian sources of religious practice and ritual. Religious culture remains an element part, as a cohesive factor for maintaining tradition in the Third World. The religious expression of the value of leisure over work, the sharp distinction between the sacred and the profane, and the separation between castes reinforces the fatalism often linked to ideas opposing development.

The Third World is an area where there are few competing religious

28. See J. K. Zawodny (ed.), "Unconventional Warfare," *The Annals of the American Academy of Political and Social Science,* Vol. 341, 1962.

institutions, since nationalism and patriotic fervor supersede linguistic and religious preferences. Whether Christian, Moslem, Hindu, or Hebrew, a national church often accompanies the national state. Where different religions coexist, there is usually strong conflict. The India-Pakistan partition was made inevitable by religious differences; and the Buddhist-Catholic rift in Vietnam is long-standing and severe. Many of the non-Christian religious organizations do not have established church hierarchies separate from the state bureaucracy. This is particularly true in the Middle East; it was true of prewar Japan and China. Also, since leadership in the Third World is tied to ethnic values rather than to religious values as such, the "secularization" process appears more accentuated than it is in fact. The parochial nature of religions in the Third World tends to force the individual to choose between religious belief and non-belief, rather than between competing religions. Socialist-secularist ideologies, rather than Western-Christian religions, compete with the established religions in Asia and Africa. And in a slightly modified sense, the same is true of Latin America—where socialism is more tolerated than Seventh Day Adventism.[29]

A large majority of people in the Third World had little, if any, primary or secondary school training prior to their political independence. It is almost axiomatic that once the Third World nation passes through its first ordeal of development, the main push is toward cultivation of its people; at least the technical and primary training that a population needs in order to enter any socially developed world.[30] There is a modifying factor to be considered. Prior to the achievement of national independence, there is a heavy premium on ideological leadership. The post-colonial ruling class tends to be recruited from the political elite. In the second stage, once sovereignty and a level of primary education are also achieved, concern for technical proficiency promotes the demand for higher education for all, a new bureaucratic ideology replaces the conventional ideology of revolutionism. This took place in Russia. The first stage was experimentation and freedom followed by an emphasis

29. It should be noted however, that the use of religion for promoting drastic changes has reached sizeable proportions in Latin America. On this, see Emilio Willems, "Religious Mass Movements and Social Change in Brazil," in *New Perspectives of Brazil*, edited by Eric N. Baklanoff. Nashville: Vanderbilt University Press, 1966, pp. 205–32.

30. On this, see Frederick Harbison and Charles A. Myers, *Education, Manpower, and Economic Growth: Strategies of Human Resource Development*. New York: McGraw-Hill, 1964, esp. pp. 49–130; also Adam Curle, *Educational Strategy for Developing Societies*. London: Tavistock Publications, 1963.

on heavy industrial growth, which in turn slowly adapted revolutionary Marxism to technical needs rather than developed a technological ideology as such. This same path seems to be pursued in such far-away places as Romania, Tanzania, and Cuba, where increasingly the political leadership is recruited from technical engineering-trained personnel.

This changeover from a militant ideological point of view to a technological point of view is accompanied by large-scale cultural reorientations. Hence, in all Third World nations, one finds a continuing struggle between political traditions and growing technical predilections between traditional values and scientific innovation. Each newly formed nation is working out the conflict between these "two cultures" that Charles P. Snow has described,[31] and Theodore Roszak has tried to resolve.[32] As a general rule, the conventional revolutionary ideology lasts longer at the cultural level than at the economic level. Since Marxism, socialism, and the variants thereof represent a pre-tested way of life, an effort is made to rationalize technical change within the conventional ideology, rather than to risk raising questions about the ideology. Hence, there is considerable disparity and lag between mass sentiments favoring the conventional ideology and technological demands for economic innovation. This in itself can be an important factor in the emergence of nations, as has been plain in the cultural debates which have taken place in Cuba, almost without letup, since the Castro Revolution of 1959. Nonetheless, if the problem of two cultures is not quite resolved by the evolution of the Third World, thus far it has become a meaningful base for the re-examination of scientific and cultural integration.

"Natural" geographic and demographic factors also directly affect the structure of the Third World. Many Third World areas have unfavorable climate and/or soil resources. Extreme heat, bacteriological infiltration of the soil, heavy rainy seasons, and the like, seriously impede sustained and rapid growth. There is no question that technological advancements such as air-conditioning and artificial irrigation can compensate for these natural deficits, but it would be a mistake to deny the grave effects of geographical and ecological impediments in Third World areas.[33] Indeed, such a natural phenomenon as water supply has played an immense part

31. C. P. Snow, *The Two Cultures and the Scientific Revolution.* Cambridge: Cambridge University Press, 1963.
32. Theodore Roszak, *The Making of a Counter-Culture.* Garden City, N.Y.: Doubleday & Co., 1969.
33. See Wladimir S. Woytinsky and Emma S. Woytinsky, *World Population and Production.* New York: Twentieth Century Fund, 1963.

in the political and economic development of China, determining the character of political control no less than who rules at any given time.[34]

Complicating the tasks of development still further are the demographic imbalances that exist in the Third World. There is today a definite trend toward overpopulation in Asia, Africa, and, more recently, in Latin America. It is a vicious circle, in effect: an agricultural economy can sustain large populations, and large extended families are a requirement for the maintenance of an agricultural economy. The facts and figures on life-expectancy rates, infant mortality, and per capita daily intake of calories are too well known to require elaboration. Yet, the demographic factor is complicated by the fact that medical and scientific innovation extends the life span, and in turn places a higher value on life. At the same time that mortality rates are steadily declining, there is no corresponding increase in family planning.[35] Dobzhansky has even claimed that the resources of the earth are insufficient to give the present world population the living standard now existing in the United States.[36]

The problems created by the transition from rural to urban life styles leave no aspect of social life untouched. They affect everything from food tastes to cultural preferences. The impact of urban form—the first contact with foreigners and foreign ways—has profoundly shaped the attitudes of social classes in the Third World. People feel as strongly about mass leisure or political participation in Jakarta and Buenos Aires as they do in London or New York.[37] The transitional process is of a special nature. Third World nations generally have a single metropolitan center, without either middle-sized cities or competing metropolitan centers within their boundaries. Thus they represent highly developed city-states, with a backward countryside surrounding them. This promotes a great unbalance in migration patterns. Class and cultural dissonance produce inevitable transition problems for migrants who move to the city.[38]

34. See Karl Wittfogel, *Oriental Despotism: A Comparative Study of Total Power*. New Haven: Yale University Press, 1956.
35. See Ralph Thomlinson, *Population Dynamics: Causes and Consequences of World Demographic Change*. New York: Random House, 1965. Such problems are not unlike those faced by the poor in the developed nations. See, for example, Lee Rainwater, *And the Poor Get Children: Sex, Contraception and Family Planning in the Working Class*. Chicago: Quadrangle Books, 1960.
36. Theodosius Dobzhansky, address before the United States Conference for the World Council of Churches, 1970 (mimeograph).
37. See Philip M. Hauser, *Population Perspectives*. New Brunswick, N.J.: Rutgers University Press, 1960.
38. See Rodolfo Stavenhagen, "Classes, Colonialism and Acculturation," *Studies*

In addition, the large urban centers of the Third World are parasites rather than promoters of development. They tend to exploit, through the domestic bourgeoisie, the labor and produce of the countryside. And in turn, this parasitism is extended to the international sphere. The cities are not favorably located with respect to further industrialization of the nation but develop in relation to their position as import-export centers. Latin America is a particularly good example of this gap between urban and rural frameworks.[39]

It is obvious that the broad outlines of the Third World are easier to define than the precise contours. Thus, if we select "non-alignment" with either the United States or the Soviet Union as the chief criteria, such nations as France and China might well fall within the Third World. However, if we select the structure of the social system as central, then France is clearly aligned with the Eastern bloc.

If we try to simplify the definitional problem by asking the "showdown" question—that is, where would the Chinese communist regime or a bureaucratic France stand in the event of military hostilities between the United States and the Soviet Union?—a clearer focus is possible. From a showdown perspective, it is evident that France is as much a part of the First World as China is of the Second World. The likelihood of a shift at this level in any near future is quite slim. The tensions in the United States and Soviet orbits alike are a consequence of the spread of thermonuclear power, of a general military affluence that has taken place. Thus, France may be considered not so much outside the American power bloc as attempting to set up a countervailing leadership in that bloc. Similarly, ideologically, institutionally, and politically, China remains dedicated to the ideals and principles of communism, and hence can scarcely afford to allow its criticism of Soviet *policies* to spill over into a general critique of the communist system.

Nonetheless, the selection of other sets of variables would clearly make China in particular a leader no less than a member of the Third World. China has so many topographic, economic, and sociological fea-

in *Comparative International Development,* Vol. I, No. 6 (1965), pp. 53–77; and for a theoretical exposition of the effects of the urban and industrial processes, see Herbert Blumer, "Early Industrialization and the Laboring Class," *The Sociological Quarterly,* Vol. I, No. 1, Jan. 1960, pp. 5–14.

39. Irving Louis Horowitz, "Electoral Politics, Urbanization, and Social Development in Latin America," in *The Urban Explosion in Latin America: A Continent in Process of Modernization,* edited by Glenn H. Beyer. Ithaca: Cornell University Press, 1967, pp. 215–73.

tures in common with the Third World that it must be said that the Chinese communist regime seems just as concerned with achieving a directorate in the Third World as it has been in developing a leadership role within the international communist movement. France for its part is not simply attempting to redefine the relationship between itself and the United States within the First World, but is also attempting to man the bastions of a fourth position—an orientation which sees a "United Europe" as equal in capacity and strength to a "United States." The dilemmas in the Chinese position are greater. China is committed to a socialist economic system built on standardized Marxist-Leninist positions (indeed, China's ideology is more dogmatic than that of any nation in the Soviet orbit), and thus its leadership pretensions are circumscribed by its ideological commitments.

In this discussion of three worlds in development, little emphasis has been given to the "re-emergence of Europe" in the past decade. Indeed, there is a new literature speaking of the "fall and rise of Europe," [40] and various theorists turned enthusiasts now speak of the "New Europe." [41] Perhaps it is a personal bias, grounded in little else than idiosyncrasy, but it seems that Europe, even while engaging in spectacular changes in social relations and scientific inventions, gives the appearance, as one writer put it, of an "antique shop" and a "well-protected aquarium." [42] The continued emigration from Europe, its traditional, unimaginative politics (of both Left and Right), the way that the European culture has become a response to events in either the United States or in the Soviet Union, the relative stagnation of the economies of England, Italy, and France—all these factors weaken the leadership potential of Europe. This is not to deny the new and vigorous role of Europe in East-West relations. But in a paradigm built upon a "natural triad"—with the three worlds of development—Europe does tend to lose a pivotal function.

Nonetheless, one cannot negate the persistent influence of England and France ("good colonialists") or of Belgium and Portugal ("bad colonialists") in Africa and Asia. There is also the persistent German influence in North Africa and in Latin America. To be sure, Western Europe continues to be the largest buyer of African produce. It is pos-

40. John Lukacs, *Decline and Rise of Europe.* Garden City, N.Y.: Doubleday & Co., 1965.
41. Stephen R. Graubard (ed.), "A New Europe?" *Proceedings of the American Academy of Arts and Sciences,* Vol. 93, No. 1 (Winter 1964).
42. See Gianfranco Corsini, "American Culture and the Italian Left," *The Correspondent,* No. 33 (Winter 1965), pp. 45–52.

sible that the widening latitude of European commercial activities will have great bearing on the future forms of African development.

France, for its part, has harnessed its archaic middle-sized capitalism to the possibilities of bureaucratic technological domination. Even if France could continue an independent economic position, it could do so only through the sufferance and forbearance of the United States. United Europe is a dream; the United States is a reality—the French posture has confused dream and reality. It is scarcely likely that this will affect other European nations—which, if they are not satellites with respect to the United States, remain economically dependent. Even if Europe continues to move away from the United States, which it shows every indication of doing, the likelihood is that Europe will expend its energies forging a new economic synthesis between East and West. When this relatively short-run task is achieved, in some ten to twenty years, then Europe will be likely to have a deeper impact on development in the Third World.

This is not to minimize the difficulties posed by France or China in working out a statement of developing areas. There are certainly new features at work which modify any definition of the Third World—but what is underscored by these schismatic developments within capitalism and socialism is not so much the growth of different systems of political economy but alternative control agencies within each system. Whether capitalist or socialist economic organization is favored in the allocation of national resources for purposes of full industrial development, new strategies are circumscribed by the social classes and political means used to exert control over the development process. Doctrines favoring the bourgeoisie and the working class are being rejected in favor of pragmatic appraisals of who can and will win leadership. Humanitarian or authoritarian preferences are balanced against national needs and sacrifices required. As Third World nations are driven by the power struggle between the First and Second Worlds, they have to adopt such postures that enhance their own options. There is no one set of premises which can encompass this whole portion of the world. Perhaps the surest guide to the existence of a Third World view is its continuing perceived interest as a bloc, despite an exasperating range of variation.

2

Ideology of Three Worlds

As a reaction to the concept of an inevitable succession of stages, social scientists have turned "anti-historical"—erecting a barrier between social change and social development. This is the counterpart of the fact-value dualism in methodology. Change can be conveniently linked to "matters of fact" and hence studied, while social development entails matters of judgment and "statements of value" and hence cannot be scientifically valid. Given such a methodological injunction, it is no wonder that contemporary efforts in the field of social development do not compare with such "nineteenth-century" works as Bury's *The Idea of Progress* or even Lecky's *History of European Morals*. Instead, current textbooks treat social change as an "area" of sociological investigation. This tendency toward compartmentalization violates the essential nature of change, which occurs in all aspects of social life.

The reasons for neglecting the question of *change as development* are manifold. First, sociology has so sundered history from the social sciences that *development* is considered an accoutrement rather than a necessary aspect of the study of any society. Second, empirical sociological studies tend to focus on internal structure and consistency, stressing pattern maintenance, models of equilibrium, consensus systems, structural hegemony, and so forth. This approach leaves little place for conflict situations, forms of radical change, spontaneous and unstructured behavior, and other "unstable" forces producing change and development alike. Third, there is a fear that to discuss human development leaves one open to charges of utopianism. This is an age which takes forward strides self-consciously. Fourth, there is a widespread doubt that the concept of development is scientifically definable since it has for so long exclusively been the rallying cry of political ideologists.

In our age the struggle for development takes place in the context of a developing social struggle. The question of what constitutes development has itself become part of the general ideological struggle. Facts and figures on everything from consumer production to rates of capital reinvestment now serve as "evidence" for the superiority of capitalism over socialism or socialism over capitalism. In such circumstances the social scientist hesitates to leap into the controversy over what constitutes development. This is the most important single reason why sociology has been so tentative about the question of human development.

Before examining differences between ideological and sociological definitions of development, we can look briefly to historical concepts of change. Ancient Greeks provide some anchor-points. Running parallel to the rather sophisticated Platonic and Protagorean notion of the basic unreality of change is the concept that changes take place in "appearances" only, while a "substratum" remains essentially one and unchanging. For Plato change in space or time meant decadence, and objects which change were intrinsically worthless. His identification of the good and the true with a changeless state represented a conservative position, which opposed all forms of development as threats to the established order.

The Aristotelian tradition removed the pejorative connotations from things which change. Thus, while Aristotle also held that there is an essentially unchanging substratum or reality (the categories of logic and mathematics), there exists an empirical reality, which is not quite as worthwhile and which is subject to laws of birth, growth, maturity, and decay. From a social point of view, Aristotle shared Plato's mistrust of things subject to alteration and progression. Empirical change was thought to "actualize" the "potentialities" inherent in all things rather than to create new phenomena.

Among the pre-Socratics, Heraclitos was the first to express a general theory of change. Several cardinal principles are offered in his dialectical picture of the world: (1) change is real, and therefore all reality must be defined in terms of change; (2) there is no aspect of physical, biological, or social life that can resist the general process of change—birth, development, and decay; (3) change is patterned and proceeds in accordance with well-defined general "laws"; (4) these general laws are "dialectical," that is, they proceed in a struggle of contrary and internal forces until a new stage of reality is achieved. Contrary to the Protagorean-Platonic view, Heraclitos placed exclusive emphasis on change and growth as the essential elements of reality.

Democritus took another approach to the problem of change. He considered atomic particles the ultimate stuff of the universe. All complex organisms are built up from these atoms, with the type and level of clusters determining the characteristics of the object. Change takes place through the combination and dissolution of basic atomic entities. The Epicureans advocated "reductionism," or an explanation of change in terms of uncomplicated material entities. Change was authentic and development feasible. But the basis of social change was still considered "physical" in essence; social laws were extensions, albeit complex, of principles of atomism and mechanics.

Although the ancient Greeks developed some highly refined and imaginative general theories of change and development, they evolved no working set of principles to account for social change and social progress. Throughout the feudal period, and until the start of the Industrial Revolution, concepts of development remained highly abstract; rooted in one or another medieval doctrine of salvationism and millennialism. Roger Bacon and Ibn Khaldun in particular, and others here and there, gave expression to development as an earthly problem. There evolved a variety of notions of what constitutes development: in one conception development signifies innovative possibilities of discovery. Development is also viewed as the unfolding in definite stages of the new in place of the old. There is also the "aesthetic" approach which views development as the working out of a theme or of variations on a theme. Finally, in the humanist tradition, development depended on knowledge and the bringing to light of new information.

The variety of these developmental theories should caution the social scientists from viewing development merely as a matter of "common sense." Such an attitude, which sociologists call "self-definition" or "auto-perception" of change, is dangerously limited—witness the endless multiplications and subdivisions in the "self-definition of social class." [1]

1. See Ruth R. Kornhauser, "The Warner Approach to Social Stratification," *Class, Status and Power: A Reader in Social Stratification,* edited by Reinhard Bendix and Seymour Martin Lipset. Glencoe, Ill.: The Free Press, 1953; and also C. Wright Mills, "The Social Life of a Modern Community," *Power, Politics and People: The Collected Papers of C. Wright Mills,* edited by Irving Louis Horowitz. New York and London: Oxford University Press, 1963, pp. 39–52.

The rise of modern industrial society gave new and robust dimension to the concept of development. Raw materials were turned into finished artifacts en masse; machines replaced human labor as the essential agency of production; organic, for example, feudal societies gave way to capitalist societies, classes capable of producing for a marketing network. The perception of change quickly followed the fact of change. There was an intense interest in new forms of social production, ownership, and consumption to fit the changing circumstances in the industrial world. Standards of "normal" life span and infant mortality were no longer accepted by growing numbers of market-oriented people; public health and hygienic improvements to guarantee maximum growth and life were demanded. Salvation became naturalized, and "man's lot" was no longer necessarily synonymous with "man's fate." The feudal contentment with the status quo now crumbled before the onslaught of the capitalist world's concern with how things might and ought to be. Capitalist society fostered new standards of achievement no less than new forms of production.

Development becomes a general human concern only at the point of dramatic changes in material culture. With the Industrial Revolution, population burgeoned, inventions proliferated, and colonization intensified. There was a transformation from the colonization for plunder characteristic of the Spaniards to a more sophisticated colonization of markets engaged in by Northern European powers. The new social forces of production and the economic reorganization of life affected the whole mass of English people as had no prior political or religious event.[2] There was a great shift from rural to urban life, a change of emphasis from agricultural to commercial production. However, this transformation in the character of production did not automatically lead to abundance for all. Quite the contrary, the early years of industrialism, in nation after nation, became identified with travails and miseries even greater than those known under the older societies. The "iron law of wages" developed by Ricardo and Malthus expressed in colorful language the intense demand for profits. This qualitative gap between industrialization and consumerism is still not clearly appreciated by those newly developing areas that perceive the end products of industrialism much more precisely than the difficulties in reaching such goals.

2. See Gordon Childe, *Man Makes Himself*. London: Watts & Co., 1941, pp. 12–14.

There seems to be a three-step process: industrialization, holding down modernization; followed by modernization at the expense of rapid industrialization; and if all goes well, a new wave of industrial growth promoted by demands for better living standards. This at any rate is the view of Myrdal, and one which probably holds for the Third World as a whole, and not just Southeast Asia.

> Substantial improvements in levels of living must be postponed for some time to come in order to permit capital accumulation and even higher productivity and levels of living in the future. This need would assume a partial conflict, at least in the short run, between higher consumption and higher production. But there is also a positive relationship between these conditions to which we shall often call attention—that improved levels of living are a pre-condition for higher labor input and efficiency and, generally, for changes in abilities and attitudes that are favorable to rising productivity. This interdependence between productivity and levels of living is much stronger in the countries of South Asia than in Western countries, though the relationship is mostly obscured by application of the Western approach in the economic analysis of South Asian development problems.[3]

The problem, one that Myrdal himself senses, is that the rhetoric of socialist and classless societies comes much earlier than the realities of industrialization; and hence only frustrates the originating demands for development.

The precondition for the scientific study of social development is the fact of social change, just as a theory of development can arise only in a changing world. These social changes wrought by industrialism turned traditional men into pragmatic risk-takers. Though the advantages were not the same for all men, opportunities for many were greater than ever before. The Industrial Revolution also highlighted problems and obstacles to change. Thus, Protestantism, Enlightenment, liberalism and socialism can each be viewed as responses, at the ideological and philosophical levels, to the problems made evident by the facts of industrial development.

Weber's classic studies of the interrelations between the Protestant ethic and the capitalist economy attempted to show how the traditional bourgeois belief in the curative power of work and the Protestant notion

3. Gunnar Myrdal, *Asian Drama: An Inquiry into the Poverty of Nations.* New York: Pantheon-Random House, 1968, pp. 58–59.

of "a calling" were fused into a monumental frontal assault against traditionalism.[4] This fusion of industry and religion was not made solely on grounds of abstract principles (for example, the need of capitalism for integrity and honor in contract relations and the parallel need of Protestantism to link salvation to a practical work-ethic). It was based on a shared belief that if the individual as an active agent were to count at all, there would have to be a break with feudal "collectivism," which assumed that the things which could be changed were not worth changing, while the things worth changing were unchangeable.

The pietistic puritan and the worldly ascetic each saw development as apocalyptical rather than historical. Nonetheless, development was deemed necessary for grace. Man's redemption became more important than man's fate. The bourgeois consciousness likewise viewed development in apocalyptical terms—that is, "windfalls," "good fortune," "business shrewdness," or just plain "luck." But even though the Lutheran concept of the calling remained traditional and the capitalist view of success remained utilitarian, both strongly hinted at a scientific view of change. In place of supernatural intervention as a means of attaining either Divine Grace or Nature's Wealth came a stress upon hard work, patient effort, and slow and tedious results. Such attitudes paved the way for the establishment of a doctrine of social change in place of the stratified and stultified view of the medieval feudal and religious world.

Social and economic development could not emerge until traditional and transcendental notions of change inherited from the feudal epoch were discarded, and development could be seen as a natural process proceeding independently of providential design. The French Enlightenment, characterized by Turgot's *Tableau philosophique successif de l'esprit humain,* Helvetius' *De l'esprit* and Condorcet's *L'Esquisse d'un tableau historique des progrès de l'esprit humain,* gave the industrial world its first fully articulated theory of social development. This theory incorporated both Protestant and bourgeois modes of social explanation. The *philosophes* expounded a new humanism, extending the concept of development to include every department of human activity and every class of people.

4. See Max Weber, "The Religious Foundations of Worldly Asceticism," *The Protestant Ethic and the Spirit of Capitalism.* New York: Scribner and Sons, 1930; also "The Protestant Sects and the Spirits of Capitalism," in *Max Weber: Essays in Sociology.* New York: Oxford University Press, 1946, pp. 302–22.

The French Revolution thus established a new view of social realities. History was no longer to be written in terms of dynastic emperors, individual genius, or self-proclaimed spiritual leaders, but in terms of the flow and thrust of mass man. By conceiving of development as a secular process, historians like Michelet and, earlier, Condorcet fashioned a theory of change which was simultaneously "scientific" and "moral" from illiteracy to universal education; from the rule of autocracy to a democratically oriented oligarchy and universal suffrage; from a law based on power and prestige to equality of all before the law; from *pax romana* to national sovereignty; from concentration to rational distribution of wealth; from women as slaves to women as partners. In this new humanism history became the story of man's progress, and true morality was said to consist of a radical critique of the present.

Some noted historians[5] have presented us with a sophisticated denigration of Enlightenment achievements, claiming that the philosophers confused religious belief and rational faith and muddled the idea of progress with that of redemption. But we still owe the Enlightenment the first significant formulation of a general theory of social development. The social scientists continue to frame the question of what constitutes development in Enlightenment terms. The Enlightenment not only took seriously the realities of development but predicted that the problem of development would become increasingly urgent. For example, Condorcet anticipated an era in which statistical and scientific methods would be enlisted to support the cause of progress.

While the French Enlightenment produced a theory of *social* development, it did not evolve a causal basis, a historical accounting, by which social science could be liberated from arbitrary forms of utopianism. French formulations viewed development as essentially a matter of *esprit, Zeitgeist* and moral imperatives. Thus it tended to ignore the concrete, historical locus of development. Historically there has been decline as well as growth, decay as well as achievement. Rather than face the problem of decline, the Enlightenment chose to cast development in anti-historical terms, pitting human reason against the dead hand of the past. The French *philosophes* in particular were troubled by discrepancies between the fact of inequality and the idea of equality. Unable to resolve this divergency empirically, they resorted to a moral

5. See, for example, Carl Becker, *The Heavenly City of the Eighteenth Century Philosophers.* New Haven: Yale University Press, 1932; and also, Crane Brinton, *The Anatomy of Revolution.* New York: W. W. Norton & Co., 1938.

posture. The progress of mankind was said to culminate in the final fusion of reason and self-interest—in short, in hedonistic utopianism.

The German Enlightenment tradition of Lessing, Herder, and Novalis managed to fuse the Protestant doctrine of millennialism and the rationalist faith in progress into a historical theory of development. This was made possible by a concerted effort to connect reason and revelation in a general theory. Revelation is a moment in time which takes on meaning only through a painstaking process whereby reason connects one great moment with another. By framing laws governing both the continuities and discontinuities in social life, the German theorists supplied the missing link to the French Enlightenment theory of development. In the highest stage reached in pre-sociological discourse on the problem of development, change is seen as linked to the religion of humanity. Development as progress became identified with the religious basis of human evolution. The German Enlightenment conceptualized problems in terms of the general organic "progress" of morals and reason, and did not, as the French had done, polarize them. With this, "philosophical anthropology" was born. Change was no longer an accidental property of society but its very essence. Feuerbach, by bringing about materialistic theology, gave the summation of this entire tradition and, more important, the first glimmer of the critical spirit upon which nineteenth-century scientific theories of progress came to rest.[6]

The socialists, from Saint-Simon to Marx, connected the concept of development with that of particularized class interests and thus introduced the first full-fledged ideological (in contrast to religious) note to development. Progress in human affairs was no longer a total undertaking of society but a class enterprise. The "great man" was transformed into a "great class" rather than "society" as a whole in the Enlightenment. The socialist tradition sought to strike a balance between the individualist and collectivist traditions. The mechanism for accomplishing this was the interest group or sectional group or class formation. The agencies and the bearers of change became the hitherto anonymous proletarian collectivity.

If Marxian and socialist tradition represents the substitution of ideology for religion, it no less represents the replacement of philosophy

6. See Irving Louis Horowitz, "Lessing and Hammann: Two Views on Religion and Enlightenment," *Church History*, Vol. 30, No. 3, Sept. 1961, pp. 344–48.

with science. By viewing development as a social question, a secular question, and insisting on the specific, interest-laden dimensions of the problem, Marxism made it unfeasible to consider development in terms of Hegelian historical categories. Marx himself developed a parallel theme: one side of development is seen as occurring in the "natural society" in which "man's own act becomes an alien power opposed to him, which enslaves him instead of being combatted by him"; development takes place also in "civil society" and actually constitutes the history of class society, the history of the division of human labor. These lines of development are resolved and synthesized in socialism; the communism of "natural society" is joined to the material achievements of "civil society." Marx waxed rhapsodic on this theme; through socialism, man's nature is "restored to himself." [7] Marx, however, clearly saw the problem of development as one which must account for both continuities and discontinuities in social life; and more specifically at the political level, development signified the replacement of state power with social authority.

At the same time Marx sought to enunciate principles of development in terms of the natural history of socioeconomic production. The concept of an inexorable progression from slavery to feudalism, capitalism, socialism, and ultimately to communism arose out of Marx's conviction that social development is the key to prediction and explanation in the social sciences. Just as the appearance of capital announces a new age in the process of social production, the appearance of labor (and the laborer as a class affiliate) signifies the next higher stage of development—socialism.

Marx's was the first system of social science framed primarily (if not exclusively) in terms of developmental models; particularly important is the fact that by relating development to social interest this system fed the streams of both modern political ideology and modern sociological inquiry. Marx asked the scientific question: What is development? But he did so in the context of ideology, and he tried to promote specific agencies to stimulate development. Under the impetus of Marxism, development became a class task; hence development did not proceed harmoniously or mechanically, since there were always classes which depended for their existence upon the status quo. Only after the down-

7. See Karl Marx, *The German Ideology,* edited and translated by Roy Pascal. New York: International Publishers, 1939; and also his *Economic Philosophic Manuscripts of 1844,* translated by M. Milligan. Moscow: FLPH, 1957.

fall of bourgeois society and bourgeois consciousness could there be national, and even international, development as a general, social phenomenon. With the discovery that power and status are independent variables that continue to divide men in post-capitalist societies, Marx's vision of economic cooperation based on a classless society has receded to a distant future.[8]

Until now we have discussed general orientations toward the question of social development. But the metaphysical orientation loses relevance when we make a clear distinction between sacred and profane. When analysis hinges upon specific problems—for example, who progresses, at what rate, and at what cost—we leave behind such issues as how we know we have progressed or how we should progress.

It should be understood that we do not view the ideological approach as bad and the sociological as good; indeed, sociology often lags behind ideology in the promotion of useful and beneficial goals. The ideological approach, which rests on the standpoint of particularized interests, has generally asked the right questions.[9] The difficulty is that it asks such questions in a biased way, with specific ends in view, irrespective both of the instrumentalities employed and of any contravening evidence. If sociology followed the reverse approach—that is, if it were unbiased, not influenced by personal or social interest factors, and always operated according to scientific canons of evidence—then our problem would be considerably eased. The fact is that both sociological and ideological discussions of development contain many unscientific and sometimes even anti-scientific formulations. Thus, while in theory it is clearly superior to argue from a sociological rather than an ideological standpoint, these two modes of thought interpenetrate to a significant degree.

Sociology confronts a human complex which is of two minds on the issue of development. Public attitudes are split not only on the worth of development but on its facts. If we distinguish between change and progress, we can see more clearly why this split has occurred—that is, in distinguishing social development from simple change in the physical sense of movement in space and time, and from growth in the biological sense of alteration in the nature of an organism.

8. See in particular, Stanislaw Ossowski, "The Concept of Social Class," in *Class Structure in the Social Consciousness*. London: Routledge & Kegan Paul, 1963, pp. 71–88; and Ralf Dahrendorf, *Class and Class Conflict in Industrial Society*. Stanford: Stanford University Press, 1959, pp. 124–29.
9. See Irving Louis Horowitz, *Philosophy, Science and the Sociology of Knowledge*. Springfield, Ill.: Charles C Thomas, 1961; and *Historía y Elementos de la Sociología del Conocimiento*. Buenos Aires: University of Buenos Aires, 1964.

For the social scientist, physical or biological processes do not constitute development, for such changes occur in the deterministic nature of things and are not subject to alteration by human decision, that is, by conscious determination. The orbiting of the earth about the sun, the growth of a fetus or of a human being—these are indeed changes, but not development processes. Human development, however, reflects at some level culture and consciousness and factors which are "unnatural" (electricity to defy the night, airplanes to defy gravity, machines to defy the limits of human labor-power, etc.). In human development alternative forms of social structure are not only possible but almost inevitable. But to conclude from these facts, as some sociologists have, that it is impossible to arrive at a scientific statement of human development is simply to abandon the major question posed for social science. The separation of "facts" and "values" is not a mandate restricting the sociologist to the former "realm" alone—but only a methodological caution for avoiding undue subjectivity. When this separation becomes a sanction for avoiding the problems of human development, it is no longer a heuristic tool but a positive hindrance.

The sociologist confronts social forces which are contradictory or at the very least ambivalent. For every utopian dream of a world of technological innovation, social justice, and material abundance, there is the sober warning of those who envision the same future as a robot-age, inhabited by technological idiots and political scoundrels. To further complicate matters, the sociologists themselves are divided in their judgments of the content and meaning of human development. One current commentary indicated that "recent developments in technology suggest heretofore unimagined possibilities in the way of human well-being." [10] Though the author pauses to indicate the dangers of such developments, he concludes that "we are only on the threshold of the possibilities and problems occasioned by these technological developments." For another contemporary sociologist the dangers far outweigh the advantages of technological achievement, which has "degraded man to the level of a mere reflex mechanism, a mere organ motivated by sex, a mere semimechanical, semiphysiological organism, devoid of any divine spark, of any absolute value, of anything noble and sacred." [11]

10. J. O. Hertzler, *American Social Institutions: A Sociological Analysis.* Boston: Allyn and Bacon, 1961, p. 220.
11. Pitirim A. Sorokin, "Social and Cultural Dynamics," in *The Making of Society: An Outline of Sociology,* edited by Robert Bierstedt. New York: Random House, 1959, p. 481.

Nor should it be imagined that only sociologists differ in their attitudes toward development. The industrial world itself exhibits similar doubts and dichotomies. Managerial attitudes toward automation are often dictated by a blithe optimism: "Guided by electronics, powered by atomic energy, geared to the smooth, effortless workings of automation, the magic carpet of our free economy heads for distant and undreamed of horizons." In contrast is the conclusion drawn recently by a labor leader:

> I am not reassured by those who tell us that all will work out well in the long run because we have managed to live through radical technological changes in the past. Human beings do not live long enough for us to be satisfied with assurances about the long-run adaptation of society to automation. And while it is true that radical technological improvements have been introduced in the past, it is well to remember that they were accompanied by vast social dislocations, recurring depressions and human suffering.[12]

Within the social sciences, no less than between social science and political ideology, development is variously defined. The demographer may measure development in terms of gross population growth or declining rates of infant mortality; in geriatrics the problem may be considered primarily in terms of human longevity; the economist may use indices of industrial reinvestment, consumer goods produced and bought, or the like; the psychiatrist may see the situation in terms of increasing the percentage of "normal" people or decreasing mental illness; and for the criminologist development may mean either the care and treatment of criminals or the abolition of the causes of crime. If there were a harmonic coalescence of all of these developmental elements, then there would be no problems. But this is not the case. The uneven distribution of wealth in the affluent society is often coupled with a high incidence of mental sickness and criminal behavior, especially among the poor. Therefore it is the maldistribution of wealth, rather than the absolute annual earnings, which most significantly affect "deviant" patterns.

Development can be seen as an aspect of human will. It can be viewed as a particular kind of planning aimed at transforming an underdeveloped country into one which will eventually resemble either

12. Both statements are contained in Robert P. Weeks (ed.), *Machines and the Man: A Sourcebook on Automation*. New York: Appleton-Century-Crofts, 1961, pp. 171–76 and 202–17.

the First or Second World or some combination of the two. According to this viewpoint, all planning is done by a dedicated development-oriented elite supported by loyal, self-sacrificing masses.

Another approach emphasizes the products of advanced technology, or some concrete evidence that machine power is displacing human energy. These products can be the types of social structures, levels of technologies, and life styles found in the First or Second World. Mass production, for example, can yield intermediary forms of social structures, technologies, and life styles. Specifically, these intermediary consequences of mass production can produce a dedicated elite, can stimulate a self-sacrificing mass, and can change handicraft activities into large-scale automated factories.

From this perspective, total social planning is not a necessary condition for development. The intermediary products of the development process, as well as the "terminal" products or stages, may or may not be produced by a dedicated elite. This open-ended view of development allows us to consider as a developing nation one which has little central planning by a dedicated elite but a plethora of modern factories and well-clothed, well-fed citizens who are politically, economically, and socially mobilized.

This viewpoint makes it possible to distinguish between a modernizing country, with few or even no factories, and a mobilizing nation that accentuates factory production at the expense of commodity goods. This "product" way of looking at the developmental process forces us to say that Venezuela is a modernizing nation, since it has shown a marked degree of industrial development, particularly in the oil industry. It is possible that Venezuela will ultimately surpass Cuba's economic development. At the present time, however, Cuba is further along the road of development than Venezuela, for Cuba has the political forms and a mobilized dedicated mass suitable for sustained development. Thus far, Venezuela has neither.

Countries may remain underdeveloped for opposite reasons. Guinea, for example, has a dedicated elite which has done an extraordinary job of mobilizing the population politically. While the elite has tried and is still trying desperately to develop the country economically, it is unlikely to succeed. Poorly endowed in resources and population and with little to offer her own people or the world, Guinea is little more than an unfortunate accident of imperialistic map-making. Only if it can unite with richer nations will Guinea become part of a developed state.

Venezuela, on the other hand, is rich in both mineral resources and population, but it may never develop if it is not successful in producing a dedicated elite supported by self-sacrificing, loyal masses.

First: A developed society is one made up of the social structures, technologies, and life styles that exist today in the First and Second Worlds. In other words, these two worlds, represented by the United States and the Soviet Union in particular, will be used in this work as models of developed nations. There are obvious "pitfalls" in treating these two countries as models. And with all due respect for the possibility of employing ethnocentric and even arbitrary criteria, the fact that the peoples and leaders of developing areas employ the big powers of the East and West as models must itself be viewed as part of the developmental process. Perhaps all we can do is agree with Myrdal that there is a need to provide a precise definition of development, without forgetting that such vagueness as remains may not simply be a problem in definition, but may interfere in the processes of development itself.[13]

Second: The concept "developmental process" refers to those planned and unplanned activities which produce the social structures, technologies, and life styles found in the First and Second Worlds, or else the means for obtaining these advanced forms. The developmental process includes those social and economic changes which tend to make the nations of the Third World more closely resemble the nations of the First or Second Worlds or some combination of the two.

Third: Whatever form development may take, it is universally an asynchronous process. The political, economic and social sectors of a nation do not advance at the same rate. The economic sector of a Third World country such as Brazil or India may be rapidly approximating the economic sector of the First World, while the masses continue to live in a state of poverty unknown to the lowest classes of the United States.

Fourth: The asynchronous nature of the developmental process makes it extremely difficult to determine whether a nation is developing or stagnating. Such a judgment assumes that the investigator has measures for determining the degree of development in the various sectors which make up the nation as well as some kind of technique for weighing the "development scores" assigned to each sector. The techniques for measuring economic development are fairly adequate; those for measuring

13. Gunnar Myrdal, *Asian Drama: An Inquiry into the Poverty of Nations,* p. 186.

political and social development are relatively crude. While we cannot be precise, we can still speak with a fair degree of certainty as to whether a particular sector of a nation is developing. However, no generally accepted method exists for weighing and averaging the "scores" accorded to each sector. Consequently, any judgment as to whether a nation rather than a sector is developing or stagnating, while not entirely arbitrary, ultimately rests on the technique the investigator sees fit to use.

Fifth: The ideological viewpoint of development attempts to determine in advance not simply the goals but the instruments, tactics, and strategies of planning social change. The sociological viewpoint, while readily granting ends in view, does not have a determined scheme for the realization of such ends. It contains a pragmatic dimension which enables it to shift its theoretical focus if plans do not work out in practice. Developmental ideologies tend to compel types of change along pre-directed channels.

These are modest steps in the clarification of meaning. But if the issue of development is raised within a perspective which recognizes both a common humanity and diverse culture patterns, then this can serve as a starting point for constructive social action. Under certain conditions there is a relative absence of any perception, much less conception, of social development. An understanding of developmental processes is inhibited by two factors:

(1) An absence of comparative criteria between nations and over a period of time. Under conditions of social or group isolation within a larger community spatial comparisons between social subsystems become difficult. Similarly, the absence of historicity or self-consciousness blocks a society from judging itself in terms of both past and future goals.

(2) Extended periods of structural equilibrium without external, counterbalancing challenges. Since primitive societies neither retrogress nor progress, they maintain a belief in the fixity of social relations. Thus, while what we term underdeveloped societies change slowly, traditional societies lack not only the fact but the very idea of human development; that is, they do not possess a plan, a direction, or a goal.

This distinction between traditional and underdeveloped societies is pivotal. The traditional society is characterized by little change from generation to generation; a behavioral pattern governed almost exclusively by custom; status determined almost entirely by inheritance (ascriptive); low economic productivity; and a social organization and life style grounded on the principle of hierarchical command. The under-developed society has a great deal in common with the developed society; the phrase "underdeveloped" is used as a measure of technical and technological inferiority vis-à-vis the developed society. This society ex-hibits rapid change; behavior governed by law as well as by custom; status based on achievement as well as on inherited patterns; low eco-nomic productivity in some sectors of the economy, high productivity in other sectors; and a life style geared to rapid social mobility, despite intensive stratification, though not defined by it.

Conceptions of social development depend therefore both upon the facts and upon the consciousness of change. These in turn owe their existence to a consciousness of being different, that is, an awareness that shared values do not necessarily represent shared wealth. The rise of rapid, universal communication and transportation systems is fast transforming traditional societies into "underdeveloped" societies—if not through structural shifts, then certainly through the rise of consciousness and the growth of spatial and temporal comparisons.[14]

We can now turn to the "developed" society in which change is first and foremost a social fact. In considering the theories advanced for or against development, we become involved in the effect of ideology on the theory and practice of development. Ideology is not concerned with the ethical aspects or the morality of development. The ideological posture naturally assumes a general dissatisfaction with the present and the necessity and feasibility of change. Though the ideologist does not consider the ethical question of whether development is worthwhile or needed, he must still evaluate the worth of available types of develop-ment. Ideological debates over such slogans as "revolutionary socialism" and "evolutionary socialism," or in American society over "government control" versus "laissez faire," take on a strong ethical flavor. It is patently clear, however, that there is a huge difference between those arguing the worth of change (the moralists) and those arguing in a taken-for-granted manner over the types of change which are worth-while (the ideologists).

What should not be lost in the fog of competing political loyalties is the similarity between capitalist and communist industrial ideologies: material abundance, rapid urbanization, educational facilities, military

14. For a dissection of the problem of change in relation to traditional societies, see Everett E. Hagen, *On the Theory of Social Change: How Economic Growth Begins.* Homewood, Ill.: The Dorsey Press, 1962, esp. pp. 55–58.

strength—these indices define both American and Soviet notions of development. This is not to say that all differences between capitalist and communist ideologies have been eliminated or that this would be advantageous. The similarities do, however, far outweigh the dissimilarities. The Russians and the Americans must face a similar set of social questions: Are large-scale changes best accomplished spontaneously or through planning? What mixture of persuasion and coercion most facilitates progress? How can the growth of a particular society be turned into a model for "underdeveloped" areas?

The ideologists tend to obfuscate and distort fundamental similarities between systems for the sake of preserving the separateness of their own, whether it be called "The American Way" or "The Communist Road." Ideologists tend also to assume a world of total voluntarism, as if human development were dictated exclusively by choice and consensus, without limitation imposed by national boundaries, traditions, political systems, or economic potential. If the sociologist is not himself to become an ideologist, he must cut through the ideological rhetoric and search out areas of convergence as well as differentiation. At the same time, due recognition must be accorded the role of ideology in defining developmental goals.

We are now in an age dominated by a common industrial ideology which is just as much the property of the Soviet Union as it is of the West. In large measure, this is a consequence of the technological rationality imposed by similar industrial processes, rather than the desire to be modern in attitudes and orientations.

Industrial demands are sufficiently potent to win out eventually over traditional political forms. This may not be obvious in the short run, since Soviet and American societies share not only an emphasis on technological and scientific achievements but also a willingness to absorb the human losses which will ensure them world leadership. A cardinal feature of any definition of "Western culture" is anchored to the notion that human development results from scientific achievement. The present competition between Russia and the West comes about precisely because there is so much (rather than not enough) common ground. A statement by Sorokin seems particularly relevant:

> Both nations are fairly similar in scientific knowledge and technological progress. In normal conditions, without the misuse and abuse of scientific and technological achievements by the governments and militarists, both countries would have mutually profited from scien-

tific discoveries and inventions of each other. This means that science and technology as values do not give any ground, any reason, any justification for continuation of the belligerent policies "for Salvation of Science and Technology from the Destruction by the Russians (or the American) Barbarians." The scientists of both countries are quite successfully taking good care of scientific and technical progress, especially if they are not hindered by governmental interference in their highly important research.[15]

The definition of economic development in terms of per capita output and rates of capital investment has become standard currency for both "Marxian" and "Keynesian" economists.[16] The convergence of East and West has proceeded so rapidly and at so many levels since World War II that there remains an ideological lag. Apologists for capitalism expend their energies discussing the pre-revolutionary *political* ideology of Marxism instead of the functioning Soviet system.

In terms of the concept of development, the ideological struggle is not between East and West but between two styles of Western thought.

> We must not forget that Marxism and Communism are also Western ideas, and that modern Russia is also culturally, intellectually, and socially in the Western tradition. Indeed, the Russian Revolution can be seen, in part, as the Westernization of a formerly "Eastern" peasantry. . . . In their general drift into the mainstream of Western history, the leaders of the underdeveloped world will have a choice between divergent currents of Western development: the one represented by the free-enterprise, free-dissent nations of the Atlantic, and the other by the planned enterprise, limited or no-dissent nations of the Soviet orbit.[17]

The choice for other nations is not between capitalism and communism—or perhaps between oligopoly and state capitalism—(the growth of the economic "mix" in both societies makes a choice implausible if not entirely impossible) but rather between the industrial ideology shared by Americans and Soviets and the pre-industrial ideology of the

15. Pitirim A. Sorokin, "Mutual Convergence of the United States and the U.S.S.R. to the Mixed Sociocultural Type," *International Journal of Comparative Sociology,* Vol. 1, No. 2, Sept. 1960, pp. 143–76.
16. Compare, for example, the capitalist apologetics of John K. Galbraith, *American Capitalism.* Boston: Houghton Mifflin Co., 1952, with the socialist apologetics of Paul A. Baran, *The Political Economy of Growth.* New York: Monthly Review Press, 1957.
17. Robert L. Heilbroner, "The Revolution of Economic Development," *The American Scholar,* Vol. 3k, No. 4, Autumn 1962, pp. 541–49.

Third World countries. Indeed the very emergence of what Trotsky emotionally termed a decadent workers' state in the Soviet Union, one that parallels Engels' notion of the "bourgeoisified workers' State" in the West, underscores the convergence hypothesis in a less than flattering way. This choice may be singularly unpleasant for those reared in inherited political ideologies. But nostalgia, while comfortable, simply does not face up to the realities of functional and ideological convergence.

The accent on development is ingrained in technological societies exhibiting high degrees of social mobility. For an American trade union leader turned businessman this signifies "self-development for everybody, everywhere." [18] For a Soviet engineer turned manager such self-development involves "the radical improving of the management of enterprises and institutions through the extensive automation and mechanization of engineering and administrative jobs." [19] In each case, the price of change is a disruption of older norms and even older patterns of culture, and development is justified in terms of the same goals, for example, higher productivity, shorter working hours, increased leisure time, more goods to consume at lower prices. What emerges is a two-fold typology of ideological preferences which rationalizes the retention of maximum profits by the supposed belief that excess consumption prevents industrial reinvestment. The situation in both the United States and the Soviet Union demonstrates that a technological society requires an ideology based on expertise, that the "debate" over inherited political ideologies such as liberalism and Marxism is most furious in the traditional nations merely supports the contention that Russia and the United States represent alternative means for reaching the same industrial goals. Nonetheless, it might be kept in mind that, even when an ideology is built upon a well-defined principle, that principle does not necessarily dominate behavior. The "experts" do not completely dominate in the United States, and the same is undoubtedly the case in the Soviet Union. The ability to allocate and distribute the wealth is still in the hands of the politicians.

It has been particularly painful for the "American way of life" to come to terms with the problem of the costs of development, and to

18. F. J. Roethlisberger, "Introduction" to Elton Mayo, *The Human Problems of an Industrial Civilization.* New York: Viking Press, 1960, p. xi.
19. A. I. Berg, "Cybernetics and Society," *The Soviet Review,* Vol. I, No. 1 (1960), pp. 43–44.

understand that traditional patterns are not necessarily and always inimical to development.[20] For the American, for the proponent of the liberal rhetoric, the idea of progress through science has become, as Robin Williams noted, "a slogan to defend the course of technological innovation and economic rationalization and concentration. If small entrepreneurs, farmers, or urban workers felt economic distress, their condition could be considered a regrettable but necessary and temporary by-product of the triumphant march of progress." [21]

Given the combination of provincial ingenuousness, Puritan piety, and a technological definition of progress, which in large measure defines the present American mood of self-congratulation, a sociological study of the negative aspects of social change borders on a subversive reading of American history.

W. F. Cottrell's brilliant analysis of the death of a railroad town in the southwestern United States illustrates the costs of development and the potential social consequences of technological changeover. In this town of "Caliente" everything was predicated on the railroad's need for continued growth.

> Men built their homes there, frequently of concrete and brick, at the cost in many cases of their life savings. The water system was laid in cast iron which will last for centuries. Business men erected substantial buildings which could be paid for only by profits gained through many years of business. Four churches evidence the faith of Caliente people in the future of their community. A twenty-seven bed hospital serves the town. They believed in education. Their school buildings represent the investment of savings guaranteed by bonds and future taxes. There is a combined park and play field which, together with a recently modernized theatre, has been serving recreational needs. All these physical structures are material evidence of the expectations, morally and legally sanctioned and financially funded, of the people of Caliente. This is a normal and rational aspect of the culture of all "solid" and "sound" communities.[22]

"Rational" economic forces and laws of technological development worked to undermine this well-defined urban structure. When the rail-

20. Ralph J. Braibanti and Joseph J. Spengler, *Tradition, Values and Socio-Economic Development.* Durham, N.C.: Duke University Press, 1961.
21. Robin M. Williams, Jr., *American Society.* New York: Alfred A. Knopf, 1960 (2nd rev. edition), p. 433.
22. W. F. Cottrell, "Death by Dieselization: A Case Study in the Reaction to Technological Change," *American Sociological Review*, Vol. 16, 1951, pp. 358–65.

road converted from steam to diesel power, Caliente, totally dependent on its water and repair facilities, was shorn of its reason to exist. The victory of technology, of the very industrial ideology of progress which the citizenry of Caliente espoused—since they were by all standards good Americans—paradoxically substantially destroyed their carefully nurtured social structure.

Development, in other words, is often preceded by social disorganization. There is a dialectic to socialization, namely, privatization. The end of the parochial rural and semi-urban standards leads to Jean Gottmann's *Megalopolis*. But it also feeds a collective anomie, a drive for escapism and frenetic leisure-time activities, and a nihilist attitude about the future, as described in Leo Srole's *Metropolis*. The overdeveloped society is tentative about the future and cynical about the present—characteristics to which the Third World societies would do well to pay closer attention.

The enormous increase in the types and rates of technological growth has created other immense problems. Even if we accept the business ideology that technological change does not create large-scale unemployment, the problem of mass mis-employment remains. As one writer recently stated:

> The underlying assumption is that one job equals another, that income is the sole criterion and it makes no difference what you do or become in order to get it. Technological unemployment may be a myth, but what about technological mis-employment? From 1880 to 1940, the percentage of Americans who were self-employed declined sharply. The percentage employed in clerical work, or in more or less parasitical service activities, rose sharply. The percentage employed in actually making useful articles declined; and even among the productive workers, millions were downgraded from skilled craftsmen to mass-production hands, with little skill or responsibility.[23]

However, this unabashed labor-oriented posture has its own difficulties. For it addresses itself only to the most obvious managerialist ploys. First, there is no need to assume that the shift from blue-collar to white-collar activities is either harmful or parasitical. Second, the problem of mis-employment is largely mythical insofar as an advanced industrial economy maintains an appropriate rate of the gross national

23. Geoffrey Ashe, "Technological Mis-employment," in *Machines and the Man*, edited by Robert P. Weeks. New York: Appleton-Century-Crofts, 1961, pp. 200–202.

product. Third, neither the union position nor the managerial position seems capable of distinguishing between economic and non-economic factors, that is, between the problems of subsistence and those of alienation.

The problem for the sociologist, one which the ideologist dare not recognize, is to discover the forms of creativity possible in a highly impersonal and mechanized society. The real failure of industrial ideology is that it provides a false alternative to traditionalist-conservative ideologies. For while the latter seem solely preoccupied with the costs, the former is exclusively concerned with the benefits of industrial change. The scientific problem at one level is the relationship between the price of change and who has to pay this price. The decision to orient a society toward rapid industrial and technical development is a value decision, most often made by an elite group for the mass of people. But the second level of the development problem is precisely the relationship between volitional and deterministic aspects. The transformation of society proceeds through a consideration of interests, no less than values, from the tendencies of social classes no less than the choices of special elites. This double interchange system defines the main parameters to the problem of development; were either missing, were development issues linked exclusively to choice or to necessity, then the tasks of science would indeed become simplified.

A decision in favor of industrial expansion may entail large-scale and long-range hardships, and short-run costs may well outweigh long-term results. An agricultural-export economy, which satisfies consumer demands by buying rather than making automobiles, television sets, washing machines, and the like, does not necessarily have to be reoriented toward industrialism. Often industrialization is demanded in the name of nationalism, the common assumption being that affluence and greatness are synonymous with industrialism. Doing without the products of General Electric or General Motors because they come from an imperialist nation may be materially damaging to a nation which could trade wheat for radios and beef for cars. The problem does not exist only in capitalist economies; the dogmatic application of the industrial ideology, of the assumption that home-grown goods are always cheaper to make than imported goods are to obtain, has boomeranged in Yugoslavia, Hungary, Poland, China, and Cuba.

This is not to be construed as a nostalgic critique of industrial society.

To recognize the weaknesses in industrial ideology is not to condemn industrial values. A modern and efficient agricultural system must basically have industrial values. It does point up the need to distinguish between absolute underdevelopment, when the basic tools whereby a citizenry can survive are lacking, and relative underdevelopment, when rates of social change are slower than in developed societies. Surely, there is a vast difference between a form of underdevelopment which witnesses mass starvation (as in parts of India) and a form of underdevelopment in which industrial capacity is low while everyone is essentially well fed and well clothed (as in Argentina and even peacetime Vietnam). Precisely because the word "underdevelopment" is charged with emotive meanings, it is doubly necessary to distinguish the actual, empirical contents of underdevelopment in any given society.

It should be noted that the nineteenth-century liberals' prophecies of progress through science were, indeed, realized. The extent of modern creativity would surprise and delight even an Edward Bellamy. Why then should there be such widespread disillusionment and dismay in the developed societies? The very giganticism of our achievements has made it possible for the individual to be overwhelmed and for whole populations to be annihilated. In short, technical and industrial development is not total development and does not settle the major problems of politics, economics, war and peace, and the like, but only raises such issues to a new pinnacle of desperation. For human development we still require some kind of "science of values," some analytical tools for expressing the new situation in meaningful terms.

Granting the increased exacerbation between the impulses toward development and the actual gains registered, there remains a remarkable consistency in the popular belief that development will take place, and even should take place. It is somehow far easier for wealthy nations than for poor nations to bemoan the failures of development. For many the costs of development are well worth the price. Most "backward" tribal associations—such as the Sironis in Bolivia, the Guayaki in Paraguay, the Macu of Brazil—join with their brothers in La Paz, Asuncion, and São Paulo to demand entrance into the gateways of tomorrow.

Development will have its price. The task of the sociologist is not only to indicate the dangers of social dislocation but to anticipate and work out solutions for potential problems. Traditional relations between parents and obedient children and between male and female may likewise have to be altered. The idea of the state as a dispenser of welfare may indeed supplant the older notion that a government governs best which governs least. The sociologist must become a physician of society.

The sociologist considers the problem of development in terms of various methods, rates, directions and consequences, while the ideologist thinks of development as a matter of national pride, and is mainly concerned that his society reach development before others. Mills made a very pointed statement in this connection.

> When we think about the "underdeveloped society" we must also think about the "overdeveloped society." There are two reasons for this: first, if we do not do so, we tend to think of everything as moving towards the developed. It is the old notion of nineteenth century evolutionism. And this is no longer a very fruitful idea. Second, to think of the polar types leads us to think about a third type—an ideal which we should always keep in mind: the properly developing society. We need all three types, not just the two.[24]

The underdeveloped society is characterized by a limited standard of living, whereas in the overdeveloped society the life style is dominated by the living standards. The fetish of production becomes a fetish for consumption. And without adding a theological note, social science should maximize human possibilities by helping to design, no less than understand, the proximate future. It is this maximization that is the substance of "proper" development. More pointedly, as an economic issue, the main task is to make sure that people have the opportunity to purchase what is produced.

We know considerably more about the difference between development and underdevelopment than we do about differences between development and overdevelopment, or what may just as readily be called mis-development. The latter is a more recent phenomenon. Also, it is easier to describe the sociology of scarcity than of affluence, since there are so many illustrations of the former and so few of the latter. Nonetheless, the need for a clear view of overdevelopment is urgent; for otherwise we shall be providing instruments to developing nations which can reproduce the worst rather than the best features of modern civilizations. Thus far, the best definition of overdevelopment is that concept common to Marx and Keynes: the realization of surplus value, or what

24. C. Wright Mills, "The Problem of Industrial Development," in *Power, Politics and People,* edited by Irving Louis Horowitz. New York and London: Oxford University Press, 1963.

is now called aggregate demand, and the inability or incapacity to dissolve such surplus among large numbers of people.

Overdevelopment cannot be equated with that social condition in which material wealth is maldistributed, since there probably has never been a society that distributed such wealth "properly." Rather, it has much more to do with large-scale availability of human skills that are not used to their fullest potentials. Structural imbalances only accentuate personality deformations. This occurs when there are social impediments —for instance, when there exist radical imbalances between social classes; or when there are organizational impediments—for instance, when available energy and power sources are not properly utilized. Further, an overdeveloped society is one in which failures at both the social and technical levels lead to breakdowns in production and in distribution and create a perennial crisis in the political institutions and educational establishments. Like underdevelopment, overdevelopment is relative to a given type of socioeconomic organization, one that has the technical capacity to satisfy basic human needs but is lacking the social instrumentalities to utilize such a capacity.

Thus, while the United States can by no stretch of the imagination simply be relegated to the realm of overdevelopment—by the above-named criteria at least—it does reveal certain properties of overdevelopment, which, if not curbed, could lead to exaggerated mis-development. For example, there has been a vast slowing down in the development of inexpensive electrical power for rural regions. There has been no follow-up to the TVA (Tennessee Valley Authority) and MVA (Missouri Valley Authority). Regional planning continues to be viewed as something the nation does only in times of economic crisis. Similarly, despite a long-term upward trend, admittedly punctuated by depression strains, United States industries continue to operate below maximum capacity— often by as much as 30 to 50 per cent—except during artificially induced crisis periods. Agricultural underproduction is encouraged to keep market prices inflated, federal subsidies given for not planting certain key crops, and tax write-offs for failing business enterprises.[25] Nor can we leave out of this inventory the military build-up. Military expenditures have most often been measured exclusively in terms of the benefits to labor and management, without a corresponding regard for the ultimate

25. See L. N. Naggle, "Scylla and Charybdis of Engineering Education," *Proceedings of the 1961 Syracuse University International Conference on Electrical Engineering Education.* Syracuse, N.Y.: 1961, pp. 52–53.

social costs involved. Galbraith has put the risk of overdevelopment succinctly:

> As matters now stand, we have almost no institutions that are by central design and purpose directed to participation in modern scientific and technological progress and its large-scale application. We have no organization capable, for example, of taking on the large-scale development of atomic power generators or radically new departures in passenger-carrying aircraft in advance of knowledge that these will be commercially feasible. Much has been accomplished by research and development, not immediately subject to a commercial criteria, under the inspiration of military need. This has done more to save us from the partial technological stagnation that is inherent in a consumers' goods economy than we imagine. But it is also a narrow and perilous prop, and it has the further effect of associating great and exciting scientific advances with an atmosphere of fear and even terror.[26]

What this should teach newly emerging nations is that the problem of development is not exclusively one of technological or natural resources or exclusively one of sociological or human resources, but rather the interrelation and interpenetration of the two. Indeed, the more "mature" a society becomes, the more it needs instruments for orderly social change and the less it provides for such agencies. Similarly, the greater the technological achievement, the more the social system is pressured to accommodate such achievements. Any prolonged and exaggerated imbalances between the social and technical sectors lead to stagnation. And the pressures for development are such that stagnation is intolerable over a long period. This is what revolutions are all about.

26. John K. Galbraith, *The Affluent Society*. Boston: Houghton Mifflin Co., 1958, pp. 354–55.

3

Morphology of Three Worlds

Any effort at typification at a universal level is bound to create many problems. It is evident that old nations of the Third World (Latin America) differ profoundly from new nations of the Third World (Asia and Africa) in everything from religion to military organization. Such variabilities will be examined in subsequent chapters, when the social subsystems are discussed. It is important to establish a cross-sectional view of how the three worlds in development are organized, before explaining their interactional patterns.

FIRST WORLD

Dominated by the United States, including allies in Western Europe and satellites in Latin America and elsewhere.

Economy: Capitalist system; based on private ownership in a free market; development of corporate wealth and strong tendencies toward monopolistic controls of large private power blocs. The typical economy is capitalistic, based on individual entrepreneurial initiative, with little centralized planning (generally only in social welfare sectors). Emphasis on services and consumer goods production. Open internal market; high international integration created by financial and commodity markets, with slight regulation. Savings policies are individual-voluntary and/or based on democratic tax system. Investment is private, unrestricted, uncoordinated. Source of funds is variable; based on decisions taken by household, business, bank credit, and international capital market. Currencies are stable. While establishing terms of trade that are mutually favorable is difficult, given protectionist ideologies, they are much less fatal than for underdeveloped countries. Growth rates tend to be low, although the 1960's showed much more vigor in this regard than the 1950's. Such rates, however, seemed adequately balanced for the needs of industrial society. The agricultural sector is 5 to 20 per cent of the GNP, and anywhere from 6 per cent of the labor force in the United States to a high of 25 per cent in France. The contraction of this sector is aided by international competition (market forces) and by government subsidy. Industrial level of development is high; growth rate has, with such notable exceptions as Japan and Korea, leveled off. Consumption orientation, encouraged as necessary stimulus for growth; restricted by market fluctuations and private savings. Labor unions strong, highly organized, constituting an economic force; but only in the sense of maintaining the status quo.

Polity: Parliamentary democracy, which is established by legal authority and based upon economic law of market. Ideologically conservative and centrist. Accepts conflict within rules of game. Emphasis on nation-state is moderate to slight; most prominent in reaction to external threats. Tendency to have few major political parties, with strategic rather than ideological differences between them prevailing. Policy formulation is by these parties and/or associational interest groups. Range of party activity is narrowly political. Party elite membership is small and inactive except at election times. Organization for the most part is highly bureaucratized, and in the more vigorous portions of the First World, membership is across class and racial lines.

The basic unit is the caucus. Elected representatives forming party leadership tend to come from traditional classes and form oligarchical control, while remaining sensitive to public desires for policy-making. Policy implementing achieved by bureaucrats functioning under political executives. Independent judiciary. Non-participation of religious organizations in governmental or political functions (separation of church and state). Subordination of army to government, though pressure to have voice in international political policies.

Society: Highly urbanized; large growth of medium-sized cities (250,-000–1,000,000) in addition to several large cities. Moderate pace of industrial growth, leveled off at a high rate of development. Rapid growth of middle class, both professional and entrepreneurial; contraction of lower and working classes. High degree of vertical upward and downward mobility (more upward); increasing specialization of occupations; great status differentiation through occupation and income. Main avenue of mobility is through education, in highly bureaucratized society. Liberal, mass education; education has high income yield and is greatly in demand. Increase in leisure activities, decrease in work activities; considerable separation of occupation from private life. Increased social welfare programs and benefits. High level of mass consumption. Greater geographic mobility. Family unit: small, nuclear; increase in emotional role. Proliferation of highly organized, functionally specific, independent groups. Low birth rate, low death rate; few official demographic policies. Immigration: by quotas; emigration: no restrictions. Religion: Christian. Racial composition: white. Ethnic preeminence: Northern European. Cultural affinities: Puritanism and secular enlightenment.

Military: The basic property of the military is its professionalization; that is to say, its general confinement to the execution of decisions made by a non-military, civilian body. The armed forces do not have any specific ideological commitment apart from the defense of the nation as this is interpreted and defined by the civilian political elites. The armed forces operate within a well-defined organizational code, with minimum emphasis on personalities, except in wartime and for propagandistic purposes. The standing peacetime army is generally small to modest in size, with large-scale conscription confined to crisis periods; although it might be added that the definition of crisis period tends to be elongated in the present epoch. The centers of actual military power are dispersed throughout the nation, with a bureaucratic core located in the capital city. Engagement in formal, open political activities is consciously eschewed, and considered a conflict of interest. Service rivalries exist; but such rivalries are normally confined to which sector of the armed forces gets what and when. There is a noticeable absence of friction between ranks, of "barracks uprisings" against higher military echelon, or open rivalries between military leadership. Requirements for admission and promotion are clearly defined and broadly accepted. Esprit de corps is very high, providing a cohesive element in critical junctures.

SECOND WORLD

Dominated by the Soviet Union, including allies and/or satellites in Eastern Europe and parts of Asia.

Economy: Socialist system; based on public (state) ownership in a strictly controlled internal and external market; centralization of all sectors of the economy by political elites; based on total planning. The typical economy is geared to proletarian values. Emphasis is on heavy industrial production. Highly regulated internal and external markets, determined primarily by economic considerations. Trade agreements are largely within Eastern bloc countries; not subject to severe trade fluctuations. Savings policies are non-voluntary, state-determined and government-controlled. Investment is through the public sector; highly restricted and coordinated. Source of funds is stable; based on internal budgeting. Currencies are generally stable. Growth rates are high; imbalances controlled through economic regulation. Agricultural section 15 to 30 per cent of GNP, 40 per cent of labor force; contraction due to prohibition of individual private agriculture. The factors making for land speculation are strictly regulated in order to release resources and increase output at a rate integrated to industrial expansion. Industrial level of development is high, and growth rates have just begun to level off. Direct and manifold controls on production and distribution of consumer goods; discouraged as deterrent to industrial development. Labor unions perceived as part of state directorate, worker councils play minor role.

Polity: Democratic centralism; legitimated by rationalized authority, and based upon economically grounded ideology of communism-socialism, interpreted through ruling elite with very high doctrinal rigidity. Very strong emphasis is put on building common forms of economic socialism in a brotherhood of political nation-states; most prominent in times of independent political dissension of a member nation-state. Prohibition and suppression of opposition. Strong one-party system dictating all interest articulation. Discipline tends to be very strong and centralization is from the top. Basic unit is the cell. Although working class oriented, party elite membership is rather large (up to 10 per cent of population); leadership based on bureaucratic principles of selection, and elites rising solely through party lines. Party activity is all-encompassing and continual: no separation of policy-making from policy-implementing, no separation of powers, legislation from above, achieved through bureaucrats functioning under political executives, judiciary not independent. Army entirely subordinate to civil control. Subordination or repression of religion and church. Enthusiasm and commitment are highly praised and broadly based, emphasizing community as well as national affairs.

Society: Highly urbanized; large growth of medium-sized cities, generally with several large ones; still a sizable peasant sector. High pace of industrial growth, just beginning to level off at a high rate of development. Rapid growth of working class, moderate increase of middle professional class (increase in non-bureaucratic white-collar workers). High degree of social mobility, with a greater amount than in First World due to technological change; slowly increased specialization of occupations; lower degree of status differentiation. Main avenue of mobility is through occupational hierarchy, although education is becoming more important with increased specialization, complexity, and bureaucratization of industrial structure. Technical-scientific, mass education is emphasized. The educational sphere is unique in that it alone can claim manpower priorities over economic production. This is based on notion of education as postponed economic improvements. Slight increase in leisure activities, little decrease in work activities; general separation of occupational and private spheres. High social welfare benefits. High level of mass communication; low level of mass consumption. Slight geographic mobility. Family unit: slightly extended nuclear family (often due to limited housing). Low birth rate, low death rate; variety of policies to integrate population increase with industrial growth rate. Immigration and emigration prohibited. Religion: Christian. Racial composition: white. Ethnic preeminence: Slavic-Central and Eastern European. Cultural affinities: Byzantine and secular enlightenment.

Military: The basic property of the military is its professionalization; but while it is generally confined to executing rather than formulating policy, it works closely with the political elite at the decision-making level. The armed forces do not have a specific ideological commitment apart from the general social commitment to the socialist ideology as defined by the civilian political elites. The armed forces operate within a well-defined organizational code, with a minimum emphasis, except in wartime and for propagandistic purposes, on personalities. On the other hand, the political elites often simulate military modes of dress and behavior. The standing army is generally larger than in the First World; but again, large-scale conscription is confined to crisis periods. The centers of actual military power are dispersed throughout the nation, with a bureaucratic core located near capital cities. Engagement in political activities is part of the role of the higher military elites, but eschewed among the rank and file (with the exception of political commissioners, either civilians attached to the military base or non-commissioned officers of political orientation within such bases). Service rivalries are frowned upon, and the organization of the branches of the military are made in terms of functional activities. The political system further discourages such rivalries by insisting on a higher military loyalty to state and party. There is a noticeable absence of friction between ranks, barracks uprisings against higher military echelons, or open rivalries between military leaderships. Requirements for admission and promotion are clearly defined and broadly accepted. Esprit de corps is very high, and provides a cohesive element in critical junctures.

However, just as the First World has exhibited an increasing tendency toward politicalization, the same pattern is unfolding in the Second World, especially the Soviet Union. The revelations by the post-Stalin leadership of political appointments which led to disastrous bureaucratic bungling during World War II are indicative of a far from smooth running military establishment. The very insistence on ideological criteria for advancement to high military positions adds a strain to the separation of the political and military elites that is perhaps somewhat less pronounced in the other parts of the world.

THIRD WORLD

Non-aligned and non-satellitic nations with a general tendency toward clustering in Africa, Asia, and Latin America—a spectrum conventionally covering Algeria to Yugoslavia in economy and India to China in polity.

Economy: Mixed economy; with both private and public sectors, but moving toward some form of socialism. Economy reveals conflict between desire for integration based on self-sufficiency, and need for aid in development. There is a dilemma between attempts at strong internal regulation (foreign/internal investment ratio) and moderate external regulation (freedom of block trading) and ability to implement development schemes. One additional problem in this connection is the difficulty in controlling the wealthy nationals, which in turn magnifies the problem in arranging for a better overseas arrangement. There is a decline in terms of trade; and a balance-of-payment problem. Variety of planning techniques also exist (total, national flow, national budget, project, labor, etc.). The typical economy is based on the peasant sector; basic level of economic production is agricultural; although emphasis is on basic industry. Desire for contraction of primary sector: mechanization of agriculture, overwhelming push factors, and imposed plans (rate of collectivization is presently reducing); agriculture often neglected in favor of emphasis on basic industrial development (the highest premium is placed on heavy industry whatever the costs in terms of man-hours) to create import substitute mechanisms. Successful integration of shift from agricultural to industrial sector is therefore uncertain, and dependent upon national planners' ability to control. Compounded by "demonstration effect," which government often tries to dampen through inflationary policies. Source of funds is variable and generally short term; foreign aid and investment supplement domestic savings (which are mitigated by unstable currency). Savings policies mostly voluntary and due to the inability to control. Growth rates are high in percentage but not in terms of per capita yields. There is an attempted control of imbalances through political regulation. Short-run private-sector gains often vitiate effects of long-run public-sector planning. Labor unions are radical and unstable, with little economic role.

Polity: Mass democracy; legitimated through highly articulated and politically grounded ideology of nationalism and socialism, with a strong charismatic leader. Ideology is radical and socialist; but with considerable variation; polycentric rather than monolithic. Basic unit is the party branch. Highly centralized state, under virtual one party rule. Elite desire for total control and suppression of conflict groups, with no disjunction between policy-makers and policy-implementers. This is mitigated by: low level of party discipline; enthusiasm and commitment often attached to party personages rather than to party policies; absence of institutionalized charisma; responsiveness to masses' desires. Source of change in policies due less to minority parties than to multiple interest articulation and application. Often independent and over-participant role of military, executive branch, and/or prematurely overdeveloped bureaucracy (sometimes much too underdeveloped). Although oriented toward the "popular" class or the nation as such, party membership is somewhere between the First and Second Worlds. Leadership often based on educational-technological-military criteria; except under highly revolutionary circumstances, leadership alliances with elites of traditional prestige where latter not resistant to development.

Society: Rapidly urbanizing; problem of developing middle-sized cities, often the major city more powerful than nation as a whole. Industrial growth still attaining "take-off" stage. Social mobility: still low in traditional areas; occupational mobility slowly increasing in industrial areas. Labor market still unspecialized. Traditional status differentiation diminishing. Main avenue of mobility is through occupational and political hierarchy.

Education: Emphasis on mass literacy, technical-scientific secondary education, with planning to integrate industrial needs into educational programs. Few leisure activities; increase in work activities; often no clear distinction between occupational and private spheres of life. High social welfare benefits. Development of mass communication; low consumption rates. Individual geographic mobility is low; occasional shifts of large groups in population (due to force, planning, natural disasters, etc.). Family unit: extended family, deteriorating. High birth rate, and declining death rate (although severe problems of mortality still exist in major Asian countries like India, Pakistan, and Burma). The Third World also exhibits great difficulties in establishing birth-control policies. Immigration and emigration: generally restricted by occupational skills. Religion: Moslem, Hindu, Buddhist, Christian (in Latin America). Racial composition: yellow, black, brown, red; in short, basically non-white. Ethnic preeminence: Negroes and Indians. Cultural affinities: philosophical rationalism closely linked to religious expressions. No clear separation between the secular and the sacred as in the Western tradition; but rather close fusions between theological doctrines and political credos.

Military: The basic property of the military is its politicalization, that is, its role as a formulator and executor of political decisions. The "new nations" witness the rise of military politics, either as a prime mark of sovereignty or directly, as the ruling political group. The armed forces have specific ideological commitments—in pre-revolutionary Third World countries to conservative Caesaristic models and in post-revolutionary Third World countries to radical-charismatic models. The organizational code of the military is ambiguously defined, with an extreme emphasis on personalities, on the military leader as a national redeemer. The standing army is relatively small in numbers, but with a "top-heavy" ratio of elite to rank and file. But the level of financial expenditure is quite high considering the size of the standing army—in part this is a consequence of the necessity of purchasing arms from foreign industrial powers, and in part the consequence of maintaining a potential agency of maximum coercion with minimum numbers. The centers of military operations are usually highly concentrated in or near the capital cities or the industrial centers, hence enhancing the possibility of "palace revolutions"; also a symbolic reflection of the military near the centers of political decision-making. Political activity is most noticeable at the elite level, but in periods of discontent, rank-and-file leadership will oftentimes manifest itself. Service rivalries are exceptionally high, with the navy and air force often representing a posture to the political right of the army. Friction among military elites is considerable. Factionalism oftentimes becomes noticeable in pre-coup d'état situations. Esprit de corps is not particularly strong—except within "ingroup" or barracks factions.

4

Psychology of Three Worlds

Some men are more anxious than others to increase their standard of living, while others are more deeply rooted in the world of their ancestors, childhood, and kinship ties. But it is safe to say that most men are complicated enough to represent, in their persons, a combination of achievement and ascription—that is, personally sought-after gains and advantages derived from birth. It may have some value to determine which type of men can be galvanized into social mobility, but it is more pertinent to examine how all such men have come to expect from their societies answers to dilemmas which in past ages were viewed as purely personal or determined by a supernatural force.

The distinction between social and personal responsibility is not confined to the industrial epoch. In early Christianity there was a great debate between those who saw in the scriptures a mandate for the militant pursuit of justice in the world and those who saw private renunciation of the world.[1] In Greek culture, competition pervaded all

1. Despite the vigorous critique by Kurt Samuelsson of the Weber thesis, based on the view that "no matter what the church or sect, the guiding principle is the renunciation of the world," there is the other strain of involvement with, no less than estrangement from, things temporal. In truth, what particular version of Christian doctrine prevails is contingent on non-religious events. But for a religion to make an appeal to the sacred through a negation of the profane would doom it in an industrial-urbanized complex. And Christianity shows no signs of such a form of ascetic death. On this topic, compare Kurt Samuelsson, *Religion and Economic Action: A Critique of Max Weber,* edited by D. C. Coleman. New York and Evanston: Harper & Row (The Academic Library), 1964; and Ephraim Fischoff, "The Protestant Ethic and the Spirit of Capitalism: The History of a Controversy," *Social Research,* Vol. II, No. 1, Feb. 1944, pp. 53–77.

aspects of non-slave social life. The mutual acceptance of a hier-archically ordered system which had obtained in Egyptian society was broken by the city-states. The evolutionary process may be considered in the following way. The allocation of responsibility in traditional society relied upon institutions which functioned only to satisfy the needs of masters. Dominant classes were deeply separated from ex-ploited masses. Or in neutral value terms, the dynamic classes were far removed from the underclasses.

In the process of a nation's development, its search for identity be-comes pronounced and the classical distinction between classes and masses dissolves. In a very advanced stage of development discontent becomes channelized along altogether new lines. Problems of class membership give way to problems of professional association. The link in this process is the growing responsibility of government to rationalize the social system.[2] In a Weberian world, the problem of bureaucracy, especially in a world of legal-rational legitimacy, transcends the prob-lem of class. But there exists another approach to bureaucracy, one that is much more skeptical about the concept of a bureaucratic class. It maintains that ownership still retains a veto effect on managerial activity, particularly within capitalist modes of production. Nonetheless, whatever the theoretical merits of debates on the nature of bureaucracy, it is clear that, in societies with a high bureaucratic input, individual intelligence and initiative are seriously thwarted. Routine replaces tradi-tion as the chief obstacle to innovation.

The individual is rarely permitted to select his ends—particularly if there is reason to believe that such ends are in violation of the funda-mental rules of the "game." Knowledge is reduced to expertise. This instrumentalization of man makes it difficult to blame any one person; hence the individual thinks he can forget about self-blame or self-loathing. If man may turn his self-doubts and self-loathings toward an impersonal object of discontent, such as the organization, the party, or the state, his own shortcomings become transformed into the general ills of society. This emphasis on depersonalized ways of solving prob-lems, on automatic operations in production, on maximizing formal rules and roles, compels each individual to engage in a struggle for self-

2. See an interesting statement on this subject by Richard Korn, "The Private Citizen, the Social Expert, and the Social Problem," in *Mass Society and Crisis: Social Problems and Social Pathology,* edited by Bernard Rosenberg, Israel Gerver and F. William Howton. New York: Macmillan & Company, 1964, pp. 576–93.

reclamation. The rise of social movements which are anti-bureaucratic and anti-organizational indicates that psychological problems persist, whatever the level of economic productivity.

The bureaucratic strain is particularly prevalent in classical capitalism: its industrial output is nearly always less than its actual capacity. Personal savings are liquidated through market fluctuations and inflationary spirals, and the capitalist as an entrepreneur is unable to survive without direct assistance from the bureaucratic organization. The image of the capitalist as a swashbuckling investor with a devil-may-care attitude has given way to the cautious manager who can be induced to take risks only with government assistance, and whose sense of the social commonweal and its needs is rarely more elevated than that of his employees. Even the entrepreneurial class has taken to blaming failure on the government, on the impersonal laws of the market, on the inequities of the tax system, rather than on the corporate self or the corporate image.

There are two quite distinct problems: ideology and reality. To some extent the entrepreneur as the swashbuckling investor of Schumpeter's dreams never quite existed even under classical nineteenth-century capitalist conditions. Further, the problem of insufficient aggregate demand had to be met by Keynesian mechanisms of building into the economy levels of demand that were linked to psychological rather than economic necessities. Thus, it was little wonder that by the present century, few social sectors had any retentive faith in the automatic mechanisms of market adjustment. This was the case especially during the post-World War I period.

Under such conditions it is little wonder that freedom and liberty have increasingly come to mean security for the person. When such security is not forthcoming, the situation becomes ripe for social rebellion. This is particularly so in industrial society. Here sectional and sectoral imbalances are at their maximum. Educational advancement can be very high and social mobility relatively stagnant, as in Argentina. An urban complex may advance at the expense of the rest of the nation, as in England. A program for agrarian reform may be promoted by civilian government, but carried out under militaristic rule which leaves the democratic aspects of this reform unachieved, as in Brazil. A nation may achieve high political integration, yet continue to be economically stagnant as a result of military over-commitment.

The developmental process is a major cause of the deterioration of the traditional society. This discontent is in turn blamed on the society rather than on the self. For this reason the need to stimulate achievement motivation is far less significant than the need to channelize already-existing discontent. In the economic system the industrial states show to the emerging nations the psychological face of their own future.[3]

There must be dissonance observed between general economic growth in contrast to one's own comparative stagnation. There must be a *cognitive* awareness of the gap between advancement at one end of the social scale—say, education—and stagnation at the level of economic opportunity. There must be a conception of a social order, not only different, but morally superior and politically more inclusive than the one men presently live under. These psychological states cannot be artificially induced. Disequilibrium in the fabric of society must precede any widespread demand for reorganization. Inducements to discontent may boomerang. There may result a thorough insulation from social realities.[4]

Social classes quite often attempt to escape from social realities. The frustrations inherent in social change can readily produce an unwillingness and unreadiness to assume the primacy of an external world in shaping inner needs and desires. There is a growing tendency to devalue *both* the traditional position of the poor and the conventional life styles of the wealthy. Such social escapism not only erodes the values of traditional society; it also brings into disrepute and then destroys the familiar relations which are almost omnipotent in maintaining traditional patterns of authority. The retreatist himself may prove incapable of mustering the effort needed to show an achievement orientation, but those of the next generation, aware of the discontent their parents have suffered, may develop a strong achievement orientation. The drive for achievement does not necessarily guarantee that alienation will not take place. To be sure, such neo-Freudian syndromes may not work out in many cases, but the forms of dis-

3. An exposition of the problem of channelizing discontent is in H. H. Gerth and C. Wright Mills, *Character and Social Structure: The Psychology of Social Institutions.* New York: Harcourt, Brace and World, 1953, pp. 456–80.
4. See David C. McClelland, *The Achieving Society.* New York and Princeton: D. Van Nostrand Co., 1961, for a perfect illustration of the confusion which can exist in the investigator's mind between achievement and development orientations, esp. pp. 36–61.

sonance and disequilibrium, whether they yield aggressive involvement or retreatist isolation, are less important to the development
process than the existence of such forms themselves.[5]

Just as retreatism may be an aid in development, overdedication to
development may actually hinder it. A man may make a great deal
of money quickly but still have no idea of social savings and business
investment. This process has been described in many novels about
Mexico before the revolution. In Bolivia, after the 1952 popular revolution, the mine workers retained their arms and used their populist
control as a demonstration of their power, not as a symbol of hard
work. The working time in the mines was drastically cut and the
amount of mineral wealth actually produced dipped far under what
it had been during the previous rightist dictatorship. These examples
illustrate the complexities in the relationship between an achievement
orientation and a developmental orientation.[6] An achiever can remain
egoistic, and a promoter can remain rooted in traditional values. Indeed, these are usually the case, which is why the role of the state
ultimately supersedes the free actions of private individuals in the
development process.

The psychological characteristics of developing man directly affect
the economic take-off point. It is widely presupposed that, however
diverse the motives for development may be, dissatisfaction with the
existential condition and some sort of program for an optional approach
are both necessary. What that option is and how it can be induced in
others and extended to future generations remain the real task. One
economist reported that in order to induce the peasantry of Northeast Brazil to work hard for long hours, he had to retain, and even reinforce, the methods of exploitation used by the latifundists.[7] It is manifestly untrue that to reveal to a person his "true interests" guarantees

5. See E. E. Hagen, *On the Theory of Social Change*, Homewood, Ill.: The
Dorsey Press, 1962, pp. 175–85.
6. On this range of questions, see Kalman H. Silvert, *The Conflict Society:
Reaction and Revolution in Latin America*. New Orleans: Hauser Press, 1962.
7. This was reported by the Brazilian economist, Celso Furtado, who as the
Director of SUDENE, the Northeast Redevelopment Program in Brazil, found
the the method of democratic persuasion yielded fewer results and was more
widely mistrusted than traditionalist methods of authority. This is a kind of
empirical confirmation of Charles Sanders Peirce's famous declaration that of
the three methods for fixing belief, none is more satisfactory for mass consumption than authority. See Charles S. Peirce, "Method of Fixing Belief," *Collected
Papers of C. S. Peirce*, Vol. 5, edited by Charles Hartshorne and Paul Weiss.
Cambridge, Mass.: Belknap (Harvard University Press), pp. 233–48.

his participation in the mass participation in the mass society or in the modernization process. The line between action and interests is far from straight. Even if we ignore the dilemmas arising out of a direct correlation of actions and interests, there is a policy issue involved: the degree of social unrest necessary to stimulate a person to think along developmental lines without creating complete revolutionary upheaval.[8]

A myth has been propagated that external stimulants are necessary to place the masses of Third World nations into a "take-off" position. While there are certainly great differences between levels of achievement and aspirations, the poor do not require much motivation for change beyond their own existential situation. If we take the "case histories" of two slum people—Carolina Maria de Jesus in the São Paulo *favelas* and Jesús Sánchez in the Casa Grande of Mexico City— what emerges is a picture of dislocated, no less than developing, people in changing circumstances. We might outline the common characteristics among the poor who are part of the development process: (1) ability to move from a rural society to an urban society, and also from a society based on barter and property to one based upon money and contract; (2) discontent with low-grade economic status, which is expressed in a variety of ways—shifts from house to house and from job to job, concern with the education of children, willingness to postpone immediate gratifications; (3) politicalization, as expressed in voting, concern with candidates and party issues, and even membership in organized political groupings; (4) secularization of personal values, as expressed in "free" love patterns, a lessening of the bonds of religious fervor, or even sometimes conversions to other faiths, and a general acculturation to the impersonal, anomic life of the large industrial city; and above all (5) an unwillingness to return to the agricultural communities from which they have immigrated.[9]

Carolina Maria de Jesus did not escape from the *favelas* from whence she emanated. The elder Sánchez, for his part, held firm to his desire

8. Rex D. Hopper has raised the interesting proposition that revolution-making is inevitably in the control of socially displaced and marginal people and that the process of automation, insofar as it accentuates the distinction between integration and marginality, accelerates the revolutionary process. See his paper, "Cybernation, Marginality, and Revolution," in *The New Sociology,* edited by Irving Louis Horowitz. New York and London: Oxford University Press, 1964, pp. 313–30.
9. Carolina Maria de Jesus, *Child of the Dark.* New York: E. P. Dutton & Co., 1962; and Oscar Lewis, *The Children of Sanchez: Autobiography of a Mexican Family.* New York: Random House, 1961.

for personal advancement, and for the success of his children, within the new urban world of Mexico City. Even when there is an achievement motivation in common, it is difficult to distinguish between those who succeed in making the great ascent and those who return to the source of their discontent. Indeed, this is further complicated by the fact that the second generation offspring of *papá* Sánchez turned out to be far more uprooted and anomic than the original pioneer to the outskirts of Mexico City. Displeasure with the old way of doing things does not guarantee successful adjustment to the new way. It may be a necessary ingredient in social development, but it alone is not sufficient.

The classical traditions within economics and sociology give little insight into the solution of such development problems as generational disputes, marginality, transitional stages, norm deviations, and anomie as a form of social discontent. Yet, they have set the stage for an independent variable. Earlier discussions of the mental set of developing man have emphasized class and status, imaginary and real.

Prior to the rise of the Third World, the psychological aspects of development were embedded in a maze of sociological and economic doctrines. Within Weber's sociology of religion, for instance, an entire series of psychological criteria, what might be termed his notion of the psychic economy, were evolved. Protestantism was made to appear more as a strategy for capitalist development than a religious revolution. The concepts of delayed gratifications, trust in fellow religionists, and salvation through hard work rather than otherworldly faith were introduced in such a way as to demonstrate the unique connection of capital formation and religious salvation.[10] For Werner Sombart, writing at approximately the same time, the Jews were the "original Calvinists"; they possessed in perfect combination those psychological characteristics of frugality, thrift, conservatism that gave them a "positive attitude" toward development in the capitalist economy.[11] In Georges Sorel and the Franco-Italian school of power sociology generally, the notion of the capitalist as a "Creative Apache" was used to show that

---

10. See Max Weber, *The Protestant Ethic and the Spirit of Capitalism,* translated by Talcott Parsons. New York: Charles Scribner's Sons, 1958; and "The Protestant Sects and the Spirit of Capitalism," in *From Max Weber: Essays in Sociology,* edited by H. H. Gerth and C. Wright Mills. New York: Oxford University Press, 1946.
11. See Werner Sombart, *The Jews and Modern Capitalism,* translated by M. Epstein. Glencoe, Ill.: The Free Press, 1951, esp. pp. 157–90.

the Robber Barons were actually the heroes in the developmental drama, and not the villains portrayed by the muckrakers. Their "constructive violence" made them the elite of economic development. Unlike the European bourgeoisie, they retained their energies, their will to victory, and their characteristic class interests.[12]

The economists came earlier, but they have persisted in rendering clumsy service to the psychological theory of development. In the world of Adam Smith and his moral economy, it was not "benevolence" but "regard to one's interests" that prompted economical growth. Indeed, the desire for such growth was so great on the part of "men of inferior wealth" as well as "men of superior wealth" that they always joined forces when the sovereign order as such was threatened.[13] Marx still retained a psychological insight toward social change, even though his vision of class struggle in industrial society prevented him from perceiving the grounds of class accommodation. Marx was a historicist. The capitalist class was pursuing its purpose: primitive accumulation. Like those in every class before its own ascendancy, the members of the bourgeoisie were too involved in their own affairs to appreciate the widespread effects of their actions. The Great Depression made them raise their heads and appreciate the liberal welfare state that could control their class caprices and avarice. Marx was profoundly ambiguous about the degree of altruism on the part of the working class necessary to bring about socialism. Just how historical and voluntary features of social change intersect to promote a general good is just as much a problem for the proletariat as it is for the bourgeoisie, or any social class with basic class interests and impulses. Terming such interests as rational or historical did not remove the problem of action, it only postponed matters for another epoch, specifically the Russian revolutionary epoch.

Interest in the psychological aspects of economic growth has not lessened since the classical period. Indeed, from Marshall to Keynes the concern with non-rational factors in economic production and consumption has sharply increased. There has been a strong tendency to recognize and accept the psychological as a necessary, if inexplicable,

12. See Georges Sorel, *Reflections on Violence,* translated by T. E. Hulme. Glencoe, Ill.: The Free Press, 1950.
13. See Adam Smith, *The Theory of Moral Sentiments,* in *Adam Smith's Moral and Political Philosophy,* edited by H. W. Schneider. New York: Hafner Publishing Co., 1948; and *An Inquiry into the Nature and Causes of the Wealth of Nations,* edited by E. Cannan. New York: G. P. Putnam's Sons, 1904.

factor in any economy. Thus, we are told about the necessity of "confidence" in a stable economy—whether there is an objective warrant for such confidence or not. We are told of how irrational commitment to style changes promotes general innovation—without being told how such emphasis on style apart from function is manipulated. Consumer spending becomes equated with faith in the economic system itself.[14]

The rise of psychological theories of society, therefore, is not simply an effort to evolve an "applied" approach to achievement motivation, but in the larger sense, and on the theoretical side, a reaction against a deterministic view of history, which assumes the primacy of a single factor in individuals who make up any given group.[15] The emphasis on individual psychology also serves to minimize any faith in collective mysterious forces operating behind men's backs. On the other hand, the psychological turn away from history still left intact the doctrine of man uncovering rather than discovering, and in fact, stimulated anew explanations of dissatisfaction with personal fate.

It is not sufficient just to declare that social mobility and high aspirations exist or are important or that they differ from person to person. Some men are blind to the values of literacy, while others will give up all comforts to learn how to read and to write. Some men could not care less about the length of time it takes to repair or replace commodities in a backward region; while others react with impatience and demand high efficiency. Some women find their traditional roles comforting, while others view them as repressive and oppressive. In short, to locate the main sociological variables in the developmental process is not to explain *why* some men are ambitious, driving, and adventurous, while others are not.[16]

We have mentioned that all developing men appear to place responsibility for achievement on society rather than on themselves. This is to say that the traditional orientation toward self-resignation and away from social responsibility represents a fundamental commitment to "na-

14. See R. F. Harrod, *Economic Essays.* New York: Harcourt, Brace & Co., 1952. Harrod's studies on the ethics of imperfect competition are an excellent summary of Keynesian economics, particularly its psychological network.

15. For a useful summary of the controversies between "sociologism" and "psychologism," see Alex Inkeles, "Personality and Social Structure," in *Sociology Today: Problems and Prospects,* edited by R. K. Merton, L. Broom, and L. S. Cottrell, Jr. New York: Basic Books, 1959, pp. 249–75.

16. Perhaps the most resourceful and impressive, presentation of these problems is contained in H. G. Barnett, *Innovation: The Basis of Cultural Change.* New York: McGraw-Hill, 1953.

ture" as something to be accepted and lived with, rather than a series of hurdles to be overcome. Traditional culture in Latin America has frequently been identified with procrastination. Traditional men suffer from a poverty of wants as well as from a poverty of ideas for satisfying them—a fundamental attitude common to pre-industrial styles of living rather than a special religious or ethnic property. This is the case in contemporary Korea. One study points out that in

> East Asian culture, man typically has not been so concerned with gaining mastery over his environment as he has been with living in harmony with it. Mountains that might obstruct travel and rivers that might be impassable during certain seasons have not been viewed as merely frustrating inconveniences. Rather, these are historical facts to which man must discipline himself.[17]

This attitude was expressed during the classical Greek period. The philosophy of Epictetus and of the Stoics in general reveals a resignation in the face of nature.

Equally significant is the traditional attitude toward time—both as an empirical measure of change and as a moral measure of worth. In the first case, the attitude toward time is distinctly a creation of our own culture, where "time is money." In underdeveloped regions, however, things do not run "on time," only "more or less on time." Centralized planning is viewed with suspicion, not simply because it is usually connected with totalitarian political slogans but also because it disrupts traditional patterns. In Italy, the fascists made much of their boast that under their regime "the trains ran on time." Under such conditions, it is easy to see how the opposition might well argue against being on time.

The industrial attitude toward time, motion, and nature differs even within the First World. The search for high achievement indices has obscured the different work habits in European and American industrial plants. The best response to this issue was made by Samuel Gompers in 1890, when he gave testimony to the United States Industrial Commission on Capital and Labor. He noted that in

> every mechanical trade, when European workmen come over to this country and stand beside their American fellow workingmen it

17. Don Adams, "The Monkey and the Fish," in *Dynamics of Development: An International Development Reader,* edited by Gove Hambridge. New York: Frederick Praeger, 1964, pp. 362–63.

simply dazes them—the velocity of motion, the deftness, the quick-
ness, the constant strain. The European bricklayer, the European
carpenter, the European compositor-printer, the European tailor
comes over here and works in the shop, or factory, or office, and
he is simply intoxicated by the rapidity of the movements of the
American workingmen, and it is some months, with the greatest
endeavor, before he can at all come near the production of the
American workingman.[18]

Gompers was no monistic theorist; in trying to explain the reasons for
this gap, he went into everything from climatic conditions ("the changes
in weather make the people more active, more nervous; accelerates
their motion, accelerates their thought") to the absence in America
of a hereditary condition of slavery and serfdom. But, above all, it
was his contention that the gap is best explained by the superior condition of the American workingman. He was the arch advocate in
labor ranks of class cooperation. Like his counterpart, the enlightened
capitalist, he insisted that more wages and better conditions make for
greater output and superior quality. Gompers bridged the gap between
labor and those sectors of enlightened management who advocated
class cooperation in the interest of greater productivity. The success of
the Gompers approach to unionism can be measured by the extent to
which the American worker defines his goals in terms of a "fair deal"
rather than the assumption of power. This confrontation of American
working-class experience with European traditions reflects the different
psychologies of development between the two capitalist spheres.

In terms of the ethics of time, we often find a profound psychological
nostalgia reinforced by religious observances. The good life is defined
in terms of living in the past, especially at a time when man was closer
to nature. Respect for ancestors is common in the East, while in the
West there is an equivalent notion of redemption in the next world.
It must be noted, however, that explanations for the rise of capitalism
have revolved in part around the secularization of religion. In this
sense, the Protestant Reformation weakened effective belief in other-
worldliness by stressing greater productivity. Indeed, such attitudes have
always been attractive, for all societies have identified virtue with events
in the dim past: "Good old days" that never were, and "men who were
men" in contrast to an effete culture of the present. These frequently

18. See Samuel Gompers, "The Philosophy of Organized Labor," in *The Nation
Transformed,* edited by Sigmund Diamond. New York: George Braziller, 1963,
pp. 206–17.

uttered banalities clearly show that such habits of mind are not the property of any single religion or culture.[19] With a century of hindsight, the good-old-days argument used by the feudal aristocrat, the petty bourgeois, and the Luddite worker were misplaced. Yet, when they were uttered, they had an element of truth. Until the last quarter of the nineteenth century, living conditions of the urban working class were probably no better, and quite likely worse, than the condition of the peasantry one hundred years earlier. Thus, what in retrospect were feeble arguments against the inevitable were in prospect outrages at the miseries brought about by planless progress.

An orientation based upon the inviolability of nature involves at least an implicit commitment to the idea of stability. In judging human affairs, this orientation rests on the theme of "eternal return"—a changing world without growth, lacking novelty and even chance. Human change is said to follow a principle of steady recurrence. Nature affords a spectacle of change within repeating cycles. Growth tends to be measured in geological terms: the layers upon layers of striated rock which form the age of the universe. The societal orientation, for its part, often involves some commitment to the idea of history in the sense that changes which occur are fragmented, nonrepeating, and under at least partial control of human agents and agencies. Society offers the unique spectacle of change which is constantly being evaluated for its "worth," that is, for its developmental properties. It may be that the view of nature as a stable entity is itself metaphysically conditioned by social norms and expectations. Be that as it may, this classical vision of "living close to Nature" involves results which are sharply different from those which start with a societal bias.

The nature orientation offers slender inducements for taking high risks, since the "natural history of men" is part of an enormous cycle of *corso* and *ricorso* that rewards the high risk-taker and the low risk-taker in the same way—by destruction, dismay, and death. Similarly, since the societal orientation sharply demarcates man from other animals, and certainly from inanimate nature, it offers reasons for taking risks. The notion of human uniqueness is so welded into the major Western religions that cautions and prohibitions against excesses of

19. On the subject of the contrast between underdeveloped and developed, see Charles J. Erasmus, *Man Takes Control: Cultural Development and American Aid.* Minneapolis: University of Minnesota, 1961; and for a more specific study, Kasum Nair, *Blossoms in the Dust: The Human Factor in Indian Development.* New York: Frederick Praeger, 1962.

materialism are the foundation of Western theology. One of the essential properties of Western religions is their utopianism. This longing for a perfect future is the basis of what has been called "positive mysticism" in Western society-oriented religions.[20]

Developing man has a great propensity toward taking risks. He has a great gambling instinct as compared with non-developing peoples, rooted as they are in nature. He also believes the world is imperfect as it is; and further, he believes that he can better himself or better the world as such. In the very notion of society there is the idea that it is imperfect and exists in time and that the world order can be improved. Optimism or pessimism are not necessarily connected with risk-taking. One might be optimistic about the possibility of changing the social world, and on the other hand, one might be pessimistic about the chances of success. Nonetheless, the willingness to take risks is stimulated by a faith in the perfectability of man.

This same attitude is reflected ecologically in the willingness of a person to risk his position and possessions and move elsewhere to an unknown place. The stimulus may be materialistic or religious. The religious factor may become an important surrogate for an ideology which justifies risk in terms of ultimate reward. People might move from comfortable surroundings, as immigrants on the eastern seaboard of the United States did when they headed west to frontier lands. Such people may brave many hardships and take all kinds of risks as the result of a theological commandment. Thus, a belief in the perfection of a heavenly order does not necessarily entail a belief in the necessity of improving the temporal world. But, as in the case of Judaism or Christianity, it sanctions a search for perfectability of man in this world.

Those who take risks are sometimes spurred on by a strong theological sanction against failure. There may be a lesson in this for developmental theory. It might be possible to stimulate risk-taking by minimizing the advantages of standing pat; by penalizing, in effect, those who do not take risks. In the Soviet Union this has been a particularly important aspect in the colonization of the relatively unpopulated "virgin soil" territories of Asian Russia, and without the earth-shaking violence characteristic of earlier epochs.

The major difficulty of risk-taking is that the more developed may

20. See David C. McClelland, *The Achieving Society*. New York: D. Van Nostrand Co., 1961, pp. 367–88.

be penalized on behalf of the less developed; hence there is a danger that those engaged in the development process will become alienated and disenchanted. But, still, risk-taking does indeed seem characteristic of rapidly developing areas. And whether this spills over into threats or coercion against those unwilling to make sacrifices of comfort or unwilling to take the risks necessary for achievement of rapid and high development is an administrative question, not a problem for psychology or religion.

We need to emphasize that the mental set of developing man includes a philosophical (no less than a religious) component. One could call this a nominalistic or empirical metaphysic. In some sense even the religious divines exhibit a belief in the material, scientific world as primary rather than otherworldly gratification. Here we immediately face the contradictory situation where, under the early Protestantism of Luther and Calvin, rapid *social* development seems to be connected with the rewards of the *spiritual* world, the rewards of Paradise. But, on close inspection, these notions are not incongruous since the idea of betterment is really the secular expression of the idea of the calling. Betterment is what the good man strives for in this world. It has not yet been resolved whether or not there is a theological sanction, or whether the theological ballast has to be overthrown entirely along with other traditionalist residues. Algeria is described as both Moslem and as socialist, whereas Ghana is called materialist in philosophy and socialist in economy. The fact remains that the emphasis on scientific measurements is part of the societal orientation of developing man. He needs something "objective" and impersonal that can be measured so that he can determine what is or is not developing.

The concept of nineteenth-century progress, so severely criticized, is a perfect illustration of a material scientific orientation. One measured development by the number of buildings that went up each year; the amount of money one had in the bank account; the size of the population of the industrial center; the size of the political apparatus. Such quantitative measuring of social entities became extremely important to the mental set of societal man. Progress became not only a subject for liberalism but also an object for scientism. This is seen most clearly in the matter of numbers. Developing societies exhibit a fetish for numbers, which may serve as indices of wealth and power. There is an equation between numerical size and rates of development. Some theorists have even taken to speaking of symbolic power "banks" as analogous to real economic banks.[21] Oftentimes this assumes a grotesque giganticism, a desperate search for the bigger and better. This was typical of late nineteenth-century United States, and reaches its present culmination with phenomena like the Empire State Building and the World Trade Center. The same phenomena are now being reproduced and replicated in the Soviet Union with the largest rockets, the highest payload, the maximum thrust into outer space. The quantification of science serves as a guide and a measure for economic development, quite apart from the social problems such giganticism creates.

Perhaps the question of second thoughts ought to be considered. What happens when and if upon inspection the social "contract" no longer meets one's needs? Should rules then be violated? In taking risks, one must have some end in view. Such risk-taking must not become disengaged from economic rationalism. The problem thus shifts back to what is meant by rationalism: a definition of the situation based on specific class interests, or an alternative model built on the concept of class cooperation for national goals.

ATTITUDES TOWARD TRADITIONALISM AND MODERNISM

Even where a people is already committed to the idea that society can be brought under greater control, there is often still a strong commitment to traditional social patterns. Far from collapsing in the presence of modernist ideologies, traditionalism retains its vitality, not only among the aristocratic classes but also among large segments of the working classes.

The poor argue that by working longer hours they are doubly exploited. They are exploited in the amount of time they work and their inability to enjoy what leisure time they have. A more sophisticated version of this is that the notion of savings is not so much an alien concept as it is a foolish one, given the inflationary spiral of most underdeveloped economies. Also modernism, far from releasing human energies for creative acts, reproduces the anomie and alienation so typical of advanced nations. Hence, the arguments by which developmentalists advo-

21. Talcott Parsons, "Some Reflections on the Place of Force in Social Process," in *Internal War,* edited by Harry Eckstein. New York: The Free Press, 1964, pp. 33–70.

cate modernism are unrealistic in terms of behavioral patterns exhibited by the working classes.

Traditionalist arguments are better known; they have existed longer. Essentially, they point out the illogicality of the argument that what is modern is good. The displacement of conventional myths, mores, and mysteries with modern science and technology only creates a higher form of mythology. Modernism replaces one form of superstition with another, but it by no means eliminates the gap between the haves and have-nots. It is further reasoned that substitution of aristocratic exploitation by middle-class or even proletarian exploitation shows little evidence of reducing man's inhumanity to man. Thus, the argument concludes, the conflict between traditionalists and modernists is essentially ethical rather than economic—one that takes place between permissive (traditional) and coercive (modernist) factions. That the bourgeoisie is on one side, and the aristocracy and working class on the other, it is held, represents only an accident of history and will not last.

The difficulties in equating the developmental process with the presence of modernism or modernization may reflect a lack of precision in terms. Even if it is an asset to be modern, attempts to define modernism still introduce a new set of ideas that differs noticeably from the original concept. A standard definition of modernization usually includes at least the following: a belief in the primacy of science, or at least in the products of applied engineering; belief in a secular way of conducting affairs; and belief in the need for continuing changes in society and economy. Beyond that it often means the intensification or the destruction of local and regional cultures in the name of a national culture, and the elimination of native language clusters in the name of national identity. Thus modernization may be science for some and internal imperialism for others.[22]

Let us summarize the objections to modernism thus far introduced. First, faith in scientific causality is no different from faith in providential teleology, even though the consequences of these beliefs may differ. Second, the materialism reflected in the worship of commodity goods is hardly different now from what it was a hundred years ago—the kind and cost of consumer items may be different, but not the psychological motivation. Third, the components in secularism are hard to define.

22. On this question, see the perceptive essay by Charles F. Andrain, "Democracy and Socialism," in *Ideology and Discontent,* edited by David E. Apter. New York: The Free Press, 1965, especially on the psychological expression of independence, pp. 189–91.

Is secularism the reduction of religious worship and church attendance to one day per week, or the transformation of the church into the social center for seven days a week? Fourth, and of a different magnitude, modernism may be present in one sphere and not in another without impairing the quality of development. A father may be traditionalist in child-rearing, beating his children as a regular part of their growing up, and yet be quite daring and modern in his business or managerial decisions. The same person may also be daring and radical in business practice, and an arch-conservative in his political orientation. The concept of modernism tends to lose its explanatory character in such a situation. Contradictory attitudes are customary: the Chinese peasant may refuse to spare his son for the educational process, since he wants the additional farm labor; yet this same man will insist on calling the Chinese Revolution his own. The American businessman who denounces the size of the federal budget may be first in line for federal contracts and government allocations.

It is not always clear how modernism replaces traditionalism. Frequently, it is a surrogate for the maintenance of traditional class patterns by the infusion of modern techniques of distribution and trade. In economic terms, modernism stands for the primary exchange economy, for the importation of commodity supplies and the export of raw materials and farm goods to pay for them. This "international division of labor," while ostensibly a move toward greater economic rationalization, in fact strengthens the economic and political position of the supplier nation. Modernism is thus often little more than an injection into the traditional agriculturally dominated society. It provides the gloss of contemporaneity and of self-determination without its substance. The social structure remains what it was, while the economic system of exploitation changes its locale.

Interestingly, where modernism has been extensively applied, industrialization has had little success. Far from serving as a demonstration effect of the advantages of industrialization, modernism serves to reinforce the existing social structure by showing how it is possible for a small section of the population to share in the goods of the scientific-technological world, without altering the forms of human relations or the character of social production. Thus, modernism may serve, ironically, to underwrite traditionalism and not to displace it. The United States has often fostered this sort of modernism as a way of curbing the marked propensity of Third World nations to seek industrial identity through economic autonomy. Many sections of the Third World have become veritable cornucopias of up-to-date goods. Such sectors satisfy the craving for modernity and, not incidentally, function as a solution to overproduction within the United States. Thus, the international division of labor continues to work to the disadvantage of the Third World, for while the instinct for modernization seems to be satisfied, no real social structural change takes place.[23]

Actually traditionalism is just as consonant with revolutionary approaches to social problems as modernism is. This is evident in the case of Japan. Indeed, the relation between tradition and revolt may be even closer, since science and secularism may turn men away from holistic and mystic solutions and toward pragmatic and partial solutions. The modernist drive lacks a cohesive ideology and hence tends to minimize revolutionary potential. Traditionalism, especially in newly emerging nations, may function to stimulate revolutionary action. For example: Kwame Nkrumah refers continually to a traditional "African personality," which in turn is defined by a "cluster of humanist principles which underlie the traditional African society." This "African personality," in its search for revolutionary principles, chooses socialism over capitalism because the latter "might prove too complicated a system for a newly independent country," not to mention the added fact that capitalism would be "a betrayal of the personality and conscience of Africa." [24]

Here one can see clearly how traditionalist orientations, far from handicapping revolutionary sentiments, may in fact serve to stimulate them much more than modernist orientations. Revolutionary groups are "social inventions" which arise as a response to an immediate crisis situation. Their political character is independent of their social functions —at least to the degree that "left," "right," or even "center" revolutions are possible in a traditionalist or in a modernist framework. The "blockage" of social change, not the nature of the social values, ultimately determines the size and the extent of revolutionary sentiments. And the transformation of these sentiments from personal protest to organized acts determines the effectiveness of the revolutionary situation.[25]

23. See William Paddock and Paul Paddock, *Hungry Nations*. Boston: Little, Brown & Co., 1964.
24. See Kwame Nkrumah, *Consciencism: Philosophy and Ideology for Decolonization and Development*. London: Heinemann Educational Books, 1964, pp. 79, 74–75.
25. See Paul Meadows, *The Masks of Change: Essays on Development Roles and Actors*. Syracuse, N.Y.: Center of Overseas Research (Publication No. 13), 1964, pp. 66–74.

THE "SPIRIT OF WORK" VERSUS THE
"SPIRIT OF REVOLUTION"

The variables of revolutionary upsurge often differ from development.
Revolutionary movements based on "rising" new classes invariably come
after the first phase of the economic development thrust is well under
way. This was the case in France, which witnessed the triumph of the
economic bourgeoisie long before its political ascendancy, and in Russia,
which witnessed the steady growth of industrialization from late in the
nineteenth century until the 1917 revolution. There are few cases on
record in the classical epoch where this has not been the case. In the
Third World nations, particularly of Africa and Asia, however, there
is often a political preliminary to economic take-off. Indeed, it might
be said that the more backward a country, the more likely it is to have
a political revolution which precedes efforts to carry out economic
development.

It is after an initial economic spurt that revolutionary sentiments
are crystalized and mobilized.[26] The condition of the peasants in France
was worse in 1788 than in 1789. The condition of the factory proletariat
in Russia was worse in the first years of World War I; by 1917 it was
improving. The condition of the American tradesman of 1775 was
superior to that of 1773 or 1774. King George had agreed to rescind
much of the oppressive taxation legislation when the colonists assumed
insurrectionary measures. What this means is that if development is
encouraged successfully, a revolution may not be avoided or even delayed. Quite the contrary, development often makes the chances of
revolution higher, and the chances of successful revolution higher still.
In each of these cases, we have a striking illustration of rich societies
with impoverished governments.[27]

The making of revolution does not guarantee rapid growth. The
"spirit of work" is bound in a dialectical relation to the "spirit of revolution." Where the spirit of revolution prevails in the post-revolutionary

26. See the study by Alexander Gerschenkron, "Reflections on Economic Aspects
of Revolution," in *Internal War,* edited by Harry Eckstein. New York: The Free
Press, 1964, pp. 196–97.
27. On this point, see Crane Brinton, *The Anatomy of Revolution (1938).* New
York: Vintage Books-Random House, 1957, pp. 30–31.

period, and where the spirit of work does not replace these revolutionary energies, stagnation can easily occur.

The Hungarian Revolution of 1919 and the Bolivian Revolution of 1952—an admittedly unlikely comparison on any number of counts—are nonetheless highly instructive. The regimes of Béla Kun and of Víctor Paz Estenssoro created post-revolutionary situations in which "direct worker control" was immediately translated into workers' establishing their own norms of work, controlling the armed forces, and disregarding established technical personnel and bureaucratic elites. The result in both instances was a curtailing of production, an immediate extreme inflation, and monetary speculation. The collapse of the Hungarian Revolution took place in less than a half-year. The collapse of the Bolivian Revolution was delayed for over a decade—but only by an incredible pump-priming that made the Bolivian worker the most heavily subsidized person in the world. While there are many factors involved in the collapse of each revolution—the lack of cooperation of the bourgeoisie with the Béla Kun regime, the incomplete way in which the traditional military was controlled in Bolivia—it remains the case that in both the Hungary of 1919 and the Bolivia of 1952 the spirit of revolution never was transformed into the spirit of work.[28]

The First World is still guided by concepts of the French Enlightenment, namely, that each person, following his own self-interests, will somehow serve the goals of society. This he will do through the rationalizing agencies of education and legislation. This doctrine asserts that self-interest maximizes profits. The businessman would produce at the lowest possible cost and sell at the highest possible price, while the laborer, for his part, would work the longest possible hours for the highest possible salary. In this way, the operational classes would contiguously, if not cooperatively, produce the largest amount of goods in the best possible society.

The Soviet variation of the enlightenment theme served only to trans-

28. On the Bolivian situation, see Robert J. Alexander, *The Bolivian National Revolution*. New Brunswick, N.J.: Rutgers University Press, 1958; and the interesting "reactionary" document written by Gonzalo Romero, *Reflexiones para una Interpretación de la Historia de Bolivia*. Buenos Aires (privately printed), 1960; and on the Hungarian Revolution, see Arpad Szelpal, *Les Cent Trente-Trois Jours de Béla Kun*. Paris: A. Fayard, 1959; and Leo Pasvolsky, *Economic Nationalism of the Danubian States*. New York: Macmillan Co., 1928, esp. Section 5.

form the theme of ego-gratification from a personal level onto a public plane. Self-interests were found embedded in the social interests. In this way, personal striving would produce an automatic rise in the welfare of society. This Second World variation, based upon Marx, fused the French Enlightenment notion of social interests to the English economists' notion of personal welfare. But it came to terms with the ego-drive as being essential to the study of social processes. For despite the utilitarianism of the French materialists, it was the English who better worked out the utilitarian psychology of maximizing personal gain and yet simultaneously producing the best of societies. The French produced the theory of the general will, whereas the English produced the theory of the economic will, and this meant a great deal in the concrete evolution of socialism in the Second World.

While significant distinctions in the social psychology of the First and the Second Worlds exist, neither area has fundamentally questioned the value of work and money. At the economic level this has been reflected in the emphasis on thrift, savings and banking, and fear of inflation, while at the sociological level it has been reflected in an automatic assumption that the purpose of making a revolution is to establish a basis of individual independence that coincides with individual wealth. In the United States, economic motivations produced the movement to end colonial status. In Russia, similar economic motivations were put forth to end the czarist dependence on the European West. In both nations the revolutionary period soon gave way to a period of high productivity. Now much of the Third World must choose between revolutions which yield chaos, like Hungary in 1919 and Bolivia in 1952, and those that create a higher social system, like Mexico and Russia after 1910 and 1917. There is strong pressure in the Third World for gratification through leisure rather than through work—through having "enough" money for survival of self and family, rather than through savings, increased labor output, and efficiency. In each case, there existed before the revolution a set of counter-desires for independence and rapid national development. Whether the same rates of growth can be achieved depends in some part on the capacity of people to adopt this persistent psychology of ego-gratification or to transform it to larger social needs.

There is a general ethical cast of mind in sectors of the Third World, especially where traditionalism prevails, which considers accelerated development an evil. This is so, the argument goes, precisely because development accentuates the drive for personal, worldly possessions. To work at fulfilling ego demands is sinful; it is a substitution of worldly possessions for spiritual redemption. In addition to which, such material goods are thought of Pyrrhic value, useless in the long run. The drive to possess goods creates a *new* man but not necessarily a *better* man or one responsive to permanent verities. Extreme traditionalists promote the sort of spiritual "inner tranquility" which makes even the enjoyment, much less the production, of material goods difficult. This argument—enunciated by tribal leaders, religious elders, university thinkers, and a host of middle- and higher-echelon elites—serves to corrupt and confuse the masses eager for the rewards of industrialization. Traditional classes, typically connected with rural life, often want development without incurring either the risk or penalities of industrialism and urbanization.

Even without the urgings of such leaders, there may still be widespread hostility to greater output and increased savings. In certain instances, those who are members of the urban proletariat may see little reason to earn more money, since such earning power may actually result in a decline of status within the "member group." The local manufacturer, for his part, may see little reason to reinvest his profits in capital goods. His drive for self-gratification can be met without fulfilling the relatively abstract demands for socially useful investment in the national economy.

Since the First and Second Worlds have insisted on reading the history of development in terms of either the private accumulation of great fortunes or the public acquisition of such fortunes, it should occasion little surprise that this insistence, reinforced as it is in a barrage of advertisements, periodicals, pictorials—in short, the entire cultural apparatus of mass society—would serve to stimulate the drive for increased social control over the use of personal wealth, and for greater productivity within the entire society.

The leading international powers not only want to define the character of development but also insist upon setting forth the proper ground rules for development. Thus, the United States will have foreign-language editions of its leading weeklies flown to every village and hamlet in the Third World, and expect the "achieving orientation" to take only acceptable—that is, capitalist and parliamentarian—forms. But a psychological imbalance pervades Third World politics. What occurs is in the nature of a boomerang effect: the goals of Americanization, material wealth, and quality merchandise do indeed become internalized, but the means for achieving these goals remain highly traditional and even authoritarian. This is one psychological basis for the seemingly strange economic and political combinations scattered throughout the Third World, especially the combination of developmental ends and coercive instruments, and industrial values and paternalistic norms.

The development process itself is placed in jeopardy by the heavy human costs involved and by the confusion and chaos often produced by modernization procedures. The conflict between immediate gratification and hard work is resolved by social pressures to maintain at least the same level of life style that existed prior to a revolution. The rapidly declining death rate and the maintenance of the birth rate have combined to produce a population increase which can be held in check only by greater economic productivity per person. Furthermore, the desire for more goods and more education has stimulated huge shifts in family and kinship patterns. Old patterns of marriage and family collapse; respect for elders is turned into competition with them; the nuclear family replaces the extended family in importance; the general society performs more of the roles once played by the immediate family. These trends, admittedly set in motion and stimulated by the advanced nations, impinge directly on the everyday life of Third World peoples and produce a conflict between traditional values denigrating hard work and celebrating subsistence life styles.[30]

The classical economic explanation of these polarities is in terms of the marginal trade off between leisure and work. A marginal increment in the time spent working provides benefits of the goods that can be bought with the wages minus the costs of the unpleasantness of the work and the lost pleasures of leisure time. At equilibrium the costs and benefits are judged subjectively equal for the individual. This much is true for the developed and underdeveloped laborer alike. If one assumes the constancy of unpleasant work conditions and the sacrifice of leisure, wage increases will prompt the worker to work more. But here is where the worker in developed and underdeveloped lands shows a marked divergency. The worker in underdeveloped areas works less not because

30. The most useful information on the question of attitudes toward work and money is contained in the economic literature. See in particular Robert Theobald, *The Rich and the Poor: A Study of the Economics of Rising Expectations.* New York: Clarkson N. Potter, 1960; and at a more technical level, Peter Bauer, *Economic Analysis and Policy in Underdeveloped Countries.* Durham, N.C.: Duke University Press, 1957.

of any innate laziness but because money earned in extra hours worked exceeds its power to purchase useful commodities. In any event, whether at the level of ethics or economy, the conflict between work and leisure is by no means confined to overdeveloped societies. The emphasis in China on the "heroic economy" and in Cuba on the "moral economy" are two efforts at coping with problems of production in developing societies.[31]

THE MAKERS OF DEVELOPMENT: MANAGERIAL VERSUS MASS TYPES

People are engaged in the developmental process in different ways. Some individuals in a sleepy rural town desire to move to big cities; others do not. But which ones? Some members of the business community have the capacity for disinterested investment for the good of the nation; others do not. Which ones? Some factory workers are content with their "station" in life; others desire higher remuneration or "cleaner" work. Which ones?

Unfortunately, the literature seems more concerned with demonstrating the entrepreneur's, theologian's, or revolutionist's role in development than in settling upon criteria to be used in solving the knotty issue of the kind of person who contributes to development. This may simply represent a long-standing gap between "personality" and "systematic" explanations of human events. Or it may be that to single out developmental "types" involves the researcher in the kind of "intervention" which may be viewed as interference with the sovereignty of a community or a nation, or may be considered as adding to the stress and strain of a given situation.[32] But we must still answer the question —what special class is most concerned with development?—before taking account of the kinds of people within these classes who are most likely to concern themselves with development.

31. See, Robert J. Lifton, *Revolutionary Immortality: Mao Tse-tung and the Chinese Cultural Revolution*. New York: Random House, 1968; and Robert M. Bernardo, *The Theory of Moral Incentives in Cuba*. University, Ala.: The University of Alabama Press, 1971:.
32. For excellent papers on research problems of this type, see *Reflections on Community Studies*, edited by Arthur J. Vidich, Joseph Bensman, and Maurice R. Stein. New York: John Wiley & Sons, 1964.

Modernism is often an argument for middle-class elitism. The First World bias has often tended to consider industrial development as a function of managerial preeminence. Originally, this was done in a critical spirit by James Burnham.[33] More recently, the same thesis was asserted as a positive and necessary correlation of industrial development.[34] Aside from how correct it is to speak of a managerial "revolution" [35] the decision to invest in managerial talent definitely presupposes a competitive social system. For better or for worse, education of engineers, physicists, and mathematicians was given top priority, and these men began, with increasing frequency, to fill managerial assignments. Thus, while it is an indisputable fact that development requires a high educational input to gain industrial take-off, there is no significant evidence that emphasis on managerial training is a necessary component of the developmental formula. The decision to invest funds in managerial training clearly involves weighing the level of inefficiency resulting from poor management against the level of the production gained from mass scientific training.

From the psychological viewpoint, one must ask what kinds of innovation can be expected from what manpower sources. Here the Soviet experience is quite relevant. The decision to invest in natural and engineering science personnel resulted in all kinds of managerial errors: giganticism, arbitrary norms, bookkeeping mistakes, industrial cheating on goods, misallocation of raw materials.[36] Furthermore this approach dehumanized the industrial pattern and produced anomie far beyond the levels reached in Western countries. Industrialization is in its essence a process of dehumanization.[37] These factors notwithstanding, Soviet industry was a success by all standard economic measurements. That such success entailed gargantuan investment projects made with-

33. James Burnham, *The Managerial Revolution: What Is Happening in the World.* New York: The John Day Co., 1941, esp. pp. 71–138.
34. See, for this interpretation, Frederick Harbison and Charles A. Myers, *Management in the Industrial World.* New York: McGraw-Hill, 1959, esp. pp. 21–24; and Clark Kerr, John T. Dunlop, Frederick H. Harbison, and Charles A. Myers, *Industrialism and Industrial Man.* New York: Oxford University Press, 1964.
35. See H. H. Gerth and C. Wright Mills, "A Marx for the Managers," in *Power, Politics and People,* edited by Irving Louis Horowitz. New York and London: Oxford University Press, 1963, pp. 53–71.
36. See Naum Jasny, *Soviet Industrialization: 1928–1952.* Chicago, Ill.: University of Chicago Press, 1961.
37. On this subject, see Norbert Wiener, *The Human Use of Human Beings.* Boston: Houghton Mifflin Co., 1954; and more recently, *God and Golem, Inc.* Cambridge, Mass.: M.I.T. Press, 1964.

out reference to interest costs was compensated for by discounting the value of labor costs. The crucial question is how much non-essential investment should be tolerated in the drive toward development. The real issue is to what degree alienation and anomie can be checked. The long-range problem is to what extent machine labor can replace human labor without creating mass unemployment, fear, and panic. By so doing, advanced industrialization makes possible new forms of creative work.

The sophisticated notion that there are "industrializing elites" does not give proper weight to the possibility of working-class or peasant elites. All elitist theories fail to take into account the social psychology of the masses as a chief agency in promoting revolutionary development. Too often the assumption is made that development is a process moving from top to bottom. In this way dynastic reactionaries come to be linked to intellectual revolutionaries in a sophisticated way. All men become part of the "elite" through which the impulse to development is asserted. Managerial activity is broadened to include every form of elitist sentiment, and thus comes to be identified with development as such. Managers "create" and workers "respond" to the industrializing process. The idea of revolutionary change is neatly divorced from that of industrial change. Even worker protest, when it is mentioned at all, is discussed in terms of how elites can harness such protest to the industrialization process. The mass unrest is converted into a problem of "industrial strategy." The problems posed by socialist parties, guerrilla warfare, and revolutionary ideologies simply fall by the wayside. Managerial doctrines treat mass unrest as "unsponsored decisions," which is another way of saying it is not treated at all.

Development as a function of managerial activity reveals a "class consciousness" that is not one whit less assertive than the Marxist notion of development as an exclusive function of the revolutionary. Indeed, at the psychological level, scholars like Hagen, McClelland, and Kerr are seeking to provide the kind of "non-Communist" manifesto which W. W. Rostow provided for the economic realm. For Hagen, there are two personality types: the "authoritarian," which prevails in present underdeveloped economies, and the "creative outsider," found in advanced industrial economies. In this system, change is induced from the outside, from marginal creative elites.[38] In McClelland, achievement

38. Everett E. Hagen, *On the Theory of Social Change*. Homewood Ill.: The Dorsey Press, 1962.

motivation is directly related to entrepreneurial types. "High-achieving mystics" are to be found among these business-oriented types, while "low-achieving traditionalists" are to be found in the peasant sectors.[39] In the work of the Kerr group, development occurs through the interaction between industrializing elites and managerial types. This relationship is held to be the creative force underlying development.[40]

It has been succinctly and convincingly pointed out that managerial elite doctrines of "goal setting" fail to account for several critical variables: (1) Economic development is a highly selective and uneven process. A developing region may exhibit a marked growth in one sector of the economy—transportation and communication, let us say—but not in heavy tool-manufacturing industries. Is this a function of creative elites being present in one sector of the economy and not in the other? Or is it not more likely that prohibitions imposed by the strength of colonial powers are responsible for this "creative imbalance"?[41] (2) Managerial elites tend to be conservative in their economic policies for underdeveloped regions. The assumption that such elites are high achievers omits the critical variable—that is, the different notions of achievement that can be entertained. (3) Personal aggrandizement may be a reflection of high achievement, but it certainly is not necessarily conducive to high development. One ought not to confuse a *petite* bourgeoisie with a *haute* bourgeoisie and drown both in the language of creative "types."[42] There are other objections to the elitist formulations. The main point to note, drawn most recently by McCord, is that latent entrepreneurial talent exists in almost every region and in every economic class.[43]

The conflict between managerial and mass types is more than an intellectual plaything of social scientists; it is a reflection of crucial differences which exist. The problem of class stereotype contributes to the imbalance between social forces. The middle classes, when questioned about their attitudes toward the urban proletariat (of Chile and

39. David C. McClelland, *The Achieving Society*. Princeton, N.J.: D. Van Nostrand, 1961; also, David C. McClelland and David G. Winter, *Motivating Economic Achievement*. New York: The Free Press, 1969.
40. Clark Kerr (ed.), *op. cit.*
41. For criticism of Schumpeter's doctrine of development, see Arthur Lewis, *The Theory of Economic Growth*. Homewood, Ill.: Richard D. Irwin, 1955, and Benjamin Higgins, *Economic Development*. London: Constable & Co., 1959.
42. Thomas Bottomore, *Elites and Society*. New York: Basic Books, 1965.
43. William McCord, *The Springtime of Freedom: Evolution of Developing Societies*. New York: Oxford University Press, 1965, p. 143.

Mexico), uniformly answered that the workers were good-hearted and lazy, indifferent rather than shiftless. When the same workers were polled as to their attitudes toward the middle classes, their attitudes were vague and undefined. Nonetheless, they possessed a self-definition of themselves and of the nation that was more optimistic than was that of the middle class. They held to a hard-working, virtuous self-definition, and to a mobile, dynamic vision of their society.[44]

Stereotyping has blunted consideration of important aspects of society, such as demography. Most middle-class people interviewed in one sample felt that the problem of overpopulation rested with the absence of restraint on the party of the working class, when in fact, in a nation such as Mexico, the middle classes tend to be less concerned, and consequently more tradition-bound, than the poor.[45] It may be that the formula that the "rich get richer" while the "poor get babies" is preferred by the rich. It is evident that the psychology of development is unevenly spread in a nation or in a community. More important, it is not self-evident that middle classes and entrepreneurial sectors are a genuine vanguard in the reorientation of attitudes toward industrialization. But, like the bourgeoisie of Victorian England, they frequently tend to equate poverty with indolence, and, correspondingly, wealth with wisdom.

The emphasis on linking social achievement to individual motivation is itself representative of a large-scale ethnocentricism characteristic of Taylorist (First World) and Stakhanovite (Second World) styles of work introduced by the managerial castes in the United States and the Soviet Union. Each culture has a different way of socializing responsibility for achievement. In the United States, social security, old-age pensions, privately administered health programs, check-off plant insurance programs, and unemployment compensation systems serve, each in their own way, to underscore and to underwrite the responsibility of society for the individual. In Japan, the system of socialization is considerably different. Japanese workers rarely, if ever, are fired. Promo-

44. I owe this information to Raúl Benítez, who is working on this material concerning class stereotypes. At the same time, Benítez's findings corroborate similar early findings made by Eduardo Hamuy. See Eduardo Hamuy, *Educación Elemental, Analfabetismo y Desarrollo Económico*. Santiago de Chile: Editorial Universitaria, 1960.
45. See Joseph Kahl and J. Mayone Stycos, "The Philosophy of Demographic Policy in Latin America," *Studies in Comparative International Development*, Vol. 1, No. 2, 1965.

tions are made on the basis of seniority rather than of efficiency. Pay is determined by a complex set of social factors in which the number of dependents and length of service are prominent. In the Japanese system, the industrial decision-making process is socialized through a vast paternalistic set-up. Lower and middle echelons make their decisions on a group basis, which allows for no one to lose face or be ashamed.[46] However, important business decisions are made in more conventional individualistic terms.

The forms of social responsibility may differ from culture to culture. But given the fact that the rate of growth of Japan has been equal to that of the United States throughout most of the twentieth century, it should be clear that these forms of social control may be different and yet yield the same over-all productivity. The "peculiar" characteristics of development in Japan are not explained by the "inscrutable" oriental face-saving mind. A more ready explanation is that in Japan the lower nobility absorbed capitalist businesses. In the absence of a productive and independent middle class, this traditionalist sector assimilated the corporate phase of capitalism to the feudal ways of the noble and military elite.[47]

IMITATION AND INNOVATION

The process of development which relies upon foreign assistance can never be the same as the process of autonomous industrialization of the past. Models of an earlier period have not so much grown spontaneously in new environments as they have been adapted to non-Western conditions. Third World social or cultural systems build upon each other in symbiotic fashion. This is clear even regarding the imitative element present in the basic vocabulary of development. What was formerly a product of chance now becomes a matter of planning. The "demonstration effect" allows for the most developed to show in advance the face of the future to the least developed, while the "law of combined development" permits a sampling by underdeveloped nations

46. See James Abegglen, *The Japanese Factory.* Glencoe, Ill.: The Free Press, 1958. For a keen anthropological study, see John W. Bennett and Iwao Ishino, *Paternalism in the Japanese Economy.* Minneapolis: University of Minnesota Press, 1963.
47. See E. Herbert Norman, *Japan's Emergence as a Modern State.* New York: Institute of Pacific Relations, 1946.

of those features and processes of development that they feel are most suitable, without regard to the place of origin of any given process.

The notion of Western democracy became important in Third World thinking when it accepted some improvisation in its own ideology, and because it demanded that the West adhere to Western political codes. The Third World has very consciously embarrassed the West by calling attention to the latter's failures to live by the principles it advocates.[48] Consider the following report given by Malinowski:

> Nationalism in the sense of a conservative reaction and the recognition of the integral value of its own culture by each nation is spreading like wild fire all over the world. We, the members of the white race, are primarily responsible for that, and we have been giving our religion, our education, and many other spiritual boons to other races and peoples, with an implied promise that once they accept our civilization, they will become our equals. This promise has not been redeemed. We are beginning now to see how dangerous it is to speak about the white man's burden, and to make others shoulder it and carry it for us. We give all the promise implied in our concept of human brotherhood and of equality through education, but when it comes to wealth, power, and self-determination we refuse this to other people.[49]

Furthermore, even the use of the military to bring about colonial domination created a boomerang effect. Those that came with the gun did indeed conquer. But in turn the colonizing powers created the basis for a new consciousness, which is dramatically described by Ndabaningi Sithole.

> World Wars I and II helped the cracks of the white myth to widen. Thousands of African soldiers went abroad on active service. . . . They were ordered by the white commanders to kill white enemy soldiers. The African soldiers from Southern and Northern Rhodesia, Nyasaland, French Equatorial Africa, the Gold Coast, and Nigeria,

---

48. One must appreciate the fact that this psychology of embarrassment can work both ways. It may inhibit the use of totalitarian forms of development deemed feasible in times of lower levels of communication transmission. On this, see the perceptive paper by R. P. Dore, "Japan as a Model of Economic Development," *Archives Européennes de Sociologie*, Vol. 5, No. 1, 1963, pp. 138–54.
49. Bronislaw Malinowski, *Freedom and Civilization*. New York: Roy Publishers, 1944, p. 219; also see Irving Louis Horowitz, "Crime, Custom and Culture: Remarks on the Functional Theory of Bronislaw Malinowski," *International Journal of Comparative Sociology*, Vol. III, No. 2, Dec. 1962, pp. 229–44.

found themselves at the front line of war with one purpose in view: to kill every white enemy soldier they could get hold of. Many German and Italian soldiers fell victim to shots fired by African soldiers. The African soldiers saw white soldiers wounded, dying, and dead. The bullet had the same effect on white and black alike. This had a very powerful psychological impact in the African. He saw those whom he used to call his betters suffer defeat, though not conquest, at the hands of the Germans and Japanese, and once more he was impressed by the fact that it was not being white or black that mattered but the necessary training in these things. The veil between him and the white man thinned to a point of transparency, and at other points it disappeared altogether. After suffering side by side with his white fellow soldiers the African never again regarded them in the same light. After spending four years hunting white enemy soldiers the African never regarded them again as gods.[50]

Thus what was provided, in the instance cited by Malinowski, was the political ideology and, in the example given by Sithole, the military cast of mind. In both cases it was indicated that the colonial exploiters were not simply hypocritical but subject to the same laws of nature as black and yellow peoples, or of people in general. Work style and life styles were imitated and adopted to new environments by post-liberation nationalists. But this absorption was always accompanied by an assertion on the part of the colonialists that they be produced and developed under circumstances which simulated conditions in the cosmopolitan center. In short, innovation, whether large or small, is a necessary part of the ideological rearmament which the Third World undertakes. The way in which the Russians adopted American techniques of industrialization represents an outstanding example; it was not done by applying mimetic principles but with the idea that adaptation is also innovation. For example, Stalin, in his lecture entitled "Styles of Work" in the *Foundations of Leninism,* claims that the Russian revolutionary sweep must also include a place for what he calls "American efficiency." The latter is necessary to prevent the revolution from degenerating into empty sloganeering; whereas the socialism is necessary to humanize the industrialization, and to prevent it from turning into a narrow empiricism.[51] Whether in fact the Stalinist model was the same in reality as in rhetoric is not at issue. However, its stated

50. Ndabaningi Sithole, *African Nationalism.* New York: Oxford University Press, 1959, pp. 155–57.
51. Joseph V. Stalin, *Foundations of Leninism.* New York: International Publishers, 1939.

goals were clearly intended to innovate without losing the advantages of development in the capitalist sector.

The extent to which the early founders of the Soviet Union kept the United States as their model of development has been underestimated. It was manifested not only in "electrification" and "mechanization" but also in Soviet emphasis on American work styles. Stakhanovism is little more than an adaptation of Taylorism—programs of scientific labor management or manipulation—to Russian industrial conditions. Lenin indicates that

> the Taylor system, without its initiators knowing or wishing it, is preparing the time when the proletariat will take over all social production and appoint its own workers' committees for the purpose of properly distributing and rationalizing all social labor. Large scale production, machinery, railways, telephone—all provide thousands of opportunities to cut by three-fourths the working time of organized workers, and make them four times better off than they are today.[52]

The only hitch in Lenin's prediction is that this automation has not exhausted its possibilities within the framework of capitalism. Whatever modifications required in the Stalinist system of Stakhanovism— the system of private ownership proved equal to the innovative challenge. Taylorism was understood as a managerial device from the outset. Stakhanovism was not so clearly understood. Indeed, it was presented as a response to worker initiative. What is interesting is the extent to which labor opposition to Taylorism, to piece-work payment, and to managerial determination of working conditions not only failed to slow up but actually promoted increased labor output in capitalist centers.

It becomes increasingly apparent that there is a great deal of tension between imitation and innovation in the "take-off" period. Innovation is based upon the existence of political and cultural variety, coupled with technological needs and capacities to absorb novelty. Collective resistance to social change is first manifested by the reluctance of individuals to accept novelty. These may come about in several ways. First, the introduction of a new product or tool may completely disrupt traditional relations between men and women. Consider this example cited by W. Arthur Lewis.

52. See V. I. Lenin, "The Taylor System—Men's Enslavement by the Machine," in *Collected Works,* Vol. 20. Moscow: Foreign Languages Publishing House, 1964, pp. 152–54.

The introduction of central mills for extracting oil from the oil palm fruit doubles the yield of oil, but it also deprives the wives of West African farmers of the perquisites they get when they extract the oil for their husbands, and is therefore strongly and effectively resisted by them; it also alters the devision of labor between husband and wife, and anything which does this has far reaching and unforeseeable consequences.[53]

The "Luddite syndrome" of resisting innovation in the name of maintaining social order is repeated endlessly and everywhere. Sometimes such resistance is individualistic, as in the case of aristocratic intellectuals; sometimes collectivistic, as in the case of whole agricultural settlements moving from one nation to another, such as the Kurdish Jews' migration to Israel. But the problem of resistance to change is not simply traditional; it is increasingly modern—a fear that development in itself is not a justification for uprooting traditional ways.

The success or failure of an innovation may well hinge on its source. One can mimetically reproduce the behavior of "rich foreigners" if they are admired, or "powerful elders" if they are feared. But this imitation is severely restricted, or dissolved entirely, if foreigners are loathed as imperialists, or if elders are viewed as obstructionists or internal colonialists. At some critical juncture either imitation is replaced by innovation, or the latter is rejected and falls into disrepute. Thus, the mechanism by which an imitation is transformed into an innovation itself constitutes a special form of development.

Innovation is the near-exclusive property of advanced nations. Technological novelty is a function of technological proficiency. Third World nations continue to remain imitative in technology, however innovative they may be in adapting new styles of work and industrial relations. The special drive for innovation in fully developed regions has multiple sources: the desire of entrepreneurs for social success, the hope of big profits or large wages, or, negatively, a fear of economic loss if innovative schemes are not used. The newly emergent states have serious problems providing substitute stimulants. They have instilled the ideology and ethos of equality. Planning must therefore avoid creating reserve armies of unemployed; otherwise it is economically as well as culturally disastrous.

Planning cuts down or eliminates to a considerable degree the hope

53. See W. Arthur Lewis, *The Theory of Economic Growth*. Homewood, Ill.: Richard D. Irwin, 1955, pp. 178–79.

of quick profits or high wages. Further, it leads to a situation in which prestige can be measured not only through entrepreneurial activities—but just as often through bureaucratic and political activities. Thus, the impulse to innovate in the economic sector is often weakened. The fear of economic loss is lessened through a system of production and payment often guaranteed and underwritten by the public sector, but in exchange for this public-sector underwriting the hope of great profits also vanishes. Public subsidy can and oftentimes does save failing or ailing industries in the Third World. But it also creates problems of motivation as well as innovation.

Thus Third World nations have specific problems with innovation incentives beyond difficulties involving imitation. It is almost impossible for them to restore competitive, laissez-faire norms, and, even if possible, such norms might create even worse social imbalances. Hence, the task is to stimulate innovative behavior despite the absence of direct monetary rewards. One way this is done is through political, bureaucratic, or cultural payoffs. The case of the Soviet Union with its Stakhanovite movement indicates that such non-monetary payoffs can be effective. But this non-economic approach seems to become increasingly effective with the passage of time and the growing affluence of the society involved. Thus, the maturation of the socialist system may witness the increase in "capitalist ego-incentives" to maintain work norms and to stimulate further innovation. At the same time, capitalist nations are witnessing a growing socialist trend in their innovative processes—that is, the rise of automated machinery has made plain the need for central planning procedures on a vast scale. Automation has increased efficiency requirements, and with this comes a demand for more, not less, planning.

Innovation serves to fuel arguments about socialism. In the developing states, demands for innovation seem to trigger utilitarian solutions at the economic level and command approaches at the political level. The dialectics of development are such that the transformation of imitation into innovation is essential to the Third World. While limits to innovation remain cultural, technology and economic organization in the Third World are badly suited to innovative work styles. At the same time, in the competition between the First and Second Worlds, the arguments for capitalism and socialism often come to rest on their innovative potential. Perhaps the destiny of the Third World will be to resolve this outstanding antinomy between competitive and cooperative doctrines of economics, or at least to tip the scales decisively one way or the other.

DEVELOPING MAN AS A PERSONALITY TYPE

For development to take place, growth must be desired. We have attempted to fill in the substance of this mental set—scientific attitudes of mind, societal orientations, achievement motivations, and so forth—but people themselves must be committed to development. There may even be an "irrational" decision to support development although the private sector is thwarted. And "gratification" may be derived from cooperative rather than competing acts. In all societies nonconformity may lead to social reorganization, no less than political disorganization. As a result, the division from industrial norms cuts both ways; it might prove to be an enormous asset, but just as often it is a burden to the planning nation.

Where there exists a large number of "positive-oriented" deviants, there is also generally a high developmental impulse. It is hardly accidental that crime rates have increased, rather than decreased, as the economy of the United States has expanded. Similarly, the extent of mobility in Soviet society may better be tested by the increased extent of "normal" crime, and the minimization of punishment for such crime, than by the organized channels of legal expression. Many basic forms of crime, such as professional and white-collar crimes, become legitimized business enterprises after a time. Waterfront activities, trucking, and, earlier, railroads are examples of industries in the United States which went outside the law to expand rapidly. Later, they became legitimized in terms of their social standing by virtue of their economic importance.

Criminal behavior and radical political behavior are often consonant with efforts toward rapid development. Part of the institutionalization of marginal groups in a nation such as the United States represents a wide tolerance of nonconformity. There is a deep recognition that everyone is deviant with respect to some other outside group. Thus the degree of movement from a member group, the amount of discontent within a member group, and the availability of other reference groups to which one can move are useful indicators of the psychological components in development. There is an absence of development as such when there is no division of organizational life and where there are no voluntary organizations of different persuasions with contrasting social functions or conflicting economic interests. Therefore normative standards, no less than deviations from such standards, interact with one another to define the psychic economy of developing man.

Not only is there a process of socialization involved in the division of labor, but the need for specialization produces a corresponding recognition of the role of the individual. The individual begins to act as an agent for himself, setting up *agencies* over and against a backward and stagnant society. The developmentally oriented "deviant" has a highly refined sense of goals. He accepts allegiance to professional groups rather than to society as a whole. The developing man thus has a basic affiliation to the particular kinds of activities he engages in, rather than to the locus or the place where these activities occur. If someone is a machine-tool operator, what is important is that he have the expertise needed for maintaining his position, not that he works for a particular tool and die company. Small companies oftentimes slow down the rates of mobility by committing the loyalties of the employees to personal factors.

The transition from corporate to professional loyalty has to be seen as part of contemporary bureaucratic styles. Associations based on professional affiliation increasingly displaced the web of association traditionally identified with the place of work.[54] This is one of the big changes between the mid-nineteenth and the mid-twentieth century. Collectivism increases; planning increases; allocations of materials and of men also increase. These events, while giving an indication of the growing breakdown of the traditional forms of social control, compel a growth of anti-organizational attitudes. The degree of resistance to collectivism has now shifted from the factory to the profession. Social interaction increasingly takes place outside the work environment. In the struggle for achievement, mobility is stimulated to the extent that social life is professionalized. Greater individuation depends on extending socialist forms of work.

In speaking of the mental set of developing man, we are in part dealing with intangible items, which go under the name of self-sacrifice, altruism, dedication, purpose and even "divine madness." These are not the same things, but in sum they add up to a willingness to submit the personality to some abstract principle that is socially accepted rather

54. An excellent anthology covering this theme is Sigmund Nosow and William H. Form (eds.), *Man, Work, and Society*. New York: Basic Books, 1962.

than to a privately defined good. This does not mean that such factors are in every situation the key to development. Changing technological requirements, new class formations, new scientific discoveries, and the like are still needed in order to underwrite what is known as achievement orientation—for that orientation may be a necessary but not a sufficient condition for development. This is where the Weberian and Marxian traditions sharply diverge. For a truly developing society to be matched by an equally developing personality means a growth not simply in the intangible values but also in the tangible goods. Marx understood this relationship well when he pointed out that the key problem is not only one of the standard of living but of the relationship between the standard of living and the style of living.

The quest for development persists because problems of the mind are less urgent than problems of the stomach. Further, there is no evidence to prove that every malevolent industrial practice must be reproduced in all its ghastly details. The terrors of development often turn out to be imaginary. The failure to put discovery and invention to the good of the commonweal is after all a human failing, not a failure of science. It only offers the Third World a greater challenge—to harness the sciences for human ends. But the human uses of the natural sciences involve a deeper appreciation of the scientific uses of the human sciences, and a further appreciation that democracy, like development, is a process, not a fact. The inordinate sacrifices made by peoples in emergent nations—years of civil war, famine, separation from families, sacrifice of material comfort—attest to the existence of a transcendent factor, a binding psychological commonality in development.[55]

If such superordinate goals were not present, the actual process of development would be slower and much less meaningful. Famines in China, civil war in Algeria, blockades in Cuba, blunders of management, investment, and allocation—these are typical of all newly emergent societies. On strictly "rational" grounds any one of these factors would be enough to topple many, if not all, revolutionary regimes. But such collapses are infrequent. Indeed when they did occur, as in the case of Nkrumah and Sukarno, the external pressures seemed less significant than the internal pressures; that is to say, these regimes were

55. C. Wright Mills, "The Problem of Industrial Development," in *Power, Politics and People,* edited by Irving Louis Horowitz. New York and London: Oxford University Press, 1963, pp. 150–51.

far too elitist to command the necessary popular support. And as a result, they became easy marks for dissidents. Where genuine "movements from below" are in control, adverse conditions may often create renewed effort and lead to a sense of rededication. The case of China is typical. The post-revolutionary period was filled with hardships, but also with commitment. Although this is a chapter on the psychology of development, it is important to bear in mind that in countries like China the revolution produced vast improvements in mass living standards. The economic stability of the new China, relative to the Kuomintang, greatly helped legitimize Mao, just as instability in the continued level helped delegitimize Sukarno and Nkrumah.

> At no stage in its history has the Chinese Communist Party had a more positive popular appeal than during the first six years of its rule. There is of course no doubt about the significance of 1949. During that year there was a drastic acceleration in the collectivization of land, which seems to have quantitatively changed the relationship between the regime and the majority of the peasants. In the late forties and the first two or three years after the establishment of the new government, Communist Party members and cadres urged or compelled the peasants to expropriate the landlords and to punish them often by death. Their land was then distributed among the poorer peasants. Therefore, in China, unlike Russia, the Communist Party could claim credit for having distributed the land.[56]

There are of course dangers and obstacles in these sentiments of self-sacrifice, altruism, and patriotic feelings. The examples of Nazi Germany and Stalinist Russia stand as a steady reminder of this. And, further, these "psychological factors" are often euphemistic ways of taking account of irrational and abnormal elements in development. To cite a few examples: nations as confined in their culture and traditions as Canada, Belgium, the Philippines, India, and Puerto Rico view bilingualism as an imperialistic hangover rather than as a novel opportunity. Language becomes a basic vehicle for expressing the ultimate in nationalistic sentiments. This is so despite the fact that the double-language system actually provides a decided cultural advantage. Another

56. See Martin Bernal, "The Popularity of Chinese Patriotism" (a review of A. Doak Barnett's *Communist China*), in *The New York Review of Books,* Vol. IV, No. 2, Feb. 25, 1965.

case of irrationality is the immense movement of people into cities, a movement all out of proportion to actual economic opportunities available in the cities. Indeed, families are often willing to endure all sorts of personal privation and even starvation to participate, however marginally, in the benefits of urban living.

A final example of such irrationality is the population boom, which is encouraged by traditional patterns of extended kinship ties. These no longer can effectively compensate for the profound economic loss occasioned by large families. In short, farming patterns, where children were significant units of economic production, continue to promote the population incline despite the changeover to industrial production. This "lag" is just as evident in contemporary China as it is in Puerto Rico. Thus, the psychological study of development must be in good measure a study of irrational elements in the stagnation and acceleration processes, and not just operational definitions of how to provoke or induce greater output per person. The lag here has been increased by the complete schism between "experimentalists" working in laboratory conditions and "practitioners" working out in society. At the theoretical level, it has divided social scientists into competing schools.[57]

Noble sentiments are fragile. Those ready to betray such sentiments, to substitute pieties for ideals, must surely be aware that they run the risk of upsetting the developmental process as such. This very knowledge enables, in fact compels, the elites of developing nations to continue to be responsive to the demands of their own peoples. When this is not the case, the slightest disturbance in the economic process causes friction. When mass participation in developing nations exists, then all sorts of blunders can be absorbed. This is another way of saying that mass social changes "from below" can absorb error, while elitist revolutions can crumble at even slight strain.

In the modern epoch at least, commentators have recognized that development takes a personal toll. As Freud put the matter: "civilization obeys an internal erotic impulse which causes human beings to unite in a closely knit group." But this group existence can be achieved only "through an ever increasing reinforcement of the sense of guilt." And when the individual moves from the family to society at large, he

57. On this, see Alvin W. Gouldner, "Explorations in Applied Social Science," in *Applied Sociology: Opportunities and Problems,* edited by A. W. Gouldner and S. M. Miller. New York: The Free Press, 1965, pp. 5–21.

suffers "a loss of happiness through the heightening of the sense of guilt." [58] This fact is confirmed by sociological literature, which indicates that suicide rates vary directly with urban and industrial development. To be sure, whatever suicide is to be found in underdeveloped nations is centered chiefly among the middle and upper strata of the population.[59]

However much we would like to subject development to scientific control, it produces unanticipated results. For the romantic tradition of Freud, the losses outweigh the gains of development, since the maturation of civilization carries with it not simply the threat of increased guilt feelings for the individual but the annihilation of civilization itself. Whether this extreme outcome predicted by psychoanalysis is accurate or not, it remains clear that development affects personality structure even more decisively than personality structure affects developmental decision. Perhaps this very fact may help ease the destructive potential in social change. From this vantage point, personality is not simply a critical factor in development, but may often turn out to be the sacrificial offering to the "needs" of the developmental process.

CONCLUSIONS

We opened our discussion of the mental set of developing man by indicating that its main feature was the shift in responsibility for welfare from the individual to the collective society. In closing, we must also indicate another radical change which characterizes developing man— his replacement of ethical problems with strategic problems. He does not ask, as men before him have asked, whether economic growth is desirable. He takes for granted the negative features of retardation or stagnation—which from a comparative economic standpoint is the same. His thoughts are now firmly fastened on another line of reasoning: since change cannot be prevented, at what rate should it be ac-

58. See Sigmund Freud, *Civilization and Its Discontents,* translated by James Strachey, in *The Standard Edition of the Complete Psychological Works of Sigmund Freud,* Vol. XXI. London: Hogarth Press, 1961–62, pp. 96–101.
59. See Richard Quinney, "Suicide, Homicide, and Economic Development," *Social Forces,* Vol. 43, No. 3, Mar. 1965, pp. 401–6; and Leo F. Schnore, "Social Problems in an Urban-Industrial Context," *Social Problems,* Vol. 9, No. 4, Winter 1962, pp. 228–40.

celerated, and at what costs, and who must bear the primary burden of this "transitional" period—which might be called the "interminable" period?

W. Arthur Lewis has tried to explain why this displacement has taken place—why indeed men of the Third World do not seem to raise with any urgency the question of the value of development as such. He locates his answer in two items: first, as a result of the rapid communication of information and ideas, human aspirations have grown faster than economic production. Second, death rates are falling faster than birth rates. These factors therefore create the need for rapid economic growth, if for no other reason than to maintain present life styles.[60]

To this might be added a third item—a value question. Men are always faced with making choices between what they determine are good things. At certain times, the redistribution of property arrangements is deemed important enough to justify revolutionary turmoil. It is not that revolution in itself is good but that the objects desired override normal social inhibitions. The same wish holds true for the developmental race. Men want the commodities which result from development rather than a part in the ownership of these products. In this sense, socialist demands are a means of gaining such ends as desirable commodities. That in the process of development certain precious political or ethical standards, such as free elections or the rotation of elites, may be sacrificed is merely viewed as the price one has to pay for higher goods. In any revolutionary situation, the death of certain innocents, or the excessive application of curfew laws and food rationing, are viewed as a necessary by-product of the revolutionary process. That such "aberrations" may come to be permanent features of the new social order is only one further risk inherent in the development process. They only emphasize how arduous and painful development now is; but they do not invalidate the ends development seeks.

The point of this chapter is not so much to locate a psychological explanation for the facts of colonialism or "deficiencies" which are purported to be a function of underdevelopment, for these facts are economic, political, and social in nature. Rather, we have offered some guidelines to the psychological consequences of colonialism—for the developmental process as a whole no less than for the imperial and

60. W. Arthur Lewis, *op. cit.,* pp. 35–42.

colonial publics in particular.[61] If the mental set of developing man appears to us to be excessively focused on feelings of inferiority based on racial differences, we must remember that the highly developed societies have brought this racialism down on themselves through their own peculiar notions of superiority. The marks of oppression remain implanted on the "liberated" peoples of the Third World, but in some measure this is because the habits of the oppressor remain implanted on the peoples of the "enlightened" First and Second Worlds.

As we enter the 1970's, it is clear that race in some measure can be treated as an independent variable and not simply as a function of class in the developmental process. No doubt sound and useful arguments can be made explaining the obvious income differential between blacks and whites—as due to a combination of educational, geographical, and political factors—but the real issue at stake is the degree to which the question of the Third World's psychology is no longer a matter of the mark of oppression as much as it is the identifying physical mark of liberation. In this chapter we have tended to treat economic class phenomena as being more basic than anthropological race phenomena. But whether in fact this is the case or not, is of far less significance than the high correlation of low economic status and low social status occupied by peoples of color. For a theoretical settlement of the race and class dichotomy may take a far longer period of time than the practical settlement of the fused liberation movement of peoples of color and peoples of poverty.

61. This distinction is well made by O. Mannoni, *Prospero and Caliban: The Psychology of Colonization.* New York: Frederick Praeger, 1964, esp. pp. 197–209.

II

Models and Modes
of Development

5

The First World of
United States Development

There are two ways of assessing life in the United States with a minimum margin of error: the quantitative way is to rely exclusively upon decennial census reports; the qualitative way is to rely upon omnibus summaries of the American national character, culture, and political system. But when one attempts to fuse economic statistics with ethnographic reports, there does not seem to be much of a match.[1] The difficulty is that economic reports are optimistic, indicating a rate of growth based on increased spending, greater production, higher profits, and more people working shorter hours. But reports emphasizing the quality and content of life are pessimistic, indicating such factors as crime and divorce as social problems, the displacement of concerned interest groups by manipulated masses, political apathy among broad sector of minority and racial groups, and the high incidence of mental illness and drug abuse; then the contradiction between economic and sociological types of information is revealed.[2] To put the matter in bold relief, the rate of unemployment in the United States moves downward from 17.2 per cent as late as 1939 to an average of roughly 4.0 per cent during the 1960's. But within the same period, a military-industrial complex takes root that rockets military expenditure from a little more than $1.2 billion in 1939 to an average of $78.5 billion by the late 1960's. The percentage of the

1. For a parallel analysis of the difficulties in fusing values and evidence, see Gunnar Myrdal, *Objectivity in Social Research.* New York: Pantheon Books, 1969, esp. pp. 39–49.
2. Compare, for example, the "quantitative" income papers with the "qualitative" life-style papers issued under the auspices of the Brookings Institution, in *Agenda for the Nation,* edited by Kermit Gordon. New York: Doubleday & Co., 1968.

GNP has shown a parallel rise. Thus it seems that the solution of one set of economic problems tends to stimulate an entirely new set of military problems that are different, but no less complicated, than the original ailments.[3]

Let us begin by examining the historical judgments of Europeans about the United States. This is little more than an application of the norm of reciprocity; for we shall apply throughout the standards of the United States in judging the rest of the world. We shall also see how nineteenth-century European historical judgments have been rendered inept by the passage of time. It is strikingly characteristic of apologists for the United States that they place an emphasis on its historical continuity which is all out of proportion to historical evidence. A peculiar type of conservatism refuses to face the implications of radical departure from tradition. Thus one writer has even observed the seeds of current Latin American revolution in the Lincoln-Douglas debates of the 1850's,[4] while another writer can observe the traces of George Washington's legacy in the current political behavior of the political elite.[5]

Another historical format for expressing the specific dualism of the American dream is the peculiar approach to problems of land. The United States was conceived of and brought into unity as a result of a constant Western expansion at the expense of English, French, and Spanish colonialists. But at the very moment that such a national consolidation takes place, the ideology of expansionism also takes root, so that the United States begins to behave with respect to Asia and Latin America in much the same way that it had condemned. What began as a huge act of anti-colonialism ended in colonial expansion itself. The "new West" came to signify the Mississippi River, then the California coast, and then the Phillipines to the West and Panama to the South.

3. For information on United States GNP, military expenditures, and unemployment rates from 1939 to 1970, see *Economic Report of the President.* Jan. 1969, pp. 227, 252; *Survey of Current Business,* May 1970, pp. 6–13. For various interpretations of this structural transformation of the country, see *Super-State: Readings in the Military Industrial Complex,* edited by Herbert I. Schiller and Joseph D. Phillips. Urbana-Chicago: University of Illinois Press, 1970, esp. pp. 1–28.
4. Harry V. Jaffa, *Equality and Liberty: Theory and Practice in American Politics.* New York: Oxford University Press, 1965.
5. Seymour Martin Lipset, *The First New Nation.* New York: Basic Books, 1964. For a discussion of this, see Irving Louis Horowitz and Seymour Martin Lipset, "The Birth and Meaning of America: A Dialogue on the First New Nation," *Panamoras,* No. 17 (Aug.–Sept.), 1965.

The dream of national consolidation, once fulfilled, became a matter of spoiled identity since it was soon locked into the politics of international control.[6]

To presume breaks rather than continuities helps us to speak with some objectivity about the United States as a First World in a historically new international setting. Such a frame of reference should enable us to avoid the extreme relativism of considering the United States as "a nation among nations"[7] or the extreme absolutism of the United States as one nation with a manifest destiny over all other nations.[8]

There has been a remarkable consensus about the United States in Europe. One critic may be more friendly than another. Another may be more or less elitist in orientation than others; but in the main, what European observers have chosen to praise or condemn about life in the United States follows strikingly similar patterns. Generally, the United States is recognized as embodying a synthesis of European traditions. This synthesis is precisely what European commentators most respected and were most troubled by. Here was a society which indeed absorbed many pluralistic strains, yet demanded very exacting loyalties.

The most common recurring theme was America as a "wave of the future." The United States was viewed as that nation which would carve the path for all other yet unborn civilizations. It attracted curious onlookers and observers because its historical leadership was recognized early. It would show other nations and peoples what their own future would look like. This has been a prevalent theme since Tocqueville designed his study of the United States with the express purpose of seeking there "the image of democracy itself, with its inclinations, its character, its prejudices, and its passions, in order to learn what we have to fear or to hope from its progress."[9] Tocqueville and other educated commentators were so convinced that the United States embodied the future of the democratic spirit that in Tocqueville's masterpiece he oftentimes dropped

6. See the remarkable extension of the Turner thesis to the international domain, by William Appleman Williams, *The Roots of the Modern American Empire: A Study of the Growth and Shaping of Social Consciousness in a Marketplace Society.* New York: Random House, 1969, pp. 351–81.
7. See, Hans Kohn, *American Nationalism: An Interpretive Essay.* New York: Collier Books, 1961.
8. See *The Works of Theodore Roosevelt.* New York: Charles Scribner, 1926. Volume 19 in particular contains perhaps the most bellicose pronouncements, coupled with an extreme paternalism, representative of turn-of-the-century American policy.
9. Alexis de Tocqueville, *Democracy in America,* edited with an introduction by

the term "America," even when describing a peculiarly American characteristic, and simply used the word "democracy." He employed the
United States throughout as a surrogate for democratic "social conditions." [10] Beyond that he drew the irrational conclusion that democracy
was the wave of the future just as mass society was the inevitable replacement for an elitist society. While Tocqueville may have said this
with a certain caution and aristocratic nostalgia, others who followed
him abandoned caution and merely assumed that America plus democracy equalled progress; that this was a magic formula for development.

This notion of the United States as the vanguard of industrial nations
has been so common that a tone of admiration persists even when the
faults of American development are discussed. André Siegfried points
out, for instance, that

> the assimilation of things of the spirit is the real lesson offered by
> the study of the humanities but America appears to consider this
> old-fashioned. In an examination for the recruitment of adminis-
> trative staff, 80 per cent of the questions were on scientific and tech-
> nological matters, while 20 per cent reserved for general culture were
> not allotted to literature or philosophy but to sociology—a very
> significant replacement. There is a whole new conception of life
> there, and it is one toward which our century is moving with the
> United States in the vanguard.[11]

These same sentiments are still frequently expressed by humanists
such as Howard Mumford Jones.[12] But whatever is most expressive,
whether the spirit is critical or celebratory, it is taken for granted that
the United States remains the wave of the future—insofar as the future
entails industrialization, urbanization, and mass dissemination of information.

The United States was seen as the land of equality in both eighteenth-
and nineteenth-century literature. Foreign observers noted the egalitarianism and the conscious dedication to minimizing stratification. The
United States represented social equality—equality of status, of manners,

Henry Steele Commager. New York and London: Oxford University Press, 1947,
p. 16.
10. Alexis de Tocqueville, *ibid.*, p. 41.
11. André Siegfried, *America at Midcentury*. New York: Harcourt, Brace, 1955,
p. 355.
12. Howard Mumford Jones, *One Great Society: Humane Learning in the United
States*. New York: Harcourt, Brace, 1959.

and of deference. What is more interesting is that, until the twentieth century, there was much emphasis upon political equality. There was also a strong emphasis on economic equality—not seen so much as an achieved fact but rather as an aspiration. The emphasis on equality did not preclude the desirability of an unequal distribution of ambition. Tocqueville attributes all equality to a basic equality of economic conditions, in contrast to the psychological inequality of talents. This dynamic tension is reinforced by the laws of equal inheritance which obtained in the United States in the nineteenth century. He saw in division of inheritance the elimination of the ultimate barrier to equality. He speaks of juridical safeguards of economic equality as "tending powerfully to destruction of large fortunes and especially large domains." He notes that in the United States the last trace of hereditary ranks and distinctions is destroyed. This is why "in a foreign country two Americans are at once friends, simply because they are Americans." This, in contrast to the English, for whom "the same blood is not enough; they must be brought together by the same rank." [13]

Harriet Martineau provided a most powerful second to this when she indicated in the mid-nineteenth century that it was an "admitted truth" that for Americans "enormous private wealth is inconsistent with the spirit of republicanism. Wealth is power; large amounts of power ought not to rest in the hands of individuals . . . the popular feeling is so strong against transmitting large estates, and favoring one child, that nobody attempts to do it." [14] The completeness of this egalitarianism strikes the present-day observer. The irony is not only how far the United States has moved away from an image of egalitarianism, but how it was possible for European observers to see in the nineteenth-century United States such exaggerated egalitarian strains while at the same time the crystallization and the encroachment of class, race, and ethnic distinctions of a rather profound type were occurring. What was also missed is the extent to which egalitarianism in the United States was linked to interest-group political economy so that all definitions of activity were linked to specific class, race, and ethnic factors which themselves were meaningful only in a community rather than in a national context.

By the mid-nineteenth century the leveling effects of the frontier

13. Alexis de Tocqueville, *op. cit.,* pp. 370–71.
14. Harriet Martineau, *Society in America,* edited with an introduction by Seymour Martin Lipset. Garden City, N.Y.: Doubleday & Co., 1962, pp. 263–64.

were still able, to some extent, to maintain the equilibrium between economic equality and psychological drives for wealth, for if the pursuit of money did not yield real wealth or, better, make many people wealthy, it at least provided a framework of shared developmental rules. But by the twentieth century, serious commentators ceased to raise the image of economic equality in the United States. Yet whether or not social equality has been based upon economic equality, the classless society has been a major ideal for Americans. Tocqueville began his second volume on America with a discussion of the American passion for equality and the American neglect of liberty. He noted that in the United States men endure poverty, servitude, and barbarism, but they will not endure fixed class differences.

The characteristic egalitarianism of the American stems from three types of rejection. First, because of the "continual movement which agitates a democratic community" family ties are severely loosened and "every man readily loses the trace of the ideas of his forefathers or takes no care about them." Second, there is no respect for the ideas of a master class, since "there are no longer any classes, or those which still exist are composed of such mobile elements that their body can never exercise a real control over its members." Third, egalitarianism is a consequence of a society in which intelligence is "placed on the footing of a general similitude, and men see each other as not being incontestably greater than each other." Because of this extreme independence the search for equality through economic freedom began tragically counterimposed with the search for liberty or that spirit that would permit the private citizen to lead a private life independent of the main stream of economic development.

The egalitarianism Tocqueville speaks of is primarily one of manners and mores. What he fails to see is that this sociological egalitarianism, curiously enough, has become a major bulwark against economic egalitarianism. But in this he was only expressing a common American dream. For, as long as Americans perceive themselves as politically equal, and as long as each American has a theoretical chance of rising out of his economic class as an individual, huge differences in economic status are not only tolerated but become the mark of distinguishing the achiever from the non-achiever, the "successful" man from the failure. This view maintained intact the idea of personal, rather than societal, responsibilities for development. As Bryce noted:

There are no struggles between privileged and unprivileged orders, even that perpetual strife of rich and poor which is the oldest disease of civilized states. One must not pronounce broadly that there are no classes, for in parts of the country social distinctions have begun to grow up. But for political purposes classes scarcely exist. No one of the questions which now agitate the nation is a question between rich and poor. Instead of suspicion, jealousy, and arrogance embittering the relations of classes, good feeling and kindliness reign. Everything that government, as the Americans have hitherto understood the term, can give them, the poor have already: political power, equal civil rights, a career open to all citizens alike. . . . Hence the poor have had nothing to fight for, no grounds for disliking the well-to-do, no complaints to make against them.[15]

How interesting this sounds in retrospect, to have someone a century ago indicate that the poor have no common denominator which would give them class consciousness. Indeed, the "war on poverty" was largely waged by the relatively well-to-do to pull the poor up as if by an Archimedean lever. It is by no stretch of the imagination illustrative of the poor hoisting themselves up by their own bootstraps. The war on poverty assumes that everyone has an equal desire for advancement, while the structure of poverty is based on motivation or lack thereof. Hence, even at this stage, there is no common consciousness of poverty or common destiny which unites the poor against other classes. Instead, there is a belief that being poor is just punishment for being uneducated.

Simone de Beauvoir has pointed out that, even in the present epoch,

no class hierarchy has been superimposed on top of any qualities of wealth and the average standard of living is high enough to prevent wealthy people from creating an inferiority complex. The rich American has no grandeur. The poor man has no servility. Human relations in daily life are on a footing of equality. Pride in the title "American citizen" which is common to all makes for understanding.

Here one detects the huge gulf which exists between the United States as a land of social equality and as a land of economic inequality; and how one serves to undermine much concern for the other. As Beauvoir herself indicates:

15. James Bryce, "The American Commonwealth (1888)," in *America in Perspective: The United States Through Foreign Eyes,* edited by Henry Steele Commager. New York: Random House, 1947, p. 224.

Each individual can disguise the poverty of his lot by believing he shares in the life of a great nation and each sees himself in his neighbor and wishes him to enjoy the dignity of man and the rights to which he is entitled just like himself. Americans have never demanded economic equality so much as economic opportunity. They admit of different standards of life so long as each citizen can by his own efforts climb from one rung of the ladder to another. Of course a few accidental successes maintain the cherished legend of the self-made man fluttering on the horizon, but this hoax is like comparing a lottery ticket with a treasury bond; any ticket may be the winning one, but only a tiny percentage of them actually do win. The equivocal meaning of the word "chance" is exploited, for its precise statistical meaning is very different from the vague meaning it has for the individual dazzled by doubtful promises.[16]

The United States has been adopted as the prime example for the liberal economists' thesis that production is more important than distribution. In the works of Alfred Marshall, for example, the nation was seen as a place where there is an emphasis on making the economic pie bigger, and not worrying about who gets shares in this pie. The argument was that raising levels of production made possible incorporating the working classes into the goals as well as instruments of American society. The United States was seen as a land of plenty and opportunity. The abundance of the United States has been held by observers to account for its liberality of spirit and for its egalitarianism as well. From the time of its first discovery, visitors were bewildered by the vastness of the United States and the bounty of its harvest, which was in such stark contrast to the nations of Europe. Cobbett looked with wide eyes on the table of the unperturbed American farmer: "You are not much asked, not much pressed, to eat and drink; but, such an abundance is spread before you, and so hearty and so cordial is your reception, that you instantly lose all restraint." [17] As the wilderness revealed its great wealth of raw materials and as the United States began to expand industrially, her riches became legendary.

By the second half of the nineteenth century, when Harriet Martineau visited America, there was a virtual rhapsody of praise for the natural wealth of the new land.

16. Simone de Beauvoir, *America Day by Day*. New York: Grove Press, 1953, pp. 260–63.
17. William Cobbett, "The Material Well-Being of the Americans," in *America in Perspective, op. cit.*, pp. 28–29.

The United States are not only vast in extent: they are inestimably rich in material wealth. There are fisheries and granite quarries along the northern coast; and shipping from the whole commercial world within their ports. There are tanneries within reach of their oak woods, and manufacturers in the north from the cotton growth of the south. There is unlimited wealth of corn, sugar-cane and beet, hemp, flax, tobacco and rice. There are regions of pasture land. There are varieties of grape for wine, and mulberries for silk. There is salt. There are mineral springs. There is marble, gold, lead, iron and coal. There is a chain of mountains dividing the great fertile western valley from the busy eastern region which lies between the mountains and the Atlantic. These mountains wield the springs by which the great rivers are to feed for ever, to fertilize the great valley, and to be the vehicle of its commerce with the world. Out of the reach of these rivers, in the vast breadth of the north, lie great lakes, to be likewise the servants of commerce, and to afford in their fisheries the means of life and luxury to thousands. These inland seas temper the climate, summer and winter, and insure health to the heart of the vast continent. Never was a country more gifted by nature.[18]

Here a decent living standard was to be had for the common man. Here lay unlimited raw materials and opportunities making both overseas expansion and revolutionary civil strife unnecessary. This wealth made inconsequential if not inevitable wastage of natural resources. When man has to conquer nature rather than adapt himself to it, he tends to become more concerned with exploiting nature. He is eager to harvest its wealth by transforming natural objects into raw materials for the industrial process. But Harriet Martineau was perceptive enough, and knowledgeable enough in economics, to realize that the greatest material wealth of America was in its diverse and developed peoples.

The notion of American abundance is classic, but its existence was not a challenge in itself. How it would be used to maximum capacity was what intrigued and interested observers from other shores. And here the first announcement of the American ideology was to perform its role.

Opportunities for work and business activity were richly abundant. Idleness and shiftlessness, when associated with poverty, were condemned as moral delinquencies. The resultant mentality developed

18. Harriet Martineau, *op. cit.*, pp. 130–31.

in this environment was one which glorified the "hustler" and the "go-getter" and deprecated devotion to anything which was not immediately practical.[19]

In brief, every social fact was also translated into moral currency, into what Perry termed the "moral economy." The American past was thus pegged to a divine mission; success was not a social good so much as it was a proof of moral competence. The "moral economy" was strangely linked to the "moral athlete," which made for the "ultimate individual." [20] In such a scheme, society could never be more than instrumental to the drives and directions of the person. And the laissez-faire economy served as a model for the fusion of material plentitude and human opportunity. This is made clear in Mackay's interesting observation on American stratification, his basic point being that, while the love of money may be a universal psychological characteristic, the availability of money is a particularized social characteristic.

> The love of money is regarded by many as a striking trait in the American character. I fear that this is a weakness to which humanity must universally plead guilty. But it is quite true that it is an absorbing passion with the Americans. This cannot be denied, but it may be explained. America is a country in which fortunes have yet to be made. Wealth gives great distinction, and wealth is, more or less, within the grasp of all. Hence the universal scramble. All cannot be made wealthy, but all have a chance of securing a prize. This stimulates to the race, and hence the eagerness of the competition. In this country England, however, the lottery is long since over, and with few exceptions the great prizes are already drawn. To the great bulk of the people, wealth is utterly unattainable. All they can hope for is competency, and numbers fall short even of that. Men soon flag in a hopeless pursuit. Hence it is that, in this country, the scramble is neither so fierce nor universal.[21]

A strange ambiguity about American political structure prevailed throughout the nineteenth century. Practical politics in the United States was most frequently described as corrupt and subject to the whims of

19. Morris Raphael Cohen, *American Thought: A Critical Sketch*. New York: Collier Books, 1962, p. 33.
20. Ralph Barton Perry, *Puritanism and Democracy*. New York: The Vanguard Press, 1944, esp. pp. 245–96.
21. Alexander Mackay, "Every American Is an Apostle of the Democratic Creed," in *America in Perspective, op. cit.*, p. 119.

the ignorant masses.[22] Political morality often shocked foreign observers. Elected officials were rarely found to be people of higher sensibilities; and even less often, appointed "Tammany Hall" type officials. They were rarely businessmen who were inspiring, and even less frequently were those in the political ranks drawn from men of intellectual substance. Dicey noted that the less "Anglo" and the more "American" the United States became, the less interest educated men took in American politics. In contrast with the colonial period, quality of leadership went down and mass consensus, what Dicey bluntly called "uniformity," went up. In other words, in setting the democratic framework, the nation paid the price in the form of a less obedient public servant.[23] What Dicey was reflecting upon was the transformation of the American value system under the impact of the double process of urbanization and industrialization. However, what Dicey did not appreciate was the extent to which this very same process of the massification of politics also resulted in the development of a less servile civil servant and more rational if less servile public official.

Lord Bryce found the same condition of public immorality widespread among administrators and legislators. Since they were in fact "average men," and thought of by themselves and by others as "average men," a sense of high purpose rarely went along with their high responsibilities. What most disturbed Bryce was not its effects on the society as a whole, but its reinforcement of the democratic ethos. Political corruption produced a certain apathy among the ruling classes and among fastidious types. Since they perceived themselves as being no more important than the ordinary voter, and since they were disgusted by the superficial vulgarities of public life, they ostensibly retreated into non-political, cultural activity. Bryce's vision of America was mostly confined to the large cities he visited.[24]

Despite the vulgarities of American political life, it became apparent to most commentators that the American had an extraordinary faith in his formal political institutions. Not only was the American

22. This was a profound motivation in even the best analysis of the American political system. See, for instance, M. Ostrogorski, *Democracy and the Organization of Political Parties,* Vol. II: *The United States,* edited and abridged by Seymour Martin Lipset. Garden City, N.Y.: Doubleday & Co., 1964.
23. Edward Dicey, *Six Months in the Federal States* (two volumes). London: Macmillan Co., 1863.
24. James Bryce, *The American Commonwealth* (two volumes). New York: Macmillan Co., 1888.

loath to challenge the political order; he was hardly prone to challenge even its sordidness. The American saw in the exaggerated displays of political appeals to lower and working classes an emerging populist spirit that would thereafter menace establishment institutions.

Ostrogorski saw the way out of this dilemma of political formalism and political populism through the widest possible use of populist sentiments of the Americans.

> The moral basis of political action was laid in the struggles for emancipation throughout the United States, in the form of "committees of seventy" or of "one hundred," of the "citizens' movements," all of the "mugwumps," or the "leagues," or "civic federations" all of which represented free associations of men brought together for a particular cause, and completely setting aside, for the nonce, their views on other political questions. In these movements the new method received its baptism of fire and showed what it could do. By its means it has been possible to combine all the living forces of American society for the struggle against political corruption, and to win victories which enable us not to despair of American democracy and of the government of the people by the people. In the sphere of the great national questions, as well as in municipal life, everywhere the "leagues" have been the instigators of the civic awakening; all the great reforms which have been passed to purify political life, beginning with that of the civil service, are due to their initiative or to their efforts; they have broken the prescription set up in favour of party tyranny and corruption, by opposing to the traditional conventions and the rigid forms that congeal and stifle everything that falls into their grasp, liberty of movement for the citizen in public life and the full light of free consideration.[25]

Whatever the contemporary significance of Ostrogorski's suggestions, he did pinpoint the achievement as well as the dilemma of nineteenth-century American politics. In retrospect it might be said that the conflict between political corruption and mass participation had a stimulating effect on the developmental process, for it kept the political machinery from hardening into an obstacle to development. The necessary price was paid but the work got done. This was true at the national level and at the ward level, and because of this, economic development in America was not fettered by an admittedly cumbersome political process. In a European context, deviance was viewed as developmental only if linked to middle-class ambitions thwarted by aristo-

25. M. Ostrogorski, *op. cit.,* p. 365.

cratic pretentions. Hence, the notion of what constitutes legitimate departure from tradition was confined to middle-class values. In the United States, deviance was linked to crime, graft, payoffs, and the like. As a result, developmental programs were unhindered in large measure by "bourgeois morality" seen as entrepreneurial niceties. And this made for a wide-open world of development.

One of the most frequent charges against Americans is that they are dominated by monetary values. Charles Dickens claimed the American was infatuated with the real to the exclusion of the ideal. Tocqueville, for his part, explained American materialism as an inevitable and natural consequence of an egalitarian state of mind. The Polish writer Adam deGurowski saw the emphasis on material acquisition as something every American could be proud of. All observers, however, sensed one distinctive peculiarity in American materialism, namely, that the passion for money-making did not stem from an innate propensity toward avarice, nor from a desire for opulence, but resulted from Americans' love for the game of chance. And this game plan was a manifestation of the will to power. But in a nation free of ascribed status, the pursuit of wealth became all the more important.

> With all the numerous and dark drawbacks of this propensity for money-making, it does not generate avarice in the Americans. If generally they are infuriated in the pursuit of money, they spend it as freely as they make it. If they are called men of the dollar, at any rate they are not hunters of cents. Parsimonious economy is not their characteristic, and in general the racing after dollars, the thirst for gain, does not make them contemptible misers or calloused to others.

As deGurowski sees it, this drive is basically autonomous, what in modern terms would be called a search conducted anomically, that is, independent of any firm frame of reference or set of goals.

> Money is made not merely for the sake of becoming independent and rich or enjoying both, but from habit—on account of finding any other congenial occupation impossible. It becomes an intellectual drilling, and a test of skill. It becomes a game, deeply combined, complicated—a struggle with men and events, exciting, captivating, terrible, hand-to-hand, man-to-man, cunning-to-cunning.

Interestingly, deGurowski sees this drive for material acquisitions as taking place in an atmosphere of cultural scarcity. "The socially passionate life in Europe, diversified, and full of various enjoyments, gives to a successful winner, new scopes, attraction, and pleasures, such as society does not proffer, yield, or create in America." [26]

The American "will to conquer" or "risk-taking" was viewed by Schumpeter as the essence of capitalism. The gaming analogy permitted a wide-open universe of bets, side bets, and the attendant corruption involved in a world where winning defined all rules, rather than the other way about. The rise of state-protected monopolies occurred only in the late nineteenth century, and by that time the basic style of American development through risk and venture capital had been set.[27]

For Hugo Munsterberg this economic materialism ends up as a philosophical idealism. He sees the money-making orientation involved in a transference of values.

> The real attraction which the American feels for money making does not lie in the having but only in the getting, from the perfect equanimity, positively amazing to the European, with which he bears his losses. To be sure, his irrepressible optimism stands him in good stead; he never loses hope, but is confident that what he has lost will soon be made up. But this would be no comfort to him if he did not care much less for the possession than for the getting of it. The American chases after money with all his might, exactly as on the tennis court he tries to hit the ball, and it is the game he likes and not the prize.

One can see that the gaming analogy is almost endemic to the American scene; it is surprising how many nineteenth-century observers used the game metaphor to describe the American way of life. But they also emphasized that idealism prompted the performers. "It is fundamentally false to stigmatize the American as a materialist and to deny his idealism," Munsterberg concludes. "The economic life means to the American a realization of efforts which are in themselves precious. It is not the means to an end but is its own end." [28]

George W. Steevens saw American materialism in much less flattering terms. It was not an illustration of philosophical idealism so much as

26. Adam G. deGurowski, "The Practical Genius of the American," in *America in Perspective, op. cit.,* pp. 157–70.
27. Joseph A. Schumpeter, *The Theory of Economic Development: An Inquiry into Profits, Capital, Credit, Interest and the Business Cycle.* Cambridge, Mass.: Harvard University Press, 1934, pp. 93–94.
28. Hugo Munsterberg, "A Philosopher Explains the American Passion for Money," in *America in Perspective, op. cit.,* pp. 261–69.

an adolescent empiricism. The keynote of this materialism is its impulsive need to express all sentiments externally by the crudest and most objective means.

> The Americans are the most demonstrative of all the peoples of the earth. Everything must be brought to the surface, embodied in a visible, palpable form. For a fact to make any effect on the American mind it must be put in a shape where it can be seen, heard, handled. If you want to impress your fellows you must do it not through their reasoning powers but through the five senses of their bodies.

Steevens also sees his materialism as the foundation for the peculiar type of patriotism the American exhibits:

> The most patriotic of men, his patriotism seems always to center rather on his flag than on his country. He can see the flag but he can't see the country. Why does he cover his person with childish buttons and badges? Because you can see them and you can't see the sentiments in his mind. They do not read Shakespeare but would think it almost a sin to visit England without seeing Shakespeare's house. In business they are the most unwearied and ingenious advertisers in the world. In dress they appear vain, out of just the same reverence for the concrete and indifference to the abstract.[29]

In sum, American materialism is actually equivalent to development as an economic notion, that is to say, concepts of development in terms of cultivation or culture did not impress the American citizen. It was not that the Americans did not believe in art. It was that their view of art was itself functional. The aesthetic was embodied in the object—in the object as a performing instrument. The continued awe in which the American holds automobile shows or boat shows is certainly not different from the awe with which an Italian holds the Sistine Chapel. The aesthetic is different, but it is there. It was this genius for linking aesthetic judgments to practical judgments that so fascinated men like Tocqueville, who indeed not only saw the influence of democracy on science and the arts but also appreciated the degree to which the arts and science influenced the structure of America.[30]

This practical materialism thus gave rise to a whole new aesthetic

29. George W. Steevens, "The American Is an Electric Anglo-Saxon," in *America in Perspective, op. cit.,* pp. 254–60.
30. Alexis de Tocqueville, *op. cit.,* pp. 265–78.

quite different to and alien in spirit from the European system. Americans were not known as people of artistic or intellectual excellence, and therefore they have not been judged by their cultural productions, at least not in the nineteenth century. Not only was there a general decline in the number of upperclass "cultivated gentlemen" in America from the days of the founding of the Republic, but the educated men themselves seemed to treat the intellect quite differently from the Europeans. Thus it might be said that the American became educated as he became massified—less concerned with cultivation and manners and hence unaffected in his developmental goals by education. Madariaga says in a rather whimsical fashion:

> They are hungry and thirsty for information—facts, stories. But they dislike thought, as all sound, healthy children do. None of your highbrow stuff for fine lads who can enjoy themselves making toys and playing with them. Knowledge, yes. By all means. Some boys must know all about how toys are made and moved to and fro and distributed fairly in the nursery, or there would be no fun. Knowledge is all right. It can be checked and put to some use, both made something of and kept busy, so to say. It can be turned into a toy, so that by means of little machines with colored lamps and buttons and switches the springs of the soul-machine may be shown to the whole nursery.[31]

Madariaga, however, undoubtedly has in mind twentieth-century American history. In the formative years there was indeed a deep desire to educate people and not simply to manufacture fact machines. There was not yet the kind of professionalism which now pervades education. The division of labor did not extend to the sphere of learning, where the notion of general education, liberal arts education, and all-around competence prevailed throughout the nineteenth century. The rise of professional training did not take place till the end of the nineteenth century with the consolidation of the American industrial system. The concept of knowledge as a bank account, as something one can dip into according to how much wealth of information is stored, corresponds to a stage in American development where industry overshadows agriculture as the main source of wealth.

What eased this transition from humanistic learning to professionalism was an emphasis on methods of work rather than on products of

31. Salvador de Madariaga, "Americans Are Boys," in *America in Perspective, op. cit.,* pp. 297–309.

work. Lack of abstract knowledge never prevented the American from plunging ahead on an experimental and operational basis.[32] As Siegfried put it,

> The new world is in no way hostile to the general idea used as a source of inspiration, but, though the American feels in spite of everything that there is an empty space to be filled, his response is not that of the classicist. He is not tempted to consider educating specialists in general ideas, that is to say, another class of experts. In everything he seems to be interested in methods rather than things themselves.[33]

The methodological orientation was the bridge over which the American crossed from an agricultural to an industrial basis. The leisure, educated class of an agrarian society was replaced by specialists and the "usefully" educated, thus encouraging a "particularistic" over a "universalistic" approach to things.

In the nineteenth century, criticism of the United States from within was mainly confined to the grafted aristocracy, that minute portion of Americans which remained unabsorbed and which preferred the culture of France and England and the courtesy of Spain to the roughhewn philistinism of America. The critique of the American system by rural populists from Andrew Jackson to Henry George was limited because of its relative isolation from mass protest movements, and from its denial of considerations of race and class. The American intellectual has a largely conservative tradition in contrast to the European intellectual, who, since the period of eighteenth-century France, has been classically a radical, isolated from other classes and even from members of his own class. By contrast, criticism of the United States by Americans during the nineteenth century tended to be imitative and almost trivial in character. Not until William James' anti-imperialism near the end of the century is there a meaningful liberal criticism of American foreign policy. It is necessary to use the European writers' image of America because of this peculiar divorce of the American intellectual from the industrialization process.

32. Irving Louis Horowitz, "Professionalism and Disciplinarianism: Two Styles of Sociological Performance," *Philosophy of Science*, Vol. 31, No. 3, July 1964; also Everett C. Hughes, *Men at Work*. Glencoe, Ill.: The Free Press, 1958; and C. Wright Mills, *Sociology and Pragmatism: The Higher Learning in America*. New York: Oxford University Press, 1965.
33. André Siegfried, *op. cit.*, p. 356.

It is remarkable how uniform the interpretation of the United States has been from within. Allusion is nearly always made to American initiative, optimism, materialism, faith, and devotion to hard work. Even when interpretations of these variables sharply differ, few challenge the facts surrounding the First World *Weltanschauung*. Perhaps the reason why this is so has less to do with the facts than with the projections of what constitutes Americanism. Few nations on earth, overdeveloped, properly developing, or underdeveloped, have such a passion for a teleological goal as the Americans. They pursue "purpose" with the same zeal, though with less assurance, than the religiously devout reach out for Providence and the politically devout reach out for utopia. The spate of literature on the "national purpose" which appeared in the late 1950's demonstrates clearly the collective anxiety of Americans unsure of their purpose. As Riesman notes: "There is something oddly regressive in the spectacle of the United States reducing itself to the size of a new nation that needs a manifest destiny." [34] Perhaps in this search for a future role one aspect of United States leadership of the First World becomes clear: from the pragmatic, pluralistic, and uncertain orientation claimed for the United States by Tocqueville, the country has evolved into a monolithic unity. It has sought out a singular purpose characteristic of historic bureaucratic world empires.[35]

The American self-perception remains fixed, atrophied, characterized by buoyant optimism about the future, by concern for material well-being, moralizing, a faith in egalitarianism, and an egalitarianism of faith. As Boorstin indicated, it is a society whose members are still convinced that they are misunderstood by everyone, and that this misunderstanding arises out of a basic jealousy of have-not peoples.[36] Interestingly, even those who do their utmost to revise this "image," who are dedicated to the elimination of "ethnocentrism" in American thought, are not infrequently guilty of moralizings which read like a catalogue of false stereotypes. Thus, in one recent effort along the lines of self-purification, "a manual for Americans overseas," [37] we find out

34. See David Riesman, "The Concept of National Purpose," *Council for Correspondence Newsletter,* No. 27, June 1963, p. 11.
35. See S. N. Eisenstadt, *The Political Systems of Empires.* New York: The Free Press, 1963, esp. the conclusion, pp. 361–71.
36. Daniel Boorstin. *America and the Image of Europe: Reflections on American Thought.* New York: Meridian Books, 1960.
37. Conrad M. Arensberg and Arthur H. Niehoff, *Introducing Social Change: A Manual for Americans Overseas.* Chicago: Aldine Publishing Co., 1964.

everything but what counts: Why are millions of Americans overseas in the first place?

Perhaps the greatest single study of the United States was made by Alexis de Tocqueville over a century ago. Nevertheless, Tocqueville is done no honor by a number of recent writers who are remarkably jejune in their uncritical acceptance of his work. These are the writers who present themselves as implacable foes of dogmatism when it comes to Marx's writings.[38] In some measure this is simply a response to an impulse to celebrate those who praise the United States and criticize those who condemn it. Tocqueville spoke well of the United States. Even his aristocratic criticisms of American democracy were made with generous respect for the revolutionary achievements of the first new nation and could hardly irritate the devoted believer in manifest destiny.

There is little advantage in basking in the judgments of the nineteenth century, unless we are prepared to say that the empirical conditions which prevailed at the time of the writings of Tocqueville, Martineau, and Ostrogorski still obtain. But if the situation is radically different, as I maintain it is, then judgments must similarly be cast in terms which reflect the present. Indeed Tocqueville himself knew this. He wrote of democratic government in America, "The foreign policy of the United States is reduced by its very nature to await the chances of the future history of the nation, and for the present it consists more in abstaining from interference than in exerting its activity." [39] Such abstinence came to an abrupt end with U.S. overseas expansion in Latin America and the Far East at the turn of the century; and this isolation was thoroughly eliminated by U.S. participation in World War I. At this point the United States became the leader of the highly industrialized part of the world.

Hans Kohn appreciated this and indicated that World War I "linked the destinies of the two shores of the North Atlantic again as closely as they had been in the eighteenth century." But this time the superordinate and subordinate positions were drastically altered.

> Though the Europeans were not aware of it, and continued their struggle to maintain a European balance of power, bidding for European hegemony as if no fundamental change had happened, the

38. See, for example, Seymour Martin Lipset, "Political Sociology," in *Sociology Today: Problems and Prospects,* edited by R. K. Merton, Leonard Broom, and L. S. Cottrell, Jr. New York: Basic Books, 1959, pp. 81–114.
39. Alexis de Tocqueville, *op. cit.,* p. 138.

> end of the war marked also the political eclipse of Europe. It was
> a misfortune for both Europe and the United States that neither
> realized it or wished to acknowledge it. Yet in 1917 only the en-
> trance of the United States into what had been until then a war for
> the maintenance of the balance of power in Europe saved Europe
> from the consequences of a German victory on the eastern and
> western fronts and from German hegemony over the whole con-
> tinent.[40]

If the United States "saved" Europe from German hegemony, it made
clear its own stake in the affairs of the world. From that point on, the
United States has in fact been the leader, acknowledged or otherwise,
of the First World.

The United States becomes leader of the First World (and not just
the industrial world) only when there are comparisons to be made with
the Second World of Soviet development and the Third World of Latin
America and the Afro-Asian bloc. As long as the United States represented one part of a homogenous Europeanized world, it had no reality
as a First World: it had no leadership possibilities. It was a radical
break, then, when the United States became the leader in an expansive
phase of what has to be known as Western civilization.

Despite the wars carried on in the name of democracy, economic
inequality has become more pronounced. The gap between rich and
poor nations has become greater. At the same time the main center of
traditional economic wealth has moved from Europe to the United
States. European nations—especially England, France, and Germany—
have declined as world powers. Europe, not merely the Axis powers,
was defeated in World War II. Militarily, economically, politically, and
culturally, the United States has become the power center of the Western
bloc. At this point it consolidated its substance and style into a veritable
First World—a measure of universal wants as well as universal needs.

In the process of rising to the fore of a First World the United States
paid an indirect tribute to the power and the potency of the Second
World of Soviet development. The First World maintains a string of
international military and political affiliations, a network of associations calculated to prevent the Second World from expanding its powerful international influence; and in a more ultimate sense it is intended
to keep the Third World from adopting concrete anti-Western "socialist" strategies or principles. The emergence of the First World as a
conscious entity has been accompanied by a drastic inflation of nation-

40. Hans Kohn, *op. cit.,* pp. 205–6.

alism and nationalistic rhetoric. Precisely to the extent that the First World has become mobilized and homogenized into an "Atlantic Community," a "Western democratic" orbit, a "civilized front against barbarism," the United States itself has been transformed from a nation-state into a world civilization.

The United States has become an international purchaser of "good will." Economically, it has sealed off its orbit; and in various ways it deploys its economy as an instrument to gain political and military ends. Even the trade union movement has become professionalized, and in the process fully incorporated into both the national economy and America's larger nationalist designs.[41] Those strata not yet absorbed, such as Negro and other ethnic minority groups, have had their protest movements severely circumscribed. Often they seek only participation in the national celebration rather than real equality.

Louis Hartz has described the impact of the United States' sealing itself off from developments in the rest of the world.

> The American failure to understand revolution derives not merely from the formal experience of fragmentation. It derives from the point at which the American detachment from the European development took place, the bourgeois point, which by the complicated mechanism of fragment evolution cut off the socialist "future." Hence it is an inability to understand the appeal of socialism itself which is involved. McCarthyite virtue at home is accompanied by bafflement with respect to the origin of sin abroad. But it is precisely the promise of modernity which socialism offers, in the context of the traditionalist order, which is the root of its appeal. . . . Life within the American fragment, which does not know that ethos, as either a burden or a lure, as either something to forget or something unforgettable, cannot seize the meaning of this promise.[42]

Perceptive as this formulation is, one important point is left unanswered: The United States has not simply "fragmented" or become

41. See Irving Louis Horowitz, "The Condition of the Working Class in the United States," *New Politics,* Vol. VIII, No. 3 (1970), pp. 13–27.
42. Louis Hartz, "The United States History in a New Perspective," *The Founding of New Societies.* New York: Harcourt, Brace, 1964, pp. 119–20. A similar argument about America as a socialist fulfillment is contained in Seymour Martin Lipset, *The First New Nation: The United States in Historical and Comparative Perspective.* New York: Basic Books, 1963. My own arguments against this position are to be found in "Another View from Our Left," *New Politics,* Vol. II, No. 2 (Winter 1963), pp. 77–88; and "The Birth and Meaning of America: A Discussion of the First New Nation," in *The Sociological Quarterly,* Vol. 7, No. 1 (Winter 1966), pp. 3–20.

"detached" from the mainstream of development; for it offers to the
Third World a highly successful model for further development. And
here is where the contradiction becomes especially apparent. It is not
just American failure to understand revolution that is at stake, but
its failure to come to terms with social revolution. What is truly novel
in the twentieth-century American experience is that nearly all definitions bear on the technological, while few innovations in economic organizations can be claimed.

Even those social changes that have taken place are largely a consequence of technological and scientific invention. The constitutional
basis of American society serves to undermine social revolution just as
assuredly as it serves to promote technological innovation. It is then
this internal contradiction which makes the United States a difficult
"model" for the rest of the world, and in turn makes it so impermea-
ble to internally induced social revolutions.

The United States role as a model for the future has been subject to
competition from other styles of economic and social development and
other forms of political organization. On the internal scene it has been
severely circumscribed by the closing of the frontier and restriction of
immigration. This dramatic change is underscored by a recent report
issued by the Rockefeller Foundation:

> The picture of the United States held at least unconsciously in the
> minds of Americans is that of a large continent, endowed with vir-
> tually unlimited resources, enjoying an easy power and favored with
> a comfortably large and growing population. That picture will change
> in the decades ahead. In comparison with the vast, amorphous new
> regional groups now obtaining political expression, the outstanding
> fact about the United States may come to seem its compactness.
> Notable among its characteristics will be a high degree of skill, elab-
> orate organization, a refined technology. Its conviction of self-suffi-
> ciency will be replaced by awareness of how greatly it is dependent
> on its relations with other countries for essential materials and for
> a supporting atmosphere in which it can breathe and be itself.[43]

As long as the United States had open frontiers, unexplored regions,
and free land it retained many of the values of an agricultural society.
The first hundred years of American experience were unique in that

43. *The Mid-Century Challenge to U.S. Foreign Policy,* Panel 1 Report of the
Rockefeller Brothers Fund Special Studies Project. Garden City, N.Y.: Doubleday
& Co., 1959, p. 58.

they revealed little anxiety over economic development. The doctrine of inevitable progress covered everyone. Even if we explore the character of technological innovation and invention in this early period we often find its orientation directed toward farm machinery and ways of creating crop efficiency. While there can be no doubt that these technological developments stimulated the movement of men toward cities and in themselves generated technological unemployment on the farm, their consequences were almost wholly absorbed by lateral mobility, by movements to fresh lands and new territories. Conservation, for example, was of no concern between 1780 and 1870 precisely because of the abundance and fertility of virgin territories.

The real end of the frontier coincided with the growth of mutually incompatible economic systems in the United States. From an economic viewpoint the Civil War involved an acute confrontation of the emerging industrialism represented by Northern interests and the declining agriculturalism represented by Southern interests. Considered in this way, slavery was a hindrance to the North and to the West, for it prevented the rapid mobilization of primary factory labor, while for the South it was a necessity because it alone of all forms of economic relationships was cheaper in cost than technological substitutes. The liquidation of slavery meant that whatever form the economic question took in the post-Civil War period, it would have to be based on the triumph of machine over human labor, of "scientific technology" over "natural law." The humanitarianism of the Civil War, the outcry against slavery, was thus a response to the needs of an industrial society.

The issue of how important the relative scarcity of labor in the United States was in encouraging technical progress remains unsettled among economic historians. America had to make the most out of its labor since land was abundant. In this sense, the Civil War rationalized the economic condition, not only by bringing about an end to slavery but by hastening the end of the agricultural epoch precisely through the encouragement of the settlement of new frontiers based on free lands. Furthermore, the elimination of the Southern plantation system was politically necessary as well as economically necessary. The dominance of the slave system extended to the national political structure, and hence hampered legislation that would positively bring about industrialization.[44]

44. Harold Underwood Faulkner, *American Economic History* (8th edition). New York: Harper & Row, 1960, esp. pp. 211–12; 306-26.

The post-Civil War drive for economic maturity, which extended from 1870 to 1914, brought about an immense industrial growth in the north and central regions. The industrial belt was fused to an urban ring. Megalopolis extended from New York to Chicago westward, and from Boston through Philadelphia along the coastal plain. States such as Pennsylvania, Ohio, and Massachusetts were the great beneficiaries of this sectional development, since their cities represented, as they still do, what is known as the industrial heartland.[45] During the same period, and with the contributing factor of chronic agricultural stagnation in both the South and New England, the total agrarian sector simply failed to expand anywhere near as rapidly as the industrial sector. Thus, in 1850, the value added to the over-all economy was $1.6 billion in the agrarian sector as compared to $4.7 billion in the manufacturing sector. By 1900, the agricultural portion had increased to $4.7 billion, while the manufacturing sector had increased elevenfold to $11.4 billion.[46] Thus, what has been taking place in the Third World, the sacrifice of the agricultural to the industrial sector, had already taken place in the United States by the end of the nineteenth century.

The exploitation of agricultural workers in the post-Civil War period corresponded to the needs of a growing industrial empire which was at the same time an urban empire. The agricultural portions of the community were made intolerable, driving excess labor into industry. At the same time concentration was placed on the mechanization of industry, the application of this mechanization to the farm lands further weakened the agricultural sector. What is amazing about American development is that the agricultural sector continued to yield higher productivity in the face of a rising urban labor force recruited into relatively well-paying jobs in an expanding industrial economy. This is in marked contrast to development in the Second World of the Soviet Union and in most portions of the Third World. One significant fact in this may have been the Homestead Act, which gave legislative sanction to the efficient farmer who needs and deserves machinery, railways, and better communications facilities.

The genius of the United States was expended in devising ways and means of making capitalism viable. There was nothing to indicate that

45. For a significant work covering these trends, see Jean Gottman, *Megalopolis: The Urbanized Northeastern Seaboard of the United States.* New York: The Twentieth Century Fund, 1961.
46. Harold Underwood Faulkner, *American Economic History,* p. 392.

this was possible. The peculiarities of American capitalism can be seen in the electrical engineering field. Despite the fact that the basic scientific discoveries had been made, with Faraday showing in 1831 how to convert mechanical power into electrical current, mass electricity was not made available to a mass public until the end of the century. The problem was not how to produce electrical energy, but how such energy was to be marketed and sold. Selling energy reached its pinnacle in the natural resource monopolies of the United States. Through the dual process of industrialization and urbanization, such new energy sources could be commercially marketed. And they were. Even at present, the "electrification process" has nowhere reached the degree of achievement it has in the United States. Furthermore, the profits from such electrical activities were partially used to sponsor new research and new styles of research. "Edison's Menlo Park laboratory may have been a crude affair, but it was the prototype of the great governmental and industrial research institutions of today. It is in the electrical industry that we can see most clearly how economic success can, so to speak, *fix* and establish scientific *development*." [47] In some measure, this new prototype was not unique to electrical industries, for it applied equally to those parts of the technostructure that were unencumbered by traditional ways of doing things, like the automobile industry in its earlier experimental days.[48]

Despite this remarkable achievement of converting society from agriculture to industry without political revolution, and despite this technological compensation for problems of the transition period, the United States has still failed to capture, in ideology at least, the imagination of Third World leadership. Paradoxically there seemed to be more enthusiasm and more interest in the genius of America when it was less developed than today when it is more developed.

To some degree the answer must be sought in the economic operations of American society, particularly its inability to operate at maximum capacity, which has given rise to underutilization of resources coupled with overproduction. The dynamics of this contradiction has placed financing in American society on a shaky credit basis in which the ability to repay is constantly being threatened by underutilization,

47. See J. D. Bernal, "Science, Industry and Society in the Nineteenth Century," *Essays on the Social History of Science,* edited by S. Lilley. Copenhagen: Ejnar Munksgaard, 1953, pp. 138–65.
48. John Kenneth Galbraith, *The New Industrial State,* pp. 100–103.

and the capacity of the lender to foreclose equally threatened by the vast problems of overproduction. The gap gets larger. Even with this new reservoir of credit the industrial complex in the United States operates at between one-half to three-fourths of its capacity. At least $10 billion worth of goods and services have been lost in the last decade alone. Thurman Arnold in a recent updating of his study on *The Folklore of Capitalism* has pointed out that:

> For the past ten years we have been able to use only about 75 per cent of what we produce. As a practical matter, it would not be difficult to avail ourselves of that unused production. As an ideological matter it is a present impossibility to carry on the public works and services which our economy could so easily afford. This is because private money and credit are not available for such things as conservation of our water supply, our health, our recreational facilities, and so on, through a long list of public necessities. Things which cannot be bought and sold for dollars on the marketplace cannot be financed by private credit. Therefore we must do without them even though this means a colossal waste of our real production resources.[49]

Even if we adjust Arnold's version to account for huge philanthropic activities, his criticism is forceful, since the underutilization of planned capacities is itself the cause in holding down the public works required for further development of the economy. The idea of setting in motion a free-floating private sector is for this reason unappetizing to most nations entering the developing stage.

One problem with the interest sector idea motivating much past United States development is the often-buried assumption that benefits and costs do not go to the same people because they should not go to the same people. In the United States, the assumption of consumer sovereignty underwrites the notion that the rich get proportionately more than the poor because they count for more in the economic marketplace. The rich are more interested in public services (especially with coercive public functions such as the police) than the poorer classes. Hence an arrangement based on the elimination of profits is not only unacceptable on ethical grounds but untenable on economic grounds as well, since it would liquidate current growth and investment priorities.

49. Thurman W. Arnold, "The Folklore of Capitalism Revisited," *The Yale Review,* Vol. LII, No. 2, Winter 1963, pp. 188–204.

Ideologically the United States no longer functions as the wave of the future. But technologically this country has never been more of a model for the rest of the human race. Admiration for the United States has been transferred from its political institutions to its industrial capacity that provides immense quantities and high-quality creature comforts, mass electrification, super-highways, consumer goods, and a host of other technological specialties. At this level the United States serves as a prime model of efficient modernization for the developing regions and for Western Europe and the Soviet bloc as well.

Compared to the Soviet Union the United States is more aware of what is and is not important in the technological order. In the 'twenties and 'thirties the United States emphasized the tallest, the largest, the most gigantic. This was particularly so in the fields of electronics and architecture. Such items as enormous cabinets for minute radios or one-hundred-story buildings, the top fifty floors of which were unoccupied, were proof of the limitations of giganticism. Ironically, in the Soviet Union one still finds an emphasis on the gigantic. It is exactly at the point when technology in the United States has become interested in "miniaturizing" that the Soviet Union has adopted the braggadocio of greatness through bigness.

The egalitarian spirit in the United States has undergone a trans-formation. The relative completion of achievement-oriented tasks has served to bring about a new concern for ascriptive values. Thus there remains enormous upward striving among Jews but with intense at-tachment to Jewish identity. Similarly there is an increase in striving on the part of Negroes but with developing attachment to the virtues of Negritude. The Protestant Establishment, for its part, has remained firmly intact. It has consolidated itself around the banking and financial interests of the country. And the existence of Catholic separatism has been well documented in all areas and walks of life.[50] Within the frame-work of the United States there is taking place a crystallization of three religious power groups focused on different spheres of activity. Broadly, one might say that the Roman Catholics have a higher-than-average involvement in the political arena; the Jews have a concentrated leader-ship in the academic and intellectual areas; and the Protestants have become the administrators of the general economy and the big organi-

50. See Will Herberg, *Protestant-Catholic-Jew*. New York: Doubleday & Co., 1955; and Milton M. Gordon, *Assimilation in American Life: The Role of Race, Religion, and National Origin*. New York: Oxford University Press, 1964.

zations of the nation.[51] The extent to which religion in America hinges on considerations of status remains to be explored, but their increasing intensity is no longer in much doubt. With the individual pressured to "climb," and the immense modern environment pressing him down, he resorts to "group mobility," uniting group identification with individual ambition.

One way of putting the model of America in meaningful perspective is to note how radically the United States has become "sociological" in its fundamental values. Membership in a church has tended to rise over the years, with upwards of 50 per cent claiming membership or affiliation of one kind or another, and over 90 per cent professing a belief in one religion or another. But the quality of such affiliation has drastically altered. In a recent study of church commitment in the American suburb, the following results were obtained. (1) It was found that one of the chief reasons for joining a church was "familism," promoting family unification and children's religious needs through authoritative agencies. (2) A central factor was belonging, social affiliation on the basis of the commercial advantages of certain friendships. (3) Peace of mind—religion as a psychoanalytic surrogate, providing mental well-being in a tormented and aggressive society—was also frequently mentioned by new parishioners. (4) Moral orientation, the belief that to identify with a church is to achieve a degree of value orientation which is absolute and meaningful, was important. (5) Success, the church is a means of validating and legitimizing already-achieved economic or political gains, was a further motivation. Two other items, often emphasized in classical sociological literature—a need for ritual and a corresponding need for religious and ethical understanding—ranked lowest on the scale of reasons for church affiliation. Thus, contrary to a religious revival, there is a tendency to subvert religion by converting it into a sociological celebration, by employing religion as a role.[52]

The trade union movement has also undergone a large transformation

51. See E. Digby Baltzell, *The Protestant Establishment: Aristocracy and Caste in America.* New York: Random House, 1964.
52. See Dennison J. Nash and Peter L. Berger, "Church Commitment in an American Suburb: An Analysis of the Decision To Join," *Archives de Sociologie des Religions* (Centre National de la Recherche Scientifique), Vol. 7, Whole No. 13, Jan.–June 1962, pp. 105–20; and for a more detailed study, see N. J. Demerath III, *Social Class in American Protestantism.* Chicago: Rand McNally & Co., 1965, particularly the theoretical discussion, pp. 177–204.

with serious consequences. It has moved from a search for redress of grievances derived from poverty to a search for economic security within the hierarchy of positions. This is particularly evident in craft unions, which have changed their goals from the total unionization of employed labor to the practice of rigid exclusion of the unorganized portions of labor from the benefits of unionization. The American union system, like the religious system, has itself become a mark of ascribed status. In certain unions the union card is virtually passed on from generation to generation.

Differentiation has been enshrined as the doctrine of the functional necessity of stratification:

> If the rights and prerequisites of different positions in a society must be unequal, then the society must be stratified, because that is precisely what stratification means. Social inequality is thus an unconsciously evolved device by which societies insure that the most important positions are conscientiously filled by the most qualified persons. Hence every society, no matter how simple or complex, must differentiate persons in terms of both prestige and esteem and must therefore possess a certain amount of institutionalized inequality.[53]

This kind of position is not a defense of conservative virtues so much as a reflection of a generalized apathy that has spread throughout the American social system, in which conditional statements are taken for immutable laws. The American ideology has accepted the canons of consumer sovereignty as being natural to capitalist development, just as in the previous century it relied on capitalist development to prove the necessity of social equality.

The land of plenty and opportunity has become classic and mythic. While lush abundance has increased dramatically, its distribution has remained remarkably uneven. The most noticeable gap, for example, that between black and white, has not appreciably changed in relative terms over the past thirty years despite the fact that the actual condition of the Negro has improved.[54] According to the 1970 census figures, Negro personal income in the South varies anywhere from one-third

53. Kingsley Davis, *Human Society.* New York: Macmillan Co., 1949, pp. 367–68; see also Kingsley Davis and Wilbert E. Moore, "Some Principles of Stratification," *American Sociological Review,* Vol. 10, 1945, pp. 242–49.
54. Alan B. Batchelder, "Decline in the Relative Income of Negro Men," *The Quarterly Journal of Economics,* Vol. LXXVIII, No. 4 (Nov. 1964), pp. 525–48.

to one-half that of white personal income.[55] Most notable also is that the rates of upward mobility along racial lines are relatively constant. This seems to be true generally of the gap between affluence and poverty. If we take three variables—race, ecology, and family income— and combine them, the result is a dramatic picture of atrophied economic inequality coupled with significant social gains for the bottom end of the class scale.

Despite wide industrialization in the South, Negro job opportunities have hardly improved in the last fifty years. During the twentieth century any increase in Negro purchasing power has been due to the family shift from the rural to the urban centers of the South and of the North. As a result, the Negro urban family has more income than the Negro rural family.

This increased circulation of personal income stimulated the growth of and provides the material basis for the Negro bourgeoisie.[56] Shopkeeping, real-estate and insurance activities, and in general those commercial establishments primarily connected with everyday needs of the Negro form the hub of this marginal middle class. The kind of work that the Negro jobseeker in the city receives is linked to low status and low pay. The new industries identified with recent economic growth in the South, such as clothes manufacturing, aircraft manufacturing, and communications industries, have followed the traditional Southern practice of confining Negroes to the same low-wage job categories. At the same time the introduction of various automation processes in the older industries is eliminating the kind of unskilled and semi-skilled jobs that Negroes have traditionally held. As a result, the income gap between the average urban Negro family and the urban white family is narrowing, as the gap between Negro and white rural families seems to be widening. According to the recent sattistics, farm labor reveals a three-to-one white-to-black salary ratio, while non-farm earnings show a slightly less than two-to-one ratio.[57] The substantial growth of the Negro bourgeoisie and professional stratum has indeed altered the classical pattern of underdevelopment. It has done so by creating a sector

55. U.S. Bureau of the Census, *Families and Unrelated Individuals*. Washington, D.C., 1970.
56. See E. Franklin Frazier, *Black Bourgeoisie: The Rise of a New Middle Class in the United States*. New York: Collier Books, 1962, pp. 42–55.
57. Current Population Reports, *Income in 1966 of Families and Persons in the United States*. Series P-60, No. 53, Dec. 1967. Washington, D.C.: USGPO, 1967.

of a minority group that is large enough and affluent enough to gain its ends within the American social system. Thus internal colonialism operates within the minority group itself, no less than between majority and minority clusters.

A "great war on poverty" was, in fact, an attempt to stave off economic class struggle as an irritant in an already difficult racial conflict. But "a war on poverty" without a concomitant critique of opulence only performed a double role: on one hand it reasserted the existence of class barriers, and on the other hand it provided a stimulus for high achievement among the present generation of wealthy who have not lost the desire nor economic drive of their forefathers. The war on poverty did not prove to be an exceptionally satisfactory way of stimulating an achievement orientation among those who thus far have not been touched by the American dream. As Kolko points out:

> From the point of view of access to economic status symbols, the position of the upper tenth of the nation's income earners should be the dominant concern of students of social inequality in America. For in almost any given year the average dollar income of the upper tenth of the income earners will be twice as high as the average income of the next highest income tenth; and about 25 to 30 times higher than the average income of the lowest income tenth. Recent assertions on the purported tendency towards income equalization have concentrated on the position of the upper fifth of the income earners and the decline of the number of annual tax returns at very high figures—$100,000 and up. This latter assertion is of little relevance, since if it can be shown that the centralization of economic power and status symbols has not moved out of the control of a small economic elite, then the problem of the elite's relation to society remains with us despite minor shifts within the elite itself.[58]

The possibilities for realizing great wealth with little effort have not only vanished for the poor but are rapidly vanishing for the middle classes.[59] As one writer pointed out:

58. Gabriel Kolko, "The American Income Revolution," *America as a Mass Society,* edited by Philip Olson. New York: The Free Press, 1963, p. 107. It is interesting to note that the situation in the United Kingdom shows no more of a trend toward leveling than that in the U.S. See Richard M. Titmuss, *Income Distribution and Social Change.* Toronto: University of Toronto Press, 1962.

59. It has been claimed that Kolko's statistics are exaggerated; but even his most severe critic admits that the top 20 per cent earn one-half the national income while the bottom 20 per cent earn less than one-twentieth. See Herman P. Miller, "Factors Related to Recent Changes in Income Distribution in the U.S.," *Re-*

Even among the highly paid and responsible businessmen and salaried executives only a small fraction were actually able to reach the top. Thus, insofar as the American people were committed to the American ideology of personal success, they were attempting to accomplish something that for most of them was impossible. Judged by the prevalent standards of American society, most Americans were compelled to regard themselves as having failed and to attribute their failure to some shortcoming within themselves.[60]

While social mobility has slowly increased, it has not kept pace with the actual growth of the economy. There is enormous pressure to participate in the American celebration and to gain a measure of plenty while at the same time there has been no dramatic or significant change in social mobility since World War II. The formal educational apparatus which was intended to further social mobility and economic opportunity has served at the same time to stratify the American society. As one group of findings show, the stratification process is reinforced by the educational system no less than the mobility process.[61]

The American educational system fuses social mobility to personality rather than to knowledge as such. As Fromm points out:

> The gospel of working loses weight and the gospel of selling becomes paramount. In feudal times, social mobility was exceedingly limited and one could not use one's personality to get ahead. In the days of the competitive market, social mobility was relatively great, especially in the United States, if one delivered the goods one could get ahead.[62]

Popular American political character has significantly changed. At the "mass" level it has revealed an increasing response to questions of

view of Economics and Statistics, Vol. 33, No. 2 (Aug. 1951), pp. 214–18; for the response to this, see Gabriel Kolko, Wealth and Power in America: An Analysis of Social Class and Income Distribution. New York: Praeger Books, 1962, pp. 46–54.

60. Henry Bamford Parkes, The American Experience: An Interpretation of the History of Civilization of the American People. New York: Alfred A. Knopf, 1955. See also Chap. 11.

61. See Murray Gendell and Hans L. Zetterberg, A Sociological Almanac for the United States (2nd edition). New York: Charles Scribner's Sons, 1964, pp. 21–22; also Elton F. Jackson and Harry J. Crockett, Jr., "Occupational Mobility in the United States: A Point Estimate and Trend Comparison," American Sociological Review, Vol. 29, No. 1, Feb. 1964, pp. 5–15.

62. Erich Fromm, Man for Himself. New York: Holt, Rinehart, & Winston, 1947, pp. 81–82.

section, race, age, and family. Citizens participate in the political process by working for the civic culture, in such activities as the passage of a local bond issue or a highway construction plan. Politics as a general system of governing or a critique of that general system has been transformed into policy-making; a system in which expertise (real or imaginary) displaces elective office in the legitimation of power.

Apart from the radical movement, politics is now concerned with parochial matters. In the process, politics based upon universal values has disappeared.[63] There remains the question to what extent the public accepts the narrowing of political choice, the sameness of the different political factions and parties in the United States.[64] The growing strength of conservatism as an organization no less than as an ideology would indicate that ideological politics may increase with the sharpening of the internal crisis.

Despite enormous fissures in American society, specifically the "national" issue of black power and the "international" issue of Vietnam, the basis of the conduct of politics has remained a maneuvered consensus. Politics has dissolved into the political sciences. Elective offices are giving way in importance to the appointive offices. Few elected officials in the history of the United States have had anywhere near the power and the prestige of such appointed officials as the Secretaries of Defense and State; leaders who for the most part have never run for office yet exercise enormous political controls. In this large-scale shift from competitive politics to policy-making, from elective to appointive styles, and in the corresponding rise of the expert as arbiter in the decision-making processes, nineteenth-century political styles seem outmoded and even quaint.[65]

The debate over whether there is in fact a power elite which runs the United States or whether there are countervailing veto groups has become, in the span of a decade, an outmoded question. Bramson has shrewdly noted that the liberal pluralists in opposing theorists of mass society posit the importance of local "influentials" as intervening variables. But the final liberal picture is about as undemocratic as the ap-

63. Gabriel A. Almond and Sidney Verba, *The Civic Culture*. Boston and Toronto: Little, Brown & Co., 1965.
64. Daniel Bell, *The End of Ideology: On the Exhaustion of Political Ideas in the Fifties* (revised edition). New York: Collier Books, 1961, pp. 393–402.
65. See Henry A. Kissinger, "The Policy Maker and the Intellectual," in *International Politics and Foreign Policy*, edited by James N. Rosenau. New York: The Free Press, 1961, pp. 273–78.

proach taken by the mass society theorists inasmuch as most of the influentials, the "locals," are unenlightened and as mindless as their blind followers among the "masses." [66]

If one examines in some detail the arguments of Riesman, it becomes evident that, while there is a series of groups, each of which struggles for and finally attains a power to stop things conceivably harmful to its own interests, the ability to start things is something Riesman fully recognizes as the responsibility of those who are the strongest, namely, those who have power within such veto groups.[67] Likewise, if we examine Mills' position, we find something more sophisticated than a blunt representation of the Franco-Italian concept of power. For what he does is to divide the power apparatus into three sections: a mass which lacks political power and lacks the agencies for attaining such power; a middle stratum which does indeed settle matters of local issue and is in what Mills calls a "semi-organized stalemate" condition; and at the third level, the power elite, which is not issue-bound but rather value-oriented and makes decisions affecting national and international policies independent in large measure of democratic norms.[68] This is not to minimize the existence of differences between Riesman and Mills. Nonetheless, it has become clear that the genius of two-party systems, multi-party systems, or of a democracy of the top based on veto groups does not alter the fact that in larger institutional and international matters the policy of the United States is as unitary as that of any other great power.

The technological innovations which distinguish the United States in the twentieth century have at the same time produced profound effects on American politics, for they have streamlined the agencies of power and in so doing minimized the exercise of popular political control of that power. In place of the responsive politician there arises the mandarin expert.[69] Political distinctions are blurred rather than banned. As Seligman notes, "American political debate is increasingly conducted

66. Leon Bramson, *The Political Context of Sociology.* Princeton: Princeton University Press, 1961.

67. David Riesman, Nathan Glazer, and Reuel Denney, *The Lonely Crowd: A Study of the Changing American Character.* Garden City, N.Y.: Doubleday & Co., 1953, pp. 246–59.

68. C. Wright Mills, *The Power Elite.* New York: Oxford University Press, 1956, pp. 3–29.

69. See Irving Louis Horowitz, "Social Science Mandarins: Policymaking as a Political Formula," *Policy-Sciences,* Vol. I, No. 3 (Winter 1970), pp. 339–60.

in a planned, even tempered atmosphere, and extremists of any kind are becoming rarer." [70] Nor has this process of political disintegration been confined to political agencies alone; there have been large-scale social and psychological consequences. Basically it has meant the collapse of the pragmatic, innovative political style. If pragmatism meant anything in the past, it required at the very least participation, action, a statement of commitment. But what we now have is political behavior manipulated to such a degree as to create what Lazarsfeld and Merton have referred to as a "narcotizing dysfunction." As they point out, vicariousness sets in, a rarefied removal from actual commitment. The modern American

> comes to mistake *knowing* about problems of the day for *doing* something about them. His social conscience remains spotlessly clean. He is concerned; he is informed; and he has all sorts of ideas as to what should be done. But after he has gotten through his dinner and after he has listened to his favorite radio programs and after he has read his second newspaper of the day it is really time for bed. In this peculiar respect mass communications may be included among the most respectable and efficient of social narcotics.[71]

To what then have the attentions and ambitions of the American mass been drawn, now that its mind has been relieved of political considerations? Here it should be recorded that it is not simply mass culture or mass leisure that defines the new situation but the character and quality of present-day work styles. For culture and leisure are still defined in terms of the labor process, and not the other way round. It would be erroneous to think that the search for alternatives to work means an end to the definition of the labor process as central.

In a generalized celebration of "American values" political ideologies have lost competitive fervor and have increasingly become economic ideologies. Perhaps the most perfect representation of this economic determination is American unionism, which paradoxically exhibits a violent history of labor class struggles accompanied by an early lack of political direction. The goals which unionism set for itself were dis-

70. Daniel Seligman, "The New Masses," in *America as a Mass Society, op. cit.*, pp. 254–56; see also Richard E. Neustadt, *Presidential Power.* New York: John Wiley, 1960.
71. Paul F. Lazarsfeld and Robert K. Merton, "Mass Communication, Popular Taste, and Organized Social Action," *Mass Culture: The Popular Arts in America,* edited by Bernard Rosenberg and David Manning White. Glencoe, Ill.: The Free Press, 1957, p. 464.

tinguished by the almost exclusive concern with economic well-being. Although this is mitigated by political affairs committees in recent history, political concerns center on economic issues. Thus, while there was a very high degree of political consciousness, there was a simultaneously low degree of political consciousness, the reverse of Marxist expectations. This ideological economism served to stimulate socioeconomic development rather than, as in Europe, act as a brake on its development. The ideology of "bread-and-butter" unionism corresponds to the recruitment of large numbers of skilled workers. What are these ideological needs?

(1) That labor is to be rewarded for the amount of work done, with harder work and more productivity deserving better rewards. Thus, at the outset, the working class of the United States is tied to the ideology of a rewards system, which was what the owning classes attempted to inspire in them. (2) The ideology of economism rarely led to the formation of political parties along class lines. When such parties were formed, they were generally farmer parties or farmer-labor coalitions and not industrial working-class parties such as have existed in Europe since the nineteenth century. This made possible a consensus at the political level which emphasized inter-class interests and needs in terms of more industrial wealth rather than in terms of new social relationships. (3) The ideology of economism was not confined to the trade union movement. It was in fact characteristic of business and professional groups as well. From their point of view, it seemed natural and organic to lay emphasis on the economy, since they were the prime recipients of its benefits. On the other hand, where class feeling took on a political cast, it was strongly colored by nostalgia, by the desire for the return of a former condition on the part of a newly displaced or threatened class. American society has been unique in the degree to which it separated the "political" from the "economic." Politics in America is run not so much by a "power elite" or by "veto groups" as by businessmen. But quite unlike the predictions of Marxist "economic determinism," the proletariat takes an active part, and in certain instances a leading part, in the maintenance of the American power structure. Politics increasingly becomes, in an American context, a formal science, while the politician is that person in possession of the keys of truth.

Anti-intellectualism in American life has taken on nuances that distinguish it from past forms of the "knowledge-through-experience" doctrine. Whereas in the last century to be anti-intellectual was to be anti-educational, this no longer holds. What is distinctly modern is the way in which education has been sundered from intellect. That is to say, mass education, even higher education, has been given an enormous impetus by those technological innovations which require more refined skills. But the professional and occupational emphasis of the educational plant leads not so much to cultivated personality as it does to a higher philistinism.[72] The learning process becomes instrumental to economic goals. Knowledge itself becomes subservient to acquisition. Money is its measure. Occupational choices, based as they are on high monetary compensation, become the goal of education, and in this way the liberal arts tradition is destroyed with more certainty than by any directly anti-intellectual assault. Instrumentalized education is perfectly in accord with bureaucratized labor. But any critique of the new educational style must still take into consideration its success with respect to the developmental process.

Much importance has been attached to where and how one is educated, and thus education has become not only a means of achievement but recently a means for guaranteeing one's family status. When education as such becomes less meaningful than the process of certification, the divorce between intellect and practice is particularly noticeable and alienative in its effects.[73]

Occupations of middling status become elevated when a college degree is required as a prerequisite. Even occupation and education lose their connection in the race for status. When the raison d'être for education is money or status, there is a tendency for an educational system to become crisis-ridden; the break-up of education along class lines between academic schools and trade training centers is itself symptomatic of a crisis.

Even with its current emphasis on leisure time and reduced work week, America still remains a productive society; and the definition of its wealth is hardly more Veblenesque now than it was at the turn of the

72. For a detailed historical account, see Richard Hofstadter, *Anti-Intellectualism in American Life*. New York: Alfred A. Knopf, 1963; see also his "Reflections on Violence in the United States," in *American Violence: A Documentary History,* edited by Richard Hofstadter and Michael Wallace. New York: Alfred A. Knopf, 1970, pp. 3–43.

73. See Irving Louis Horowitz and William H. Friedland, *The Knowledge Factory: Student Power and Academic Politics in America.* Chicago: Aldine-Atherton Publishing Co., 1970, pp. 89–117.

century.[74] The wealth of America, while visible in terms of a search for status, is still measured in terms of economic productivity. The worth of the person is measured not in terms of leisure but in terms of his working capacity and productive skills. Although the rise of a technological order has changed relationships between labor and leisure, production and consumption, machine labor and manual labor, it only alters the mix, it does not alter the facts. The facts are plain enough. The measure of American worth in foreign eyes is its immense material wealth and its high degree of skilled labor, not the way in which non-working time is employed.

Development in the United States in the twentieth century is almost exclusively about technology, for the characteristic stamp of the First World is its technology. Standardization, automation, and a host of technological cultural influences, such as the tendency toward miniaturization and interchangeability of parts, are all innovative devices calculated to make work less severe and life easier. The processes involved in standardization are absolutely essential to development, since they allow for the richest production diversity with minimal confusion or retooling. At the same time, automation is a long-range process in the United States. Factory assembly-line techniques have incorporated every possible device to liberate labor from the burdens of manual work and of course to liberate management from the burdens of labor even at the administrative level.

Standardization maximizes output and minimizes the labor necessary for it. It makes machine tools available for multiple uses and cheapens costs of repairs and replacements at the same time that the cost of labor rises. It brings forward new machine goods to such a state of mass production as to make unnecessary and even burdensome repair work as such. Therefore the process of standardization accelerates and accentuates the problem of obsolescence. The very notion of economic stability or instability involves the ability of a society to manage such changes in the technostructure. Old goods in a modern United States are not so much obsolete as they are simply too expensive in contrast to new commodities. The same is true at the production level, where it is cheaper to buy new machinery than to maintain used machinery.

Automation cuts labor costs by cutting the time necessary to produce commodities, while at the same time it expands the energy output of

74. See Eric Larrabee and Rolf Meyerson (eds.), *Mass Leisure*. Glencoe, Ill.: The Free Press, 1958.

machines. At least short-range planning is necessary with automation, for the level of productivity must be correlated with the level of consumption needs and the ability to pay for these goods and services.

Together standardization and automation lead to new types of laboring man and managerial man. The distinction between the technician and the professional tends to be minimized, since the processes they are engaged in, and the skills needed to harmonize such efforts, often become isomorphic. Thus, the Galbraithian technostructure affects not only the objective functioning of the social order but the subjective relationships between men in the social order.[75] These twin processes of the technological society have made possible the first consumer-oriented society in the world, the first society which consciously dedicates itself to solving the problems of consumption and takes for granted the solution of problems of production.

Technological processes also tend to transform men into instruments, commodities, or things which are themselves measured by the products they create, and thus give an "anti-human" and "pro-machine" quality to society. Human valuation may become converted from a human act into a technological fact. Thus a person may come to be defined in terms of an all-purpose computer, which is easy to produce but difficult to control.

The mechanical age has succeeded in displacing human labor power, but this displaced labor power has not developed into new creative channels. On the contrary, it has become fragmented, alienated, and deeply torn from the social fabric. At the least, displaced labor searches out new mechanized jobs. At worst such labor power falls into aggressive and anti-social forms of mental and social disorder.[76]

In light of this, it is not surprising that the American celebration has turned sour before it has begun. It is remarkable that in the light of United States development, criticism of it by others has been so restrained, so imbued with good will.[77] Perhaps this is the ultimate cut. The rest of the world may still consider the United States an adolescent

75. John Kenneth Galbraith, *The New Industrial State,* Chap. XIII, pp. 159–68.
76. Joseph Bensman and Bernard Rosenberg, "The Meaning of Work in Bureaucratic Society," in *Identity and Anxiety: Survival of the Person in Mass Society,* edited by Maurice R. Stein, Arthur J. Vidich, and David M. White. New York: The Free Press, 1960, pp. 181–97.
77. See the pleasant rendition of Third World attitudes toward the United States in Richard B. Morris, *The Emerging Nations and the American Revolution.* New York: Harper & Row, 1970, pp. 178–223.

society rather than a developed nation. In this case the adolescent holds the ultimate possibility of life and death; therefore he must be humored as well as cajoled. Seen from this point of view the absence of criticism may not be so much an absence of resentment as a fear that we have not grown mature enough to absorb criticism without recourse to armed violence.

Little more than a decade ago, nothing seemed more important than knowing what the future of the United States would bring. There was a sense of urgency which derived from the central position of America in the world scheme of things. The kinds of questions posed by Commager in *The American Mind* seemed especially vital. The Americans "had created an economy of abundance; could they fashion a political mechanism to assure the equitable distribution of that abundance? They had become the richest people on the globe; would they use their wealth to prosper society or to display power? They were democratic in law; would they be democratic in fact? They were equalitarian by conviction; would they be equalitarian in conduct? They had developed technology to its highest point; would they learn to make technology their servant rather than their master?" And then there were yet the newer questions. The Americans "had made the atomic bomb; would they use it for purposes of civilization or of destruction? They had achieved such power as no other nation had ever known; would that passion for peace . . . triumph over the temptation to establish a Pax Americana by force?" [78]

Two observations deserve to be made on such typical (and rhetorical) remarks. One, that the answers remain as obscure as they were then. And this very fact indicates a certain stagnation in the American style, if not in the American soul. But more significant than the fact of stagnation is the implication that the answers to such questions lack the urgency they once possessed. This is because the United States lacks the urgency it once had. In its assumption of the leadership of the First World it indicated its power, but a power over only a small sector of the universe. There remained the Second World of the Soviets, who noted how rapidly and readily development in the United States had come. And there came into being a Third World either indifferent to or indignant about the "American century." It became apparent that the "dialogue"

78. Henry Steele Commager, *The American Mind: An Interpretation of American Thought and Character Since the 1880's*. New Haven: Yale University Press, 1950, esp. pp. 442–43.

of Americans was more with themselves than with the rest of the world. Thus, it is less important whether these questions receive immediate answers than that the questions be placed in a universal context. The United States came into being through an anti-colonial revolution. Because it had only this one revolution, it must continually make it symbolically and realistically relevant to the present. Perhaps Nehru summed it up best when he pointed out that the birth of the United States was a consequence of the revolt against economic injustices and, secondarily, against the social consequences of these injustices. "The colonists did not begin fighting for the sake of independence. Their grievances were taxation and restrictions in trade." As a consequence of the Revolution, independence became a rallying cry and a unifying idea among the colonies. "The United States republic was a new kind of country. It had no past as the countries of Europe and Asia had. It had no relics of feudalism except in the plantation system in the South. It had no hereditary nobility. The bourgeois or middle class had few obstacles to its growth and it grew rapidly." [79]

As a matter of record, there are few policy-launched attacks emanating from the Third World against the United States. An exhaustive survey of the literature will turn up a wide spectrum of sentiments about the United States but, with the exception of the war in Indochina, little open condemnation. As a general rule, there is an inverse correlation, strangely enough, between the weakness of a participant nation in the Third World and the strength of its condemnations of the United States. Thus one finds the most powerful and forthright criticisms of United States policy emanating from Latin America; and the most cautious and reserved statements emanating from Africa. One explanation for this difference is that in Africa anti-American statements are modified because the rulers themselves speak for the official position of the entire nation, while in Latin America such statements often come from those out of power. In addition, of course, the United States does have a colonial "tradition" in regard to Latin America.

Instead of showing militant anti-Americanism, African leaders such as Robert Sobukwe of South Africa and the late Patrice Lumumba of the Congo have advocated a United States of Africa.[80] While the merits

79. Jawaharlal Nehru, *On World History*. Bloomington: Indiana University Press, 1962, pp. 69–70.
80. See on this Rolf Italiaander, *The New Leaders of Africa*. Englewood Cliffs, N.J.: Prentice-Hall, 1961, esp. pp. 121–22, 155, 209–10.

of the phrase as well as its actual meanings have often been debated, it demonstrates an obvious respect for the achievements of the American federated union and, also, a symbolic recognition of the United States opposition to *apartheid* and Congolese separatism.[81]

The Third World is not so much hostile to the United States as it is disenchanted with it. The disenchantment has come from high expectations; it is not the kind of resentment reserved for implacable enemies. The Third World was irritated during the years when the United States equated neutralism with betrayal and treated neutrals as surreptitious enemies. A recent symposium on *The Dynamics of Neutralism in the Arab World* makes this point. Friendly Egyptian-Western relations were greatly harmed by American policy during the first two years of the Eisenhower administration. The United States aroused Afro-Asian as well as Arab resentment by demanding their participation in American-sponsored Cold War pacts. The passionate "pactomania" ascribed to Dulles was as irritating to proud and pressure-sensitive new nations as was its corollary "neutrophobia." The latter dashed the cherished hopes of the Third World for speedy economic development, for the United States, acting on the belief that "he who is not with me is against me" and treating neutrality as immoral, translated this into the maxim "I am against those who are not with me," which meant in practical economic and political terms that there were no military pacts or economic assistance available to neutralist nations.[82]

Non-alignment has become a cornerstone not only of Third World policy but of a great many advanced industrial nations as well. Thus, a leader of the European Economic Community has noted that "the road for real completion of national independence is the road of non-alignment, of non-polarization." [83] For the African nations, non-alignment does not imply a passive neutralism but rather the active pursuit of international peace through the mediation of the claims of the big powers. "Our foreign policy has never been one of neutrality, but rather non-alignment. We have never, for instance, been neutral in African affairs, nor can we be neutral in matters pertaining to world peace." [84]

81. See Pierre L. van den Berghe, *South Africa: A Study in Conflict.* Middletown, Conn.: Wesleyan University Press, 1965, pp. 257–62.
82. Fayez A. Sayegh, *The Dynamics of Neutralism in the Arab World.* San Francisco: Chandler Publishing Company, 1964, pp. 194–95.
83. Vassos Lyssarides, "Socialism, Non-Alignment and Under-Developed Countries," *Voice of Africa,* Vol. 4, No. 2, Feb. 1964, pp. 15–16.
84. Abubakar Tafawa Belewa, "Nigeria Looks Ahead," *Foreign Affairs,* Vol. XLI, No. 4, Oct. 1962, pp. 19–39.

The United States has been reluctant to see that the Third World's alternative to non-alignment is not alignment with the West but a perennial anti-colonial crusade under the auspices of mainland China. To understand the attitude of the Third World one does not start with the peculiarities of individual nations. Nations of the Third World behave as nations generally do, in terms of their self-interest and general area-wide interests. It is inevitable that these will from time to time conflict with the interests of the United States, a fact which should be viewed as a normal part of international relations. In addition, this conflict of interests does not necessarily have to spill over into a conflict of values, which is to say that American values can be held in very high esteem, and most often are, without making it necessary for them to support a free-enterprise economy. And, conversely, the conflict of interests does not necessarily raise the specter of long-term animosity. This said, let us now turn to the spectrum of sentiments expressed in the Third World about the United States.

Basic to the Third World "profile" of United States shortcomings is its economic policies, and the effects of such policies in weakening the process of development by draining the poor nations of their already-limited capital. The main lines of criticism made by Third World leaders about the conduct of the United States can be summarized as follows: (1) Under various forms and in various degrees, the United States maintains, by the selective manipulation of the international economy, various kinds of military, political, and cultural privileges which encroach upon the sovereignty and independence of Third World countries. (2) Although Third World industries are nominally free, American business firms often control the major branches of production and technology, which means they can influence the political structure and the internal social life of each nation. (3) The First World, especially the combination of the United States and the European Common Market, controls the international trade market and, not the least significant, the money market. In this way it manipulates world prices and arbitrarily lowers the values of primary products or the kinds of products manufactured in the Third World. With equal arbitrariness it manipulates the prices of finished manufactured goods, thus creating a constant drainage on the developing nation. (4) The United States is able to raise interest charges at will; and even when it does not do so, its credit position provides it with a constant economic edge, since, given the unequal starting point of the Third World, its member nations can barely repay the interest, let alone the principal on loans issued. (5) The United States controls and monopolizes a considerable portion of the communications and transportation industries and by so doing controls a good deal of what can and cannot be traded and between whom. For example, it uses its maritime shipping as a political weapon against opponents.

These charges against United States *economic policies* do not in any way imply criticism of its *value system*. Nor is there any negative reaction to its social system. The political literature of the Third World shows that there are more pointed criticisms directed against the social system of the Soviet Union than against that of the United States. What preserves the Soviet Union from even more damaging criticism is precisely its positive economic policy toward and political identification with the Third World.

The United States is repeatedly called the most developed nation in the world. From the technological point of view, it holds up the future to the rest of the world. With the exception of a relatively small but articulate group of European intellectuals, with whom a relatively small and articulate group of Third World intellectuals identify, there is little criticism of United States technological achievement, either at the production or at the consumer level. Similarly, the Soviet Union tends to be viewed as that society which has best resolved the question of economic organization. This is so, if for no other reason than it is a society based on planning. At the same time the Soviet Union has the moral advantage of having introduced a non-competitive economy. But this initial advantage has been largely liquidated by the political repressions of the Stalin era. Interestingly, there is far sharper criticism in certain sections, particularly in Africa, of the Soviet achievement than of the American achievement. This is due in part to the acceptability of criticism of a political system and the relative inaccessibility of a technological system to the same sort of criticism. It also reflects the extent to which the many and varied definitions of African socialism are made with an eye toward distinguishing socialism from Soviet communism no less than from American capitalism. Men like Tom Mboya have said so openly; others like Julius Nyerere have only whispered this truth.

There is a constant din of intellectual talk in the Third World concerning folk values, regional conditions, and national cultures. Oftentimes the concepts of Negritude, Moslemism, and regionalism represent a disguised fear of the impact of both the United States and the Soviet Union on the traditionalistic aspects of Third World cultures. For example, in many areas where there has been a successful liberation movement, traditionalism seriously retards the developmental process. In India it is the caste system and Hinduism as an economic philosophy. In Tunisia it is the Moslem culture. In many instances there is a tendency to revert to a type of theocratic state, or tribal social order, similar to what existed before the European conquest began. Thus the form of anti-colonialism can be reactionary insofar as it views liberation as a return to a pristine pre-conquest era. But reactionary anti-colonialism does not represent a direct assault upon the United States so much as an attempt to prevent the more militant marginal sectors, such as the radicalized military and the socialist intelligentsia, from taking complete charge of the developmental process. In other words, anti-Americanism can have a backward content, and is not always illustrative of the revolutionary sectors.

The three parts of the Third World react differently to United States involvement in their affairs. For Latin America the main fears tend to be economic encroachment; in Africa, political encroachment; in Asia, direct military encroachment. Each form of United States involvement produces profound negative sentiments throughout the Third World. The character of the criticisms tend to be slightly different, depending on the nation's stage of development, the historical relationship between a particular nation and the United States, and whether the nation is within the United States sphere of influence. The attitude of the Third World as a whole and in its parts toward the United States is richly textured and widely varied. Nothing could possibly be more dangerous than to flatten out the Third World and imply a uniformly implacable hostility. But in the absence of significant distinctions and refinements on the part of United States foreign policy between various forms of communism, between various types of economic mixes, between one-party states which encompass and engage opposition within their structure and multi-party states that may really be more autocratic than a one-party system, and ultimately between neutrality pertaining to matters of world peace and non-alignment pertaining to economic-power blocs, we may expect a continued increase in anti-Americanism as a surrogate for anti-colonialism.

As a result of World War II, the United States sought to provide maximum leadership to the emerging nations—as indeed it did in relation to India—but as a result of its obsessive return to European politics it forfeited its opportunity. The only real question seems to be whether the Soviet Union or China, each representative of variations upon classical socialist tactics, is best suited as a model to be emulated. The Soviet Union is moving rapidly to build an image of itself as an Asian nation. Not only is two-thirds of its land mass in Asia, but its political, economic, and military aid, however tentative and halting when made, has been on the side of revolutionary factions.

Thus, even the forces of "conservatism" in Asia and Africa are more likely to be demonstrating support for Soviet foreign policy than for the United States.[85] The United States has avoided the implications of the Sino-Soviet rift, not because, as its official spokesmen declare, it does not want to upset the course of that rift, but because it is unable and unwilling to make a real dent in the socialist bloc by a positive policy of support for the economic phase of revolution in the Third World. The United States has recognized the distinction between nationalism and communism when such recognition was clearly a disadvantage to the Soviet Union—as in the case of such Eastern European nations as Poland and Hungary. But the same distinction has not been made for the emerging nations because the United States would then be placing at a disadvantage its own large foreign investors. This diplomatic appreciation of the difference between the needs of the American nation and the needs of private commerce has not yet registered. Until the United States puts its own interests ahead of the protection of private American business overseas, the Third World will remain suspicious that the first new nation seeks to establish a claim to being the only new nation.

85. Sékou Touré, "Africa's Destiny," in Charles F. Andrain, "Democracy and Socialism," in *Ideology and Discontent,* edited by David E. Apter. New York: The Free Press, 1964, p. 194.

6

The Second World of
Soviet Development

The development of the Soviet Union holds a certain fascination for the Third World which no amount of dismay at communist political patterns can quite deter. First, the Soviet Union represents a civilization which became powerful in the twentieth century. Second, the Soviet Union withstood the challenges of foreign aggressors and emerged from a condition of "encirclement" as a world military power second to none and equal to or better than all. Third, the Soviet Union demonstrated that social and state planning, whatever their political deformities and technical deficiencies, can create full economic mobilization and complete integration of a society in a very short period of time relative to the experience of most capitalist countries. Fourth, the Soviet Union demonstrated that historical "stage-skipping" is not only possible but necessary. This point, since it contradicts some basic ideological tenets of Marxism, is often underplayed by the Soviets. Fifth, if socialists come to power in an underdeveloped country they have no choice but to play the role of a nationalist bourgeoisie and that entails exploiting the masses and keeping consumption levels at a minimum so as to provide the maximum for investment.[1] Planning and socialization, when joined to urbanization and industrialization, reveal the extent to which the processes of development can be consciously manipulated. This is precisely what the elites of the Third World are searching for. And this is in marked contrast to the pragmatic daring of the development process in the United States.

1. For a brief but useful overview, see Robert Sharlet, "The Soviet Union as a Developing Country," *Journal of Developing Areas,* Vol. 2, No. 2 (1968), pp. 270–76.

With the consolidation of state power in the Soviet Union, the Marxist theory of class struggle tends to be forgotten in these circumstances. Marxism becomes a theory of national liberation from foreign exploitation, instead of an ideology or social-science technique for the liberation of masses from ruling classes. The Soviets have themselves encouraged this construction. Increasingly, the Soviet elite has at least admitted the fact that social distinctions exist inside Russia. Through the ad hoc notion of compatible classes, Soviet officials, by sending business and managerial personnel all over the Third World to elicit support and negotiate trade agreements with their business and professional elites, have created an appeal to the Third World across class "barriers"—although this technical appeal is seriously restricted by the fear that Soviet wealth is compromising Soviet policy. Thus the very "realism" of present Soviet policy may create suspicion as well as admiration, and the Chinese communists stand ready to exploit this.

The most obvious fact about the Soviet Union is at the same time the most impressive. In less than a half-century, Russia has gone from a backward peasant economy based on rural life styles to the second largest industrial complex in the world. However, this rapid development should be distinguished from its relative power position with respect to the United States. Development includes a whole range of measures related to consumption patterns and consumer goods, whereas the power position is better measured by selective investment patterns in heavy machinery, armaments, and other goods and services that are vital from the perspective of national power.[2]

The development of a military machine capable of enormous offensive action, no less than a defensive series of actions, should not be undervalued.[3] As has been noted,

> as a country considerably less powerful than the USA, the USSR is generally satisfied with less complex apparatus and equipment than the USA and is more inclined to concentrate on relatively few

2. See Henry J. Bruton, "Contemporary Theorizing on Economic Growth," in *Theories of Economic Growth,* edited by Bert F. Hoselitz. New York: The Free Press, 1960, pp. 239–94.

3. I have not included charts and tables from this chapter, since statistical information is available in great abundance about the Soviet Union. Further, a review essay of mine contains what I believe to be essential information about present-day Russian industrialization and urbanization. See Irving Louis Horowitz, "The Political Sociology of Soviet Development," *Il Politico,* Vol. XXIX, No. 1, 1964, pp. 28–47.

projects, whereas the USA can afford to invest in a great diversity of programmes. All this points to a somewhat less expensive Soviet military and space research and development programme, although the great progress made by the USSR suggests that the difference cannot be enormous.[4]

Thus, there has arisen a widening gap between the two super powers at the level of "modernization" (consumerism) and a narrowing gap at the level of "industrialization" (especially in the military aspects).

Like many nations of the Third World, the Soviet Union has been subject to considerable foreign intervention and invasion. And the size of the military establishment represents an extremely considerable factor in Third World nation evaluations of the Soviet system. At the same time, the Soviet Union has transformed an essentially rural society into a "citified" one. Because of the productive emphasis, it has done so with a minimum of the kind of economic drainage represented by high-priced automotive production, expensive televisions, status buildings, and such. Of course, it has been argued that this absence of consumerism has created a chronic constraint on consumption as such. Nor is this urbanization process a simple consequence of a population boom. Despite the extraordinarily high casualties sustained, especially by the decimation of the male population in World War II, the Soviet Union has maintained a large but well-balanced population. Militarism, industrialism, and urbanism are magic words for the Third World, and they represent the achievement of the Second World.

The Bolshevik Revolution was the first time in history that a society consciously dedicated itself to the realization of an ideal model of social change, namely, the Marxist model. True enough, this model was designated a scientific plan. But for our purposes, whether Marxism represents an ideology or a science or some combination of both is irrelevant to the overriding significance of a society dedicated to the realization of a blueprint blanketing all *social* sectors.[5]

In previous revolutions the connection between the pre-revolutionary ideological build-up and the actual course of revolution were, at best,

4. David Ingram, *The Communist Economic Challenge.* New York: Frederick Praeger, 1965, p. 163.
5. See Lewis S. Coser, "Prospects for the New Nation," *Dissent,* Vol. X, No. 1, pp. 43–58. For the further development of this theme, see Dennis H. Wrong, "Economic Development and Democracy," in *A Dissenter's Guide to Foreign Policy,* edited by Irving Howe. New York: Frederick A. Praeger, 1968, pp. 260–72.

tenuous. In discussing the relationship between the French Enlightenment and the French Revolution, for instance, one must carefully distinguish ideological stimulants to the Revolution itself from the ad hoc manufacture of a pre-revolutionary tradition after the fact of revolution. Let us turn, therefore, to Marx's discussion of the nature of past social development. Essentially, he uses the dialectic as a method somewhat akin to a bookkeeper's balance sheet. Every social system Marx describes has positive and negative factors. The ultimate positive factor in each social system is that it gives rise to "its other" or to some other form of social existence potentially more advanced than itself. Even within each social system, Marx adapts a "trial-balance" approach to history. Feudalism may have been an evil in terms of the increased misery of the masses and in the formalization of the gap between servant classes and noble classes; however, Marx recognized in feudalism an advance over slavery with regard to social relations. This does not mean that the medieval period represented a linear progression in economic technique or technology. It did mean, however, that feudalism produced a multiplication of economic classes and new occupational roles and the development of a system of rights and obligations which, however uneven, was at least mutually shared and reciprocally understood by wide sectors of the population excluded under slavery.

Capitalism, for its own part, rationalizes the fragmented state of social affairs of the feudal period by producing once again two great class contenders for power—capitalists and proletarians. It is a system which introduces mass industrial innovation and which substitutes secular for theological values, which in its latest stage moves people from rural to urban forms of existence and makes possible, for the first time, abundance and affluence. As with feudalism, capitalism is said to have its negative aspects. This system estranges men from the source of creativity and alienates labor from the values embodied in productivity. Capitalism is a system which indicates how the tower of massive wealth no less than the abyss of poverty can be reached. It is a system which intensifies both strife between social classes and achievement by human beings. Thus, capitalism for Marx is the ultimate dehumanization of man, precisely because the distance between humanity and inhumanity is never so plain as it is under the modern, privately operated industrial factory system. It is Marx's unique contribution that he saw the process of social change emanating from "below" rather than instigated from "above."

The massive contribution of Lenin to this theory of historical development was to enlarge the scope of the class struggle from a European to an international context. This was made necessary in part by the backward conditions of Russia itself and in part by Lenin's awareness that the advanced countries would not go through the various stages of development in the phases blueprinted by nineteenth-century Marxism. At the very time that class struggles within Europe seemed to be displaced partially by national struggles, it became even sharper between emergent nations and established imperial powers. Hence the class struggle in the Leninist view becomes internationalized, becoming a conflict between have and have-not *nations* rather than have and have-not *classes*. As a matter of fact, there is substantive support for this. According to a United Nations report, the gap between rich and poor nations is steadily widening. From 1950 to 1970 poor nations had the slowest growth rate and the rich ones showed moderate growth. Middle-income nations, however, had the fastest growth—and this is a fact easily overlooked. The per capita annual increase in the gross national product is 1.3 per cent for India and 0.4 per cent for Pakistan. Latin American nations such as Ecuador and Colombia show a parallel low growth rate of between 1.0 per cent and 1.6 per cent. To this must be contrasted the growth rates of Japan with 7.2 per cent and West Germany with 6.1 per cent. More damaging still is the fact that 87.1 per cent of the world's total population has an annual income of $700 or less, with 64.5 per cent of these earning less than $200.[6] It may well be theoretically stretching the point to transfer the Marxist concept of class struggle to the international arena. However, the political consequences of perceiving an uneven distribution of poverty has been an unrelenting search for a radical means to eradicate it. This is particularly so since Marxists consider capitalist wealth to be at the cost of Third World resources, whereas liberal economists argue that the industrial countries are merely reaping the benefits of internal processes such as thrift, entrepreneurship, and technology.

When we turn to Marx's description of socialism, this dialectical bookkeeping procedure breaks down. There is no longer an analysis of the cost of socialism, of negative factors in development once polit-

6. On this problem of the "widening gap," see Raúl Prebisch, *Nueva Política Comercial para el Desarrollo.* Mexico-Buenos Aires: Fondo del Cultura Económica, 1964, esp. pp. 125–43; also International Social Development Review, *Unified Socioeconomic Development and Planning.* New York: United Nations, 1971, pp. 1–22.

ical power is transferred to representatives of the working class, or of the possibilities of socialist exploitation of peasant economies. Analysis turns into rhetoric, and the language of distant ideal refutes that of dialectics. No longer is there stocktaking of real material costs, and new social problems, but only the movements of men from the realm of necessity (which is the realm of economic determinism) to the realm of freedom (which is the realm of political indeterminism). In essence, socialism is made synonymous with the good life. In consequence of this, Marx's analysis is no longer balanced in the same way. As equality replaces stratification, science gives way to a longing after paradise. A moral goal is substituted for scientific law. Socialism is not subject to the iron laws of economic evolution the way all previous social systems are said to have been. The justification for the breakdown of these iron laws is that freedom itself replaces necessity as social ownership of production replaces private ownership.[7] But while Marxism offered few guidelines on how to plan an industrial empire, this in itself had a liberating effect in a Russian context. Once capitalism created the productive basis necessary to rid society of want, people could get to more important tasks, namely, creating the good society, a society characterized by the conflict between the administration of things rather than the ordering of people. In its ideal form, this was the goal of the Soviet Revolution.

The attraction of the Russian Revolution for the Third World is heightened by the fact that it occurred under economically backward conditions. This attraction is most forceful in those areas where development has become increasingly difficult due to the existence of a highly developed and competitive industrial capitalist social system in the West. Even for many Western European nations, the process of economic take-off was preceded by an earlier process of national consolidation and organization. And while this phasing-in of political modernization was slow and less abrupt than it was in the Soviet Union, the fact remains that nationalism, far from being the enemy of development, proved to be the precursor of development.

The development of Russia more nearly approximates the obstacles faced by developing areas in the modern world. Here, too, was a backward nation with an uneducated, illiterate peasantry. Here, too, there was an imbalance between the agricultural and the industrial sectors.

---

7. Ralf Dahrendorf, *Class and Class Conflict in Industrial Society*. Stanford: Stanford University Press, 1959, Chap. 1.

And here, too, there was a heavy investment of foreign capital in those areas which, prior to the revolutionary build-up, had already been subject to some degree of industrialization. Hence, the developing areas of the Third World would be magnetized—perhaps even hypnotized— by the Soviet model. The classic model of economic development employed the Ricardian model of international trade, whose key concept was "comparative advantage." A country producing and exporting what it is "best at" and importing only what it is not "good at" is most likely to succeed. Liberal economists in particular have developed this theory; its policy conclusions are free trade. The Soviet model, on the other hand, is a variation of the "infant industry" argument, first offered by List and Schumpeter.[8] Neither Germany nor Russia concentrated on those industries it was best at or even necessarily what it was good at. Instead, they isolated their economic systems by means of tariff walls and political decisions, insulating them from other nations. They attempted to create a self-sufficient system which would protect their relatively inefficient industries from foreign competition. The liberals argue that this is enormously inefficient; the radicals reply that liberals ignore questions of time and therefore remain static. And that were they, the radicals, to permit free trade, the already developed countries would continue to dominate the technology and economy of the underdeveloped nations. Radicals talk about the interdependence of nations due to trade; but some are more interdependent than others. Hence in a world of excess supply of primary goods, the bargaining position of a country depends on having an industrial economy. In other words, manufacturing output is considerably more valuable than mineral or agricultural supplies.

What we should note is that, contrary to those economic diagnoses concerning the advantage of those who come last in the developmental race,[9] the Soviet Union's model for development is important for precisely the reverse reasons. There are, in fact, powerful economic and sociological disadvantages for those who develop last. For example,

8. See Joseph A. Schumpeter, *History of Economic Analysis*. New York: Oxford University Press, 1954, pp. 504–6.

9. This refers to the avoidance of reduplicating historical forms of development. For example, in transportation the move from horse and buggy to jet airliners is direct. Ostensibly, the Third World nations do not have to cope with each intermediary stage of problems in transportation. This was anticipated in the Russian Marxist literature by Trotsky's "law of uneven and combined development." See Leon Trotsky, *The History of the Russian Revolution*. New York: Simon and Schuster, 1932, pp. 264–68.

the conception of development in the United States and in England comes attached to the revolution of political liberties and the rise of humane industrial relations. In the older European civilizations there is no contradiction or conflict between political liberties and economic growth.

The first full-scale model of development through planning came out of a supposedly "non-Western" area. The specific geo-political conditions which backward Russia had to confront proved to be magnetic. This magnetism stems from a belief in the Third World that Russia faced and resolved; first, the problem of foreign occupation; second, the problem of internal colonialism; and third, the relationship between rural and urban working sectors. The structural similarities of Russia to the underdeveloped areas of today cannot be dismissed by making loose statements about political freedom and political liberties. Soviet attempts to break feudal relations by means of peasant mobilization and land appropriation provide the impetus for rapid development in the Third World. The Soviet revolution was unique not because it worked out a theory of socialist economy or implemented the Leninist theory of the state. It did neither. Rather the consequences of the Russian Revolution were to place in the forefront of discussion the matter of priorities and allocation: in short, a manipulation of the economy by the polity, and hence the reversal of base and superstructure. In the Soviet Union politics once more became central and the economy residual.[10]

It must be understood, but rarely is, that Marxism in a Russian context does not so much represent an economic as a political determinism.[11] The ideology derives its power and its strength not from the economics of social equality but from the politics of mass movements. The limits of Marxian theory include a description of the forms of making a successful revolution, the means for mobilizing publics in the capture of state power, and the kind of political structure (euphemistically called dictatorship of the proletariat) which is necessary for the solidification of government power. In its political and social planning aspects, Marxism can be described as a rational action system of society, and not simply a theory of economic growth. It is a science

10. See S. Swianiewicz, *Forced Labour and Economic Development: An Enquiry into the Experience of Soviet Industrialization.* New York and London: Oxford University Press, 1965, esp. pp. 208–35.
11. See Stanley W. Moore, *The Critique of Capitalist Democracy.* New York: Paine-Whitman Publishers, 1957.

of the seizure of power, or, rather, a science of political relations. The justification of Marxism is that the chief goal of socialist revolution—human liberation from the class system—is at the very outset separated from the political instruments for achieving this democratic end. But Marxism as Leninist practice provides a series of contradictory propositions for reaching the free society. It uses a theory of dictatorship to arrive at practical freedom, a theory of political coercion to justify a historical withering away of the state, and a theory of mass affluence to be brought about by an organization of select political elites headed by a "vanguard" party.

It was inevitable that the socialist tradition would cleave. Those who called for a socialist revolution prior to settlement of anticipated negative consequences and those who insisted on settling the purposes of a revolution before engaging in any actions, which could have unanticipated negative effects, were inevitably pitted against each other. The ideological controversies *between communism and socialism,* between the ideologies of the first and second internationals, thus form the essential background of contemporary discussions on development. Actually, there is no such thing as "plain Marxism" because Marxism is ambivalent about socialism as a form of freedom and socialism as a form of control.[12]

The economic history of the Soviet Union provides ample verification that Marxism contains the incompatibilities of social democracy and social authoritarianism. The Civil War period temporarily delayed consideration of internal problems of development. Revolutionary euphoria and party slogans carried the government a long way. But underneath the superficial activities of the Communist Party, the Red Army, and the Council of Soviets, the broad outlines of economic crisis were looming. As one observer reported:

> "War Communism" could be defined as follows: firstly, requisitioning in the countryside; secondly, strict rationing for the town population, who were classified into categories; thirdly, complete "socialization" of production and labor; fourthly, an extremely complicated

12. The inability of C. Wright Mills to see that the problem of Marxism inheres in its ambivalence permits him to set up a trichotomous distinction between Social Democracy, Bolshevism, and Plain Marxism. In point of fact, what Mills describes as Plain Marxism is precisely the kind of pragmatic makeshift view of life that was alien to the spirit of both the founders of Marxism and its Russian and German advocates. See C. Wright Mills, *The Marxists.* New York: Dell Publishing Co., 1962.

and chit-ridden system of distribution for the remaining stocks of manufactured goods; fifthly, a monopoly of power tending toward the single Party and the suppression of all dissent; sixthly, a state of siege, and the Cheka.[13]

But once war communism ended, and problems of succession to bolshevik leadership came to the forefront, an open schism between social democratic factions and social authoritarian factions emerged.

The Social Democrats could properly argue that the Russian Revolution was rapidly becoming an aberration; that Marx would never have called for a revolution merely for the sake of a change of rulers; that he would never have offered intellectual sanction to a revolution made in the name of humanity that required so much sacrifice and so little possibility of the political realization of popular liberties. On the other hand, the bolsheviks could argue, just as righteously, that everything about the later Marx was geared to the seizure of power and the mobilization of the population. The long-range liberation of men was held to be subordinate to the necessary tasks of forging a socialist society and a political party which would be responsive to this new society. Thus to jeopardize the *Russian* Revolution on behalf of an abstract principle of *Socialist* Revolution was held to be an irresponsible form of nihilism.[14] However, the codification of socialism under Stalin was bought so dearly by the bureaucratization of politics that the political leadership itself became captive to the bureaucratic network.

The codification of Soviet ideology under Stalin also resulted in a series of confusions concerning the role of the Communist Party in the life of the Russian nation and immense setbacks in the economic performance of the society. Giganticism in engineering, falsification of basic statistics in industry, misallocation of scarce resources in research and development, and careerism in the bureaucratic hierarchy itself— each of these accentuated the fact that the new Soviet man was much like the old Russian peasant. The recognition by Stalin that this was the case gave him a definite advantage over his competitors for power, who believed in the need for moral redemption as a prerequisite for material achievement; whereas Stalin clearly perceived the idea of

13. Victor Serge, *Memoirs of a Revolutionary, 1901–1941* (translated and edited by Peter Sedgwick). London and New York: Oxford University Press, 1963, p. 117.
14. Maurice Dobb, *Soviet Economic Development Since 1917.* New York: International Press, 1947, pp. 261–63.

coercion, symbolic or real, as the key for moving the "mujik" behind the modernist.[15]

The Soviet assertion and insistence on the monolithic appearance of socialist politics, particularly as this developed under Stalin, was a response to the absence of genuine theory, and the inability of Soviet leaders to make useful generalizations concerning strategies for social development. The bitterness of early policy strife within the Soviet leadership, as well as the continued, agonizing ideological discussions within Soviet rank-and-file Communist Party members throughout the 1920's, indicated powerfully that "plain Marxism" was nowhere to be found inside the Soviet hierarchy. As a matter of fact, the choice had to be made between two types of Marxism: one humanistic and emphasizing continuity with Russian agrarianism; the other authoritarian and emphasizing the break with tradition as symbolized by industrialization.

The Soviet Revolution announced the liberation of women from marital bondage, but twenty years after the revolution (by 1936) the Soviet Union became the most difficult country in the world in which to get a divorce, with the possible exception of Ireland. Marriage, which Marx called a form of legal prostitution, became sacrosanct in the Soviet kinship system. In every aspect of cultural activity, the same pattern reveals itself, a task of social development irrespective of social costs; and without considering the positive consequences of developing "social deviance."

The positive results of the bending of all portions of Russian society toward a common goal are not to be minimized. It resulted in Russia's rapid industrialization. It compelled the Russian peasant to abandon his small primitive holdings and to set up collective farms. It ruthlessly tore primeval plowshares from the hands of the peasant and forced him to come to terms with the modern tractor. It transformed a society of illiterates into a society with bulging schoolrooms. It compelled adults to enter technological and industrial plants where for the first time reading and writing were essential. It made the factory a learning experience, and brought science to factory management.

Deutscher dramatizes the pre-industrial nature of peasant agriculture and the death of social change implied by the early five-year plans. The peasants had been accustomed to work in their fields according to Russia's harsh ecology, to toil from sunrise to sunset in the summer,

15. See Herbert Marcuse, *Soviet Marxism: A Critical Analysis*. New York: Columbia University Press, 1958.

and to drowse on the tops of their store during most of the winter. The purpose of the plan was the rationalization of the labor process and hence a break with the structure of the traditional agrarian framework.[16]

It is important to point out that the rate of growth of Soviet agriculture has been remarkably stagnant over the last two decades, both in terms of millions of tons of grain harvest and over-all agricultural production. In some measure, the deficiencies of Soviet farming are precisely a result of this break with tradition. Planning involved collectivization; collectivization involved social farming; and social farming had a tendency to underprice goods in relation to demand.[17] As a result, this syndrome led to an undervaluation of agrarian labor in relation to industrial labor. Ultimately, the rate of industrialization itself has been drastically slowed by the various difficulties encountered in the industrialization of farming.

The rewards of the Soviet Revolution were astonishing. It succeeded in transforming a rural society, in which peasant masses and other social classes were clearly rent, into an industrial society, in which all sectors were linked through the instrument of planning. Part of this reorientation involved the partial detachment of Russia from Europe. This detachment did not rest exclusively on the confiscation of the business holdings of European capitalists, but was also a spiritual detachment from political agencies and institutions of European democracy. As Isaac Deutscher indicated, this political detachment was not at all inherent in the early program of bolshevism. The idea of a multi-party system was readily assumed.[18] But there was enough evidence in the history of Marxist ideas and in the conduct of Western socialism to offer precedence for both economic confiscation and political totalitarianism.

The disputes and disagreements among early leadership of the Russian Communist Party convey the impression of men amazed rather than aware of having actually concluded a successful revolution. That they were little conscious of just how unique and rocky an enterprise the Russian Revolution represented is reflected in their obsession with

16. Isaac Deutscher, *The Unfinished Revolution: Russia, 1917–1967.* New York: Oxford University Press, 1967, p. 44.
17. Alec Nove, "Soviet Farming: No More Campaigns," *New Society* (Feb. 12, 1970), pp. 262–63.
18. Isaac Deutscher, *Stalin: A Political Biography.* New York: Vintage Books-Random House, 1960, pp. 224–25.

ideology and the lack of concern about empirical necessities.[19] Even after the revolution and the conclusion of the civil war period, its leaders spoke in terms of compromise and conciliation. Lenin, speaking on February 2, 1920, before the All Union Executive Committee of the Communist Party of Russia, addressed himself to the Social Democrats. He pointed out that terror was perhaps a necessary part of the victory over the foreign enemies of Russia who were occupying its soil during the period of revolutionary ferment. But he declared that, with the simultaneous achievement of three aims—the victory over the foreign enemy, the successful completion of the capture of state power, and the mobilization of the basic elements in the productive apparatus —terrorism was no longer necessary.[20] From Lenin's point of view, terrorism was not compatible with the needs of the country. He encouraged open debate and criticism with the anarchists, social revolutionaries, and Mensheviks, and even utilized portions of the old czarist apparatus in the armed forces and the civil service. It is useful to divide Soviet terror between that aimed at stifling liberal freedom of speech on the grounds that liberalism dissipated revolutionary energy and that form of terror aimed at recalcitrant classes as a means of boosting economic development. Lenin was optimistic that classic liberalism was unnecessary, but at the same time he was extremely ambiguous about whether to pursue a soft or hard line with respect to internal class resistance to change. In a sense, the distinctions between Stalin and Trotsky were not over the worth of classic liberalism—neither had a high view of that—but rather over the worth of consensus versus coercion with respect to the factory proletariat and laboring peasantry.

What took place is indicative of the inability of an ideology to think outside of its own ideals. Two major events, little reported, occurred in the years 1921–22: the victory of the Communist Party apparatus *over* the Soviets, or the Council of Workers; and an intensification of tension between rural and urban interests. The victory of the Communist Party over the Workers' Soviets was first announced in the debate over the Red Army which took place at the close of the civil war period. The concept of a professional and permanent standing army was against all

19. This is the distinct impression left by the most knowing observers. See, for instance, E. H. Carr, *The Bolshevik Revolution,* Vol. I: *A History of Soviet Russia.* London: Macmillan & Co., 1950, esp. pp. 70–101.
20. Vladimir Lenin, *The Essentials of Lenin.* London: Lawrence and Wishart, 1947, Vol. II, pp. 683–86.

socialist tradition. However, as John Erickson shrewdly observed: "Armies feed and fatten themselves on men, not on phrases." [21] Hence, at the conclusion of the civil war period there were demands for a transition to a national militia in the hands of the Soviets. Leon Trotsky advanced a proposal under which the future militia would be based in the industrial centers so that the leading army cadres could be organized through the close cooperation of the army and trade unions, both under the direct control of the Soviets. This proposal, which amounted in effect to an operational military dictatorship of the Soviets, was approved in principle but never carried out. The Kronstadt sailors' uprising, peasant rebellions, and the unrest among industrial workers all combined to make any thought of developing an army of Soviets too dangerous to contemplate. There was also opposition to a Soviet militia on principle. The professional officers regarded such a system as less efficient than a standing army and impotent in the face of foreign encirclement.[22] Others felt that a national army was necessary in order to lend support to socialist revolutions elsewhere. Russian communists, it must be remembered, felt revolutions were as imminent as they were desirable.

Once Trotsky's plan for a proletarian Soviet armed guard was abandoned, it was inevitable that the army should be thoroughly under the control of the Communist Party leadership, particularly the Central Committee of the Communist Party. The possibilities of terrorism became manifest once a "Party army" (or a Soviet Army) triumphed.[23] It had its first opportunity to exercise this national power in the conflict between the urban and rural sectors. In the early 'twenties, the situation between the two sectors grew increasingly desperate. The distribution of goods was dependent on private traders. The peasants clamored for more and cheaper goods, while at the same time they

21. John Erickson, "The Origins of the Red Army," in *Revolutionary Russia,* edited by Richard Pipes. Garden City, N.Y.: Doubleday & Co., 1969, pp. 286–328.
22. The theory of imperialistic encirclement, which rationalized the "party army" at the time of war communism, still persists in Soviet Communist statements. However, the concept of the Red Army as an instrument of internal repression has ceased. The Red Army has, in fact, been transformed into an instrument of the Party for the guardianship of the nation. See on this V. D. Sokolovskii (ed.), *Soviet Military Strategy.* Englewood Cliffs, N.J.: Prentice-Hall (A Rand Corporation Research Study), 1963, pp. 82–83.
23. Leonard Schapiro, *The Communist Party of the Soviet Union.* New York: Random House, 1959–60, pp. 325–27.

demanded higher prices for their own products. Industry, only slowly rising from the ruins of revolution and civil war, produced few goods at high prices. Indeed, the idea of socialism as *immediate* gratification of wants served to reinforce industrial confusion. Factory laborers clamored for cheap food and inexpensive raw materials, but could not see the need for a corresponding effort on their part.

Given this situation, the solutions proposed by the communist leadership were desperate. The group around Bukharin was willing to have a degree of capitalism in the peasant sector in order to maintain some kind of social peace, while the group around Zinoviev was anti-peasant and vowed "no compromise" on the issue of socializing the rural sector.

The Bukharin faction reasoned that the organs of state power were in the hands of the socialist sector. Therefore the drain of a private-sector agricultural economy would not be sufficient to upset the basic economy. At the same time, compromise with the peasant groups would give the public sector of the economy a necessary breathing space for consolidating its power. In contrast to this, the Zinoviev faction stressed the incompatibility of a private sector in the agricultural sphere with a public-sector-dominated industrial sphere. The reasoning of the ultra-left faction was that inevitably the rural sector (particularly the wealthy landholders) would increase their wealth at the expense of the factory workers. In long-range terms, they feared that appeasement of the peasants would undermine the revolution. Moreover, they saw the peasants' demand for a greater return for their produce as an attempt to reintroduce private enterprise, free-market economy which would in effect be a betrayal of the Socialist Revolution. It would stimulate the economic conditions of class warfare and cause strife among the disenfranchised. These factors, the Zinoviev faction felt, far outweighed the short-run gains which the Bukharin plan would bring. The Bukharin faction was essentially non-violent in its strategic position, moving to an opening up of the private sector and a surrender to peasant demands. The Zinoviev group was ready to engage in the slaughter of the rich peasantry as part of a meaningful termination of war communism. At the same time, this would bring about the collectivization of the poor peasantry and help start the socialization process.

This controversy also has a significance in relation to contemporary strategies of development. The kinds of responses held to be available are still important today. Stalin makes his entrance into Soviet politics as the great compromiser between the two factions. It must be understood that prior to the mid-'twenties there was no such thing as Stalinism. There is no ideology which can properly distinguish Stalin's from that of his colleagues. As a matter of fact, his position as Secretary of the Communist Party was the most ambiguous one within the Councils of the Soviet ruling elite. It was thought to be the least likely position from which ideology could emanate. The early image of Stalin the organizer did not include any comparable image of him as a theorist.

Throughout the period of Lenin's rule, Stalin represented the perfect bureaucrat, the man who executed the plans of others and went to the "field" only to file efficiency reports. But he scarcely made plans of his own. Since Stalin had an abrupt, brusque character and clearly lacked charismatic qualities of leadership, it appeared unlikely, all things being equal, that he would ever be in a policy-making position.[24] All things were not equal. And in this controversy between compromise and coercion, between the public sector and the private sector, was born the hybrid phenomenon of Stalinism.

The argument regarding industrialization was unyielding. The rightists, supported by professional economists in the bureaucracy, argued for moderate growth of industry, leaving the peasant sector relatively untouched. They argued for emphasis on more economic goods and on a productive network that would take into account the productive output of the peasantry. However, if this were to be done, foreign capital would have to be imported. If the capital was to be in the form of direct payments rather than in the form of foreign investments, the Soviet Union would then be in a position to step up exports. But all they had to export at the time was grain, because this was the only portion of Soviet production, apart from primary mineral products, against which Western economies were willing to advance funds. As a result, the leftists argued that this would make the Soviet Union permanently subservient to Western economy as well as Western political influence. They took the position of a need to extract a larger agricultural surplus from the peasantry before anything else; in this way the country would be in a position to mount a heavy industrial investment, which could be offset by the grain fed to the urban sectors. Agricultural supplies during the 1920's were the main bottleneck to the Soviet Union. However, the first five-year-plan advocated only slow collectivization. It was Stalin's program to accelerate the rate of collectivization on the

24. See Bertram D. Wolfe, *Khrushchev and Stalin's Ghost*. New York: Frederick Praeger, 1957, p. 263.

basis of its successes during the early 1920's. The assault on the kulak class, by this time a class which had become identified with the independent peasantry as a whole, came to be a high point of Stalinist repression.[25] The plain fact of the matter is that Stalinism became a basic form of making industrialism rather than of buying industrial produce. And that of course is the major fact of Soviet experience that has permeated the Third World. It is precisely this point that Deutscher indicates by pointing out that terror has to be considered a function of two entirely separate entities—political repression and economic development—and the confusion of the two was really dysfunctional and not simply the employment of unpleasant devices to bring about social change.[26]

There developed in Russia a phenomenon over and above what Stalin as a leader or an individual implied or advocated. When the peasants had been crushed in 1930, Stalinism was victorious. But Stalin the leader backed away from the implications of his own adoption of the methods of terror. At this point, we find him advocating caution and avoiding a revolutionary euphoria which made regional bolshevik cadres "dizzy with success." Throughout his whole career, Stalin showed a political ambivalence, an inability to face up to the theoretical implications of his own policies. He had little faith that the rapid development he was encouraging, contingent as it was on the high risks he was taking, would produce the desired developments, but in the absence of a theory of development Stalin became a desperate pragmatist—like so many before and after him.

Development in modern Russia is ironically a matter of an economy of haunting politics. Even under the socialist regime planning becomes willy-nilly subject to the "iron laws" of "surplus value." The political commissariat lagged behind economic transformations at every stage of Soviet development. Stalin himself lagged behind the phenomenon of Stalinism. In effect, then, when we speak of Stalinism, we are not speaking of the individual capacity for terror. Terror is not a new phenomenon in the social or economic history of Europe. What we are speaking of is a method for control of the economy through the political apparatus. Insofar as this method was successful, and real de-

25. Merle Fainsod, *How Russia Is Ruled* (revised edition). Cambridge, Mass.: Harvard University Press, 1963, pp. 443–61. See also Maurice Dobb, *Soviet Economic Planning*. New York: International Press, 1946, pp. 228–29. Dobb sees this as the turning point in European economic history.
26. Isaac Deutscher, *The Unfinished Revolution*, p. 45.

velopment could be accelerated through central-planning agencies, socialism represented a new phenomenon. Bureaucratic socialism, where planning, party, and politics are fused into one gigantic machine presided over by an industrializing autocrat, is similarly unprecedented.[27] Thus, the victory of the Soviet Revolution represented the triumph of bureaucracy no less than of socialism.

We cannot measure development exclusively or even primarily in terms of agriculture. The Russian Revolution only rationalized, but did not eliminate, the uneven nature of the developmental process. But even this asymmetry has made its "economic experiment" fascinating to Third World leaders. The drama of one sector surrendering its sovereignty to another sector has been played out in all post-Soviet revolutions. It is in this context that the essence of Stalinism was realized. There were by-products of development in the Soviet Union, accidental features Stalin contributed, which can hardly be overlooked. But it is doubtful that such features are organic to the nature of the planning system involved. Terrorism, for instance, formed part of the package. Development for Russia represented a recognition that industrialization is war-like. It was a war against famine, hunger, illiteracy, potential foreign enemies. It is also true that development was seen as a war to prevent war. This image of a military undertaking helped to legitimize the political control of economic development. In a sense then, Soviet Russia has from the outset been on a wartime footing. The Soviet regime trained a generation of educated men, a generation of literate men, and a generation of machine-oriented men. By what it excluded (the liberal arts, for instance) this training furnished exactly the kind of selective information geared to prevent any bottlenecks in the process of social development. Nonetheless, this education in technology produced an uneven form of development. It dehumanized Marxism and led to grotesque and arrogant notions of Party members as "engineers of the soul" and the Russian people as the engine. The effect of this bureaucratic corruption by the Party, which was greatly facilitated by the liquidation of the old intelligentsia, produced a generation geared to false claims and improper estimates of Soviet industrial output.

The reliance on terror itself proved to be a partial bottleneck. As

27. This is certainly the main conclusion which emerges in the critique of Stalin reputed to have been made by Khrushchev. See *Khrushchev Remembers,* with an introduction, commentary, and notes by Edward Crankshaw. Boston: Little, Brown, 1970.

Fainsod has pointed out, a secret police develops its own laws of conduct. The concept of secrecy breeds an atmosphere of fear even in the leadership which created the instrument of terror. It tends to preserve the fiction of permanent dangers since the bureaucratic apparatus of terror, like any other, seeks to survive and extend its domain, even when it becomes dysfunctional.

Terror may have helped bring Russia into the modern technological world while at the same time it cut down industrial efficiency; but the important point is that it did not disturb the momentum of industrialization and urbanization. The very success involved and implied in Stalinist developmental strategy is its greatest source of weakness. Stalinism created new forms of unevenness, new bottlenecks to development, that were unknown in the capitalist sectors. We may list some of these contradictions in Soviet socialism: (1) The rise of a preferred political bureaucracy, unchecked by popular control; (2) the loss of labor incentives prior to the institutionalization of the socialist system; (3) a toleration of regional subnational groups which offered but slight allegiance to the Soviet Union as such.

If we look at the dislocations of the forced labor system, many of the lesser contradictions can be put in perspective. The institutionalization of police terror, aside from its other functions, provided a cheap source of labor—prisoners, political or otherwise, for the industrial march. Large-scale arrests put a large reservoir of labor at the disposal of the state and its supervisory organs. Penal and conscript systems were fused in the "labor camps," and "labor therapy" was prescribed for "criminal" offenses. The chief virtue of this conscripted labor force was its "cheapness." Conscript labor was used "entirely without investment of capital." Industrial equipment to a great extent had to be bought abroad at a time when export opportunities were limited by the small amount of *valuta* on hand. Forced labor was largely manual labor and did not require modern industrial equipment. And what is more, an iron-bound discipline "can be imposed upon the personnel, both technical and staff workers." [28]

Providing a system of incentives, rewards, and even awards for this conscript labor system may have maintained a relatively high level of output, but it did little to refine or advance individual productivity. Since there was little concern about the physical maintenance of con-

28. David J. Dallin and Boris I. Nicolaevsky, *Forced Labor in Soviet Russia.* New Haven: Yale University Press, 1947, pp. 89, 91.

script labor, there was a permanent problem of "recruitment." Even when periods of high arrest and confinement solved the "personnel problem," the efficiency of this labor was minimal. There was a general lack of human incentive and an equal lack of modern equipment. But in terms of the whole Soviet system, the use of conscript labor was an undoubted success—given the circumstances in which Russian development took place. Thus, while the average efficiency of conscript labor was perhaps half that of free labor, its value in Russia's "take-off period" can hardly be questioned.[29]

In Russia the system of conscript labor has been reduced, if not entirely eliminated. This was not only for humanitarian reasons. With the introduction of more complicated machinery requiring greater technical skills, such labor has become obsolete. Russian conscript labor may be considered a substitute for the immigrant labor flow in nineteenth-century America. In the absence of a flow of free labor, it provided the Soviet Union with a cheap labor source for rapid industrialization. But when the relative advantages of free and skilled labor far outweighed those of conscripted and unskilled labor, the developmental process underwent drastic changes.

The basic dilemma of the post-Stalin period is that few measures exist for dismantling the coercive apparatus—a task made doubly difficult by the Soviet's insistent denial that such an apparatus even existed.[30] Strong discipline will be necessary to raise consumer production and create better living standards. The growth of differences between incomes and positions of power, wage rises, and increasing professional and labor specialization, has made "inequality" widespread. Thus, achievement of social mobility in a Soviet context required an increase in social stratification. And what this shows is that the degree of mobility is not uniquely determined by the presence or absence of broad social distinctions in rank and earnings.

With all of its pitfalls, the field of economic statistics remains the most reliable single indicator of the paradoxes of the post-Stalin period. The Soviet regime promised an improvement of more than 250 per cent in per capita consumption between 1960 and 1980. But this would have necessitated an increase at a compound annual rate of more than

29. *Ibid.*, pp. 105–6.
30. This is the main reason that the transition from totalitarian to authoritarian models, while real, is extremely uneven. See Isaac Deutscher, "Kosygin's Economic Counter-Reform," *Russia, China, and the West.* London and New York: Oxford University Press, 1970, pp. 309–13.

6.4 per cent. Yet, the Soviets achieved this growth rate in only one period of their existence, between 1948 and 1958. And even this high rate of growth may have been due in part to the destruction caused by World War II, for the real starting urban wage for 1948 was less than half that of 1928. Thirty years later, by 1958, the real urban wage barely reached that gained in the 1928 period. And by the mid-1960's, the Soviet growth rate had decreased to approximately 4.0 per cent.[31] This is while the rate of economic growth in the Soviet Union slightly exceeded that of the United States. During this period the fact that the starting points are quite different prevented the Soviet Union from realizing the premise of its leadership to achieve a high enough per capita production to equal that of the United States. Indeed to "catch up" would mean an abandonment of many wasteful features of Soviet production. It did mean above all the capacity to modernize and industrialize at the same time—a feat which so far has eluded the Second World but is quite the norm in the First World. In Soviet Union there exists at present an uneasy balance between a Stalinist model based on an economy of primary production and the revisionist model based on the writing of Liberman which emphasizes consumer production and exact cost accounting.[32] In either case, this would occasion pressures on the regime from many and diverse social sectors. And as long as present Soviet commitments to the world socialist bloc and to the developing regions must be moderated in terms of internal pressures for greater consumer satisfaction, there is unlikely to be any radical shift in Soviet economic strategy.

The backwardness of Soviet agriculture is the perfect illustration of the nation's uneven economic development. It reveals in the most acute form the problems Soviet policy planners now face with respect to the acceleration of growth and the corresponding relaxation of tensions inside the Soviet Union. As of 1960, the distribution in the Soviet Union was 40 per cent in agriculture, 38 per cent in industry, and 22 per cent in service industry. Given approximately 2.5 per cent annual decline

31. See Oscar Gass, "Soviet Economic Developments," *Commentary,* Vol. 37, No. 2, Feb. 1964, pp. 54–69; and for more recent data consult the Senate-House Joint Economic Committee, *Current Economic Indicators for the U.S.S.R.* Washington, D.C.: United States Government Printing Office, 1965.
32. "Libermanism" refers to the unorthodox approach to the Soviet economy advocated by Yevsel Liberman, Professor of Economics at Kharlov University. The basis of his approach is that any great improvement in the quality and the quantity of national production can best be brought about by making profits the principal indicator of the success or failure of any enterprise.

in agricultural labor force between 1958 and 1968, and a 2 per cent annual rise in the industrial working force by the present decade, there are more industrial than farm workers in the Soviet Union. Nonetheless, this still compares quite unfavorably to the United States, where by 1970 there were roughly six farm workers for every hundred factory workers. While there has been a decline from 71 per cent to 40 per cent of the Russian population on farms between 1928 and 1958, the absolute number of farm workers has continued to increase.[33]

Soviet planners hoped to reduce the size of the agricultural labor force while increasing the yield per acre through increased efficiency. But a number of serious problems arise: First, the Soviets have yet to make industrial existence as attractive as it is in the West, although slowly, over time, the social goods and services are beginning to have their effect. (We really don't, however, have any information on the voluntary migration from rural to urban areas.) Second, the geography of the Soviet Union makes it difficult for agriculture to increase its yield beyond present capacities for areas of comparable climate. Grain yields in the Soviet Union are considerably lower than those in the United States, and further, the output per worker in the Soviet Union continues to be much lower than the American counterpart.[34] On both scores, Soviet development will probably not only remain uneven but become even more so. The much vaunted liquidation of the distinction between farm and factory labor or between manual and intellectual labor will probably not only fail to be realized but will most likely become greater.

This raises the question of what is considered legitimate in the process of development and what must be viewed as illegitimate. The moral question in a sense precedes the social question. Stalinism in one country has become an accepted political formula despite the inevitable corruption of the bureaucratic state. But Stalinism as an economic program is not obsolete in the same sense. Terror was vindicated as a necessary feature of accomplishing the tasks of the social revolution. Once these tasks were accomplished, once it was demonstrated that the socialist revolution was possible, it became a desired goal for other countries. Given this new high value, terror was no longer a main source of contention but became only a necessary consequence for

33. Simon Kuznets, *Modern Economic Growth: Rate, Structure, and Spread.* New Haven: Yale University Press, 1966, p. 107.
34. Lloyd G. Reynolds, *Economics: A General Introduction* (3rd edition). Homewood, Ill.: Irwin Publishers, 1969, p. 839.

social development and social planning in a backward economy. This is counterposed to the capitalist ideology of agricultural development through technological innovation and scientific management.

Soviet development was greatly helped by the pre-revolutionary domestic bureaucracy, one which was thoroughly Russian, and thus could not easily be removed as was the colonial bureaucracy in so many parts of Africa. At the same time, the Russian bureaucracy was sufficiently separated in fact and in function from the rest of the Soviet class system so as to be able to give its direct allegiance to the political apparatus. The social basis of Stalinism was this bureaucracy, which gained disproportionately in the industrialization process.[35] We can appreciate this factor when we note that the traditionalism of the Chinese bureaucracy drastically reduces China's potential for rapid development after the Sun Yat Sen Revolution of 1910–11. As one writer recently pointed out:

> The weak point lay in the reluctance of the Chinese bureaucracy, imbued with the ethical standards of the mandarin system, either to allow effective management to pass into the hands of those competent to exercise it or to adapt their own ideas to changed circumstances. It was exacerbated by the inability of the Chinese government to maintain order and political unity, a defect which persisted until 1949.[36]

In Russia, the bourgeoisie bequeathed a "value-free" bureaucracy to the Soviets, while in China the examination system, based as it was upon class privilege, was unable to liberate the bureaucracy from traditionalism.

It is useful to compare modern China and the Soviet Union with respect to the use of terror. True to the predictions of Stalinism, party strife, while low in the early years of the post-revolutionary ferment, grows after the initial consolidation period. The consensus of the earlier years gives rise to an inner party conflict in the second decade of the Chinese revolution, as it did in the second decade of the Russian revo-

35. H. Malcolm Macdonald, "Revisionism and Khrushchev," *The Southwestern Social Science Quarterly*, Vol. 44, No. 4, Mar. 1964, pp. 335–45.

36. C. D. Cowan, *The Economic Development of Southeast Asia: Studies in Economic History and Political Economy.* New York: Frederick Praeger, 1964, pp. 17–18. For a particularly relevant statement of the current status of Chinese polity and economy, see Franz Schumann, "China's 'New Economic Policy'—Transition or Beginning," *The China Quarterly*, Jan.–Mar. 1964 (reprint no. 134, Institute of International Studies, University of California at Berkeley).

lution.[37] Although there has been a considerable amount of rhetoric concerning new laws of development through the art of self-criticism, the science of terrorism ultimately reared its head. The cultural revolution and the post-cultural revolution period reveal several major features of both Chinese and Russian development: that the attempt to prevent a bureaucratic sloth from taking place resulted in an assault on the political hierarchy and scarcely disrupted or disturbed the basis of economic production. The dependence on terror remains a moot point, since, whether violence against the internal proletariat is high or low, the rate of economic development seems to be remarkably unaffected by such political devices. What does affect production is rationalization through planning, particularly in the agricultural sector, and not the simple exercise of terror.[38]

The Chinese have not avoided certain forms of terrorism which took place in the Soviet Union. They too have made a huge purge of the peasantry, with large numbers of wealthy peasants having been killed in the process of collectivization in the two decades since the Chinese communist seizure of power, but they did so without convulsing the political apparatus to the same degree. So that basically the Chinese model, although showing vast innovative potential and great technical independence, tends to resemble the Soviet model in its process of development, however dissimilar the two models are in political ideology at this time. That is to say in both China and Russia, the internal peasantry was made to pay a heavy price for the industrialization of the nation.[39] And this kind of uneven development based on sectoral sacrifice remains a stronger model for the underdeveloped areas than it did when only the Soviet model was available.

It has been pointed out that, although the Chinese pattern has not shown quite the same degree of ruthlessness as the Soviet pattern under Stalin, the effects of the "cultural revolution" and its bureaucratic aftermath will be as devastating and long standing as its Soviet counterpart. "Like Russia in the last years of the Stalin era, so China has now plunged headlong into a self-centered isolationism and nationalism and has shut itself off more hermetically than ever from the outside

37. Choh-ming Li, "Economic Development," *China Quarterly*, Vol. I (Jan.–Mar. 1960), pp. 35–50.
38. Alexander Eckstein, *Communist China's Economic Growth and Foreign Trade*. New York: McGraw-Hill, 1956, pp. 267–74.
39. See W. K., "Soviet Agriculture as a Model for Asian Countries," *The China Quarterly*, Vol. 2 (Jan.–Mar. 1961), pp. 116–30.

world and from all its political and cultural influences. To achieve this Mao had to organize a program of the intelligentsia, whom he suspects of being vulnerable to foreign, especially 'revisionist,' influences." [40]

Socialism as set forth in the Marxist program does not answer the questions of nationalism, racism, and militarism. It is on these grounds, not on the argument of alternative roads to development, that socialism faces its most severe challenge from the Western capitalistic democracies. While problems of electrification, military build-up, and steel and iron-ore production are central to the major large nations of the world, these are not the biggest problems in the underdeveloped or developing regions.

Behavioristic manipulation through the propagandistic obliteration of political memory has displaced outright terrorism. Stakhanovism, the Soviet blend of time, motion, and terror, has given way to psychological manipulation, to a mechanical scheme of punishment-reward incentives. Leading technicians of the new socialist society concentrate on making the productive process work rapidly and precisely. Through punishment and reward, incentive schemes are designed to end criticism. Some technicians have assumed that the economic norms set by the politicians are often self-defeating. However, the difficulty with most forms of technocratic thinking both in the Soviet Union and elsewhere in the socialist bloc is that it tends to lose sight of non-economic factors in the development process. And while this produces tension between the technocrats and the politicians, it also is part of the ongoing dialogue within socialist society. While subject to high personal risk, the technician's autonomy from the political planner has never quite been obliterated and therefore never quite resolved either.[41] Mechanical validity, or prima facie accomplishment, becomes the basic characteristic of practically all automated societies. The power of the automated socialist society to reward its members depends upon their uncritical acceptance of what is offered in the form of those signals which mean "well done" or "how right you are." But this travels the

40. Isaac Deutscher, *Russia, China, and the West*. London and New York: Oxford University Press, 1970, p. 334.
41. The recent dismissal of a Soviet public health inspector for failing to approve newly constructed buildings because of structural and operational defects has publicly raised the conflict of interest between an honest bureaucrat and overanxious politicians trying to meet their planning norms. See Bernard Gwertzman, "Ouster of Soviet Official Stirs Protest," *The New York Times* (June 26, 1971).

full circle. What is wrong with Soviet life is thus closely connected to what is wrong with industrialization as an ideology.

The power of the machine to condition the populace would be decreased if it were suspected for a moment that the rewards given to workers in particular planning tasks did not correspond to those expected from the general population. This assumption of perfect economic rationality is a key reason why the development of the Soviet system has been so uneven. Actions which might prove to be unrewarding or even fatal in a wider context might be the most rewarding within the planning zone. But any suspicion that the plan might not be perfect would tend to destroy the popular faith in the artificial forms of manipulation held necessary for development.

Clearly, the Soviet development has given enormous stimulus to new forms of controlled development. But it has also bequeathed to the Third World new forms of uncontrolled terror. The final question here is not an easy one: To what degree is the terrorism warranted on pragmatic grounds? And for a partial answer, we must necessarily compare the Soviet Union and the United States.

There is an obvious difficulty in establishing standards for such a comparison. In the first place, the United States is a mass-consumption society, while the Soviet Union is a mass-production society. The United States and the Soviet Union both think that their differences are far greater than their similarities. This has led them to be more intensely competitive in the struggle for world influence than any actual economic differences warrant. Third World countries similarly see them as antithetical, yet major powers like France or England may see their similarities as important. The United States and the Soviet Union can really be only imperfect models, for their own history and experience are in many ways unique.

The difficulty with much political and economic analysis of similarities and dissimilarities between the Soviet Union and the United States is the tendency to maximize ideological factors; to take at face value statements about the extent of differences in means and ends between the two economic goliaths. While there is no doubt that differences of ideology permeate the social structure, and even serve to define the differences between some leadership groups, the serious observer cannot help but feel that ideological differences have been overtaxed and freighted at the expense of structural similarities. If we eschew ideological self-definitions of the international political situation and move to some statistically and empirically based generalizations, then we'll see that the variations are due to differences in geographical and historical background rather than ideological adversity. This is not to deny real differences, even structural differences, between the two systems. In the United States, an economic class rules with a subordinate polity, whereas the reverse is true in the Soviet Union. The very fact that egalitarian reforms in the Soviet state come directly from the political apparatus would indicate how substantive these differences are. Nonetheless, even such differences can be expressed as a time lag rather than as a structural deficiency in either society.

The American Civil War took place between 1861 and 1865, and its outcome guaranteed the victory of industrialism over agrarianism. The Russian Civil War took place between 1919 and 1922, and its outcome made possible the institution of planning and in this way guaranteed a long-range victory of industrialism over agrarianism. If we take the civil war in each countries as the trigger for its rapid economic development, then the gap between the United States and the Soviet Union can be considered a function of the period in which each civil war took place, rather than as a consequence of the social system.

Even if we place a positive assessment on the convergence of the two systems, Brzezinski and Huntington properly caution against a bland assumption that convergence at the economic level guarantees consensus at the political or military levels:

> History shows that socio-political uniformity and peace need not go hand in hand. In fact, the latter may be a more comforting conclusion than the proposition—shared by both the Marxists and the "convergists"—that peace depends on uniformity. The theory of convergence minimizes or ignores the totality of the Russian and the American historical experience—political, social, and economic —and exaggerates the importance of one factor alone. It minimizes also the uniqueness of the historical process and forces it into a common pattern with fundamentally the same outcomes for all. It asserts the repetitiveness of the historically familiar and ignores the probability that the future will see in both the United States and in the Soviet Union novel forms of government which will evolve out of the present on the basis of the *uneven* importance of political and social-economic determinants in the two countries.[42]

42. Zbigniew Brzezinski and Samuel P. Huntington, *Political Power: USA/USSR*. New York: The Viking Press, 1964, pp. 429–30.

The United States developed in a military atmosphere relatively free from foreign pressures toward conquest. The profound isolation of nineteenth-century United States from "European involvements" placed minimal pressure on the industrial machine, for it did not have to divert a portion of factory production for such non-valuable goods as military hardware. The Soviet Union was born in the midst of World War I, and the extent of military adventurism against it in its formative stages has now passed over into mythology. From the "imperialist cordon sanitaire" of 1920 to the "ring of bases" which Stalin saw in 1950, the Soviets have developed with the fact as well as the psychology of being surrounded by hostile military forces. While this undoubtedly rendered the Russian worker more willing to engage in the rituals of self-sacrifice for the fatherland, it also served as an effective drain on Russian economic growth roughly between 1918 and 1948. In recent post-World-War-II condition, military expenditures have continued to plague Soviet efforts at greater commodity productivity. In point of fact, the United States has been far better able to cope with the problem of guns and butter than has the Soviet Union. Despite the leveling off of military investments, with respect to total economic output, the Soviet Union still spends roughly 14 per cent of its GNP on defense, whereas the United States spends roughly 10 per cent. This, coupled with a higher living standard at the start of the arms race, provides a significant edge to the United States economy.

In comparing the relative advantages and disadvantages of the developmental process in the United States and the Soviet Union, special mention should be made of the role of organized labor. The arguments at the ideological level between worker representatives in each nation often reflect the different character of labor and the different notion of success. Despite the high costs of class conflicts, labor organization in the United States served as a vehicle for rapid development. In the nineteenth century, unions served to maintain labor discipline more than to elevate mass labor rights. In the twentieth century, the continuing pressure by unions for higher wages has provided one of the absolutely essential underpinnings for expanding mass demand and has thus served to accelerate the nation's economic growth. It is worth noting that the popular Keynesian analysis of spreading income and the power to spend over broad masses runs counter to free enterprise ideology. The institutionalization of industrial unionism, a process functional to capitalist stability, was irrationally fought by the very class it was designed to protect in the long run, the bourgeoisie.

The pressure of labor costs has also become one of the main reasons for increased productivity. Above all, unions, their leaders and members alike, have had a shared value in the fundamental transformation of the worker's status. The goals of the workers themselves are close to those of other parts of American society, thus guaranteeing a formal consensus between Americans on the appropriate developmental goals.[43] Hence, industrial unionism contributed to the general developmental process.

The Soviet Union, for its part, was so bound by Marxist formulas concerning the cooperative nature of social classes under socialism that it suppressed all displays of labor independence and labor strife as indicative of counter-revolutionary activity. There is no doubt that the forced labor system had advantages in the earliest stages of the Soviet regime, and, similarly, it is quite possible that the suppression of independent labor agitation led to a higher rate of production. But if the Soviets hoped to achieve by their methods the full liberation of productive energies in a cooperative situation in replacement of the American system of formal consensus, it failed dismally.[44] The Soviet Union was forced to increase externally inflicted terrorism, constant propaganda, and postponement of hopes to arrive at the same point which the United States managed to gain by being more tolerant and, at times, more sensitive to the role of labor independence and its stimulus to development. This is one reason why the Soviet Union, in its formative period, has advanced at a rate parallel to, rather than in advance of, the United States. And this with higher social costs.[45]

While we are on the subject, it should be said that the coexistence of the United States and the Soviet Union as major industrial powers has served to puncture some favorite myths about developmental ideology. The idea that Protestantism per se represents the driving force of development, rather than only one strain or variety of de-

43. See Sanford Cohen, *Labor in the United States*. Columbus, Ohio: Charles E. Merrill Books, 1960, pp. 68–94.
44. See S. Swianiewicz, *Forced Labour and Economic Development*. London and New York: Oxford University Press, 1965, pp. 50–53.
45. A significant beginning of such comparative-historical study is contained in Reinhard Bendix, *Work and Authority in Industry: Ideologies of Management in the Course of Industrialization*. New York: John Wiley & Sons, 1956.

velopment in the West, is now firmly put to rest. It is not only that the Soviet Union has few if any Protestant worshippers, but, more to the point, no religion has dynamized the USSR toward development. Indeed, "delayed gratification" can be urged on religious grounds (as in England or the United States), but it can also be urged on nationalist grounds (via the medium of the Communist Party as in the Soviet Union and China). It is also quite clear that, whereas the elite in the West was indeed touched by the Protestant Ethic, this elite did not labor in the vineyards of God. This was left to Irish hod-carriers, Jewish garment workers, Italian brick-layers, and the whole universe of a non-Protestant labor force in the United States.

Another fairy tale exposed by the examination of the USA and the USSR is the idea that development is somehow a consequence of political liberalism—of a belief in progress through free choice and free science. Development may be quite rapid under dictatorship or military rule. Political pluralism necessarily minimizes the effectiveness of planning, and it makes the decision-making process so complex and subject to countervailing pressures as to slow down substantially the rate of industrial growth, while on the other hand, totalitarianism minimizes precisely these types of obstacles to development. Stalinism was not simply rule by terror. Rather, terrorism was the consequence of an approach to development in which planning, decision-making, and policy-determination were all centralized and expected to be realized—whatever their human cost. Thus, the choice is really the other way around. Political liberalism has turned out to be less viable with respect to sustained high industrial growth rates than totalitarianism at least in the context of a less than fully educated or fully cultivated underclass. This is far from the naïve notions prevalent—at least until Sputnik—that economic liberalism is the best possible state for high rates of development in all social contexts, and that dictatorship is somehow incompatible with modern industrial life or scientific achievement. Fascism and socialism alike have dispelled such myths.

Another myth punctured by the coexistence of the United States and the Soviet Union is that high growth rates require, as a metaphysical necessity for their realization, the destruction of the middle classes. It may be true that the liquidation of the Russian bourgeoisie as a social class was necessary to achieve high levels of social production, but it is also clear that in the evolution of the United States the bourgeoisie performed the significant role as the directorate of development. Through significant investment procedures, industrial combinations, foreign holdings, and philanthropic services, the bourgeoisie of the United States proved its exceptional qualities—its capacity for self-sacrifice to gain development. Too often the talk about American exceptionalism has focused on the character of the labor force. In fact, what has made the United States "exceptional," at least with respect to Marxist "laws" about socioeconomic transformation, is its bourgeoisie.

It is simpler to assume that the similarities between industrial organization in the United States and the Soviet Union drive them both to similar economic peaks and plateaus and lead to a convergence of productivity rates, than it is to argue the opposite. Indeed, both the United States and the Soviet Union are rapidly growing, in like manner, and the gap between them and the rest of the underdeveloped world is widening sharply. Both are self-sustaining economies; both are exporting economies; both are industrial economies. The Third World nations, for their part, tend to reveal less of a capacity for self-sustained growth. They are importing economies (of finished goods), while they export their materials. Furthermore, they are pre-technological, in both scientific and industrial senses, and hence it scarcely pays for these nations to "nationalize" one isolated economic sector, since the finished goods are usually bought far more cheaply abroad than domestically.

What is actually taking place today is the very slow growth of industrial parity between the two giant powers. But since the starting points differ significantly, and since other independent variables favor the United States in terms of high growth rate, the actual date of coalescence is much later than the Soviet Union has envisioned it. The target date, the rendezvous with economic destiny, is more likely to be around the year 2050 than 1980. The industrial gap, with great crudity, may be expressed in terms of about fifty years, and by 1980 it may, all things remaining equal (meaning no major shift in balance of political power or no thermonuclear war), be about thirty years. Again, this suggests the striking structural similarities between the United States and the Soviet Union—similarities which Khrushchev has been more ready to grant exist in the military sphere than in the economic sphere; even though one might expect that from a Marxian point of view, the military capacity of a nation would be considered directly linked to and forged by a nation's economic potential.

The statistical information adds up to a bright picture for both the

United States and the Soviet Union. True, there are dark spots in each. The Soviet agricultural system is in a shambles—but the declining importance of this sector and the introduction of scientific technology can overcome this handicap. The United States, for its part, continues to avoid making full use of its industrial potential. But this can also be rectified through "welfare" investment or by raising the threshold of consumer wants and demands by new products and services.

Despite the similarities between the two nations which advanced industrialization has produced, there is little point to First World and Second World characterizations if existent structural likenesses are the only focus. Methods, traditions, and types of development—in other words, "procedures"—still make of both nations two distinct entities in world political culture. Third World countries attest to these differences by the sheer fact of being driven back and forth between "the camps" for aid, for "models," for support. Perhaps both their similarities and differences are best illustrated in this fact.

The most important point to note about the political structure of Soviet life is its high degree of bureaucratization and rationalization. It has managed to solve the problem of succession, what Marxists refer to as the transference of power, without resorting to blood-letting and without a coup d'état. And it is done so outside the customary framework of parliamentary politics or multi-party politics. And if Brezhnev and Kosygin do not exactly represent charismatic authority, they do represent legitimated authority, which in a Soviet context is not just a confirmation of Max Weber's notion of the movement from ideology to bureaucracy, but more important, a statement of potential stability within present Soviet life; a stabilization based upon conservative "businesslike" decisions.

Whatever this shift in the Soviet command posts is taken to signify, one point stands out above all others: this change is a revolution and not a restoration in the forms of Soviet political life. Basically, the fall of Khrushchev signified changes in Soviet life even more profound than the shift from Malenkov to Khrushchev. Indeed, if the fall of Malenkov carried with it the collapse of Stalinism, it might well be that the fall of Khrushchev entails the demise of Leninism—not, to be sure, as the saviour of Mother Russia, but, quite surely, as the author of Divine Truth and Providential Good. Hence, whatever regressive features exist in the policies of the Brezhnev–Kosygin leadership, they appear utterly unable to curb the pluralization of socialism abroad and the fragmentation of the Communist Party monolith at home.

It is important to note the major role of Khrushchev in bringing about the current move from a totalitarian to an authoritarian regime. Khrushchev was first of all the last of the old bolshevik leaders. He embodied a good deal of revolutionary fervor, populist virtue, respect for peasants, even a streak of egalitarianism; and his educational reforms eliminated many of the paramilitary trappings of the Soviet bureaucracy. He was also the first modern Soviet leader capable of the most serious criticism of his predecessors, and yet because of his long years of service to the Stalinist regime, he provided a legitimacy to his criticism that the contemporary rulers of Russia could not possibly command. And perhaps Khrushchev is at least as important in his post-rule period as in his rule period, since he is also the first ex-leader of the Soviet state to remain at liberty and alive, beyond the period of his dominance. It is for this reason that a certain emphasis on his role is unavoidable in understanding the current situation in the USSR.

In every sphere of life, Khrushchev excoriated those who wanted to operate within traditional modalities, but he stopped short of instituting new, more modest norms of political behavior. Khrushchev was the very best product of the Stalin era: a believer in the goals of collectivization without terrorism. That is why, while denouncing the "personality cult," Khrushchev did not find it possible to limit his own political power. Because Khrushchev still retained the Stalinist fusion of Party and government functions in one person, Bulganin's fall became inevitable. It is precisely this partial, incomplete aspect of Khrushchev's legacy which has been focused upon in the policy statements which have been forthcoming from the Soviet press since Brezhnev and Kosygin came to power.

The concern with style in Soviet politics is more properly a concern with maturity in human behavior. From the adulation and adoration of the Stalin period to the capricious and even boorish qualities of the Khrushchev era, the new Soviet technical elite has had to wince, grin, and bear it. It is most important to note that Khrushchev was the most successful Soviet leader in trying to prevent the technical bureaucratic elite from transmitting from one generation to its next the special privileges, particularly in the areas of education and salaries, and that the attack on him is in large measure a bureaucratic impulse rather than an ethical one.

But with the Brezhnev-Kosygin regime, the term "business-like" has become the byword in Soviet political behavior. For example, in the closing session of the Supreme Soviet held in December 1964, Premier Kosygin spoke without the usual accompaniment of "thunderous ovation" or "stormy applause" so characteristic of bolshevik politics. Also missing were the usual flamboyant phrases about the "building of communism" and the "victories of socialist labor." So radical a departure was this that the *New York Times* in its report was moved to point out that "Mr. Kosygin sounded more like the president of a big Western corporation than a Communist politician."

But the question of style, of the sophistication of Russian political behavior, has an authentic sociological content. The changes in the organization of Soviet life are far-reaching in their consequences, both for the Russian people and for the peoples of the whole world. It would be tragic were the rhetorical demands of the Cold War allowed to obscure these new beginnings. During the Khrushchev era precise legal restrictions and limitations were placed on the political machinery, and beyond that, some distinction between the art of rule and the science of government. While there has existed since the "Stalin Constitution" of 1936 a formal recognition of the differences between government functions and the Communist Party apparatus, the differences were more observed in the breach than in observance. The leadership of the Party and of the government were fused at the very top of the political hierarchy, with the Party leadership also in charge of the principal (if not of all) administrative posts.

The new attitude is signified in two key words: *autonomy* and *exactingness*. Gigantic planning agencies, with their outmoded methods of production and distribution of goods, are giving way to a new autonomy. The critique of centralism, of the inability of centralization to determine volumes of output, changing consumer orientations, level of profitability, and the like, in the early post-Khrushchev days has already been pushed into a wider critique of the politicalization of areas of economic life that are better left in the hands of knowing experts. This brought about a second word: "exactingness"—what might be called "expertise" in the West. The demand for "high exactingness" was coupled by the Communist Party ideological organ with a "Leninist style of work." To be sure, every Soviet leader since the death of Lenin has demanded a style of work in keeping with the supposed demands of the founding father of bolshevism. For Stalin it meant primarily an "inner party struggle" with which to achieve a *Gleichschaltung,* a co-ordination of the various social sectors which would render unswerving (and uncritical) fidelity to the leader. For Malenkov, adhesion to Leninism meant adhesion and identification with the Party apparatus as a whole. During the Khrushchev period, Leninism signified an identification with the nation-state no less than with the Party. The present leadership marks a further development toward the liberalization of all that Leninism included.

In other words, Kosygin and Brezhnev represented the successful take-over of "the new class." The Party has finally been forced to recognize the autonomy of the administrators; the "new turn" also had a profound economic aspect. Khrushchev's agricultural emphasis was a failure: the crops in the early 1960's were bad, and this natural accident accentuated technocratic dissatisfaction. Finally, the aggregate growth rate went down in the 1960's precisely because of the attempt to placate consumer desires no less than industrial demands. It has come to signify attention to details of administration and organization, and, no less, to an avoidance of any linkage of personal achievement with political infallibility.

The new turn in Soviet politics emphasizes means no less than ends. It is no longer sufficient to "pursue the plan." The new, new Soviet Man must behave "correctly" in interpersonal relations. "Boorishness" or a "lack of composure" or "negative" psychological attitudes attributed to the past leadership of the Soviet Party by the present leadership are to be replaced by the technocratic virtues: "composure, discipline and industriousness."

These are not simply mandates for the behavior of Communist Party cadre, but more significantly, warrants for distinguishing between partisan political functions and non-political bureaucratic functions. The technical aspects of a planned economy require a separation of functions to mesh gears satisfactorily. In this respect, it is significant that traditional communist clichés about Party loyalty have given way to demands for technical competence. This represents a considerable shift from personal styles to legalistic modes of judgment. "Moral judgment" has given way to "practical judgment." But this transition from charismatic to bureaucratic modes of rule entails serious limits upon the role of the communist cadre.

The colossal changes in political structure are already widely reflected in changes in political ideology. True enough, these changes are being introduced cautiously and with circumspection—lest they become objects of the controversies now raging within the communist sphere of influence. The main shift is from a "party of the proletariat" to a "party of the people." Yet it is difficult to imagine how such a phenomenon as the "Africanization" of the Soviet Communist Party can fail to come under critical gaze—even if this phenomenon of an all-peoples' party is veiled under the discussions concerning modernization of economic practices.

For a long while it has been apparent that the leaders of the Third World have refused to accept the idea that their parties are class dictatorships, and therefore maintained that they are caretakers of transitional regimes and transitional economies. The ideological leaders of the Third World have insisted that their respective national liberation movements are "parties of the whole people," in this way fusing bureaucratic and charismatic features into a single dominant party.

Soviet intransigence on this point has, in the past, cost its leadership serious losses in the Third World—both with respect to the indigenous revolutionary high command, and also by advocates of the broad-based national liberation ideology adopted by the Chinese communists in their overseas policies. Thus, the recent announcement in *Pravda* that "the socialist state has ceased to be an organ of the dictatorship of the proletariat and has been transformed into a state of the entire people" serves a dual purpose. It serves to underscore the new Soviet policy of limiting the role and function of the Communist Party, and, second, it serves to bring Soviet political ideology into line with the major "national liberation" ideologies of the Third World nations of Africa, Asia, and Latin America. However, the continuing difficulties of the Soviet Union with its own minorities has muted the impact of its new policies.

The internal affairs of the Soviet Union reflect this new focus on emergent nations. There is much current discussion in the Soviet Union on merging Communist Party organizations based on the principle of territory, and those based on industrial plants, and this represents much more than a criticism of Khrushchev's belief in regional-territorial councils, or multiplication in the number and costs of administrative agencies within the Party. In its most complete form this view is part of the process of decentralization; of separating Communist Party functions from administrative functions as such.[46] Nonetheless, the fact that for the first time in dim recollection a public *parliamentary debate* took place inside the Supreme Soviet, with the Party leader of Leningrad, Georgi I. Popov, actually speaking against the reorganization proposals, and for the expansion of industrial management councils set up under Khrushchev, is a powerful indication that the "state of the entire people" notion is already being put into substantial, albeit limited, practice.

The standard Soviet guide to problems of power and organization has been the principle of monolithic unity. This notion of single-party and single-purpose was supposed to ensure against selfishness, opportunism, and deviant politics generally. It was on the basis of this dogma of the monolith that all forms of opposition, potential and otherwise, were eliminated with Stalinism. First, local party organizations (such as those which existed in Leningrad, Kiev, and Moscow) were deprived of their autonomy, in favor of an all-knowing central committee. Second, the potential threat of the Red Army to Communist Party leaders was minimized by professionalizing and, in this way, isolating the armed forces from the Party organization. Third, the Party elite periodically purged the military elite, thus ensuring the allegiance of the soldier through the assignment of a cadre of political instructors. Fourth, the separate republics which comprise the Soviet Union were deprived of their "states' rights" in a manner different from that employed in the United States, but without much difference in substance. Any show of a real thirst for local power, or of autonomous political decision, was severely condemned as "bourgeois nationalism" and/or "petty-bourgeois separatism." Fifth, the Soviets, the actual council of workers, were devitalized in the early 'twenties, and never again became an effective countervailing agency. True, the Soviets were revitalized later in the decade—but only as an instrument of aiding higher production, as an instrument of the State, rather than as a spokesman of the workers. Sixth, the leadership of the bolshevik movement was badly

46. It should be noted that this position is not uniformly shared. More common is the "undulating" thesis in which Soviet politics is described in terms of power shifts rather than social changes. But such a view does little to resolve or to explain how the present Soviet leadership views the problem of succession or the larger problems of dictatorship as one of several forms of managing crisis. On this problem, see Myron Rush, *Political Succession in the U.S.S.R.* New York: Columbia University Press, 1965.

fragmented organizationally and ideologically. The Lenin cult somehow made it unnecessary to pay attention to problems of succession. Thus, although the schisms between Trotsky, Zinoviev, Bukharin, and the other Politburo hierarchy served to enhance the magical force of Lenin during his lifetime, they created havoc afterward—making possible the bureaucratic surge to power of Joseph Stalin.[47]

The reasons for the Stalinist consolidation, however, derive not so much from his singular pursuit of terrorism as a tactic but from his purposive bending of terror toward developmental goals. Over time, Stalinism came to signify five prongs: (a) rapid industrialization, (b) societal planning, (c) collectivization of agriculture, (d) socialism in one country, specifically nationalism in Russia, and (e) inner party struggle collapsing the organs of State and Party power into a single combined leadership.[48] But if this program served the take-off period well, it proved less than satisfactory in handling more sophisticated problems of political succession and economic decision-making.

These various changes in the political structure may finally solve the problem of political succession—the central dilemma in the single-party and/or single-leader state. By emphasizing the separateness of Party and bureaucracy, by going even further and emphasizing the technical requirements of Party membership, the Soviet political elite undoubtedly expects to create the internal checks and balances within the Party which can lead to pacific resolution of future political issues, without leading to a multi-party system. The emergence of a science of government in institutes of higher learning, independent of an ideology of Marxism, is a clear indication that the problem of succession is foremost in the minds of the present Soviet ruling elite. The increasing attention to the social sciences, particularly social sciences such as sociology and political science which have a clear potential for policy statements but were formerly denounced as bourgeois, coincides with an effort to have every Party member resolve questions with precision. "The Party teaches boldness and daring. But it also calls for circumspection, a sober analysis of the pluses and minuses of every phenom-

47. The whole of volume six in E. H. Carr's *A History of Soviet Russia* can be interpreted as a study in the problem of succession under communism. See *Socialism in One Country: 1924–26* (Part Two). London: Macmillan & Co., 1959.

48. For a succinct summary of the Stalinist polity, see Barrington Moore, Jr., *Soviet Politics: The Dilemma of Power*. New York: Harper & Row, 1965, pp. 108–16.

enon, of the objective conditions, the real situation." This is a far cry from the "partiinost," the unthinking partisanship which undoubtedly had a divisive effect on the Communist Party apparatus. The ancien régime, which placed loyalty above truth, made every major bureaucratic shift in the power base a cathartic event.

It has long been apparent that in the trinitarian class world of "workers, peasants, and intellectuals" the intellectuals have grown enormously with respect to the rest of society. A self-definition as "intellectual" has become an all-encompassing road to high upward social mobility. The term includes a broad sphere of government bureaucrats, engineers, professionals, scholars, and the technical expert as such. The demand for sophistication—in matters of culture as well as politics—stems from these diverse sectors. It might well be that the current developments in the post-Khrushchev era are a cross between pragmatic responses to practical exigencies and a natural working out of bureaucratic requirements in industrial society.

Whatever the more distant meanings of the silent Soviet Revolution, some immediate consequences are evident. First and foremost, the new Soviet posture is a continuation of the struggle with Chinese communism for the loyalties of Third World nations. Whereas Khrushchev conducted this struggle at an ideological level, the new Soviet leadership is conducting it at the technical level. It is attempting to solve some outstanding issues of the relationships between democracy and development, politics and economics, in a way that will enable the Soviet Union, like the United States before it, to reveal the "face of the future" to the new nations, that is, to serve as a "demonstration effect."

The Soviet Union's desire to "normalize" its relations with China, without at the same time altering its fundamental attitudes toward the Mao Tse Tung regime, indicates that the present leaders, Brezhnev and Kosygin, perceive certain clear advantages in its struggle with China for preeminence in the Third World. The disadvantageous aspects have long been known and assessed: the Chinese were a people who endured classic and modern forms of colonialism; they are a colored people and an Asian people. Above all, they share in the general syndrome of impoverished "have-not" nations: a cycle of underemployment, overpopulation, food crisis, communication and transportation lags, and so forth. As against such "ascriptive" advantages for the Chinese, there are "achievement" advantages for the Russians in their struggle for worldly preeminence. The Soviet society cannot only claim to be a socialist state, but as the first and most successful socialist state it is a prototype of every other twentieth-century "revolution from below." Soviet society shows a concern with problems of democracy and total participation, which are close to the hearts of Third World militants, however much repressed. Above all, the Soviet Union is in a far better position to render economic and technical assistance than is China. And in a world of increasing nationalistic loyalties, the Soviets promise more in way of what the current situation demands.

With respect to the United States the new changes in the Soviet political structure will mean a continuation of "correctness" in diplomatic relations. It has long been plain that the Soviet Union is seeking a détente with the United States and is not in search of any rapprochement at the ideological or social levels. More than ever, the Soviets seem to believe that "history is on their side"; and that these new changes in political form and style only intensify the contradictions of the United States. The more attractive the Soviet Union becomes, the less appealing is the United States; or so at least the theory would have it. To be sure, the continuation of Soviet policy along present lines seriously weakens any outright control of its satellites. But this "turn to the West" has already gone beyond the point of recall. The Soviet Union is now so forcefully committed to the national style in politics and the regional style in economics that the social transformations taking place in Eastern Europe, or even in Western Europe—in and out of Communist Party circles—may themselves serve as an insurance policy to the West that the Soviet Union has no future designs for a *pax sovietica*.

It is significant that the internal movement toward a less coercive and less restrictive regime does not necessarily mean that the Soviets were willing to hold out the same kind of reformism for its satellites. Events in Hungary in 1956, Czechoslovakia in 1968, and Poland in 1970 all indicate that the Soviet Union does not view its portion of the European empire as party to the reform occurring in Soviet life. In part this is simply a function of a fear that social change in Eastern Europe is beyond control, and in part reflects the fact that the Soviet Union comes from a totalitarian background, whereas most East European nations come from less restrictive and sometimes democratic backgrounds. Nor is this phenomena particularly unique in European history; England evolved as a major democratic force during the nineteenth century at the very time it was massacring Zulus, dominating trade with Latin America, and colonizing Southeast Asia. The fact is that colonialist behavior or imperialist behavior does not always reflect precisely the character of the state machinery of the cosmopolitan state. Therefore, the incongruity between the softening up of the Soviets from within while the hardening up process continues from without remains consistent with the history of dominant nations throughout history.

The word "revolution" with respect to current events in the Soviet political hierarchy might seem to be exaggerated. For those who view the word as a concept akin to revelation and redemption, this would be the case. However, in a world of political lag, of slow growth in administrative norms, the transformation from autocracy to technocracy is of considerable value. It illustrates the limits and even the reversibility of Lord Acton's famous dictum. For if "power corrupts, and absolute power corrupts absolutely," the interesting question from the present viewpoint is the possibility of moving from absolute power to limited power. The Soviets have been at the abyss twice: with Hitlerism from the outside and Stalinism on the inside, they have seen the future, decided that while it worked, the principle of socialist survival is itself insufficient either to define the goals of a mass society or to delimit the immediate policies of that society.

What the Soviet Union has really demonstrated is that the power of nationalism is far greater than the power of socialism, and the power of a Russian is far greater than the power of a worker. That nationalism should turn out to be more operational than internationalism, and that the ethnic factor should be more decisive than the class factor. has had a jarring impact within the Soviet Union, not because of the uniqueness of the situation—quite the contrary: this is the case throughout the whole world—but rather because it is at odds with classic socialist ideology, which places preeminence on the brotherhood of working men, wherever they may live. In a sense, therefore, the current malaise within the Soviet Union is not over the exceptionalist features of that nation, but, quite the reverse, its ordinariness in the light of world history. That is to say the Soviets like the Americans have not delivered on the promise of mass democracy—an even more serious problem for the Russian Communists since their ideology does not permit any real options to such egalitarianism. Thus, the Soviet Union stands at a crossroad: it can either promote greater political freedom as a stimulus to higher economic production or scale down its economic goals to suit its political framework. Whatever the results, the current absence of isomorphism between Soviet politics and economics weakens its international posture no less than its internal possibilities.

7

The United States, the Soviet Union, and the Third World: Triad in Turmoil

Economic change and development are taking place throughout the world at a dizzying pace. Everywhere old institutions and values are being eroded and shattered while new ones are being erected in their place—and the economic factor is ever present. Once proud, England and France are relegated to a "second-place" position because they have not been able to keep pace with the United States and Russia in economic development. In the United States social issues such as alienation, status-seeking, conformity, leisure, confrontation, mass society, and the like, are all associated with economic changes. The values of the society of scarcity are giving way to the values of the society of affluence, and the emergence of achievement conflicts reflect these changes. The rise of Soviet Russia to its position as a world superpower is the product of its fantastic economic growth over a period of fifty years. But even this may be only transitory, for the wind from the East—the wind that tells of the beginning of the biggest economic push in the history of the world among the Asian-African nations—foretells a new shift in the center of economic gravity, and a realignment of political power. In those under-developed nations just entering upon their era of modernization and economic development, traditional patterns of culture are being destroyed under the grindstone of economic change. But old traditions do not die gracefully; and they in turn try to hold back and destroy the enemy, change. But it is hopeless. The fuse of economic change has been ignited and explosion must inevitably follow. But meanwhile there is toil and turmoil.

Freedom versus slavery, democracy versus totalitarianism—these are the terms in which economic issues are couched. The conflict may be between capitalism and socialism, or between Chinese Maoism and Soviet Revisionism, or between white and colored peoples, but always the undercurrent of economic issues can be discerned. In this chapter we shall attempt to gain some understanding of the influence upon institutions and individuals and how the latter in turn affect economic change.

CLASSIFYING SOCIAL SYSTEMS

Of the many ways in which socioeconomic systems have been classified, three seem to present dimensions that are most significant to an understanding of what is taking place in the world today. One way in which we can distinguish between economic systems is in terms of how economic decisions are made. The actual economic systems functioning throughout the world are a mixture of three types: traditional, market, and command economies.

Traditional economies are those where economic activity is embedded within a ritualistic and religious framework. All contemporary primitive peoples and many underdeveloped economies are basically of this type. Economic life is circular with no progress or change. Natural phenomena of some sort or other may occasion a retrogression in well-being, and at other times some improvement, but the form of economic life remains constant.[1] The economic role of the individual is rigidly determined by hereditary factors such as caste, sex, age, and there is no such thing as upward mobility. Every type of economic behavior—consumption, savings, taxes, tribute, investment—is determined by inherited culture and unquestioned custom. In the tradition-directed economy, economic progress has little meaning, and although people may spend most of their time in economic activity just to garner a meager existence, economic behavior is seen to be primarily religious behavior; and if it is done correctly the people are pleased. By and large this is the state of affairs in the vast and populous areas of the Third World. But the spark of economic change has been ignited, largely through the impact of relationships with the First and Second Worlds, and mainly as a consequence of the effects of imperialist expansion and penetration by the West.

Command economies are those in which economic decisions are made

1. See Daniel Lerner, *The Passing of Traditional Society: Modernizing the Middle East.* Glencoe, Ill.: The Free Press, 1958.

by a central authority. These are societies which have a conscious purpose, be it political, military, economic, or social, and the central authority organizes the economy in such a way as to maximize the possibility of achieving its goal or goals. Command economies are largely identified with the Second World, for example, the Soviet bloc, China, and Cuba. The goals of these societies may be manifold, for example, the achievement of communism, political power in international affairs, military supremacy; but the power to bend the economy toward these needs, to the extent that it is possible, rests with a central authority. Unlike traditional economies, command economies facilitate change. They force it—through economic policies that determine, in accordance with the planner's requirements, what the level of consumption, savings, investment, and taxation shall be. Command economies operate on the principle that the social welfare is best determined by central planners and that, if the population is left to its own devices, change-resistant custom will take over and progress will be stifled. However, central authorities do not have carte blanche, for not only must they take account of tradition even when they are attempting to destroy it, but they are also the victims of the new customs and mores which they create in the process of change that they have instituted. When we deal with Soviet society the importance of this factor will be manifest.

Market economies ideally optimize economic welfare and development without any central direction whatsoever. Individuals, striving to maximize their economic welfare, respond to a system of prices which is in itself the result of their interaction. The market economy largely exists in the First World. In brief outline form, this system works in dealing with the major economic problems in the following ways. *Consumer Sovereignty:* In the market economy the consumer is king. Whatever is produced is done so in response to or in anticipation of consumer demand, since the only way in which the producer can maximize his own position is by selling his wares to the consuming population. *Efficiency in Production:* Competition between producers ensures that the most efficient supply the consumer market since only they will be able to provide goods cheaply. The consumers, in maximizing their economic welfare, purchase only at the lowest available price. *Technological Innovation:* Since producers can improve their economic position by expanding their market, each producer will be in constant competition with every other one. Seeking to expand one's market can be accomplished only by reducing prices (price competition), and this can be achieved only by reducing production costs via technological innovation. The system, then, has a built-in force which generates motivation for technological change and development. *Equity in Income Distribution:* Those whose services or products are in strongest demand by the consuming or producing population receive the highest prices for their labor power or goods. The market system provides for an automatic mechanism by which income is distributed (unequally) in accordance with the social evaluation of the benefits of income received to society as a whole. *Full Employment:* Should there be an outbreak of unemployment for any reason whatsoever, for example, displacement via the introduction of machinery or errors in judging the market on the part of employers, automatic forces are set into motion to re-establish full employment. For instance, there might be an increase in demand resulting from lowering prices based upon an increase in productivity from technological innovation. Further, competition between workers, who must be employed for their own survival, may lower wage levels to a point where it becomes profitable for employers to use them. Finally, labor and capital can shift from low demand to high demand where they may once again be employed.

Since we are dealing with the United States as predominantly a market economy and the leader of the First World it is important to note the underlying conditions which are necessary to make this system a smooth-functioning apparatus. The most important of these conditions is competition. Any interference with free competition between economic units will defeat the system's ability to provide automatically the advantages described above. A corollary of this condition is an absence of monopoly. No firm or group of firms nor any group of laborers may be powerful enough to be able to fix prices by virtue of their control of a necessary good or service.

Rapid and smooth shifts of labor and capital must be possible from one industry to another and from one area to another. Anything which interferes with such movement (for instance, the desire to stay in a given community, or hindrance to the entry of new firms into an industry) will tend to prevent full employment and the optimal allocation of resources. People are motivated by material well-being, by economic gain. Obviously, to the extent that they are not, the entire First World mechanism breaks down since then economic inducements to action become meaningless; or at the very least seriously compromised as a basis for allocation of goods and services.

DIGRESSION ON DETERMINISM

The significance of economic life in determining the nature of all other aspects of social and individual behavior has been the subject of much debate in the social sciences. For a number of reasons, the idea of economic determinism—that is, the notion that economic life has primacy and works independently of our will in the determination of social and individual behavior—exercised a great deal of influence in intellectual circles from the late eighteenth to the early twentieth century. The reasons for this orientation may be summed up as follows: The rise of secularism brought forth the need for non-religious explanations of human behavior and institutions. Since economic affairs are the sine qua non of biological existence, the fundamental nature of economic life seemed self-evident. The replacement of one monistic orientation (religion) by another (economics) was intellectually attractive. A unifying center of gravity was preserved. The independent influence of the economy upon social life was in fact more pronounced during these years than at any other period in the previous history of the Western world. This was the period of the Industrial Revolution and the rise of the market economy. Economic change was taking place at a pace never before experienced, and the staid, traditional system that existed before was being shaken to its roots. Since in a market economy (in contrast to the other two types) military or other non-economic sources of control over economic change were relatively weak until the present century, it is patently true that there is more economic determinism under this system than under others. But if the First World operationalizes economic factors, the Second World ideologizes such factors.

Classifying economic systems according to the manner in which economic decisions are made does not provide a dynamic model with which to explain the process of change from one social system to another. We turn now to the system developed by Karl Marx, who did construct a dynamic model and whose work is of great significance in the history of social science, since it was he more than anyone else who emphasized the interdependence and interrelationship between the economy and other aspects of social and individual life.

Marx posited three major factors underlying and determining the form of any socioeconomic system and socioeconomic change. These he called forces of production, relations of production, and class conflict.

The first is equivalent to productivity and is based upon changing technology. The second describes a socioeconomic system in terms of the relations of persons and groups to ownership of the means of production. For example, in the system of slavery, relations of production are those of master and slave in which the masters own all means of production including both land and slaves. Class conflict refers to the struggle between various classes over the distribution of economic output as well as over control of the means of production themselves. Class conflict takes both economic and political forms. Thus, in First World countries, class conflict exists on the economic level, for example, in union strikes and collective bargaining, and also in the political sphere as the labor movement attempts to gain its goals via parliamentary action.

According to Marx, the forces of production are constantly increasing throughout history—more or less rapidly depending upon the socioeconomic system itself. Productivity, or output per man per unit time, moves steadily upward. Different socioeconomic systems (relations of production) are harmonious with different levels of development of the productive forces. As such forces of production develop within any existing socioeconomic system, that system becomes less viable as a means of maintaining stability and development. Existing relations of production are incapable of incorporating increasing productive power. Crises ensue and class conflict sharpens as the beneficiaries of the existing system attempt to hold back change in the relations of production which will displace them and put new groups into the seats of economic power.

Marx projected five basic social systems in the process of socioeconomic development. They are primitive communism, slavery, feudalism, capitalism, and communism. In the beginning, the forces of production are so little developed that cooperation in economic activity is necessary for survival. A division of society into economic classes whereby some groups receive a share of the social output merely by virtue of the fact that they own the means of production is impossible. The low level of productivity precludes the possibility of such a class extracting surplus from a non-owning producing class. A classless society, primitive communism, is necessary under such conditions. Ultimately, however, productivity does rise to levels where the division of society into classes is possible. The three intermediate economic systems between primitive communism and advanced communism are the forms that such societies take. Basically, Marx held that in each of these societies the class that owns the means of production uses the power derived from such ownership to extract for itself the entire surplus production over and above the subsistence needs of the producing class.[2] In the slave system this process is obvious. The slave owner returns to the slave the bare means of subsistence and appropriates to himself everything else that slaves produce. In essence Marx felt that the same process was also taking place in the capitalist system, except that it was veiled by the wages system. Marx held the freedom of workers to be illusory in the sense that workers are compelled to work for the capitalist in order to survive. In the communist society, the surplus above agreed-upon subsistence levels, instead of going to an owning class, is invested for the public good.

Since Marx did most of his detailed and concrete studies about the development and decline of capitalism, it might be well to take his analysis of this process as an illustration of how the disharmony between developing forces of production and existing relations of production arises and causes a change in socioeconomic systems. Capitalism, according to Marx, is a system which is characterized by increasing polarization of society into two classes (there may be many intermediate groups but their significance is held to be relatively unimportant). These classes are the capitalist class, the owners of the means of production, and the working class, who, precisely because they own no means of production, are compelled to hire themselves out to the capitalist class for wages. All feudal and religious and traditional restrictions upon the use of the property owned by the capitalists have been shattered, and the naked economic drive for profits and accumulation pushes the development of the forces of production forward to previously undreamed-of heights. Technological development is unchained. In this respect Marx held capitalism to be an enormous step forward in the progress of mankind.

In the process of this development of the productive forces, two phe-

2. One of the great conceptual difficulties in the Marxian system derives from the fact that Marx assumed that subsistence itself was determined by the level of development of the productive forces so that the owning class could be extracting the entire surplus above subsistence while the subsistence level itself was "rising" absolutely. Subsistence is a cultural-psychological phenomenon. The television set, for example, is part of the subsistence level of the modern American family.

nomena are taking place which spell the ultimate doom of the system. On the one hand, industrialization and mechanization greatly increase the division of labor in society. The interdependence and complexity of the economy grows rapidly. Marx held that it would be virtually miraculous if such an intricately interrelated economy could be stabilized on the basis of individual capitalists making individual decisions about what to do with their businesses. Marx called this situation "anarchy of production" and indicated that the chronic breakdowns in the system would tend to become increasingly severe as the economy became more complex. This growing contradiction between socialization of the economy and private ownership must inevitably be resolved by the socialization of the means of production. Further, the increase in size and concentration of the working class as capitalism develops is creating the force that compels the resolution of the contradiction. The increasing concentration of the working class in large-scale industry facilitates the formation of unions as workers strive to maintain and increase their share of the economic product and to defend themselves against the effects of periodic economic crises. Ultimately, the working class develops a political point of view, and its leadership realizes that only a transformation of capitalism into socialism and the establishment of a planned economy can deal with the problems facing them. Class conflict now takes political form, and eventually power is transferred from the capitalist class to the working class and the means of production expropriated and socialized. Since it is always true that the ownership of means of production requires the owner to plan for the disposition of what he owns, the social ownership of the means of production requires over-all economic planning, since this is the only rational way in which the complex economy created by capitalism can be stabilized and its development brought to service society as a whole.

While there is much to criticize in Marx's examination of the development of capitalism, the development of the Welfare State in Europe and the New Deal in the United States in response to the deep economic crisis of the interwar period verifies Marx's prediction that increased economic planning would be necessary as the capitalist system developed. Marx believed in the primacy of the economic factor in the determination of individual and group behavior, but he was also cognizant of the interaction between economic and non-economic forces in social development. He believed that the human being was primarily a product of his environment and that the economic environment was of particular significance. Thus, the selfish and competitive aspects of capitalism tended to create a selfish and competitive human nature. At the same time, the need for cooperation on the part of the working class in trade unionism provided an economic basis for cooperation. Radicalism would be more characteristic of the working class because it needed to change the system, whereas conservatism would be the characteristic attitude of the capitalist class. Sociological research in recent years has tended to raise doubts about this.[3] Yet, even Marx's severest critics admit the desire for private property is itself a function of the system and not of human nature. Marx considered the entire history of society from slavery through capitalism as an age of barbarism in which man exploited man. Civilization would come into existence only with the advent of communism, when such exploitation would be ended and man would cooperate with man in the exploitation of nature. Under this system for the first time, cooperative, humanistic man would emerge.

Marx divided communism into two stages which have come to be called socialism and communism. The ultimate stage, communism, would function according to the principle "from each according to his abilities, to each according to his needs." Since people's needs differ, this represents the only system of true equity. Under communism all status distinctions between mental and physical labor would be eliminated, as well as distinctions between rural and urban life. In other words, whatever human problems may exist under communism, there would be none stemming from scarcity and class distinctions. In order for the utopia to be possible, two conditions would be necessary. One is an economy of abundance based on a very high level of technological development, so that not only will goods be available for distribution according to need, but also machines will have eliminated menial labor. The second is bringing into being a new "communist man," so that when goods are distributed "free," people will not hoard them for resale as capitalist man presumably might. The first stage of communism, socialism, is the system which aims at paving the way for this transition by harnessing economic resources inherited from capitalism for the big technological push, and creating the cooperative institutions in a social-

3. Concerning working-class conservatism, consider the works of Seymour Martin Lipset, *Political Man: The Social Basis of Politics.* Garden City, N.Y.: Doubleday, 1970; and John C. Leggett, *Class, Race and Labor: Working Class Consciousness in Detroit.* New York: Oxford University Press, 1968.

ized economy for the transformation of human nature.[4] The socialist economy works on the principle of "to each according to his work," which is considered to be the only way in which capitalist human nature turned socialist can be induced to exert itself for economic development. When we discuss the Soviet Union in the next section we shall see how a society which considers itself to be at the socialist stage is facing these issues and what sorts of problems have arisen in the Second World as a result of the uncritical acceptance of the Marxian model.

UNDERDEVELOPED AND ADVANCED ECONOMIES

Socioeconomic systems can be classified according to level of economic development. This involves lumping together nations of very different per capita income—Venezuela, whose per capita income is about $500, with Burma, whose per capita income is $60, as underdeveloped; the United States, per capita income about $3000, with Western Europe, per capita income about $1000, as advanced. Yet in terms of the level of industrialization, economic independence, composition of work force, and types of problems and aspirations, Venezuela is in fact closer to Burma than it is to Western Europe. In a nutshell, the problem of underdeveloped economies seeking development is how to mobilize their resources of land, labor, and capital for investment in industrialization and diversification. If the population in these countries is all working in agriculture and merely eking out a subsistence at low levels, how shall people be made available for building of steel mills, electric power plants, and so on? The answer, in simplest terms, must be either that some means must be found to increase productivity while living standards are held relatively constant (an increase in agricultural productivity with living standards held constant would permit a proportionate number of peasants to be drawn off into industry), or that living standards must be forced even below their already miserable levels so that a nonagricultural labor force may be sustained. If an increase in agricultural productivity is simply eaten up in higher living standards for the peasantry, then no industrialization is possible. An intermediate alternative

4. On this, see John H. Kautsky, "The Appeal of Communist Models in Underdeveloped Countries," in *Developing Nations: Quest for a Model,* edited by Willard A. Beling and George O. Totten. New York: Van Nostrand Reinhold Co., 1970, pp. 101–15.

is that living standards shall not be permitted to rise as rapidly as productivity, with the surplus going into industrialization. This involves the problem of how the savings that are required for investment can be created among people already on the brink of starvation.

Standing in the way of achieving this goal are a host of economic, social, and political problems. Most Third World nations are not politically unified, having been carved out by former imperialist powers. Many of them are made up of a number of traditional tribal societies so that not only tradition stands in the way of national economic mobilization but tribal rivalries as well. Most of them have distorted "one-crop" economies as remnants of their colonial or semi-colonial period so that whatever revenues the government is able to collect from exports for social programs are constantly threatened by vagaries in the international market as well as by overseas political blackmail. This fear of external control is a major reason why diversification is an important goal for Third World countries.

Underdeveloped nations have difficulty industrializing for several reasons: (1) increases in productivity are swallowed up by maintenance of the living standards of an increasing population, and, in fact, rapid development is necessary just to maintain the existing standards; (2) it is difficult to find qualified, trained, and skilled personnel, while illiteracy is common; (3) tax collection is difficult because there is no agency to do it, which means there is no forced savings and no social investment; (4) the distribution of income is unequal so that a small number of people with high incomes, such as landowners, drain the surplus and live in luxurious consumption, virtually immune from taxation because of political influence; (5) finally, the leadership of these nations must contend with a traditional peasant culture suspicious and resistant to change. Therefore, if development is to take place it must come on the basis of a many-pronged attack on these problems simultaneously. It can hardly be doubted that this will involve a great deal of centralized direction in the form of a high degree of economic socialization. Indeed, the leading figures of the world-wide revolution of the underdeveloped nations are professed socialists of one sort or another.

Advanced socioeconomic systems are those that, due to high levels of industrialization and the ability to employ advanced technology, have crossed the line from mass poverty. For the first time in history, the majority of the population of these nations do not have to work long hours to provide themselves with the bare necessities of life. It is cer-

tainly not subjective to note that this fundamental shift in life has occurred in the twentieth century for the nations of Western Europe, the
North American continent, the Soviet Union, Japan, and a few other
countries. We are the witnesses of one of the most profound transitions
in the history of mankind. How the world handles the problems raised
by this change is an issue of the greatest importance. Among the problems raised by this transition, we might list seven that appear to be the
most striking:

(1) The major mass religions and ideological systems developed in
history were, in one form or another, responses to the needs, problems, and anxieties of populations in a condition of poverty and unend-
ing toil for physical survival. These deeply ingrained values come into
conflict with new ways of life created by developing affluence.

(2) The shortening of the work day and work week via the effects of
technological innovation and the prospect of this trend continuing create
problems in connection with the functions of work itself. The adjustment to increased leisure is a difficult one, and is accompanied by deep
personal anxieties. As Freud noted, work is valuable for the opportunity
it and the human relations connected with it provide for a considerable
discharge of libidinal component impulses, narcissistic, aggressive and
even erotic. Work is indispensable for subsistence and justifies existence
in society.[5] The breakdown of this balance becomes a major problem.

(3) Highly industrialized economies require extensive bureaucracies
in order that they may function. The majority of individuals, with their
television sets and automobiles, are confronted with a sense of powerlessness in decision-making. Further, the high level of technological
development, based as it is on modern science, tends also to separate
the society into experts and mass. The extreme specialization and division of labor of such societies implies that the individual is just a cog
in a big societal machine and partly dependent upon those who are running the big machine for his well-being. The development of science and
technology in the means of communication and manipulation of people
increasingly reduces the stature of the individual as the maker of his own
destiny. All these phenomena add up to the problem of "alienation,"
the sense of loss of power, significance, and freedom. It also produces
mass political movements which seek to resolve such alienation—such
as fascism and communism.

5. See Sigmund Freud, *Civilization and Its Discontents*. London: Hogarth Press,
1957.

(4) The affluent society brings with it the massification of former symbols of status. This breakdown in means of status differentiation creates the problem of "status anxiety" and leads to the hysterical, and quite often ridiculous, chase for new status symbols. The psychological tensions associated with this phenomenon have been too well popularized to require repetition.

(5) The increased ability of individuals to provide for their own economic needs in advanced economies has also led to the breakdown of communalism in social life and the rise of privatization, a painful experience for those still influenced by the older value systems. The same is true for the shift in national character from "inner-directed" to "other-directed." The conflict in the values of older and newer generations in our time is particularly severe on this account.[6]

(6) Imbalance in the economic development of affluent societies also presents interesting and difficult problems. The concentration of population in urban and metropolitan areas in response to economic concentration has created chaotic conditions in such areas as housing, transportation, education, sanitation, and the like. Further, the taste for consumer goods of the sort provided en masse in the affluent society has whetted the appetite for still more of the same, and has affected the ability of the society to care for its social needs.[7] This is as true in the Soviet Union as it is in the United States. In the United States it boils down to an unwillingness of the population to support increased taxation—necessary if the resources for social expenditure are to be made available to all sectors; in the Soviet Union, even in the command economy led by the Communist Party, the leadership must respond to the demands of the population for more consumer goods, since these have become important work incentives. One of the effects of this pressure in the Soviet Union is that it tends to slow down the rate of growth of the economy as more resources must be thrown into consumer goods' production and are therefore not available for investment.

(7) Finally, the highly advanced economies of the First and Second Worlds have the industrial-technological-scientific capacity to create and use nuclear energy for constructive or destructive purposes. How they will manage this power is of vital concern to the entire world. But this

6. See David Riesman, *The Lonely Crowd: A Study of the Changing American Character*. Garden City, N.Y.: Doubleday, 1950.
7. See John Kenneth Galbraith, *The Affluent Society*. Boston: Houghton Mifflin, 1960.

monopoly on hardware is itself a crucial variable in the triad of world turmoil.

These and other problems stemming from the transition to highly industrialized mass-consumption societies may very well be the growing pains of societies in transition, and the new conditions of affluence may merely require a period of adjustment until balanced adaptation takes place. They may be short-run phenomena. But as the famous economist, Lord Keynes put it: "In the long run we are all dead." But it is also true that utopia of economic plenty for all can now be realistically envisioned for the first time in history—as a matter for present examination.

PRIMARY, SECONDARY, AND TERTIARY ECONOMIES

A socially significant feature of societies in the process of development is the changing occupational distribution of the work force and the changing composition of economic output. The Australian economist, Colin Clark, has shown that economies change in specific ways as development takes place. Economies at a low level of per capita income have their labor force and output largely concentrated in what he has termed "primary" industries, that is, primarily agriculture, fishing, and hunting. As development continues and productivity increases, the percentage of the economy's resources devoted to primary industries declines and that of secondary industries—manufacturing, mining, electric power production, building, and construction—rises. Development brings with it a shift to "tertiary" industries, largely services, finance, recreation, and education.[8] These changes are exactly analogous to what takes place in family expenditures as income rises. Families with low incomes spend the largest part of their money on food. As incomes increase, the proportionate share of family funds going to food declines rapidly. Thus, in underdeveloped countries about 70 per cent of income goes for food alone, while in the United States this figure is about 20 per cent.

This way of looking at change is important because it indicates that a developing economy, especially one that is moving rapidly, is going to have severe social problems associated with shifting occupational needs.

8. See Colin Clark, *The Conditions of Economic Progress.* New York: Macmillan Co., 1960.

A rapidly shifting occupational pattern is going to upset status relationships, the pattern of income distribution, and the sociopsychological correlates and values of previously dominant types of work. In turn, these factors become obstacles to be overcome in the process of rapid economic change. In a society such as that of the Soviet Union, for example, the massive movement of peasants and women into the industrial work force during the early 1930's created grave difficulties in industry because the style of life of an economy which was essentially "primary" was not suited to the secondary economy which was being created. Similarly, in the United States at the present, the effects of the shift to tertiary occupations is having a most profound effect. Automation is leading to the obsolescence of formerly skilled craftsmen and to concomitant losses in status and shifts in the distribution of income. The trade-union movement is losing its significance because of its heavy concentration among blue-collar manufacturing employees whose proportionate share of the labor force is declining in favor of white-collar and service workers. On the other hand the incomes of teachers, scientists, and others associated with tertiary occupations are growing. The crisis in education in the United States is the product of shifting occupational requirements, as is the problem of the permanent unemployables who have been thrown upon the economic scrap heap because their skills are no longer required and they cannot or will not be retrained for new occupations. These people and school dropouts whose lack of education makes employment in the new occupations impossible account for a good deal of the poverty and unemployment in the United States. Similarly, as an increasing percentage of the nation's output shifts to tertiary commodities and services, styles of life, national character, and values and attitudes in general change accordingly. Former means of status differentiation, such as differences in dress, housing, education, and the like, are destroyed as productivity in secondary industries level consumption patterns in these basic areas. Problems of leisure, work satisfaction, and mass society surface. The age of economic man is replaced by the age of sociological man.

Changing Economic Systems in Action

The United States is the First World's prime example of an advanced market capitalist society. If we examine the American economy in terms of its own standards and values, or in terms of the "rationale" of such a system, it becomes a study in contrasts and contradictions.

The United States has by far the highest average per capita income in the world, yet it is relatively unequally distributed, and pockets of poverty, relative to the average American standard of living, are widespread. The growth of the American economy has projected it to the first position in world economies, yet it is having great difficulty maintaining a growth rate consonant with full employment. A significant and growing unemployment problem plagues the American economy. The United States is the richest nation in the world in its production of consumer goods and services, yet it is far behind much poorer economies in the provision of social services. The American economy is the possessor and user of the most advanced technological and scientific achievements—but much of this is the by-product of governmental military needs during World War II and the Cold War, rather than of the vigor of the capitalist economy per se. The United States ideologically is the foremost defender of the ideals of the free competitive market economy, yet it has rapidly been moving away from this position in practice. A good deal of its advances in recent years can be traced directly to the activity of highly monopolistic industries. Further, its recent prosperity can be traced to high levels of government expenditure, again largely for military and defense purposes.[9]

The Concentration of Economic Power

Five hundred corporations, or less than one-tenth of 1 per cent of all corporations in the United States, produce over two-thirds of the nation's non-agricultural output. And less than 1 per cent of the corporations own some 53 per cent of all of United States major industries' corporate assets. In many major American industries—aluminum, auto, electricity, steel, computers, and the like—a small number of large firms produce virtually the entire output of the industry. The reasons for this concentration of economic power are twofold. On the one hand, bigness is necessary to make possible the utilization of advanced technology, and on the other hand bigness has developed out of a desire for economic power. The consequence of this concentration of economic

9. See Michael Harrington, *The Other America: Poverty in the United States.* New York: Macmillan Co., 1962.

power is that there is no doubt that big business, precisely because of its ability to utilize the advantages of large-scale production, has been the major force in the development of America's affluent society. But in the process it has also been responsible for what some consider to be very harmful distortions in American values.

MONOPOLISTIC COMPETITION AND AMERICAN VALUES

In the ideal competitive model of the market capitalist economy, competition via price reduction leads to the elimination of the least efficient firms from an industry so that the consumer purchases his products only from the most efficient, low-cost firms at the lowest prices. But where an industry is dominated by a few giant corporations, such competition is manifestly impossible. Because of the huge assets available to each of the firms, price reductions can hardly be counted upon to drive any one out of the industry. They can result only in lowered profits for all concerned. Therefore, the few large firms in an industry have been driven by considerations for their own welfare to collusive agreements of various sorts to eliminate competition in prices.

If price competition is not feasible, other forms of competition are. These forms are discussed under the heading "monopolistic competition" by economists. Basically, in the area of consumer products, this competition takes the form of each firm attempting to differentiate its products from those of the other firms in the industry via advertising, packaging, styling, or some other superficial means—since all firms are equally capable of producing the basic product itself.

One of the effects of the increase in concentration of economic power has been the sharp increase in advertising by large corporations. By 1970, for example, total annual advertising expenditures are over $12 billion. To convince the population of the importance of their products to their health, status, sexual attraction, and so forth, the advertising agencies of the large corporations utilize the latest scientific achievements in the area of mass influence and manipulation.

Largely as a result of this, the American people in the post-World War II period have become extremely "goods" conscious, strongly oriented toward the consumption of the products of large private corporations.

PROBLEMS OF THE AFFLUENT SOCIETY

The felicitous phrase "social imbalance" is from *The Affluent Society*, and refers to the growing discrepancy between the amassing of privately produced goods by Americans and the development of the social services needed to make their use comfortable.

> The family which takes its mauve and cerise, air conditioned, power steered and power braked automobile out for a tour passes through cities that are badly paved, made hideous by litter, blighted buildings, billboards, and posts for wires that should have long since been put underground. They pass on into a countryside that has been rendered largely invisible by commercial art. (The goods which the latter advertise have an absolute priority in our value system. Such aesthetic considerations as a view of the countryside accordingly come second. On such matters we are consistent.) They picnic on exquisitely packaged food from a portable icebox by a polluted stream and go on to spend the night at a park which is a menace to public health and morals. Just before dozing off on an air mattress, beneath a nylon tent, amid the stench of decaying refuse, they may reflect vaguely on the curious unevenness of their blessings. Is this indeed the American genius? [10]

This value orientation has created a situation where Americans are largely unwilling to support increased taxation for any social purpose except defense, so that even those political figures who might wish to do something about this problem find it impolitic to press for it. The notion that American interests are better served if Americans spend money for their own consumption rather than hand it over to the government for public expenditures is very deeply entrenched. Yet the contradiction between this attitude and the desire for better schools for children, for example, is not readily appreciated.

Most middle-class Americans are inclined to underestimate the extent of poverty in the country. The majority of Americans have crossed the poverty boundary since the Great Depression, and that is why the description "affluent society" is an apt one. But it also dulls the consciousness of the scale of poverty in existence. New patterns of living (suburbia) have made the low-income population increasingly invisible

10. John Kenneth Galbraith, *The Affluent Society*, p. 253.

to the middle classes, who by-pass areas of urban blight in commuter trains that bring them almost directly into their newly air conditioned offices. Many Americans have been taken in by their own films and television programs which invariably depict the "typical" American family. And the passage of time has tended to erase from memory the years before World War II when the majority of today's middle class were part of poverty-stricken families themselves. The compassion for the poor which forced the reforms of the New Deal has been increasingly replaced by a tendency to blame the poor themselves for their condition.

The fact is that poverty is still extensive. Depending upon what income is taken as a level below which we wish to consider a family as living in poverty ($2500 to $3500 for an urban family of four), the number of persons in this condition ranges from 32 million to 50 million, or roughly from 19 per cent to 25 per cent of the American population as we enter the 'seventies. A good deal of this poverty is directly due to rapid technological changes in the American economy that have created a growing pool of unemployed and supernumeraries with inadequate education and training. Much is due to discrimination against minority groups such as Negroes, Puerto Ricans, Chicanos, and others. Inadequate social security provisions for the growing population over sixty-five years of age is yet another factor. This has created the basis of an American "underclass" quite distinct from the American "working class."

The onset of the age of automation in America has also brought with it many problems to accompany its blessings. In many industries, such as mining, automobile, chemical, railroad, and others, the labor force required to meet the existing demand for their products has been sharply reduced. This problem is closely associated with the lagging rate of overall growth of the American economy, as well as with the inadequate social policies for aiding the unemployed to re-establish themselves.

During the 'sixties the American economy grew at a rate of approximately 2 per cent to 3 per cent per year. It has been estimated that a rate of at least 5 per cent would be necessary to absorb the increase in the number of Americans seeking to be employed. Thus, the number of unemployed has been steadily growing. The recession of 1954 produced 4 million unemployed, but the boom of 1955–57 reduced unemployment barely below 3 million. Then, the recession of 1958 created an unemployment of about 5 million, and the subsequent recovery still left it at about 4 million. The recession of 1961 produced unemployment among 6 million, and the latter recovery still left it hovering about the 5 million mark. The same pattern seems to obtain in the recession of 1970, with an additional rise in *under*employment as well as *un*employment.

The impetus needed to produce the kind of expansive boom that would re-create conditions of full employment seems to be missing in the United States economy, and, should the trend continue, this country may be in for severe social problems attendant upon conditions of high unemployment levels. Another facet of the lagging rate of growth is that in the United States' competition with the Soviet Union the gap between the two is rapidly being closed in the face of the Soviet's rate of growth of somewhere around 7 per cent per annum.

Let us therefore turn to Soviet society directly and evaluate its own performance at the socioeconomic level.

THE INDUSTRIALIZATION OF THE SOVIET UNION

The economy of the Soviet Union is the world's prime example of an advanced command socialist economy. In the years since over-all economic planning was initiated in 1928, its rate of growth has been unprecedented in economic history. Because of this, the Soviet Union's mode of development has been particularly attractive to those under-developed nations seeking early achievement of affluence and power in the modern world. Unfortunately, they often fail to appreciate properly the bitter price paid by the Soviet citizenry for this development, in severely restricted living standards, in the massive upheaval in social structure and institutions, and in foregoing various democratic rights.

At the present time the Soviet Union also faces problems in maintaining its growth rate, some of which are analogous to those experienced in the United States, and some of which are peculiar to its own development. Furthermore, in terms of the anticipated transition to communism, many features of Soviet development have created attitudes and values that have presented new obstacles to that movement. Just as in the American economy, economic development in the Soviet Union brought with it many economic benefits as well as accompanying social problems.

From 1928 to 1940, the Soviet economic leadership produced a shift of its labor force into industrial occupations, a movement that took thirty to sixty years in most of the Western capitalist nations. The key forces in this development were the collectivization of agriculture, the large-scale utilization of female labor, and strict control of consumption and a high level of public investment in industry.

The collectivization of agriculture in the Soviet Union between 1928 and 1937 released large numbers of peasants for industrial occupations.[11] By merging small farms into larger units, the Soviet agricultural community was able to maximize the limited mechanical and scientific resources available to increase agricultural output and to use fewer workers per acre. The marketable surplus thus obtained could be used by the government to provide subsistence for the growing industrial labor force. The collectivization program also increased the control of the planners over agriculture, eliminated the growing politicoeconomic power of wealthier peasants whose number was increasing during the 1920's, and reinforced ideological commitment to socialization.[12]

During the period of the Soviet industrial revolution, the agricultural segment of the labor force dropped from about 85 per cent to about 60 per cent of the total labor force. The absolute number of persons in agriculture declined from 70 to 60 million. (By the mid-1960's these figures were 48 and 50 million, respectively.) Meanwhile, the non-agricultural labor force increased from 1928 to 1940 at a rate of about 8.7 per cent per annum, a rate above the maximum rate in American economic history of 5.1 per cent in the decade between 1840 and 1850. By restructuring the agricultural economy, by underpricing them in relation to demand, the Soviet planners were able to produce "free"—except for the costs involved in collectivization itself—a considerable surplus of labor that could be diverted into industrial pursuits.

A second major source of industrial labor came from the wholesale introduction of women into the labor force. Communists have always believed that women's liberation could come about only as a result of

11. A Soviet collective farm is *formally* a cooperative in which farmers merge their land and equipment and in which decisions are made by the farmers themselves. Income is distributed in accordance with an incentive system based upon the individual's contribution to the work. In addition, each farmer is permitted to farm a little private plot of his own. Collective farms today farm about two-thirds of the plowland of the Soviet Union, while state farms— agricultural factories in which the farmers work for wages and, apparently, the truly communistic form—cover the remaining one-third.
12. See Alec Nove, "Soviet Farming: No More Campaigns," *New Society,* Feb. 12, 1970, pp. 262–63.

her achieving economic independence, so this shift corresponded to their ideological orientation as well as to immediate economic requirements. This goal was achieved by structuring the wage system so that it was virtually necessary for the subsistence of the family that the wife should work. In this manner, and through intensive internal propaganda, the percentage of females in the Soviet nonagricultural labor force increased from about 10 per cent in 1928 to some 27 per cent in 1940, and it stands at about 45 per cent today.

Naturally, the result was considerable alteration in child-rearing practices, in cooking, dining, and other housekeeping customs, and in the entire range of attitudes about the relationship of females to males. This change was also made without cost to some other sector of the economy, as in the case of collectivization. However, one must remember that these are one-time changes. Future increases in the labor force, one of the major stumbling blocks to the maintenance of high rates of growth in the Soviet Union, can no longer be obtained by large-scale institutional shifts such as these.[13]

In order to take advantage of developmental possibilities provided by these two programs, the Soviet planners had to guarantee two other conditions: that consumption standards would be held down so that the maximum investment could be made in basic industries; and that such investment actually took place.

Intensive studies made by American scholars on wages and prices in the Soviet economy during the pre-World War II period leave no doubt at all that real wages fell drastically. Even though some of this decline may have been compensated for by increases in communal services, rapid industrialization in the Soviet Union during those years was not reflected in any positive improvements in average living standards. Since 1948, however, living standards have been rising quite rapidly, as the industrialization of the country has begun to pay off.

While international comparisons of living standards are extraordinarily difficult to express precisely, a rough estimate of present day Soviet real per capita income including communal consumption shows it to be about 35 per cent of the Soviet gross national product in comparison with 15 per cent to 20 per cent in the United States. Not only has the

13. On these details of Soviet growth statistics, see Abram Bergson and Simon Kuznets, *Economic Trends in the Soviet Union.* Cambridge, Mass.: Harvard University Press, 1963; and for an earlier, and more optimistic appraisal, Maurice H. Dobb, *Soviet Economic Development Since 1917.* London: Routledge & Kegan Paul, 1948.

total of Soviet investment been higher, but of this total a much larger share has gone into industrialization. In the Soviet Union, this share has been about 45 per cent; in the United States today it is only about 28 per cent. The Soviet rate of industrial growth has been exceptionally high. For the years 1928 to 1937, it has been estimated by American economists that the rate was about 16 per cent per year. For 1945–50, about 20 per cent per year. And in recent years about 10–13 per cent per year. By way of comparison, the average annual rate of growth of industrial production in the United States for the years 1946 to 1957 was 4.3 per cent.[14] Assuming that the Soviet growth rate remains between 7–9 per cent annually, and the United States from 2–4 per cent annually, the Soviet Union should exceed American industrial production in fourteen to thirty-two years, depending on the relative rates. For instance, if Russia maintains a 7 per cent growth rate, and the United States' rate is at 3 per cent, it should take twenty-four years to surpass the United States. At a 9 per cent rate, however, the Soviet Union could exceed United States production (at the 3 per cent rate) after sixteen years. But whether this takes place by the gruesome 1984 or the gloss year 2000, is less important than it is to see Russia as a developing nation.[15]

MARXISM AND SOVIET ECONOMIC DEVELOPMENT

While the Soviet Communist Party has hardly ever let doctrine stand in the way of practical achievement, it is perhaps a tribute to Marx that, in fact, necessity has led the Soviets to function precisely in the way in which he predicted—at least in economic matters. The Soviets consider themselves to be in the first stage of communism. In this system, as we will recall, Marx held that the society would function on the basis of need satisfaction and work performance. In the first years after the revolution, the Soviet Union tended to increase equality in the distribution of income, in large part because in the pre-revolutionary years a good deal of the attraction of communism was in its promise to eliminate inequalities. As long as organizations such as the trade unions had independent

14. Lynn Turgeon, *The Contrasting Economies: A Study of Modern Economic Systems*. Boston: Allyn & Bacon, 1964; for excellent summary comparisons of the economic systems of the United States and the Soviet Union.
15. Robert Sharlet, "The Soviet Union as a Developing Country," *Journal of Developing Areas*, Vol. 2, No. 2, Spring 1968, pp. 270–76.

power in the society, they could influence the Communist Party to accede to their long-felt desires. But for purposes of economic growth, this system did not provide the necessary work incentives.

Consequently, with the advent of the first Five Year Plan in 1928 (the actual beginning of wholesale socialism), an elaborate program of wage and income differentials was instituted to ensure a system of maximum incentives. Studies comparing Soviet and American wages show that for the prewar years inequalities in Soviet wage patterns exceeded those in the United States. Wage differences were based, first, on the social evaluation of type of work—for example, in order to induce people to become coal miners, miners' wages were raised sharply—and, second, on the output produced per person. Thus, those who worked at more necessary occupations as well as those who worked harder were differentially rewarded. Since the vast majority of Soviet labor has always operated in a free labor market, such a system helped the planners to allocate the labor force in accordance with their economic goals. This system certainly worked to help achieve these goals, but it is important to consider to what extent the movement helps subvert development toward creation of the new "communist man"—a question asked with increasing frequency by such "heroic" economies as those of Cuba and China.[16]

PROBLEMS OF THE SOVIET ECONOMY TODAY

The major institutional changes which gave the Soviets a big boost in their economic development have already been made. Today the big pressures are for the increase of productivity by means of the introduction of scientific and technological innovation. This pressure has been doubly felt because of the great manpower losses which the nation suffered during World War II as well as the low birth rates of that period. Consequently, in the 1960's, in order to increase the nonagricultural labor supply, the Soviets have had to institute a program whereby many students are compelled to work for a period between graduating from high school and entering college. Premier Khrushchev has pleaded with the Soviet people to have more children, and subsidies are offered for large families (the decline in family size accom-

16. On this, see Joseph A. Kahl, "The Moral Economy of a Revolutionary Society," *Cuban Communism*, edited by Irving Louis Horowitz. Chicago: Aldine Publishing Co., 1970, pp. 95–116.

panying rising living standards has begun to affect the Soviet Union). But basically, the new technology will have to be relied upon to do the job, and the pressures for its introduction are much greater in the Soviet Union than in the United States. The Soviet problem is shortage of labor rather than unemployment, but it is an equally serious obstacle to achieving national goals. The rise in Soviet living standards in the past decade has also made the Soviet population less willing to work under the austere conditions that produced their industrial revolution. They insist that the Communist Party begin to make good on some of its promises for the better life and are no longer content with visions of a utopian future. To the extent that the leadership is forced to give in to these sentiments—to that extent will the percentage of national output available for investment be decreased. If the high rates of growth are to be maintained, this is a further pressure for the rapid introduction of new technology. Another factor that may slow the Soviet rate of growth is that many of the consumer goods that were largely neglected during the Industrial Revolution and are now most in demand are items that are themselves heavy users of capital, such as housing.

On the favorable side is the fact that in the Soviet Union there are at present few social obstacles to the introduction of automation. Union bureaucrats are not struggling to exclude labor-saving devices, nor are monopolistic corporations quashing innovations to protect previous investments as both do in the United States. While there are certainly dislocations resulting from the displacement of labor by machinery, and while plant managers may be hesitant to push for drastic changes, on the whole the fact that the planned economy is capable of providing full employment is somewhat of a cushion against these problems. The counterweight to this is what Milovan Djilas has called the "new class" in the Soviet Union. This refers to a bureaucracy of the Communist Party, plant managers, and a military, scientific, engineering elite who are able to appropriate for themselves a disproportionate share of the national income. These forces have a vested interest in preventing any sharp institutional changes that might upset their favored apple cart. That there are considerable differences in living levels in the country is hardly to be doubted, and it is understandable that such vested interests attempt to hold back social change. The children of this favored group have better opportunities both as a result of their higher living standards and of the power of their parents, and the dangers of a sharpening elite-mass dichotomy in the country are significant.

In the Soviet Union today discussion about the transition to communism is widespread. To some degree this is a form of propaganda to induce continued exertion on the part of the population to increase output. The proposed procedure seems to be one of gradually placing one commodity after another on the "free" list as production of it reaches the level of "abundance." As production reaches high levels in a particular commodity, its price will be gradually reduced until it approaches zero.[17] So far, this has not yet occurred for any commodity, and it may be that the possibility of doing this may be a long way off. One interesting problem has already occurred in the process. A number of years ago, the Soviet Communist Party began price reductions on bread and announced that bread would be the first item to be distributed free in the nation. What a significant propaganda stroke this would have been in the economic competition of the Cold War had it actually been done! But what happened was that as the price of bread became increasingly lower, it gradually fell below the price of animal feed, and the peasants began to purchase bread to feed to their livestock. Unfortunately, the Soviet productive apparatus had not yet reached the point where they could provide communism for animals too, and very strict punitive measures had to be introduced to prevent this practice. It seems that the transition to communism is going to be much more complex than the more utopian-minded had originally envisioned. A second approach to the transition is to increase gradually the percentage of consumption that is provided socially, but one of the effects of the rising living standard in Soviet Russia, as in the United States in recent years, has been to increase the trend toward "privatization"—to reduce the revolutionary zeal and in other ways to set the population psychologically against communalism.

The competition and differences in incomes that were the product of the rigorous incentive system that was considered necessary to achieve high levels of output in the past have also created attitudes that are not conducive to the cooperation necessary to implement the communist ideal in which people are not rewarded according to their contribution to the society but according to need. In order to cope with this problem, the Soviets have recently begun to make changes in their wage system

17. It should be clear that production always costs something—the resources that go into the production process. It is distribution that is free and people may take as much of the free commodity as they wish. See P. J. F. Wiles, *The Political Economy of Communism*. Cambridge, Mass.: Harvard University Press, 1963.

so as to create greater equality in the distribution of income. Similarly, rising living standards, rather than helping to wipe out differences in attitude toward various types of labor, have instead created a situation where most people desire to do "white-collar" work and disdain manual labor. Since, as has been indicated, the Soviets maintain a free labor market, the economy currently faces a crisis in fulfilling its needs for manual labor. How the Soviet Union will deal with these and many other issues in the future has profound implications for the socioeconomic development of the Third World as a whole.[18]

INDIA AND CHINA

In the postwar surge for development among the Third World nations, none have excited the imagination more than China and India. The basic similarities between these two potential world powers and the different paths of development which they have undertaken are a natural object of discussion by people and nations throughout the world. Both India and China are densely populated in the more habitable parts of their countries. Together their population comprises more than one-third of the world's people, and the population of both is rapidly increasing, with attendant needs to raise per capita incomes. Both began their development at about the same time: India achieved independence in 1948 and the Chinese communists came to power in 1949. Both began with very low average per capita incomes, about $65 per annum. And both nations are rich in untapped natural resources covering large geographical territories.

China's development, under the leadership of the Communist Party, is taking place under rigorous command conditions. The socialization of the Chinese economy has proceeded much more rapidly than did that of the Soviet Union. In this manner, the state has been able to seize control of the land, labor, and capital resources of the country and mobilize them for economic growth. In fact, in terms of institutional changes, China has already gone further than the Soviet Union toward some of the sociological features of a communist society.

One of the key economic facts about densely populated underdeveloped nations is what is called "disguised unemployment." This means

18. See Harry Schwartz, *Russia's Soviet Economy*. Englewood Cliffs, N.J.: Prentice-Hall, 1963.

that in the agricultural economy, the population is so dense (large families on relatively small plots of land) that output would not suffer if some of the population were removed. In fact some economists feel that these excess "hands" are a negative economic force and that their elimination would actually increase output. Such circumstances mean that there is actually a reserve of labor which the society as a whole may put to more productive use if it is able to organize it. As it is they are a drain on the society's economic output.

In non-command economies, the tapping of this type of resource usually awaits the development of industry, which then automatically attracts the excess farm population to the city. But China has made the unique decision to mobilize this excess labor directly. In this manner, even though the capital implements were not yet available to the economy with which these hands could work, China has been able to put them to good use without decreasing the food supply from which they were fed.

China has adopted a severe austerity program to keep consumption levels low so that all surplus productivity can be channeled into industrialization. The rate of investment has been very high—about 22 per cent of total output in recent years—and her industrialization has been proceeding very rapidly.

From 1952 to 1959, industrial production increased at an annual rate of 21.3 per cent, electric power at 28.3 per cent, and steel output 38.7 per cent, while during the same period population increased only 2.4 per cent annually.[19]

Another aspect of the massive socialization of the economy, in line with the Chinese communist's program of radical advance to communism, was the organization of virtually the entire rural population into about 26,000 communes in 1958. These communes were largely self-contained societies producing everything from agricultural products to small-scale industrial commodities (including the famous backyard steel mills). The population of the commune was organized for work on virtually a military basis. And, in the beginning, a large part of consumption was communal in nature, that is, was supplied free by the commune. The commune movement, however, seems to have gone too

19. However, food production increased very little more than the percentage increase in population: food grains at 3.4 per cent and agricultural production at 3.1 per cent annually. See Choh Ming Li, *Economic Development of Communist China: An Appraisal of the First Five Years of Industrialization.* Berkeley: University of California Press, 1959.

far too soon in upsetting established institutions. This, coupled with severe agricultural failures due to natural factors, has led the communist leadership to lower its aims somewhat. On the communes themselves, for example, the percentage of consumption provided socially has dropped from about 80 per cent to 20 per cent and the percentage provided by each family out of its own personal income appears to have risen from 20 per cent to 80 per cent. In other words, the Chinese have found it necessary to re-establish individual work incentives on a large scale. While little is known about Chinese economic progress for recent years, it is a fairly safe guess that agricultural difficulties may have led to a shift in investment in the direction of agriculture—a fact that may have slowed down the rate of industrialization in the mid-1960's.[20]

India's economic development, in contrast to that of China, has proceeded to a larger degree under market conditions, even though the Indian leadership is socialistic. India has tried to preserve not only political democracy but also to maintain the rights of capitalist ownership of means of production. It has tried to operate with the public sector restricted mainly to basic industry of strategic importance for development, public utilities, and to aiding those industries of importance requiring public aid for growth. The development of private enterprise outside these areas is encouraged. India's land reform program has not included large-scale collectivization of agriculture but the redistribution of the lands of many large landowners to the peasantry, along with technical assistance. India's industrialization program has been considerably hampered by its inability to mobilize its resources for development. Unemployment, for example, rose from 5 to 10 million in the decade from 1951 to 1961. Voluntary saving in such a poor country is obviously an unlikely means of restraining consumption. And it has been difficult for India to raise its taxation levels in such a way as to provide large sums for government programs. India, to a much larger extent than China, has depended upon foreign aid to provide its investment margin.[21]

The institutional differences between Indian and Chinese development have meant that Chinese development has been much more rapid

20. See Edgar Snow, *The Other Side of the River: Red China Today*. London: Victor Gollancz, 1963.
21. John Badgley, *Asian Development: Problems and Prognoses,* pp. 20–75. New York: The Free Press, 1970.

than that of India. At least until the 'sixties, China's per capita income increase, by conservative estimates, was more than double that of India's 1.5 per cent. Should India's democratic path prove unable to produce results for the country in the near future, it may very well be that she will be compelled to take up the Soviet method. And, indeed, India's increased reliance upon military mobilization would indicate precisely such a turn toward a command system and away from the free-market system.

Economic Change and Social Democracy

The reciprocal interaction between economic change and social democracy is an important issue of our time. The power that an individual or group has to support the meaningfulness of his participation in the making of social decisions involves his ability to withhold something significantly necessary to the welfare of others in the group. One source of such power is the control over economic resources necessary to the society as a whole or to individuals in the society. Democracy is related to the distribution of power in society. The more concentrated power is, the less democratic is the society. Contrariwise, the more widely and evenly power is distributed, the more democratic that society is likely to be.

This argument implies that the economic circumstances which are optimal for democracy are either those in which a society is made up solely of small property-holders, and the significance of any individual property-holding is roughly equal to that of any other, *or* a completely communistic society where all are equal with respect to property-holding, since no one owns any property and no distinctions are made as to the value to the society of the different forms of labor power.

This association of democracy with economic power is strengthened by even a cursory examination of the historical background of modern democracy. Marxists refer to what they call "bourgeois" democracy to indicate the connection between Western democratic institutions and the struggle of the middle-class property owners for freedom from feudal and mercantilist restrictions during the seventeenth and eighteenth centuries. Much of the ideology of contemporary American democracy stems from the association of a set of political principles with the economic requirements of property owning groups in years prior to the

American Revolution. In a word, political liberty was needed to obtain economic liberty. The American Revolution is a case in point. The cry for liberty arose on the heels of a long period of economic suppression and discrimination. The antagonism to the Navigation Acts, the Stamp, Hat, and Tea Acts, and many others, were ultimately formulated in the slogan: "Taxation without representation is tyranny." And the structuring of political struggles in economic terms has become a basic legacy of the Third World.[22]

The economic development of the United States has been marked by a shift from an economy of small producers to one of large-scale production—from what has been called "family capitalism" to corporate capitalism. In the process, economic power has shifted from individuals to groups. "Town Meeting" democracy has lost its economic base. In this sense, there has been an inevitable loss in meaningful participation in decision-making by individuals qua individuals. And for a long time, the increasing concentration of economic power on the side of the business class without any countervailing influence from the laboring class produced a one-sided distribution of economic, and therefore political, power. Since the 1930's, primarily as a result of the rapid growth of the trade union movement, labor participation has taken a more important part in United States political life, and one may regard this development as an extension of democracy. To the extent that the interest of any individual is represented in the interest of the group, to that extent does the politicoeconomic power of the group make him a meaningful participant in decision-making.

More recently, and this is especially true of the years since World War II, economic changes are bringing into play forces with the contrary effect of reducing democratic participation. Technological changes, the rise of the expert (expertise is an economic power), and the development of forces of manipulation are leading to an elite-mass relationship. The effect upon the labor unions of the changing composition of the labor force is reducing the significance of their power in the political process. This is one of the crucial problems of our time, and it is a good illustration, visible to all of us, of the impact of economic change upon political relationships.

In a socialist economy, the means of production are socially owned. This includes, of course, the means of communication—radio, tele-

22. Richard B. Morris, *The Emerging Nations and the American Revolution.* New York: Harper & Row, 1970, esp. pp. 178–223.

vision, newspapers, and so forth. This last fact is an important issue in the discussion of democracy, and we shall return to it shortly. Clearly, where the means of production are socially owned, the existence of a bureaucratic structure to manage and plan for the disposition of the economic resources of the society is an immediate necessity. This position is taken by the state, and in the Soviet Union, by the Communist Party. Destroying the economic power of the capitalist via socialization, of the peasant via collectivization and of the labor unions by absorption enabled the Communist Party to eliminate effectively the economic basis of political power of these various groups in the society. Thus, while the Soviet Union has many of the formal aspects of democratic participation—elections, a parliament, and the like—these have very little significance in the actual formulation of decisions, especially on the national level. And since no one can get his hands on the means of mass communication, which are all owned by the state, any effective political organization for ends contrary to those of the Communist Party leadership are effectively ruled out.

In tracing through the effects of economic change in the Soviet Union upon political life, one can discern tendencies promoting an increase in democracy as well as anti-democratic tendencies in the United States. Even in a centrally planned command economy the government (read Communist Party in the Soviet Union) does not have carte blanche in the making and carrying through of decisions. There is always a kind of *passive* democracy at work. The population can sabotage the plans of the government by refusing to respond to the incentives offered for cooperation. Therefore, in addition to the use of such force and terror as may be applied, the government must, if it is to be successful in achieving its goals, take into account the attitudes and motivations of the population. In the Soviet Union the peasantry has been a particularly difficult group to harness, and in recent years one concession after another has been made to the peasant, even though at no time has there been a peasant party representing their interests.

Furthermore, as economic development takes place and brings in its wake an increase in literacy, education, living standards, and all the other concomitants of a more affluent society, the conditions develop for greater insistence by the people upon participation. People of this caliber will be more resistant to being pushed around, and the planners will be increasingly required to take their needs into account. Of course, this is a far cry from having a national debate on foreign policy, but it does represent a step toward greater democracy. On the other hand, the same technological imperatives of an industrially advanced and rapidly developing economy, together with their sociopolitical correlates, exist in the Soviet Union as in the United States. The rise of expertise is rapidly creating a class of individuals with a great deal of economic power residing in the technical and scientific ability upon which political figures are becoming increasingly dependent. And the elite-mass problem faces the Soviet Union as well and in the same manner as in the United States.

In the Third World economies, the sorts of issues confronting the advanced economies lie in the future, awaiting the culmination of the process of development. Instead, Third World problems center upon the relationship between democracy and development; for instance, is a democratic political structure conducive or detrimental to the requirements of economic development? Both views have been advanced. Those who hold that a non-democratic way is the only way to guarantee economic development look to the conflict aspects of democracy. Rapid industrialization requires that the entire nation be mobilized for a united effort; and converting the society into a debating club, it is held, is more likely to dissipate this unity than to achieve it. Furthermore, it is held that the masses of the Third World nations are so backward and their immediate needs so pressing that it is unlikely that they would willingly consent to the sacrifices necessary to provide the means for economic growth. The Soviet Union is accepted as the example par excellence of rapid economic development on the basis of a non-democratic society. Had the Soviet masses been granted the right to vote, say, on whether to choose consumer goods now or later (in 1928), they would have assuredly voted for them now, and the investment which made the Soviet Union the second most powerful nation in the world, economically, would never have taken place. It is not unreasonable to speculate that the course of World War II itself might have been modified, to the detriment of the anti-fascist nations, had the democratic path been taken in the Soviet Union.

This strong view has considerable force in most Asian and African nations. Since the leadership of these nations has been largely trained in the advanced democratic societies of the West, and therefore has a strong personal attachment to the democratic ideal, the undemocratic period is usually considered to be a temporary expedient—just until the nation rises above some reasonable level of economic development.[23] The Third World appears to be conscious that the means may become the end, but whether they will be able to deal with this problem remains to be seen, and the future development of the Soviet Union is an important future portent for them.

A contrary view, well expressed by Myrdal, holds that democracy is conducive to rapid economic growth in underdeveloped nations. Myrdal believes that democracy will make possible the more widespread dissemination of the benefits of development which will in turn speed development forward more rapidly. But he is cognizant of the difficulties involved:

> The underdeveloped countries need real democracy even at this early stage in order to break down the existing impediments to economic development. But undoubtedly democracy, at the same time, makes it more difficult for governments to hold down the level of consumption in the degree necessary for rapid development. The tendency toward dynamic dictatorships of a Fascist, or Communist type, visible in most parts of the underdeveloped world, should be viewed in the perspective of this basic political dilemma.[24]

In considering this problem, one should also be mindful of the historical fact that in most of the advanced countries democracy—for instance, universal suffrage—was severely restricted to upper-income persons and property-holders during the formative stages of economic growth.

A theme of considerable interest, which everyone seems to deny and no one can seemingly refute, is the convergence thesis: the notion that all developing societies are inevitably coming to be similar to each other. Insofar as social institutions and value systems are related to the economy, it is held that there is convergence at the productive base. A corollary of this idea is that international conflict today is not merely the result of economic conflict per se but of sharply divergent value systems between nations at distinctly different levels of development.[25]

23. This view has been ably expressed by African leaders in particular; see Ndabaningi Sithole, *African Nationalism* (second edition). New York and London: Oxford University Press, 1968, esp. pp. 169–88; and Léopold Sedar Senghor, *On African Socialism*. New York: Frederick A. Praeger, 1964, esp. pp. 67–103.
24. Gunnar Myrdal, *Beyond the Welfare State: Economic Planning and Its International Implications*. New Haven: Yale University Press, 1960, pp. 132–33.
25. An excellent summary of papers on this theme of mutual convergence is con-

With this theory, one can go a long way toward explaining the Sino-Soviet dispute as representing the conservative-pragmatic orientation of a relatively rich society confronting the radical-moralistic-ideological outlook of a poor society. The power of the Soviet Union rests upon its growing affluence and technological development, while China, not having reached this stage as yet, puts its power position forward in terms of revolutionary ideology. Similarly, the developing United States-Soviet rapprochement can be seen as reflecting the merging interests of two highly developed societies seeking to preserve their achievements. To put it another way, neither in the United States nor in the Soviet Union are radical political movements liable to develop and have political leverage. The deepening radicalism in the conflict between the underdeveloped and the advanced economies may also be seen as a form of status- and power-seeking among nations that have not yet reached a high level of economic development. The assumption is that once the affluent society is approached, the "irrational" expressions will no longer be necessary and will disappear.

This point of view holds out much hope for the world *in the long run*. Should the world survive until affluence catches up with the developing countries, there is great hope for that one world in which the problems of society will at least not include the physical survival of mankind.

The convergence thesis rests primarily upon the further assumption that technologically advanced, high mass-consumption societies require similar economic organization and breed similar social institutions and attitudes. Cultural differences in the background of nations are gradually submerged, that is, they are powerless in the face of the shattering force of modern economic development and at most constitute a temporary "holding action."

The shift from primary to secondary to tertiary economies appears to be an inevitable change. Inasmuch as the rate of economic development of less developed nations (especially those proceeding under command economies) is more rapid than the developed nations, they will be catching up, and one of the ways in which the catching-up process will show itself will be in convergence of occupational and consumption patterns and their associated cultural features.

Many of the problems and attitudes in the socioeconomic systems of

tained in Paul Hollander (ed.), *American and Soviet Society: A Reader in Comparative Sociology and Perception.* Englewood Cliffs, N.J.: Prentice-Hall, 1969, pp. 561–89.

the United States and Soviet Union may be attributed to the impact of affluence, regardless of the difference between capitalism and socialism. And the instabilities of the capitalist economies have led them increasingly to move toward the "welfare state," a kind of half-way house between capitalism and socialism. Strachey in his work has suggested that the capitalist democracies are moving irreversibly toward socialism and that the necessary responses to each succeeding recession represent a small step further in the socialist direction. In this respect, the capitalist societies are converging toward the socialist.[26] In other ways, the advanced socialist societies are converging toward the capitalist ones. This is particularly evident as they develop into economies of high mass consumption and the values associated therewith. Khrushchev nostalgically recalled the romantic days of early post-revolutionary Russia. He deplored the demise of the old spirit in much the same way as our inner-directed parents deplore the ways of their other-directed children. Similarly, the bureaucratic requirements of large-scale industry, the elite-mass dichotomy related to technical-scientific advance, and all the other attributes of the affluent society are phenomena which the Soviet Union is now beginning to experience.

The need to study the Third World in depth is underscored by the possible convergence of the two major powers within the First World and Second World. For if it is correct that dyadic relations tend to be much more stable than triadic relations, the new dyad may be polarized in terms of the convergence into a single entity of the old worlds, and their coming to grips with the problems and aspirations of the Third World.

26. John Strachey, *Contemporary Capitalism.* New York: Random House, 1956. A similar if less pleasant reading of the convergence hypothesis is contained in Pitirim Sorokin, *Basic Trends of Our Times.* New Haven: College and University Press, 1964, pp. 78–130.

8

The United Nations and the Third World: East-West Conflict in Focus

The unvarnished fact is that the United Nations is little more than a theater in which certain inter-nation scenarios are sometimes played, a stage on which historical events can be recorded rather than an organization making history. To say this is not to criticize the United Nations so much as to cast doubt on exaggerated expectations for the organization as an effective keeper of the peace. My purpose is to tease out a set of serious contradictions which limit the effectiveness of the United Nations. There is no need for a lengthy analysis of the United Nations formal organizational components because studies of the charter are readily available and because the most interesting sociological aspects of organizational life concern what takes place at the operational and informal performance levels.

The United Nations illustrates two principles of organizational theory well known to the social sciences. First, the formal rule structure by no means serves as the operational codebook of the organization. Rather, it defines only the outer limits beyond which the informal system cannot transgress. Second, the United Nations demonstrates, beyond a doubt, that the size of an organization in no way uniquely determines its power. Thus the simple fact of broad membership, or even the relative status of member nations, is not in itself a measure of power. The proportions of United Nations power are not indicated by either its formal structure or its size. Let us then consider six contradictions which have limited the organization's effectiveness.

First and foremost is the contradiction between the peacekeeping functions and the developmental goals of the United Nations. It is obvious that the peacekeeping role was largely responsible for maintaining a relative state of tranquility between Israel and Egypt from 1956 to 1966. It is also clear that the peacekeeping activities of the United Nations have been instrumental in preventing regional wars over Cyprus and the Congo. But these peacekeeping functions, which we are repeatedly being urged to strengthen, in effect conflict with the United Nations role of stimulating social and economic development. In spite of the fact that these roles are spoken of as corresponding ones, the plain fact is that they do not correspond at all. The United Nations encourages the spread of capital to underdeveloped areas both through its own programs and through pressure exerted upon advanced nations to work toward reducing the gaps between poverty and wealth throughout the world. In these underdeveloped areas, two things occur as a result: economic development and destabilization of traditional societies.[1] Groups within underdeveloped countries seeking the advancement of these two processes often see violence either as good policy or as an absolute necessity.

The perception of development held by the developing nations differs from that held by the United Nations. But, more importantly, the developing nations' perception of the developmental process conflicts with the United Nations peacekeeping goal. Violence, when it has occurred, has had a high probability of inviting foreign intervention with the attendant possibilities of escalation and general war involving the intervenors and other nations. Of course, in the cases where violence and intervention have occurred, the United Nations has often been called upon to exercise its peacekeeping function. The United Nations seems to have overlooked this goal conflict, for it continues to underwrite and advocate both development and peacekeeping, that is, it continues to weigh its goals from the viewpoint of the developed sectors rather than the newly emerging nations, which often perceive a high stake in violence.

The effect of the contradiction between development and peacekeeping functions is aggravated by the fact that the United Nations peacekeeping role is not wholly restricted to preserving peace among nations. The Congo crisis of 1960 plainly represented an intervention by the United Nations forces within an essentially civil-war situation. The strained definition of the Congo problem as linked to the "mer-

1. On this, see J. P. Nettl and Roland Robertson, *International Systems and the Modernization of Societies*. New York: Basic Books, 1968, pp. 124–25; 150.

cenary intrigue," in this case by the Belgians, simply does not over-come the obvious fact that intervention in this case reflected a restriction of internal conflict rather than a restriction of conflict between nations.

Second, a contradiction arises from the conflict between the United Nations' cosmopolitan intent and its effect of legitimating national identities. The United Nations in some sense was organized as a savior from the complete rule of national interest in world politics, yet it is precisely limited to being a forum for the expression of such national interest. This contradiction was written into the charter itself in the form of an organizational division between the Security Council and the General Assembly. The function of the General Assembly as a forum for the expression of national interests is frequently noted. What is rarely appreciated is that, insofar as the United Nations expresses national interests, it serves to legitimate those interests. It reinforces the very kind of national identities which the organization was established to overcome. Indeed, the symbols of national identity are set forth in righteous dress to a world public, appealing for legitimacy on a scale otherwise unavailable to an individual nation. Nations such as Israel and Cuba, for example, which are denied a considerable number of normal diplomatic channels of expression, require the United Nations, both as a forum for expression of their national sentiments and as a basic acknowledgment on the part of the world community that there is in fact a nation such as Israel or Cuba.

Further, the concessions made to national identity effectively deprive the United Nations of any role in handling intervention in civil strife. The group in rebellion, lacking national status, has no formal means to utilize the United Nations forum. The position of the government claiming national sovereignty over internal affairs, however, is reinforced by its position in the international forum. The cosmopolitan intent of the United Nations is subverted by the very legitimizing effect it has upon nationalistic claims.

The third contradiction is between the democratic aims reflected in the organization of the United Nations and the political domination by the major powers which denies rule by democracy.

While the organization of the United Nations is very much in keeping with the spirit of Montesquieu—that is, faith in bicameral legislative devices and the idea of checks and balances—the Security Council and General Assembly relationship is more nearly a stimulus-response situation. What was overlooked by the founders of the United Nations, and has long since been forgotten by present-day jurists, is that bicameralism and the theory of checks and balances against the undue exercise of power must rest on an independent constituency with strong electoral power. The source of authority has to be differentiated from multiple agencies of power if it is to be effective. In the case of the United Nations, this very assumption breaks down; for the source of power in the General Assembly is the large nations. Separation of functions and checks and balances formally operate in the United Nations, but the substance is lacking. And without distinct and different constituencies, the democratic options desired by all nations remain unattainable.

The contradiction, of course, defies an organizational remedy. The problem is that world politics has bypassed the organizational machine. The United Nations itself has seemed to become aware of this in its new approach to membership of China in the world body. However, even this may be viewed as a recognition that genuine political power cannot be exercised by the United Nations but, rather, lies in the hands of the major world powers, who decide even what absurdities should and should not be followed.

The fourth contradiction arises from the conflict between the foundation of the United Nations upon the nation-state system and the emergence of regional alliances with significant power in themselves. Since World War II there has been a steady growth in regional organizations.[2] Just what legal arrangements exist between larger-than-nation organizations and the United Nations remains unclear and, for the most part, unexamined. The attitude of the United States is demonstrated by the fact that, even though NATO, SEATO, and other defense pacts contain boilerplate language subordinating the organization and its goals to the United Nations, in practice they are carrying out many of the functions reserved to the United Nations in the charter; for example, they are characterizing conflicts and embarking upon intervention in the name of the charter.

Interest politics, including intervention, goes on at the international level largely uncurbed by what is ostensibly an organization providing sufficient security to cancel the need for such purely protective self-

2. In Latin America, for example, there are the United States-supported Organization of American States and the newly formed Cuban-sponsored Organization of Latin America Solidarity. At another intermediary level, there are regional economic associations, such as the Latin American Free Trade Association and the Central American Common Market.

interest mechanisms. Both major world powers conduct their affairs through such regional agencies rather than through the United Nations. The likelihood of any clarification of the United Nations jurisdictional role in conflicts involving these regional organizations seems remote.

We have covered contradictions between large nations and small nations within the United Nations and between the United Nations and regional bloc associations. We turn now to perhaps the most agonizing contradiction of all, that between member nations and non-member nations. Whereas one might dismiss the previous contradictions as simply different levels of operationalizing diplomatic and political relationships, this contradiction drives right to the core of the United Nations problem.

The final contradiction is that between expectations and performances in the United Nations. Although the United Nations twenty-two-year-old record is superior to that of the old League of Nations, part of the superiority stems from the less presumptuous goal the United Nations set for itself: more stringent limits on the violation of national sovereignty. Above all, the United Nations peacekeeping function benefits from the escalation in the price of general war. In the cases in which the United Nations performs its peacekeeping operations, it is on a limited scale approved by the great powers. However, the role of the big power sovereigns is usually more direct and critical in bringing about a suspension of armed hostilities than United Nations resolutions.

Even in the cases where United Nations intervention is foreseeable, it is unclear whether strife is inhibited by that possibility. When the issue of basic limits upon United Nations functioning is raised, the response is often intellectually petulant. It is as if every success is to be counted a blessing and every failure a consequence of nationalism. An often cited apology for United Nations peacekeeping defects is that any organization reflecting varied and diverse interests must count its blessings that it may perform peacekeeping functions even on the limited scale made possible by tacit big power approval. Thus, credit for the settlement of the Middle East crisis, the Congo crisis, and the Cyprus struggle are all chalked up to the "Miraculous Value" of the international organization. Aside from the fact that in each case the role of big power sovereigns was much more direct and critical in bringing about a suspension of armed hostilities than the United Nations resolutions, there is a covert possibility that the United Nations may actually serve to stimulate limited warfare.

Since a group engaged in, or intent upon, conflict can program hostilities only for a short period of time, the very foreknowledge of United Nations intervention can itself be programed. It is hardly a matter of doubt that Israel was able to synchronize its military response to the Arab blockade by anticipating United Nations actions. Thus, inter-nation rivalry is not necessarily inhibited by United Nations operations. Indeed, they may be but another variable to consider in calculating the possibilities of victory or defeat. Of course, the programming of a short-run struggle is good only with respect to anticipated United Nations action and resolution. When the conflict has become protracted and widespread, as in Vietnam, United Nations intervention is simply not serviceable as a meaningful preventive to further war.

The genuine failures of the United Nations at the peacekeeping level should be recognized. With respect to the war in Vietnam, the United Nations role has been ineffective, restricted by and large to informal attempts by the Secretary General to limit the scale and scope of the conflict.[3]

Though there have been measurable degrees of success by United Nations organizations in areas of technological cooperation, education, and health, it would be a dismal climax to reduce the worth of the United Nations to the work of its specialized agencies. Nor is this altogether necessary. One can recognize at least four valuable functions of the United Nations on a macroscopic organizational level.

First, the United Nations does represent a forum for expressing disagreements. Men talking, after all, tend to be men not shooting. The longer they talk, the less likelihood there is of open military hostility. Furthermore, a neutral forum promotes a quicker resolution of actual conflicts, for it is often easier for belligerents to deal with a "Mediator Rex" than with one another.

Second, the United Nations is a diplomatic equivalent to the old-fashioned international Swiss (now West German) spy center. There is an informal trade-off of new policies between nations. Trial balloon proposals can be sent up indicating sentiments and currents at work that for one reason or another cannot be part of the public dialogue.

3. For a juridical analysis of these shortcomings, see Alf Ross, *The United Nations: Peace and Progress.* Totowa, N.J.: Bedminster Press, 1966, esp. 395–408; and Michael Barkun, "Integration, Organization, and Values," in *The United Nations System and It's Functions,* edited by Robert W. Gregg and Michael Barkun. Princeton: D. Van Nostrand Co., 1968, pp. 450–60.

For example, there have been indications of several attempts at quiet diplomacy concerning the war in Vietnam.

Third, the United Nations functions as an informal early-warning system by defining the limits of national sovereignty. The definition of these limits serves to apprise nations of potential conflicts and of the threshold for greater violence in already-existing conflicts.

Fourth and finally, the United Nations serves as an ideal typification of international consensus. As an ideal, it serves as an informal limitation upon the worst excesses of nationalism, self-righteous chauvinism, and unbridled military response. The Secretary General has seemed particularly well suited to bring this informal limitation to bear on potential conflicts. From Dag Hammarskjold to U Thant, the goal of international tranquility between nations has been expressed by the giant men of the small nations.

Although real power is not exercised within the juridical framework of the United Nations, real sentiments are expressed there. Insofar as there is a desperate need for exact information on the nature and sentiments of those who have power, the United Nations serves as a major forum and, at the same time, as a realistic measuring device of both where the world community of nations is and where it seeks to go. This is particularly so in the area of economic activities. In fact, one might say that just as there has been a displacement of power in the United Nations by the Third World over the First and Second Worlds, in equal proportion the United Nations has become a forum for socio-economic tasks rather than the solution of political tasks.

In the very process of a transformation in its size and character, the United Nations has become the locus for the emergence of the Third World as an organized, institutionalized bloc. Curiously, through the legitimizing functions of the United Nations, the Third World is no longer a loose confederation of ideological formulas, as was the case at the first Bandung Conference in 1955. Indeed, so far has this process evolved that the need for the United Nations has itself become minimized. Conflict in the Congo and then in Nigeria has also served to expose the racial nerve separating the old colonialist powers from the rising tide of African and Asian nationalism. Similar strains are revealed in France's call for a summit meeting to revise and update the United Nation charter, in the Soviet Union's demands for a reorganization of the Secretariat, and in the incapacity of United Nations agencies to finance their peacekeeping efforts.

The most powerful schism of all was revealed in the various postures evident at a little summit meeting on trade and development held in 1964. At this Geneva conference the United States found itself in splendid isolation on matters concerning the economic and social life blood of the Third World. Few significant events in recent times have received so little journalistic attention. For what the conference reflected was not simply a mounting pressure for multilateral economic relations, but a deepening rift between the American and Russian haves and the Afro-Asian have-nots.

The United Nations does not serve so much as a problem-resolving agency as it does a problem-focusing agency. The triadic nature of the world is nowhere illustrated with greater clarity than in the United Nations. First, there is the United States-Western Europe–dominated Organization for Economic Co-operation and Development (OECD). Second, there is the Soviet-dominated Council of Mutual Economic Assistance (COMECON); and finally the Group of 77 Third World-sponsored United Nations Conference on Trade and Development (UNCTAD). And while the formal organizational lines between the three are much less clear and decisive than the informal norms governing their origins and operations, it becomes evident that in policy and program, the needs of the three worlds in development are hardly isomorphic. The Third World-sponsored UNCTAD is characterized by large membership, heterogenous composition, great political and ideological diversity, and the absence of the leadership role of a great power. The Group of 77, or the UNCTAD group, is an instrument to enhance the negotiating position of developing countries vis-à-vis the developed countries. The former realize that through individual efforts exercised separately, they can do little to change the adverse effects of world conditions and trends on their own economies.[4]

The profound schism between the Third World and the advanced economies is reflected in specific areas. While the issues raised may in time produce a general schism between the Third World and the fully developed world, there is no doubt that at present the central focus of the animosity is the United States. What follows is a catalogue of grievances which form the background and prelude to the public rift which took place at the United Nations Conference on Trade and Development.

4. See Branislav Gosovic, "UNCTAD: North-South Encounter," *International Conciliation*, No. 568, May 1968, esp. 14–30.

(1) *Bilateralism versus Multilateralism:* Third World commentators, like Raúl Prebisch of Argentina and Edmundo Flores of Mexico, claim that the character of United States aid is strictly bilateral, and that this aid often deteriorates into idiosyncratic assistance based upon tests of political allegiance. In addition to driving political bargains, bilateralism helps the advanced nation drive economic bargains as well, by setting up favorable terms of credit, shipping surplus goods in place of purchasing power, demanding certain raw material advantages, and determining with whom and under what conditions trade with others is to take place. Finally, the bilateral approach often limits recipient countries from extending their trade lines with other nations.

(2) *Modernism versus Structuralism:* Both of these assume the middle class to be the prime force in development. The argument for modernism is that if the local entrepreneurs realize that they can personally enjoy a mass consumption life style they will be prepared to engage in productive investment with their wealth, rather than attempt to "beat the system" with Swiss bank accounts, hoarding, and corruption. The structuralist position amounts to one of "tricking the capitalists" into engaging in productive investment by inflationary pressures. If the middle classes only have a choice, with respect to how they allocate their wealth, they will more likely opt for modernism, since structuralist arguments assume that inflationary pressures would effect the wealthy disproportionately, when in fact, they would simply increase the money value of the goods produced, and the costs passed along to the other sectors of the populations. That as it may be, it is the contention of many Third World nations that the basic posture of the United States is to discourage self-sustaining economic units in favor of heavy consumer-oriented economies. Thus, the United States lends its weight and prestige to nations securing finished consumer products, with little or no emphasis on the costs, in independence and growth, of such an arrangement. The hub of the argument is that the United States, in advocating modernism, in effect supports the relatively small elite within the developing nations that is able to pay for the import of manufactured goods, while it ignores the needs of the large mass who would be aided much more substantially if the country emphasized industrial goods for public use rather than commodity goods for private use.

(3) *Agriculturalism versus Industrialism:* In general, Third World nations dislike the role they are being assigned as agricultural and raw materials areas. At the present time most of the Third World is

forced to import expensive finished consumer goods and export relatively inexpensive farm and mineral raw materials. Such a trade pattern saddles a nation with a deepening inflationary spiral due to the imbalance between high-price consumer goods and low-cost raw materials and with perpetual poor-nation indebtedness, also because of the price differential. These countries "export" on capital account by selling their industrial potential to the United States. These countries have a chronic inability to acquire the foreign exchange they want because of their unfavorable export position. Thus they are always trying to get loans in foreign currency. The trade pattern can be broken only if the United States gives meaningful across-the-board trade and tariff concessions. At the present time the United States appears reluctant to offer such assistance. Such a condition contributes greatly to social unrest in the Third World. It is ironic that the United States' very insistence on the present international division of production helps sustain social unrest which it feels compelled to treat as a military threat.

(4) *Private Sector versus Public Sector:* While the Third World recognizes that the United States, like every other dynamic economy in the world, is a mixed economy, it is still viewed as a predominantly private-sector economy. What is more, the United States does little to disabuse the Third World of this impression. Indeed, its official posture is private enterprise. This stands in profound contrast to the economy of most Third World nations, which are debating what type of public-sector economy they prefer rather than assessing the degree of public or private enterprise they should adopt. Third World nations are upset that the United States fails to understand their needs and demands on adhesion to an economic philosophy of private-sector preeminence which even the most highly industrialized nation can itself no longer pursue.

(5) *Economic versus Political Determinism:* The Third World views the United States as a parliamentary democracy. At the same time it considers the introduction of such a system into less developed regions an impossibility. The historical conditions which have given rise to the Third World, particularly the lack of a mature and self-sustaining polity and the demands for rapid economic acceleration, seem to imply the need for much more centralized authority than was present in the United States at the time of its take-off. The failure on the part of the United States to appreciate the need for political centralization and economic planning is held to be a key abrasive in the situation.

(6) *Integration versus Fragmentation:* Third World nations tend to be racially homogeneous, have a high density of population, widespread illiteracy, and a relatively large rural population; and caste, class, and tribal sectors which make them fragmented and ascriptive societies. The United States does not sufficiently appreciate their lack of structural solidarity. The problems of the modern world presuppose participation in international relations; and this is hard to achieve in societies still bound by class, caste, and racial schisms. Yet it is true that Third World nations cannot obtain their legitimate role in the international arena while the United States hinders their efforts.

The factual bedrock upon which the Third World position (as illustrated by UNCTAD) rests is that the gap between rich nations and poor nations is steadily widening.[5] Perhaps the most succinct statement of this gap was offered by David Horowitz, governor of the Bank of Israel:

> Economic growth is to a very great extent a function of investment. As long as per capita investment in developed countries is 12.5 times higher than in underdeveloped ones, the gap between the two parts of the world will probably increase. This problem is aggravated by every technological step forward which increases the volume of capital to be invested per head in order to achieve significant economic growth. Moreover, the composition of investment in this technological age of ever-increasing sophistication necessitates an increase in skill, know-how, and higher education, which are almost non-existent in underdeveloped countries. Economic growth in our time is tantamount to a larger unit of equipment per head and a larger proportion of skilled manpower, expertise, and specialization.[6]

A strongly related reason for this gap is the intense fluctuation of the world price of raw materials, a fluctuation often manipulated by fully developed industrial nations. The increasing cost of purchasing finished commodities from fully industrialized nations is a primary cause of the gap. The trends in the prices of manufactured goods is half the problem

5. For empirical confirmation of the widening gap between the economic growth of industrial countries, in contrast to underdeveloped "primary producing areas," see Alfred Maizels, *Industrial Growth and World Trade.* Cambridge: Cambridge University Press, 1963.
6. David Horowitz, "Development Strategy in Developing Countries," *Middle East Development: Some Current Economic Problems* (Truman Center Publications, No. 3). Jerusalem: The Hebrew University, 1968, p. 5.

of the deteriorating terms of trade agreements between advanced and underdeveloped nations. The other half is the foreign ownership and participation patterns in underdeveloped industries. It was the gap rather than any question of ownership which united the bloc of 77 nations in UNCTAD.

The work of Raúl Prebisch and other Third World economists directly challenges the classical assumption that progress which results from technological innovation will automatically benefit industrialized and non-industrialized nations alike through the mechanism of free trade. The assumption that "the first positive aspect of private foreign investment in the developing nations is precisely the fact that it is foreign," assumes that foreign investors bring new capital, new management techniques, and new technology at a nominal cost.[7] In point of fact, it is precisely the cost factor in modernization through foreign capital that serves to accentuate the gap rather than overcome it.[8]

Prebisch accepted this widening gap as the major fact of the current international situation, and consequently it became the primary subject to be accounted for by his economic explanation. The basic premise of the Prebisch thesis is the differential market power of the have versus the have-not nations. It is important to state explicitly the thesis propounded by Prebisch—and now by Hirschman—since it forms the basis of so much Third World thought in the United Nations.

First, the haves and the have-nots are not converging. The rich continue to get rich and the poor either improve at a slow rate or not at all. This is the basic fact of the international situation.

Second, a principal effect of this is the differential power in international trade and other political areas related to trade—such as foreign aid—between the rich and the poor.

Third, the reasons for this power differential are to be found in the nature of the products manufactured by these two factions, and the market institutions each have at their disposal. The underdeveloped nations are primary producers of goods which are, with a few notable exceptions like tin, in excessive supply and subject to inelastic demand and which are furthermore threatened by obsolescence due to technical

7. See Herbert K. May, *The Effects of United States and Other Foreign Investment in Latin America.* New York: The Council for Latin America, Jan. 1970.
8. Raúl Prebisch, *Towards a New Trade Policy for Development.* New York: United Nations Publications, 1964 (E/Conf/46/3); see also Nicholas Kaldor, *Strategic Factors in Economic Development.* Ithaca: New York State School of Industrial and Labor Relations, Cornell University, 1967, esp. pp. 66–70.

progress. The rich produce manufactured goods which reflect elastic demands and exhibit extremely high salability in developing "modernizing" countries.

Fourth, the international market for manufactured goods is not characterized by competition but by institutions assuming monopoly profits to the rich. Granted, some of these profits are shared with the domestic middle and working classes; but conversely, this very situation serves to further isolate the poor of the underdeveloped nations, since they cannot exert equal leverage over the prices of wheat or rice or sugar. One factor is their large numbers, making cooperation between the poor—in market terms at least—exceedingly difficult. Bilateral trade terms between wealthy and impoverished countries is another source of imbalance, since unlike manufacturing countries, many primary products are subject to domestic variations in supply that place a strain on any multilateral price agreements. Assuming that the agreement specified is a "true" average price, then in times of glut, there are tensions that arise from the buyer trying to lower the price—a situation far more likely to occur in primary or agricultural markets than in manufactured goods.

Fifth, there is a differential market power which manifests itself in terms of trade between the products exported and imported by rich and poor nations. These have steadily shifted to the disadvantage of the agrarian producing sectors, and to the Third World as a whole.

In recognition of the first development decade, the United Nations General Assembly set a *minimum* target to be achieved by newly developing countries by 1970: a minimum annual economic growth rate of 5 per cent. This turned out to be an immense exaggeration; even in per capita terms it meant roughly 2 per cent because of a 3 per cent annual population increase. This minimum target has instead turned out to be the rarely achieved maximum.

The United Nations Conference on Trade and Development was designed to create an international trade environment which was to offset the trade disadvantages to developing countries. And as we have seen, the emergence of UNCTAD did not unify developed and underdeveloped countries, but rather re-emphasized their polarization. The response of the second development decade has been to develop a more modest yet more realistic estimate of the possibilities. As was recently pointed out:

ever since the period of decolonization began some twenty years ago, the mistaken impression has been prevalent in some public opinion circles—as well as among those responsible for providing them with adequate information—that economic development is a relatively simple and natural process which ought to take place almost as a matter of course. Experience has clearly demonstrated that this assumption is wrong and that the problem is far more complex.[9]

Thus far, however, the second decade of development has shifted from a program of economics to one of education; and this means a shift to an interest-group orientation on the part of Third World nations.

While underdeveloped countries have an increasing need to import industrial equipment, their exports do not earn enough to pay for basic capital imports. The result is a trade gap, which gold and foreign exchange reserves have not been able to bridge. The gap must be then filled by capital import. Neither foreign loans nor foreign investment provide a permanent solution. Eventually the richer nations will refuse to lend to or to invest in nations with faltering economies. Even in the short run, the expenses incurred in servicing external debts diminish the stop-gap effect of capital import. Many developing countries are faced with declining prices for their exports of primary commodities at a time when the prices of their imports of manufactures, especially of equipment, have greatly increased. Their dependence on primary commodity exports has reduced their capacity to import. This trend represents a major obstacle to their efforts to diversify and industrialize their economies. Recognition of this trade pattern as a barrier to development led to the Conference on Trade and Development which convened at Geneva on March 23, 1964, and continued until June 16.

The 1964 conference was based on the following findings: (1) World export has more than doubled since 1950 through over-all expansion of the "world economy" aided by socioeconomic change and scientific and technological progress. (2) The countries of the world do not share proportionately in this expansion of international trade. Although exports of developing countries nearly doubled between 1953 and 1965, the expansion of exports from these countries proceeded at

9. Centre for Economic and Social Information of the United Nations Office of Public Information, "The Mobilization of Public Opinion for the Second United Nations Development Decade," in *International Associations*, Vol. 22, Mar. 1970, pp. 154–56.

an appreciably lower rate than that of developed countries. Indices of export and import quantum reveal that imports have largely absorbed these upward spurts in exports. Further, the share of developing countries in world exports declined during this same period from one-third to one-fifth.[10] Concurrently, the developed market economies increased their share from three-fifths to two-thirds, and the centrally planned economies from 8 per cent to 13 per cent. (3) The rate of expansion of world exports declined from 8.5 per cent per annum in the early 'fifties to rather less than 5 per cent in the early 'sixties. One reason for the decline is the inability of the developing countries to attain a higher rate of export expansion.[11] (4) The demand for the export products of underdeveloped countries is relatively inelastic. And they have little chance of gaining ground, not only because they are faced with artificial tariff restrictions, but also because raw material substitutes are being created, for example, the replacement of rubber, leather, and fabrics by plastic goods. (5) The monopolistic elements in developed nations channel technological innovation into higher profits, shorter working hours, and higher wages for their own populations. Thus, technological progress does not automatically become an advantage for the developing regions. (6) Finally, because their exports are not expanding significantly, developing nations are unable to increase their purchases of capital goods from the developed countries.

World trade was aggravated by deterioration in the terms of trade between 1950 and 1963:

> The slower growth in the quantity of exports of the developing countries and the adverse movement of their terms of trade were largely the reflection of the present commodity composition of their trade, consisting, as it does, predominantly of the exchange of primary product exports for manufactured imports whose relative positions in world markets have undergone significant changes. World trade in manufactures has been increasing at an annual rate more than twice that of trade in primary products.[12]

Increasing technological efficiency in primary products of advanced countries, increasing productivity, low consumer demand for food com-

10. Department of Economic and Social Affairs, *World Economic Survey, 1965,* Vol. I—*The Financing of Economic Development,* Vol. II—*Current Economic Developments.* New York: United Nations, 1966, pp. 41, 169, 185.
11. *Final Act. United Nations Conference on Trade and Development.* E/Conf/ 46/L.28, June 16, 1964, p. 8, Section III.
12. *Ibid.,* pp. 8–9.

pared to increases in consumer income, the widespread use of substitutes and synthetics in advanced countries where incomes and food consumption are high—all of these exaggerate the imbalance between the developed and underdeveloped nations. The gap between import requirements of Third World countries and their export earnings has been widening. "According to United Nations Secretariat estimates, this gap could be of the order of $20 billion a year in 1970, on the basis of a five per cent per annum rate of growth set as the target for the United Nations Development Decade, assuming no change in the trends of the 'fifties upon which these estimates were based." [13]

In other words, Prebisch creates a situation in which the "gap" is a figure which is derived from an analysis that assumes a 5.0 per cent growth-rate target and various other international trade assumptions. This 5.0 per cent rate, however, is just a hope of the Third World and in this sense the "gap" is more ephemeral than real.

As a result of the somewhat artificial nature of international measures, Third World countries have begun to emphasize internal rather than comparative rates of growth. To do this effectively they have turned to economic and social planning as a technique for satisfying demands whether the international gap is narrowing or widening. Whatever the weaknesses may be in various planning devices, from a strictly economic point of view, such planning mechanisms serve to stimulate structural changes within each society, and mobilize previously untapped human and technical resources. In this way many developing countries hope to succeed whether or not changes in the structure of international trade provide them with ample opportunity to expand their foreign exchange. In a sense therefore, nationalism is economically feasible no less than politically necessary.

In spite of the risk of antagonizing the United States, Third World nations have turned to communist bloc countries. At the present time, however, trade between Third World countries and centrally planned economies remains but a small part of the trade turnover of developing countries as a whole. "In 1962, $1,630 million, or 5.6% of the total exports of the developing countries went to the centrally planned economies, while imports from the latter into the former totalled $2,150 million and formed 7.3% of total imports. This trade has, however, shown a tendency to increase in recent years." [14] For while the Third

13. *Ibid.,* p. 9.
14. *Ibid.,* p. 11.

World registered its main absolute increase in exports to the First World, the largest proportional increase was to the centrally planned economies of the Second World.[15]

There are obvious economic advantages in Third World countries trading with the centrally planned economies of the socialist bloc. The establishment of "normal relations" between these blocs becomes an important factor in the creation of an international push to improve the trade balance of developing countries with advanced countries in general. The General Principles of the United Nations Conference on Trade and Development underline this point: "There shall be no discrimination on the basis of differences in socio-economic systems. Adaptation of trading methods shall be consistent with this principle." [16]

The most striking aspect of the resolutions presented at the conference is the voting patterns of the United States, tacitly supported by France and Britain (though they abstained from voting whenever possible and whenever they felt no direct economic stake), and of the Soviet Union. The United States consistently opposed the resolutions of the conference, even where it was the only nation at the conference to do so. The Soviet Union consistently supported the claims of the developing nations. It is therefore necessary to explore further the economics in back of these resolutions.

A 5 per cent minimum growth target would be extraordinary if in fact it were reached. However, even with such a growth rate the composite wealth of Third World nations would lag behind developed nations. Since the rate of increase in consumer imports continues to be 6 per cent, payments for these imports more than absorbs any growth in the national economy. It is a simple mathematical result that if the GNP gross is at 5 per cent, and consumer imports is at 6 per cent, then the latter will at some point be constrained by the former. But this becomes a serious problem only given appropriate current magnitudes of consumer imports, and assuming that loans and other forms of aid do not supply the difference between growth rate and consumer rate. Prebisch points out that "any acceleration in the rate of growth requires additional investment; and the import content of this investment is normally higher than that of income as a whole. Consequently, it is

15. See Department of Economic and Social Affairs, *World Economic Survey, 1965.* New York: United Nations, 1966, pp. 146–47.
16. *Final Act. United Nations Conference on Trade and Development.* Second Part, Section I, Principles, p. 17.

not going too far to conclude that imports would have to rise at a rate somewhat higher than that of total income." [17] This is valid given Prebisch's market-economy assumptions, but not otherwise. For if capital can be internally generated, or involving sectors of low capital intensity, then the balance of payments constrained on importing foreign capital would be less severe.

One major dilemma involved is that two different strategies emerge from the foregoing bleak economic picture. The first is to move toward austerity, high taxation, and the push of investment capital at the expense of consumer needs. The second is an alternative strategy which does not move in the direction of expropriation or austerity but rather views high trade as a substitute whereby mass consumption and productive entrepreneurship redress the trade balance. And while Prebisch clearly leans toward the more classical structural model, the fact is that emphasis upon external responsibilities for Third World deficits only obscures rather than resolves the problem of the "gap."

The Third World has repeatedly emphasized, although judiciously and politely, that it opposes present trade associations and agreements such as the General Agreement on Tariffs and Trade and the Common Market. The first Trade and Development Conference, held in Havana nearly thirty years ago, took place in a context of a world economic crisis and impending involvement of advanced countries in World War II. At that time the developing nations could not exert sufficient pressure to produce trade agreements designed to encourage their economic development. The code of rules and principles of that conference are still, with slight modification, embodied in the General Agreement on Tariffs and Trade. The GATT agreement, as it is called, is based on an abstract notion of economic heterogeneity, just as were regional protectionist measures before it. GATT simply internationalizes protectionism.

The GATT agreement does not take into account the considerable structural differences which exist between big industrial centers and peripheral countries. In particular, it fallaciously assumes full employment, complete elasticity of supply and demand and homogeneity of economic systems. In other words GATT's philosophy is a free trade one. It assumes that a country can easily adjust its resources to maintain full employment in the face of rapidly shifting world demand unprotected by high tariffs. In point of fact, regional and bilateral trade agreements have not benefited the Third World as much as they have

17. Raúl Prebisch, *op. cit.*

market economies of the developed world. GATT is a product of immediate post-World War II diplomacy, which came about through demands for the economic restoration of Western Europe as a principal goal. The GATT negotiations were not designed to expand world trade but rather to develop the aggregate income of the Atlantic community. It was reciprocal, based in the main on rationalizing trade between major centers. In the Common Market by contrast, the member countries grant each other, by means of industrial pooling, preferences which are expected to convert their reciprocal trade into higher industrial production.

The General Agreement on Trade and Tariffs, and the European Common Market, although both instruments of large-scale business, differ in the sense that the former is "universalist" whereas the latter is "particularist" and concerned with maintaining barriers against nonmembers. This preferential system offers a powerful impetus to trade among member countries. However, it does not do very much to change the basic disequilibrium which exists between "donor" and "recipient" nations. Third World countries have attempted to demonstrate that preferential trade systems need not conflict with those which encourage development in disadvantaged nations. But the developed sector's actual attitude toward the agricultural products of the Third World underscores the disparity between the interests of the two sectors.

The highly restrictive Western European policy toward agricultural imports is a major source of irritation to "wealthy" countries like Canada as well as to "poor" countries like Argentina. Both serve to underscore the difference between the Third World and Europe, whatever may be the level of economic development of the Third World countries involved.

> Agriculture is a declining sector in the Six, as it is in most countries. The level of agricultural income has not kept pace with other sectors of the economy. Moreover, the share of agricultural income in total national income is markedly lower than the proportions of people working in agriculture would lead one to suspect. This lag in agricultural income is due to two sets of factors, first the relatively low productivity of agriculture resulting from such structural deficiencies as too many small holdings, the fragmentation of farms, the lack of available capital, and the poor mobility of agricultural manpower; and, second, the inelasticity of demand for agricultural products and the unfavorable relationship between the prices received

for agricultural products and those paid by the farmer for his means of production.[18]

This conflict of interests is further heightened by a high degree of political participation of French agricultural groups. The same holds true for German agriculture. Trade becomes based on a preferential system between industrialized nations, and is very difficult to change because of political as well as economic reasons. The declining importance of agriculture in these developed economies may bode well for future agreements which can support a principle of an "international division of labor." But this rationalization in the world economy depends on a rationalization of economic systems as such. Presently constituted preferential systems—the European Six, the United States, and the Atlantic Community—have not been able or willing to liberalize terms of trade to take account of other "preferential systems."

Until developing countries have sufficient capital formation for economic take-off, preferential systems established on regional grounds will have limited value for them. Such attempts as the Latin American Federation of Trade Associations have value mainly for articulating economic claims in political terms. At best, Third World regional systems tend to allocate resources more efficiently. But their supply and demand, shortages and abundance, are similar to each other. They cannot satisfy one another's needs for the materials offered by developed countries. Regional organization among poor countries cannot truly relieve economic pressure. As a result, aside from some minimal good effects, such associations serve to organize Third World business interests for the purpose of articulating their claims. And conferences sponsored by the United Nations, which present these issues as a matter of world concern, serve as a platform where trade and financial policy of all the great blocs can be compared and perhaps adjudicated. It is a way for Third World nations to take fresh initiative in making their multilateral image of the economic world a reality.

Western objections to such multilateralism of Third World economic aims seek, at the very least, to purchase time for favored nations. Such aims, whatever the moral implications, are quite specious. Nor can the underdeveloped and developing nations be assuaged with token aid

18. Leon N. Lindberg, *The Political Dynamics of European Economic Integration.* London: Oxford University Press, 1963.

measures. Multilateralist trade arrangement is considered by Third World nations to be a virtual model for slow and modest change since their governments and business classes wish to avoid total renovation of their social structures. Hence, Western objections based on accusations of haste merely reveal the speciousness of such opposition. Such a position fails to take into account the precipitous haste with which colonial empires were forged to begin with. It has been pointed out that "in the ten years 1880–1890 five million square miles of African territory, containing a population of over 60 million, were seized and subjected to European states." [19] Furthermore, what appeared to be a "scramble" for colonies was, in fact, a relatively well-integrated program of the advanced European powers to adjust their "spheres of influence" to their actual economic and political roles. Thus, by the beginning of the twentieth century, Asia and the Middle East were absorbed in the colonial fold, along the classical lines evolved in Africa.[20] If the process of colonization were rapidly worked out, it is no wonder that demands for decolonization should now be insistently presented before the pivotal United Nations agencies.

Demands for preferential economic treatment and for multilateral decision-making in economic affairs have an obviously "anti-capitalist" content. However, these demands also reveal a clear desire on the part of the Third World to avoid an exaggerated dependence upon the socialist bloc as well. The principal of self-determination therefore, permits Third World countries, especially those unencumbered by tradition, such as the sub-Saharan Black African nations, to invite major First World private enterprises to invest in their countries at favorable trade and exchange rates, and do the same with trade missions from Second World planned enterprises. Development may be redefined by rapid industrialization but this does not exclude the role of foreign capital. Many Third World nations zealously guard their political sovereignty without at the same time closing their economic doors to foreign investments. It might well be that the price of such investments will take its toll on political independence in the long run, but this is a gamble most Third World nations have no alternative but to take.

Despite the highly liberal tone of the general principles recorded at

19. Leonard Woolf, *Economic Imperialism,* pp. 33–34, as quoted in Maurice Dobb, *Political Economy and Capitalism.* New York: International Publishers, 1954, pp. 243f.
20. On this subject, see Maurice Dobb, *Political Economy and Capitalism,* pp. 242–44.

the Conference on Tariffs and Trade, liberalization to Third World countries means new preferential systems based on the profitable sale of their goods in the advanced sector of the capitalist economy. Unless this "liberalization" occurs, developing countries will turn increasingly to trade arrangements and exchange with the centrally planned economies of Eastern Europe. This in turn would help relieve the economic pressures the East feels from the West.

After World War II, the centralized economies of the Soviet type had twin aims: reconstruction and industrialization. They were obviously designed to change the character of these societies and to solve their basic problems—surplus population in agriculture, accelerated investment rate, and the need to curtail private consumption. Certain priorities were set which ultimately produced unintended strategic imbalances. Industry as a whole was emphasized as against agriculture, heavy industry over other industry, and heavy machinery within heavy industry. East European countries increased their investments in industry by 50 per cent and placed very low priorities on light industry and agricuture.[21]

The nations of Eastern Europe were not so much harmed by the Soviet Union's insistence on a heavy industrial basis as they were by the relative inability of the Soviet Union to maintain a decent agricultural base at the same time. The modified Stalinism of the post-World War II period did in fact increase industrial production, but it also seriously jeopardized agricultural life, which is one of the main reasons Yugoslav communists broke with the Stalinists in 1948. Despite attempts to coordinate labor, serious inefficiencies and imbalances in output and trade developed within the planning bloc itself, and even led to alarming food shortages. During the 1950's, and after the death of Stalin, the Eastern European nations sought a new economic course—a course involving a shift in favor of light industry and agriculture. But this move toward light industry and away from heavy industry in some measure seemed more a response to external Soviet pressures than any felt internal needs of Eastern European nations.

But from time to time, pressures to secure these "low-priority" goods through trade mount and it is clear that to head off these pressures from finding Western channels, it is to the advantage of the Soviet Union that the claims of the underdeveloped bloc be used economically.

21. Nicolas Spulber, "Planning and Development," in *Resources and Planning in Eastern Europe,* edited by N. J. G. Pounds and Nicolas Spulber. Bloomington: Indiana University Publications, 1957.

Because there is no rift in Soviet policy then, between its economic and political aims with respect to the Third World, it can afford to carry out common assistance programs. The Soviet Union has assisted developing countries not just with consumer goods, but with industrial equipment and technical knowledge. Vast numbers of Third World technicians and workers are currently studying in Soviet universities and technological colleges and learning industrial skills in Soviet factories. As Deutscher notes,

> This is the cheapest and most effective assistance. It costs less than does American aid in consumer goods; and it helps the underdeveloped nations to help themselves. The effect of American assistance is largely ephemeral. This is why it earns so little gratitude. The results of Soviet assistance are lasting; and those who receive it have the sense of being raised up from backwardness and dependence. The Russians say: "We can do all this because we are not afraid of foreign competition; we do not tremble for our markets; and we are not afraid of sharing industrial know-how." Western capitalists cannot afford to do this.[22]

Quite aside from the obvious political advantages of such moves, the Soviet Union also has much to gain from expanded trade with underdeveloped countries. It is in a position to allocate long-term loans and monies on a more efficient basis than the United States, since it is not faced with the "problem of perversity" from business or Congress as the United States is.

But more important, the Soviet Union does not have a favorable trade balance with Eastern Europe. If Eastern Europe could import a large supply of foodstuffs, raw materials, and primary commodities from the underdeveloped countries instead of perpetuating its dependence of the Soviet Union, and if it could then ship its increasing surplus of "engineering products" to them instead of to the Soviet Union, Eastern Europe would obviously gain considerable economic maneuvering space.

However, the unfavorable trade balance of the Soviet Union with Eastern Europe is an economic problem that the USSR solves by its superior political power over Eastern Europe, that is to say, the "dependence" of the Eastern European bloc on the Soviet Union is rooted in power, not production. The industrialization of Eastern Europe has

22. See Isaac Deutscher, *The Great Contest: Russia and the West*. New York: Ballantine Books, 1961, pp. 117–18.

not been a drain on the Soviet Union. For example, it has managed to exploit the well-developed consumer goods industry of Czechoslovakia by underpricing such goods that it imported. Similarly, one reason for Roumania's present frustration with the Soviet Union is that its economic planners wanted to develop Roumania's industry, whereas the Soviets wanted to concentrate on producing agricultural surpluses that could easily be tapped. It is assumed by the Soviet Union that such a policy would reduce the present drain on Soviet resources involved in directing the industrialization of Eastern Europe. Granick has pointed out that "the Eastern European countries would also gain, in the sense that they would have several eager trading partners instead of one reluctant one." [23]

Many development specialists of the United States have argued that American economic interests are compatible with the trade interests of the underdeveloped nations.[24] It is further assumed that the generosity represented by aid from the American taxpayer to underdeveloped nations will in the long run benefit the United States by opening up new credit lines on favorable terms. However, this supposed moral softness is more mythical than real, since the funds made available are smaller than generally believed. Aid figures often indicate commitments and authorizations rather than actual disbursements. Furthermore, amortization and interest payments must be deducted from gross aid figures; as indeed a further deduction must be made, since many payments are in the form of military aid rather than economic support. With respect to Latin America, disbursements are often in the form of Eximbank loans, "Whose funds are derived from the sale of Treasury bills to investors." [25] "These loans have realized a profit for American investors. And with the aid of the Inter-American Bank potential investors are provided with new channels for development funds open to Latin American governments." [26] Disbursement in part is made in the form of surplus commodities which would otherwise remain idle and subject to storage costs or deterioration.

23. David Granick, "Economic Relations with the USSR," in *Resources and Planning in Eastern Europe, op. cit.*
24. Eugene Staley, *The Future of Underdeveloped Countries* (revised edition). New York: Frederick A. Praeger, 1961, esp. pp. 397–441.
25. Irving Louis Horowitz, *Revolution in Brazil: Politics and Society in a Developing Nation.* New York: E. P. Dutton & Co., 1964, esp. pp. 196–223.
26. Tad Szulc, *Winds of Revolution.* New York: Frederick Praeger, 1963, esp. pp. 275–77.

The performance of the United States, with respect to the Third World in the United Nations and outside of it, represents a rational extension of United States economic policy combined with United States foreign policy. It is in fact a continuation of politics by economic means, nothing unusual in the annals of Western civilization. Earlier there was France and its doctrine of Liberty, Equality, and Fraternity —which in effect primarily served its *mission civilisatrice*. Then there was England whose liberal virtues were considered too important for the sun ever to set on the British Empire. Before that there was Holland with its protectionism that freed itself from Spain, only to serve Dutch exploitation of the East Indies in much the same way.

The United States, since entering international politics as a major force, has been confronted by a duality within its tradition, no less blatant than what confronted England, France, and Holland before it. On one side there is its revolutionary background—a belief in a democracy where each man counts as one and no man counts as more or less than one. On the other side there is the United States of the manifest destiny of the Monroe Doctrine and of the Puritan conviction that the fate of the world is pre-determined by the march of American hegemony. These political contradictions were no more deterrents to American economic growth than was totalitarianism to Russian economic growth or liberalism to European growth.

The confusions are well stated by Hans J. Morgenthau: "The traditional anti-imperialism of America was without a political objective either by virtue of its very nature or else because the radius of an active American foreign policy was limited to the Western Hemisphere." In contrast to this,

> the new anti-imperialism can no longer afford to condemn the suppression of liberty from afar and limit its tribute to freedom to charitable deeds. Committed to the containment of communism, to the preservation of national freedom wherever it is threatened by Soviet imperialism, the United States can reconcile itself to this loss of national freedom only if it altogether ceases being anti-imperialistic.[27]

In other words, anti-imperialism, by taking on anti-communist pretensions, has become tough-minded instead of tender-hearted. But even

27. See Hans J. Morgenthau, "The American Tradition in Foreign Policy," in *Foreign Policy in World Politics,* edited by R. C. Macridis. Englewood Cliffs, N.J.: Prentice-Hall, 1962, pp. 206–11.

Morgenthau shrinks away from the *Realpolitik* of this anti-communist framework. He has to see United States interests as eternally linked to European allies in particular and to a "common civilization threatened by an alien and oppressive social system" in general. In other words, the classic stress between "interests" and "ethics" is seen as a uniquely American problem, and for that very reason, a certain jejune quality is manifested in United States international policies with respect to the Third World.

The United States when faced with responsibilities and problems of world leadership has shown that it is no more and no less ethical than those leading nations which came before it in time. The specific character of the confrontation rather than the universal moral goals which, after all, define the nature of the contradiction within the United States, and its inability to reconcile power and morality. Perhaps the youthfulness of the United States is attested to by the fact that it has not yet awakened to the possibilities that in important ways the two are irreconcilable. Every imperial nation has an ideology that muddles reality: from civilizing missions to white man's burden and now anti-communist crusades. The motives undergirding this rhetoric is an attempt to build an American empire on the basis of a counter-imperialism; a far cry from the early American pledge of anti-imperialism. The United States conceives the efforts of other nations to extend territorial influence as imperialistic; its own efforts to do so are often conceived as rescue operations. It is therefore blind to its own imperialism and considers the efforts to extend its own power as the height of justice.

With perfect moralistic consistency it can pursue policies which seek to extend its spheres of influence in the name of justice and deliverance from tyranny. The United States is an imperialistic democracy. But it cannot reconcile the nature of the terms. It could perhaps wield its power more ruthlessly in certain areas, but then it would not square with a democratic self-image. It could allow for the full autonomy of weaker nations, but then it would not be powerful. While it attempts both, it loses ground on both fronts. It cannot be frankly imperialistic as England and France were in earlier generations. Neither can it be truly just. It is ambivalent because it feels now the needs of one, now the needs of the other. Thus, it has never developed a satisfactory imperialistic style, nor a meaningful moral posture.

Every great nation has a sense of mission. It has often been noted that a great nation is both expansionist and imperialistic because it is in the nature of power that it be driven thus. The Soviet Union also has this divided self-image. It too is exporting democracy, economic if not political democracy. It also conceived the extension of its influence in the name of freedom from tyranny. It has sought to store immense power in its organs of government, and notions of its ethical mission have guided its foreign policies. It too has undertaken to solve the white man's burden. It acts in the name of moral justice, often sincerely. The Soviet Union amasses power to extend the areas of freedom, though its conception of this term is largely economic. Like the United States, it is sensitive to reactions to its policies from those whom it tries to influence. It perceives itself as anti-imperialist.

The United States defines justice in terms of political liberty. The Soviet Union defines justice in terms of economic welfare. The latter best suits the needs of the Third World. The United States defined imperialism as a form of injustice. According to its political libertarian definitions of justice the Soviet Union is unjust and imperialistic, the former because of the latter. The Soviet Union defines injustice as attempts to practice political libertarianism without solving economic dilemmas of poverty. Injustice of this kind can be engaged in legitimately only by an elite. Hence efforts to spread this false democracy are imperialistic and unjust, the former because of the latter. The ideologies of the First and Second Worlds are therefore mirror images of each other's shortcomings in practice.

The underdeveloped countries conceive it to be their sovereign right to make their own choice between the First and Second Worlds. And the United Nations is in some sense their instrument for limiting the imperialistic variations of both worlds, while holding both accountable for their ideal claims. Efforts on the part of the United States to obstruct United Nations conference decision-making are seen as unjust and imperialistic. For part of the Third World shares with the Soviet Union an economic conception of democracy and justice. The successes of the Soviet Union in the economic sphere seem to be confirmation of this belief. Hence the Soviet Union does not seem to be imperialistic. The Soviet Union, like the United States, is seen as powerful, but United States power is viewed as necessarily restrictive of the sovereignty of underdeveloped nations. This is defined as imperialist. American attempts to combat the imperialist image, by such programs as the Alliance for Progress and the Peace Corps, have aimed at paralleling its interests with altruistic actions, but have never made a significant sacrifice of the former, and therefore such institutions as the Peace Corps come in for particular derision because of the hypocrisy involved—if not by the practitioneers then by the Washington political establishment. The Soviet Union is not in a similar bind at the present historical moment. The United States can attend a conference at which the underdeveloped countries present a number of proposals and resolutions for implementing programs to relieve their economic distress, and out of the simple fact that the Russians can support these proposals without serious sacrifice to its positions, the United States seems peculiarly colonialist and, hence, unjust. To counter this imperialism the United States has to surrender some part of its own immediate interest. When the United States does not give support to the Third World, it gives the classical argument of the rights of power. The United States balances these factors "pragmatically," issue by issue. It cannot surrender any part of its interest, nor will it recognize other legitimate definitions of justice. It cannot see the temporariness of these given issues, and tends to stand therefore for "eternal truths" when it votes as when it fights.

That this "self-interest" doctrine is gaining support is shown by the tendency of at least one wing of American policy-makers to consider foreign aid in militaristic rather than in developmental terms. One authority has summed up this position most candidly: "American policies regarding aid and trade may legitimately be employed as strategic weapons in the Cold War, and that in such employment, flexibility is both appropriate and necessary." [28] In short, all trade and aid must be viewed in terms of enhancing the security of the United States, while any humanitarian concerns must be considered as a by-product of national objectives. The startling voting pattern of the United States, with respect to Third World trade demands, can be considered a response to the growing self-consciousness of America as a world power—something not in evidence during previous decades. The American dialogue between considerations of power in contrast to those of justice remains in evidence. It is also clear that the power factions within the political hierarchy now occupy command positions with respect to the issuance of foreign assistance.

The perverse voting pattern of the United States at the Conference on

28. James R. Schlesinger, "Strategic Leverage from Aid and Trade," in *National Security: Political, Military, and Economic Strategies in the Decade Ahead,* edited by David M. Abshire and Richard V. Allen. New York: Frederick A. Praeger (for the Hoover Institution on War, Revolution and Peace), 1963, pp. 688–89.

Trade and Development shows it to be combatting Soviet influence in the name of justice. It is, it believes, acting cautiously or out of principle. To the rest of the world, which does not share this dialectic of self-definition or self-interest with the Soviet Union, the United States is seen to be acting against its own interest. Hence, the United States is often looked upon as an imperialist which cannot extend the borders of democracy. The United States stands alone with irritating suspicions as to why, but with few explanations. This kind of political behavior, this incapacity to surrender anything but taxpayers' money for foreign aid, reveals it to be blind to the image cast. The United States cannot adopt colonialist positions as equivalent to justice. Modern imperialism is built into the American system of political democracy. This paradox cannot be easily removed by a new vocabulary or a new dedication to national purpose.

Perhaps the cruelest cut of all is that the political posture of the United States has itself become a unifying agency of Third World nations. What might easily deteriorate into national rivalries, regional jealousies, and social distinctions are prevented from doing so, in some measure at least, by the fear of United States policy formulators that a positive line toward the Third World is tantamount to a betrayal of national interests. Thus the purposes of United States moral aims are contradicted not so much by the communist challenge as by United States political decisions.

For all the confusions and ambiguities which exist in the interaction of the United Nations and the Third World, the fact is that the latter increasingly has come to define the operational characteristics of the former. The United Nations for its part has enshrined the concept of the Third World in the very organization of its data, if not its decisions. The First World has come to be labeled the "developed market economies"; the Second World is called the "centrally planned economies"; and the Third World is identified simply as the "developing countries." Whatever organizational relationships may obtain with the United Nations, the obvious need to organize information on the premise that there are three spheres of development serves to legitimize the triadic nature of social and economic relationships in the world.

III

Third World
in Development

9

Community and Society:
Alternative Developmental Models

What is required for understanding models of development is a combination of linguistic analysis and sociological analysis. What indeed may be needed is a combination of the logical skills of Wittgenstein and the sociological capacities of Weber. It would be presumptuous of me to claim to have effected such a synthesis.

The concept of *model* is as slippery as any currently in use by the social sciences. Even if we can settle on a formal definition of the word, namely, an isomorphic representation of objects that leads to an unmistakable identification of the expression of the object with the physical object, we are left with a host of substantive issues.[1]

There are at least three different fundamental meanings which attach to the term "model," each which almost puts the word in a different universe of discourse each time. First, "model" is used as a surrogate for "levels," or an epistemological statement of how the world is carved up. Second, "model" is used as a surrogate for "strategies." This entails the pragmatics of social change, or how one goes about carving a world up. Third, "model" is often used as a surrogate for "theory," or how the explanation of changes in the world can best be made. What I should like to do is provide at the outset a framework showing what is entailed in each of these types of models of development and then show the implications of model-construction for social change.[2]

1. See May Brodbeck, "Models, Meaning, and Theories," in *Symposium on Sociological Theory,* Evanston, Ill.: Row, Peterson, 1959, pp. 373–403.
2. For a serious cooperative effort in this direction at model-building, see Willard A. Beling and George O. Totten, *Developing Nations: Quest for a Model.* New York: Van Nostrand Reinhold Co., 1970, pp. 207–25.

THE MODEL AS A SOCIETY: THE COMMUNITY CONCEPT

Let us begin with the study of how models are used in terms of levels. What one finds is that models of development extend from personality development, or how the individual unfolds by progressive stages, to international development, which generally refers to how agencies of a supranational character evolve to handle problems of economic, exchange, legal-diplomatic norms, political sovereignty, and demographic-ecological boundaries. At the same time, when social scientists deal with models of development they oftentimes imply intermediary levels at a range extending from the little community to giant nation-states. It is customary for each of the social-science disciplines to have a relatively precise model of development, and in this sense to carve out an explicit level at which types of research are legitimized. Thus, in general, anthropologists have as their model the community. Political scientists have as their model the nation and the problems of sovereignty. Economists have as their model the class of problems related to the interaction of those groups within a society most responsible for industrial production.

It is evident that this linkage of models to levels has a great bearing on the kinds of results which are obtained. What is implied is not simply a model as a level of development, but a set of assumptions indicating the main human carriers or the key institutions of the developmental process. Thus a social psychologist may write a text on human development with the explicit assumption that *human* in this instance refers to the biosocial patterns from childhood to adulthood, while an economist may use the concept of development in terms of how the wealthy classes within a nation are able to manipulate changes either for their personal profit-taking or for the general productive norms.

It would not be possible, nor for that matter feasible, to provide an exhaustive analysis of the concept of models as it relates to levels. However, by taking one well-worked model for one well-articulated level (in the first case the community level of development), it is immediately evident that several kinds of conceptual problems arise when one studies the developmental process.

The community as a form of social organization is the most amorphous model from a geographical perspective, and therefore it charges the anthropologist with considerable conceptual dilemmas. Nonetheless, it is my view that the use of a model of development based on the community level really has no fewer and no greater problems than those encountered by scholars working with a concept of national development.

Generally speaking, those who use the manifest concept of community employ a latent model of "true" community. By community one usually means: (1) people who share in similar activities and in unfolding similar values and virtues; (2) people who share common problems and act jointly and amiably to solve them; (3) that they may individually engage in dissimilar activities but that many of these prove to be interdependent, and (4) that there is a strong psychological identification among members of any true community. Insofar as the isomorphic properties of the community model go, it cannot be faulted. The difficulty intrudes itself at a different angle; namely, the assumption that a true community implies a fixed geographic terrain no less than a psychological condition. The model of a true community tends arbitrarily to fuse two realms of reality (the psychological and geographical), and it is at this point that the problems of the community model of development become insurmountable.

The first and main charge that one could make is that at the psychological level the definition of a true community has no more warrant behind it than the definition of a true nation. That is to say, the nineteenth-century Germanic historians define nationhood in precisely the same terms of "community of fate" as twentieth-century community developmentalists define progress.

A second, and scarcely less damaging, critique is that the psychological notion of community, even if taken at face value in its pure *Gemeinschaft* form, created by the German sociologist Toennies, is not necessarily found in the kind of geographical terrain generally connected with agricultural production that the model implies. One can find a true community in any slum block of any large city—such as Whyte's *Street Corner Society*—if the stipulations adduced in the community model are confined to their psychological indicators.

This brings us to our third criticism. The notion of true community, as it is commonly used, is in fact a model of agricultural scale-enlargement and not an attempt to explain the characteristics of community life in an industrial setting. The agricultural bias found in the concept of community development creates a double bind for those who do field work at this level. On one hand there are the *nostalgists* who think of community development as some return to paradise, that is, an organic civilization.[3] On the other hand are the *utopists,* who perceive of the true agricultural community as something to move forward to.[4] But whether in its nostalgic or utopian form, the model of development implied by community studies often denotes a singular level of development, namely, the level of agricultural technology. It further rests on a negative appraisal of what industrial society either has done or can do to mankind.[5]

Invariably, those who adhere to the community model are found to be the severest critics of mass society and the alienation it engenders. The imputation of negative motives is usually accompanied by a vocabulary of alienation. The list of bad words usually contains "disorganization," "decline," "insecurity," "breakdown," "frustration," "anxiety," "dehumanization," "depersonalization," "bureaucratization," "anomie," and so on. In contrast, the model community is charged with the heavy responsibility of providing organization, progress, security, organic living, humane behavior, and *Verstehen.* In short, the problem of the community level involves a stereotype, the assumptions of which are highly dubious and made obscure by the very model which underwrites the stereotype.

Even those defenders of the community development model most appreciative of the need for structural change in the macrosociety remain caught up in a set of implausible contradictions. On one hand, they want community development to entail scale-enlargement, that is, to link smaller communities into larger units. Yet, on the other, they still want to retain the township-community as "the natural seat of development" without explaining what is so natural about town or village existence.[6] Indeed, the demise within the last several years of several leading community development journals such as *International Review of Community Development* and *Community Development Bulletin* indicates the inability of any single level of social organization to constitute a meaningful model for social development.

3. See Robert Nisbet, *The Quest for Community: A Study in the Ethics of Order and Freedom.* New York: Oxford University Press, 1953.
4. See Allen R. Holmberg, "Changing Community Attitudes and Values in Peru: A Case Study in Guided Change," in *Social Change in Latin America Today.* New York: Harper & Row, 1960.
5. See, for example, Henry Winthrop, "In Quest of Community," *Journal of Human Relations,* Vol. 14 (1966), pp. 457–72.
6. See J. A. Ponsioen, "In Defense of Community Development," *International Development Review,* Vol. 7 (Sept. 1965), pp. 15–16.

The community development model is historically anchored. It arises in connection with the growth of village life and early city life, where the psychological characteristics of a "community of fate" were in fact fused to the economic characteristics of a "concentration of production." But the present situation is one in which urbanization and industrialization have simply displaced the community development idea in most parts of the developing world. It is strange and a trifle anomalous to find social scientists speaking of community development when the criteria invoked would seem to indicate it was equally necessary to deal with the notion of tribal development. Clearly this is not the case—development does not simply mean the expansion of a level of social organization. It may (and often does) imply the destruction of old organizational modalities. In this sense, I am suggesting that the community, like the tribe, represents an archaic form of social organization and hence an awkward style of sociological explanation.

The city as well as the community might be placed in the category of the historically obsolete. This is surely the implication of the work of Jean Gottman, whose concept of "megalopolis" definitely entails a version of development that moves beyond the confines of the city—either in its juridical or informal definitions—into a network of interlocking associations based on new levels of transportation and communication.[7] To speak of urban development may soon be as obsolete as speaking of community or rural development. For social scientists to get beyond the mechanistic equations of development to the progress of any single level of social organization, they should give closer attention to the relationship between obsolescence and innovation as the essential dialectic of development. In that way, the special issues arising from urbanization will be placed in the larger focus of industrialization and modernization.

THE MODEL AS STRATEGY:
THE CONSUMER-PRODUCTION CONCEPT

Models can also be used as a surrogate for development strategies or, as I have indicated, the pragmatics of change—how one plans the future. At this level the types of personnel involved are planners, engineers, and

7. Jean Gottman, *Megalopolis: The Urbanized Northeastern Seaboard of the United States.* New York: The Twentieth Century Fund, 1961.

technicians more often than they are social scientists. These are models based not on scientific requirements but rather on therapeutic requirements, on getting the job done, on clearing away the debris of traditionalism.[8]

At this second tier, the concept of models is directly linked to an indicator or set of indicators, which, taken as a whole, is said to provide a basis for rapid development. As in the case of the community, we shall confine ourselves here to one commonly used illustration: the equation of development to consumer production.

On this count, we can take recourse to the Rostovian model, in which the key indicator is consumer production, particularly automotive production,[9] and at the other end of the scale, a Prebisch model, in which the key indicator becomes national industrial production.[10] While Prebisch appears to adopt the neo-Keynesian model more critically than Rostow, in point of fact, for him, no less than for Rostow, the consumer is the touchstone. In both cases, the drive to technological maturity presupposes the existence within a national economy of a sophisticated industrial system, possessing a high consumer orientation, which in turn can be plugged into a developed transportation and communication network. The implication of the model is a unitary outcome of a high energy productive system, that is, the equation of rapid development based on modernization and a high level of consumer response.

Such models employed as guides for planning work on roughly the same kind of technological premise; namely, the presence of a heavily industrial basis becomes prima facie evidence for developing a strategy of rapid development. If every effort is bent to develop a domestically owned and controlled heavily industrial basis, development then appears within the reach of all. In the case of Rostow, it is assumed that what works well for the United States can be both simulated and assimilated elsewhere in the world. In the Prebisch model, it is assumed that a capital intensive model which has worked well for Western

8. A good indication of this type of model-building is contained in John McHale, "The Future of the Future," in *Architectural Design*, Feb. 1967, pp. 64–101.
9. See W. W. Rostow, *The Stages of Economic Growth: A Non-Communist Manifesto*. Cambridge: Cambridge University Press, 1960; and more recently, "Unsolved Problems of International Development," *International Development Review*, Vol. 7, No. 4, Dec. 1965, and Vol. 8, No. 1, Mar. 1966.
10. See Raúl Prebisch, *Nueva Política Comercial para el Desarrollo*. Mexico—Buenos Aires: Fondo de Cultura Económica, 1964.

Europe will work well for underdeveloped areas. Neither assumption can be sustained by evidence. As a matter of fact, these models are often tried but rarely work.

Let us look at these models more closely. In the case of Rostow, the use of a consumer indicator—automotive production, for example—introduces the dilemma (for Latin American nations at least) that a high rate of automotive production can occur, and yet the nation involved can still find itself in the intense grips of underdevelopment. One might go further and say that extreme consumer orientation may deepen the economic crisis and forestall development. The Rostow model often is dependent upon credit and deficit-spending policies that induce the nation to maintain its agriculturally based economy as a means of paying for these modernization programs through the export of primary goods. The real decision, however, is not so much whether to increase automotive production or heavy industrialization as it is whether to produce automobiles for consumers or trucks for the use of the agricultural market.

The problems with the Prebisch model are as serious as those in the Rostow model when applied against the practical means for achieving full development. It might be that for any given society the costs in any change-over from an agrarian to an industrial basis are far too heavy to justify the transformation. This is especially true in small nations, as the East European bloc and many nations of Latin America have discovered. If the goal of many nations is not a self-sustaining economy but rather the greatest surplus of per capita wealth, then one cannot declare a priori that agricultural production is less efficacious than industry in achieving such goods.

The Prebisch model also assumes that industrial production will constantly be more profitable than agricultural production. But this is not necessarily so. Particularly in the present era, when increasing food shortages go together with increasing secondary commodity abundance, it might turn out that those nations which maintain their agricultural basis on sound social and technological principles instead of transforming it to increased consumer production will have a significant edge.

In Latin America there has been a serious obstacle to the application of this approach. Agricultural predominance has meant the predominance of a landlord class. Thus, even when land reform is advocated most forcefully, it tends to be linked with radical changes in industry and the urban regions. For the most visible demonstration of nationalism are brand names carrying a local national and linguistic identification. Therefore, it is essential to appreciate the extent to which any rational model—and in this sense "rational" means economically advantageous —must come to terms with the political culture.

The model of industrial production usually meshes with a doctrine of technological society. In both the "conservative" Rostow and "liberal" Prebisch variants, the index of progress remains the rate of increase in consumer products, an appeal to "materialistic" and acquisitorial attitudes rather than to long-range social programs. Rostow makes a direct appeal to industrial technology and economic growth, while Prebisch makes an indirect—almost elliptical—appeal by emphasizing the high cost of consumer imports and the low yield from agricultural products.

The model of industrial production equates maturity with mass consumption. It has as an underlying premise the fusion of capitalist and socialist economic sectors. This model is based on three false assumptions: (1) It is empirically incorrect to speak of the fusion of capitalism and socialism, or for that matter of the United States and the Soviet Union. (2) Even if the model covers the Third World nations, the notion of industrial production as the unique road to mass consumption fails to recognize the possibility that agricultural production may become more important than industrial production, and hence more profitable. (3) The model not only puts too much emphasis upon the unity between the capitalist and socialist sectors but also upon the unity of the capitalist bloc and the socialist bloc. The fissures within each major bloc indicate that no over-all agreement between them seems possible.

Actually it is quite certain that one does not get similar attitudes between nations by mimesis or by simulation techniques (as Rostow's position strongly implies). Nor can any general agreement result from appeals to rich nations to work out more equitable trade and tariff levels for poor nations (as Prebisch strongly implies). In many instances of model-building at this intermediate strategic level, there is an assumption that underdevelopment is the same as feudal ancestry and hence that advanced nations—capitalist and socialist alike—have a vested interest in helping underdeveloped nations achieve models for growth that could place them in a take-off position.

Too rarely is it appreciated that underdeveloped conditions may be the consequence of the developed sectors. The fully developed nations have actually helped foster undevelopment through the policies of intervention that they have followed.[11] What would the history of Latin America be if the colonization of the area by the Spaniards in the eighteenth century, the British in the nineteenth century, or the United States in the twentieth century had never taken place? Surely, the so-called "feudalistic" aspects of the hemisphere can just as well be viewed as an essential attribute of foreign colonization as a lingering consequence of feudalism, Catholicism, geography, or any one of a number of other factors said to explain the backwardness of Latin America. In this instance, as in many others, the model of developmental strategy disguises nostalgia on the one hand and the role of foreign intervention on the other.

The failure to acknowledge even the possibility that a "revolution of rising expectations" is directly related to a "revolution of falling profits" has given most strategies of development a Pollyannish glow in "advanced" nations while leading to bitter responses in many "backward" nations. The fanaticism of consumer production has led to a different kind of crisis that has been no less deep for many other developing areas. Nations have been producing pots and pans at twice the world market price and half the quality, all in the name of nationalism. The model of strategic development may start with pragmatics, but it ends with dogmatics—which leads the Third World to a permanent condition of satellite-subordinate relationship. The series of historic failures that have occurred reveal what exaggerated faith in model-building has cost.

THE MODEL AS A THEORY: MONETARISM AND STRUCTURALISM

Finally, we have the use of models as a surrogate for theory. Here the purpose is not so much to carve up or to change the world but to understand the mechanisms involved in the developmental process as part of a more general socioeconomic system, which in turn creates certain structural tensions because of the systematic framework. What is often involved is not simply an explanation of change, but, more usually, an insistence that change take place in a certain way.

11. One significant effort to overcome the consensual model of development, at least on the hemispheric level, is Andrew Gunder Frank, *Capitalism and Underdevelopment in Latin America*. New York and London: Monthly Review Press, 1967.

The theoretical models used by economists and sociologists are brothers under the skin. One group of sociologists speaks of modernization, while economists speak of monetarism. But what is meant is roughly the same thing: a consumer-oriented society in which basic creature comforts are available on the basis of the capital derived from the sale of agricultural and light industrial goods. Another group of sociologists will speak of industrialization, while economists deal with structuralism. In each case what is involved is a transformation of the industrial basis of the satellite nation. Profits are held to derive from import-substituting activities rather than from the export of crops to, or the import of finished goods from, the cosmopolitan centers. The structuralist approach insists that the production model rather than the consumption model be considered primary in the developmental process.

There has been scant attention given to what has aptly been termed the "explosive" model of development.[12] Increasingly, a theory of revolution is seen as a prelude to development rather than as a postscript to underdevelopment. This is meant to explain the activities of private entrepreneurs. For instance, most Latin American private investors will not invest in either labor-saving or capital intensive activities unless they really do save labor and capital. Most fully developed nations have been able to avoid the explosive model because investment choice was made with little effort to calculate either costs or rates of return. Both in the United States and in the Soviet Union, investment allocation quickly became a matter of political decision-making—with priorities set by the state rather than by private investment returns. But in Latin America, where the public sector has been singularly unable to harness the private sector, revolutionary preconditions may arise if for no other reason than to break the bottleneck of economic laissez faire. Thus, the explosive model of development might be a necessary prelude to the full-fledged urbanization and industrialization of Latin America, and perhaps of other parts of the underdeveloped world suffering from this same static condition which obtains between private and public sectors.

This kind of model-construction creates intellectual polarities that have few, if any, distinguishable payoffs in developmental economics. The controversy between monetarists and structuralists in economics illustrates this. For the monetarists, the most significant indicators are a

12. For this point I am indebted to the paper by Alec Nove, "The Explosive Model," *The Journal of Development Studies,* Vol. 3 (Oct. 1966), pp. 2–13.

stable price level and a stable rate of exchange. It is held that where these are present, savings will be encouraged, and it will be easier to promote exports; foreign capital will be attracted and domestic capital will invest in the home economy; and investments in long-term projects will increase. The key to achieving these ends is a non-inflationary situation. For the structuralists, the most significant indicators of economic development are an equitable distribution of wealth and a meaningful redistribution of property. It is held that when these two factors are considered, savings will be encouraged, it will be easier to promote exports, foreign capital will be attracted and domestic capital will invest in the home economy, and investment in the long-term projects will increase. The key to achieving these ends is sound policy-making.[13]

It is interesting how each doctrine considers itself a way out of revolution and views the other as resulting in a revolution. This was put most bluntly by Dudley Seers when he wrote: "The paradox is that though the monetarist is normally far from a revolutionary, and his preference is for peace and quiet, his policies may lead to social disorder and eventually regimentation of one form or another." The dilemma arises (and this Seers does not address himself to) that the same sort of regimentation is involved on structuralist premises, perhaps even more clearly, since Adam Smith's "invisible hand" is to be replaced by Lenin's "guiding plan."

It is difficult to understand how a theoretical resolution can be made for this sort of problem. How can the economist answer whether growth is more important than stability any more than the sociologist can theoretically resolve whether modernization is more important than industrialization? In the case of our economists it leads them to postulate the incompatibility of growth and stability, while it may lead the sociologists to postulate the incompatibility of industrialization and modernization. It is not that incompatibility does not exist; it is only that such an outcome cannot legitimately be derived from model-construction.

Nor can this point be reduced to the banal proposition that the truth of every controversy is to be found somewhere in the middle. For that too is clearly fallacious, as improper a deduction from the model as

13. See the masterful presentations of the monetarist and structuralist positions respectively by Graeme S. Dorrance, "The Effect of Inflation on Economic Development," and Dudley Seers, "Inflation and Growth: The Heart of the Controversy," in *Inflation and Growth in Latin America,* edited by Werner Baer and Issac Kerstenetzky. Homewood, Ill.: Richard D. Irwin Co., 1964, pp. 37–103.

reification. Indeed, the real dilemma in model-building is that while it generally starts with arbitrary polarization it ends with false synthesis. In the case of Latin America, at least, it might well be that revolutionary solutions are requisites for either monetarist or structuralist strategies or both. For while it has properly been noted that "one can be a structuralist at a five per cent a year inflation rate and a monetarist when prices are increasing at fifty per cent per annum," it is hard to be anything but a revolutionist when inflation reaches beyond 50 per cent, or when there is a corresponding stagnation in levels of production.

At the level of theory, one can see the essential weakness of model-construction, for it offers an ideological substitute for those who most passionately eschew ideology as such.

The same is true with the respective languages of political science and economics. Some political scientists speak of nation-building, while more traditionally oriented ones speak of nationalism. What is involved in both cases is the fusion of economic development and agencies of political planning for the purpose of legitimizing the forms of rule, and no less galvanizing growth projects of national proportions. From the point of view of political development this kind of model applies to an economy based on national rather than regional needs. This tends to be a large-nation model; and thus the "fit" of the model is once more seriously impaired by the assumption of parity and simulation.

Social scientists could offer (but rarely do) a revolution-making model in place of a nation-building model. This model would make the achievement model at the psychological level into a change model at the political level. The assumption that certain institutional forms have to be broken before full developmental "take-off" can be reached seems to fall outside of "disciplinary" boundaries. The assumption that illegitimacy rather than legitimacy has become the basic fact of twentieth-century development, or at least development within the Third World, is rarely entertained by social scientists whose essential model derives from equilibrium and consensus doctrines. The political and the economic point of view coincide in advocating mending existing economic orders rather than making over the old economic system. The fusion of politics with economics is made complete by transforming the revolutionary elite into heads of planning agencies. This might involve the destruction of those economic sectors that are non-productive, and hence might involve a revision of conventional models of how development occurs.

The range of phenomena described by the rubric of modernization, which is itself little else than a surrogate for urbanization and industrialization, which is little more than a surrogate for capitalization and nation-building, which itself is nothing more than a surrogate for socialism, all present stereotyped explanations of how the world changes. They explain development within a rationalized vision of what the world ought to be. The dilemma at the stage of model construction is that if explanation is simply a form of prediction, and prediction is simply the reverse of explanation, we come upon a difficult moment. In the social sciences, explanation is often a form of exhortation; if the exhortation is successful, it may then be called a correct prediction. The exhortations in favor of any type of model previously mentioned, when successful, become incorporated with the hope that they will justify the inevitability of national building, modernization, socialism, or any other deterministic "model." Such models do not, however, take variables into account or provide a warrant for manipulation, but merely provide a means of insinuating moral desires or ethical commitments into the social structure. The deterministic system becomes a form of consecrating the future into the present.

This is not to say that the social world is pure volition or that there is an absence of determinism in the long run (although the wider use of stochastic models in place of deterministic models might prove just as fruitful). However, the models that support theories of development oftentimes rest upon an ideological frame of reference improperly equated with an explanatory frame of reference. It is difficult to distinguish between explanation and ideology at the social levels precisely because ideological exhortation can be effectively translated into manipulation of the social system. The developmental ideology can then be shown to demonstrate the rightness of any given model of society.

The entire concept of models as they relate to social development ought to be seriously reviewed for their ethnocentric and ideological content before mechanically being applied to every level of society, to any strategy for bringing about changes in that society, or to any theory offering an explanation of the society. Invariably, the most interesting aspect of any model is what is *excluded* rather than what is *included*. Herein is the essential weakness of deductive systems used in predicting or prodding social development; and herein is the tale of why the best-laid plans of men and machines often go astray.

10

Expropriation and Taxation: The Economic Pivot

The main problem in development from the economic viewpoint is not the need to "break out" of stagnation. This is a politically inspired decision. The economic issues enter at that point where the initial political decision has to be sustained and upheld by economic action. The hub of the matter for Third World nations is this: how can they amass the savings necessary to bring themselves into the modern world. Of course, the language used to express this sentiment varies widely. Some might talk of achievement values, others of the need to break up feudal property holdings. Even within strictly economic terms the path of development might be viewed in terms of constraints on foreign exchange, human capital resources, investments as a percentage of the gross national product, and the like. But this latter is the same process of "savings" viewed from the standpoint of domestic investments. Such savings can be created either through taxation or expropriation. Taxation can be called "forced savings," "guided investments," "reallocation of profits"; expropriation can be called "land reform," "urban renewal," "popular control"—but the fact is that an economy can be grounded either in evolutionary principles of mending existing social structures, or in revolutionary principles of smashing and replacing these structures. There is a third approach—retaining surpluses from state-run enterprises. However, such an approach presupposes a resolution of inherited forms of savings and investments.

The concern here is with the place of taxation, involuntary savings, and other fiscal measures in stimulating the economy. We will consider types of expropriation-confiscation of land with the aim of establishing individual proprietorship or collectivist ownership. The decision to re-form a society or conduct a revolution against it from an economic perspective means choosing whether to mend or to smash the social structure.

Various governmental and international agencies employ a convenient shorthand in describing development. Social development is indicated by such criteria as improvements in the fields of education, health, nutrition, housing, and social security. Economic development is in-dicated by such criteria as increases in production, in per capita use of electrical energy.[1] However, the fact is that with a 3 per cent world birth rate, underdeveloped nations will have to do better than the United States in the 1970's merely to avoid getting poorer. Thus even if such nations satisfy the positive criteria for economic growth, they must also be in a position to prevent an erosion of their relative positions vis-à-vis population increases.

As the late Paul Baran well understood, economic development has always been propelled by classes and by groups interested in a new economic and social order. It has always been opposed and obstructed by those interested in, and deriving innumerable benefits from, an existing fabric of society, and from the prevailing mores, customs, and institutions.[2] Given the interrelation between social and economic de-velopment, we may begin the discussion of taxation and expropriation with an appreciation of the complexities involved. Taxation often rep-resents the transfer of real resources from the private to the public sector and from personal consumption to social saving.[3] And while taxes can be spent on such items as social security payments, and hence do not always and necessarily change the net balance between consumption and savings in the total economy, they do tend to be used in this way. The tax base also serves to stimulate investment and minimize private "idle capital" precisely to the extent that the tax structure reinforces invest-ment and not idleness. Moreover, taxation legitimizes the political ap-paratus by "rationalizing" the social system. Economic improvement carries with it the right and even obligation for the political apparatus

1. *Report on the World Situation*. New York: United Nations, 1961, p. 41. In this connection, see an earlier report, *Measures for the Economic Development of Underdeveloped Countries*. New York: United Nations, 1957.
2. Paul Baran, *The Political Economy of Growth*. New York: Monthly Review Press, 1957, p. 3 *et passim*.
3. *Economic Survey of Asia and Far-East*. New York: United Nations, 1961, p. 210.

to purchase or produce many goods and services, and to redistribute income among different sections of the community.[4] This perspective has further meant the crumbling of the older ideology that only the savings of the capitalist counts.[5] The very extension of the principle of savings to include all economic sectors means that in some sense a model of development, which would be liberated from the structures of any one sector, would, in part, be liberated from the restrictions of economic competition as such.[6]

A basic factor determining the rate of economic development is the ratio of investment to income, or the percentage of current income transformed into new productive uses. The strategy of increasing such investment capital is a political chore. Governments in the Third World survive or collapse by the decisions they take concerning the stimulation of development. To "tax" the poor through denial of wage increases or through austerity programs is one way; to "tax" the rich directly through government collection of funds gained as a result of business profits is another way. To do nothing results in stagnation. To burden the poor may stimulate revolution. To focus on the wealthy may lead to industrial demoralization and the flight of capital. Therefore to mend or to smash is at the basis of any taxation approach. The economics of development is thus linked to the politics of risk-taking. The strategy of taxing the poor indirectly, by charging exhorbitant prices for a restricted supply of consumer goods, while at the same time expropriating the rich in more direct, conventional terms, was successfully tried in the Soviet Union in the 1920's. The difficulty, as we shall see, in this double pronged approach of taxation and expropriation is that it entails a high degree of centralized authority and effectively managed coercion.

To accomplish a mobilization of financial resources, governments

4. A. R. Prest, *Public Finance in Underdeveloped Countries.* London: Weidenfeld & Nicolson, 1962, p. 17.
5. W. Arthur Lewis, *The Theory of Economic Growth,* Homewood, Ill.: Irwin Publishers, 1955, pp. 225–27.
6. A basic problem economists frequently encounter is that while they see the possibilities for moving beyond the laissez-faire assumptions in the idea that only capitalists save, they fail to appreciate the possibilities, even the likelihood, that when the state imposes universal taxation, it gives us a model of development which is no longer economic in character; that is to say, one which no longer relies on the free play of free-market forces to amass savings. See Albert O. Hirschman, *The Strategy of Economic Development.* New Haven: Yale University Press, 1958, pp. 38–39.

often use fiscal manipulation. An important part of this program is taxation. An extensive and effective fiscal policy is indispensable to the acceleration of the "take-off" point. Government revenue and expenditure policies have a significant effect upon social and economic life, and upon the rate of economic development in particular. Such policies affect the allocation of resources, alter the distribution of income, promote capital accumulation, and restrain inflation.

In the Third World, government expenditure in a particular section of the economy tends to attract resources, whereas taxation tends to repel them. This is especially the case where the governing agencies choose to support enterprise, rather than to give themselves a monopoly over a given sector. Obviously, where the government expropriates an industry or a service, the likelihood of private capital investment is all but eliminated.

Land and property taxes can affect the system of land tenure; tax exemption and tax discrimination can influence the direction of investment to particular sectors; taxes can serve as a break on consumer-oriented industries; and subsidies can encourage industries that provide for wide social benefits.[7]

Fiscal measures alter the institutional environment which determines the distribution of income, or directly changes the resulting distribution. Government expenditures on health and education may increase occupational mobility and can upgrade workers; land taxes can alter the distribution of land ownership; and a system of taxes and subsidies can alter the degree of competition in various sectors of the economy. On the other hand, the distribution of income can be made more equitable through progressive taxation. This can be done by re-allocating monies directly and providing expenditures to lower-income groups. Value-free Keynesians are at pains to insist that they are not interested in income redistribution. However, "fiscal" is linked to liberalism in opposition to monetary economics and conservatism. Hence, progressive taxation is a frequent policy recommendation of the liberal "fiscal" economists. It is they who have best appreciated the extent to which taxation is linked to wealth re-allocation.[8]

Fiscal reform measures, particularly taxation, can serve to accelerate

7. A. R. Prest, *op. cit.*, p. 27.
8. See the particularly fine collection of essays contained in *Readings on Taxation in Developing Countries* (revised edition), edited by Richard M. Bird and Oliver Oldman. Baltimore: The Johns Hopkins Press, 1967.

economic and social growth. These proposals, while basically mending ideals, when carried "too far," can bring about the demand for smashing tactics and hence forestall the implementation of even modest reforms by the ruling economic elite.

To be effective in social development, fiscal measures of a newly developing area should satisfy the following conditions: (1) They must penalize non-essential consumption and encourage savings and investments. (2) They must channel an important percentage of the increments in national income to the public sector for further investment. This is not because of any unique moral advantage of the public sector, but simply because the private sector seems less capable of undertaking fiscal reforms on a massive scale. (3) They should not promote inflationary spirals or curtail savings unless they have a clear idea of converting inflationary tendencies into a means of reducing poverty by penalizing the wealthy. (4) Fiscal measures will unquestionably have some sort of pronounced bias in favor of particular economic classes; thus it is important to convert the grounds of such bias from moral rage to empirical statements of creating a better mixture in the graduations of wealth. (5) They must be administratively feasible for the country involved, since, failing this, non-economic factors will serve to frustrate fiscal changes. (6) They must be capable of reducing and curbing economic inequalities without at the same time stimulating social chaos. When these six propositions about fiscal equity are examined, it will be seen that the changes suggested must be initiated and carried through by political leadership, for if the political elite is unwilling to pursue such policies, then fiscal measures become inadequate as an end, and simply become a set of instruments used by more militant political actors. (7) They must promote inflationary spirals or curtail savings or investment. (8) They must not have any pronounced bias in favor of or against any particular economic class unless there is a socially recognized justification for it, such as wide graduations in wealth. (9) They must be capable of reducing and curbing economic inequality without at the same time stimulating social chaos.

The basic fiscal characteristic of Third World countries is that the largest percentage of national income exists in the agricultural sector. The majority of the population still gains sustenance through agriculture. But for various reasons—illiteracy, primitive agricultural methods, overpopulation, overdivided lands, lack of transportation, and the lack of mechanization—farms are not economically productive. Agricultural cycles often accentuate the subsistence level of the economy.

It is worth noting that capitalists, from small merchants to large entrepreneurs, are only marginally hurt by a general rise in the price level (although if specific prices rise, those for whom this inflated pricing are costs will suffer). In a situation of general inflation, what the capitalist needs, as well as what he buys, increases. Therefore, there is no a priori reason for him to be worse off. In fact, an expectation of sustained inflation will provide a significant boost in stock values well above the rate of inflation, as the market internalizes such expectations.

The landlord classes of Latin America and Asia, and the tribal rulers of Africa, while small in size, own a substantial part of the land. But their contribution to the public revenue is even less than that of the small proprietor. In nations like Brazil and India the landlord class transforms its economic power into political power, and thus can avoid paying taxes. In so doing, this class can influence fiscal policy as a whole, and determine the distribution of income, the direction of public expenditures, and the form of economic development. Recent United Nations data collected from fifty-five nations show that there is a very great difference in personal income tax between developed and underdeveloped countries.[9] In the United Kingdom and the United States, for example, from 30 to 40 per cent of the total population pays income tax each year. In the Caribbean territories, on the other hand, less than 3 per cent does. In Africa and Asia, a country is doing relatively well if 1 per cent of its population pays. Whereas income subject to personal income tax amounts to some 75 per cent of gross national product in the United Kingdom, it amounts to only 10 per cent in the Caribbean and 5 per cent or less in African territories.[10]

Taxation is made difficult by these factors: First, and most significant, is the disproportionate distribution of wealth. Second, most taxes are of the indirect variety—import duties, export taxes, excise taxes, sales taxes, and public utilities taxes—which affect the poorer classes disproportionately. Third, inflation, which is itself a form of taxation, increases the disparities between those who live on relatively fixed in-

9. *Economic Survey of Asia and Far-East.* New York: United Nations, 1961, p. 211.
10. A. R. Prest, *op. cit.,* p. 28.

comes, such as factory workers and lower-echelon bureaucrats, and those whose income is pegged to an informal sliding scale, such as shopkeepers and industrialists. Fourth, economic problems tend to become political problems.[11]

According to the most recent reports of the *International Labor Review,* in Venezuela, 50 per cent of the total income was in the hands of 12 per cent of the families; in Chile, prior to the nationalization projects of Frei and later Allende, at least two-thirds of the national wealth was controlled by 5 per cent of the population; in Colombia, 41 per cent of the national income was received by 5 per cent of the population; in Mexico, which has undergone considerable modernization, 16 per cent of the population received 56.5 per cent of the total income (as late as 1957); while in Brazil, despite a huge public-sector orientation, 63 per cent of the wealth went to 17 per cent of the population.[12] Given this data, the relative weakness of the present tax structure is evident. It is a failure of underdeveloped regimes to collect and graduate the tax structure. It means that the very rich are even wealthier in relation to the rest of the population as a whole than even the damaging statistical information reveals.

Because of the unfavorable taxation schemes, lower-income groups are responsible for a very high percentage of the fiscal expenses. As Luis A. Monge has declared: "The privileged minority groups have managed to guide fiscal policy along indirect taxation lines, largely to escape direct taxation." [13] Indirect taxation amounts to more than 70 per cent of the federal revenues in Brazil, Costa Rica, Ecuador, Guatemala, Honduras, and Nicaragua, while every other nation of Latin America, except Venezuela (which has a ratio of 58 per cent direct taxes to 42 per cent indirect taxes), has more than 50 per cent of its revenues collected from indirect sources. These indirect taxes are clamped on everything from the manufacture to the importation of goods. Such forms of taxation affect the poor much more than the rich,

11. For a general account of the distinction between direct and indirect taxation, see A. R. Prest, *op. cit.,* pp. 27–79.
12. *Economic Survey of Latin America.* New York: United Nations, 1957, p. 138; see also Celso Furtado, *The Economic Growth of Brazil.* Berkeley: University of California Press, 1963; and Albert O. Hirschman, *Journey Toward Progress: Studies of Economic Policy-Making in Latin America.* New York: Twentieth Century Fund, 1963, esp. pp. 11–91.
13. Cited in Luis Alberto Monge, "The Labor Movement and Economic Development," in Mildred Adams (ed.), *Latin America: Evolution or Explosion?* New York: Dodd, Mead & Company, 1963, pp. 185–86.

for the poor have even less opportunity to save than they would have under an equitable and direct tax structure.

The indirect effects of inflation are harder to verify statistically, but it is evident that those tied to a fixed wage scale are simply not in as advantageous a position to cope with the inflationary "tax" as merchants whose prices change when the market value of their currency changes, or the banker who adjusts his interest rates on a daily basis. Thus, inflation, whatever its positive effects on the investment and circulation of funds by those who have large sums of money, has a deleterious effect on those who have no savings, or those whose savings are linked to insurance policies or pension programs. Indeed, what appears as inflation from the top down often emerges as depression from the bottom up. Since, especially for the Third World, there is a constant crisis in fluidity, that is to say, money is in perennial short supply, every pressure toward increasing costs reflects itself in an intensification of working-class impoverishment and lower-class marginality.

Given these factors it may be unrealistic to expect that an economic development program can be financed to any large extent from taxation or from subsidiary forms of taxation such as import and export duties. As Paul Baran says,

> For backward countries to enter the road of economic growth and social progress, the political framework of their existence has to be drastically revamped. The alliance between feudal landlords, industrial royalists, and the capitalist middle-classes has to be broken. . . . Such progressive and enterprising elements as exist in backward societies have to obtain the possibility of leading their countries in the direction of economic and social growth.[14]

Otherwise the existing class system and power structure will again manipulate a debt policy advantageous only to the status quo. Foreign economic aid cannot substitute for domestic change. Such aid only postpones a settlement of the issues of mending and smashing—indeed, it makes any solution more wrenching than its consequences.[15] Expropriation means the displacement of private ownership of lands and

14. Paul Baran, "On the Political Economy of Backwardness," in A. N. Agarwala and S. P. Singh (eds.), *The Economics of Underdevelopment*. New York: Oxford University Press, 1963, p. 90.
15. Paul Baran, *op. cit.,* p. 91.

factories by public ownership. It reduces the net consumption of the economy by reducing the incomes expropriated. Expropriation may result in savings, but in and of itself expropriation is a transfer of control of resources rather than of savings.[16]

Expropriation should be considered in two different aspects. One is the case of land-tenure reforms to lessen the unequal distribution of real income and to relieve the peasantry from the burden of a land which fosters inequitable and distinctly undemocratic conditions.[17] There is also what political authorities in some countries refer to as collectivization. Virtually all Third World countries have progressive income-tax systems. However, tax evasion is the rule, which is why political transformations are often a prelude to economic equity.

Since the economies of poor countries are largely based upon agriculture, the conditions of land tenure have great significance.[18] These conditions vary considerably. The ownership unit may be a tribe, village, family, or an individual. Different types of ownership may also exist in combination, as in the Middle East. In most sections of the world, particularly Latin America, the land is in the hands of a few owners. In Brazil, Syria, and Iraq, for example, it is estimated that about half the land is owned by large landowners, and cultivated by small share tenants.[19] Where tenancy exists, the land is often fragmented into strip parcels and scattered holdings. Systems of inheritance, according to which every son receives a parcel of land, or every daughter is given land as a dowry, also make for a continual division and scattering of lands over wide numbers of already-poor farmer-owners. Moreover, all tenure systems are custom-bound and semi-feudal. There are very few well-defined juridical rights and obligations between landlords and tenants. Feudalism regulates human relations through a system of custom and mutual acceptance of obligations. While most experts agree that there is an urgent need for land reform in the Third

16. See Maurice Dobb, *Political Economy and Capitalism*. London: Routledge and Kegan Paul, 1937, pp. 277–85.
17. Kenneth Parsons, Raymond J. Penn, and Philip M. Raup (eds.), *International Conference on Land Tenure and Related Problems in World Agriculture*. Madison: The University of Wisconsin Press, 1956, p. 44.
18. See Gustav Ranis and John C. H. Fei, "A Theory of Economic Development," *The American Economic Review*, Vol. LI, No. 4 (Sept. 1961), pp. 533–38.
19. *Land Reform*. United Nations Department of Economic Affairs: New York, 1951, p. 14.

World, just what constitutes land reform is a complex matter. Land reform is an issue charged with political emotion, and it is often viewed as an economic panacea. It is vital that there be some evaluation of what it can and what it cannot accomplish.[20]

In the rural sectors of Japan and South Korea, efforts have been made to eliminate the abuses of the feudal social order. In these countries genuine attempts at land reform were made after World War II. The system of private ownership of land was not only retained but emphasized. In sharp contrast, the communist pattern, which emerged in China and North Korea, viewed the reform movement as a means to abolish the existing land-tenure systems and collectivize the agricultural sector.[21] Japanese reform was externally guided by the United States, whereas Chinese reform was internally guided by the revolution.

In Japan and South Korea a modern land-tenure system was achieved with a minimum of confiscation. In Japan the area under tenancy was reduced from nearly 50 per cent to approximately 10 per cent of the land under cultivation. As a result, owner-farmers and owner-tenants operated up to 50 per cent more land than before the war. On the small area remaining under tenancy, rents were reasonable, rental contracts were in writing, and local land commissions corrected any abuses and prevented a feudal backlash. This drastic change took place with relatively little disturbance to the existing farm management pattern, without interruption of farm operations, and without serious disruption of the psychological pattern of the farm population.[22]

The political disturbances caused by the reform were very significant. Japanese society was radically altered. Land reform, however smoothly it was carried off at the technological level, meant a drastic change in existing social relationships, traditional values, and vested interests.[23] The informal power structure of agrarian Japan was transferred from military overseers to middle-sized farmers. Land reform produced the following results: First, most of the farmers acquired the one thing that farmers the world over want: land of their own. This private

20. Arthur T. Mosher, "Research on Rural Problems," *Development of the Emerging Countries.* Washington, D.C.: The Brookings Institution, 1962, p. 86.
21. Sidney Klein, *The Pattern of Land Tenure Reform in East Asia After World War Two.* New York: Bookman Associates, 1958, p. 189.
22. Sidney Klein, *ibid.,* pp. 50–51.
23. John W. Bennett and Iwao Ishino, *Paternalism in the Japanese Economy.* Minneapolis: University of Minnesota Press, 1963.

property "instinct" proved to be the chief incentive for improving the land.[24] Second, the reform narrowed the traditional differences between classes in the villages. The Japanese landlords who lost much of their affluence also lost much of their influence. Land reforms may not have done away with the network of social exploitation common to the agrarian sector, but it did in fact have the effect of displacing one class with another. The fact that the Japanese landlords have lost out to petty bourgeois independent farmers is a case of class displacement, although not necessarily an end to class exploitation as such. Large- and small-scale peasant owners now serve on agricultural committees, cooperatives, and school boards.[25] Third, the distribution of land ownership among the multitude of farmers contributed to the foundation of a more satisfying rural life and to the beginning of local control of the decision-making processes.[26] This was all made possible by a corresponding rise in the industrial sector and a broad trend toward urbanization and occupational specialization.

Taiwan and South Korea followed the Japanese lead, but with different results. In Taiwan, the area of land cultivated by owners increased by nearly 50 per cent, while the area cultivated by tenants decreased by more than 60 per cent. By 1954 only 16 per cent of the total cultivated lands was left to share-cropping tenancy. Significantly, land productivity did not show any noticeable increase. The conditions of tenancy were also put on a de jure foundation as in Japan. As for the South Korean experiment, the redistribution of land ownership seems to have been the sole achievement of the reform efforts of this country. The number of half-tenants and full tenants was reduced by 77 per cent, while the number of half-owners and full owners increased by 170 per cent. Ownership of approximately 26 per cent of all the cultivated land of South Korea was transferred to the tillers of the land.

Land reform in South Korea was essentially a failure. The conditions of tenancy were little improved. Rents remained high, paid in kind rather than money. Tenants were burdened with many expenses of cultivation which should have been borne in whole or in part by the landlord. Tenants were still insecure because landlords failed to put their leases in writing and to register them at the local land office.

24. Wolf I. Ladejinsky, "Land Reform in Japan: A Comment," in Parsons, Penn, and Raup (eds.), op. cit., p. 225.
25. Sidney Klein, op. cit., pp. 19–52.
26. Ibid.

Tenants remained dependent upon the good will of their landlords. During the first three years of agricultural reform (March 1951–December 1954), 235,000 farm families, were unable to meet the payments due on 253,000 acres of land and had to give up their ownership rights and revert to their former tenant status. It seems certain that, unless some way is found for the new owner-farmers to meet their cash needs other than by the sale of their land, this reversion to tenancy will continue.[27] Thus, we see two different outcomes of externally induced land reform without land revolution.

While it is clear that great new advances in social life are now taking place in agricultural nations, and that problems of land, rather than problems of population, more nearly approximate the over-all social situation of the Third World, the above discussion is designed only as a historical backdrop.[28] Land reform in the Third World can be defined as a series of strategies designed to break the mold of those land relationships as existed under the colonial period. In the main, when land reform is undertaken without reference to general industrial change, as in South Korea, the developmental process is abortive— even in the agricultural sector. When land reform is undertaken as a general consequence of industrialization, as in Japan, the development process is highly successful, even in the agricultural sector. This is because in Japan, as in most European countries, agriculture was improved by technological advances linked to industrialization. By contrast, in countries like India, Vietnam, and other Asian nations, where an agricultural solution has been attempted without a sufficient industrial basis, the results have been extremely disappointing.

This does not mean that agricultural solutions are out of the question. Nothing could be further from the case. Nations as different as Yugoslavia, Cuba, and Malaysia have succeeded in bringing great increases in food and mineral production. But it is much easier for a society to "sacrifice" the agricultural sector to industrialization than the other way around. And when industrialization process is abandoned,

27. The same situation has developed in Mexico's small farms where the absence of liquid assets often compels the independent peasants to resell their lands to the ever-waiting large landowners. Often land is sold illegally, and just as often, small farmers are not aware of credits available to them from government sources.

28. For a brilliant examination of agriculture in developing nations, see Doreen Warriner, *Land Reform and Economic Development*. Cairo: National Bank of Egypt, 1955.

it is usually done so as a "temporary maneuver," a "concession" to economic realities, not as an abandonment of the long-range ideal of achieving self-determination through industrial production.

Despite the urgent need for land reform in most of the underdeveloped countries of Asia, Africa, and Latin America, it has either not yet been undertaken or has not been done so satisfactorily. This failure has often been justified on the grounds that there are technical difficulties in working with uneducated people, or that exceptional geographic features affect the programs. But Japan's experience would seem to indicate that the problems of land reform are more political than technical. In many countries land reform is thwarted not because of any lack of technical knowledge but because the political apparatus is wedded to the economic status quo.[29] It is no accident that in both Japan and South Korea land reform was externally induced.

Under the political stimulus of a foreign military government Japan succeeded in separating out, once and for all, military functions from landholding functions. Neither militarists nor landlords were "liquidated." They were simply provided with separate social roles. On the whole, land reform in Japan emphasized innovation rather than investment. In the past other innovations had been undertaken; members of the functionless samurai became the business leaders of industrial Japan; students of literature were shifted to scientific skills by means of a clever manipulation of rewards and awards; economic efficiency increased through machine technology, and disciplined farm laborers formed the backbone of an enlarged migrant proletariat.[30] The growth of per capita income was not the result of rapid capital formation, for the growth of capital barely exceeded the rate of population growth. Hence, the role of innovation and the mode of utilizing savings in Japan goes far to explain why Japan succeeded where South Korea failed.

For the strategy of smashing old ownership patterns as an answer to agricultural development, North Korea and China provide two interesting models. In the former, the property of landlords was confiscated and distributed. The peasants, however, did not acquire the rights of ownership but merely title to use the property. The redistri-

---

29. Parsons, Penn, and Raup (eds.), *op. cit.*, p. 228.
30. Richard R. Nelson, *Growth Models and the Escape from the Low-Level Equilibrium Trap: The Case of Japan.* Santa Monica: The Rand Corporation, Jan. 1959 (P-1537), pp. 1–23.

bution of the land did not result in an increase in the income of North Korean peasants nor in their having a feeling of ownership. The tax rates set by the government on agricultural products effectively siphoned off revolutionary enthusiasm. All surplus production became state-owned, and subsistence became the norm. North Korean officials exercised a high degree of control over peasant cooperatives. The control and supervision of the peasants were excessive even by Soviet standards under Stalin. Given the constant threat of civil war and counter-revolution, this is perhaps understandable. But it is economically unsatisfactory, since production continued to stagnate.

China has become the focal model for take-over as the basic strategy of social development. The main impulse and support of the Maoist revolution has been the peasantry. China had its revolution in the countryside, the way Bakunin predicted, and not in the cities, the way Marx imagined. The special role of the Chinese landowner, who also had administrative power, made any formal scheme of taxation quite out of the question. The central government under the Kuomintang was supported by the wealthy landowners, not the other way around. Under such circumstances, the Chinese communists engaged in a policy of staged take-over.

The first period (1948–52) saw an emphasis on private land ownership. The large peasant mass became enfranchised, albeit in an unprofitable economic maneuver. Parcels handed out varied from only 1.15 to .45 acres per person. This had the effect of uniting the peasants behind the revolution, but it did little to improve the productive capacities of agriculture. The second period (1952–56) saw the introduction both of persuasion and coercion in a change-over from individual proprietorship, first, to mutual aid teams, then to elementary cooperatives, and finally to producers' cooperatives. The advanced cooperatives were based on the collectivization of the village economy. But each person was allowed to own property which he could voluntarily cultivate. By the end of 1956, 96 per cent of the peasantry had pooled their cooperative shares. The state thus controlled the productivity of the land, without actually owning any of it. The third period (1957–60), commonly referred to as the commune period, sought to rationalize agricultural production by linking the peasant sector to the general life of the Chinese society. Mao Tse Tung is reported to have said: "It is better to run people's communes. Their advantages lie in that they can merge industry, agriculture, trade, culture, education, and military affairs into one entity, and make it easier for leadership." [31] The communes represented the final stage in the confiscation of private lands and private ownership, and in addition the commune system provided a case study in gentle terror—also known as the "Asiatic Form of Communism." The fourth period (1960–63) rescinded many of the harsher features of commune life by restoring personal possessions to their rightful owners: by putting a limit on the working day and by returning to private dwellings as the basic mode of living, that is, the three-generation system of housing.[32]

There can be no doubt that land collectivization in China, whatever its shortcomings, has made impossible a return to past feudal relations. But it is also clear that enforced communization, like other land tenure systems, must deal with the problem of taxation. In the case of China, the tax problem was dependent upon that part of production (translated into wages) held in reserve for state allocation. At present, each peasant brigade is guaranteed 60 per cent of its product. This guarantee still represents a "taxation" of 40 per cent of the yield. A central program of confiscation was to establish the ground rules of taxation. Thus the very phenomenon which causes governmental instability, the failure to collect and receive a portion of production or services for general allocation, continues to exist in the post-revolutionary period.

The individualist solution in Japan and the socialist solution in China have worked with relative success not because of the unique advantages of private or public ownership of land but because of their unique ability to fuse nationalist values and peasant demands. This is borne out by the relative failure of the South Korean and North Korean economies alike, even though they have great structural and ideological differences. Thus, whether the strategy of taxation or that of take-over is adopted, success depends upon the general processes of economic development and not on any single policy-making decision.

In developed countries, there have been various degrees of governmental participation in the initiation and direction of the developmental

31. Choh-Ming Li, "The First Decade: Economic Development," *The China Quarterly* (London), No. 1 (Jan.–Mar.), 1960, pp. 35–50.
32. Edgar Snow, *The Other Side of the River*. New York: Random House, 1962, pp. 418–38. For comparable information of Chinese agricultural production during the first decade of communist rule, see Ta-Chung Liu and Kung-Chia Yeh, "The National Income of the Chinese Mainland, 1952–59," *American Economic Review. Proceedings of the American Economic Association* (May 1961), pp. 489–98.

process. In countries like Imperial Japan, Weimar Germany, and Soviet Russia the political apparatus has played a large part in initiating and activating an entrepreneurial role.[33] By contrast, development in England and the United States occurred with much less deliberate governmental action.[34] The epoch of take-off, rather than the type of social order, determines the extent of political intervention.

Most observers agree that in the newly developing regions the very tardiness of the developmental process, coupled with the absence of a responsible economic elite, makes governmental intervention necessary for economic take-off. The situation in which the have-not countries find themselves is far different from the situation of those countries which developed during the nineteenth century. The obstacles for underdeveloped countries are now greater than they were in developed countries precisely because the developed countries in the past achieved their preeminence through economic and political imperialism, while developing areas today must rely exclusively upon their own population resources. Consequently, political action tends to unite around the theme of nationalism and anti-imperialism.

When we depart from the mending-smashing dualism and look at specific situations, vast differences arise. For a particular country, private-sector advocates suggest limiting the government's role to over-all allocation of funds for research and development, where government intervention can easily be minimized. Public-sector advocates would have the government interfere directly with the market mechanism and exercise specific control over (and prepare for the eventual elimination of) private enterprise. In its more extreme form, this would mean that the market mechanism would be totally supplanted by central planning, and the state would replace private enterprise as the moving force in social development.

The current pessimism with respect to development has polarized developmental theorists into Stalinists—cum-Maoists on the one hand and laissez-faire conservatives—cum-Keynesian reformists in favor of native industry on the other. As a result, the middle-of-the-road positions—ranging from import substitution policy through encouragement of foreign capital—are being squeezed out. This position encourages

33. See Reinhard Bendix, "Preconditions of Development: A Comparison of Japan and Germany," in *Nation-Building and Citizenship: Studies of Our Changing Social Order*. New York: John Wiley, 1964, pp. 177–213.
34. G. M. Meier and R. E. Baldwin, *Economic Development: Theory, History, Policy*. New York: John Wiley, 1957, pp. 360–61.

public intervention because it encourages the idea that change has benefits that accrue beyond the boundaries set by developmental planners. Public intervention becomes palatable when and if private investors withold their capital for projects deemed to be publicly worthy whatever the scope of the marginal private benefits. As a result, the very arguments used by conservative economists are also used by the Marxist economists to prove the necessity of revolutionary change.

Differences in strategy generally arise when estimates differ on the sequence and tempo of development. Socialists maintain that obstacles to development in poor countries are so formidable that they can be overcome only by deliberate and immediate industrialization on the part of the state. The political apparatus should engage in programing and planning, assume most of the entrepreneurial activities, and attempt to achieve a high rate of capital accumulated as soon as possible.[35] Only then can the private sector be contained, if not confiscated. Capitalists, on the contrary, advocate gradual industrialization, which would limit the degree of specific planning, rely mainly on the market mechanism, and approach development problems in a step-by-step fashion.[36] In this way, the specific market mechanisms will not be aborted by arbitrary state planning; and industrialization will be both a stimulant and a response to increases in social mobility.[37] One must not be overwhelmed by the import substitution thesis—a position that argues against all gradual industrialization theories as if they were apologetics for imperialism. In point of fact, socialists as well as capitalists can advocate gradual industrialization. In the main, there is a sound case to be made against gradualist industrialization theories, and this case has been made herein. However, the situation in Asia, where there are successive droughts, overpopulation to a catastrophic degree, and all sorts of natural as well as social inhibitions to modernization, it is only common sense to emphasize agriculture as a step toward industrialization.

Those who favor rapid and deliberate industrialization have two main arguments. First, in order to gather sufficient momentum, a development program must ramify widely in space and rapidly in time throughout the economy; but only a large country can develop an industrial base

35. Meier and Baldwin, *op. cit.,* p. 362.
36. Meier and Baldwin, *op. cit.,* p. 363.
37. See Gino Germani, "The Strategy of Fostering Social Mobility," *Social Aspects of Economic Development in Latin America,* edited by Egbert De Vries and José Medina Echavarría. Paris: United Nations Educational, Scientific and Cultural Organization, 1963, pp. 211–30.

adequate to most of its needs. Unless the program involves large changes in class relations and social structure, the development process can never be self-generating and cumulative. If rapid development is desired, certain steps must be taken. Regarding capital accumulation, investment must be on a scale, and of a type, that is facilitated only through the joint efforts of the underdeveloped country and large-scale investments from willing advanced countries. Socialists tend to believe that heavy industrialization in itself lessens obstacles to development and dependency on others. If ambitious capital and technical assistance programs are undertaken, social and cultural obstacles may disappear without being directly attacked. But industrialization will be obtained only if the scale of such assistance is large enough to provide a "shock treatment" for the traditional ruling classes, and flexible enough to turn present large-scale part-time unemployment into an asset.

Second, only through large-scale development can old distinctions between rich and poor be broken down. Unless class extremes are blunted, political agencies would be unable to regulate the total economy for social purposes. In short, if the strategy of forced savings is to be institutionalized, political power must supersede economic power. Thus, in the newly developing areas, confiscation is a necessary prelude to any real growth of the public sector. If rapid and accelerated development is to be undertaken, the nation must be prepared to rely on internal sacrifice instead of external foreign assistance.

What aggravates this situation is that a government that chooses to confiscate risks alienating its capitalist class, which in turn may do everything possible to resist such confiscation. To forestall this response, the government must have political power that can make possible the transferring of economic power. Conversely, for the government to avoid conflict with entrenched wealth, it must forego plans for confrontation and concentrate, as do structuralists, on liberalizing or ameliorating the economic environment in order to encourage the productive use of private wealth. This was certainly the attempt of Ayub Khan in Pakistan. The failure of his regime demonstrates that there is at least as much danger in toying with an economy as in transforming it.

"Mixed economies" such as India and Brazil have used a good deal of central planning to convert an agrarian economy into an industrial economy. But a more gradual and decentralized approach has gained increasing favor in these countries. Instead of seeking deliberate industrialization through direct political intervention, such nations tend to concentrate on agricultural improvements, the promotion of social services, the extension of public overhead capital, and the establishment of small-scale, dispersed light industry.

The rationale behind these more moderate programs is varied: First, the agricultural sector of the economy is predominant, and this is where extreme poverty exists. But the possibilities for rapidly increasing agricultural output are highly favorable, precisely because the disorganized state of farm labor makes the introduction of advanced machine technology easier than in the developed industrial sectors. Furthermore, welfare projects such as schools, hospitals, and disease control involve a relatively small investment in exchange for a high return in reducing human misery. Second, concentrated heavy industry is not immediately required because there are inadequate market opportunities, lack of capital, scarcity of skills and administrative capacity, and an insufficient supply of managerial expertise. Small-scale light industry may, on the other hand, be linked to local handicrafts. Small rural industry does not need many urban services, and savings can be made in capital expenditures which would otherwise be applied to the cost of urbanization. A revitalization of the land must take place. It has the advantage of moving industry to the labor supply, which despite urbanization remains largely immobile. This gradual approach to industrialization is characteristic of development plans in Latin America (such as the Alliance for Progress) and in parts of the Near East and Asia.[38]

Once a nation has achieved some kind of high-level industrial productivity in such areas as basic tools, iron and steel, automotives, then the problem shifts from taxation to reinvestment, since the developed nation must shift from a reliance on borrowing capital to a reinvestment of surplus. While it remains extremely difficult to extract taxes from industries in newly developed societies which have entered into an advanced phase of the Industrial Revolution, it may be even more difficult to get the upper classes to invest their profits properly. Thus, it is estimated that in Mexico, no less than in France, the collection of taxes has long been viewed as quixotic, with only an estimated 25 per cent of the due taxes actually collected. But with extension of the franchise to urban working classes, as in Mexico today, it is possible to institute equitable tax reform. A new Mexican law will have the effect of giving workers 9 to 13 per cent of the profits of the companies for which they work. In short, bureaucratic capitalism, such as one finds in France and Mexico, is a

38. Meier and Baldwin, *op. cit.,* p. 365.

political approach to economic change which involves planning without revolution.

Under the new Mexican law, profits must be made public, and every company's statement of profits will be subject to approval by its employees, who will scrutinize it carefully because it will determine their share. The tendency of the monied classes in Latin America is to bank their profits abroad, rather than to plow them back into the business. In Mexico, reinvestment will be made virtually mandatory, for businessmen will receive a 30 per cent deduction in taxes if they invest in national enterprises. After further deductions for capital investment and labor costs, the remainder of the profits will be subject to a 20 per cent share for the workers.

It must, however, be borne in mind that such legislation came more than half a century after the commencement of the Mexican Revolution, and that its effectiveness is still largely subject to the wishes of the private sector of the economy. Legislation of this kind does indicate, however, that development can be "gradual" only after political and economic revolutions have taken place; and such development is largely managed by the political agencies in ways that a considerable public-sector economy will coexist with the private sector.

This gradualist approach has prima facie advantages over comprehensive planning. But social expectations now run very high, and the gradualist approach delivers results only over the "long haul." By concentrating on agriculture it promises to increase national income and to distribute the increase to those people who need it most; however, it comes up against the established resistance of traditional landholding power. This approach is less inflationary because the efforts to achieve full-scale industrialization are likely to encounter fewer problems of capital absorption and scarcity of raw materials. It is not disruptive of the entire culture as is large-scale industrialization. It does not mean a rapid urbanization with its attendant social problems. And even if this approach should not achieve its ultimate goal, the cost of failure will not be as burdensome as would the failure of a grandiose industrial development plan. In terms of human discontent, the costs of abortive development programs would be much greater. However, urbanization is an ongoing process brought to a point of crisis by the constant pressures of industrialization. And the problems created by industrialization will have to be faced in any event, either in the short run or in the long run. The types of government intervention required by gradualism have advantages over those required by large-scale industrialization. The latter implies centralized planning, comprehensive specific control over economic life, and government operation of industries. The gradual approach, in contrast, involves relatively mild state intervention. In limiting its activities to general allocations of resources, and to providing a favorable atmosphere for private entrepreneurs, the nation avoids the administrative problems, irreversible decisions, cumulative errors, and undemocratic controls associated with thoroughgoing industrialization. However, the gradual approach, precisely because it seeks to disarm opponents of industrial development, makes it easy to sabotage such development. Precisely because it leaves political agencies in a backward stage, the gradualist approach is not likely to nurture or promote those indigenous forces that are necessary to sustain economic development nor to allow the process to become self-generating and cumulative. Hence, the political agencies are in danger of collapsing before the rising tide of private property interests.

In fact, the same problem arises with gradual communism as with gradual capitalism: the self-limitation which the state imposes upon itself to provide a feasible atmosphere for various forms of decentralization by an autonomous enterprise may so weaken the fabric of the economy in the short run that the society as a whole either falls under a tutelary relationship once again, as in the case of Poland and Bulgaria, or gradually begins to harden its political directives for the economy, as in Czechoslovakia and even Cuba. The point is that, given an adequate amount of time, which is almost a tautological necessity for gradualism, many societies like Yugoslavia and even India can work out their problems. But in the absence of this time factor, or, better, given competing pressures, the mild consensus society approach tends to be ineffectual and even to yield to a command society.

Even with the gradualist approach, rapid economic progress is not possible without painful adjustments. Inherited philosophies of life and colonialist institutions have to be scrapped; old social institutions have to be fought; bonds of caste, creed, and race have to be eliminated; and people who cannot keep up with the canons of development may find their expectations of a comfortable life frustrated.[39] In short, in so far as latifundism remains a force in traditional societies, it generates tremendous social antagonism. Whether evolutionary or revolutionary techniques are utilized, the problems to be overcome remain the same.

39. *Measures for the Economic Development of Underdeveloped Countries.* United Nations, Department of Economic Affairs, New York, 1961, p. 15.

The chief fact to be recognized is that very few "have" sectors of a society are willing to pay the full price for rapid economic progress. Thus, the policy of confiscation is not necessarily a spiteful insistence on ideological purity but often the quickest way to achieve rapid development, once there is a sufficient agreement in favor of development as such. Where economic and political power is concentrated in the hands of a small group, whose main interest is in the preservation of the status quo, prospects for economic progress are very slight unless a social revolution effects a shift in the distribution of income and power.[40]

The argument that only a policy of democratic consensus can be sanctioned has to be rejected. This argument greatly oversimplifies the problem of development by assuming that development hinges on constitutional norms rather than on a more rational allocation of resources. In any expanding society the political system must cope with a wide range of conflicting demands. Even an authoritarian regime must recognize such demands. Significantly, most demands do not entail reform of the political system but are largely concerned with the allocation of material resources.

Development may prove to be a basic demonstration of the viability of mass democracy. The emergence of mass democracy may be a long-range consequence of the failure of authoritarian rule. A one-party system primarily oriented to economic development may find that it can satisfy demands only in areas affecting the use of economic resources. Under such conditions all aspirations must be translated into party terms, and thus an excessive political strain is placed on the limited resources of the country. Totalitarianism remains a clear and present danger. Mass terror is not as powerful a method of extracting loyalties as mass propaganda is. The theory of small groups demonstrates furthermore that a developmental consensus based upon force does not provide the same powerful individual or group motive as does government recognition of status to outstanding persons within the group.[41] However, such techniques of persuasion are used just as effectively by totalitarian forces as by democratic ones. Therefore, any recourse to the achievement orientation school of development adds little to the mending or smashing strategies

40. *Measures for the Economic Development of Underdeveloped Countries,* p. 16.
41. George C. Homans, *The Human Group.* New York: Harcourt, Brace and Co., 1950, esp. pp. 288–312. For a more recent extension of this view, see Peter M. Blau, *Exchange and Power in Social Life.* New York: John Wiley, 1964.

that have to be decided upon. Decisions must still be made on the basis of objective circumstances rather than of personal situations.

There can be no rapid economic development unless the various groups within a country—politicians, teachers, engineers, business leaders, trade unionists, religious figures, journalists—support economic progress and are willing to sponsor a successful economic take-off. Many groups will support developmental projects only when these projects maintain rather than transform traditional class or caste privileges. For this reason, powerful political leadership is necessary in order to institutionalize public support for far-reaching developmental projects; otherwise the public is likely to support only projects that simply continue or improve on traditional schemes. The problem before political leadership of developing nations is not only one of mass support, but of class support as well; that is, support from those sectors of society that have established privileges built into current operations.

The Third World increasingly has to choose between types of take-over, not between taxation and take-over. Traditional landed classes have never accepted a progressive tax structure. But as speculation on scarce goods rises, as excessive profiteering takes place, as consumer spending rises, the capacity for self-imposed limits sharply declines. The wealthy classes become incapable of the sort of effort necessary to impose economic rationalization since they are themselves caught in the inflationary spiral. The growth of intermediate classes and intermediate elites, such as the military or white-collar sector, has the effect of further isolating the very rich and making confiscation a broad-based and necessary strategy for the nation's political survival.

Confiscation has been successful because the process of industrialization depends on the elimination of social classes, which make such planning mechanisms impossible, and on the rationalization of production as a whole. In Japan, planning agencies were externally introduced as a result of the collapse of the empire in World War II; in China such agencies came about as a result of the civil war. Nonetheless, from a Western frame of reference, confiscation goes against the grain of economic morality and economic interests. And the resort to direct take-over is usually a sign that weaker forms of restraint on private drainage of public wealth (such as taxation) have failed.[42]

42. M. Bronfenbrenner, "The Appeal of Confiscation in Economic Development," *The Economics of Underdevelopment*, edited by A. N. Agarwala and S. P. Singh. New York: Oxford University Press, 1963, p. 487.

The obstacles to confiscatory policies in the agricultural sectors of the Third World are considerable. Factors impeding confiscation stem not simply from the latifundiary character of much agricultural ownership but also from the international ramifications of such bold measures. Furthermore, most land tenure systems in the Third World generate lethargy, backwardness, suspicion, and the inability on the part of the huge peasantry to distinguish its interests from those of the ruling classes. The romantic image of the peasant fighting for possession of land is, it must be remembered, the exception. The peasant is suspicious of new forms of production, fearful of innovation and crop rotation, and opposed to government intervention. Thus if there are "natural" reasons for supporting confiscation and collectivization of the land, there are equally powerful social reasons for moving with caution and circumspection in the direction of take-over.

But in the industrial sector matters are quite different. Here, where it would seem that taxation and the promulgation of a private sector would fulfill the norms of development, there are powerful social reasons for confiscation. If the class adversaries of confiscation are potent, so too are the class agencies which support it. We might cite three basic categories of production which by their very nature are highly socialized:

(1) Monopolistic and oligopolistic enterprises attract the attention of the state, the "guardian" of the public sector, because they are usually engaged in a highly critical enterprise (such as machine and electric products). Since competition is conspicuously absent, the traditional laissez-faire argument of free enterprise is inadmissible.

(2) These basic commodities, or what might better be called infrastructures or natural monopolies necessary for community wants, naturally fall into the public sector. Hence, forests, roads, water supply, dams, canals, and post and communications systems tend to be placed under public directorship. The character of public control may vary from local-township control to large-scale state control, but even where basic utilities are privately run, they are very heavily supervised and controlled by the state. The very complexities of a modern supply system make a powerful argument for public ownership. In countries under colonial domination the initial action is often to attack foreign ownership and control of utilities—the telephone systems in Brazil, natural gas and oil in Argentina, electric power in Algeria—for on such matters a clear consensus exists among the various classes of the country, which is not the case with agriculture or commodity production.

(3) Defense establishments and military production also tend toward public ownership, because the function of such production is directly tied to the policies of the national state. In addition, research and scientific technology in this area tend to be profitless unless they are under state supervision. Investment in military hardware may sometimes be politically necessary, but at the same time it is a drain on the economy. In any case, the higher the degree of economic rationalization, the more a society is able to engage in military production.

The arguments against increased emphasis on the public sector come down to the following: First, an absence of the profit motive leads to waste and results in inefficiency and sluggishness in production. Second, efficient economic activity is hampered by bureaucratic red tape. Third, there is a tendency to make appointments to major positions from political considerations extrinsic to job qualifications.[43] The interesting aspect of each of these three objections is that they are basically arguments concerning efficiency and management, not arguments in favor of private enterprise. As such, the counter to such arguments is not an increase in profit incentive or private capitalization and funding but scientific management procedures. Such procedures are consonant with healthy organization, whether public or private, and therefore cannot legitimately be employed as an argument against expropriation or public operation or ownership. The achievements of "private socialism" of the sort to be found in any major corporation in the United States are not dependent upon private ownership of the instruments of production and distribution. They are a direct consequence of the rise of mass production techniques in the early part of the century and automation in the middle part of the century. In other words, the problem of organizational management is directly tied to the level of technology a society has achieved and not just to class relations within a society.

No discussion of the political economy of mending and smashing would be complete without some historical accounting. First, in the last days of the old colonial regimes the rulers of these regions became increasingly intransigent and corrupt. They were drawn from a class of landowners who had hardly any interest in developing an industrial basis but who did consume on a large scale commodity products manufactured by foreign nations. Second, once the colonial economy snapped,

43. For a cogently argued and modern critique of expanding the public sector, see Wilbert E. Moore, *The Conduct of the Corporation.* New York: Random House, 1962.

old solutions became dysfunctional. Laissez-faire and marginal adjustments through a private enterprise system could not in most instances cope with problems of development, since what was needed was not marginal but fundamental growth. Third, the process of take-over was directed by a revolutionary and nationalist regime, whose first action was to curtail the political influence of the rich.[44] It limited their wealth and income and then later gave in to "reality" by permitting huge irregularities of wealth and income to persist into the post-colonial era. These stages are rarely simultaneous. Indeed, they may take decades to coalesce. And it is on this historical level that national differences make themselves felt and give peculiar shape to expropriation policies throughout the Third World.

One must not overlook the marginal advantages of expropriation, advantages which oftentimes determine the time table of development, if not the structural changes in a society as such.

(1) In many of the developing regions, particularly in the Middle East and Asia, there exist long-established traditions of strong central government. The tradition of central control in the Indian subcontinent, for example, was provided by the British. The post-independence trend has been the reverse. The process of decentralization may even ultimately involve the break-up of India along religious, ethnic, and even political lines. Given material conditions of poverty and inequality of opportunity, state authority increases, if only to prevent the unleashing of economic competition and the pursuit of self-interest, could lead to a breakdown of society. Of course, the permanent threat of mass violence will prevent the middle classes from abandoning national economic policy.

(2) The Third World can dramatically show its independence by trading with the socialist nations of Eastern Europe and Asia; this is particularly true for such states as Egypt, Algeria, Indonesia, and Cuba. In dealing with centrally planned economies of communist countries, Third World nations sometimes gear their own planning activities to those of the communist bloc in order to make such dealings effective. Beyond the nuts-and-bolts stage, Third World government organizations adopt slogans of peaceful coexistence and even national socialism as a

44. R. C. Agarwala, *State Enterprise in India*. Allahabad, India: Chaitanya Publishing House, 1961. This work contains extremely valuable materials on the process of nationalization in India after the 1948 independence period. The chapters on industrial enterprises owned by the government, and the problems of administration and financing that they create, clearly reveal the managerial level at which the problem of the public sector is encountered.

means to accommodate socialist ideologies and as a more effective handling of problems of trade and commerce. The pressure for such adjustments depends in part on Third World political affinities to the socialist bloc, and upon the extent of trade agreements with the Western bloc. The coexistence of capitalist and socialist features should not be overlooked as a factor which paves the way for any easy transition from confiscation to state socialism.

(3) Many Third World countries have been drawn closer to socialist bloc countries on the basis of a common political rhetoric: nonalignment in the Cold War, the development of nuclear-free zones, common strategies for dealing with larger states, and the like. Thus, the political postures of such countries as India, Yugoslavia, Egypt, Algeria, Indonesia, and others are intense at the level of national development but are equally temperate in terms of big power struggles between the First and Second Worlds. This itself becomes a technique of Third World management.

The sharp dichotomy between capitalist and socialist worlds has given way to polycentrism in the socialist sphere and pluralism in the capitalist sphere. The existence of mixed economies even within self-declared capitalist and communist countries has proved stimulating for the Third World. By absorbing the latest techniques a society can achieve new combinations and variations on the development theme.

(4) Civil and international wars have also accelerated the drive toward confiscation and public-sector domination. The immediate consequence of the Suez crisis and its aftermath led into the "Egyptianization" of the large British and French economic holdings.[45] The conclusion of the Algerian conflict brought about a similar confiscation of foreign landholdings and industrial wealth which was then followed by a declaration of the socialist character of the Algerian Revolution. The settlement of the first civil war in Vietnam, which was hardly an all-out decisive victory, made possible the development of a socialist economic sector in those areas "liberated" from the old regime. In short, the outcome of warfare has served to stimulate socialist public-sector economies where none before existed, or to consolidate such a public-sector economy where it may have existed in a shaky condition.

What these economically marginal factors suggest is that the strategy of confiscation blends invariably with an immense outburst of state activity leading to consolidation of the public sector.

45. Saiah El Serafy, "Economic Development by Revolution: The Case of the UAR," *The Middle East Journal*, Vol. 17, No. 3, Summer 1963, pp. 215–30.

(5) Confiscation, when part of a communist victory, may produce such economic advantages as higher production through standardization of manufacturing procedures, decentralization of the center of production, and orderly transition from rural to urban living. However, such confiscation does not affect capital requirements. It does affect the consensus on how to use the confiscated capital. That is, it means an end to overseas dividend payments, excessive consumption out of these profits, and so forth. But it bears repetition that confiscation does not lessen the need for capital in the economy. The judgment of Henry Villard is particularly instructive in this respect. In comparing the advantages of the Chinese approach, based on total confiscation, to the Indian approach, based on partial and differentiated confiscation, he notes that the fear of Western politicians and sociologists that communist development rests on perpetual coercion may be exaggerated.

> It may well be that, when starting from a low level, an initially larger amount of resources devoted to development will "pay off" very rapidly indeed even in terms of available consumption, so that it is not certain that the present Chinese generation will be "exploited" for very long. In fact, the reluctance of the Indian government to reduce present consumption, which presumably explains why it is unwilling to devote a larger percentage of the national income to development, could conceivably mean that the present Indian generation will receive, over its lifetime, less consumption than the present generation in China.[46]

We have already seen the large extent to which the "democratization" procedures in the Soviet Union followed hard on the heels of peacetime on the one hand and a degree of material abundance on the other. Thus, the traditional dialectic of personal "costs" versus social "gains" in development may be less significant than has usually been estimated.

(6) The following remarks made by Isaac Deutscher have undoubtedly been used on many occasions in Third World nations, especially those which aspired to some sort of political and military "greatness." The central point—that a private enterprise economy is inadequate to meet the challenges of the East-West struggle, that, in fact, the West has had to become socialized in some measure—cannot fail to impress factions advocating evolutionary approaches in the Third World.

46. Henry Villard, *Economic Development* (second edition). New York: Holt, Rinehart, and Winston, 1963, pp. 200–201. Compare this with Paul Baran, *The Political Economy of Growth*. New York: Monthly Review Press, 1957.

> The new technology tends to outgrow our inherited institutions and to render obsolete the frameworks within which we have been accustomed to act, think, and live our lives. It grows above the head of private property. Even in the West atomic power has not been the child of State enterprise. Henceforth nearly every act of the technological upheaval is likely to strengthen the trend toward public ownership and enterprise; the gigantic scale of the new inventions and scientific ventures puts these beyond the resources of private investment. . . . The more rational and concentrated use of resources in a nationalized economy follows from the organic integration of its elements.[47]

If the Third World learns from the Soviet Union that absolutist government is not a spark to development but instead an impediment, it learns from the United States that its system of private enterprise may prevent Third World nations from making the most effective and concentrated use of their economic resources. Destruction of the small property-owners may therefore create a prima facie advantage for a public-sector economy. But one has to be careful here, since a public-sector economy does not necessarily represent the total destruction of the class system.

(7) A powerful "international" reason for confiscation is that the intermediary classes of the economy are unlikely to advocate anything more effective than budget surpluses to fill the gap resulting from increased taxation of the wealthy. A policy of inefficient taxation inevitably invites foreign investments for the wrong reasons, that is, for keeping the social system "going." The savings derived from taxation, even under optional circumstances, can scarcely pay for necessary social services, much less stimulate new investments and capital plant expansion. Insofar as foreign capital is needed for economic expansion and not for maintaining a political equilibrium, the arguments in favor of confiscation are strengthened. This is because money agreements, particularly as they affect interest charges, can be negotiated more advantageously by independent states than by nations under foreign control. A policy of inefficient taxation invites foreign investment, and such investment adds to the instability of the economic sitation, for it drains off the nation's wealth.

(8) A public-sector economy has no difficulty in appropriating much of the fruit of economic development for capital accumulation rather

47. Isaac Deutscher, *The Great Contest: Russia and the West.* London and New York: Oxford University Press, 1960, pp. 110–12.

than for increasing consumer demands. As long as some areas of capital formation are in the hands of large-scale entrepreneurs, it is inevitable that there will be an outright struggle between the monied sector and the rest of society. There is no simple way of resolving this conflict to satisfy both private interests and provide for a proper distribution of income among the people at large. Hence, from an economic position, a choice must be made between mending and smashing.[48]

(9) Confiscation also has certain political and sociological advantages. But it does not necessarily provide a license for authoritarian modes of politics. Indeed, totalitarianism may be more necessary to induce the wealthy sector of the economy to pay taxes than to induce the poor to march on the latifundists. However, only communists seem prepared to face up to the problems of authoritarian politics created by a policy of confiscation. Democratic socialism has underestimated the degree of traditionalism inherent in feudal and capitalist classes, and this has produced a sharp difference regarding the advantage of smashing or mending within the socialist camp no less than between socialist and capitalist blocs. By the same token, it would be a mistake to equate confiscation with the appeal of socialism, since very often land take-over represents a delayed liquidation of feudal sectors under the aegis and sponsorship of the national bourgeoisie. Nationalism and radicalism ought not to be equated, either by friends or enemies of the Third World.

(10) Confiscation unites a sizable portion of the population in a common historic endeavor, mobilizes the masses behind the political system over and against the entrenched economic system, and makes it possible to introduce changes such as urbanization and rapid mobility which have been thwarted by conditions of economic control from abroad and monetary scarcity at home. It is easy to see why confiscation has become a principal feature of the national revolutions of our age. That such policy directly affects foreign credit arrangements and threatens existing securities is a small matter when put against the country's need to "close the gap" and enter the modern world. The ideological advantage of take-over is based on the mobilization and integration of anti-imperialist forces; the economic substance of such take-over is basically antitraditional. This strategy produces political independence from the old ruling classes and creates a nationalism which serves to unify the masses.

48. See the following papers on this necessity of choice: N. Belshaw, "Economic Development as an Operational Problem," *Civilizations*, Vol. II, No. 2, 1952, pp. 159–60; and I. G. Patel, "Mobilization of Domestic Resources for Economic Development," *Civilizations*, Vol. II, No. 4, 1952, pp. 487–95.

Confiscatory policies cannot of course in themselves solve the "social question," that is, the relationship between social classes. Economists, particularly those with an orthodox left-wing bias, tend to overestimate the role and function of agrarian confiscation and redistribution and to minimize drastically the nature of the obstacles which face a nation attempting to advance toward an even partially functioning industrial economy.[49]

Most countries are not economically self-sustaining and indeed tend to be single-crop economies. The sale of the crop involved and the use of the cash surplus thus realized for industrial expansion depend heavily on who controls the international market price of the crop. Thus, sugar prices can, without too much effort, be manipulated by the former colonial country long after actual colonial status is dissolved. An agrarian reform policy based on confiscation which is not followed by crop diversification is likely to run into serious difficulties. Problems arise in particular if the crop cannot be exported in its entirety, and if the pricing of the crop cannot be externally manipulated by the colonial powers. Yet, diversification is costly. In itself it may act to delay industrialism rather than to accelerate it. The degree of actual national sovereignty, while in part demonstrated by the ability to redistribute the national wealth, may be limited by other factors, such as the degree of external control of the over-all economy. It may be that subsidization and cash grants are still required, and that whatever the sources of such foreign loans, the actual indebtedness is great enough to cast doubt on the ability of the nation automatically to move from land confiscation to a socialist revolution. I am not asserting that such a transition cannot or should not be affected but only that the transition cannot be effected by any one master plan for agriculture. Indeed, it may be necessary to reverse the process and move from industrialized centralization to agricultural decentralization. While Cuba represents the centralization process, Yugoslavia represents the decentralization process. Nonetheless, both can reflect the radical socialist approach to development. While both taxation and expropriation can guarantee the stability and well-being of a society, the ability of a nation to make its own choice is in itself the best index of its own stability and well-being.

49. See Paul A. Baran, *op. cit.*, esp. pp. 271–83; and Edmundo Flores, *Tratado de Economía Agrícola*. Mexico City: Fondo de Cultura Económicia, 1961, esp. pp. 300–345.

11

Party Charisma: Political
Practices and Principles

Democratic dogma has it that the two-party system, with a legally sanctioned change-over of political power, is not simply functional in certain Western cultures but organic and universal to any definition of democracy. True enough, this is more of a populist than a professional view; yet academic sanction is not lacking. Perhaps the most direct expression of this position was made by Maurice Duverger when he wrote that "the two party system seems to correspond to the nature of things, that is to say that political choice usually takes the form of a choice between two alternatives." [1] This proposition contains two distinct and not necessarily connected premises. First, that the two-party system is "natural" because contradictory interests tend to polarize. Second, that political choice entails a choice between alternative party organizations.

Since *Political Parties* was written, much has happened to demonstrate that, while politics does indeed involve choice and while the need for oppositional elements within the political process is constant, the need for choice and opposition in itself does make a two-party system necessary. Even democracy is just as adaptable to a single-party apparatus representative of the major interest groups and factional elements as it is to a multi-party system.[2] There is increasing evidence that even in such a classic two-party nation as the United States there

1. Maurice Duverger, *Political Parties: Their Organization and Activity in the Modern States* (second edition). New York: John Wiley & Sons, 1959, p. 215.
2. On this, see John H. Kautsky, *Political Change in Underdeveloped Countries: Nationalism and Communism*. New York: John Wiley & Sons. 1962, pp. 116–17.

is probably more difference between factions within each party than between Democrats and Republicans as such.[3] Indeed, commentators have taken to speaking of the American "four-party" system, with liberal and conservative groupings within each political party.[4]

The number of parties does not necessarily determine the presence or the absence of democracy—the word is used here simply to denote the extent and impact of public opinion on policy decisions. This asymmetry between democracy and the party system is essential to any discussion of political behavior in Third World nations; in such "one-party democracies" as Mexico (*Partido Revolucionario Institucional*) and India (Congress Party), no less than in such "two-party dictatorships" as Morocco, the Union of South Africa, and Paraguay.[5] As Apter points out,

> New nations tend to have either a great many parties, or a single dominant party with the opposition purely nominal. The Sudan was an example of the first, with the two main parties divided over the issue of closer union with Egypt. Government was a shaky coalition between large and small parties. India and Ghana are examples of the second. They possess a large mass "Congress-type" party which grew out of the nationalist movement, while competing parties remain small and relatively helpless.[6]

Thus, to examine seriously political principles and practices in the Third World one must shed parliamentary preconceptions regarding democratic and totalitarian processes.

Max Weber went far toward anticipating the instability of personal rule, or pure charisma. Because of the idiosyncratic potential of "godlike" rulers, bureaucratic institutions emerge not so much as a "higher stage" in political life but as a consequence of the need for rationaliza-

3. See Hugh P. Williamson, "The Two Party System, Its Foibles and Follies," *The American Journal of Economics and Sociology,* Vol. 23, No. 1, Jan. 1964, pp. 85–93.
4. See on this James MacGregor Burns, *The Deadlock of Democracy: Four Party Politics in America.* Englewood Cliffs, N.J.: Prentice-Hall, 1963, pp. 280–322.
5. For a useful discussion of this question of multiple parties and singular dictatorships, see Fred R. van der Mehden, *Politics of the Developing Nations.* Englewood Cliffs, N.J.: Prentice-Hall, 1964, pp. 61–62.
6. David E. Apter, "Some Reflections on the Role of a Political Opposition in New Nations," in *African Politics and Society,* edited by Irving Leonard Markovitz. New York: The Free Press, 1970, p. 229.

tion through routinization. While Weber did allow for charisma of office, he did not apply this concept to political systems today, that is, to the present context of bureaucratic regulation and rationalization. For him, there was an ultimate choice between "the sovereignty of the charismatic man" and the "superordination of the institution." While Weber notes that the "conflict between discipline and individual charisma has been full of vicissitudes," the polarities between discipline and individual charisma remain hard and unyielding. Discipline, "like its most rational offspring bureaucracy, is impersonal," while charisma, which often reveals itself in military or semi-military situations, "uses emotional means of all sorts to influence followers through 'inspiration' and, even more, to train them in 'emphatic understanding' of the leader's will." [7] What has become apparent but thus far remains relatively inexplicit in the literature of political sociology is how discipline and charisma, rational authority and personal appeal, are fused in the political party which is at the same time the national party.[8] This party, which embodies the charismatic leadership responsible for making the national *revolution of development,* in effect transforms the Weberian duality into a search for a "higher unity"—into what is herein called party charisma. Party charisma is related to what Shils has called "charisma of office." Following Weber, he argues that in a bureaucratic society the bureaucracy is more than profane, but is still somewhat short of sacred. Charisma is afforded to the higher offices of the bureaucracy. The shift from the "revolution of independence" to that of "development" involves bureaucratization, which is analogous to party charisma. The relationship between charismatic top roles in a bureaucracy and the bureaucracy as a whole is roughly similar to what is herein considered the relationship between the charismatic party and other non-charismatic institutions of the state.[9]

There is scarcely a Third World nation which is not caught up in a political bind. This is becoming clear only now, after liberation. On one

---

7. H. H. Gerth and C. Wright Mills (eds.), *From Max Weber: Essays in Sociology.* New York: Oxford University Press, 1946, pp. 254–55; see also their introduction, pp. 51–55.

8. An important early attempt to work out the sociological component of the psychological concept of charisma is contained in William H. Friedland, "For a Sociological Concept of Charisma," in *Government in Black Africa,* edited by Marion E. Doro and Newell M. Stultz. Englewood Cliffs, N.J.: Prentice-Hall, 1970, pp. 58–68.

9. See Edward A. Shils, "Charisma, Order and Status," *American Sociological Review,* Apr. 1965, Vol. 30, No. 2, pp. 199–213.

side, nearly every nation in the Third World exhibits a strong principle, a *Führerprinzip,* in which power is seen to reside first and foremost in the leader, since he contains within his person the sum and substance of the aspirations and sentiments of the whole people. There is thus a significant tendency in the direction of charismatic authority, particularly since the leader is identified in the minds of the people with liberation from colonialism. But at the same time the people themselves have become greatly interested in participating in the creation of the post-independence political apparatus. Socialist rhetoric serves both to accelerate demands for mass participation and also to channelize such demands through the one-party ideology. Huntington has correctly noted that

> the creation of a one-party system redefines the scope of the political community. The basis of that community is the "chosen" social force, and other social groupings must either be assimilated to it or permanently excluded from the scope of politics. Legitimate political participation is limited to the members of the constituency social force, and the party which speaks for that social force monopolized, at least in theory, legitimate political activity. Every one-party system comes into existence with a concept of the community of the chosen and of the party as the political expression of that community. The community may be in part a social fact pre-existing the creation of the one party system, and it may also be in part the product of political action by the leaders of the party. If that community does not pre-exist the establishment of the party, the first task of the party is to bring it into existence.[10]

In the light of the tensions produced by these contrary trends, a unique political form has evolved in some emergent states. This new form, however "transitional" it may turn out to be, can be summed up by the phrase *party charisma.* Yet, the number of new states reflecting the crystallization of party charisma would indicate that it is anything but a passing fancy. The single party assumes the "god-like" features of leadership, which in the medieval world belonged to a series of popes, in the seventeenth and eighteenth centuries to a series of monarchs—some enlightened, but all absolute—and which in the present century has been raised to a new level by such secular rulers as Hitler, Stalin, and, on a lesser level, Mussolini and Perón. Nonetheless,

10. Samuel P. Huntington, "Social and Institutional Dynamics of One-Party Systems," in *Authoritarian Politics in Modern Society,* edited by Samuel P. Huntington and Clement H. Moore. New York: Basic Books, 1970, p. 13.

in the past charisma was most often lodged in living rulers rather than in the institution per se, although, as Weber showed, the Catholic Church attempted to lodge charisma in the institution rather than in the person.

I

Every social institution has an ideological rationale. As long as the colonial powers held ultimate power, they could support the growth of European types of institutions against the pressures exerted by the internal society to resist such institutions with stubborn parochialism. The civil service ethos increased steadily under the sponsorship of co-lonial powers.[11] Indeed, as in India, the bureaucracy is often considered a colonial achievement in the underdeveloped areas. But with the com-pletion of the anti-colonial phase, we find what seems to be a curious political reversion to traditionalist ways of sanctioning public authority. This is especially noticeable in Africa.[12] Thus, the new leaders, who may appear as demagogues to Westerners, are often considered democrats by their own peoples. The maximum leader is someone whose authority is permanent, personal, pervasive, and above all, "legitimized." It is a power not necessarily destroyed by being out of office, as is made clear by the career patterns of men like Patrice Lumumba and Jomo Ken-yatta, and to lesser extent by Juan Perón and Getulio Vargas. Indeed, it might be argued that political exile aids resistance to new political leadership and may actually prolong the life span of obsolete political institutions.[13]

Recently James S. Coleman divided party systems into three distinct types—one-party dominant systems, comprehensive nationalist parties,

11. See Irving L. Horowitz, "A Formalization of the Sociology of Knowledge," *Behavioral Science,* Vol. 9, No. 1, Jan. 1964, pp. 45–55. Paul P. Van Riper, *History of the United States Civil Service.* Evanston, Ill.: Row, Peterson and Company, 1958, esp. pp. 533–64.

12. On this clash of universalist and particularist political norms, see David E. Apter, *The Gold Coast in Transition.* Princeton: Princeton University Press, 1955; and James S. Coleman, *Nigeria: Background to Nationalism.* Berkeley: University of California Press, 1958.

13. The idea that there is a correlation between the growth of charisma and the decline of colonialism was first put forward to me by my former colleague Alvin W. Wolfe. This idea is being further developed by him in a work in progress on African conceptions of authority.

and competitive party systems—but they seem more academic than real.[14] First, most of the big nation-states fall into the category of one-party dominant systems. Second, comprehensive nationalist parties are functionally one-party systems only without the protective gloss of minority parties. Third, even competitive party systems are rarely competitive, since the dominant parties invariably have more than 65 per cent of the total electoral vote, the minority parties rarely more than 25 per cent. Hence, only in rare instances can sub-Sahara Africa be said to exhibit a genuine two- or multi-party system. Thus, party charisma is a more fundamental occurrence than can be revealed by examining only the political doctrines or organizations.

It is significant to note that this phenomenon of pseudo-competitive parties is by no means strictly African. The Mapai has withstood the onslaught of its own charismatic founder, David Ben-Gurion. He was able to muster only small support against an "organization" candidate. The Congress Party in India has clearly become an omnibus ruling party, despite the tolerance of other political parties. The P.R.I. in Mexico encourages the widest differences and divergences of opinion, but only so long as they occur within the party. Hence, the shift from multi-party to one-party domination is a world-wide phenomenon. The end of traditional society, the rise of modernization, has been accompanied by a decline in competitive party politics.

Charisma, however vague a concept it may be, is a factor in the "national liberation struggle." We must satisfactorily explain what takes place after this revolutionary phase. On the whole, the social functions of charisma radically shift after the successful conclusion of the national liberation effort. The revolutionary period is characterized by a heightened personal charisma. The revolutionary leaders take advantage of the weakness of the established social order to intensify the mass sense of bewilderment and confusion resulting from the revolution; beyond that, however, such leadership provides real alternatives and options for action. The new leaders establish their credentials not simply by exposing weakness or by asserting principles of an alternative social system, but by the process of mobilizing popular support to remedy either the real or assumed defects in the old system. Although

14. See James S. Coleman, "The Politics of Sub-Saharan Africa," *The Politics of the Developing Ideas.* Princeton: Princeton University Press, 1960, pp. 286–95. It should be noted that Coleman's paper makes explicit reference to sub-Saharan Africa, but he leaves no doubt that his categories can be extended to other regions of the world.

revolutionary leaders often assert historical necessity, they are successful largely in terms of their ability to exploit the confusion and chaos of the moment.

Charisma in the post-revolutionary period must respond to an entirely different set of needs: it must respond to the need to make order out of revolutionary chaos; it must reconcile the social sectors that have become antagonistic during the revolutionary period; it must resurrect the nation's disintegrated personality by welding it to a higher collective purpose. Through the process of symbolic identification of the masses with the leadership, the individual can realize his sense of fulfillment. Charisma makes the fusion of mass aspirations with leadership demands much simpler, if for no other reason than that party charisma is a more stable and reliable guide to action than personal (and inevitably capricious) leadership.

Earlier I spoke of party charisma as being a transcendental "ideal type" above the simple polarities of charisma and bureaucracy. The charisma of office illustrates the point. Bureaucracy exists alongside charisma of office, but because of its inefficiency or its attempt to control consumption, it cannot appear like General Motors or American Telephone and Telegraph as the bountiful provider of goods and services. Therefore, bureaucracy must legitimize itself in the Third World not on utilitarian grounds but by appeals to symbolic and irrational needs for unification and cohesion. In a historical context the bureaucracy is primary in that it manipulates the charismatic leadership; but in a concrete setting, party charisma serves to mediate the claims of the political elites and the technical elites. So if party charisma is to succeed, it must harness the polity to the tasks of development without dissolving the political activism which generated the revolution in the first place.[15]

Charismatic authority is not only a stimulus to change; it may also act as a brake on social change. As Hirschman has shown, the idea of

---

15. A serious deficiency in the sociological literature is that while "pure" charismatic leadership and bureaucratic structures have been well described, the intermediary, transitional systems have not been appreciated. On pure charisma, see Leo Lowenthal and Norbert Guterman, *The Prophets of Deceit.* New York: Harper & Brothers, 1941; and Erich Fromm, *Escape from Freedom.* New York: Farrar and Rinehart, 1941; on pure bureaucracies, see Robert K. Merton, "Bureaucratic Structure and Personality," and Alvin W. Gouldner, "Introduction," to *Studies in Leadership,* edited by Alvin W. Gouldner. New York: Harper & Brothers, 1950, pp. 3–49.

change may be a prime obstacle to development.[16] The charismatic leader promotes an ego-focused conception of progress which hampers economic development by placing the responsibility for it on political rather than technological means. In the United States, development has historically been accomplished in a "human-engineering" light, whereas in many of the emerging nations' struggles for political popularity tend to reinforce charismatic features of rule. To summarize this point, a highly accentuated charisma is dysfunctional in that it puts tremendous emphasis on the ability of leadership to make use of fate and fortune, but it underestimates political skills based on using actual data for action while at the same time discouraging development of a mass educational and political socialization apparatus.

Charismatic leadership often degenerates into personal tyranny because it must rely on the symbolic value of the ends sought and make little consideration for the means necessary to achieve such ends. The charismatic leader must turn to terror in order to make good his pledges and promises or to run the risk that his followers will quickly turn from disillusionment with him to active opposition. Even more moderate leaders find themselves subject to intense pressures to eliminate opposition. Factionalism and corruption seem to be inherent in all opposition to leadership. As Apter indicated, "the opposition is often blamed for producing a situation which in fact is inherent in the post-independence period of a nation." [17] In such a situation, party charisma serves to maintain the dynamism of personal leadership, while absorbing oppositional tendencies within the single party structure.

Party charisma is a synthesis of practical political considerations and symbolically laden personalist leadership. While it is unappealing to those reared in a culture stressing constitutional norms, it is an outgrowth of pressures to limit the excess of pure personal charisma. What is more, party charisma can more readily absorb defeat, or a series of defeats, than can the individual leader.

The Catholic Church long ago understood that the fallibility of popes had to be distinguished from the infallibility of the papacy if the charisma invested in Catholicism was not to deteriorate into sectarianism. However, the church understood this point better before Pope Leo IX

16. See Albert O. Hirschman, *The Strategy of Economic Development*. New Haven: Yale University Press, 1958, pp. 16–18.
17. David E. Apter, "Some Reflections on the Role of a Political Opposition in New Nations," in *African Politics and Society*, edited by Irving Leonard Markovitz, New York: The Free Press, 1970, p. 228.

put forward the infallibility thesis. The adaptability of the church in this century, with the remarkable exception of Pope John XXIII, has been severely hampered because of it. Many conflict-ridden exercises in "reinterpretation" might have been avoided if various claims to infallibility were eschewed in favor of a regressive insistence upon a pure charismatic form of church leadership. But this digression into church ideology simply underscores the existence of a form of organization that is something more than charisma and something less than bureaucracy.

II

Party charisma is hardly a new phenomenon. While it has achieved considerable refinement in African nations, many of its aspects can be seen in the revolutionary movements of Latin America. Here the "science" and "art" of leadership are dedicated to moving beyond the legacy of Western parliamentary democracy and socialist centralism. Capitalism and socialism, mass action and creative leadership, worker and peasant, male and female, and so forth, are all summed up in the party of the "whole people." In Argentina it bore the name *justicialismo* under Perón. The party became the "mediating power." The party is also the "perfect organization." For whatever the defects of the maximum leader may be, such "human defects" (as Perón called them) do not carry over to tarnish the party. Unlike Africa, however, old and well-established political parties do exist in Latin America. But the charismatic party claims that these traditional parties are riddled with self-interest and fraud and hence are too weak to integrate the nation. The "políticos" go nowhere; they lack a sense of destiny, which is what *Justicialismo* claimed to have. For it is not simply an "old-fashioned party" but a movement—an activity going somewhere, responsible to somebody, headed by someone.[18]

The extent to which Peronism is a party phenomenon rather than a simple charismatic condition has been revealed by the survival of the party, even though the leader has been in exile for a decade and is scarcely likely to resume power.[19] Personal leadership does not by any

18. See Juan Perón, *Conducción Política*. Buenos Aires: Ediciones Mundo Peronista, 1952, esp. pp. 205–12, 295–97.
19. See on this dichotomization of Perón and Peronism, Irving Louis Horowitz, "Modern Argentina: The Politics of Power," *The Political Quarterly,* Vol. 30,

means disappear. The revolutionary party persists even though the revolutionary government may be overthrown. And this is a significant fact, since party charisma seems evident in the *apristas* of Peru and the Brazilian Labor Party (PTB) of Brazil. In Cuba, despite the monumental personal authority of Castro, the elevation of the United Party of the Cuban Socialist Revolution (PURSC) to a supreme place necessarily means that Castro has been willing and able to place himself under its authority.[20] Perhaps this is the only way to prevent factionalism from openly breaking out.

Strangely enough, the Peronist movement in the Argentina of the 'forties is more a prototype of what took place in Africa a decade later in the 'fifties than an imitation of fascist Italy of the 'thirties. Peronism was directly linked to the transformation of a rural society into an urban society; it served as a catalyst for the industrialization of the nation; it served to give the drive toward economic development a base in a socially revolutionary doctrine and ideology.[21] But perhaps the most perfect symbol of charismatic authority is the unique relationship the "leader" is said to have with the "people," a uniqueness underscored by the "anguish" of the past and the "joys" of the present. Eva Perón wrote:

> The Argentine people does not forget those days of anguish and death. Why should it not celebrate the First of May, now that it can do so without fear and anxiety? Instead of screaming with clenched fists in front of the closed doors of Government House, the Argentine working people now celebrate May Day with a magnificent festival, at which their Leader presides from the balconies of Government House in his character of the first Argentine worker, the title which, without any doubt, Perón appreciates most. And the marvelous thing is that, instead of fearing death on that day,

No. 4. Oct.–Dec. 1959: in this connection, see Gino Germani, "El autoritarismo y las clases populares," in *Política y Sociedad en una Epoca de Transición*. Buenos Aires: Editorial Paidós, 1962, pp. 127–46.

20. See the report by Richard Eder on Castro's urging of an easing of tensions between Cuba and the United States, in which Castro's plans for a "constitutional regime in Cuba by 1969" are reported. *The New York Times,* July 6, 1964.

21. For contrasting views of the significance of Peronism as an ideology of development, see Marcos Merchensky, *Las Corrientes Ideológicas en la Historia Argentina*. Buenos Aires: Editorial Concordia, 1961, esp. pp. 215–30; and Jorge Abelardo Ramos, *Revolución y Contrarrevolución en la Argentina*. Buenos Aires: La Reja, 1961, esp. pp. 435–45.

the people are wont to offer their lives, yelling a chorus which always moves my soul: "Our lives for Perón." [22]

The role of the leader is to purify the hearts and cleanse the minds
of his followers. There is always much to purify and cleanse! The
culture of poverty is difficult to celebrate when it is realized that its
asking price is the surrender of the political processes to the benevolence
of wealthy classes. Up close, within sight and touch, the culture of
poverty evaporates into a poverty of culture. For want of a resistant
and sophisticated political system, the mass of the poor is prey to
promises of deliverance. For this reason, the leader can be charismatic,
can appear god-like in his presentation of self to the undifferentiated
mass. But when the poor are newly mobilized, uprooted from older
patterns and former life styles, then "working-class authoritarianism"
becomes a factor. The process of development cannot be judged by
whether it avoids charismatic appeals but only by its achievements.
Hence, the real measure of party charisma is, first, in the successful
execution of the tasks of social development and, second, in its ability
to satisfy the claims of the masses.

This "role confusion," in which the leader identifies with the nation
in an almost tautological fashion, has been carried to perfection in
Latin America. We have a clear illustration in the suicide of Getulio
Vargas in the mid-'fifties. In his suicide message, Vargas declared he
would enter history by this act of identification with the "people."

> My sacrifice will maintain you united, and my name will be your
> battle flag. Each drop of my blood will be an immortal call to your
> conscience and will maintain a holy vibration for resistance. . . . I
> fought against the looting of Brazil. I have fought against the loot-
> ing of the people. I have fought bare-breasted. The hatred, infamy,
> and calumny did not beat down my spirit. I gave you my life. Now
> I offer my death. Nothing remains. Serenely I take the first step on
> the road to eternity and I leave life to enter history. [23]

One can see here, as in the words of Eva Perón, the powerful strain
of messianic fervor, a fervor which gives rich substance to the charis-

22. Eva Perón, *My Mission in Life,* translated by Ethel Cherry. New York:
Vantage Press, 1953, pp. 101–2.
23. Getulio Vargas, "Farewell Message to the Brazilian People," in *Revolution in
Brazil: Politics and Society in a Developing Nation,* by Irving Louis Horowitz.
New York: E. P. Dutton & Company, 1964, pp. 132–33.

matic aspect of this ostensibly altruistic identification of person with nation, and, through this identification, with the gods, with immortality.

From the more profane side of things, it is evident that this "old-fashioned" Latin American personal charisma is not easily transferred into party charisma. In the case of Perón, through *justicialismo,* and in the case of Vargas, through the *Partido Trabhalista Brasileiro,* the image of the personal leader was a handicap rather than a help to party charisma. What Lipset refers to as "left fascism" occurs in countries undergoing, but not completing, the rapid social changes of urbanization and industrialization.[24] In the absence of a completed social revolution, the mystique of charismatic leadership cannot readily be transferred to a party as a bearer of principles. Therefore, when personal charisma collapses under such circumstances, there is a return to traditional political processes, albeit in a truncated and usually sterile form.

Political party leaders often see themselves as the "vessels of universal truth" while manipulating their party machinery "as simple mechanisms with which to gain power." [25] But in fact, this approach is more common to the "old" underdeveloped nations of South America than to the "new" underdeveloped nations of Africa. In Latin America, the artificial grafting of a libertarian political code onto a soft underbelly of feudal socioeconomic relations often accentuated pure charisma, just as it also accentuated pure bureaucratic norms. It is precisely the kind of permanent crisis of dependency evident in Latin America which many of the new nations of Asia and Africa have sought to overcome through party charisma. In those cases in Latin America where more or less successful changes in the social structure have been brought about—Cuba, Mexico, Chile, and to a lesser extent Venezuela—the party apparatus becomes the vessel of universal truth, while the leadership draws its inspiration from the claims of the party. Developing nations tend to become the model, replacing that of the most developed "first new nation," the United States, and avoiding the well-advertised problems of the Soviet Russian bureaucratic state.

In Brazil, precisely because its present military leadership is charis-

24. See Seymour Martin Lipset, *Political Man.* New York: Doubleday and Co., 1959, p. 135.
25. See Kalman H. Silvert, "The Costs of Anti-Nationalism," in *Expectant Peoples: Nationalism and Development,* edited by K. H. Silvert. New York: Random House, 1963, pp. 355–56. See also his article on "National Values, Development, and Leaders and Followers," *International Social Science Journal,* Vol. XV, No. 4, 1963, pp. 560–70.

matic without party, political parties often follow the ways of United States politics by stressing electoral function and providing bureaucratic careers for popular leaders. In these instances the leadership often turns to the bureaucracy or military to build up power reserves. This intensifies the political seizure. Real power bases are created through control of the "bureaus" at the administrative levels and by alliances with military and other sectors. The direct power relation is between personal leadership and the state machinery. The Brazilian political party is the leader's vehicle, but it does not become enmeshed in government as such or enjoy the mass following of a "movement." It lies outside the state to a greater degree and control of it is only peripheral. It does not become fused with charismatic dimensions except in revolutionary "movements." Even then, party organization, being essentially "non-ideological," is likely to overpower or modify charismatic party tendencies. It is a commonplace for the Brazilian intellectual to decry the opportunism of Brazilian parties and their lack of solid ideological lineage and loyalty. Because of the tenuous connection between leaders of the party and those of the state, political reorganization may be stifled. Politics may then be fragmented into many parties representing different interests.

III

One of the peculiarities of authority in the Third World is that party ideology is generally much more inflexible than the criteria for party membership. While the ideological features of the political apparatus are often highly centralized, the actual organization allows for a wide variety of ideological types. Lipset has noted that

> such parties tend to be loosely structured, more like a *rassemblement* than a party of ideology or interest. They combine a number of interests and strata, either through the charisma of the leader or through the original need for unity in the struggle for independence. Charisma is necessary if the system is to survive in its early stages, and the absence of opposition may prove beneficial if it preserves the often frail mystique upon which authority depends.[26]

It is not so much the "frail mystique" which determines the situation, since it rests on the frailties of power, but rather the inability of any

26. Seymour Martin Lipset, *The First New Nation: The United States in Historical and Comparative Perspective.* New York: Basic Books, 1963, pp. 314–15.

one social sector to dominate the political context. The foundations for legal authority are strengthened when one well-defined social-economic sector is in control of the state. The American bourgeoisie in the nineteenth century (notwithstanding the rubrics which may be employed to show the aristocratic tastes of that class) gave legal shape to society because they were able to generalize their class interests so that they became identified with the national interest. Since the emergent nations of Latin America, Asia, and Africa have never witnessed a complete crystallization of modern class relationships, there has not been a properly installed rational-legal superstructure. The irony is that in many nations of Latin America law has been revered rather than obeyed. On the other hand, in those nations where the national movement was initially based on charismatic force, such as Mexico and Cuba, there are strong grounds for anticipating the long-range success of rational authority, as was the case in the United States between 1775 and 1865.

If we take Japan between 1860 and 1940 as typical of the "pre-Third World" developmental process in Asia, we find that disillusionment with multi-party processes does not necessarily resolve itself in party charisma but may result in personal charisma, which in this context meant the emperor.

> Despite the growing popular participation in elections and extensive parliamentary experience, a politically mature middle class, with demands and expectations, did not develop. There was not enough time for this adjustment: rather, politicians came to be regarded as corrupt, parasitic, somehow un-Japanese, and "politician" took on a pejorative ring in prewar Japan. Essential power remained entrenched in a small elite, civilian and military, with the latter having direct access to the Emperor and able to use him to sanction its objectives without reference to the wishes of the popularly elected Diet.[27]

One must be cautious about assigning the "anti-political" spirit to nations like Japan, as if this were an exclusive occurrence in Asia. From the Civil War to the Great Depression the word "politician" had a pejorative ring to it in the United States. To some degree, there is a residue of this sentiment in the current American climate as well, for

27. Lawrence Olson, "The Elite, Industrialism and Nationalism: Japan," in *Expectant Peoples: Nationalism and Development,* edited by K. H. Silvert. New York: Random House, 1963, pp. 409–10.

instance, among "alienated youth" and sectors of the "blue collar." It might be argued that the institutionalization of multi-party politics in the United States prevented the formation of a political elite out of its military and economic ruling components. In the First World, it seems that it was the parties at least as much as the politicians that were labeled as corrupt and parasitic: Boss Tweed, Tammany Hall, the Prendergast Machine. Because of this, transference of party allegiance (note the reticence of members of the same party to attack colleagues of widely different persuasions) becomes more difficult than in many parts of the Third World. In such a situation, the two-party apparatus is more than a stratagem of rule but a necessary means for avoiding total elitism on one hand and total anarchy on the other. In Japan the tensions between the needs of a mass society and that of a neo-feudal economy did not have to be resolved by party charisma. Stability was supplied by custom and tradition, the hierarchical rigidity of Japanese political leadership, and its close identification with military order and religious sanction.

Recent scholarship has persuasively argued that the single party system is the functional equivalent to traditional forms of monarchism.

> A strong one-party system appears to meet certain functional needs for a society in the early to middle phases of modernization. In an era when modernization involves the expansion of political participation, the single party is the functional equivalent of the absolute monarchy of seventeenth century Europe. The absolute monarchy centralized power to promote modernizing reform, but it then proved incapable of expanding power to assimilate new groups into the political system. The one-party system, however, is unusual among political institutions in providing significant capacities for both the concentration and the expansion of power.[28]

This sense of hierarchy is precisely what is absent in most Third World nations, where there is extreme fluidity in both the definition and execution of leadership. Charismatic leaders are often under pressure to establish a principle of rule that is based on the political party as such. In Kwame Nkrumah's Convention People's Party (CPP) in

28. Samuel P. Huntington, "Social and Institutional Dynamics of One-Party Systems," in *Authoritarian Politics in Modern Society,* edited by Samuel P. Huntington and Clement H. Moore. New York: Basic Books, 1970, p. 12; see also Ali A. Mazrui, "The Monarchial Tendency in African Political Culture," in *British Journal of Sociology,* Vol. XVIII, No. 3 (Sept. 1967), pp. 231–50.

Ghana, this transference of charisma from the person to the party was nearly complete:

> The party must become at once the symbol and the focus of the national consciousness towards which loyalty can be directed above and even irrespective of loyalty to particular persons. Thus the agents of the party's authority may be acknowledged to fail or defect and ministerial heads may be seen to roll, but his must never be equated with any failure by the party as such. When the source and agency of authority are successfully separated in this way, it can then become true that *le parti regne mais il ne gouverne pas.* Charisma will become successfully routinized once the separation of the source from the agency of authority immunizes it against the failure which would bring about the collapse of a "pure" charismatic system.[29]

And, of course, such routinization never happened. The CPP never dissociated itself from Nkrumah. But there is a danger that problems of political stability, when viewed from the standpoint of charisma, can be overstated on psychological grounds. With respect to Ghana, such an approach might overemphasize the personal obsessions of Nkrumah, his failure to maintain his charisma, and the like, and as a result underemphasize such structural features as the power of the Ghanaian bureaucratized military and the antagonism against Nkrumah by the Western capitalist bloc.

Even where personal charisma is exceptionally powerful, as in Cuba, we find direct appeals to party charisma. In an address delivered in May 1964, Fidel Castro said: "If the imperialists should invade this country, you would have to realize that the majority of the leaders of today would die in the struggle. But the people will remain, and the party would remain. There would be no need to ask for names or for men. Each one of us would do his duty in the way demanded of him and do it well." [30] There is no question of the sincerity of the emotions herein expressed. It is obvious that under stress and duress the appeal to the rank and file is made in the name of the people and the party. The rhetoric does indicate a clear distinction between transient elite and permanent mass. Cuban leadership displays a passionate involve-

29. W. G. Runciman, "Charismatic Legitimacy and One-Party Rule in Ghana," *Archives Européennes de Sociologie,* Vol. IV, No. 1, 1963, p. 159.
30. Quoted by Dave Dellinger, "Cuba: Seven Thousand Miles from Home," *Liberation,* Vol. IX, No. 4, June–July 1964, pp. 11–21.

ment rather than an Olympian detachment. In this fashion the party serves to solve the succession of leadership without destroying personal charisma. To say that this is simply a clever and modern way of reinforcing personal charisma misses the point that the cult of the party is quite commonplace. If we examine the history of the Soviet Union, it will be found that the extreme cult of personality came, not at the outset of the revolution, but only at a late stage when the goals of political revolution hardened and became goals of economic development; and only at that point when the fight over control of the party apparatus became uppermost.[31]

One of the chief functional by-products of charismatic leadership is that traditional economic sectors are made subordinate to state decisions. The kinds of independent class struggles engaged in by trade unions and business associations in the highly developed capitalist nations are intolerable for the Third World. They are viewed as obstructions to the task of social development, and in this way, the conduct of the union or the corporation has to become subordinate to state power. This was perfectly expressed by the deceased African leader Tom Mboya. Speaking of both union and management separatist tendencies, he wrote:

> The lesson they have to learn is that if their beliefs are to be respected in our new countries, they will need to show a response to government and nationalistic requirements. If their stand appears to be negative and unnecessarily obstructive, then it is inevitable that, with this sense of urgency in our new countries, they will be overridden and completely set aside. If they show they are cooperative and become partners in the urgent need for development, then they will survive.[32]

This is a way of pointing out that, in the Third World, economic power is not equivalent to political power. But the "partnership" Mboya pointed to is obviously far from neat. One should not confuse the aims of sincere charismatic leaders with social reality. Assuming that the charismatic ideology cannot be the opiate of the underdeveloped masses,

31. See Myron Rush, *Political Succession in the U.S.S.R.* New York: Columbia University Press, 1965.
32. Tom Mboya, *Freedom and After.* Boston: Little, Brown & Company, 1963, p. 197; also pp. 56–57.

it would be nonsense to suggest that Bombay's charismatic V. K. Krishna Menon was more powerful that the combined might of Bombay's textile owners. Thus, if there is a certain peculiar leverage in the political process, the same can be said for the power of economic processes.

Class competition is blurred, but not replaced, by the doctrine of the "unity of the whole people" or by variations on the theme of consensus. This doctrine makes multiple parties superfluous, since the whole people can obviously be represented by the whole party.[33] Yet, the conception of the whole people, or the myth of the mass, imposes severe limitations on totalitarian possibilities in the Third World. For any party which is compelled to make its appeal by crossing class lines has clearly limited its cohesive potentialities. Yet party charisma is also the product of a relatively unstable equilibrium, an instability created by the fact that the very social forces which contributed to the formal political independence of the emerging nation are not compelled to choose between socialism and capitalism. Since experimental attitudes do prevail, they create a political atmosphere that is far from rigid or totalitarian.

Many Third World countries place great emphasis upon the mobilization of the working classes and union movements in support of the national leadership. In this, the nations of the Third World have incorporated selective features of other radical movements to further consensus between the various classes in the society. Unionism becomes the most powerful bulwark of the nationalist elites. The working classes thus believe they have attained power rather than acted as a mere factor in the power arrangement. This variety of "national socialism" is made possible by the rational division of the economic spoils. Since large-scale capital is held by foreigners, internal economic fissures between classes will be dissolved, or at least drastically minimized. This creates the *development ideology* of class struggle.

The formal independence of many Third World nations makes possible greater economic penetration by the older colonial powers. Formal freedom liberates the ex-colonial powers of the necessity of rule, and ensures greater productivity, greater output, and greater interaction

33. The most impressive study of this phenomenon of socialism of the whole people, and its effects on political processes in the new nations, is Emile R. Braundi, "Neocolonialism and the Class Struggle," *International Socialist Journal,* Vol. 1, No. 1, Jan.–Feb. 1964, pp. 48–68; see also, Hamza Alavi, "Imperialism: Old and New," *The Socialist Register,* edited by Ralph Miliband and John Javille. New York: Monthly Review Press, 1964, pp. 104–26.

with foreign powers.[34] The new middle classes which emerge in post-colonial situations move in the direction of the kind of formal authority which characterizes advanced middle-class societies elsewhere; but they are thwarted by the overt sentiments of the revolutionary leadership. More important, middle-class political consolidation stands in contradiction to the stated socialist objectives of many emergent nations. Therefore, the political elite tries to continue to exercise the special prerogatives of office, lest the middle class and proletariat jeopardize through social conflict the thorough mobilization and integration of the nation.

In the light of the fall from power of such titans as Nkrumah, Sukarno, and Ben Bella, party elites are increasingly cautious in making exaggerated claims for themselves as purveyors of universal truths; they now prefer to invest such claims in their party. In a new nation like Mali, for example, the Political Bureau, made up of a dozen men, makes all decisions, and these decisions are binding for all Malians. It is the *Union Soudanaise* party which "holds in its hands the destiny of the country and has absolute power." The danger in this situation is that it fails to "surround the party with guarantees of popular agreement." There is a genuine concern about keeping connections to the mass, and this is resolved by an unnatural consensus—a demand for collectivity as a way to avoiding errors. But this often leads to an avoidance of decision-making.[35] Party charisma enables the new nation to combine maximum organizational efficiency with the greatest mobilization of the masses. It becomes a way of establishing the paradoxical claims of a consensus built upon mass participation and of a coercive apparatus built upon elitist drives toward development. And to the degree that such paradoxical claims are matters of ultimate interests and are "non-negotiable," then party charisma may turn out to be an unstable and temporary equilibrium. But then again, the entire Third World may be in this position in relation to the advanced industrial-military complexes of the world.

The new nation-states provide an extremely fertile area for observing

34. However, even this is not uniformly true. In per capita terms at least, a number of nations have probably become poorer in post-independence times. The cases of Burma and India are most important illustrations of the lack of correlation that may exist between formal independence and real growth.
35. On this subject, see William J. Foltz, "From French West Africa to the Mali Federation: The Background to Federation and Failure" (Ph.D. dissertation). Yale University, 1963.

party charisma. The problem might be posed in the following way: Why is there a need for charismatic rather than rationalistic types of political authority? First, there are very few educated people in the new African states; very few whose background and qualifications alone could help create non-charismatic rule. Second, people feel frustrated that development has come so late and been so difficult; party charisma therefore serves as a ready-made tool to accelerate this process. Third, most African states have a long history of acceptance and response to raw power. In both British and French former possessions the lines of authority were clear, however much they were hated.[36] With the departure of the colonialists, this clear demarcation between ruler and ruled also ended. Party charisma thus overcomes the problem of political succession in the most feasible way possible within a context which exhibits a high degree of traditionalism among the masses and a no less marked modernism among the elites.

In response to the cry of treason which has been heard with increasing stridency from socialist elements in the Third World and Western Europe alike, the leadership of many emerging states has asserted that the national liberation phase has not yet been concluded (at least this is held to be so in Africa); only when nations like Angola and South Africa are liberated from white domination will it be possible or desirable to focus attention on internal imbalances between social sectors within the continent. It is further stated that for relatively advanced nations such as Ghana and Nigeria to intensify the conflict between the new urban proletariat and the new urban bourgeoisie would only postpone a settlement of accounts with the remaining imperial powers. Thus, the spokesmen of these new nations claim that a class struggle would prove to be sectarian and self-defeating, at least at this historical juncture. Indeed, they point to Biafran "separatism" as having failed because of its devisive aspects. This demand for consensus has come to define not only nations but has been extended to the rest of the continent. It seems to underly the insistence on the unique properties of African socialism.

The growth of party charisma in the Soviet Union was thwarted by two important factors; one practical and the other theoretical. On the practical side, the Soviet Union inherited a relatively complex, if not especially well-organized, bureaucratic apparatus from the czarist regime

36. See Aidan Crawley, "Patterns of Government in Africa," *African Affairs,* Vol. 60, No. 240, July 1961, pp. 393–94.

(as did India from the British some thirty years later). Unlike the post-colonial situation in the new nations of Africa and Asia, the technical functions of this pre-revolutionary bureaucracy were left intact. From the outset, it was a distinctively Russian entity, not a colonial import which could be expanded or withdrawn at the pleasure of the foreign governing body. It was not necessary for the Bolshevik Party to incorporate unto itself all the features of organizational life. On the theoretical side, the separation of power between government and party was a Leninist canon. It represented the Communist Party way of establishing a one-party system of checks and balances. The fact that under Stalin the role of government was profoundly weakened, and federal and party functions combined, made possible the kind of personal charisma which sapped the strength of Soviet organizational life. One may characterize, therefore, the Khrushchev and Kosygin eras as a time of restoration—the re-establishment of lines of authority which are in some measure traditional, while in other respects legalistic and rationalistic.[37] In any event, the post-Stalin period in Soviet political history has been one in which bureaucratic norms have replaced charismatic leadership at the top of the political elite, no less than within the rank and file.

IV

The underlying assumption that "man" will eventually assert his individuality in the face of tyranny takes for granted that people of the Third World share the Western cultural conception of "man against state." There is no evidence that the powerful disposition in favor of constitutionalism exhibited by the British working class in the nineteenth century is a valid guide to action for the recently liberated colonial working classes. To assume that a charismatic mobilization system is undemocratic while a parliamentarian reconciliation system is democratic, simply turns constitutionalism into an article of faith.[38]

37. Irving Louis Horowitz, "The Second Soviet Revolution," *The Correspondent*, No. 33, Winter 1964–65.
38. For a conventional "Western" position on this, see David E. Apter, "Political Religion in the New Nations," *Old Societies and New States: The Quest for Modernity in Asia and Africa*. New York: The Free Press, 1963, pp. 57–104. It is interesting that the references Apter uses to prove the existence of personal charisma and "political religion" better demonstrate an impersonal or, better, depersonalized charisma lodged in the authority of the party.

Until now, constitutionalism, when employed in underdeveloped nations, has not operated to create or broaden the consensual basis but has become a basic instrument for popular wants and needs. By contrast, party charisma establishes a basis of authority which is at one and the same time personal and legal, one that focuses on the party and not on either the individual or the law as such. It should not be assumed that the Third World is one in which personal authority is exclusive and dominant. This is, as a matter of fact, rarely the case. Party authority is not simply a rhetorical device used to disguise the fact of personal power. It is itself a limitation on personal power, though not yet legal or universally acknowledged. The actual transitory character of political parties stands in the way of the complete rationalization of the social systems in the Third World.

Party charisma does not do away with problems of bureaucracy and formal organization. On the contrary, such problems are multiplied to the degree that authority takes on multiple social roles: a portion of power remains with the leader, and another portion with the party directly. Leaders and parties can attempt to legitimize power, that is, to gain authority on the basis of fulfilling requirements.

Historically, a greater measure of power has been invested in the personal leadership *prior* to the revolutionary period and a greater measure of power invested in the technical-professional elite *after* the revolutionary phase. The charismatic party functions as the clearing house for ideologists and technologists alike, deriving its own momentum from the unstable equilibrium they create. The ability to perform a particular task may appear to rest on "rational" grounds, while the choice and allocation of such tasks may appear to rest upon "irrational" political grounds. Actual political interaction is far muddier, since as a matter of course the line between task and decision is constantly shifting, and it is in the areas between that friction arises.

The problem becomes particularly acute because so many of the new nations have one-party arrangements. All major decisions and tasks must be funneled through this single-party channel. The battle for control of the party apparatus becomes especially bitter. To lose control of this apparatus may mean to lose out in the over-all sense, to forfeit the opportunity to move the nation. Thus, the battle for control is not only severe, but invariably subversive.[39] Seen in this way, we can under-

39. See Colin Legum, "What Kind of Radicalism for Africa?" *Foreign Affairs,* Vol. 43, No. 2, Jan. 1965, pp. 237–50.

stand how personalism and constitutionalism are tactical responses to an unstable historic situation, and historical stages in the unfolding of nationhood.[40]

There is a growing literature dedicated to proving that not all of the emergent nations fit this pattern. Sir James Robertson has cited Nigerian "exceptionalism" based on the long precedent of compromise, the slow maturation of political responsibilities under the Crown, and the development of three strong parties.[41] This sounds more like an apologia for the superiority of British imperialism than an example of significant differences between Nigeria and other new African states. There is also the literature attempting to prove that constitutional monarchy resolves the problems of Middle Eastern bureaucracy. The argument is that, given the background and context of Middle Eastern history, a cultivated, Westernized notion of democracy can be brought about only by the modern counterpart of the eighteenth-century benevolent despot. This seems to place Middle East nations, like Iran, in a more backward political condition than that reflected by party charisma. The latter at least has the advantages of depersonalization of the political machinery, and the legalization of the bureaucracy over and above kings and monarchs.[42] Nonetheless, it is dangerous to draw a fixed line between feudal monarchy and party charisma. The Meiji restoration in Japan was not necessarily a backward political step, despite certain monarchical manifestations. Again, certain objective factors, such as foreign capital and border insecurity, play a vital role in determining the essential character of politics in emergent nations.

V

Ideology has become a particularly powerful force of rationalization in the newer African states. It can be seen with striking voice in Sékou

40. The various papers in Gwendolen M. Carter (ed.), *African One-Party States.* Ithaca: Cornell University Press, 1962, provide a solid basis for my judgment that charisma and bureaucracy ought not to be viewed as historical stages in the unfolding of nationhood, but extremes between which choices are constantly made and unmade. The difficulty with the Carter analysis is that it develops an analysis of empirical worth without a corresponding theoretical framework for making sense out of the single party state phenomenon.
41. See James Robertson, "Sovereign Nigeria," *African Affairs,* Vol. 59, No. 239, Apr. 1961, pp. 145–54.
42. Mohammad Reza Shah, *Mission for My Country.* New York: McGraw-Hill, 1963.

Touré's explicit rejection of the classic struggle in favor of the anti-colonial struggle, even after the successful conclusion of the national liberation phase of the revolution. He speaks of unionism in Guinea as "specifically African . . . an authentic expression of African values." [43] This means that European socialist standards of labor relations are to be replaced by the ideology of development as such. Speaking for Senegal, Léopold Sedar Senghor says that this Africanization of socialist ideology will eliminate the "one-sidedness" of European socialism and nationalism problems of social development. This development is to take place through "Community Development Centers." In this the Senegalese Party (UPS) is to be the "echo of the popular aspirations" and also the "scientific expression" of peoples' needs. In this apocalyptic vision of socialism and negritude, the party of the whole people may even become the party of the whole race.[44] The Third World has produced a party ideology as well as a political strategy. However mythic the synthesis of European socialism and African nativism may be, it would be foolish at this early stage to assume that the doctrine of the whole people led by the single, unified peoples' party, headed by the knowing and responsive leader, who is furthermore the choice of the whole people and the unified party alike (the two are not always distinguishable), is either transitory or lacking in practical application. But it would be equally risky to assume the opposite, that the poet of Negritude (Senghor), who worked closely with French colonialism, will develop Senegal. For whatever else they are, the leaders of the emergent African states are sharp-eyed and razor-tongued, and above all practical men, concerned with political survival in extremely rugged social-economic circumstances.

Party charisma also represents a response to the division of power between local or tribal units and national units. Speaking of Ghana, Dennis Austin makes precisely this point. "If one asks how such an aim [of resolving the cosmopolitan-local duality] is pursued, the answer is clear—through the party, which dominates the contemporary scene. It remodels the State in its own image—reducing the power of the chiefs, centralizing the trade unions, legislating against tribal and regional

43. Sékou Touré, *L'Expérience et l'Unité Africaine*. Paris: Présence Africaine, 1959, pp. 390–91.
44. Léopold Sedar Senghor, *On African Socialism,* translated by Mercer Cook. New York: Frederick Praeger, 1964, pp. 154–59, and 165.

parties, and centralizing power within the constitution." [45] According to
Kwame Nkrumah: "There must be no stress on local, separatist
loyalties. . . . in Ghana, in the higher reaches of our national life,
there should be no reference to Fantis, Ashantis, Ewes, Dagemgax, etc.
We should call ourselves Ghanians—all brothers and sisters, members
of the same community, the State of Ghana." [46] However, contrary to
the wishes of Nkrumah and national socialists of his type, ethnic
heterogeneity does not disappear over time. Indeed, it might be argued
that the "principle of self-determination" is counter-productive of nationalist trends, since it serves as an ideological reinforcement of precisely the sort of separatistic tendencies that resolve themselves in civil
warfare rather than civic culture.

However reluctant the inherited oligarchical system is to surrender
its traditional power, and however desirous the political rulers are to
avoid a direct confrontation with these traditional classes, the introduction of an industrial system compels these rulers to fight the oligarchy.
The two forms of legitimation inherited from the past—personalism and
constitutionalism—are historical and structural at the same time. Personal charisma, while a mechanism of transition from colonialism to
independence, is not something which yields automatically to rational
authority. While party charisma may be unstable, with the leader having to choose between absolute dictatorship and benevolent despotism,
it remains an ongoing force in many Third World nations, long after
some system of rational legal authority has been created and long after
the collapse of the initial post-independence leadership cadre. The
dialectic of the situation dictates that a charismatic figure must stay in
power long enough to permit the crystallization of those opposing factions which can debate the character of the legal system. Charismatic
parties thus make possible discussions on laws of political succession,
divisions in the power structure, and relations between social and
economic sectors. The growth of rational authority should allow for the
kinds of innovations by the leadership that will not produce rigidly
opposed political factions. There should be enough fluidity to permit the
existence of highly personalized relations between leaders and fol-

---

45. See Dennis Austin, "The New Ghana," *African Affairs,* Vol. 59, No. 234,
Jan. 1960, pp. 20–25.
46. *Ibid.,* p. 21. See also Kwame Nkrumah, *I Speak of Freedom: A Statement of
African Ideology.* London: Heinemann, 1961.

lowers in the revolutionary movement for national development. This
is the proper function of party charisma.[47]

47. In the first edition, the chapter on party charisma included two parts of an
appendix: one on distinctions between ideological and institutional bases of
party charisma, and the other on intra-country variations in party charisma. I
have decided to eliminate this appendix, first because the distinction between
ideological justification and counter-arguments based on institutional considerations
are roughly analogous, although they emphasize different parts of the political
process. Second, the variations in the application of party charisma in Latin
America in contrast to Africa and Asia have sharply diminished over time. There
has been a strong propensity toward Latinization, with the military take-over of
established political machines. This has taken place in such pivotal areas as Pakistan, Nigeria, Ghana, and Indonesia. In fact, the instability of many regimes
throughout the Third World, regardless of how old the regime is, indicates that
the transitional properties of party charisma do not, in themselves, serve so much
to maintain stability as they serve to prevent democratization. This process of
the homogenization of the Third World permits a simpler type of analysis, although it indicates the growth of non-democratic political outcomes that are reinforced rather than resisted by the existence of party charisma.

12

The Organization and Ideology of Militarism: From Revolution to Nation-Building

I

To say that we live in an age of rapid development is more of a truism than a significant observation. What is of critical importance is the exact character of the transitional process—not only in the sense of where we were and are now heading, but how we will get there. To favor "indeterminism" is not to deny the possibility that some factors are more important than others in the development process.

It is evident that from the social science perspective there are some variables which are more important than others. The political apparatus of sixteenth-century Italy and the economic foundations of eighteenth-century England are obvious cases in point. It is my belief that the military apparatus of twentieth-century civilization has the same kind of "deterministic" properties—to be sure, like any system of determinants, it has its limits and perhaps even its deficiencies as an explanatory system.

But the basis of my remarks, and of my continued concern with problems of the military, is that the rise of military establishments throughout the Third World, as well as the vigorous pursuit of counterinsurgency techniques and weapons among the major powers, represents a greater readiness to generate social and economic advances through military means than through conventional industrial processes. The sheer capacity of military power to cancel any and all "processes of history" by canceling society gives weight to the term "military determinism." This is not an attempt to deny multi-causality, for without a certain level of industrial production, modern armies are impotent.

But this does not seem to apply to guerrilla forces. Furthermore, unless legal codes are sanctioned, armies tend to militarize civilian populations. But is this true in developing Third World regions?

The Latin American complex offers an excellent laboratory for showing the extent to which the military determine the game of politics in the Third World. In the past decade, nine countries have experienced one or more military coups (Argentina, Peru, Ecuador, Guatemala, Dominican Republic, Colombia, Honduras, and Brazil); three more have seen the military continue preeminence from the previous decade (Nicaragua, Paraguay, and Haiti); in one country a guerrilla army has been constituted into the regular army (Cuba); and one country has transformed its essentially pacifist civilian-oriented militia into paramilitary, counter-insurgency units (Costa Rica). There are also nations in which the military perform back-stage pivotal roles—an omnipresence rather than a simple presence (Venezuela, El Salvador, and Colombia). Mexico, Chile, and Uruguay are the only nations in which the military has minimal effect on policy. They are also probably the only ones in which guerrilla insurgency units are non-existent. The score card for Africa and Asia is scarcely less impressive.

The rise of guerrilla activities throughout the Third World has been spectacular. Yet, it might well be an irony that counter-insurgency units precede in time the formation of insurgency units. This, at any rate, seems to have taken place in the Dominican Republic and in Cambodia. When the legitimate aspirations of the people are frustrated by military action, and when newly formed, foreign-sponsored counter-insurgency units spearhead the ouster of legitimate regimes, then a rise in guerrilla action is likely to follow. The exact causal sequence is important. If it is the case that counter-insurgency precedes the formation of insurgency units, then the self-fulfilling prophecy of United States foreign policy may well turn into self-destructive actions.[1]

It might well be that for ecological, sociological, and political reasons, insurgency forms of revolutionary activity will either be unsuccessful or simply unfeasible. Its patent failure in the big nations of the hemisphere, particularly in Brazil and Argentina, makes it clear that insurgency warfare, as outlined by Mao Tse Tung or Ernesto Guevara, is not necessarily operational in highly urbanized and industrialized sectors. Given

1. On this, see the work by Edwin Lieuwen, *Generals vs. Presidents: Neomilitarism in Latin America.* New York: Frederick Praeger, 1964, esp. pp. 7–9, 126–29, 136–41.

the concentration of Latin America's population and resources (not to mention political power) in the urbanized coastal regions, it is unlikely that the strategy of surrounding the cities with a peasant mass would be successful. On the other hand, it must also be borne in mind that the deployment of regular troops, either of a home-grown or colonial-imported variety, does little to resolve fundamental demands made by revolutionary movements.[2] If it takes between 20,000 and 30,000 troops to maintain a cease-fire agreement in one small Caribbean nation, it becomes evident that it would take at least one hundred times that number to maintain an equilibrium in the face of revolutionary tides and sentiments in Southeast Asia. All of which should provide sober food for thought to those devotees of *Realpolitik* who still believe that those who rely on international, legally sanctioned organizations are dazed romantics.

Several things we do know and several things we do not know about the organization and ideology of the military in the contemporary period. Let us first consider what we know, or at least what we know to be wrong, for this in itself constitutes a kind of necessary prelude and background for discussion.

First, the nuclear stand-off, far from creating any delicate or indelicate balance of terror, only creates the basis of a more sophisticated conventional arms race in the absence of any peace-keeping arrangements.

Second, the rise of a scientific military technology does not in itself lead to the "civilization" of the military in industrially advanced societies, but rather to the militarization of the civilian population.

Third, the central dynamic in present-day war-making concerns the relationship between the fully developed (and over-developed) nation-states to the semi-developed (and under-developed) nation-states.

Fourth, the "rule of Law" which was to replace the "rule of force" is no more a reality with the United Nations than it was with the League of Nations. Indeed, regional and inter-regional military blocs constitute the major legitimate forms for intervention in the affairs of other sovereign states.

Finally, while the potentiality for total destruction is far greater than at any previous time in history, the actual types of destruction now

---

2. For a useful expression of problems in, as well as solutions of, a revolutionary military approach, see Régis Debray, *Strategy for Revolution*. New York and London: Monthly Review Press, 1970.

taking place as a result of military engagements are "minimal" and have not necessitated anywhere near the sort of total mobilization evidenced in World War II.

There are, doubtless, many other factors and items not herein taken account of. But these do help set a framework for coming to terms with our more pressing problem: What do we not know about the military structure of the Third World that makes analysis a hazardous, if not a downright dangerous, undertaking?

First, perhaps the most serious shortcoming in the study of Third World military establishments is the absence of a significant body of empirical information concerning their internal performances or perceptions. Unlike studies of the United States military, such as those by Stouffer[3] and Janowitz,[4] we have no comparable studies of the actual mechanisms of command and consensus, or bureaucracy and ideology, in the Third World military.

Second, what we know tends to be restricted to general studies on the interaction of military rulers with government functions, and some crude data on the size of military budgets, the allocation of these budgets to various branches of the service, and the number of people engaged in military service. But even here our knowledge is for the most part more official than real.[5]

Third, we know very little of the rivalries between military factions or the separate services, at either the organizational or ideological levels. We know, for example, that as a general rule the army will be more liberal in its position than either the air force or the navy; however, we do not really know why this is the case. It might well be that this liberal-conservative dichotomy has nothing to do with Third World characteristics but is simply a function of the land-based nature of both army and civil functions, giving to their policies perhaps a greater

3. Samuel Stouffer, Edward A. Suchman, Leland C. DeVinney, Shirley A. Star, and Robin M. Williams, *The American Soldier: Adjustment During Army Life,* Vol. I; and *Combat and Its Aftermath,* Vol. II. Princeton: Princeton University Press, 1949.

4. Morris Janowitz, *The Professional Soldier: A Social and Political Portrait.* New York: The Free Press, 1960.

5. Several efforts at collecting basic information on a regional level have been recently undertaken. On the Middle East, see Morris Janowitz, *The Military in the Political Development of New Nations.* Chicago: University of Chicago Press, 1964; and on Latin America, Irving Louis Horowitz, "United States Policy and the Latin American Military Establishment," *The Correspondent,* No. 32, Autumn 1964, pp. 45–61.

realism than that present in other branches of the armed forces who are geared to operate in "unnatural" environments such as air or sea.[6]

Fourth, while studies are now under way to determine the recruitment practices, class, religious and ethnic backgrounds, types of educational systems, and the like, relevant to the Third World military, these have thus far not been linked to political behavior.[7] We can hardly be sure that such sociological information is even relevant to an understanding of schisms within the armed forces that now are evident in nearly every nation of the Western Hemisphere, including our own.

I propose to do two things: first, to discuss the national and international characteristics of military relationships; and, second, to develop a meaningful typology which, in bypassing certain conventional issues such as the relationship between different branches of the armed forces, gets at the core of the issue—the relationship between different types of military systems and political situations.

II

The national independence of nearly every Third World nation—the old nations of Latin America and Asia, as well as the newer nations of Africa—has been ensured through revolution and secured through the armed might and organizational skills of revolutionists. The use of coercion, when it ceases to be a monopoly of the state, heralds the arrival of the revolutionary moment; for it is at that moment when the organized use of terror is neither confined to the ruling class nor accepted by wide masses that a revolutionary situation can be said to exist.[8] The mass character of revolution in the Third World can hardly be ignored. And this requires an appreciation of the mass character of the military apparatus that either sustains or thwarts the revolutionists in their struggles. It is not helpful to conceive of these para-military

6. See the studies by Mario Horacio Orsolini, *La Crisis del Ejército*. Buenos Aires: Ediciones Arayu, 1964; and José Luis de Imaz, *Los que Mandan*. Buenos Aires: Editorial Universitaria de Buenos Aires, 1964.

7. While a number of recent studies have called attention to the socioeconomic aspects of military recruitment, to my knowledge none has thus far linked the service rivalries with differential status or mobility rates. For some first attempts, see John J. Johnson, *The Military and Society in Latin America*. Stanford: Stanford University Press, 1964, pp. 102–33.

8. E. V. Walter, *Terror and Resistance: A Study of Political Violence*. New York: Oxford University Press, 1969, esp. pp. 29–55.

movements simply in terms of insurgency and counter-insurgency as so many recent strategists have done.[9] Nor is the lofty rhetoric of viewing militarism in the Third World as simply the revolutionary phase prior to the assumption to authority of an integrating political party an acceptable alternative. For this formalistic view similarly serves to preserve conventional wisdom at the expense of the mass character of revolution.[10] In point of fact, what most often happens is that the military phase of the revolution becomes the integrating mechanism, whereas the political phase is confined to the disintegrating and residual aspects of the ruling sectors.

Within the Third World itself revolutionary action is not seen as civil warfare between the nationals but as the struggle of the underprivileged and underdeveloped areas against the direct military might or indirect economic interests possessed by the old colonial powers. Even in a "marginal" case such as the Congo, the people do not consider the conflict civil warfare but the final stage of anticolonialism. For this reason "wars of national liberation" frequently take on an "anti-imperialist" content. To term such struggles "insurgent uprisings" minimizes the national scope of such military activities and debases their mass revolutionary content. While there is by no means a direct correlation between national liberation movements and radical revolutionary ideologies, the confusion on this point, fostered by colonial apologists no less than by revolutionary romantics, tends to drive nationalists into radical channels.

For modern mass revolutions to be successful, they must assume a military character. This may take the form of a conventional military apparatus turning "leftist" as in the case of Nasser's Egypt. It may take the form of a peasant-based counter-military force, brought into existence by the continuing adhesion of the existing military establishment to the old social-political order, as in the case of China. It may be a peasant guerrilla army pressed into existence to do battle with a foreign controlled army, as in the case of Algeria. But whatever the precise form, the success of a social revolution, whether dedicated to a particular class or consecrated in the name of the entire people, depends for the most part on the level of military organization. There are, of

9. See, for example, David Galula, *Counter-insurgency Warfare: Theory and Practice*. New York and London: Frederick Praeger, 1964, pp. xiii-xiv.
10. Samuel P. Huntington, *Political Order in Changing Societies*. New Haven and London: Yale University Press, 1968, esp. pp. 315–43.

course, exceptions: for example, in nations such as India and Ceylon there were both non-military and even electoral processes which preceded the revolutionary phase. However, in many cases, especially in a nation such as India, the aftermath of a pacific revolution has been a steady rise in the military budget, to the point where India spends at least as great a percentage of its budget for its armed forces as does nearly every other nation in the Third World.

The revolutionary cadre of the pre-independence period often comprises the military establishment of the post-independent period. In fact, the consolidation of power in some measure is determined precisely by the degree to which the revolutionary faction becomes synonymous with the military apparatus. The prestige and the power of military growth is in direct proportion to the nation's growth. There is no recorded case of a Third World nation that has achieved its independence since 1945 voluntarily or consistently reducing the role of the size of its military apparatus. Any attempt at developing an operational model of disarmament or arms control must take into account the widespread belief of Third World nations that the military is its guarantor of future survival no less than the mark of its present sovereignty. This is underscored by the direct incorporation of the army into the political system.

To gain some appreciation of how radically different the shape of modern warfare has become since the rise of the Third World, we need only examine basic studies of military power made in the pre-World War II period. Even the most far-seeing of them fails to reveal even a faint appreciation of Asia, Africa, and Latin America as centers of military affairs.[11] In less than a quarter-century, the military preeminence of Europe—of Germany, Italy, France, and England—has given way to the preeminence of the United States and the Soviet Union. Just as these two evolving goliaths stood on the periphery of power during the first decades of the century, so now the leading nations of the Third World stand at the threshold of military power in the last decades of this century.

The chief reason that the military potential of the Third World remained unexplored in the pre-World War II period was that the nation-state, which is an essential prerequisite for the existence of a national military complex, hardly existed in Asia and Africa. The very absence of revolutionary fervor for independence signified an absence of indigenous

11. See, for example, Max Werner, *The Military Strength of the Powers*. London: Victor Gollancz, 1939.

military struggles. After the European destruction of original independent tribal forces, whether among Zulus of Africa or the Aztecs of Mexico, there was a virtual cessation of agitation for independence. In other words, where there is a condition of stable colonial or semi-colonial regimes, there one will find a tutelary arrangement rather than a military order. Although the role of the police and local constabularies may increase in proportion to the growth of industrialization and urbanization, there is no independent military establishment within a colonial context. This is one reason why police are rarely drawn upon as a source of revolutionary military support. The rise of a military establishment in the Third World is uniformly linked to the struggle for national sovereignty, and the strength of that military network is underwritten by the addition of revolutionary mass movements. As mentioned already, there have been minor exceptions, India for instance. On the other hand, military expenditures may be quickly enlarged in countries like Burma, the Philippines, and Indonesia, where the post-revolutionary period exhibits a wide degree of cleavage and conflict among the liberated social forces. But whatever the unique conditions which lead either to an underestimation or overestimation of military needs, the existence of this national military sector is related to a post-colonial rather than a pre-colonial condition. There have been minor exceptions: the pacifism of India's rulers prevented a big military build-up for several years after independence (a situation which has now been "corrected"), while the military expenditures of countries like the Philippines and Indonesia are more swollen than the threats to their sovereignty, real or imaginary, warrant.

In considerable measure, the pivotal role of the military in the Third World stems from the importance of military engagements in the transitional "war" period. Perhaps the case of China is the "classic" model of the formation of an army from below. But not even Maoist communists claim that guerrilla and peasant insurrections are caused by anything other than the breakdown of conventional rules and habits in the old regime. The leading general of the Chinese Revolution, Chu-Teh, noted that

> in a semi-feudal and semi-colonial country like China, the simplest democratic rights for people had to be fought for with guns in hand. In Shanghai, Handow, Canton, and other cities, workers and intellectuals were being beheaded in the streets for demanding free speech, press, assembly, and the right of organization, and for demanding the right to defend themselves in court when arrested.

The eight-hour day, increased wages, and the abolition of child labor were all branded as Communist banditry, as was the idea of free trade unions.

Because of this, Chu concludes, it was evident that "the Chinese people could win democratic rights only by the armed defeat of the counter-revolutionary henchmen of foreign imperialism." [12] Guerrilla action was thus said to be a response to three factors: misery of the masses; the inability to settle conflict in a parliamentary or legal way; and foreign control of the domestic economy and polity. But, above all, such guerrilla action took place when the old colonial powers were intransigent.

These items are as true for Cuba as for China. That is why it would be a profound mistake to describe *all* military action in the Third World as "revolutionary," or correspondingly, all revolutionary processes as military. Indeed, most of Latin America illustrates a different situation. After new nations pass through their initial consolidation stage, the military establishment remains nationalistic, while often becoming politically conservative. National revolution and social revolution are radically different phenomena. That is why the distinction between revolution from above and from below is significant. Revolutions made "from above" tend to have national orientations, while revolutions made "from below" tend to have social orientations. "National" revolutions appeal to present-day values held by the middle-class elements who see revolution as a prelude to immediate material gratifications; whereas "social" revolutions appeal to long-range values oftentimes expressed by lower-class interest groups who see the revolution in more abstract and utopian terms. It is paradoxical that those who have the least seem to have more long-range ambitions, whereas those who are closer to economic security tend to have more short-range ambitions. But this paradox is only superficial since it is a cardinal sociological axiom that those who are already upwardly mobile tend to be aggressive in the pursuit of careers and consumer satisfaction, and therefore tend to view revolution in terms of personal expectations rather than national ambitions.

Militarism in the Third World can be studied in terms of key variables which define the role of the military in the political sphere. This may extend from peripheral or arbitrational roles to paramount decision-

12. See Agnes Smedley, *The Great Road: The Life and Times of Chu-Teh.* New York: Monthly Review Press, 1956, p. 254. For a more recent account of China's turn to "military determinism," see Lin Piao, "China's Grand Strategy," *Current,* No. 64, Oct. 1965, pp. 6–9.

making roles, such as control of the government apparatus. We might analyze the military by isolating the elements of a professional and political army. We might then differentiate between these professional or political types.[13] I have chosen to divide the military establishment into component roles that also illustrate the structural characteristics of the armed forces. There is no exclusive rationale for any approach, except that the manner employed here better accounts for the similarities in the Third World military than any other. Not until a full-scale analysis of military budgets, hardware, war-making potential, and the like, is undertaken will it be possible to make a definitive choice of one set of measures over another.

III

The emergence of the Third World, both in the form of newly independent nations and revitalized old nations, has created new elites, the most outstanding of which are the party bureaucracy and the military. Often indeed these post-colonial political leaders are also military heroes of the liberation period. The easy transformation of political leaders into military heroes is common to all three continents of the Third World. It is a characteristic of Jomo Kenyatta in Kenya as it is of Fidel Castro in Cuba. What is really unusual about these men is their ability to survive the shock of further transition, from making a revolution to ruling a nation.

The military elites of the new nations function in radically different ways from conventional European military forces and yet have many structural similarities to them. New nations require new armies. And the sources of these new armies are often the popular classes. Hence these armies were often radical in origin as well as national. The military tended to recruit from formerly dispossessed sections and from elements demanding rapid social mobility. This latter group supplied the intellectual fuel to fire mass resentments. Thus the formation of a new army in such places as Algeria, Cuba, and Indonesia served as a pronouncement in favor of rapid economic development and revolutionary political structures.

13. I am grateful to John Lovell, who raised many of these points in his paper on "A Study of the Involvement of the Military in Political Problems of Achieving Conceptual Clarity," presented at the Special Operations Research Office Conference held in Washington, D.C., between May 26 and May 29, 1965.

Military power exists in its relation to state power. It is geared to defend a well-defined geographic terrain and a certain body of people having a common set of economic, psychological, and linguistic elements within this terrain. The main function of the armed forces at the outset of nation-building is to preserve and make visible national sovereignty. They "defend" and "project" the national entity into the international arena. And once actual sovereignty is obtained, they acquire a critical role with respect to the internal affairs of the state. The military revolutionists thus come to power against colonialists, but maintain power against internal threats, especially by preventing political infighting among the ruling groups.[14]

The relationship between government and the military is no less intimate than the connection between control of power and control of violence at the more general level. But whatever the main role of the armed forces at any given moment, whether toward the maintenance of the state against external enemies or against internal terrorists, the military leadership alone is assigned the right to use physical violence. Such a right does not, however, extend to legal authorization. The ambiguity in civil-military relations often resides in the separation of the use of violence (a legal-social function). Such exercise of violence in the absence of complete legitimation also remains a constant source of tension between the military and the civil apparatus. The military, when functioning properly, quickly acquires a sense of the nation and becomes sensitized toward vested interests and factional enclaves that break down the egalitarian consensus of the revolutionary period. Of course, there are many cases in which the military itself becomes a vested interest and serves to unbalance equitable arrangements that may have been made during the early revolutionary period. Furthermore, when various factions of the military cleave and adopt different ideologies toward national goals, a period of protracted civil strife usually follows. This was certainly a prime factor in both the Congolese and Nigerian civil wars. While there is no automatic rule which ensures the military maintenance of a post-revolutionary equilibrium, the military will assume such a role when no other social factor does so.

One way the military is able to serve national interests with relative equity is related to its methods of recruitment. The military gains membership from disparate groups and classes within the society. By minimiz-

14. See Albert Meister, *East Africa: The Past in Chains, the Future in Pawn.* New York: Walker & Co., 1968, p. 261.

ing the class basis of membership through a heterogenous recruitment policy, the armed forces can function as an important socializing agency.[15] This trans-class role can be performed despite the relatively pronounced class basis of military leadership. In Middle Eastern states, such as Egypt and Iran, where the class formations remain relatively diffuse and weak, the corresponding importance of the army as a national and even a class-welding agency becomes manifest.[16]

Unlike the formation of either the United States or the Soviet Union, the armed forces in the newly emergent nations are not absorbed into the civilian society but instead become partners with the society. It was one of the hallmarks of the first United States administration, that of George Washington, that it made the military subject to political control.[17] Curiously enough, in the Russian Revolution, despite urgings of the permanent revolutionists, the military was placed under the rule of the political elites.[18] In the United States civilian control had democratic consequences and in the Soviet Union autocratic consequences, but in neither case did it make much difference in terms of the functional efficiency of the armed forces. In both the First and Second Worlds the military served as a professional source of political strength and developmental orientations rather than as a ruling directorate. The same cannot be said for most Third World nations, where, as a matter of fact, the political functions are oftentimes militarized from the onset of independence. Due to this early identification with the national cause, the military is transformed from a symbolic badge of sovereignty into a decisive partner in the composition of the state.

The function of the military establishment as the mark of sovereignty is well exemplified by post-liberation India. Given its strong traditional bias against force and violence, India represents a good test case. Under

15. See Joseph La Palombara, *Bureaucracy and Political Development*. Princeton: Princeton University Press, 1963, pp. 31–32.
16. See on this Manfred Halpern, *The Politics of Social Change in the Middle East and North Africa*. Princeton: Princeton University Press, 1963; and George E. Kirk, "The Rise of the Military in Society and Government: Egypt," in *The Military and the Middle East*. Columbus: Ohio State University Press, 1963.
17. See Seymour Martin Lipset, *The First New Nation: The United States in Historical and Comparative Perspective*. New York: Basic Books, 1963, pp. 16–45; and William N. Chambers, *Political Parties in a New Nation*. New York: Oxford University Press, 1963, pp. 21–27.
18. See Klementi Voroshilov, *Fifteen Years of the Red Army (Russia)*. Moscow, 1933. Quoted passages in Max Werner, *The Military Strength of the Powers*. London: Victor Gollancz 1939, p. 36.

the reign of Nehru, the Gandhian approach to pacifism was severely modified in the name of expediency. According to Gandhi, the key to real victory is the doctrine of *Satyagraha*—the force which is born of truth and love, rather than error and hatred. Non-military, non-violent social action was pitted against all enemies.[19] But the actual conduct of foreign policy after the British left compelled a quick and uneven modification of this policy. With reference to the early stages of the Kashmir dispute, Nehru considered it his "misfortune that we even have to keep an army, a navy, and an air force. In the world one is compelled to take these precautions." [20] While the rhetoric remains pacifist, the actual chore of strengthening the military was well under way no more than two years after independence. And, by the end of the 'fifties, Nehru abandoned even the pacifist rhetoric. He noted that "none of us would dare, in the present state of the world, to do away with the instruments of organized violence. We keep armies both to defend ourselves against aggression from without and to meet trouble from within." [21] India responded to the increased military determinism of all worldly situations. It was not so much that Gandhiism was a dead letter in India by Independence Day, as that nationalism proved to be more compelling than ideology in shaping Indian society. The bitter controversy over Pakistani independence in the 'fifties and the equally dangerous rift with China in the 'sixties moved India into a much more conventional statist posture than it was in its origins. But at the same time it became more nearly a national power and lost a good deal of its claims as an international moral authority.

The increase in military spending in India has kept pace with the general militarization of the Third World. From 1960 to 1964 alone, the increase in military allocations was nearly threefold.[22] The percentage of India's budget went from 6 per cent of the gross national product in 1961 to 17 per cent in 1964. The national military cadet corps, the breeding

19. See Joan V. Bondurant, *Conquest of Violence*. Princeton: Princeton University Press, 1958; W. H. Morris-Jones, "Mahatma Gandhi: Political Philosopher?" *Political Studies*, Vol. III, No. 1, Feb. 1960; Irving Louis Horowitz, "Tolstoi and Gandhi: The Pacifist Dream," in *The Idea of War and Peace in Contemporary Philosophy*. New York: Paine-Whitman Publishers, 1957; and Arne Naess, *Gandhi and the Nuclear Age*. Totowa, N.J.: The Bedminster Press, 1965.
20. Jawaharlal Nehru, *Speeches: 1949–1953*. New Delhi: Publications Division, Ministry of Information and Broadcasting. Government of India, 1957, p. 357.
21. *Ibid.*, p. 211.
22. See Ministry of Information and Broadcasting, *India, 1962*. New Delhi: Publications Division, Government of India, 1962, pp. 72–74; and *India, 1963*, pp. 21, 64, 180.

ground of the future officers, went from 150,000 in 1958 to 300,000 in 1964. Slowly also, the military mix of army, navy, and air force grew steadily at the expense of the other branches. And with the increasing military hardware sent in by both the Soviet Union and the United States, India was transformed from a leader to a buffer zone of the Third World.

The military build-up is continuing. The rise of communist opposition to Congress Party rule in Kerala and elsewhere and the pressures from China and Pakistan only partly explain this increase. For, as in other Third World nations, national greatness is more and more linked with military grandeur. And no country of the Third World, even one conscientiously dedicated to pacifism, has been able to withstand this formula of a civil-military partnership—what can be controlled is the degree of military involvement (as in some parts of Africa) but no longer the fact of involvement.

IV

The capacity of the military in Third World nations to help establish a political system depends upon three main factors: its control of the instruments of violence; its ethos of public service and national identity instead of private interest and class identity; and its representation as an articulate and expert group.[23] In the Third World the military alone combines these factors, which may be generalized as technical skills combined with an ethic of national purpose.

These factors also help to explain why the elite of the armed forces no longer confine their allegiance to traditional upper classes. The rise of the middle class, as well as the rise of the working class, in many portions of the Third World has forced the military to become more nearly representative of the nation as a whole than its own vested interests or natural proclivities might have indicated. As long as the military maintained such alignments with the aristocracy and with religious groups, it was difficult, if not impossible, for the nation to become developmentally oriented or for the military to perform in terms of public service or its technical or professional skills. This shift has been most pronounced in those nations where the military underwent a transformation from within; especially in Asia and Sub-Sahara Africa where the inherited military establishment

23. See Morris Janowitz, *The Military in the Political Development of New Nations.* Chicago: University of Chicago Press, 1964, pp. 27–28.

had to break with this oligarchical notion of service to the upper classes in order to function as a redeemer of the popular will.

The military becomes concerned with internal security when a national revolution becomes a class revolution. Since most Third World societies are highly stratified, according to class, race, caste, or area, the possibilities, even inevitabilities, of class conflict persist. Thus the military establishment, whether it so desires or not, is compelled to align itself with either traditional social classes or modern social classes. In a concrete sense, the role of the military in maintaining internal security is impaired by the very existence of class forces, for it is subject to pressure from both sides. It is possible to overthrow military establishments as part of a general upheaval against traditional class. At the same time, if the military is identified too closely with the popular classes, it tends to bring about an oligarchically inspired counter-revolution.

The role of the military is impaled upon the horns of a structural dilemma. In the very act of serving as an instrument of national redemption, it finds itself aligned against traditional class forces that have a great deal to lose in terms of wealth as well as prestige. At the same time, the use of the military as an instrument of suppression for riot control and secret police action has the effect of aligning the military against the popular class forces it is ostensibly serving. This problem is more acute in the Middle East and in Latin America than in most parts of Asia or Africa, where the military has not been replaced in the course of revolutionary action so much as found its roles transformed in the course of the developmental process.[24] Interestingly, these former areas also contain nations where there is high tension and low stability.

There is an obvious tension between the function of military systems in the Third World that moves toward socialism and populism and those that move toward more traditionalist economics and politics. The military clearly stands closer to the class and sector which actually wields power; and only when such classes and sectors are in a condition of impotence or cleavage does the military perform overt leadership tasks. One might say that within the "iron law of militarism" the choice is to be made between the military defense of national interests and the military definition of what these interests are. This is a more realistic goal than

24. See Dankwart A. Rustow, "The Military in Middle Eastern Society and Politics," in *The Military in the Middle East,* edited by S. N. Fisher. Columbus: Ohio State University Press, 1963, p. 11; and more generally, P. J. Vatikiotis, *The Egyptian Army in Politics.* Bloomington: University of Indiana Press, 1961.

non-military solutions in nations and cultures in which politics has been and continues to be militarized. The case of the Arab nations in this connection is most significant. The analysis by Avneri of militarism in North Africa deserves serious attention. "Within the Arab context, the emergence of military regimes has not signified a breakthrough to modernization, but a reversion to the traditional, legitimate form of government accepted and revered by the Arabs and by Islam for the past fifteen hundred years." Avneri concludes the point by noting that "within the political culture of Arab society, military power equals political legitimacy, and for this reason military leaders have had very little difficulty establishing their authority in Arab countries." [25]

The political leadership in the Third World tends to be drawn from the military corps. Therefore, in the "Egyptian socialism" of Nasser, or in the "guided democracy" of Sukarno, there was extreme emphasis on providing adequate policy-making roles for the armed forces. The tendency of political leadership in the Third World to stimulate military models, and at times to adopt even the dress, manners, and bureaucratic norms of the military establishment, underscores the close kinship and partnership between military and civilian elements.

The military often function as a counterweight to the party apparatus on the one hand and the bureaucratic apparatus on the other. These two major forces of domination in the Third World are often kept harnessed and even bridled by the military acting in this adjudicatory role. The military acts to ensure a partnership between party and bureaucracy, so that if the conversion from colonial rule to independence is not particularly constitutional, it is at least orderly. Involvement by the military in the political system and in the bureaucratic system can take place by promoting developmental programs or by consolidating or stabilizing popular revolution. But, whatever mechanism, the fact of its involvement in the maintenance of the social structure is clear.

The strength of the military often reflects the absence of strength on the part of the middle or working class. This is particularly true in the new nations. When the popular classes are too ineffectual in changing obviously bankrupt social relations, the elite of the armed forces perceive themselves as capable of filling a social vacuum. The army is thus able to guarantee an equilibrium between classes through military might. The

25. Shlomo Avneri, "The Palestinians and Israel," *Commentary*, Vol. 49, No. 6, June 1970, pp. 31–44; see also Amos Perlmutter, "Egypt and the Myth of the New Middle Class," *Comparative Studies in Society and History*, Vol. 19, No. 1, Oct. 1967, pp. 46–65.

army, in virtue of its national liberation character, may not have the capacity to crush opposition, but it may prevent any successful attempts at overthrowing the new regime. It is remarkable how few counter-revolutionary or restorationist regimes have been successful in the Third World despite the large number of coups d'état. For although there has been an enormous amount of turmoil and transformation within the single party states during the post-colonial era, these have not led either to the restoration of colonial rule anywhere in the Third World, or to a particularly more advanced stage of social revolution once the nationalist phase has been achieved. On the other hand, in such multi-party states as the Congo, where there are no fewer than two hundred political parties and three different military directorates, there is far more instability than in the one-party political-military condition. Many leaders who were in charge when independence was attained in Africa remained heads of state or of the party a decade and even two decades later. Among these are Nyerere, Touré, Kenyatta, Senghor, and Banda. Even when this original leadership collapsed, as in Algeria and Ghana, the new leaders were chosen from an alternative faction of the original revolutionary group—usually from the military faction of that early leadership. This indicates how ably strains in the social system are managed by the present power hierarchy.

The military in the new nations can oftentimes exercise international power. The Egyptian and the Algerian military see themselves very much concerned with problems of the unification of all North Africa, including the training of Palestinian Arabs for the reconquest of Israel. The same kind of regional pattern is to be found with Indonesia in Southeast Asia, where it too hopes to function as a homogenizing force in the whole of the area, especially in the Malaysian peninsula. But thus far, the international role is more regional than truly world-wide. The internal role predominates.

Nevertheless, the search for regional, if not international, roles cannot simply be dismissed as artificial. The annual regional meetings within the Third World provide a show of force no less than a show of political principles. The collective military might of the Third World determines its strength in relation to the First and Second Worlds. At the same time the individual might of each nation within the Third World determines its position in relation to the other nations within that world. Even nations who are debtors before the International Monetary Fund may act as creditor nations within regional blocs. Thus, a nation like Egypt

German types of models; in many parts of Latin America there is a combination of French and German as well as United States prototypes. In other words, the actual organizational charts which describe these military organizations are based upon prototypes brought over from the former imperial power.

Even though the military in the Third World may think of itself as distinct and distinctively nationalistic, it still carries on the traditions of the old colonial armies. This is not just a cultural inheritance but a consequence of the complex nature of modern warfare, especially the complicated technology of advanced combat and the problem of training human forces so that they become a significant military asset. Thus there is rising tension between the need for autonomy and the necessity for seeking out models and materials from the advanced blocs. One way Third World nations attempt to overcome this contradiction is by the process of "spin-off," by relying on one major power for technological and military hardware and on another for its military organization charts. Many African nations, such as Ghana, Nigeria, and Sierra Leone, which exhibited total military dependence on the British style at the outset of the independence period, have moved to counteract this by arrangements with advanced countries as disparate as West Germany, France, and Czechoslovakia. At this point a three-person rather than a two-person game model comes into its own. The First and Second Worlds increasingly must respond to Third World pressures as opposed to its being simply the other way around. For example, Great Britain must provide arms to Nigeria in order to forestall the Soviet Union in the area. France must refuse to deliver aircraft to Israel in order to maintain Arab support and Arab oil supplies. However, as in the three-person game model itself, the outcomes can often be frighteningly unpredictable and, as in the case of the Nigerian civil war or in the Indian-Pakistan war, gruesome.

Another reason for the diversification of military programing derives from local factors. Thus the strength of Ethiopia compels Somalia to accept Russian military missions. Pressure from China leads India to diversify its forces by using both Soviet and United States tactical and strategic weapons. A limiting problem is that the debtor nation faces the same problems in military terms that it does in economic terms. The credit line is not irrevocable. This serves to place an economic impediment and limit to the problem of political management in the Third World. Military assistance becomes a focal point in maintaining exclusive relations with the former imperial power. For example, the fact that France remains the exclusive distributor of military hardware to most of its former African colonies can undermine the purpose of independence as much as it is undermined by exclusive trade arrangements.[27]

There is less apparent ambiguity in the military's role on the international level than in its role as an internal agency. Military organizations directly influence social structure by their allocation and distribution of power. The military decides how much violence should be used in any internal situation. Not only is the military reluctant to compete with civilian authority, but positive factors contribute to this situation. First, institutions subject to comparison, such as an army, are tested against other armies. The army can never be wholly judged in terms of maintaining internal security. The military thrust cannot completely avoid international considerations. Second, because of the long-range aspect of foreign affairs, armed forces are immune to pragmatic tests of economic efficiency. They are not subject to the pressures of private enterprise or to the rules of business and investment. They can function as a planning agency even within a "free-enterprise" social order. Third, an armed force generally has a style of its own. It is not subject to or limited by ordinary standards of behavior or legal canons.[28]

These distinctive features also have negative by-products. The role of the army as an international agency requires a highly professional group of men, capable of making and rendering decisions on strategic issues, whereas an armed force concerned with internal security requires a much more politicized orientation in which considerations of bureaucratic efficiency or separation may be secondary. Hence, the multiplicity of roles for military establishments in the Third World may involve structural incompatibilities. As Andrzejewski indicates,

> Modern military technique produced two contrary effects. On the one hand, it strengthened the centripetal forces by making subjugation of distance regions easier; but on the other hand, it fostered a disintegration of multi-nation empires, because universal conscription became an unavoidable condition of military strength, and armies

27. For a significant discussion of this point, see William Gutteridge, *Military Institutions and Power in the New States.* New York: Frederick Praeger, 1965, pp. 117–29.
28. Lucien Pye, *Armies in the Process of Political Modernization.* Cambridge, Mass.: M.I.T. Press, 1959, pp. 12–13.

raised in this way were of little value unless permeated by patriotism.[29]

V

When armed forces participate in nation-building, they are involved in a gamut of political decision-making that in point of fact carries them far into alien terrain. Perhaps the most important decision involved is whether the military itself should be directed toward the suppression of internal cleavage or the maintenance of a force potential able to cope with international struggles. This is a critical phase of the military participation in Third World nation-building, since it defines its relationship to the political regime and, even more profoundly, to the masses of people. Obviously, police functions differ from military functions: they require different kinds and amounts of manpower as well as different kinds of technology. Although most military regimes would prefer external to internal enemies, it is becoming evident with increasing frequency that internal repression rather than foreign aggression has the highest priority.

The capacity of the armed forces to act as a nation-building instrument is inherent in its structure. It is often the most "modernized" and most highly refined organization in Third World nations. This does not simply mean that it is technologically proficient. The armed forces offer the individual a conspicuous channel for advancement based on achievement and merit rather than background or ascribed status.

The army has had a historical role as a nation-building device, particularly in Japan under the Shogunate and in Germany under the Kaisers. They both provide significant cases of how a military modernizes a society in the midst of the predominance of feudal sectors. Of course, in both Japan and Germany one must not underestimate the unique capacity of paternal capitalism to secure for the ruling class an industrial labor force with a minimum of disruption of fuedal life styles. Since most Third World nations are moving from some kind of latifundism to some kind of socialism, the army can act as a surrogate for the bourgeoisie in the classical Western process of development under

29. Stanley Andrzejewski, *Military Organization and Society*. London: Routledge and Kegan Paul, 1954, pp. 83–84.

capitalism.[30] Hence from a historical as well as functional point of view, the army serves in this developmental capacity.

In societies where everyone is tardy, the military is prompt. Where the population is ragged, the soldiers are neatly uniformed. Where indecisiveness reigns supreme, the military can take direct action. This enables the armed forces' leadership to claim a mystique about its role in the developmental process. But this mystique is no mystery. Since, in such nations as Turkey and India where the mystique of civilian supremacy is even more powerful than any military metaphysics, it becomes plain that this mystique can obtain only when the military has something better than other social forces to offer to enhance social cohesion. When it does produce this unifying effect, when the nation is finally solidified, it is just as likely to be anti-military as pro-military; the popular resolution is likely to be made in terms of the relative inefficiency of the military and the civilian, not in terms of their respective rhetoric.

The military establishment can be seen also as an instrument of continuity in a context where violent breaks with the past are unsettling. In nearly all the countries of the Third World, westernization has produced the deterioration and the breakdown of traditional societies. Oftentimes the one institution that was preserved from the old order, and indeed reinvigorated, was the armed forces. This surely must rank as a key reason why the armed forces serve as a socially cohesive element in new nations. They can embody traditional values and modernistic goals at the same time and still contribute to stabilizing the political situation.

The rapidity of the developmental process enhances the desire to establish politics, especially party politics, on elitist rather than populist grounds. Populist parties are seen as handicaps to rapid development and also as crisis-provoking agencies. When in fact there is an absence of a single party apparatus with a unified goal, the military may be the only group capable of maintaining political order or preparing the ground for further economic breakthroughs. The military tends to perform all sorts of omnibus functions, whatever the size or substance of the party apparatus, or whether it is able to assume direct political con-

30. To see how this works out in a nation such as Turkey, see Dankwart A. Rustow, "Turkey's Second Try at Democracy," *Yale Review*, Vol. LII, June 1963, pp. 518–38; and by the same author, "The Military in Middle Eastern Society and Politics," in *The Military in the Middle East, op. cit.*

trol. That is why the military may be quite powerful in multi-party nations and at the same time quite restrained in single-party nations.

This situation often produces a widespread condition of atrophy. The military, powerful enough to cancel democratic norms, is not powerful enough to maintain social order over a long period of time. By temperament and by training, the military is more capable of preventing the exercise of political rule than of exercising such rule itself. Thus the armed forces have the ability to cancel democratic norms but not the political know-how or the mass support to retain power in their own hands.[31] The wear and tear of prolonged governing is likely to reduce the armed forces to the level of just another political group in the eyes of the country. The very sectionalism, or schismatic quality, fostered by military directorates would destroy the prestige which gives to the army its exceptional role in the Third World. Even where military men do rule, as in Egypt and Algeria, a process of "civilianization" has set in.

The role of the armed forces is not just dependent upon the level of industrial technological achievement. In itself the army promotes such achievements; it demands the newest technological apparatus. To function comparatively—with respect to other armed forces—it must be at the technological level of these other armed forces. Hence the army makes great demands upon the economy. The army demands a highly efficient economy while it insists on remaining the touchstone for determining the character of economic production.

In this way a point is reached at which the army serves not only as an indication of political sovereignty but as a strong influence on the economy. It may use the industrial technology for its own purposes. It may sustain a certain portion of the industrial basis by its contracts and purchases (and this is just as true for the "public sector" as for the "private sector"). It may underwrite certain industries which are weak or non-competitive either in the domestic market or in the world market if it is convinced that such industries are militarily useful. For these reasons, the impact of the armed forces on the economic sector of Third World nations is likely to increase greatly in the forthcoming period. To

31. I have documented this point in several different ways in a series of articles on Argentina. See Irving Louis Horowitz, "Revolt Against Political Mythology: Storm over Argentina," *The Nation*, Vol. 194, No. 13, Mar. 1962; "The Peronista Paralysis," *The Nation*, Vol. 195, No. 10, Oct. 1962; and "Militarism in Argentina," *New Society*, Vol. 1, No. 39, June 1963. This same phenomenon has been described for another area. See Josef Silverstein, "First Steps on the Burmese Way to Socialism," *Asian Survey*, Vol. IV, No. 2, Feb. 1964, pp. 716–22.

some degree, the public-sector character of many Third World economies will make them more subject to military pressures than if industry were to remain in the hands of even a powerful private economic sector. In a public-sector economy, the factory and shop managers have a special relation to other portions of the state, of which the military is the most obvious. And since decision-making is in the hands of the state, the ability of private industry to perform a countervailing power role is severely circumscribed. Thus, we can observe how the military reduces the threat to itself from "alien" class forces not by destroying such classes but by embracing them in an over-all national consensus based on the "needs of the whole people."

There is a need to be specific about the kinds of relationships that obtain between the military and the economy. For the most part, military demand for goods involves a corollary demand for increased imports of advanced technological goods; in contrast, much of its domestic demand is for food, building, clothing, and those items which help supply the everyday needs of a military establishment. But this diversion of surplus resources to the military means that such resources cannot be used to support an advanced industrial labor force. In this way, the military retards development. This retardation may be offset because idle soldiers are used to perform useful economic tasks. However, the fact is that idleness has spread to the military rather than thrift spreading to the industrial sector. The fact that millions of men in Third World nations perform relatively idle tasks in relation to their tanks or airplanes, simply patrol or sit in barracks, or parade before foreign dignitaries is not particularly encouraging from the point of view of economic development. The tragedy remains that the civilian sector appears even less able than the military to spur the processes of development.

VI

There are a number of contradictions in the role played by the military in the Third World. The nation-building potential of the military may in itself be a prod to other groups. But this nation-building potential must be correlated with the costs of maintaining a military establishment. In many Latin American nations, the military represents a constant drain on the national economy—anywhere from 5 to 40 per cent of the total budget. It might well be that the idea of a Latin America demilitarized, denuclearized, and protected by the United Nations directly, far from creating chaos, may actually stimulate social and economic development. But this possibility remains quite remote, since such a solution would also confirm the role of many Third World nations as permanent satellites. This may prove to be an inescapable dilemma. It may be that a permanent contradiction remains between the military as a drain on processes of economic development and as a force in the development process.

The military is geared both to national redemption and to the international expectations of big foreign powers. This is as true of Eastern European nations with respect to the Soviet Union as it is of Latin America with respect to the United States. In other words, there are competing claims of autonomy and heteronomy: the international demands of the leading powers in contradiction to the nation-building role of the military in the secondary powers. This contradiction may in time prove a more serious drag on disarmament negotiations than any of the present schisms between the United States and the Soviet Union.

The actual military strength of new nations is obscured by the fact that the definition of a military budget, while often put in terms of the gross national product, is in fact subject to immense contributions from foreign military missions, defense agreements with the major power blocs, and technical training provided by these external power blocs. The actual militarization process in the Third World is therefore far more extensive than is usually realized. And because military aid tends to be packaged and bracketed along with other kinds of aid, the difficulties in developing statistically significant devices for understanding the actual size of a military establishment are compounded.

The military in the new nations derives its power in many ways, only one of which is its ability to forge a common front against the older traditional powers of Europe and North America. This external show of solidarity is more symbolic than real. The actual sources of military power continue to be directed inward rather than outward. The Nigerian military gains its power from its ability to conduct the civil war and crush the rebellious Biafrans. The Greek military junta gains its power from its ability to suppress the domestic left wing. In fact, it may be a mistake to formulate the issue in causal terms of derivation of power. It is more likely that the military seeks to maintain and strengthen its power over other groups. One must be careful not to underestimate the role of the military as a support of the modern industrial sector. If the problem in

Egypt is the connection of the military elite with a traditional landed aristocracy, the problem in Pakistan is the relationship of the same military elite with industrial wealth. In some sense the military of the Third World, compelled as they are to derive their power from within and yet serve masters from without, are able to support the national anti-colonial phase of revolution but are rarely able to go beyond that phase into a more extensive assault on the class system or the imperial system as such. This may simply be another way of saying that the Third World is not a unified solid phalanx. But this contradiction between national independence and international dependence only accentuates rifts between the military and other sectors of society.

Many of these military establishments, particularly in Africa or Asia, function in terms of the new classes in emerging nations, while others, in Latin America, function in terms of the needs of traditional classes. Thus, in describing the Third World military, one is describing a military forged both in support of traditional class interests and in support of contemporary developmental classes. This has often produced great confusion in big-power foreign aid programs, for there has been a tendency to treat the military as either reactionary or revolutionary without evaluating the historical context of area development.

Ultimately the problem is whether the military sector of the Third World—any more than military establishments elsewhere—can function as a modernizing democratic force. The organizational and structural characteristics of the military are fairly universal: bureaucratic standards, chain of command, authoritarian traditions, sharp distinctions between enlisted men and officer corps, and so forth. It is questionable whether such an apparatus, if geared to a system of superordinate and subordinate units and particularly if unchecked by other sectional interests, can ever function in terms of democratic values or developmental needs—or can ever do so for any extended period of time. Indeed when sectional interests are reflected in the military, especially its elite, it can accentuate such cleavages by providing both sides with a potential war-making machine. This was just as true in the United States Civil War as it was true in the Nigerian Civil War. Even the most democratically organized military institution with obvious popular support, such as the Algerian army or the Cuban army, has great difficulty in maintaining both a democratic structure and a developmental orientation. The sensitivity of military institutions to political and class cleavages makes them as much part of the problem as the solution. In other words, the military are the mark of sovereignty when in fact there is a political or bureaucratic consensus, but it may also become a mark of sectional and regional cleavage when there is an absence of consensus. This is another way of saying that the military functions best when class interests are either too weak to oppose them or too strong to care about subjugating them.

To turn the matter around, can there be real development in the Third World without a military establishment committed to development? A trade-off of democratic values takes place not simply at the level of economic production but also at the level of military dominion. While the general trend is in the direction of less development and less democracy, the decision to increase the amount of militarism does not in itself guarantee successful development. This is an extremely complicated issue, one that we shall be going into in greater detail. However, it is evident that there is a definite correlation between high militarization and high development, but so too there is a real correlation between high militarization and low development. There is always the question of whether non-military means might have proven more efficacious in the development process, but this is purely speculative, particularly in early stages of growth.

The military of the Third World presents us with a set of contradictions which have not yet been resolved in theory. What we are entitled to say is that the Third World is contributing its share to the rise of military determinism in the conduct of social affairs. Further, it has been proven throughout the Third World that as long as there is a nuclear stand-off between the First World and Second World, conventional arms can serve quite readily to continue to define each and every crisis in terms of military might. Thus, the militarization of the Third World may be as large a threat to world peace as the nuclear stockpiles of the advanced industrial powers are.

VII

The process of comparative development includes a wide and real disparity between democracy and development. There exists a relatively high congruence between coercion and even terrorism on the one side and development on the other, and a far lower congruence between consensus and development. In part, our problem is that middle-class spokesmen of the Western world have often tended to identify a model of consensus with a model of democracy, and both have become systematically linked to what has taken place in North America and Western Europe in the last 150–200 years: a model of congruence in which political democracy and economic growth move toward the future in unison. The very phrase "political economy of growth" gives substance to this "bourgeois" model of development. When faced with the necessity of playing a role in the Third World and performing certain activities economically, politically, and socially in terms of the inherited model, the Third World finds that the rhetoric can be no longer sustained in performance. What one is left with, and why it has been difficult to confront so much theorizing on development, is a democratic model at the rhetorical level which is different from the capitalist model at the functional level. Further, there is a strong propensity, once this ambiguous model is accepted, to avoid coming to grips with the role of strong coercion in achieving rapid development.

If we examine the available data, and here I will restrict myself to the non-socialist sector—in part, because there is a problem of data reliability and, also, because socialist systems have their own peculiar dynamic in relation to development and democracy that requires a different set of parameters to explain relationships. Further, since there is already established a bias which equates socialist systems to extreme, political coercion, it is instructive to see how capitalist systems stand up to such coercive strains. Developmentalists are already prone to employ a Stalinist model as the basic type of socialist option. Thus there is no problem in conceptualizing the relationship between coercion and development as a natural one when it comes to the socialist sector. However, when we turn systems around and look at that Western or capitalist sector of the developmental orbit, then the absence of the same kind of coercive model creates great problems conceptualizing Third World tendencies.

When the word "democracy" is herein referred to it will be defined in terms of multi-party operations under civilian regimes. Those two variables are key. There is no point in cluttering matters up with rhetorical theorizing about nice people who do good deeds. Simply put, "democracy" refers to multi-party control of politics on one hand and civilian bureaucratic administrative control on the other. This definition is bareboned and obviously subject to refinement. However, when talking about a military leadership or a military regime we can also simplify things. Military government ranges from outright rule of the armed forces without any civilian participation to co-participation by civilians under military domination and control. Military regimes operate better within a single party structure rather than a multi-party structure; that is, if they require a formal political apparatus as such.

The data herein examined is drawn from reports issued by the Organization for Economic Cooperation and Development.[32] It concerns growth rates of the total and per capita GNP output between 1960 and 1967 on average per annum; and per capita GNP in 1968 for selected developing countries. The information, although provided randomly, does break down into three large clusters: (1) those single party countries under military rule that have high developmental outputs and a high GNP rate over the decade; (2) those countries that are democratic (or relatively democratic) and have low GNP levels; (3) those countries (approximately twenty) that do not reveal any pattern in terms of problems of conflict and consensus in development. It is not that the latter violate model construction as much as they remain undecided about economic or political techniques for generating socioeconomic change.

In the high developmental, high militarization cluster, there are the following nations: Israel, Libya, Spain, Greece, Panama, Nicaragua, Iraq, Iran, Taiwan, the Ivory Coast, Jordan, Bolivia, Thailand, and South Korea. Even a surface inspection indicates that this is hardly a line-up of democratic states. Let us directly examine the GNP figures, so that some sense of the extent of the aforementioned correlation can be gauged. On an annual per cent increase over the decade the percentile figures are as follows: Israel, 7.6; Libya, 19.2 (there are some special circumstances related to oil deposits in Libya but, nonetheless, the figure is impressive); Spain, 5.9 (an interesting example since it is a long-militarized European mainland country); Greece, 7.5 (with no slow-up in sight under its present military regime); Nicaragua, 7.5 (one of the most "backward" countries in Latin America from a "democratic" point of view); Iraq, 6.9; Iran, 7.9; Taiwan, 10.0 (a growth figure which even the Soviets have recently marveled at); Ivory Coast, 7.5 (by all odds, one of the most conservative regimes in Africa and boasting the highest growth rate on the continent in the sub-Sahara region); Jordan, 8.8; Bolivia, 4.9 (a long way from the old socialist days of high foreign subvention); Thailand, 7.1; South Korea, 7.6. This is a most interesting line-up. One would have to say that those with democratic proclivities and propensities must face the fact that development correlates well with authoritarianism. Whether

32. Edwin M. Martin, "Development Aid: Successes and Failures," in *OECD Observer*, No. 43, Dec. 1969, pp. 5–12.

this is because authoritarianism quickens production, limits consumption, or frustrates redistribution is not at issue. The potential for growth under militarism remains an ineluctable fact.

Let us turn to the other end of the spectrum. These are low GNP units: Venezuela, Argentina, Uruguay, Honduras, Ghana, Guatemala, Brazil, the Dominican Republic, Senegal, Ecuador, Tunisia, Paraguay, Morocco, Ceylon, Kenya, Nigeria, Sudan, Uganda, India, Tanzania. Within a Third World context and without gilding the lily, and admitting that there are exceptions in this list like Paraguay, this second cluster represents a far less militarized group of nations than the first list presented. It is instructive to list their GNP per capita annual per cent increase: Venezuela, 1.0; Argentina, 1.2; Uruguay (which is one of the most democratic and liberal countries in South America) −1.0; Honduras, 1.8; Colombia, 1.2; Ghana, which exhibits no percentile change over time in the whole decade; Guatemala, 1.9; Brazil, 1.2 (increasing however to 9.2 under military rule from 1964 to 1971); Dominican Republic, −7; Senegal, 1.2; Ecuador, 1.1; Tunisia, 1.5; Paraguay, 1.0; Morocco, 0.3; the Philippines, 1.0; Ceylon, 1.3; Kenya, 0.3; Nigeria, 1.6; Sudan, 1.2; Uganda, 1.2; India, 1.5; Tanzania, 1.2. The data largely show that the low rate of development corresponds to the non-military character of political mobilization in this second group of nations. Low militarization and low development are only slightly less isomorphic than high militarization and high development.

There is a most important middle group of nations. They do not partake of the nations which reveal extensive polarities in GNP. Further, they exhibit different kinds of transitory patterns of political systems. Chile, for example, has 2.4; Jamaica, 2.1; Mexico, 2.8; Gabon, 3.2; Costa Rica, 2.4; Peru, 3.2; Turkey, 2.7; Malaysia, 2.5; Salvador, 2.7; Egypt, 2.1; Pakistan, 3.1; Ethiopia, 2.7. Many of those nations have relatively stable GNP figures over time and do not easily fit the description of being depressed or accelerated in GNP rates. They are also the most experimental politically—at least during the 1960's. Certainly, experimentation (both by design and accident) characterize countries like Pakistan, Egypt, Costa Rica, and Chile. It is not entirely clear what this middle cluster of nations represents, or whether these trends are politically significant. Yet, they do represent a separate tertiary group and should be seen apart from the other two clusters of nations.

The critical level of GNP seems to be where levels of growth are under 2 per cent, and where there is high population growth rate which more or less offsets the GNP. Under such circumstances, it is extremely difficult to achieve basic social services for a population or maintain social equilibrium. For example, in India, if there is a 1.5 level of growth of GNP and a 2.4 level of population growth per annum, there will be an actual decline in real growth rates. This is how economists usually deal with the measurement of development. It may be faulty reasoning to accept ex cathedra this economic variable as exclusive; yet this measure is so widely used that the GNP provides a good starting point in our evaluation.

The fits at the lower end of the model are not as good as at the upper end. Statistically, it is necessary to point out that militarized societies like Argentina and Brazil are progessing very well economically. However, Latin Americans have a kind of "benign" militarism, a genteel quality that comes with the normalization of political illegitimacy. Thus, Latin American military regimes, in contrast to their African and Asian counterparts, have many exceptional features that account for why the fit of the model is better at the upper end of the GNP than at the lower end.

Many nations clustering in the middle seem to be the carriers of experimental political forms like single party socialism, communal living, and socialized medicine. These same nations also reveal an impressive movement toward some kind of democratic socialism that somehow cannot be classified politically. In other words, the experimental forms seemed to be clustered in that middle grouping, whereas the nonexperimental nations tend to be polarized, just as the GNP itself is polarized.

The political structure of coercion seems to be a more decisive factor in explaining the gross national product than any factor of production in any Third World system per se. The amount of explained variance that the military factor yields vis-à-vis the economic factor is much higher than the classical literature allows for. If we had comparable data for the socialist countries, and if we were to do an analysis of the Soviet Union over time, then we would see that there is a functional correlation between the coercive mechanisms that a state can bring to bear on its citizenry and the ability to produce high economic development, however development be defined, ignoring the special problems involved in definitions based upon the GNP. For example, one problem in GNP measurements is the absence of an agreed-upon cost-accounting mechanism whereby education is evaluated by input (costs) rather than output (benefits); whereas in goods and commodities there is a profit margin built into the GNP figure. But such variations are true across the board;

therefore special problems involved in using the GNP formula are canceled out in the larger picture. But the main point is that the element of coercion is itself directly linked to the character of military domination, while the specific form of the economy is less important than the relationship between military coercion and economic development.

Those critics in the West who celebrate progress as if it were only a matter of GNP cannot then turn around and inquire about the "quality of life" elsewhere.[33] Developmentalists cannot demand of foreign societies what they are unwilling to expect from their own society. Too many theorists of modernization ask questions about the quality of life of countries that themselves ask questions about the quantity of life. The military are the one sector in most parts of the Third World that is not absorbed in pursuit of consumer benefits. It is not a *modernizing* sector, but rather a *developmental* sector. Insofar as the military are autonomous, their concern is nation-building: highway construction, national communication networks, and so forth. They create goals that are not based on the increased production of commodities that characterizes the urban sectors of most parts of the developing regions. The functional value of this model is that the linkage between the military and the economy is unique. The military is that sector which dampens consumerism and modernization and promotes, instead, forms of developmentalism that may move toward heavy industry and even heavy agriculture rather than toward such consumer items as automobiles and television sets. Because the military most often will make its decision on behalf of industrialism rather than modernism, it generates considerable support among nationalists and revolutionists alike. This is a big factor in explaining the continuing strength of the military in the Third World.

The data clear up a number of points. It helps to explain why many regimes in the Third World seem to have such a murky formula for their own polity. For example, despite the brilliance of Julius Nyerere[34] it is exceedingly difficult to delineate the political economy of Tanzania. One reason for this is that there is a powerful military apparatus in nearly every expanding nation of the Third World. And this military structure, if it does not share in national rule directly, is directly involved in the nation as an adjudicating voice between the political revolutionary element and the bureaucratic cadre.

33. Chester L. Hunt, *Social Aspects of Economic Development*. New York: McGraw-Hill, 1966.
34. Julius K. Nyerere, *Freedom and Socialism* (*Uhuru na Ujamaa*). London and New York: Oxford University Press, 1968.

To appreciate the role of the military in developing nations we must go beyond the kind of economic definitions that have been employed either in Western Europe or in the United States. The murkiness of the Third World at the level of economics is in fact a function of the lack of clearly defined class boundaries and class formations. Social structure does not matter as much as social process. There is stability over time in these regimes. The political regime, the civilian-based political regime, tends to be much less stable than the military regime, and in many of these nations there are coups within the coup, that is, inner coups within the military structure that function to make civilian rule superfluous. But the military character and the military definition are not thus altered. For this reason, the relationship between military determinism and high economic growth tends to be stable over time, precisely to the degree that civilian mechanisms are found wanting.

Philips Cutright came to this conclusion through an entirely circuitous and different route. He examined a mass of information on health, welfare, and security and found that the contents of the national political system usually become stabilized at that point in time when basic socioeconomic needs are satisfied.[35] Further, there is no mass mobilization beyond such a point in time. If socioeconomic needs are satisfied within a socialist regime, then the Soviet system is stabilized. If such social needs are satisfied during a capitalist regime, then the capitalist system becomes permanent. If they are satisfied during an outright military dictatorship, then outright military dictatorship becomes normative and durable. In other words, the satisfaction of basic social services and economic wants is a critical factor beyond which masses do not carry on active political struggle. This quantitative support for the Hobbesian thesis on social order in the Leviathan has not been lost on the leadership of Third World nations, who continue to see the military as a stabilizing factor in economic development.

VIII

If this foregoing analysis is correct, and if the military are able to solve these outstanding problems at the level of the GNP, we should be able to predict continued stability of these military-dominated governments.

35. Phillips Cutright and James A. Wiley, "Modernization and Political Representation: 1927–1966," in *Studies in Comparative International Development*, Vol. V, No. 2, 1969–70.

Since basic social services will be provided for under this kind of military rule, political struggles will cease to assume a revolutionary character in much of the Third World. In point of fact, the character of socialist politics does not determine the strength of political behavior, instead it works the other way around. The critical point in the Soviet regime came during Stalinist consolidation. During the 1930's the Soviet regime achieved internal stability. The contours of socialism in Russia were thus fixed, some might say atrophied, at this specific historical juncture. True, certain adjustments have had to be made, certain safety valves had to be opened to prevent friction or crisis. The Soviet Union exhibited a move from totalitarianism to authoritarianism. However, basically the political organization is set and defined. There are no opposition movements in the Soviet Union, since there are no mass movements at the level of social discontent.

Similarly, in the United States, the point of resolution was when the political democracy became operational. Therefore, it continues to be relatively operational two hundred years later, even though great pressures have been brought to bear on the federalist system in recent times. Many Third World areas are stabilized at that point when military intervention occurs. When the initial revolutionary leadership vanishes (or is displaced) and when the bureaucracy and the polity are both contained and yet oriented toward common tasks, the military then becomes powerful. At the same moment economic growth charts start rocketing upward. Therefore it is no accident when fervor for political experimentation declines. What we are confronted with is not simply transitional social forms but permanent social forms.

Most general theories of development postulate transitional conditions in the Third World since they are bound to fail to coincide with preconceived models. We are told in effect that military regimes in the Third World are a necessary transition of "political economy." [36] Socialist doctrines of development often employ the same teleological model of politics for explaining away uncomfortable situations. Marxists declare that everything is in transition until socialism is achieved. Everything else is either an aberration or a deviation. The difficulty with teleological explanations is that they work from the future back to the present, instead of taking seriously the present social structures and political systems which exist in the Third World.

36. Warren F. Ilchman and Norman Thomas Uphoff, *The Political Economy of Change.* Berkeley and Los Angeles: University of California Press, 1969.

From an empirical perspective, social science determines what is meant by stability over time in terms of survival rates. Therefore, on the basis of this kind of measurement, the kind of network which exists in the Third World is, in point of fact, stable. What we are dealing with in many Third World clusterings are not simply permutations, or the grafting on of parts of other social systems. Third World systems are not simply transitional or derivational. They have worked out a modality of their own. In the Third World today, particularly in those nations which exhibit a pattern of high economic growth while under military rule, there seems to be acceptance of a Leninist theory of the state while at the same time a Marxist theory of economics is rejected. That is to say, these nations accept the need for political coercion as a central feature of their existence, but they deny socialist principles of economic organization.

The military state model is invariably a one-party model. Interparty struggle and interparty discipline vanishes. The party apparatus becomes bureaucratic and even its political control becomes hazy. The Leninist model is decisively emulated. The party serves the nation, but with a new dimension: the party also serves the military. The traditional Leninist model has the military politicized so that it serves the ruling party. In the Third World variation, the political elites become militarized so that they serve the ruling junta.

In economic terms this means acceptance of some kind of market economy based on a neo-capitalist model. This process might be called one step forward and two steps backward. Any series of national advertisements will point out the low-wage, obedient-worker syndrome of many new nations. The model being sold to overseas investors by Third World rulers is in large measure (whatever the rhetoric of socialism may dictate) a model built on production for the market, private consumption, and private profit and on a network that in some sense encourages the development of differential class patterns within Third World nations. But to gain such capitalist ends, what seemingly is rejected is the political participatory and congressional model common in Northern and Western Europe and the United States. There is no reason why this sort of system is transitional. On the contrary, given the conditions and background of underdevelopment, the kind of revolution made, the historical time of these revolutions, and the rivalry between contending power blocs, this neo-Leninist polity, linked as it is to a neo-capitalist economy, is a highly efficacious, functional, and exacting model representative of the way most societies in the Third World have evolved in terms of political economy.

It might well be that with a greater amount of accurate data, this theory of the militarization of modernization will have to be modified or even be abandoned. However, the prima facie evidence would seem to indicate otherwise. More countries in the Third World have taken a more sharply military turn than anyone had a right to predict on the basis of pre-revolutionary ideology or post-revolutionary democratic fervor. Therefore, the overwhelming trend toward militarism (either of a left-wing or right-wing variety) must itself be considered a primary starting point in looking at the Third World as it is, rather than what it should become.

This does not mean we are either celebrating or criticizing the good society, or blaming Third World nations for falling short of their own ideals. Few of us are entirely happy with any available system of society. It is, however, not something that one would simply use as a proof that the system is unworkable. Indeed, if anything is revealed by the foregoing analysis, it is that the Third World has evolved a highly stable social system, a model of development without tears that forcefully draws our attention to the possibility that the Third World, far from disappearing, far from being transitional, far from being buffeted about, is becoming stronger, more resilient, and more adaptive over time. The widespread formula of military adjudication of political and bureaucratic strains within the emerging society is an efficacious model for creating the kind of mobilization out of "backward" populations that at least makes possible real economic development. It might well be that the strains in this military stage of development become too great, and the resolution itself too costly, to sustain real socioeconomic stability. However, at that point in the future, the Hobbesian laws of struggle against an unworkable state will once more appear and we shall know the realities of the situation by the renewed cries of revolution: this time against internal militarists rather than external colonialists.

13

Personality and Social Structure in Comparative International Development

The tension between human volition and social necessity is central to developmental analysis. In comparative international research, the critical task is identifying equivalent phenomena, or at least analyzing the relationships between them as if things and events were consistent across national boundaries.[1] Yet, although the character of the problem and the importance of finding solutions to it are widely recognized, there have been surprisingly few systematic attempts to deal with it in comparative studies on development. It might nonetheless be useful to catalogue briefly what these systematic attempts have been until now, and where they have taken us.

Moore's attempt at the typology of comparative studies[2] underlines our present dilemma: the decision to conceptualize the developmental process in terms of one model rather than another is often made on the basis of strategy rather than on the basis of scientific warrant. What is optimal for the researcher or convenient for the scholar may be a far cry from the requirements of the field situation itself. In some sense, perceptions of development in terms of dyads, models, systems and stages take place simultaneously. Even though researchers select from a number of research strategies—which suggest that the developmental goal is already defined and evaluated and that research tasks are basically descriptive—"development" is a value still being defined rather than a goal whose means of attainment are clearly understood. The

1. Adam Przeworski and Henry Teune, "Equivalence in Cross-National Research," *Public Opinion Quarterly,* 30 (Winter 1966–67), pp. 551–68.
2. Wilbert Moore, "Social Change and Comparative Studies," *Order and Change: Essays in Comparative Sociology* (New York: John Wiley, 1967), pp. 21–32.

problem confronting social scientists is still that of determining in general and in specific times and places what developmental goals, values, and processes are.

The problems of comparative international research do not arise from anything unique to developmental studies but from inherent dilemmas of applying the methodological research techniques evolved in investigating other social areas, such as class stratification. Basic problems of social science methodology are not bypassed by emphasizing macroscopic research; the magnitude of a research task is only one factor determining a methodological choice. Nevertheless, there are methodological and systematic formulations that seem particularly significant for solving problems in the field of comparative international development, and we will concentrate on these.

There can be no precise distinction between "attitude data" and "structural data," but as heuristic devices they deserve consideration. Smith and Inkeles have written that

> the term [modernity] may refer to two quite different objects. As used to describe a *society,* "modern" generally refers to such structural factors as a national state characterized by a complex of traits including intensive mechanization, high rates of social mobility, and the like. When applied to individuals, "modern" refers to a set of attitudes, values and ways of feeling and acting, *presumably of the sort either generated by or required for* effective participation in a modern society.[3]

Smith and Inkeles appreciate the distinction between structural and attitudinal data, but choose to link both in the rubric of modernity. The difficulty with their resolution is that measures of modernization, as I shall seek to show, have been much more readily linked to changes in individual development than in the social structure. Specifically, the following will be emphasized:

(1) The different attitudinal patterns associated with modernity involve two different but related problems: the problem of consistency and the problem of sequence.

(2) The nature of the relationship between attitudinal data and structural data also involves two different considerations: the problem

3. David Smith and Alex Inkeles, "The OM Scale: A Comparative Socio-Psychological Measure of Individual Modernity," *Sociometry,* 29 (Dec. 1966), pp. 353–77.

of congruence, which basically defines the adequacy and equivalence of attitudinal data and structural data, and the nature of the explanatory relationship. Assuming that we could obtain attitudinal data that cross-culturally would typify the degree of correspondence with the structural data what could we infer about the order of causality?

(3) The qualitative aspects of the disjunction between modernization and industrialization, personal attitudes and social structures involve dual considerations: the problem of decision-making and planning and the problems of national goals in an internationally fixed environment.

THE MEASUREMENT OF ATTITUDES AND VALUES

There is an obvious correlation between individual attributes and the social structure in which they are positioned, and sociology is concerned with just this relationship. The symbolic interactionist school in particular provides insight into the social character of man, while both exchange theorists and psychoanalytic-oriented social scientists add weight to the argument that individual and structural variables are linked by the process of socialization. But beyond these established shibboleths, the two types of data stubbornly resist synthesis. There may be lack of correspondence between individual and structural information because (1) the variables are incorrectly conceptualized; (2) the indicators used are inappropriate for explanatory purposes; (3) there is a measurement or sampling error; or, finally, (4) there is a significant time lag between accumulation of data and application to problems of the future. Since the last two possible errors are easily accounted for, we will concentrate upon the first two possibilities of error.

Problems of Consistency: As the material bases of society change, human values and attitudes alter. But the question is, which attitudes change? In what direction, with what intensity, and at what rate? Will the process of industrialization of societies elicit a concomitant process of cultural homogeneity? Will world-wide processes of urbanization and industrialization homogenize the diverse cultures of the world and produce an "industrial man"? How will the population of diverse societies respond and adapt to demands of industrialization and urbanization?

An answer to these questions requires that we measure changes in the attitudes of peoples undergoing modernization.

Toward this end Inkeles describes modern man according to nine different themes.[4] He characterizes modern man by (1) receptivity to experiences and openness to innovation and change; (2) a disposition to form or hold opinions over a large number of problems and issues that arise not only in his immediate environment but also outside of it; (3) orientation to the present or future, rather than to the past; (4) planning and organizing beliefs as a way of handling life; (5) mastery of the environment in order to advance individual purposes and goals, rather than complete domination by environmental needs; (6) confidence that the world is calculable and that other people and institutions can be relied upon to fulfill or meet obligations and responsibilities; (7) awareness of the dignity of others and a disposition to show respect for them; (8) faith in science and technology; (9) belief in distributive justice, in rewards based upon social contribution and not according to either whim or special properties of the person not related to such a contribution.

The traditional man is said to hold opposite views on these nine different themes; the difficulty is that this "over-all modernity" rarely can be found in one person. Furthermore, while the scale of 119 items is said to "cohere psychologically" in the countries tested, this does not guarantee that the "structural mechanisms" are the same (even though the countries may reveal comparable levels of social development).

Smith and Inkeles show that they are aware of the dilemmas by their qualification: "Although we have stressed certain themes that cut across numerous concrete realms of behavior, some students of the problem prefer to emphasize attitudes and behavior relating mainly to certain important institutional realms, such as birth control or religion. Their position is certainly reasonable. . . . We have therefore included questions on such themes as restriction of family size, treatment of older people and obligations to one's parents and relatives, the importance of social change; the role of woman; how to bring up children, attitudes toward religion, attitudes toward the consumption of material and physical goods, social and political problems of the community, the nation and the international realm, education and social mobility; and contact with media of mass communication. For each of these realms, one can define certain themes as more traditional, although at times the process of definition becomes very complex." [5]

4. Alex Inkeles, "The Modernization of Man," in Myron Weiner (ed.), *Modernization: The Dynamics of Growth* (New York: Basic Books, 1966), pp. 138–52.
5. Smith and Inkeles, "The OM Scale," *op. cit.,* pp. 355–56.

If modern man is to be defined by such an attitude scale, it behooves us to question how consistent the attitudes of "modern men" really are along these different attitudinal dimensions. If a man is modern in one aspect (assuming that all the different attitudinal dimensions are indicative of modernity), can he also be expected to be modern in other aspects? Smith and Inkeles never explain why they use the term "modern." All living men, whether by choice or necessity, live in a contemporary world. Modernism and traditionalism may coexist in the same person, whatever the level of development of his society, since they signify approaches to the future, not approaches to real structural parameters.

Kahl has "measured" modernity with a high degree of sophistication and has demonstrated how the multi-dimensionality of modernism can be directly examined.[6] Kahl begins by setting up two ideal types: traditional and modern. From these he specifies a set of profiles in which each attribute may vary independently of the others. All sorts of combinations are possible. Instead of using all the theoretically possible combinations and permutations (Parsons' five-pattern variables alone would yield 32 types and Kluckhohn's three main relationships with five subdivisions would yield 243 types), Kahl switches from either/or attributes to *continuous variables,* which can then be intercorrelated, making it possible to derive personal profiles from modal profiles. But what can be done with such correlations?

Kahl specifies fourteen different components of modernity. Each was conceived of as a separate variable that ranged from the traditional pole to the modern pole, with a number of possible intermediate points. He chose these particular components of modernity because of their relation to work and career values, without pretending to exhaust the relevant dimensions of modernity, or to restrict the definition of modernism to all fourteen variables which were constructed as independent unidimensional scales. Kahl found that the core syndrome which he calls modernism consists of seven scales which were closely interrelated; they are: (1) activism, (2) low integration with relatives, (3) preference for urban life, (4) individualism, (5) low urban subcommunity stratification, (6) mass-media participation and (7) rigid stratification of life chances. There are additional values he associates with modernism

6. Joseph A. Kahl, *The Measurement of Modernism: A Study of Values in Brazil and Mexico* (Austin and London: Institute of Latin American Studies, University of Texas Press, 1968).

but these are operative to a lesser degree: trust in people, an attitude in favor of manual work and a distaste for traditional institutions and agencies of coercion. Kahl also noted a propensity to take risks in one's career and an attitude in favor of modern roles within the nuclear family. Surprisingly, occupational placement and low secularization were not associated with modernism.

In a general way, Kahl's study supports Inkeles' basic hypothesis that a syndrome of values remains as obscure in the quantitative rendering as it was in earlier qualitative forms. A comparison of Kahl's and Inkeles' studies is made difficult because there are differences in their definitions. Furthermore, there are problems of construct validity. As the work of Kahl and Inkeles illustrates, basic constructs may be quite similar and yet not mutually exclusive, even though the constructs are identified by different concepts and the substantive content of the concepts is organized differently. Thus various substantive components of a particular concept for Kahl (for example, activism) are embodied in a number of different concepts for Inkeles (for example, political activism, change and perception valuation, planning valuation, and general efficacy).

Every attempt to define "modernism" in terms of an operational set of variables results in the introduction of new ideas which have relatively little to do with the original concept. A standard definition of "modernization," for example, usually includes at least the following: belief in the primacy of science, or at least in the products of applied engineering, belief in a secular way of conducting affairs, and belief in the need for continuing changes in society and economy. But beyond these formulations, it often means intensified destruction of local and regional cultures in the name of national identity. Thus, modernism may be a goal for some and a handicap for others.[7] The answer will depend on who benefits from modernization, not by any intrinsic merits it is said to have.

This distinction points out a crucial problem in construct validation. Which of Kahl's fourteen scales and Inkeles' thirty themes are *substantively* and *empirically* related to modernism? Both men claim to have summarized only those values that have been associated with modernism in the literature. Unless we develop a more rigorous, theoretical, and empirical justification for the inclusion or exclusion of par-

7. Denis Goulet, *The Cruel Choice: A New Concept in the Theory of Development.* New York: Atheneum, 1971, pp. 96–108.

ticular value components in a definition of modernity, these values must be seen as another product of industrialization. In a world already parceled out among the big powers, they are neither a consequence nor a cause of the motivation to achieve.

As these studies and others begin empirically to isolate the crucial components of modernism, and as theory develops, greater construct validation may be expected. Then, descriptions of the different types and degrees of individual modernity will begin to resolve the problem of consistency of attitudinal dimensions. Kahl's study has already empirically demonstrated some over-all degree of consistency. In his identification of seven scales of variables that form the core syndrome of urbanization, he has noted, "on the average, a man who is high on some will also be high on the others, although there is room for variation." The specification of the different variations is the crux of the problem of consistency.

When controlled for socioeconomic status, Kahl's studies tend to parcel out the differences in "objective conditions" or structural indicators among the three countries he investigates—Brazil, Mexico, and the United States. This enabled each study to show the relatively high degree of frequency with which attitudes are held, as distinct from the congruence between these attitudes. But their attitude data refer only to particular groups; structural data generally refer to the whole nation. The Kahl studies lack indications of modal distributions or the standard deviations of attitudinal modernity for the whole population of three countries. Furthermore, the Kahl study illustrates that as long as "modernity" is *operationally defined* as the pattern of attitudes of "modern" groups (urbanites, for example), then the question of congruence is resolved by operational definition. A measure is needed to derive "cultural development" (changes in the values and attitudes) independently from "structural conditions." Without it, we cannot resolve the relationship of attitudinal data and structural data, since the size of the "modern" group is probably related more to the *level* of the development than to the *rate* of development.

The Sequential Problem: Modernization of attitudes denotes a growth of consciousness. There is movement from one position to another in time; from "traditional to modern." Because modernization is multidimensional, there are also problems of consistency among the different components of the concept and problems of sequence.

When social scientists describe the attitudes characteristic of traditional and modern societies, they assume a progressive transformation in the attitudes of developing man. But is such an assumption warranted? Assuming a priori that we can identify a cluster of attitudes as "traditional" and a cluster as "modern," we would then have to specify whether in fact in the process of development the "traditional attitudes" are transformed into the modern cluster of attitudes. For this purpose, longitudinal studies are needed. We need to know whether a rural person who moves to the city does in fact modify his traditional attitudes and become a "modern man."

Feldman and Hurn have begun to question the assumption of a simple sequence in the attitudinal dimension of modernism.[8] As they observe, most modernism studies deal only with cross-sectional data. The usual approach is to take a sample of urbanites and call their attitudes "modern," an approach obviously limited and biased against the "rural population." More importantly, the method itself generates the consistency found among attitudinal components of modernity. This is because attitudinal modernity is defined purely as a derivative of the structural factors, such as geographical residence or socioeconomic status. Ruralism is equated to traditional attitudes and urbanism with modernity, but the extent of ruralism (indicated, for example, by the percentage engaged in agriculture) is really a function of the structural conditions prevailing in the country.

Feldman and Hurn point out in a follow-up study of their Puerto Rico sample, some ten years later, that the process of modernization (defined in terms of the experience of mobility) does not differentiate between those who remained peasants and those who changed their status in the *direction* of their attitude change. The experience of mobility does differentiate them according to degree of attitude change. Those who were mobile (experienced modernization) tended to have higher aspirations, for instance, but there were also some reversals. For example, modernism studies assume that moderns tend to value education. Feldman and Hurn found out that those who were mobile tended to de-emphasize the value of education after their experience of mobility. But Feldman and Hurn quickly point out that an "anti-education" stance should in some cases be considered modern. More education may not imply great economic rewards if the employment-opportunity structure is not expanding. The concept of modernism tends to

8. Arnold Feldman and Christopher Hurn, "The Experience of Modernization," *Sociometry*, 29 (Dec. 1966), p. 293.

lose its explanatory power in such a situation. Contradictory attitudes become customary. They conclude by saying that the basic impact of modernism is increased cognitive awareness. "There must be dissonance observed between general economic growth in contrast to one's own comparative stagnation. There must be cognitive awareness of the gap between advancement at one end of the social scale—say, education— and stagnation at the level of economic opportunity." [9]

ATTITUDE "WAVES" AND STRUCTURAL "PARTICLES"

The Problem of Congruence: Descriptive Relationships: Cross-national studies dealing with attitudinal data show an impressively high degree of attitude convergence, considering the diversity in structural characteristics. Inkeles, for example, posits that values tend to converge in industrializing countries. Kahl writes: "These results support the position of Alex Inkeles that societal structures tend toward convergence in industrial (or industrializing) countries, creating sets of cultural values that reflect status positions and the exigencies of life that are associated with them, regardless of previously different national tradition." [10] One gets the misleading impression from Kahl that Brazil, Mexico, and the United States have similar value configurations, for the syndromes of modernizing attitudes in the three countries are similar. "Cross-national comparisons" are really comparisons across and within socioeconomic groups in different countries. They are not comparisons of objective national conditions, since it is precisely these conditions that differentiate countries. To put it differently, one cannot strictly speak of "cross-national" studies when the conditions used to compare the different countries are not representative of the three countries concerned.

To make worthwhile comparisons of attitudes one would need representative samples of the countries that would permit measurement of the respondents' subjective world, and comparison of this measure with "objective" socioeconomic indicators. One such macroscopic study is Cantril's *The Patterns of Human Concerns.* Cantril devised what he called a "self-anchoring scale." It was basically a projective type of interview scale by which the respondent's subjective world was the frame of reference:

9. Feldman and Hurn, "The Experience of Modernization," *op. cit.,* p. 294.
10. Kahl, *The Measurement of Modernism, op. cit.,* p. 54.

A person is asked to define on the basis of his own assumptions, perceptions, goals and values the two extremes or anchoring points of the spectrum on which some scale measurement is desired. . . . it was utilized in this study as a means of discovering the spectrum of values a person is preoccupied or concerned with and by means of which he evaluates his own life. He describes as the top anchoring points his wishes and hopes as he personally conceives them and the realization of which would constitute for him the best possible life. At the other extreme, he describes the worries and fears, the preoccupations and frustrations, embodied in his conception of the worst possible life he could imagine.[11]

Cantril used the ladder scale to rank the respondent's perception of his own "personal world" and the respondent's perception of the "nation" with respect to past, present, and future. He expressed the problem of congruence in these terms: "Curiosity naturally arises as to how the ratings people give themselves and their nations on the ladder are related to the indices used by economists to measure the stage of development people are in." [12]

To measure the degree of congruence, Cantril devised a composite index of socioeconomic development for the thirteen nations in his study, using eleven "structural variables." The countries were ranked for each of the eleven indicators, and their relative standing was then converted to a 1.00 to 0.00 scale. The socioeconomic index thus obtained was: the United States, 1.00; West Germany, .71; Israel, .67; Japan, .60; Poland, .45; Cuba, .35; Panama, .31; Yugoslavia, .19; Philippines, .17; Dominican Republic, .16; Brazil, .16; Egypt, .14; Nigeria, .02; India, .00.

Cantril then proceeded to obtain the rank order correlations of the socioeconomic index and the ladder ratings. Cantril explains the ratings by noting:

As would be expected, the correlation of the present personal rating with the socioeconomic indices is highest of all—in other words, an individual's personal experience now. Next in order is the person's estimate of his own ladder rating in the past and then a significantly high correlation between the present rating of the nation and its

11. Hadley Cantril, *The Patterns of Human Concerns*. New Brunswick, N.J.: Rutgers University Press, 1965, p. 22.
12. Cantril, *The Patterns of Human Concerns*, op. cit., p. 192.

socioeconomic index. When it comes to the future, both for the individual and the nation, any clear-cut relationships break down.[13]

Cantril's data yield an important point: there is an *inverse relationship* between the subjective rating and the objective rating. People in four highly developed countries tended to give themselves low present ratings, to rate their nation presently low, to rate the future for their country low, relative to their favorable position as measured by objective indices. For people in less-developed countries, the opposite was true.

The cross-national comparisons established by Cantril and his associates show a remarkable variation in the socioeconomic index and remarkable similarities in the ladder ratings, that is, in the attitude measures. And since both types of data are presumably "standardized," the differences must be attributed to something other than sampling techniques. His findings substantially bear out that there are odd disparities between structural and attitudinal data. Clearly, levels of industrial skills are built-in features of advanced countries—features which are far more difficult to "export" (presuming indeed even the intent of export) than the attitudes which emerge as a consequence of industrialism. One might say that the *products* of industrialism are largely responsible for modernization, while the *processes* of industrialism are largely responsible for economic development.

Another central problem in comparative international studies is the apparent gap between attitude research and structural analysis. If we attempt to measure differences between Argentina, Peru, and the United States, as Miller has intriguingly done, we find that distinctions between them on a scale of fifteen items relating to norms, values, and attitudes, and judged by persons intimate with each of these nations, tend to be rather small.[14] This is immediately apparent in Table 1.

Even if the comparisons are drawn on a rotation basis among Peru, Argentina, and the United States, the mean differences, while going up slightly, still remain indecisive. The differences of 59 per cent and 35 per cent, while important, are too insignificant to settle the issue either

13. Cantril, *The Patterns of Human Concerns, op. cit.,* p. 195.
14. Delbert C. Miller, "The Measurement of International Patterns and Norms: A Tool for Comparative Research," *Southwestern Social Science Quarterly,* Vol. 48 (Mar. 1968), pp. 531–47.

TABLE 1

MEAN RATINGS FOR UNITED STATES, PERU, AND ARGENTINA
AND THE DIFFERENCE BETWEEN MEANS OF PERU AND ARGENTINA, PERU
AND UNITED STATES, AND ARGENTINA AND THE UNITED STATES

Scale Item	Mean Ratings			Difference Between Means		
	U.S. N = 21	Peru N = 21	Argen-tina N = 15	Peru and Argen-tina	Peru and U.S.	Argen-tina and U.S.
1. Social Acceptance	1.66	4.48	3.18	1.30	2.82	2.02
2. Health	1.38	4.66	2.93	1.73	3.28	1.55
3. Trust	1.75	4.86	3.27	1.59	3.11	1.52
4. Security	2.33	4.95	3.50	1.45	2.62	1.17
5. Family	5.42	1.85	2.71	.86	3.57	2.71
6. Child	1.33	4.43	2.80	1.63	3.10	1.47
7. Moral Code	2.00	4.90	2.75	2.15	2.90	.75
8. Religion	4.57	2.05	3.66	1.61	2.52	.91
9. Class	5.00	1.38	3.07	1.69	3.62	1.93
10. Consensus	1.57	4.57	3.92	.55	3.00	2.35
11. Labor	5.33	3.10	2.69	.31	2.23	2.64
12. Democracy	1.42	3.66	2.81	1.85	2.24	1.39
13. Work	1.52	4.76	3.07	1.69	3.24	1.55
14. Civic Activity	1.19	4.81	3.58	1.23	3.62	2.39
15. Property	1.19	3.29	3.59	.29	2.10	2.39
Grand Mean Difference of all Ratings				1.33	2.93	1.95

Source: Delbert C. Miller, "The Measurement of International Patterns and Norms: A Tool for Comparative Research," *Southwestern Social Science Quarterly*, Vol. 48 (Mar. 1968), p. 545.

of the existence of a Latin American homogeneity or an Inter-American homogeneity. This table provides little comfort for those who argue the thesis that Latin America can be understood only in contrast to and in contradistinction with the United States, since it is clear that modernization carries with it a "demonstration effect." And in the case of the Latin American middle classes this means the emulation and incorporation of North American values of achievement.

As the tabular material shows, not only are there differences in the items taken as measures of value among the three nations, but on some very important items Argentina is more like the United States than like Peru. Miller does not adequately respond to his data; instead he calls into question the already slightly tarnished notion of a Latin American civilization. It might be argued that Miller's fifteen items are incomplete, that the inclusion of a more sophisticated set of measures of how personal satisfaction relates to political attitudes would help remove the tautological aspects in his findings.[15] While this seems a valid defense against criticism, the problem would not be resolved by merely widening the number of factors sampled, since the explanatory power of each factor would remain unexamined. Whether or not attitude factors are relevant when considered in terms of structural parameters may have more to do with the industrial organization of production and consumption than with cultural attitudes producing individuals have toward the consequences of industrialism.

Data gathered by Feinstein suggest that objective differences between Argentina and the United States are much more extensive than one would believe possible from attitude surveys.[16] For example, measuring inflationary spirals and rates of growth and using the year 1950 as the baseline of 100, the United States data show that by 1957 the cost of living index was up 17 points; for Argentina, the cost of living index in the same period of time was up 226 points. Furthermore, the United States exhibited an annual rate of economic growth of 3.5 per cent during this period; for Argentina, the annual growth rate was 1.9 per cent. One might add that GNP in Argentina has shown no marked propensity to "leap" forward during the recent years, despite the shifts in political power. Furthermore, in 1957 Argentinian income was $439 per capita, whereas the United States was $2079. The ten years since 1957 have witnessed continued growth in the United States, and an even slower pattern in Argentina. Now, Argentina shows income per person to be $680 in comparison to $4050 per person in the United States.

The United States and Argentina do have modernizing phenomena in common. For example, the literacy rate is extremely high in both nations. The percentage of the urban population in relation to the total population is high for both. The distributions are very different, however: the United States has a wide distribution of urban areas while Argentina has only one really major city and a capital area which accounts for roughly 45 per cent of the total population of the nation.

15. In this connection, see Kahl, *Measurement of Modernism, op. cit.*
16. Otto Feinstein, "A Changing Latin American and U.S. Foreign Policy," in *Two Worlds of Change: Readings in Economic Development,* edited by Otto Feinstein. New York: Doublday-Anchor. 1964, pp. 375–420.

Unionization and secondary education also rank high in both nations.

The really significant differences are in private investment of United States firms in Latin America compared to Argentine investments in North America. The constant rate of growth of United States investment in Latin America is too well known to require detailed commentary. Similarly, the near absence of any large-scale export, and certainly of any large-scale Argentine control over United States industry, is beyond contest. Use of these and many other similar variables would enable one to avoid the indeterminate kinds of comparisons with the United States that attitude surveys yield. For example, gross investment as percentage of GNP remained disappointingly stable in most Latin American countries during the past decade: only El Salvador, Guatemala, Nicaragua, and Panama succeeded in raising it. Savings in Latin America rose from 16.3 per cent to 16.9 per cent between 1951 and 1964, while income increased over 50 per cent. But during the last five years savings have either failed to increase or had even fallen slightly in spite of higher incomes per person. The most important symptom of national effort, the marginal rate of savings, at best failed to increase and remained at a level of 15 per cent, or 20–30 per cent lower than in India and Pakistan, which have but a fraction of Latin American income per capita. The marginal rate of savings must be increased by at least 50 per cent if self-sustained high growth is to be attained. The rates of industrial growth should be almost twice as high and the level of agricultural growth 50–60 per cent higher than at present if the goals of full employment and of sustained growth of 2.5 per cent per capita per annum are to be reached.

Foreign exchange also failed to increase sufficiently in the past decade. Since the mobilization of domestic savings seems to depend on complementary foreign exchange—prospective investors may not save if they see no prospects of obtaining foreign exchange for imports or machinery—the scarcity of foreign exchange may in part explain the scarcity of savings.

Lack of monetary stability combined with widespread inflation still prevails in a good three-quarters of Latin American nations. Because we have learned that stabilization should not proceed at the expense of growth, and since it normally takes several years to increase the production and supply of domestic foodstuffs, only a gradual stabilization is attempted. Yet the price in terms of growth seems to be high in some countries (Argentina, Brazil, Colombia) even though the reduction in inflation has not been as much as planned. Monetary instability may discourage savings as well as impede progress in Latin American economic integration.[17]

A series of measures that economists employ indicates that the United States and Argentina (and Latin America as a whole) stand at the opposite ends of the developmental ladder on several major dimensions. The United States exports much more than it imports; nations such as Argentina have a difficult time maintaining any sort of equilibrium between exports and imports.[18] The rates of earnings on United States direct private investments abroad in Latin America averaged during the post-World War II period more than 14.0 per cent per annum, which is considerably higher than the earnings-to-investments ratio achieved on purely domestic capitalization. The rate of earnings on Argentine direct private investments abroad during the same period averaged less than half this percentage, or under 7.0 per cent, which is considerably less than the earnings-to-investment ratio achieved on purely Argentine sources of investment, and much less than the annual inflationary rates. When we add to these factors the underdevelopment and satellitic relationships; the chronic balance-of-payment deficits; minimal investment funds from underdeveloped nations in the advanced nations; and the flow of finished goods at high prices from developed to underdeveloped nations in contrast to the flow of agricultural and mineral wealth from the underdeveloped nations, one can readily perceive that modernization is often achieved in backward areas at the cost of postponing industrialization.[19]

The case of Argentina and the United States represents a Heisenberg indeterminancy situation. Both countries exhibit similar indicators of modernization—of cultural identification—but there is little correlation between their respective indicators of industrialization and foreign trade. Germani estimates that on a cultural scale of *modernism,* Argentina

17. See Paul N. Rosenstein-Rodan, "The Alliance for Progress and Peaceful Revolution," in *Latin American Radicalism,* edited by Irving Louis Horowitz, Josué de Castro, and John Gerassi. New York: Random House, 1969, pp. 53–60.
18. This same structural imbalance between export and import also characterizes over-ripe societies such as England and France. It might be tentatively noted that a number of processes characteristic of underdevelopment are also found in the phenomena of overdevelopment.
19. See Comisión Económica para America Latina, *Boletín Estadístico de América Latina,* Vol. III, No. 1, Feb. 1966. New York: United Nations, 1966; and *The Economic Development of Latin America in the Post-War Period* (E/CN). New York: United Nations, 1964.

ranks alongside Germany, England and even the United States; whereas on a scale of *industrialism,* it ranks closer to Brazil, Mexico, and Ecuador, and even some African countries (see Table 2).[20] This therefore strongly supports the view that an immense gap exists between economic development and sociocultural modernization.

One way of working out a systematic theory that would resolve this particular variety of the Heisenberg principle would be to show how attitudes affect structures and, contrariwise, how structures affect attitudes. One might say that Lipset has already attempted the former, namely, to show the movement from attitudes to a change in social structure;[21] while this writer has emphasized the latter, namely, how structures affect attitudes.[22] Still, neither approach quite resolves the issues since the causal sequence involves trend analyses that the data themselves are not refined enough to yield up thus far. That is to say, the choice between an idealistic frame of reference, stressing the need for change in people, and an orientation toward revolutionary behavior or mass response to structural inequities is ultimately still determined by some kind of animal faith. I venture to say that lurking behind idealistic formulations is the researcher's belief in individual initiative and gradual change, while naturalistic formations equally tend to reveal a contrasting cluster of beliefs in mass organization and revolutionary change.

As far as possible, the degree of attitudes in contrast to structures has to be measured in terms of real consequences. We must ask ourselves whether modernizing attitudes toward achievement lead to a revolution in social structure or provide even a greater measure of security, wealth, power, or other indicators of development. For instance, we should examine those nations in this hemisphere that had substantial sociopolitical revolutions in the twentieth century, namely, Mexico and Cuba in the Western Hemisphere, and contrast them with those nations adopting a more evolutionary posture toward the same developmental goals, such as Chile, Argentina, and Venezuela.

Attitude surveys have difficulty in achieving true comparabilities which are not tautological. If the cultural values of South American and North

20. Gino Germani, *Política y Sociedad en una Epoca de Transición: De la Sociedad Tradicional a la Sociedad de Masas.* Buenos Aires: Editorial Paidós, 1962.
21. Seymour Martin Lipset, "Values, Education and Entrepreneurship," in *Elites in Latin America,* edited by Seymour Martin Lipset and Aldo Solari. New York: Oxford University Press, 1967, pp. 3–49.
22. "Psychology of Three Worlds" in this work pp. 72–113.

TABLE 2

INDICATORS OF ECONOMIC DEVELOPMENT AND INDEMNIZATION IN FIVE GROUPS
OF COUNTRIES AT DIFFERENT STAGES OF THE PROCESS (approx. 1950–55)

	I Mass Consumption Stage		II Industrial Revolution Stage			III Pre-Industrial Societies in Transition			IV Traditional Societies		
	U.S.	Eng-land	West Ger-many	Italy	Argen-tina	Brazil	Mex-ico	Ecua-dor	Congo	Haiti	Ethio-pia
1. Economic Development											
(a) G.N.P. per capita, U.S. $ 1955	2243	998	762	442	374	262	187	204	98	80	75
(b) Energy consumption	7834	4594	3266	992	1033	329	817	157	56	75	43
(c) % of active population in agriculture	12	5	14	29	25	61	58	53	84	—	83
2. Modernization											
(d) Gross birth rate (per 1000)	24.9	15.8	15.6	10.0	23.7	45.0	47.3	47.1	—	—	—
(e) Gross death rate (per 1000)	9.5	11.7	10.7	9.5	10.0	20.0	15.0	20.0	—	—	—
(f) Life expectancy at birth	71	71	67	65	64	45	50	45	—	22	—
(g) % living in cities of 20,000	52	67	44	30	48	20	24	18	8	2.5	5
(h) % literate (15 yrs. & over)	97.5	98.5	98.5	87.5	86.4	49.4	56.8	55.7	37.5	—	10.5
(i) % university students (per 1000)	18.2	7.7	4.8	2.9	7.5	1.2	2	1.5	0.1	—	0.3
(j) % voters among adults	63.0	78	88	94	90.0	42	50	46	—	—	3
(k) % in middle occupation strata with respect to total active population	47	34	40	29	40	17	17.0	11	—	—	5.4

Sources: (a), (c), (g), (h), (j): Yale Data Program, *Basic for Cross-National Comparisons.* New Haven, 1960; (b): United Nations, *Statistical Yearbook,* 1960; (d), (e), (f): United Nations, *Report on World Social Situation,* 1957; (k): based on S. M. Miller, "Comparative Social Mobility," *Current Sociology,* IX (1960), No. 1, and G. Germani, *Po ítica y Sociedad.* Buenos Aires: Paidos, 1962.
Note: dash indicates no data available.

American peoples are compared, and the total cross-national sample is drawn from highly urbanized sectors, the values expressed by the respondents may represent modernization attitudes rather than point up real national similarities.[23] This is made forcefully clear in a recent survey of Argentine attitudes on the Vietnam War. The sample revealed a sharp class demarcation in attitudes unlike what comparable surveys have indicated for the United States. This principle of qualitative specificity in survey questions—more often observed in the breach than in the execution—is illustrated in this survey questionnaire. When asked the causes of American intervention, the Argentine middle and lower classes tended to attribute such intervention to the nature of capitalism, colonialism, imperialism, militarism. Only 19 per cent of the upper classes saw these as causative factors, but 50 per cent of the middle class and 45 per cent of the lower class gave imperialism and related phenomena as the answer. On the other hand, the upper classes assigned the causes of the war to the need to defend democracy, liberty, and the West (43 per cent) or the status answer: the prestige requirements of a great world power (36 per cent). The lower classes credited the "defense of democracy" answer in only 18 per cent of the cases, and the status response in only 3 per cent of the cases. On the question of how the war could be solved, the lower classes and middle classes saw the resolution in self-determination and sovereignty of the Vietnamese to the extent of 65 per cent and 62 per cent respectively; while the upper classes, in 45 per cent of the cases sampled, saw the solution in restraining the expansion of communism and the totalitarian system of government.[24] This demonstrates that class factors seem much more powerful in explaining attitudinal differences than might be surmised from the customary social mobility questionnaires.

The Nature of the Explanatory Relationship: the Order of Causation: Some authors immediately assign to attitudes a causal role in the developmental process, without dealing with construct validation, consistency, sequence, and congruence. McClelland's need-achievement theory, while interesting, is difficult to accept as a stimulus for develop-

23. This seems a particularly acute problem in accepting the findings given in Gabriel A. Almond and Sidney Verba, *The Civic Culture.* Boston and Toronto: Little, Brown & Co., 1965.
24. "Encuesta: Qué piensan los argentinos sobre Vietnam," *Primera Plana* (Mar. 5, 1968), p. 28.

ment because of the problem of validating the causal chain.[25] One must assume innate drives for success to make such a theory operative. Hagen's withdrawal of status respect theory seems even more far-fetched. It would take an entire generation before the withdrawal of status respect would have significant developmental implications of shaming the rising sectors into an achievement syndrome.[26] Following them, one would have to revise all the different children's books and fairy tales so that the young would manifest high achievement patterns in their vision of the future society. And even then we would have to wait a generation for confirmation of the theory. In short, achievement theories of development postulate an idealistic predisposition to be remotely intelligible.

The causal role of attitudes and values in development continues to haunt social-science thinking. Such a viewpoint remains persistent because there are no social structures dismembered from the individuals who operate and maintain them, and there are no individuals without attitudes and values, attitudes must thus have causal roles. This syllogism is a caricature, and yet it underlies the attitudinal approach to development. Even economics, which tends to rely more on objective (structural) data, makes assumptions about the attitudinal aspects of man, such as the much debased "rationality" of economic man.

To pose the question of which comes first values or structures is really to pose a "chicken-or-egg" debate. They can be shown to be closely interlinked. The root problem for applied social science is *where* one should break into the circle of causality. Since attitudes and structures can be logically considered as either causes or consequences, we must postulate the conditions in which it is more expedient, parsimonious, and effective to consider one as either cause or effect. It should be pointed out, though, that a single attitude can lead to different kinds of behavior, just as different attitudes can lead to a single kind of behavior; an individual's behavior might not be significant unless translated into a group action, which in turn might not be significant unless

25. Even David C. McClelland, who first offered his need-achievement theory in *The Achieving Society,* Princeton: Van Nostrand Co., 1961, has considerably modified his claims in more recent work. See in particular "Personality Changes After Training," in David C. McClelland and David G. Winter, *Motivating Economic Achievement.* New York: The Free Press, 1969, pp. 324–35.
26. Everett E. Hagen, "How Economic Growth Begins: A Theory of Social Change," *Journal of Social Issues,* Vol. 19 (Jan. 1963), pp. 20–34.

translated into institutionalized behavior. On the other hand, institutionalization of processes, while rendering greater predictive validity, does not guarantee uniform effects on different people.

The need, therefore, is for "contextual types" of analysis which take both attitudes and structures into consideration. We also need to know whether the relationships between the two are multiplicative and/or additive. Furthermore, we need to know the appropriate time lags involved between the two kinds of indicators of change. We need to investigate threshold conditions. Just as in economics Rostow's "preconditions" must be attained before one can reach self-sustained growth, the take-off stage,[27] we would like to know at what points attitudes effective for social change take effect. The most promising lines of investigation are those that deal with processes, rather than static equilibrium models which have characterized social science for all too long.

The researcher must not lose sight of the limitations involved in the nature of the data utilized. For instance, attitude approaches to change and development tend to emphasize the innovative role of the middle class, but managerialism is only useful insofar as it presupposes the existence of a capitalist system of economic exchange. Klausner, in his study of total societies, writes:

> The "total society" involves linking concepts belonging to different theoretical networks. The simplest case is that of the bi-disciplinary statement. A "good" bi-disciplinary statement will involve two terms, each referring to a distinct theoretical system—for example, one referring to the personality and the other to the social system; or to distinct subsystems—for example, one referring to the polity and the other to the economy. The statement will also cite a mechanism that mediates the events in these two systems. Usually the mechanism consists of an interactive process within a specified social structure. The function of the mechanism is to transform an event in one system into an event in another system. If no mechanism is cited, the causes of the asserted co-occurrence of events remains indeterminate. The mechanism may be antecedent to the independent event, or forged by the interaction of the independent and dependent events, or be in a third system or subsystem which shares a boundary with both the dependent and independent events. A special case is that of the loop in which the independent and dependent events are

27. See Walt W. Rostow, "The Take-off into Self-Sustained Growth," *The Economic Journal,* Vol. 66 (Mar. 1956), pp. 25–48.

two states of the same system. A mechanism in another system may be called upon to explain the change of state.[28]

CONCLUSIONS

The choice between an intrinsic standpoint and an extrinsic standpoint is, at rock bottom, a decision in favor of either a theory of values (modernism) or a theory of interests (structuralism). To argue the case for underdevelopment is to argue a set of value premises related to backwardness. Whereas, to argue the case for extrinsic causes of stagnation is to argue the case for an interest theory; namely, that it is primarily in the interest of the advanced nations to exploit the less developed nations.

The literature demonstrates that this methodological dilemma creates an enormous ideological chasm between those who believe that the fully developed nations require colonialism to maintain their special status, and those who believe they do not require a huge cluster of dependent areas for their own wealth and status. The solution to such a problem cannot be made a priori; it is obviously clear that both external factors and internal factors effect the subordinate position of the colonized nation. The question is one of mix rather than either/or. In the Lipset and Solari collection on developing elites, the essays can be divided between those by social scientists who assume that internal factors and value problems are the key and those who assume that the external factors and interest problems are the key.[29] Those who assume the value standpoint are invariably those who take attitudes as their measuring device, while those who take the interest approach use structural variables to prove their points.

The problem has been compounded rather than resolved by newer forms of methodology. The introduction of multiple variables in present computer techniques of analysis simply adds factors not previously considered in attempting to explain variance. But those who manifest faith in the additive value of factors fail to provide a scale of factor intensity to explain the problems at hand. It is peculiar as well as unfortunate

28. Samuel Klausner, *The Study of Total Societies.* New York: Anchor Books, 1967, pp. 3–29 ("Links and Missing Links Between the Sciences of Man," pp. 28–29).
29. Lipset and Solari (eds.), *Elites in Latin America, op. cit.*

that factor analysis has still not yielded insight into problems such as whether the Catholic life style of most Latin America peoples is a greater factor in their state of underdevelopment than the capitalist economic system. Indeed, the relationship between religious factors and economic factors remains clouded in Weberian rhetoric. Developmentalists lack a basis comparable to the analysis of capitalism provided for Western Europe and the United States. Such a fundamental issue is further complicated because of a tendency to add to the quantity of variables employed in the analysis rather than to reduce the number by a process of statistical condensation.

It has been argued by Daland that in Brazil the notion of economic planning is basically a ploy used to mobilize the population on a national basis into the political system.[30] The main purpose of planning, then, is not economic growth but political mobilization. Further verification of this comes from that exceptional "case"—Japan, a nation which tends to confound most analyses of underdeveloped states and/or stagnant societies. Japan has exhibited a remarkable degree of internal development under a basic capitalist framework, and a remarkable degree of penetration by foreign capitalist nations. Yet its growth is not the result of the sort of revolution that one is led to expect is necessary to foster such growth. On the other hand, the structural framework points to the feudal class structure as a means of explained Japanese exceptionalism. The structural problem is thus directly connected to the nation-building issue.

Whatever the weaknesses of nation-building analysis, and there are many, it has the singular virtue of compelling an examination of the exchange system involved in bilateral national dealings. It focuses upon the direct relationship between any given underdeveloped nation and any given fully developed nation and shows how that relationship leads to specific results. Thus, the relationship between the United States and Bolivia, or between the Soviet Union and Poland, may prove to be the most important framework in which to examine underdevelopment. International comparison is not simply directed toward the connection between fully developed and underdeveloped nations, but deals with very specific bilateral relationships between large and small nations. And here, as Apter and Andrain indicate, structuralists and game theorists agree how important this international bargaining position

30. Robert T. Daland, *Brazilian Planning: Developmental Politics and Administration.* Chapel Hill: University of North Carolina Press, 1967.

can be for underdeveloped nations in their attempts to realize their own internal aims and ambitions.[31]

The structural approach permits us to use a comparative framework. It also enables us to distinguish internal problems of underdevelopment from external problems of economic stagnation. Finally, it enables the researcher to single out key connections (usually bilateral relationships) that are maintained between fully developed and semi-developed states.

Soares and Hamblin have suggested one solution to the problem of combining census and election data with survey data: for each unit—for example, national, state, or county—the survey attitudinal response should be averaged.[32] This average attitudinal response then could be analyzed along with other demographic or structural characteristics of that same unit. Thus the per cent of the survey respondents who strongly agree with the survey item measuring "favorableness to revolution" might be correlated with the per cent of unemployed (a measure of class polarization); the per cent divorced (a measure of anomie); the per cent urban (living in communities of 10,000 or more).

There remains the question of how much the survey sample allows one to generalize about each sub-unit. Some existing samples would probably be unsuitable for this purpose, since the respondents are highly clustered. However, in theory it is a simple matter to design a sample that would adequately represent each sub-unit. While presently available survey data may limit the method of analysis, there is no reason why new studies could not be made that would fulfill all the methodological requirements. These studies would have many advantages over present macroscopic analyses, since by and large the latter do not include any attitudinal data. If values, attitudes, beliefs do have an effect at the macro level, then certainly they would control significant portions of the variance in such analyses.

Coleman's *Equality of Educational Opportunity* has followed a similar procedure.[33] His survey involves many school characteristics, and in one

31. David E. Apter and Charles Andrain, "Comparative Government: Developing New Nations," in *Political Science-Advance of the Discipline,* edited by Marian D. Irish. Englewood Cliffs, N.J.: Prentice-Hall, 1968, pp. 82–126.

32. See Glaucio Soares and Robert L. Hamblin, "Socio-economic Variables and Voting for the Radical Left: Chile, 1951," *American Political Science Review,* Vol. 61 (Dec. 1967), pp. 1053–65.

33. James S. Coleman *et al., Equality of Educational Opportunity.* Washington, D.C.: Department of Health, Education and Welfare, Office of Education, 1966.

analysis he correlates these school characteristics with various attitudinal characteristics which are averages of the individual responses in the school. It turns out that these attitudinal characteristics do control significant portions of the variance independently of the school's structural characteristics. The dependent variable in this case is academic achievement. There are considerable shortcomings in this averaging process, primarily because it is possible that such reductionism fails to weigh the factors properly. Demographic and structural variables all turn out to be proportions which are averages. There is no reason why other kinds of measures, particularly attitudinal measures, cannot be averaged in the same way and thus included in the same analysis.

Whether attitudes can be viewed as simply one more variable on a structural scale of measurement is still in dispute. And this might better be resolved by psychological measures that are in fact comparable with all other forms of structural measures. If much past effort seems epigrammatic, it is simply because the levels of analysis in developmental studies thus far has rarely gone beyond aggregative data. There is a great need for more sophisticated measures than are currently available. The structural framework supplies a conceptual richness to discussions on development so that the researcher can now link strategies of social development to the history of the countries involved.

The conclusions which follow from this analysis, while tentative, are nonetheless compelling. First, the process of development involves sub-units of industrialization and modernization. Second, these two main sub-units may or may not be spatially or temporally parallel. Indeed, available data indicate that for the most part they are quite distinct and even antithetical in certain periods. Third, as in the Heisenberg wave-particle effect, it is best to analyze and generalize about discrete processes entailed in development, rather than make a monistic assumption about the nature of change in society. However, this does not necessarily mean one must rely on dualistic formulations. Within the dual processes of industrialization and modernization, it is quite possible to make decisive choices by conceptualizing attitudinal data as one critical cluster of factors. In this way we can better determine what factors are independent and interdependent in any given national decision concerning priorities for social change.

14

Politicians, Bureaucrats, and Decision-Making

Social change is never total. Even under conditions of revolutionary transformation, the need for certain types of continuity are imperative. Lenin implored the telephone and communications workers to remain at their posts as the first days of the Bolshevik Revolution unfolded, while Mao Tse Tung judiciously insisted that basic productive norms be strictly observed during the Cultural Revolution. There are people in every society who are defined as primarily organizational rather than ideological. After all, neither American pragmatism nor Soviet dialectics placed rockets in orbit around the moon—although post-lunar rhetoric would make us believe so. In any event, it is clear that some sector of a population must provide basic services while political action is taking place. The organizational problems of the Third World can be summarized as follows: (1) The inherited bureaucracy is often not a national or nationalist-oriented bureaucracy, and thus the actual number of functionaries available to the new regime may be limited. (2) While the inherited bureaucracy may be political, it quite often has a political persuasion that is at odds with the new regime leaders. (3) The inherited bureaucracy, as the only sub-class not transformed by a revolutionary situation, often serves as a fulcrum for either real or imagined counter-nationalist and counter-revolutionary tendencies. Therefore, this interaction of the two major elements of party and bureaucracy assumes decisive importance in the political structure of the Third World.

The conflict between politicians representing the popular will and bureaucrats representing efficient management is world-wide. But it has special dimensions in and for the developing areas. In the euphoria surrounding termination of colonial rule in Asia, Africa, and the Caribbean, the triumphant glow of nationalism shines most brightly on the new governments' optimistic plans for economic and social development. Particularly because the private sectors of these nations are backward or oriented toward export rather than domestic needs, their governments expect to play a dominant role in the development process. On the day after Independence Day, governments address themselves to translating their ambitions into action and their critical dependence on the bureaucratic machinery becomes painfully clear.[1]

Public administration inherited from the colonial period is in many ways unsuited or unprepared for the demands now placed on it. To some extent it suffers disorganization and demoralization as the expatriate colonial officers return to their native country, even where their departure is a gradual phasing-out instead of a rout. Routines are disrupted, projects truncated, and traditional long, thorough training programs are interrupted. Despite rapid promotion of the lower ranks and crash training programs, it proves impossible to fill all the vacancies with trained personnel.

Salary scales and benefits, appropriate to a developed nation's civil service, tax the newly independent nation's economy sorely.[2] Moreover, the structure and procedures of the bureaucracy, as well as the skills of native civil servants trained during the colonial period, are designed for the custodial tasks of colonial administration: preserving law and order, collecting taxes, maintaining transportation and communications systems. Little machinery or experience exist for the innovative activi-

1. See Henry L. Bretton, *Power and Stability in Nigeria: The Politics of Decolonization.* New York: Frederick A. Praeger, 1962, pp. 95–96, 150; Margaret L. Bates, "Tanganyika: Administration," in *African One-Party States,* edited by Gwendolen M. Carter. Ithaca, N.Y.: Cornell University Press, 1962, pp. 461–62, 465; Anthony H. Rweyemamu, "Managing Planned Development: Tanzania," *The Journal of Modern African Studies,* Vol. 4 (1966), pp. 3–9; Donald Rothchild and Michael Rogin, "Uganda: Central Administration," in *National Unity and Regionalism in Eight African States,* edited by Gwendolen M. Carter. Ithaca, N.Y.: Cornell University Press, 1966, pp. 406–8; Anthony H. M. Kirk-Greene, "Bureaucratic Cadres in a Traditional Milieu," in *Education and Political Development,* edited by James S. Coleman. Princeton: Princeton University Press, 1965, p. 401.
2. Ralph Braibanti, "Administrative Modernization," in Myron Weiner, ed., *Modernization: The Dynamics of Growth.* New York: Basic Books, 1966, pp. 172–73.

ties the bureaucracy is now called upon to perform.[3] But the greatest administrative challenge confronting the new governments is the problem of reaching an adjustment between politicians and civil servants whose relative power and status have just undergone an abrupt and drastic reversal.[4]

In the difficult and chaotic period immediately following independence, tremendous strains begin to appear between the new nationalist politicians and the government apparatus. In part, these frictions reflect the frustration of the politicians who, in seeking their goals, have to rely on an agency not of their making, outside of their control, whose loyalty to them is uncertain.

POLITICAL AND BUREAUCRATIC IDEOLOGIES

The new political leaders differ radically from the civil service in their ideological orientation. Swept to power by the high nationalistic feeling accompanying independence, they are strongly committed to lifting from their countries the stigma of colonialism. Since the slow rate of economic growth can be blamed on the colonial regime, the new leaders are faced with strong expectations that with this obstacle removed the country can anticipate rapid progress. Deferential colonial attitudes change to national pride and a feeling that the authoritarian governmental system should be democratized. Political initiative was said to rest with "the people" or at least with their representatives. The amount of hostility felt toward the departing colonial power varies, but the desire to impose political control over the governmental machinery left behind is universal. To ensure control, the new leaders reason, all policies must originate with the party in power. Moreover, the bureaucracy must be policed by politicians to guarantee that policies not be distorted along colonialist lines in the process of implementation; in one-party states this comes to mean in practice the virtual merging of party

3. Eme O. Awa, *Federal Government in Nigeria.* Berkeley: University of California Press, 1964, pp. 171–72; A. L. Adu, *The Civil Service in New African States.* New York: Frederick A. Praeger, 1965, p. 226; Abdelmalek Ben-Amor and Frederick Clairmonte, "Planning in Africa," *The Journal of Modern African Studies,* Vol. 3 (1966), p. 475.
4. Lucian W. Pye, "The Political Context of National Development," in *Development Administration: Concepts and Problems,* edited by Irving Swerdlow. Syracuse: Syracuse University Press, 1963, p. 31.

and state. So closely identified with the old regime is the bureaucracy that even its clerical and accounting procedures may become suspect and carry little weight with the new politicians.

Civil servants, on the other hand, tend to remain committed to principles of colonial-style administration. Although their organizations usually diverge in many respects from the Weberian model of rational bureaucracy, their ideals reflect the prescriptions laid down in civil service training manuals: a hierarchically structured bureaucracy with orderly progression through the ranks and strictly observed lines of authority, its personnel recruited according to merit, impeccable in its technical competence and impervious to political influence. Commitment to political neutrality and aloofness, however, is not complete, for many civil servants tend to interpret from the colonial experience that policy-making is a function, or even an exclusive prerogative, of the bureaucracy. Training for paternalistic service, they consider themselves not only the most capable but the proper agency for national progress in the post-colonial period. They feel that, when the expatriates left, the "white man's burden" descended on the shoulders of the native civil servants. Accordingly, their inclinations and ideological commitments are not directed toward democratizing the governmental system or sharing their authority with new political forces. To do so would, in their view, admit irrationality into the system and threaten the efficient, carefully considered administration necessary for national development.[5]

These differences in orientation breed considerable distrust and antagonism between politicians and bureaucrats. Now that the bureaucracy is vulnerable to open attack, political leaders are usually quick to give voice to popular resentment of the civil servants' high-handed manner. A series of interviews held with post-colonial Burmese politicians, for example, reveals general bitterness over bureaucratic arrogance: civil servants were thought to be " 'worse' than the British, acting as 'little kings,' and finding pleasure in doing the 'dirty work'

5. See James S. Coleman and Carl G. Rosberg, Jr. (eds.), *Political Parties and National Integration in Tropical Africa.* Berkeley: University of California Press, 1964; Lucian W. Pye, *Politics, Personality, and Nation Building: Burma's Search for Identity.* New Haven: Yale University Press, 1962; Immanuel Wallerstein, *Africa: The Politics of Independence.* New York: Random House, 1961; *Nigerian Government and Politics,* editor John P. Mackintosh. London: George Allen & Unwin, 1966; Walter Birmingham *et al.* (eds.), *A Study of Contemporary Ghana.* London: George Allen & Unwin, 1966; Marion E. Doro and Newell M. Stultz (eds.), *Governing in Black Africa: Perspectives on New States.* Englewood Cliffs, New Jersey: Prentice-Hall, 1970.

for the British." [6] In Pakistan, politicians continually admonish civil servants that they are now "servants of the people," not rulers, and should conduct themselves with humility.[7] The bureaucrats' caution and conservatism are ridiculed, their methods and procedures called hopelessly antique. Burmese Prime Minister U Nu succinctly put the typical politician's doubts: "The question to be asked is, 'Will the Civil Service, which has its training among the peasantry in lonely districts at least for the earlier years, and which claims to have acted as kindly fathers of the poor, rise to the occasion and throw up men capable of guiding and inspiring New Burma?' " [8] Considering the motives of the bureaucracy as questionable as its techniques, political zealots suspect native civil servants of disloyalty. In Tanzania bureaucrats are accused of being "black neocolonialists." [9] In Indonesia they are attacked as "colonial" or even worse, "liberal" in the sense of being capitalistic and materialistic.[10] In Jamaica, bureaucratic ineptitude is likely to be regarded as sabotage.[11] In Ghana, during Nkrumah's rule, civil servants were referred to as "intellectual spivs," and party newspapers editorialized that the "appointment of anti-party, anti-Socialist rascals on the basis of bourgeois qualifications alone leaves open the possibilities of creating so many agents of neo-colonialism in a State administration." [12]

Put on the defensive by politicians, civil servants are likely to cling tenaciously to status-affirming symbols of westernization, which in practice means the life style of the departed expatriate officials. Advancement into the upper ranks of the colonial civil service had usually

6. Lucian W. Pye, *Politics, Personality, and Nation Building*, p. 224.

7. Albert Gorvine, "The Civil Service under the Revolutionary Government in Pakistan," *The Middle East Journal*, Vol. 19 (1965), p. 331; Ralph Braibanti notes that "as recently as 1962 in the National Assembly, one legislator said of Pakistan's elite cadre that it possessed powers not even enjoyed by the President and that 'all the hatred in the hearts of the people against any Government is due mainly to the self-conceited and haughty behaviour of these functionaries.' " ("Administrative Modernization," p. 171.)

8. U Nu, "From Peace to Stability," pp. 34–35, quoted in Lucian W. Pye, *Politics, Personality, and Nation Building*, p. 221.

9. John B. George, "How Stable Is Tanganyika?," *Africa Report* (Mar. 1963), pp. 5–6; and Henry Bienen, "The Ruling Party in the African One-Party State: Tanu in Tanzania," in *Governing in Black Africa*, pp. 68–83.

10. Herbert Feith, "Dynamics of Guided Democracy," *Indonesia*, edited by Ruth T. McVey. New Haven: Human Relations Area File, 1963, p. 388.

11. B. L. St. John Hamilton, *Problems of Administration in an Emergent Nation: A Case Study of Jamaica*. New York: Frederick A. Praeger, 1964, p. 192.

12. David E. Apter, "Ghana," in *Political Parties and National Integration*, edited by James S. Coleman and Carl G. Rosberg, pp. 313–14.

depended on acquiring expatriate social skills, on being able for instance to "appreciate English tea and . . . intelligently discuss the fine points of cricket." [13] Even "crash programs" to train native officials in Nigeria had included instruction on "social savoir-faire and 'senior service' etiquette and mores," with careful attention to ceremonial behavior, entertaining, and the niceties of wearing uniforms and attending plays and polo matches.[14] Style became almost synonymous with technical competence, since the two qualities were usually found together, and both were essential for promotion. However thin their veneer of expatriate style, native civil servants in the post-colonial period tend to feel that their possession or at least appreciation of such social skills sets them above the politicians, who except for some at the very top levels generally lack this kind of acculturative training.[15]

Administrators typically express equal scorn for the political officials' relative lack of formal education. Senior civil servants in Burma complain, "They think they should run the district, but they haven't even been to a proper school," and say of leaders, "He is a minister, but he has never been to the university. Uneducated like all our politicians. What hope is there for us?" [16] In Tanzania "an organization of African civil servants has protested against the appointment of certain district and area commissioners on the grounds that the TANU [political] appointees are incompetent and should be required to complete a course in public administration before taking office." [17] To the politicians, this passion for Western customs and education is insufferable affectation —an attitude which only further convinces the bureaucrats of the politicians' dismal lack of culture and their general unfitness to give orders. Politicians, the bureaucrats feel, are bound to make mistakes, rush headlong into impossible projects and neglect vital tasks, bungle everything they try. Lucian Pye reports that older Burmese civil servants were apologetic for the country's problems, explaining that Burma used to be a better land. Before the war the bureaucrats ran the country; now, "the politicians have their hands in everything." [18] These mutual

13. Robert O. Tilman, *Bureaucratic Transition in Malaya*. Durham, N.C.: Duke University Press, 1964, p. 127.
14. I. Nicolson, "The Machinery of the Federal and Regional Governments," *op. cit.*, p. 186; Lucian W. Pye, *Politics, Personality, and Nation Building*, pp. 218–19.
15. Lucian W. Pye, *ibid.*, pp. 213, 217–19, 221, 246–52.
16. *Ibid.*, p. 219.
17. John B. George, "How Stable Is Tanganyika?," *op. cit.*, p. 5.
18. Lucian W. Pye, *Politics, Personality, and Nation Building*, p. 214.

antagonisms and suspicions make cooperation between politicians and bureaucrats on administrative programs a diplomatic challenge in itself.

PATRONAGE, POWER, AND PRIVILEGE

When politicians and bureaucrats clash in the ex-colonial countries, the politicians have the upper hand. The coming of national independence gives them the means of control that they feel it is necessary to have over the inherited civil service, specific sanctions that can be invoked to deal with resistance, dissention, and failure. In some countries punishment of recalcitrant officials is severe—removal from the service, fines, imprisonment, or expulsion from the country.[19] Elsewhere politicians operate under more restraints, but they have at their command subtler weapons that they can use to keep effective control. In Pakistan, for example, civil servants enjoy legal protection from dismissal for political reasons, but a noncooperative official may find himself transferred from post to post so frequently that his personal finances are ruined, or he may be retired fifteen years prematurely at "the request of the government." [20] In India, the price of offending or disputing an important politician is likely to be a hitch in one of the country's "Siberian" districts.[21] The threat of such sanctions causes many civil servants to leave the service or flee the country, and those who remain, while outwardly obedient, are often sullen and passively resistant.

The bureaucracy has little capacity to defend itself against intimidation, having lost its former prestige as well as the instruments of power. In its early stages the colonial administration had been an awesome institution in the minds of the native population. Ambitious indi-

19. Peter Worsley, pp. 177–83; J. S. Annan, "Public Servants Driven Out [Ghana]," *Venture,* Vol. 18 (June 1966), pp. 9–11; Victor D. DuBois, "The Rise of an Opposition to Sékou Touré," *American Universities Field Staff Report* (1966), pp. 1–9; Aristide R. Zolberg, *One-Party Government in the Ivory Coast.* Princeton: Princeton University Press, 1964, pp. 303–4; Elliot J. Berg and Jeffrey Butler, "Trade Unions," in *Political Parties and National Integration,* edited by James S. Coleman and Carl G. Rosberg, pp. 369–70.
20. Ralph Braibanti, "Public Bureaucracy and Judiciary in Pakistan," in *Bureaucracy and Political Development,* edited by Joseph La Palombara. Princeton: Princeton University Press, 1963, p. 385.
21. Paul R. Brass, *Factional Politics in an Indian State: The Congress Party in Uttar Pradesh.* Berkeley: University of California Press, 1965, p. 219.

viduals sought to associate themselves with it, and while its precepts of order, efficiency and gradualism may have excited resentment, they also commanded respect. The civil service represented the primary agency of westernization, endowed with superior skills and knowledge, transmitting a way of life both admired and desired. The nationalistic movements preceding independence seriously eroded this image. In the post-colonial period, it is the politicians who define and monopolize the new national symbols of legitimacy: destruction of all vestiges of colonialism, completion of national development as rapidly as possible, exaltation of the people's special mystique. The values to which the civil service could once appeal are no longer applauded.[22] They have, in fact, acquired negative connotations: they are felt to be subversive, cowardly, outmoded, and time-wasting. Thus the bureaucracy can expect little public support or sympathy when politicians pressure it into submission. Its loss of legitimacy in the eyes of the masses is frequently so great that it becomes the national scapegoat, denounced as responsible for whatever complaints the public may have.

One major point of conflict between politicians and bureaucrats is the question of personnel recruitment for administrative posts. In the newly independent nations it is common for prominent political figures to occupy the top positions in the bureaucracy which were formerly reserved for senior expatriate civil servants.[23] Where no official positions were created to replace the colonial Governor and Chief Secretary, as in Nigeria for example, direction of civil service operations has been assumed by the Prime Minister.[24] By virtue of this formal control over staffing, politicians have acquired tremendous latitude in selection of civil service personnel, and the colonial ideal of qualification by merit and experience is usually superseded by other considerations.

Staffing the civil service takes place in an atmosphere of urgency, as the new governments struggle to assert control and expand their services through bureaucracies whose ranks are reduced by the departure of expatriates. The supply of nationals qualified by official criteria is exhausted long before all new or vacant posts are filled. Native civil servants are promoted out of the lower levels, often far above the positions for which they were trained; but vacancies persist. Eventually,

22. Herbert Feith, "Dynamics of Guided Democracy," *op. cit.,* pp. 387–89.
23. Ruth Schachter Morgenthau, *Political Parties in French-Speaking West Africa.* London: Oxford University Press, 1964, p. 355; Peter Worsley, p. 182.
24. I. Nicolson, *"The Machinery of the Federal and Regional Governments," op. cit.,* p. 197.

shortage of trained manpower may leave no alternative but to employ anyone who is even remotely qualified, even men with meager administrative skill and a sketchy knowledge of the expatriate language in which affairs of state are conducted.[25] But, as the charges of a senior administrator in Burma suggest, manpower shortage becomes as well a pretext or justification for political patronage:

> It is quite true that we began with a shortage of trained personnel, but we did have the cadres and orderly expansion was possible. It is not true, as our politicians and many foreigners have said, that we had no experienced people. The politicians were anxious to make everyone believe that we had no people about trained for the jobs, for all they wanted to do was to put their friends and workers on the government rolls. By claiming that there were no trained Burmese they could put their untrained and incompetent people in all the high jobs they wanted.[26]

Whether trained personnel are available or not, political leaders find themselves under overwhelming pressure to fill administrative posts through patronage. Party followers, competent or not, demand some share in the spoils of power as a reward for allegiance. Furthermore, the new government, none too sure of its own stability, operates in a paranoid environment in which distribution of patronage is seen as vital precaution against opposition from disgruntled followers.

The political leaders' distrust and dislike of the civil service moves them to place more politically reliable and congenial men in key positions as insurance against subversion. Criteria of loyalty come to prevail over criteria of technical competence.[27] In some cases, as in Ghana, suspicion is so extreme that existing agencies are bypassed entirely and new organizations created, staffed exclusively with political appointees.[28] More typically, political appointments are made at strategic points in the old system. If the new executives are incompetent, they are forced to rely heavily on their better-trained subordinates. If they are technically qualified for their post, they are still resented by career bureau-

25. Pierre L. van den Berghe, *Race and Ethnicity: Essays in Comparative Sociology.* New York and London: Basic Books, 1970, pp. 244–57.
26. Lucian W. Pye, *Politics, Personality and Nation Building,* pp. 214–15.
27. Ruth Schachter Morgenthau, *op. cit.,* p. 335; Herbert Feith, "Dynamics of Guided Democracy," *op. cit.,* p. 389.
28. Ruth First, *Power in Africa.* New York: Pantheon Books-Random House, 1970, pp. 363–407.

crats for disrupting the seniority system.[29] The consequent hostility and lack of cooperation from civil servants only convinces political leaders that more politically appointed watchdogs are needed.[30]

Patronage can also be a response to familial pressures on politicians. Men who acquire wealth or power are expected to take responsibility for their less fortunate relatives. A politician's natural tendency to trust the loyalty of family members is thus not the only motivation for nepotism. In Africa particularly, if a successful politician does not use the administrative jobs at his disposal to provide for his relatives, they may eat him out of house and home.[31]

Some problems resulting from widespread use of patronage are obvious. The previously mentioned animosity and mutual disrespect between politicians and career civil servants are intensified. Placing inexperienced men in important administrative positions further exacerbates the government's operational difficulties. The party in power may even diminish its own strength by overburdening party members with administrative chores.[32] But the indirect consequences of patronage are even more damaging. As long as the civil service was run and largely staffed by expatriates, it was able to remain aloof from the ascriptive forces rampant in the society. This artificial neutrality, imposed and sustained from the outside, grows precarious when the system leaves expatriate control. Once civil service recruitment and promotion become openly based on non-technical criteria, that is, party loyalty, the bureaucracy's thin moral shield crumbles and ascriptive pressures begin to operate. A variety of particularisms filter into the administrative machinery—familial responsibilities, friendship, caste or tribal loyalties, regionalism, religion, and the like. In outlying districts, traditional forms of particularism may entirely obscure political as well as technical criteria, simply translating age-old frictions into a new setting of intense occupational and status competition.[33] The factions that form along these traditional

29. Henry L. Bretton, *op. cit.,* pp. 89–90.
30. Hugh Tinker, *The Foundations of Local Self-Government in India, Pakistan, and Burma.* London: University of London, Athlone Press, 1954, p. 155.
31. René Dumont, *False Start in Africa.* New York: Praeger, 1969, pp. 84–85.
32. James S. Coleman and Carl G. Rosberg, "Conclusions," in *Political Parties and National Integration,* edited by Coleman and Rosberg, p. 674.
33. I. Nicolson, "The Machinery of the Federal and Regional Governments," *op. cit.,* pp. 193–94; Henry L. Bretton, *op. cit.,* pp. 89, 150; Ralph Braibanti, "Public Bureaucracy," *op. cit.,* pp. 388–90, 394; Martin Kilson, "Sierra Leone," in *Political Parties and National Integration,* edited by James S. Coleman and Carl G. Rosberg, pp. 115–16.

lines differ from the informal clique structure usually found in modern bureaucracies. Instead of depending on factors within the organization, such as association with a particular program or office group, these factions are based on external loyalties to groups outside the bureaucracy. Bureaucratic goals are secondary to enhancing the position of the external group, and factional rivalries within the civil service take on some of the vehemence and vindictiveness of family feuds or tribal warfare. Whatever an individual's objective qualifications may be, he cannot stand alone in this ascription-saturated environment. For security as well as personal advancement, he must affiliate with some larger group within the administration. Appointment of apolitical, unattached technicians becomes increasingly threatening to this system.[34] The once-idealized slogans of qualification by merit and experience evoke suspicion, hostility, and sheer disbelief. In Pakistan, for example, the distinction between personal and impersonal modes of conduct finally broke down to such an extent that "every action of promotion, discipline, or severance, however justly based on impersonal grounds, could be deemed capricious and based on clique animosities. . . . Government employees were incapable of construing any bureaucratic personnel decision as being devoid of selfish, factious considerations." [35] Ironically, the flood of factionalism ushered in by political appointments in the civil service tends to weaken the party in power as well as the bureaucracy, since it frustrates political leaders' attempts to replace regionalism and tribalism with a transcendent loyalty to the state.

Whether the lower levels of colonial bureaucracy ever processed petty complaints and requests or dispensed minor favors with complete impartiality is questionable. Certainly with the coming of independence, ease in obtaining licenses, exemptions and the like has come to depend heavily on one's personal connections. Favoritism at lower administrative levels creates in the polity a cynical attitude toward both politicians and bureaucrats and causes ill feeling in those who lack influence. But in the deals and petty power struggles that take place, politicians and civil servants probably cooperate as much as they conflict.

At the higher levels of administration, however, pressures for special privilege generate serious strains between civil servants and politicians. The heads of the various executive agencies, as political appointees,

34. William J. Foltz, "Senegal," in *Political Parties and National Integration,* edited by James S. Coleman and Carl G. Rosberg, p. 44.
35. Ralph Braibanti, "Public Bureaucracy and Judiciary in Pakistan," pp. 388–89.

usually are committed either to some local or occupational "constituency" of their own or to other politicians who have clients to satisfy. Popular expectations of rapid development are high and, since the usual government appeals to sacrifice and selfless nationalism are rarely interpreted by the masses to apply to anyone in particular, politicians are under tremendous pressure to deliver special benefits to those they represent. Therefore ministers tend to push the specific programs of their own agencies in the specific regions to which they feel responsible, in utter disregard of any over-all development plan formulated on the basis of technical considerations.[36] If a planning agency exists, it finds itself swamped with competing politically inspired demands for special dispensations to particular agencies and areas.

Pressure on ministers to grant requests for special privilege also disrupt administration within agencies. For political figures who berate the aloofness of previous colonial governments and whose legitimacy rests on popular support, accessibility is vitally important. For reasons of ideology as well as political expediency, they must make themselves available to favor-seeking clients even at the cost of neglecting other duties. Unfortunately, a minister who becomes deeply involved in relationships with his clientele finds his days taken up with interviews and conferences, leaving little or no time for consulting and hearing reports from the officials in his agency. Unable to take action on their own authority, the minister's staff can only accumulate half-processed files and wait until their busy superior has time to make the necessary decisions and authorizations. The delay may block the operations of related agencies so that officials spend considerable working time explaining the situation to other officials. When clients' complaints reach the minister about his unkept promises of months ago, he places the blame on the civil servants, who have no means of defending themselves publicly when accused of inefficiency or deliberate sabotage.

The minister with an open door to all clients seldom has the time or opportunity to get adequate briefing from his staff prior to interviews. As an alternative, he requires staff members to leave their planned work and attend the interviews to provide any information he may need. As this pattern operates in Jamaica, the result is that

> the administrative work of the agency becomes disorganized and
> senior staff frantically seeking to overtake a backlog of work have

36. E. N. Omaboe, "The Process of Planning," in *A Study of Contemporary Ghana,* edited by Walter Birmingham, *et al.,* p. 460.

little time to supervise and direct the basic program, review what has been done, indulge in research, consult staff and other agencies, plan improvements and raise vital issues of policy that need to be discussed with the minister.[37]

In this situation, the processing of promises and commitments the minister has made previously is delayed. He is put in the position of failing his clients and becomes more harried than ever trying to deal with their grievances for the second time. In his view and that of the client, the fault lies with a stubborn and incompetent staff who frustrate the minister's attempts to serve his people. From the staff's point of view, they are being unjustly maligned by a political hack who makes a shambles of rational administration by trying to satisfy every request that reaches him.

PLANNING PROBLEMS, AND COMMUNICATION GAPS

The governments of most Third World nations have created some kind of development planning agency, if only to satisfy international lending organizations from which they hope to secure funds, and internal demands for social security.[38] The civil servants who usually draw up such plans, being trained in the cautious, deliberate procedures of custodial administration, are convinced of the necessity for rational and efficient allocation of resources, priority ranking of development programs, and regional balance. They consider the optimum government development program to be a gradual and complex phasing-in process in which some projects must be postponed and initial yields may be small.

Political leaders, on the other hand, are impatient with a gradualistic approach to development. They are interested in making a start on all fronts as rapidly as possible now that the nation is freed from colonial restraints, in order to catch up with the developed nations of the world. Even when good technical reasons exist for postponing some projects rather than choosing among poor alternatives, there is a strong impulse to make the leap.[39] The slower tempo recommended by bureaucrats is

37. B. L. St. John Hamilton, *op. cit.*, 195–96.
38. Benjamin Higgins, "Planning Allocations for Social Development," *International Social Development Review.* New York: United Nations, 1971, pp. 47–55.
39. Roberto Campos, "The Meaning of Planning in a Democratic Society," in *The Ideologies of the Developing Nations,* ed. by Paul E. Sigmund. New York: Frederick A. Praeger, 1967, pp. 422–24.

considered further proof of their foot-dragging conservatism and colonial mentality.

When a development plan is drawn up, civil servants and politicians anticipate conflict. The civil servants know their allocation and priority schemes will be disrupted by what they regard as the politicians' lack of discipline and knowledge. The politicians, suspicious of the bureaucracy's commitment to development goals, expect an unimaginative, slow-paced program that will require considerable amendment and supplementation to make it effective. The result is likely to be a general set of long-term guidelines, vague at critical points, that is largely ignored in the process of implementation. Besieged by clients clamoring for special and immediate attention, ministers make constant departures from the plan, add on special projects that do not conform to its principles, and jealously guard the planning prerogatives of their own agencies from any central planning organization that may exist. Having little time to consult technical advisers and little confidence in the information they would receive if they did, ministers initiate many projects that later turn out to be technical and economic nightmares. When such ill-advised ventures are eventually abandoned or shelved, much effort and money have been wasted and antagonisms between the programs' political sponsors and the civil servants charged with implementation is deeper than ever. The politicians and the bureaucrats blame each other for the failure to achieve the goals of national development, and there is equal bitterness on both sides.[40]

CORRUPTION

Corruption, while of course neither new nor unique to the newly independent nations, thrives in these countries with particular vigor. Graft and bribery, diversion of supplies and outright thievery are generally acknowledged to be endemic, implicating businessmen, politicians, and bureaucrats alike.[41] Speaking of the new African states, the spokesman

40. René Dumont, *False Start in Africa.* New York: Praeger, 1969, pp. 242–47; Douglas Rimmer, "The Crisis in the Ghana Economy," *The Journal of Modern African Studies,* Vol. 4 (1966), pp. 26–27; Victor D. DuBois, "The Decline of the Guinean Revolution," *American Universities Field Staff Report* (1965), pp. 1–8; Henry L. Bretton, *op. cit.,* pp. 90–94.
41. Ronald Wraith and Edgar Simpkins, *Corruption in Developing Countries.* New York: W. W. Norton & Co., 1963; Colin Leys, "What Is the Problem About

for a European business firm recently remarked that his company normally figures in a "standard" 5 per cent bribery allowance in its African operations.[42] There is no question that such illegal surcharges get essential tasks done, that would otherwise languish. But this widespread corruption in government administration generates frictions between politicians and the civil service.

In addition to the general ill-will arising from the conviction of both politicians and bureaucrats that each is more venal than the other, probably the most common kind of conflict over corruption concerns work distribution. When the illegal activities of a political appointee occupying a key post take up an inordinate amount of his time, administrative work in his agency may be obstructed and many of his duties must be assumed by his staff, who are usually already heavily burdened with their own work.[43] It is also possible that politicians may find their administrative work blocked or increased by absenteeism of staff members who are busy attending to illicit projects of their own. But since the politician has more overt means of retaliation while the civil servant does not, the reverse situation is more usual.

Involvement of both bureaucrats and politicians in illegal activities may in theory give both groups an interest in keeping government corruption from emerging as a public issue. This gentlemen's agreement breaks down, however, in struggles between politicians. Then charges of corruption are leveled against particular agencies or local offices, not necessarily with any aim of correcting malpractices, but as a pretext to injure the standing of the political figures associated with the agency in question. Since political strife is no less fierce between individuals and factions within a party than between parties themselves, this pattern is repeated endlessly even in one-party states. Where elections are held, charges of corruption are common as a campaign issue when no real policy differences divide opposition parties from the party in power.[44] These politically inspired accusations bear no necessary relation to the

Corruption?" *The Journal of Modern African Studies,* Vol. 3 (1965), pp. 215–30; Henry L. Bretton, *op. cit.,* pp. 79, 169–72; Herbert Feith, "Dynamics of Guided Democracy," *op. cit.,* pp. 389–95; Hans Rosenberg, "The New Bureaucratic Elite," in *Political Sociology,* ed. by S. N. Eisenstadt, New York: Basic Books, 1971, pp. 301–303.

42. Lloyd Garrison, "Africa's Top Nationalist—Or Africa's Prima Donna? [Sékou Touré]," *The New York Times Magazine* (Jan. 1, 1967), p. 27.

43. Henry L. Bretton, *op. cit.,* p. 89.

44. Paul R. Brass, *Factional Politics in an Indian State.* Berkeley: University of California Press, 1965, p. 223.

actual presence of corruption. However, since infractions usually do exist and the bureaucracy is generally unpopular, the public readily accepts the charges as true. Even if civil servants involved have been models of efficiency and honesty, they stand to be discredited along with the politicians who are the real target.

In the transition from colonial to native political rule, relations between politicians and bureaucrats pass through a highly fluid stage during which no agreed-upon normative patterns exist to guide interaction. In a structural sense, the administrative system is anomic. The political-civil service tensions and conflicts we have discussed produce varying degrees of non-cooperation, sabotage and reprisal until eventually some form of modus vivendi emerges.

Discredited in the eyes of the public and lacking formal power, the civil service is in a weak position to defend its inherited ideals of political and ethnic neutrality, technical competence and efficiency, especially since they assume a manpower supply and level of training no longer available. Given the propensity of politicians in power to place highest value on loyalty and nationalistic zeal, it is inevitable that the conflict should be resolved in complete politicalization of the bureaucracy. Through political appointments and pressures, the civil service fragments into rival factions. Political concerns come to dominate its operations as it abandons its role of an instrument for policy implementation and becomes actively engaged in policy formation and obstruction.

Transformation of the civil service into a political forum makes it unable to resist other forms of particularism. It becomes permeated with family, ethnic, regional, and religious divisions, aggravated by the ever-present conflict between generations. The high salary differentials and sharp status distinctions which under colonialism divided expatriates and Europeanized native civil servants from the lower ranks occupied by vernacular-speaking natives are easily adapted to this factional strife. High bureaucratic positions become the rewards of well-chosen loyalties and political skills. Even bureaucratic pathologies like corruption are transformed from administrative-legal problems to weapons of national or intra-bureaucracy politics.

The consequence of the bureaucracy's politicalization is a breakdown of internal communication. In the colonial civil service, at least within the upper levels, individuals had been able to transmit information, questions and recommendations through both formal and informal channels without fear of jeopardizing their own career interests. The general emphasis on objective performance and commitment to administrative goals, as well as the security of seniority standing, allowed communication of bureaucratic affairs to exist on a relatively impersonal process. When particularism erodes this impersonality, however, communication becomes hazardous: in transmitting information civil servants risk insulting or embarrassing superiors or persons who may someday become superiors, damaging their own standing, and giving away advantages. Thus while the communications system may survive unchanged in a formal sense in the politicalized bureaucracy, the pre-existing informal communication network based on wide-spread trust can no longer operate. A new informal system grows up along factional lines, in which information circulates freely only within each clique. Since advancing clique interests takes precedence over administrative goals, information will be denied to rival cliques.

Uneven communication in a bureaucratic system designed for free information flow seriously impairs its ability to function effectively. The prevailing suspicion and distrust disinclines those on lower levels to take initiative and responsibility, particularly in new or ambiguous situations, for fear any mistakes will weaken their position. They tend to confine themselves instead to a ritualistic following of rules. Their preoccupation with personal or factional interests precludes their making any serious identification with policy goals, and so civil servants feel no particular commitment to their work. When they must submit information to superiors, they may doctor it into palatable inaccuracy first.[45] On the higher levels, distrust of subordinates makes officials hesitant to delegate responsibility. Ministers feel compelled to work out the programing of policy decisions in minute detail and supervise projects at every stage of implementation, assuming a mountain of functions that in a modern bureaucracy would be discharged by lower level administrators.[46] Constantly seeking assistants they can rely on with more assurance, they transfer personnel so frequently that both work and salary payments fall behind. In such an atmosphere, the ordinary routine of custodial administration naturally suffers but may still be carried on. Reform of the system and effective administration of innovative programs, however, become nearly impossible.

The post-colonial conflict between politicians and bureaucrats herein

45. David E. Apter, *The Politics of Modernization.* Chicago: The University of Chicago Press, 1965, p. 385.
46. A. L. Adu, *op. cit.,* pp. 231–32; B. L. St. John Hamilton, *op. cit.,* p. 197.

may be a borrower of funds, but it is a distributor of arms to other Middle Eastern nations. As long as the First World and Second World were organized against each other for the purpose of making nuclear exchanges, the Third World could not be considered militarily significant. With the widespread acceptance of war as a game, the rise of insurgency and counter-insurgency, and the nuclear standoff created by First and Second World competition, the conventional military hardware of the Third World has come to function as a more significant variable in international geopolitics than it did a decade ago.

When there is a balance of nuclear terror between the First and Second Worlds, relatively powerless Third World countries can become influential. However, one must be cautious on this point, since in fact such a perfect balance rarely exists. What does exist is a modernized version of the sphere-of-influence doctrine that still leaves the Third World in a relatively powerless position, at least with respect to exercising a role in foreign affairs. For example, when the Soviet Union decided to crack down on the revisionist regime of Czechoslovakia in the late 1960's, or when the United States decided to break the back of radicalism in the Dominican Republic a few years earlier, they were able to do so with impunity in part as a consequence of the unwritten sphere-of-influence doctrine which was established between the United States and the Soviet Union during the 'sixties. Conversely, the prestige of the Third World, at least as a homogeneous military unit, has been seriously undercut, for example, by the failure of the Organization of African Unity (OAU) to be able to resolve civil war in Nigeria, white rule in Rhodesia, or the continued colonial domination of Mozambique. The same situation obtains with other regional Third World clusters, such as the Organization of American States (OAS), which was virtually powerless during the Dominican crisis to affect United States foreign policy. In other words, when there is in fact a delicate equilibrium between the First and Second Worlds, then the military of the Third World can be important. Otherwise, it tends to be far less significant than in fact it would like to become.[26]

The character of the military of the Third World is often shaped, symbolically at least, by the military power or powers which trained or occupied the territory during the colonial period. Thus in Indonesia one finds a Japanese and Dutch combination; in Egypt there are English and

26. See Ernst B. Haas, *Tangle of Hopes: American Commitments and World Order.* Englewood Cliffs, N.J.: Prentice-Hall, 1969, pp. 151–58.

described is not, of course, the only process that can lead to a fragmented, immobilized civil service. It has been suggested, for instance, that continuous political instability produces the same pattern in some Latin American countries.[47] The national bureaucracies of Thailand and Iran, both countries that were never under colonial rule, suffer from similar distrust and limited communication.[48] The convergence suggests that once such a pattern becomes institutionalized, it persists tenaciously —a disturbing implication for those who look to the governments of underdeveloped countries for leadership in national development.

To appreciate how much the strain between bureaucracy and polity is not simply a function of simple "newness" of a nation, the case of Israel is instructive. Given three special features it exhibits—the social solidarity imposed from a common core of religious values, a political leadership structure that derived from European centers exhibiting high social and political mobilization, and the relatively small scale of the nation—one can see that the competition of bureaucrat and politician is neither inevitable in or endemic to the Third World.[49] Perhaps an additional factor which sharply curbs such competitive ambitions and goals is a feeling of external threat. Nations like Israel, Cuba, and China live in constant fear of being surrounded by hostile forces—and whether such perceptions are accurate or otherwise, they do compel the bureaucracy and the polity to dampen their criticism of each other while battling against the common foe. In extreme cases, such as Cuba, this may actually take the form of a demand for anti-bureaucratic work styles among all levels of the population, but what apparently happens in operational terms is not the destruction of the bureaucracy but a redefinition of its structure in task terms rather than role terms. And it might

---

47. Frank Tannenbaum, "The Influence of Social Conditions," in *Public Administration in Developing Countries,* edited by Martin Kriesberg. Washington, D.C.: The Brookings Institution, 1965, pp. 33–42. On the subject of public administration in Latin America, see also Herbert Emmerich, "Administrative Roadblocks to Co-ordinated Development," in *Social Aspects of Economic Development in Latin America,* edited by Egbert De Vries and Jose Medina Echavarria. Tournai, Belgium: United Nations, 1963, pp. 345–60 and Victor L. Urquidi, *The Challenge of Development in Latin America.* New York: Frederick A. Praeger, 1964, pp. 94–97.

48. William J. Siffin, "The System in Operation: Management in the Civil Service," *International Review of Administrative Sciences,* Vol. 26 (1960), p. 262; Leonard Binder, *Iran: Political Development in a Changing Society.* Berkeley: University of California Press, 1962, pp. 138–39.

49. Leonard J. Fein, *Israel: Politics and People.* Boston: Little, Brown and Co., 1968, pp. 243–52.

be that the solution of this dilemma between bureaucrat and politician may depend on how the bureaucrats learn to handle the rhetoric and realities of the new nationalism and how quickly the politicians acquire the expertise necessary to run a nation.

It is probable that the strain between bureaucrat and politician is far higher in the major urban capitals than in the rural regions or the rural capital districts. In the latter the interaction between administrative officials and the ordinary people is often far too intimate to permit bribery and corruption to be conducted on enlarged scales. Second, those working in rural regions often seem to be motivated by stronger national feelings than the cosmopolitans, and hence probably are less concerned with personal aggrandizement. Third, the opportunities themselves are far more restricted in rural areas for large-scale corruption or for political pay-offs. And, finally, since "politics" itself is so largely a game played by the urban industrial sector to the exclusion of the rural mass or the tribal clan, one would expect less strain to take place in small village life than in large cosmopolitan activities. This is not to say that the sort of strains herein described are absent in rural areas, only that the degree of such strain seems greater at the center than at the periphery of political involvement with bureaucratic expertise.

15

Technologists, Sociologists, and Development

With remarkable consistency, early pioneers of sociology believed that engineering, as a practical art and an applied technique, offered the best supportive model of any meaningful science of society. It would seem that the situation has now been reversed. It is the engineering leaders who are beginning to look to sociology as a chief scientific source for resolving technological dilemmas. This is certainly the burden of the generous remarks recently made by Elting Morison: "The most important kind of invention for the future lies not, as in the nineteenth century, within the mechanical realm, but in another area: the way we are to deal with all the new conditions produced by the new machines and ideas." Morison concludes by making an appeal for social innovation that will permit adaptation to social change. "We should seek to become an adaptive society, detached from allegiances to specific products and procedures which will change; committed instead to engagement in the process of living, that is, in the present age, to the process of rapid change itself." [1]

To speak of interdisciplinary relations in international development is redundant because development, as a distinct field of study, is itself an amalgam of many professional and technical specialties. I will therefore try to address myself to the issue of engineering and the building of nations and will restrict my approach to the problems of technology and the social order as encountered in the developmental enterprise.

The Third World faces a range of professional technologies no less

1. Elting E. Morison, *Men, Machines, and Modern Times.* Cambridge, Mass.: M.I.T. Press, 1966, pp. 218–19.

than a range of ideologies for development. The conventional engineering perception is that changes in the technical order are more urgently needed and simpler to act upon than long-range social or political goals. The conventional sociological perception is that changes in the social order precede changes in technology in significance (if not customarily in time). It is my own belief that the assignment of causal priorities is intellectually fruitless and professionally resented.

In the decision-making process, engineers and sociologists provide different qualitative inputs. Engineers provide expertise with a tendency toward non-ideological, non-political solutions to social problems. Sociologists tend toward political solutions. The latter are usually as wary of technological bureaucracies sponsored by governments as engineers are of charismatic or patriarchal domination by governments. The problem can be stated as follows: the engineering impulse is toward rational and systematic solutions and toward impatience with the norms and values of non-rational and "ideological" class, radical, and ethnic interests. Like most professional groupings, engineers have been unwilling to perceive themselves as yet another special interest group whose claims to political preeminence are neither more nor less valid than the claims of other, albeit non-scientific, pressure groups.

The most vital issue immediately affecting engineers and sociologists alike is their joint commitment to application, to framing a language and a set of techniques widely understandable because they rest on results. Thus far, the scientific language of system design and manpower allocation has not been integrated with a political language of social revolution and decision-making. This is not to fault engineers. Indeed, social scientists have reinforced methodological divisions by assuming stylistic differences between systems engineering and applied sociology to be permanent simply because they are operational. Yet the emergence of a computer technology, widely adapted to social-science uses, and the corresponding emphasis on measurable indicators of health, welfare, fertility, crime, and so forth, clearly link engineers and sociologists so as to make new break-throughs highly probable.

Any dialogue between sociologists and engineers requires a recognition of the enormous contributions made by modern technology to social science: the engineering emphasis on the special problems involved in application and directed research, which has created a whole new field of social planning; the engineering emphasis on posing problems in soluble formulations, rejecting apocalyptic readings of events as a way of bringing about a solution to problems of the world; the engineering emphasis on design and organization—particularly with respect to the processes of urbanization and industrialization—which has led sociologists to place greater emphasis on anticipating problems of social reorganization by conceiving the larger society as appropriate for the input of system changes.

Nonetheless, engineers have exhibited little reciprocal interest in sociology, and, more specifically, in how the sociology of development might be directly relevant to overseas engineering activities. Pleas are frequently heard for greater understanding between those in engineering and those in the "humanistic-social studies." These pious wishes often take the form of urging greater sophistication upon engineers, deeper artistic cultivation, and a wider appreciation of political and historical institutions.[2]

Unfortunately, the very reference to a link between the humanities and the social sciences is itself an indicator of parochialism. Engineers still think of social studies without understanding social sciences. Further they tend to view social-science inputs as shadow rather than substance. For example, one important writer sees social problems strictly in terms that can be treated by technicians, such problems as environmental pollution, transportation, water resources, medical care, and regional development. No mention is made of problems of revolution, anomie, generational conflict, racial struggle, and the like.[3] The view of the scientist remains insular. It is clear that as long as commonplace pieties are used to describe the social sciences, the actual contributions of social science to engineering—with specific reference to developmental analysis —will remain unexamined.

There is still a strong tendency on the part of engineers to celebrate their intellectual self-sufficiency. They speak of a doubling of knowledge in the twentieth century. They refer with pride to the fact that a history of technology covering two earlier centuries may take one volume, while the same sort of historical survey of the twentieth century alone may be multi-volumed. They even manage to get some scholars to promote the heady wine of "one hundred technical innovations likely in the next

2. For a well-intentioned but tragically typical example, see George A. Hawkins, "Humanistic-Social Studies for Engineering Students in the 1980's," *Engineering Education*, Vol. 57, No. 5 (January 1967), pp. 369–71.
3. See Harvey Brooks, "Science and the Allocation of Resources," *The Government of Science*. Cambridge, Mass.: M.I.T. Press, 1968, pp. 38–39.

thirty-three years," [4] although the more judicious engineers speak in sober and cautious terms, pointing to the relative slow-down in new inventions in recent years, and the underutilization of present plant capacities.[5] What in fact has taken place, and what obscures the dilemmas, is the sophisticated refinement of established inventions. In the first twenty-five years of the twentieth century the following major inventions were realized and widely applied: plastics, automobiles, radios, and commercial aircraft. For the second twenty-five years, one may list electronic computers, television, video tape, nuclear explosives, and antibiotics. There is little in the third quarter of the century to match this output— except in the area of military technology, because of which the space industries have mushroomed. It is also possible that the lasers and masers will find multiple uses in future research. But thus far, both spacecraft and laser beams seem more useful to James Bond films than to mankind. If there has been such a slow-down as a sober reckoning would in fact indicate, and if we are getting refinement in place of innovation, then it is important that the social dimension of the problem of innovation be raised and celebrationist illusions removed.

Admittedly, my assertion that the rate of significant invention is decreasing rather than increasing moves counter to the view of those positing a twenty-first-century environment of plenitude and beatitude. But it would seem that the greatest growth is in miniaturization rather than in the discovery process. Transistor radios and televisions remain essentially what they were earlier. Jet aircraft remain airplanes. Cassettes are but a more polished form of tape-recording device. It is also interesting that areas of major breakthrough, such as artificial insemination and space travel, are direct consequences of military programing and needs. Not that the character of invention should be downgraded on this account. Rather, the real issue is that prosaic human wants have been largely displaced by dramatic extraterrestrial explorations and exotic biological investigations. The next question is, should this shift have taken place?

The most impressive fact is that the costs of new inventions and applications are increasing at so great a speed that they cannot be absorbed

4. Herman Kahn and Anthony J. Wiener, "The Next Thirty-Three Years: A Framework for Speculation," *Daedalus,* Vol. 96, No. 3 (Summer 1967), pp. 711–16. In introducing this issue of *Daedalus,* Daniel Bell cautions against such uncontrolled optimism.

5. See L. N. Naggle, "Scylla and Charybdis of Engineering Education," *Proceedings of the 1961 Syracuse University International Conference on Electrical Engineering Education.* Syracuse, N.Y.: Syracuse University Press, 1961, pp. 52–53.

at plant levels. More often than not, they require collective efforts which far transcend the capacities of any single plant, or sometimes even of an industry. No less significantly, the sorts of inventions now being brought out cannot be counted on to produce rapid returns on financial investments. Hence, private firms are reluctant to invest in large-scale research, preferring refinements of presently marketed items. Public sector enterprises, for their part, are hamstrung by lack of funds, or by constant pressures within certain societies against extended socialization. Because of this, technological sloth, at least in the area of commodities, must be viewed as structural and long-range in character, rather than representing a temporary lag in the over-all economy.

Instead of coming to terms with such essential socio-structural issues, the new utopians—those engineers turned social analysts—develop an exaggerated burst of futuristic appraisals. The shift in technocratic orientations is away from the social role of scientific specialists toward a belief that political or administrative responsibility may become a relatively minor prize in the environment game. In a new view of life within the town (interestingly a nostalgic *Gemeinschaft* view of social organization has gone along with utopianism), the task of the human engineering principle will be "the matching of the constructed environment to the man rather than vice versa." [6] Behind this ostensible humanism are Platonist echoes of the military and intellectual roads to power. Bluntly, we are never told how those doing the "matching" will be chosen. In keeping with this utopian republic is a downgrading of enterpreneurial or administrative skill because the computer makes it commonplace. Finally, in the brave new engineering complex, leadership will be done away with, since in a self-sufficient, self-confident, highly educated democracy all one wants are chairmen.

One is sorely tempted to inquire whether the *Chairman* of the People's Republic of China is really such an improvement over the *Premier* of the Soviet Union or the *President* of the United States. Just as 2000 years of political theory are eliminated at the stroke of a pen, or rather at the punch of a card, so too is sociology to be dissolved. Crimes such as theft will be largely obsolete, because with computerized accounting they will be largely impracticable and immediately discoverable. But for other sorts of crime, the most effective deterrent will be the way of dealing with

6. For a veritable catalogue of utopian sentiments cast in terms of the new technology, see Nigel Calder, *Eden Was No Garden: An Inquiry into the Environment of Man.* New York: Holt, Rinehart & Winston, 1967, esp. pp. 209–26.

it: the force of social disapproval in a closely knit community. The painfully crude resolution of social problems in abstract theory is made precisely because of the sophistication of modern technology. The magic of the machine grows in mythic proportions as the conventional legitimation processes of established societies seem to fail.

What is so often involved in the engineering approach is a consensualist vision of social life, a discounting of conflict models of behavior. This is directly traceable to the ideology of efficiency—and of course, consensus is a more efficient style of social action than a conflict model, or one which recognizes the existence of sociological interests which are divergent at their sources, and hence cannot be removed by computerized accounting systems or abstract, community-imposed standards of consensus. If the engineering vision of society is to be taken seriously, it must first sort out the vision from the myth, its limits from claims to universalism. For, as Boguslaw says in speaking of the "utopian renaissance" heralded by modern technology, what is involved are "fundamental changes not only in the value structure of Western people, but redistributions of power concentrations made possible through the use of system control mechanisms. The resurgence of intellectual and political orientations such as 'conservative' and 'liberal' must be re-examined in the light of these newly emerging, altered power relationships." [7] It would be high irony if the "end of ideology" in the West ushered in only a series of false utopianisms.

There are several specific features of engineering education that provide clues to sources of ideological negativism toward the social sciences, not only in the sense that such world-famed physicists as Dirac and Einstein started as engineers, but in the sense that engineering problems often stimulated scientific theory, while engineering theory in turn often became the basis for confirming scientific theory. But engineering has had a direct link to the world of industry. It grew to importance in relation to capitalist entrepreneurship and had to be linked to large-scale industrial undertakings with highly refined machine tools in order to realize its potential as an applied discipline.[8]

This double tradition may help to account for both its technocratic em-

---

7. See Robert Boguslaw, *The New Utopians: A Study of System Design and Social Change*. Englewood Cliffs, N.J.: Prentice-Hall, 1965, esp. pp. 29–46, 203.
8. For some preliminary, but unusual, remarks on the education of engineers, see J. D. Bernal, *The Social Function of Science*. London: Routledge & Kegan Paul, 1939, pp. 39, 366–67.

phasis and the largely conservative biases manifested in public utterances by engineers. Without the existence of any attitude surveys to draw upon for verification, it is my contention that engineers tend to represent a conservatizing force in business, political, and university life. They confront the problem of class and commitment to work as representatives of management, and the problem of liberty as representatives of order.

The insularity of an engineering approach to social life, uninformed as it is by the social sciences, results in engineers becoming prey to all kinds of social panaceas and pseudo-political movements. The most highly developed industrial nations in the world have also been the beneficiaries of the crudest forms of technocratic ideology. Whether in their overtly totalitarian forms, or in their subtle bureaucratic-managerial forms, engineering perspectives have often turned into technocratic movements, representing a distinct attempt to bypass rather than to cope with a scientific study of society.[9]

In the past, sociologists and engineers have been most at home with one another when they have attempted to carve out a future that would provide both order and progress, to use Comte's motto. Change was to be admitted (applied scientists could hardly do otherwise), yet the demons of change, given their uncontrollable aspects, were to be curbed by scientific prescription. But from Saint-Simon to Skinner these prescriptions became well-defined life styles, as intolerant of social deviance as they were of possible alternative modes of explanation. Futuristic guesses spilled over into authoritarian rules: all individual wills were to be united into one will, and all human efforts to be aimed at achieving one social goal. In this impulse toward system and order, social science strangely dropped out of the bottom. There was no room for subtlety because there was no need for differentiation. That engineers fell heir to such a legacy was more a matter of default than necessity. The social scientists could no longer live within such a "system," whereas engineering felt justified in its search for the simple.[10]

Technocratic movements seem to have several characteristics in common.[11] First, they are crisis-oriented, usually arising in conjunction with

9. This is well appreciated by Jean Meynaud. See his *Technocracy*. New York: The Free Press, 1969, esp. pp. 145–89.
10. For further discussions of the historical aspects of technological utopianism, see Frank E. Manuel, "Toward a Psychological History of Utopias," *Daedalus*, Vol. 94, No. 2 (Spring 1965), pp. 293–322; and J. L. Talmon, *Political Messianism: The Romantic Phase*. London: Secker & Warburg, 1960.
11. For an extensive discussion, see Henry Elsner, Jr., *The Technocrats: Prophets of Automation*. Syracuse, N.Y.: Syracuse University Press, 1967, pp. 186–219.

a breakdown in the economic stability or social structure of the nation and claiming to offer a quick and easy solution. Second, they take the simplistic form by advocating the elimination of political obstacles by non-political means. In so doing, technocracy, far from encouraging humane criticisms of the social order, tends to mechanize problems and perceive solutions as arising in a context of what *can* be solved rather than what *must* be solved. Third, as a result of anti-sociological biases, technocratic movements, far from leading to an "end of ideology," foster utopian blueprints that reveal few realistic social ideas on how the good society is to be reached. Fourth, if technocratic approaches begin in crisis, they often terminate in fear—in the belief that only the engineering of the soul can stave off the march of the masses to the seizure of power through violence. In this way the manifest anti-*politique* of technocracy often disguises a latent reinforcement of the social order as it is presently constituted.

Nonetheless, the technocratic movement, which took on the proportions of a scientific messianism in the industrial crisis that gripped the United States between 1929 and 1939, failed to excite or enlist the masses. There is, indeed, some question as to how the engineering profession responded to such urgings. But the old engineering spirit sought command in an era when the gap between the rich and the poor of America seemed ever-widening. It was one of many social responses to the continuing class strains within the American nation. Now, a generation later, we are faced with a parallel situation and a similar set of responses, except that, at present, the perceived gaps between wealth and poverty are not only national but international.

Although Technocracy, Inc., has yielded to Automation, Inc., which in turn has given birth to Techno-Democracy, the scale of social response has now become world wide rather than national; the same kinds of problems at the theoretical levels which the previous generation coped with now manifest themselves with painful clarity. The "Year 2000" movement and the "Futuribles" method have certainly appreciated some of the dilemmas involved in the transformation of engineering into a social movement.[12] But the response of "cyberculturalists" and "futurists" has been to intensify the elitist character of present-day automation approaches. This stands in marked contrast to the generally liberal and mass character of the earlier Technocracy movement. If this ideological shift has ap-

12. Bertrand de Jouvenel, *The Art of Conjecture.* New York: Basic Books, 1967, esp. pp. 101–42.

peared to overcome the naïve approach of the previous engineers of the soul, it has been at the expense of a critical attitude toward the political establishment as such. The Automationists seem far readier to become servants of power than the Technocrats, who held firm to a belief in becoming its masters.[13]

To describe technical innovations is simpler than to talk of social or political innovations. It is assuredly more comfortable for engineers to be conservative with respect to the social order than to be conservative with respect to the physical environment. In their search for technical innovation, engineers for the most part are truly radical; in their trained incapacity to explain the consequences of such innovation they are truly conservative.

It is clear that a laser beam represents a definite input not previously available, whereas descriptions of social innovations usually involve new mixes of old elements. The very novelty of a social innovation is in doubt. In the same vein, it is probably simpler to agree on what constitutes a technical innovation than on what constitutes a social innovation. Engineering as an ideology can be viewed as an extension of this duality. The Technocrats tend to imagine that consensus on the nature of a technical innovation necessarily entails consensus on the uses of such an innovation.[14] The rub, of course, is precisely here: the problem of uses—of operationalizing technical innovations—is rarely, if ever, dictated by the innovation itself. The discovery can open up new possibilities and even unshackle the limits of past invention. The utilization of the invention, however, remains eminently a social and political undertaking.

This may lead not only to a schism between engineers and social scientists but to further impatience with the behavior of the public. The expertise required to manufacture sophisticated goods sets a norm for public behavior and is seen as basic to the creation of a sophisticated social order. The procedures ensured by a democracy—indeed, perhaps the very nature of democracy itself—involve a certain degree of procrastination. But system design and management can see these procedural safeguards only as a series of obstacles preventing the tasks of modernization from being accomplished. Thus social scientists have not only

13. A good example of the attempt to infuse the technocratic approach with a democratic ideology is contained in Fred Cottrell, *Energy and Society: The Relation Between Energy, Social Change, and Economic Development*. New York: McGraw-Hill, 1955, esp. pp. 256–311.
14. This is certainly true for such technocratic publications as *News Analyst: Americans for a New Society*. See especially Vol. VII, No. 7 (Mar. 1969).

to instill the engineering profession with an appreciation of the complexities of the social order, but, with at least equal weight, to instill a proper appreciation of the positive values of democracy itself, even in its "irrational" or "non-logical" aspects. The irony is that this very task has proved repugnant to engineers turned sociologist no less than to sociologists turned engineer.

Sociology might be of future assistance to engineers, without sacrificing its own scientific role, by investigating problems linked to training and education in engineering. Perhaps in this way, sociology can come to be considered as an essential tool instead of a surface polish. The following lines of inquiry should be considered only as suggestive:

(1) *What* are the status rewards for engineers involved in the developmental process—for example, political power, contact with foreign cultures, revolutionary surrogates—that can compensate for leaving smooth-running, well-tooled industrial plants in the cosmopolitan centers?

(2) *Who* among engineers are likely to seek out careers in international development—people of radical political background, humanistic training, second-level proficiencies?

(3) *When* is the training of technicians working in international development functional or dysfunctional to the over-all aspirations of the underdeveloped areas?

(4) *Where* can technological achievements be transplanted intact into different social systems, and *where* must technology be adapted to meet qualitatively different environmental needs?

(5) *How* can sociology assist in accelerating the education for overseas work of engineering personnel highly sensitized to the nuances and needs of the social sciences?

The engineering profession seems unable to snap the bonds of conservatism even when its leading spokesmen promote the idea of social development around the world. Assessing the goals of engineering education, the Engineers Joint Council notes that "the world scene is troubled by the existence of new weapons of immense power in the hands of a growing number of nations," but offers not even a hint of what might possibly be done about this situation. It then notes that in the developing nations "pressures are mounting for a share in the greater well-being and security that come with advancing technology," but sees these aspirations as "hampered by many factors—economic, social, and political—that result in a continued widening of the gap between those nations which have and those which have not." It is understandable that factors of a technological nature impeding development are omitted. Even the rhetorical tone of the document might be forgiven, in the absence of specific goals, but what seems inexcusable is that the only reference to international development should appear under the rubric of "national goals" and in a proclamation declaring that engineering education is "an instrument of national purpose." [15] Aside from waiting in vain for a definition of this national purpose, the deployment of the vast resources of engineering for nationalistic rather than scientific ends places the overseas engineer more in the position of the traditional missionary than of the modern innovator.

A factor that induces conservative trends among American engineers is that a large proportion of them work in areas of military and space technology—activities directly linked to at least the tacit acceptance of United States overseas postures. Indeed, many engineers work in industries which from their inception were involved in non-commercial, governmental programming for military conflict. It is to be expected that engineers would thus tend to believe in armaments as a bulwark of social solidarity, and to support patterns of secrecy, suppression of information, and even coercion as a social norm.[16]

Given the fact that the post-war affluence of engineers is so closely linked to the Third World War industries, it is little wonder that any alteration in the status quo would quickly be interpreted as a direct assault on standards of living. With such prevalent attitudes, the overseas engineer, far from having any firm appreciation of local problems, remains fully committed to the implicit (or explicit) exploitative and extractive aims of the corporate empires for which he works.

Further, the education of engineers on overseas assignment has tended to be intensively specialized and restricted to the bachelor's degree level. Although the number of post-graduate engineers is steadily increasing, the bachelor's degree remains a terminal professional degree. This serves to limit the kinds of non-professional training an engineer receives, and

15. See the report of the Panel on Engineering Education, *Assessment of the Goals of Engineering Education in the United States,* Engineers Joint Council (Sept. 1966).
16. See Irving Louis Horowitz, "The Conflict Society: War as a Social Problem," in *Social Problems: A Modern Approach,* edited by Howard S. Becker. New York: John Wiley & Sons, 1966, pp. 695–747; and on this whole range of issues, see Thomas G. Miller, *Strategies for Survival in the Aerospace Industry.* New York: Arthur D. Little, 1964.

is particularly confining and conservatizing in relation to developmental activities. Often graduate training is geared to specific industrial tasks—with the business enterprises themselves saying and hence giving shape to graduate education. Thus, the engineering elite is siphoned off from general guidance to the field and is diverted to the narrow and often confining goals of the industrial firm.[17]

The study of interdisciplinary problems is first concerned with the ways in which this study is a response to world problems, and, second, with the degree to which it is a response to the autonomous evolution of each discipline involved. Conventional divisions between the sciences are responses more to bureaucratic needs of university auditing than to the social needs of human beings. Therefore it is to be hoped that a time will come when relations between sociologists and engineers will be *intra*disciplinary rather than *inter*disciplinary.

The social role of technology in underdeveloped nations has not yet been adequately explored. As a matter of fact, even in those rare studies concerned with "adapting the training of engineers to the requirements of economic growth," the emphasis has invariably been on greater use of applied mathematics, probability statistics, and modern computing techniques.[18] That it is now recognized that future engineers should take a greater part in the developmental process is commendable. That their training omits the social aspects of development is deplorable.

Reinforcing this situation, engineers have in some instances dismissed any "preoccupation with pre-industrial value standards" as a bad case of "nostalgia," and have made incredible statements that "material possession is no longer a source of economic power and ownership." Indeed those taking such positions are declared captives of an outdated myth.[19] Problems of development are transformed into "the world game" in which capitalism, communism, religious and ethnic rivalries will all give way to masked men flying freely about the world in plastic bubbles. In this way, the contempt for ideology is translated into a celebration of utopia.

17. See Joseph M. Pettit and James M. Gere, "Evolution of Graduate Education in Engineering," *Journal of Engineering Education,* Vol. 54, No. 2 (Oct. 1963), pp. 57–62; also Ralph E. Dunham, "Engineering Degrees (1964–65) and Enrollments (Fall 1965) in Institutions with One or More ECPD-Accredited Curricula," *Engineering Education,* Vol. 56, No. 6 (Feb. 1966), pp. 181–97.
18. See "Adapting the Training of Engineers to the Requirements of Economic Growth," *OECD Observer,* Whole No. 26 (Feb. 1967), pp. 12–14.
19. See John McHale, editor of a special supplement on "2000 +," in *Architectural Design* (Feb. 1967), pp. 64–101.

There are approximately 8680 American engineers working in foreign areas;[20] an amount roughly equivalent to the total membership of the American Sociological Association. Such a total does indicate the importance of engineering in the developmental process. The impact at engineering cannot be made an abstract accounting of the rights and wrongs of social change but must be considered more realistically on the basis of current overseas performance and future goals.

In a remarkable book, the full implications of which cannot possibly be summarized here, Jacob Schmookler has pointed out some basic truths about technology that bear on our subject: long-term economic development is primarily the result of the growth of technological knowledge; retardation in each industry's rate of technical progress is to be explained by the retardation in the rate of growth, and not vice versa; technological production not only greatly affects economic development but is itself a basic form of economic activity; social and economic demand determines the allocation of inventive effort.[21]

The implications for underdeveloped nations are quite clear: if the over-all economy is dependent, then the technology too will be dependent. A slow growth rate indicates the backward state of applied science in an underdeveloped nation. The need levels of the peoples in underdeveloped nations are a function of the demands of the two socioeconomic extremes. A tension builds up which results either in the dissemination of products that in turn results in a deepening dependence by the underdeveloped upon the developed areas, or a search for new economic forms that establishes the necessary political preconditions for technological innovation.

To speak of problems of technology in developing areas it is thus necessary to deal with the special place of interlocking corporate activi-

20. My estimate derives from a National Science Foundation Report which indicates in a ten percent sample a total of 868 out of 57,779, as working in foreign areas, including Puerto Rico. While as of 1964, there are 677,959 members of the engineers who hold multiple memberships, thus reducing the estimates on the number of engineers in the United States. A report issued by the Engineering Manpower Commission does, however, indicate that according to their best estimates, "there are currently between 500,000 and 600,000 degree-level engineers in the United States." See "Report from the National Engineers Register," *Engineering Manpower in Profile*," Washington, D.C., 1965; and Harold Foecke, *The Engineering Manpower Situation, Present and Future*. New York: Engineering Manpower Commission, 1965.
21. See Jacob Schmookler, *Invention and Economic Growth*. Cambridge, Mass.: Harvard University Press, 1966, pp. 196–215.

ties. The United States Steel Corporation, which produces one quarter of the steel output domestically, also actively engages in manufacturing thousands of products for overseas markets. It has seventeen subsidiaries through which it controls raw materials and transportation facilities in far-flung places like Canada, Brazil, Venezuela, and parts of Africa. Dow Chemical is also involved in scores of manufacturing activities throughout the world, with affiliates in every major market in the world. This situation can be replicated for many, if not most, of the largest 500 corporations in the United States.[22]

This is not the place to investigate the values of such overseas empires. It is nevertheless plain that the function of engineers as primary personnel attached to such overseas operations is much more organically linked to the American corporate structure than is the function of people who go to underdeveloped areas on work or study missions. Under such circumstances it can be seen that the problem of engineering ideology as it relates to overseas training is not simply an "educational" matter, but a "structural" characteristic built into the functional circumstances that affect engineers working in foreign lands.

The master organizational dilemma is that engineering activities are often related to managerial functions, while the structure of ownership remains keyed to nineteenth-century industrial forms. Fred Cottrell summarizes very well the engineering aspects of modern management:

> To run a railroad involves specific techniques, not generalized ones. To build a plant to produce penicillin or an atom we must call upon a different body of specific knowledge from that involved in producing cotton cloth or cash registers. Decisions, to be effective, must be based upon an enormous amount of information available only to specialists. To coordinate the operations of a large number of specialists is again a specific technique involving the cooperation of large numbers of persons.

He concludes by noting that "the system cannot be operated effectively by the hunches, guesses, fears, and hopes of widely scattered amateurs who happen to be owners." [23]

That as it may be in theory, the fact remains that in the United States,

22. See Staff Report to the Antitrust Subcommittee of the Committee on the Judiciary, *Interlocks in Corporate Management* (Subcommittee Report No. 5). Washington, D.C.: U.S. House of Representatives, USGPO, 1965.
23. Fred Cottrell, *Energy and Society, The Relation Between Energy, Social Change and Economic Development*. New York: McGraw-Hill, 1955, p. 218.

ownership functions still prevail. What is easily overlooked is that precisely because of the specialized nature of managerial functions, managerial personnel are perhaps the most easily manipulated group in modern society. Far from taking over modern industrial society, management, technical staff, and engineers remain in an insecure position with the defined property status of ownership.[24] The managerial "revolution" never took place, except in the world of New Deal rhetoric. A technological "revolution" did occur. This dualism between ownership and management is in effect a dichotomy between wealth and technique. That there had been virtually no perception of this struggle between decision-makers in ownership and middle-echelon management itself requires sociological explanation.

The sociology of technology, at least insofar as it must deal with the area of development, has to explain the relationship between underdevelopment and overdevelopment, that is, those factors which prevent the *coming into existence* of the technical means for achieving maximum production, consumption and distribution; and those factors which prevent the *utilization* of the technical means for achieving maximum production, consumption, and distribution, respectively.

In a great many ways, the problems of underdeveloped nations are analogous to problems of fully ripened industries carried over from previous epochs. The building and machine tool industries illustrate this condition. Concomitantly, problems of overdeveloped nations may be seen as analogous to those of new industries unable to find a stable place in the industrial complex, since so much depends on a thoroughly new set of categories to explain their operations. The aircraft and space industries typify this latter category. In the absence of a meaningful sociology of technology, we might perhaps work out a characteristic profile based on information we do have on the behavior of old and new industries.

The technology of traditional nations reveal the following characteristics—all of which seem present in discussing old industrial styles: (1) The technology of backward industrial nations is built on craft-based rather than science-based technology, that is to say, they derive from individual skills rather than from scientific organization. (2) Invariably, the size of factories in backward areas is far below the critical size necessary for innovation or maximizing profits. (3) Related to this is the fact

24. See H. H. Gerth and C. Wright Mills, "A Marx for the Managers," in *Power, Politics and People,* edited by Irving Louis Horowitz. New York and London: Oxford University Press, 1963, pp. 53–71.

that the size of a factory in underdeveloped areas prevents a scientific division of labor from taking place but is instead usually dependent upon the total skills of the individual. (4) Underdeveloped areas have a low research and development orientation and instead focus exclusively on production using present methods and obsolete machines. (5) Entrepreneurial and marketing techniques are usually imitative and primitive. This industrial inertia is usually reinforced by the fact that goods can be sold off rapidly, since many underdeveloped areas are labor rich and product poor.[25]

The sociological aspects of technology in traditional nations serve to reinforce existing patterns. For each of the above points, one can indicate distinct sociological consequences: (1) Because of the handicraft character of so much production, certain "feudal" psychological characteristics appear in the work process. Often these are disguised ideologically by reference to the "dehumanization" of automation and machine labor. (2) The small size of so many factories aslo serves to reinforce traditionalism. It makes possible the continued existence of family ownership of industrial life. Such family ownership is committed to the perpetuation of conventional modes, particularism in hiring policies, and a lack of merit-based promotions. (3) The absence of a scientific division of labor is reinforced by the family and patrimonial styles of ownership. In particular, it prevents managerial orientations toward production innovation, rather than perpetuating family controls. (4) The absence of funds for research and development makes the industrial plant of underdeveloped areas subject to intense competition in technique and sophistication from foreign enterprises, with which they often cannot cope. They are just compelled to purchase know-how at the expense of local ownership, or continue to issue inferior goods by the erection of high tariff walls—something less satisfactory for underdeveloped nations. (5) Industrial inertia is reinforced by localism. Lack of a planning or even a nation-wide distribution system curtails innovation even as a style.

The question then arises as to how the cycle of backwardness gets broken. And the answer very often comes from external sources. But these external sources are too rarely innovative and too often imperialistic.

25. For an excellent discussion on stagnation and innovation in United States industry, see Donald A. Schon, *Technology and Change, The Impact of Invention and Innovation on American Social and Economic Development*. New York: Delacorte Press, 1967, pp. 139–71; and also see Donald A. Schon, "Forecasting and Technological Forecasting," *Daedalus*, Vol. 96, No. 3 (Summer 1967), pp. 759–70.

Another vicious cycle builds up: backwardness in technique leads to a demand for innovation, which in turn gets frustrated by low capital investment in research and development, and in turn, this leads to an invitation to or invasion by private foreign investors—who extract ownership or managerial priorities in exchange for plant modernization. In addition, there is the constant pressure of the demonstration effect—the pressure exerted by the display of foreign goods and services—either directly, in the homes of the bourgeois sectors of underdeveloped nations, or more commonly, through symbolic forms such as direct and indirect advertising. Thus, to speak of the technology of underdeveloped areas is invariably to come to grips with the technology of fully advanced countries as well.

These fully advanced countries, precisely because of their technical sophistication, are far more aggressive in marketing and distribution, so that often foreign firms capture cosmopolitan markets abroad, while local industries are compelled to sell off goods in non-competing backward areas of the nation. Thus, national goods are often sold in rural regions, while foreign goods make their heaviest market dent in the comparatively wealthy capital centers. In other words, local industries are disadvantaged precisely because of the intensification of urbanism and a concurrent sophistication in advertising and distribution techniques.

One distinctive social input of technology concerns the difficulties entailed in patterns of investment. The successful implementation of technical innovation takes between five and twelve years. This means that very large firms, or large-scale government enterprises such as the military, monopolize the area of innovation as an organized social activity.

> Over half of public expenditures on research and development in the United States is concentrated on security projects. Even privately financed expenditures are extremely concentrated by industry: 1956, in the same country, seven manufacturing industries which accounted for only 10.5% of the national income, accounted for 56% of the research and development expenditures. Industries accounting for 31% of the national income account for 96% of all the expenditure.[26]

26. See E. F. Dennison, *The Sources of Economic Growth in the United States.* New York: Committee for Economic Development, 1962 (Supplementary Paper No. 13); and H. M. Phillips, "Science and Technology in Economic Development," *International Social Science Journal,* Vol. XVIII, No. 3 (1966), pp. 325–44. I should add that the dates derived from these two studies are interpreted differently than above. Dennison and Phillips see the dissemination of new research as a fact, rather than as a problem between cosmopolitan and peripheral sectors.

And while it is true that technological information spreads rapidly in terms of results, such "know-how" must be brought through licenses, patents, or concessions to foreign firms. Thus, the continued pressures of research and development serve to disequilibrate social relations between advanced and backward nations. For what is purchased in the form of patent rights is paid for in terms of profit-sharing with the original large corporate structures from the cosmopolitan centers.

One compensatory device which may somewhat redress the imbalance is that, since innovation is both costly and risky, there tends to be an enormous investment in maintaining a technological status quo. In such a situation, it may be easier to convince a smaller firm in an underdeveloped area to undertake an innovative device than a large private corporation in the advanced sector.[27] However, since so many innovations depend on large-scale industry for their execution, this limitation upon concentration of research and development in the hands of a relatively small group of industries cannot be viewed as a significant prop for the maintenance of small-scale levels of production.

The concentration of technological facilities in the hands of the advanced developed nations also means that such concentration spills over in research and development—to the disadvantage of the less developed nations. The latter, which earn considerable amounts of their income from the sale of raw materials such as iron ore, copper, and lead, find the trend of modern technology is to invent and employ raw-material substitutes in every area from bridge construction to automobile manufacturing. As one scholar recently pointed out:

> There is, in the industrialized countries, a tendency to employ more and more material-saving techniques. This development is certainly not news as such, but the rate at which it is progressing is quite novel. The absolute increase in raw material consumption, of course, partly offsets the tendency, but its value seems to be generally lower than that of the factors of production employed in utilizing this increase.[28]

This trend toward raw-material surpluses accentuates the gap between advanced and underdeveloped regions. The same article soberly

27. See Daniel V. de Simone, "The Innovator," *Engineer,* Vol. VIII, No. 1 (Jan.–Feb. 1967).

28. G. H. P. Aymans, "Technology and Natural Resources, The Example of Latin America," *International Social Science Journal,* Vol. XVIII, No. 3 (1966), pp. 345–61.

indicates that "the rapid expansion of material saving and substitution techniques has serious consequences for all those countries which earn their national income mainly from transforming natural resources into raw materials—primary production alone will as a rule not suffice to raise the material standard of living to that enjoyed by the more fortunate countries." [29] The likelihood is that such technological innovation, far more than any "brain-drain" of engineering personnel, weakens the social and economic position of underdeveloped lands. The decreased importance of raw-material exports causes a "money drain" that further weakens underdeveloped nations with respect to the advanced nations.

If technical innovation has a long-term weakening effect on under-developed areas, manpower drainage has a short-term effect in the same direction. This is the so-called "brain-drain." [30] The evidence is clear that acquisition of any degree of technical proficiency brings with it demands to perform in practice, and also demands for status rewards commensurate with technical training in the advanced societies.[31] The problem of invidious comparison can scarcely be overlooked in the study of engineering and nation-building. For as engineering personnel in the United States are increasingly being tooled up for work and study in the under-developed regions, these backward nations are sending forth the cream of their manpower, their developmental sector as it were, to both study and work in the United States and other fully developed nations. It is possible to break this cycle by convincing underdeveloped nations to place their technical and scientific manpower in a reward-plus situation, but this might just polarize the "experts" and the "politicians" and so place even greater burdens on the working man.

Another way of framing this dilemma is to put it in terms of the "failure of success." Engineers may assist an underdeveloped nation to reach beyond the import-substitution phase. But what are the sociopolitical consequences of market competition for sophisticated buying areas, that is, what happens when Brazil or Argentina reach out for a portion of the

29. *Ibid.,* pp. 353–54. There has been little work done on how the imbalances in research and development might be overcome. One such major effort is Murray L. Weidenbaum, "Government Encouragement of Private Sector Research and Development," *Studies in Comparative International Development,* Vol. 1, No. 9 (1965), pp. 123–31.

30. *The Migration of Highly Trained Persons From Latin America to the United States.* Washington, D.C.: Pan American Health Organization, 1966 (mimeo).

31. On this, see Morris A. Horowitz, *La Emigración de Profesionales y Técnicos Argentinos.* Buenos Aires: Instituto Torcuato di Tella, 1962.

international economy already controlled by the United States, or for that matter, the Soviet Union? In other words, technological success at the national level by no means guarantees social stability. The stress brought on by a long-term increase in market competition may stimulate the impulses toward revolution, and those working toward maximizing technological achievement must anticipate and measure the degree to which engineering serves as a stimulant rather than a brake upon violent change.

Nevertheless sociologists and engineers share the difficulties of "the natural history of the planning cycle." Actual involvement in the developmental process, apart from an analytical framework, involves, first, an untapped natural or social resource; second, individuals who perceive its high potentialities as realizable; third, an industry or an agency willing to take change on developing it; fourth, a government willing and able to manage high-level synchronization of efforts; and finally, the capacity to mobilize manpower to realize planning schedules.

In this set of relationships, the importance of organization is self-evident. Whether through model construction or through ethnographic description of case-book approaches, the sociologist of development should be able to provide relevant information at the utilization level. On the other hand, it is the responsibility of engineering personnel to take such matters seriously. This sensitivity could be much enhanced if agencies making overseas assignments prepared their people properly. For example, briefing sessions for overseas engineers, if Latin American informational services issued by the government are an indication, are still at the level of intellectual doggerel; they ill-equip the newly arrived technical personnel for the world they enter. This in turn is reinforced by the way the visiting technicians live in a foreign land: separate living quarters for the American, just a little bit of home (in the form of piped-in television and third-rate supermarkets) to make the foreign area "palatable." A major difficulty encountered by the developmental engineer is the qualitative units employed in analysis. Since engineers are most familiar with physical systems, environmental attributes tend to be taken for granted, or what could be more damaging, simply carried over from the "home" environment. In this way, engineering concepts of rationality may serve severely to impede and restrict technological innovation. This seems to occur with particular frequency in non-Western environments, where differences in religious customs and cultural rituals produce friction. Thus, many overseas technicians may resent the prohibition of meat-eating in Hindu India amidst a sea of starvation, yet few of them are prepared to examine their own biases on meat-eating. For example, few Westerners would advocate the widespread breeding of horses for meat-eating purposes, yet this is a perfectly "rational" outcome in strict engineering terms. The purpose of social science for engineers at the pragmatic level is thus to open up a range of considerations that might, once taken account of, eliminate areas of frustration, confusion, and ultimately hostility. But there have thus far been no estimates of the costs of misunderstanding, the reinforcement of nostalgia, the alienation from the physical environment, the breeding of contempt, and the like. These issues are part of studying the natural history of planning cycles.

Even beyond the problem of social adaptation is the problem of the technological "fit of units working well in one environment but not another, and the influences of this factor on social behavior." [32] For problems such as machine design, simplicity or complexity of mechanical operations, innovative employment of machinery, and the like directly affect the social dimensions of behavior, and in turn, any system design is seriously modified by such social dimensions.

The sociological dimensions of technical adaptation are not limited to distinctions between one nation and another, but occur within a given nation itself. In fact, a recent study of the introduction of new thresher machines in two adjacent Indian villages shows that this sort of problem also arises at micro levels of implementation. It was found in the study of thirty-two "adopters" and forty-four "non-adopters" that the village which adopted new techniques was receptive to the foreign personnel who came to demonstrate and diffuse the Olpad Thresher, while in the other village town factionalism and mistrust of the foreign personnel brought about not only differential utilization of the new machinery but differential net returns.[33] Religious castes, political party allegiances, and the effect of past efforts at cooperative farming would all help to explain differential results in farm technology.

The problems are not limited to the capacity or limits of machinery in a given environment. The attempt to improve agricultural production, a major issue given the food scarcity in the underdeveloped world, has in-

32. For example, "model cities" of the same technical dimensions might show great disparity or even no resolution of social stratification problems. On this, see Suzanne Keller, "Social Class in Physical Planning," *International Social Science Journal,* Vol. XVIII, No. 4 (1966), pp. 494–512.

33. J. P. Hrabovszky and T. K. Moulik, *Economic and Social Factors Associated with the Adoption of an Improved Implement.* New York: Agricultural Development Council, May 1967.

volved such different groups as resource allocation experts, agricultural economists, engineers, architects, and sociologists. Solutions are sought in terms of developing more sophisticated machinery. But even when such a direct increase in machine improvements does yield higher production, difficulties arise that require more than bigger and better tractors.

The basis of increased production, even from a strictly technical viewpoint may involve: (1) *Incentive problems*—getting the peasant sector to work better and more efficiently, which in turn hinges on rewards for agricultural effort at the market end to a land reform approach at the proprietary end. (2) *Rationalization problems*—getting the food which is produced into storage warehouses and from the rural growing region to the urban consumer region. (3) *Advertising-communication problems*—getting the food to a cosmopolitan market with a minimum of spoilage, and also to getting the most easily available food purchased, consumed, and reordered. (4) *Decision-making problems*—getting the peasant sector to produce high-protein foods in place of easy-to-grow foods; getting a government to provide incentives for growing foodstuffs with a high resale value rather than production exclusively for the home market. (5) Finally, there are *investment problems*—political and economic decisions have to be made concerning investments in the agricultural sector or investments in an industrial sector (with the hope that agricultural products can be bought with surplus funds from product sales). In all of this what is needed is personnel who perceive *human* problems by means of systems analysis.

The gap between recommendations for underdeveloped nations and developed nations rests on ideological incongruities that must be removed before any serious transformation in the present structure is possible. Take, for example, the analysis of the capitalist system offered by John Kenneth Galbraith.[34] He indicates that the present, post-1929 success of the American system rests upon: limiting the play of market factors; industries no longer being in the position of passive receptacles governed by the independent activities of consumers and market supplier of services but rather corporate agencies which themselves generate lines of power to create orderly and acceptable behavior of both suppliers and buyers; the modern corporation being more and more the name for an integrated sequence of operations that converts resources into saleable commodities.

34. John Kenneth Galbraith, *The New Industrial State*. Boston: Houghton Mifflin, 1967.

Above all, the corporate structure is regulated from within and from without, from agencies of the larger government and from internal executive divisions of industry. But the same problems are of a different order in underdeveloped nations. There the automony of industry is thwarted by foreign domination on the one hand and by internal political public sector control on the other. Hence, the social organization of factory life, so "rational" in the developed nations, becomes highly irrational in underdeveloped regions. Production can be geared to the rationality of a foreign enterprise rather than to that of a domestic one. Or, it may be tied to a domestic enterprise at the sacrifice of rhetoric more profitable to nationalism. Funds earmarked for research and development are often not present, and, hence, innovative patterns get drawn from foreign sources rather than from within. In these circumstances, it is futile to implore industry to become technologically innovative or socially modern. And the very criteria of modernity are not set, hard and fast, around technological sophistication.

For example, a major difficulty with Rostow's developmental formula is not exclusively or even primarily in his elevation of the field of automotive production as an independent variable of modernity, but rather his failure (shared by not a few social scientists) to distinguish between Cadillac economies (USA); Volkswagen economies (Brazil, Japan); and Moskvich pick-up truck economies (USSR).[35] This is not a simply automotive export-import decision but a sociopolitical decision which ramifies throughout the national and international economies. A technological decision on what to manufacture or what to purchase also entails decisions about highway construction, consumer orientations, overall transportation-communications systems. At this level, cooperation between engineers and sociologists is as absent as it is vitally needed.

Whenever the concept of "Westernization" is now introduced, there is a clear-cut implication of modernization. Whatever being "Western" meant in previous ages—religious reformation, industrial revolution, urban concentration, or even political liberalism—in the second half of the twentieth century it mainly refers to technological innovation—the unequivocal displacement of human labor by machine labor. But the

35. See Walt W. Rostow, *The Stages of Economic Growth, A Non-Communist Manifesto.* London and Cambridge: Cambridge University Press, 1960. This problem in Rostow's approach is even more evident in his recent work, *Politics and the Stages of Growth.* London: Cambridge University Press, 1971, esp. pp. 98–141.

movement from human to machine labor has been accompanied by cries of alienation and anomie rather than by a new-found integration and identity. The very success of the engineering enterprise has created a series of social failures. And even if the rhetoric about "one-dimensional man" is discounted, even if it be recognized that a technical background may well result in a plethora of different personality types and men of manifold skills, there remains a problem that can be described only as failure to achieve a true integration of engineering skills with the best of the sociological imagination.[36]

In the context of national development and engineering problems we might seek this integration by a process of sifting and winnowing, redefining problem areas confronted. First, we need to distinguish between the rise of independent nation-states in the Third World and those which depend upon the First and Second Worlds. National independence is by no means identical with economic independence, as the history of Latin America in particular (and now of Africa) shows so dramatically. Second, we must distinguish between indicators of modernization, which concern the product consequences of development, and indicators of development, which concern the production causes of social change. Third, the language of technical assistance, which has emerged with full force since the close of World War II, should not obscure the sharp differences in the terms of grants, contracts, and the wider network of unspoken and unwritten obligations which may obtain in any given technical aid package. Fourth, some appreciation of cost accounting is required by sociologists, but by the same token some respect for the qualitative aspects of international development must begin to pervade engineering approaches to social change, for both technical feasibility and social desire must be tested by human costs no less than by industrial efficiency. Such distinctions will become all the more urgent as anomalies in the developmental process assert themselves. The Soviet Union will probably reach the moon in its rocket craft before it manages to draw abreast of Argentina in automobile production. The People's Republic of China is able to accelerate its growth rate of gross national product in the midst of a civil war. The United States is able to reach fantastic new levels of employment despite automation, and yet has entered a period of racial and ethnic violence unparalleled in its history.

36. Claire Nader, "Technical Experts in Developing Countries," edited by Claire Nader and A. B. Zahlan. Cambridge, England: Cambridge University Press, 1969, pp. 447–91.

The explanation of such anomalies will require distinctions, not obfuscation; scientific integration, not professional animosity.

If physics has become something of a model for sociology, then by the same token and with the extensive difficulties taken into consideration, engineering might well serve as a model for applied sociology. The extrinsic motivation of sociology has always been a social problem for some, just as the extrinsic motivation of physics has been an engineering problem for others. As has been recently asserted:

> Mathematics originated because men had to measure, weigh and count to maintain an organized economic system. The study of thermodynamics started from Carnot's interest in steam engines. Pasteur's science of bacteriology began when he tried to prevent French beer and wine manufacturers' products from turning sour. Group theory was invented as a means of studying the properties of an algebraic equation. So to speak, nearly every pure science starts as an applied, or at least as an extrinsically motivated, science.[37]

Sociology also originated because men had to measure, weigh, and evaluate their social habitat. The emergence of urban studies came about through grants to study ghettos. The scientific study of Negro life came from economic pressures, from the need to understand migratory patterns from south to north, among other factors. The science of criminology came about through a need to explain the causes of theft, murder, and the like. Even so abstract a field as the sociology of knowledge came about as a consequence of the "Rashomon effect," that is, an attempt to answer why different people looking at the same objects develop different responses and perceptions based on their interests rather than on their cognitions. In short, in social science, as in physical science, demands for application preceded theoretical resolutions.

This is not merely true at the early stages. The same is true at the terminal points as well. The theoretical resolution of a problem means little unless applied contingencies are built into the initial design. Were it not for automatic dialing systems, the complexity of any telephone network would be such as either to convert every user into an operator or lead to a complete breakdown of the telephone system. Thus the central switching system is much more responsible for making the

37. See Alvin M. Weinberg, *Reflections on Big Science*. Cambridge, Mass.: M.I.T. Press, 1967, p. 148.

present-day telephone network work than is the discovery that sound can be transmitted from one place to another over wavelengths. And while nothing in sociology quite rivals the system design of present-day communication, it is clear that, with the development of social accounting and social indicators, the operational aspects of the social system are now being built into the theoretical design in order to estimate the proper worth of any theory. This serves as a major link between engineering and sociology—a far more sober and useful one than any metaphysical demands for efficiency and order.

The disruption caused to societies around the world by major technological innovations, particularly when they have taken place in the military sphere, has often called forth Luddite responses from both physical and social scientists. At this point, such resistance to innovation often takes the form of antagonism toward the applied sciences. Disregarding the ideological or ethical bases of such appeals, the plain fact is that there are few cases on record where nations, faced with the material advantage of technological progress, have spurned them on the grounds of potential increases in social disorganization. Since this is so patently the situation, it is imperative that social scientists accelerate their own efforts in applied research rather than demand an implausible slow-down in technological innovation.

Sociologists, for the most part, know the inexorable pressures toward technical improvement, yet, like Buridan's ass, they have preferred neither to drink nor to eat, but simply to stare at the options. There are, however, signs that the Luddite phase may be drawing to a close. Forced to confront the technical as well as societal dimensions of the growing disparities of international wealth and poverty, the imagery of Buridan's ass may at last give way to Minerva's owl.

IV

Principles and Policies of Development

16

Dilemmas and Decisions in Development

The rise of new states in old regions of Africa and Asia and the growth of new industrial complexes in old states, especially in South America, have proven to be the most volatile and vital fact of the modern age. Economic development on an international scale has not only created new varieties of social and political differentiation but is already providing channels for action in the developing societies. The stratification of future societies is clearly being shaped by the decisions taken now. Development acts to redistribute political and economic forces and determines the form that modern nationalism and internationalism take. Political control, economic growth, and social structure are related to each other as never before. The consciousness of development has revolutionized the structure of development. For this reason, certain long-standing roadblocks can be cleared away, while newly emergent issues can be satisfactorily posed.

THE UNEVEN NATURE OF DEVELOPMENT

Neither continents nor nations develop. What do develop are specific geographic areas which have particular ecological patterns, economic properties, and psychological orientations. One might speak of the rapid development of the Brazilian or Indonesian economies; but what is really more to the point is the growth of São Paulo and Jakarta—growth measured by the standard economic indices of real wealth, rate of investment, improved living standards, changed conditions of existence, and changed relationships between social groups.

At the same time, the "costs" of development are not an abstraction. Generally, what suffers most in this process (comparatively) is the agricultural sector, and the people who suffer most are the peasants. Even if we were to choose as our model the relatively advanced Soviet Union, we would find that agricultural technology and farm production lag badly. And if this is true for the advanced Soviet Union, it is still more so for such recent entries into the development race as Brazil— where the contrasts between the industrial and agricultural sectors are sharp and taut. On the unevenness of development, on this "sectorial phenomenon," a recent United Nations survey offers a most instructive contrast of the Third World to First World countries in which per capita productivity grows faster in agriculture than in manufacturing, thereby creating the dual problems of food surpluses and surplus farmers.

> Ideally, productivity in agriculture would rise at a rate meeting the cities' growing demands for food as well as the demands of export markets, while permitting the release of agricultural workers at a rate meeting the rising demand for labour in industry and services. In practice, of course, the transition does not proceed so smoothly, and in many countries today something quite different is happening: productivity is hardly increasing at all, while masses of rural workers come to the cities looking for jobs that either do not exist or from which they are barred by illiteracy and lack of skills.[1]

Thus, even during the transitional phase, when a country is shifting from rural to industrial patterns, differences between the sectors only become accentuated. There is a surplus of farm labor in most underdeveloped countries, which produces a problem of disguised rural unemployment. Further, there is no reason why farm profits should be below the national average. The English landlords of the eighteenth century pushed their tenants off the land so that they could earn more with their livestock and wool. They were quite efficient as businessmen. Indeed, the same is true for the Russian Kulaks of the twentieth century, who were doing very well compared to other small entrepreneurs. This friction-producing situation is also a situation which produces change. An entirely new phenomenon, "transitional man," has come

1. United Nations, Department of Economic and Social Affairs. *Report on the World Social Situation, with Special Reference to the Problem of Balanced Social and Economic Development.* New York: United Nations, 1961, pp. 19–20.

into existence.[2] The English peasant was rapidly absorbed into the industrial life of Manchester and London because development was a national event and there were common features making for social solidarity—ethnic, religious, and racial. The cross-over from rural to urban economic and social patterns occurred with minimum delay and without foreign impediment. The conflict between agricultural and industrial sectors in the newly developing nations often produces the sharpest kinds of differences in social norms, cultural patterns, and personal habits. Marginal, unabsorbed elements in the transitional periods tend not to disappear but to become a permanent fixture. Thus marginal sub-societies emerge outside Mexico City, Rio de Janeiro, and Buenos Aires and become permanent.

While many economists have pointed out the "advantages of coming last"—that is, the ability of current underdeveloped countries to profit by the experiences of other civilizations—too few have dealt candidly with the disadvantages of coming last. And it is precisely these disadvantages which are most apparent when one examines underdeveloped regions. We have already alluded to the fantastically wide gap between wealth and poverty as a function of the internationalization of class exploitation.

Other examples come quickly to mind: (1) The intensification of features in modern labor which produce alienation, as when "transitional man" must confront and cope with automatic assembly-line techniques. (2) The gap between skills of handicraft or agricultural labor and the highly refined knowledge necessary to participate in advanced industrial life. (3) The jarring effects of the depersonalized, bureaucratized forms of "modern" existence on the traditionalist value systems of the impoverished. (4) The rise in competition between peasant and proletariat.

It is important not to confuse the transition from feudalism to classical capitalism in Europe with the transition from classical capitalism to bureaucratic statism more characteristic of Third World processes. The Third World, for the most part, has chosen to accept the framework of capitalist economic relations and put this economy into a statist mold approximating the single party machinery. In this way, some sort of effective synthesis is made between First and Second World models that manages to reduce the social costs of change to a tolerable level. It is

2. See Oscar Lewis, *The Children of Sánchez*. New York: Random House, 1962; and William McCord, "Portrait of Transitional Man," in *The New Sociology*, edited by Irving Louis Horowitz. New York: Oxford University Press, 1964.

time to stop assuming that the costs of entering the modern world at a late stage automatically outweigh the benefits. Individual suffering may well turn out to be greater under traditionalist rather than modernist regimes. Nonetheless, unless a society is ready and able to absorb the disadvantages of being last, it will rarely be in a position to reap the advantages of being in that position.

The Irreversibility of Development

People in highly developed nations are fond of thinking about social questions in terms of human will. Even those committed to social determinism are generally hesitant, if not unwilling, to rule out the existence of options and choices—at least within a certain sphere. But the fact remains that, once the wheels of guided social change are set in motion, little can be done to halt the process.

Bluntly put, no known society has ever consciously accepted a lower standard of living as a permanent feature of social existence. Indeed, a primary cause of social revolution is the incapacity or inability of an established set of rulers to maintain or accelerate growth rates in a society. This is not to deny that for the short run, recessions and depressions may not occasion social upheaval. The American depression of the 'thirties and the British experience of crisis in balance of payments during the 'sixties indicated as much. But such reductions in life styles are deemed intolerable for a long period.

For social scientists the movement from ruralism to urbanism may be simply a matter of change, but for the mass of people it is a matter of emancipation. Women are emancipated from domestic obligations; children are emancipated from the work force; laborers are emancipated from the tyrannies of the medieval land tenure system, and human relations as such are emancipated from strict economic necessity. Yet, although there is a direct relationship between regression as the reverse of urbanization, there is no a priori linkage between them. Urban human relations in Calcutta are linked just as firmly to economic necessity as they are in an Indian village. The Soviets could afford to turn away from agriculture because it had surpluses with which to maneuver; but China paid severely with its "Great Leap Forward" that took agriculture for granted, as did India in its Second Five Year Plan. Thus, while ruralism, traditionalism, economic inefficiency, extreme levels of poverty, are often wrapped in one bundle, particularly in Latin America, they sometimes are quite divergent—particularly in Asia.

What then happens to human will under the stress of automation and rapid development? Certainly, it is a part of the growing rupture between advocates of traditionalism and modernism. To be "reactionary" in this sense implies that even though one knows that social development is irreversible, one must still do battle against the forces of development with the hope of maintaining traditional values. It is therefore no accident that conservatism has become increasingly strident, and perhaps obsolete, as it becomes increasingly frustrated by the irreversibility of developmental patterns.

There may be very sound reasons for opposing rapid development. After all, every "emancipation" is also a "hardship" for some social sector or class. The loss of domestic servants may represent a genuine deprivation to those who have been used to an "aristocratic" life in a pre-industrial world. And the utility of washing machines may offer slight consolation to those who either were or still are in a position to employ human washing machines. Nonetheless, there is little point for anyone to shed crocodile tears over the social costs of development to essentially parasitic groups. Development, in being irreversible, tends also to sharpen the competition between sectors within a nation rather than to lessen it. In this sense the unilateral direction of development is related to the sectorial nature of development to increase social pressure, and hence to emphasize social revolution as a means toward rapid change.

Actually, development today may succeed in accomplishing what often-repeated political slogans of the past were not able to accomplish: namely, to create the basis for the theory and practice of permanent revolution. It is becoming increasingly evident that to desire rapid socioeconomic development means to accept the realities of permanent social transformations on a deep and wide scale.[3] This is not to say that no options are left—indeed, they may well increase—but they all must operate within the framework of the developmental pattern. Nostalgia in its own way reflects an inability to cope with the realities of the revolutionary process.

3. See Marion J. Levy, "Some Sources of the Vulnerability of the Structures of Relatively Non-Industrialized Societies to Those of Highly Industrialized Societies," *The Progress of Underdeveloped Areas*, edited by Bert Hoselitz. Chicago: The University of Chicago Press, 1952, pp. 113–25.

NECESSARY COERCION VERSUS INTERNECINE TERRORISM

The connection between coercion and terror, in political terms, can be viewed as a choice between totalitarian models, in which there is a total appropriation of power by a single group, and authoritarian models, in which the formal apparatus, however repressive, admits of a considerable latitude at the level of informal life. This does distinguish between public and private spheres, if nothing else. But, while this model has much to recommend it, it does not quite face the issue.[4]

The main issue is not the institutionalization of legal safeguards. Such a legal superstructure is simply a consequence of development without deformities—in vacuo. Such restraints may well involve the abandonment of the revolutionary impulse toward development. In any comparison of economic growth rates between China and India, one notices a direct ratio between the rate of industrial growth and the presence of coercive mechanisms. When Baran points out that India's stagnation is due to its being "neither able nor willing to accept that challenge [of breaking the hold of the property-owning strata] and to provide the leadership in breaking the resistance of urban and rural vested interests," he has in mind the willingness and/or the capacity of the Chinese to do just that.[5] It serves no purpose to recoil in horror or employ disparaging slogans about oriental despotism and authoritarianism.

Therefore, legal safeguards are clearly going to be violated whenever a high priority is placed on rapid industrial development. It is a relatively simple matter for a citizen of an advanced country, which has long since "internalized" the necessity for judicial restraints or witnessed no serious repressive parliamentary forms, to be outraged by authoritarian measures in the nations of Africa and Asia which are now entering the modern world. To be sure, what complicates growth patterns in Latin America is precisely this long history of parliamentary cretinism, the mystical regard for formal restraints to expropriation or land redistribution that suited the interests of the vested classes.

The real issue is to distinguish between necessary coercion—that is, those forms of coercion which both suppress vested interests and also

4. See Lewis Coser, "Prospects for the New Nations: Totalitarianism, Authoritarianism or Democracy?" *Dissent,* Vol. 10, No. 1, 1963, pp. 43–58.
5. See Paul A. Baran, *The Political Economy of Growth.* New York: Monthly Review Press, 1957, pp. 225–26.

ensure the normal functioning of the productive classes—and politically inspired terrorism—that is, that form of coercion which spends itself on the maintenance of state power and the prevention of free criticism and free choice by the citizenry. Whether we start with Lord Acton's formula that power corrupts and absolute power corrupts absolutely, or a more specific sociological variation such as Roberto Michels' theory of the oligarchical tendencies of organization, or Max Weber's concept of a rise in the bureaucratic sector as a direct response to the rationalizing agencies of state power, we are still confronted by the problem of distinguishing necessary coercion from internecine terrorism.

The Soviet Union and China represent classic examples of the failure to maintain a distinction between these two factors. Once rapid industrialization was decided upon, it was also decided that to oppose this process in any way was tantamount to betrayal, treason, and "wrecking." Indeed, if any useful definition of Stalinism is to be made, it must emphasize its liquidation of the distinction between "class struggle" and "party struggle." The Stalinist period in Russian industrialization rested not simply on coercion but on terrorism. And the distinction between these two words is not inconsequential—the former may involve persuasion, education, relocation, as well as expropriation, while terrorism as an exclusive principle involves the liquidation of all private existence and the replacement of the private man with the thoroughly "integrated" industrial man.

What is herein at stake is not only a question of rules for the conduct of elites or the legitimation of politics, but something infinitely more complicated: a determination of when coercion is acceptable because it is done with a belief in some greater public good, and whence it deviates from the public good and can thus be identifiable as terrorism.[6] Admittedly, an operational definition of terror is extremely difficult to establish. But it might be seen as those acts of destruction that are counterproductive to stated ends and yet cannot be prevented by the exercise of legitimate power: for example, the destruction of the intellectuals during the Stalin period; or even more crucial, the decimation of the ranks of military leadership just prior to the outbreak of World War II at the behest of the Stalinist leadership and against the wishes of the Red Army. This is not to say that terrorism is without pragmatic

6. Maurice Merleau-Ponty, *Humanism and Terror: An Essay on the Communist Problem,* translated and with notes by John O'Neill. Boston: Beacon Press, 1969, esp. 178–89.

value for growth. No one has proven that terrorism and development are incompatible. One might argue that from the Communist point of view the two are mutually exclusive; and therefore that the revolution is "betrayed." But this is an argument which begins with the absolute need for an ideology to deliver "the goods" down to the final prophecy. However distasteful to the Western world, the position expressed by E. H. Carr and Isaac Deutscher—that Soviet society has indeed satisfied the requirements of a growing society, however deformed its method of doing so—can no longer be doubted.

From the standpoint of development the most dysfunctional feature of coercion turned inward, turned terroristic, is that the revolutionary social process thus unleashed will be aborted.[7] The "great leap forward" in Communist China, the suppression of the "hundred flowers" doctrine, had a profound boomerang effect on the developmental process. Even so sympathetic a reporter of China as Edgar Snow criticizes the bad effects brought on by the extreme pressures to "catch the West" in the shortest possible time.[8] The slipping of coercion into terror demonstrates only the political efficacy of violence, not its value for development. In this connection it is significant to note that the Chinese, who at first managed to avoid the technique of the general political purge and the internecine factional strife that played havoc with the early development of Russian socialism, finally fell under the spell of terrorism. It did so precisely at that time, during the late 1960's, when political solvency became more significant a factor, to the Communist leadership at least, than economic development.

Khrushchev's own denunciations of Stalinism, whatever else they signify, are a clear announcement that "inner party struggle" has little to do with "class struggle," and that since the latter has been resolved in favor of the combination of a worker-peasant state, development will be through "consciousness" and "harmony," or what in the West is referred to as consensus. And it is here that we can see the increasing similarities of the functional prerequisites of growth in Russia and the West—however distinct the goals of these societies may remain.

The "models" for the developing nations remain paradoxical. Western liberal styles do not seem to "deliver the goods." And while the

7. See John J. Johnson (ed.), *The Role of the Military in Underdeveloped Countries*. Princeton: Princeton University Press, 1962.
8. Edgar Snow, *The Other Side of the River: Red China Today*. London: Gollancz, 1963.

social and political traditions of many new nations remain Western-influenced, their great needs for economic and technological development make them move away from Western liberalism toward "oriental despotism." In this context the strongest argument against terrorism can be made by an authentic socialism, which fully recognizes the needs for maintenance of a coercive apparatus but at the same time seeks to distinguish class struggle from party struggle and necessary suppression from politically inspired terror. This distinction forms the very essence of the Yugoslavian experimental approach to socialism.[9]

Coercion is often necessary because private industries either fail to accelerate developmental patterns or are unwilling to alter conventional patterns of development. Even if one were to assume the sufficiency of available resources, the private investor would undertake to make investments which are profitable and directed toward short-run return on the investment rather than those which are costly (such as explorations in the technological uses of nuclear power) and directed toward the long run. The private sector in underdeveloped economies generally has neither the means nor the will to interest itself in those industries that require a large initial investment with the prospect of low returns for the immediate future. In a private-sector economy, the uncertainties attached to any given combination of factors of industrial production tend to inhibit growth patterns. Thus given the fact that in an underdeveloped country risks are infinite and the task of capital formation complicated by intervening social variables some form of coercion will undoubtedly be required. Coercion would thus be used to rationalize productivity, avoid excessive expenditures on consumer goods, create the basis of support for unprofitable but necessary lines of scientific industrialization, curb speculative spending, and minimize the exercise of power by the former ruling classes. Coercion in this sense is actually the reverse of naked power, since the former may imply a wide use of persuasive devices, while the latter eschews persuasion in favor of raw power—often used ignorantly and maliciously.

9. See Wayne S. Vucinich (ed.), *Contemporary Yugoslavia: Twenty Years of Socialist Experiment*. Berkeley and Los Angeles: University of California Press, 1969, pp. 235–65.

ACHIEVEMENT AND ASCRIPTION IN THE
DEVELOPMENTAL PROCESS

The developmental take-off is connected with a strong emphasis on achievement values. As a matter of fact, there is a powerful sense of achievement, of getting ahead in the status race by one's own efforts, implied in the developmental process. But if achievement is not to be taken as a synonym for development, it must also be recognized that this achievement motivation by no means rules out traditional values and judgments. If the right to "get ahead" within a social system is part of a developing society, it is no less the case that the social class, race, or nation also has the right to get ahead.

Development implies that for a class, as opposed to particular individuals, "getting ahead" may involve changing ascriptions and not simply abandoning ascribed status in exchange for achievement status. Among working-class people, for example, new manufacturing jobs may be considered, as were the old rural jobs, as ascriptive rights passing from father to son. Similarly, among upper classes, it may be ascriptive orientations that are involved in their performance as bank managers instead of as country squires. Thus, the connection between ascribed and achieved status is at least as important as their differences.

The ease with which national liberation efforts spill over into anti-white crusades is symptomatic of the fact that an ascriptive element not only is present in the development process, but, in its earlier stages at least, may well be the essential catalyst. Nor does this necessarily represent an ideology foisted on the masses from above. The following striking interview with a Vietnamese peasant shows this:

> The other day I [an American reporter] visited a small farmer near Saigon. Through my interpreter I asked him to tell me what he thought of the Americans coming to Indochina. He said: "White men help white men. You give guns to help the French kill my people. We want to be rid of all foreigners and the Viet Minh . . . was slowly putting out the French." I said: "Don't you know there is a white man behind the Viet Minh? Don't you know that Ho Chi Minh takes Russian orders?" He said: "In Saigon I have seen Americans, and I have seen Frenchmen. I have never heard of any white men being with the Viet Minh." [10]

10. This statement, reported by Fred Sparks, is quoted in Hans J. Morgenthau, *Politics Among Nations: The Struggle for Power and Peace,* third edition. New York: Alfred A. Knopf, 1960, p. 341.

ryphal remarks attributed to Mao Tse Tung to the effect that in Asia and Africa, at least, the race war is the class war symbolizes the powerful role of ascribed status.

If the central issue of development at the take-off point is an acute *definition* of friends and enemies, rights and obligations, then the central issue at the stage when (or if) development is undertaken is how a society attempts to *consolidate* its initial successes.

It serves little purpose to argue for the best of all possible worlds, in which political democracy and economic growth march hand in hand. Such a view is predicated on the willingness of backward social forces to accept their demise peacefully and legally. Classes simply do not accept their demise with grace, nor do new ruling groups spring into being with a full appreciation of the craft of political leadership. The mark of an authentic and democratic revolution is not the maintenance of traditional canons of law during periods of dynamic change in economic and political relations, but, rather, the degree to which the transitional stages in social development can be shortened and the amount of coercion minimized, without inviting a breakdown of the processes of social change as such.

Breakdown can thus occur from two directions: either through the excessive use of terrorism or through the absence of a regulatory machinery for enforcing developmental norms. Once the take-off stage has passed, the central issue becomes how to get people to work more efficiently and with greater purpose. Productivity is by definition output per unit of labor input. Hence, development at this level is simply the reduction of human effort with an incremental gain in material output. It is clear that by "developed" most people mean simply (and rightly) the degree and the extent to which human energy is displaced by machine technology. And in fact, highly developed societies reveal just such an ongoing process. One need simply recollect that in the 1860's the average factory work day in Western Europe was fourteen hours, while today it is between seven and eight hours and steadily decreasing.[11]

What is of even greater consequence is that factory laborers—the paid proletariat—are a constantly diminishing social class. New standards of machine technology not only shorten the work day but eliminate

11. See Georges Friedmann, "Leisure in an Automated World," *The Nation*, Vol. 195, No. 5, Sept. 1962, pp. 89–92. For a general useful estimate, see W. Lloyd Warner and Norman H. Martins (eds.), *Industrial Man: Businessmen and Business Organizations*. New York: Harper & Row, 1959.

the need for a large undifferentiated labor supply. Georges Friedmann has even suggested that some word other than "worker" will be needed to characterize the duties and responsibilities of automatic operators. However, this opinion needs considerable qualification. During the 1960's the number of production workers in manufacturing in the United States had increased. More important, the fastest growing employment sector is the service industry—which now comprises 10 to 12 million workers (or nearly three-quarters of those engaged in manufacturing). And this service sector, far from being technologically advanced, is the most backward, with low unionization, low skills, and low salaries. This sector represents a return to the non-productive labor practices of pre-capitalist times. Although this sector includes doctors and teachers at one end, most are characterized as beauty-parlor aides, laundry workers, hotel waiters, and the like. In short, the obsolescence of labor is still a considerable distance in the future.

This long-range process has given rise to a third stage in development: the revolution of achievement as a standard index of social and personal worth. It is not *who one is* so much as *what one knows* that comes to govern wages, political influence, community standing, and other types of rewards. What went by the boards in this stage is a judgment of worth or "ratings" based on class, sex, nationality, or ethnic and religious affiliation. Throughout the "classical" industrial period of development there has been a "status revolution" based essentially on intelligence or "know-how" as a measure of the degree of social worth. This does not mean that class conflict has been absent. The fight for higher wages and better working conditions still remains a primary task of unions and worker organizations. Nonetheless, even in the unions there has been a perceptible shift away from traditional concerns toward the wider implications of automation. Thus unions have become much like any other "business" protective organization—concerning themselves with retraining members for higher skilled work, protecting their members with wise and prudent investments, and guaranteeing their members some priority in available positions rather than concerning themselves with new recruits or with the non-affiliated portion of the work force.

Labor organizations, like business organizations, tend increasingly to have shared problems and hence shared values. Managerial concerns in automated factories supersede traditional schisms along class lines— and the forms of the division of labor do not so much disappear as alter. The skilled technician of "labor" and the trained engineer of "management" have more in common with each other than either has with his traditional class. This process of redefinition of work roles is far from complete and may even be said to be in a nascent stage. Nonetheless, the traditional systems of stratification have proceeded far enough along toward revolution for some general features of yet a third stage in development to be examined.

This new stage is characterized by the emergence of technical workers suffering "relative exploitation," since neither their salary nor condition of life permits these technicians to become part of the bourgeoisie. In this way, the swollen student population is seen as part of the emergent technical sectors where work roles and class attitudes are changing.[12]

As for the new features of development, they seem implicit in what has already been said. Emphasis is now placed on redefining social relationships in terms of "functional" ties rather than "class" antagonism. But more than that, the achievement process is accompanied by a rise in autonomous relations between people rather than integrated factory or office relations. The place of work becomes an accidental property of urban living, rather than the reason for the urbanization process. Urban life does not consolidate class affiliation; rather, it relates the individual worker to matters outside his work. Workers are linked to one another and develop what Durkheim called solidarity, not through factory life as such but in terms of their own skills. Scientists exhibit a concern for their profession, not for the institution in which their work is carried on. What this means is that the advanced stages of development reveal professional competence as a prime condition for work mobility. The higher the degree of professionalization, the less the attachment to any particular place of work and, conversely, the fewer the professional skills individuals possess, the greater their institutional concern. The degree of geographical movement resulting from changes in occupational activities is indicative of the acceleration of social *mobility* in the advanced stages of development.

What then happens to invidious distinctions in a world where "achievement" values prevail? This is a highly speculative question. The answers, however tentative, appear quixotic. There seems to be a

12. See James O'Connor, "Some Contradictions of Advanced U.S. Capitalism," in *Economics: Mainstream Readings and Radical Critiques,* edited by David Mermelstein. New York: Random House, 1970, pp. 577–88.

return to a fourth "saturation" stage. Problems which were supposedly transcended at earlier stages of development reappear. The process of social mobility has clearly not eliminated social stratification. Indeed, the stratification of men through skill and "knowledge" becomes increasingly difficult to maintain and gives way to stratification through ascription.

To an extraordinary degree the search for status differentiation falls back on racial, sexual, and religious dimensions. In an advanced stage of industrial development, Germany was witness to an incredible outpouring of religious hatred that led to mass genocide. The United States now exhibits problems between black and white citizens that seem to make its own class struggles appear tame in comparison. In part, this is a reflection of the force of ascriptive status conflicts, and in part, the fusion of lower-class life with marginal races in contrast to a similar fusion of working-class life with the mainstream classes.

What is more, the achievement of industrial abundance is not an automatic guarantee that all sectors of society are going to share it equally. That is why political struggles may become sharper than in the past. The choice between capitalist and socialist sectors is essentially reduced to a decision as to who can best manage the affairs of state. Economic production is increasingly subject to political control. Who then is to manipulate whom? The political platform concerned with management rights or workers' salaries simply misses the point at this stage. Parties increasingly come to win support through their public attitudes on racial equality, religious toleration, immigration policies, law and order, opposition to new taxes. In short, political parties can remain concerned with epiphenomena at the level of public discourse, while larger issues of war and peace, racial and ethnic harmony, and the like go largely unattended.

The development process has gone far enough to upset new-found individual attitudes. It can add a new variety to old ascriptive systems by intensifying group competition and shattering the individual seeking a "solid place" in the established system.

The persistence of values of ascription once achievement standards are more or less realized may be indicative of the general state of normlessness in the advanced nations. There is a growing search for forms of political control that can be said to overcome the inherited forms of stratification systems. The change from a natural market economy to a planned economy may help to settle problems of achievement motivation, but it scarcely touches the rationalization of society in terms of ascriptive values. For that reason, it must be said that development is basically an ongoing process rather than a fact. Development is no panacea. Industrialism does not put an end to human conflict. An increase in the velocity of change will accelerate conflict.[13] It is utopian in the extreme for a nation to embark on the path of industrial development in the hope of ending social struggle and political rivalry.

It is necessary to realize that the "risks" of development remain firmly intact, while there is a great increase in the number of people willing to take risks to achieve social status. The risks are worth the price only if a higher premium is placed on social transformation than on stability. The enthusiasm for the new is a contemporary Western value. It ill behooves us therefore either to condemn others for overthrowing their forms of traditionalism or to sanction only those models which have been tried (satisfactorily or otherwise) elsewhere.

RISK-TAKING AND POLICY-MAKING

It would be an oversimplification to view risk-taking exclusively in terms of willingness to upset inherited culture patterns. For instance, there is the question of the relative ease with which Cuba resolved the "religious problem" and Hungary's relative difficulty. Catholicism in Hungary has been a long-standing force and deeply embedded in the nation's traditions, while it has never gained a strong foothold in Cuba because the Vatican sent Spanish priests unconnected with the problems of Cuban society. Hence, risks must be measured against tolerable loss.

Soon after a new nation has obtained relative independence from the old colonial power, it is faced with a number of policy-making alternatives: maintenance of a favorable balance of trade with the former colonial overseer—which carries with it the danger of aborting social development and hence creating instability; pursuance of a thoroughly independent financial and trading policy, which means entering the Third World—which can abort social development through denying the country the capital goods and basic technological needs which can be

13. For a most interesting speculative thrust into the special "phases" and "multiple levels" (double orientation) of development, see Alain Touraine, "Sociologie du développement," *Sociologie du Travail*, Vol. 5, No. 2, Apr.–June 1963, pp. 156–74.

supplied only by the fully developed areas; and passage over into the "socialist bloc" directly (or conversely, from the "socialist bloc" into either a neutralist or capitalist bloc), which can abort social development through external military aggression or the prospects of further civil conflicts. The alienation of sectors within the newly formed national units is increasingly under the weight of industrial and commercial specialization.

The "simple" process of development runs grave risks no matter how smoothly internal transition takes place. For the very entrance of a new nation into the developmental race is bound to have serious consequences for established power and trade equilibriums. That is why the Third World slogan appears to be: seek ye first the political kingdom and the rest shall follow. It is not possible to understand the rise of a Third World as such without realizing that this is a mélange of nations arriving in a world turning on American-led or Soviet-led blocs.

Thus a number of Third World nations have attempted to enter the modern economic world by minimizing political risks. The fact is, of course, that variations of capitalist and socialist patterns are quite possible given the historic peculiarities of Asia and Africa. Bureaucratic militarism (Nasser in Egypt, Sukarno in Indonesia) imposing a custodial socialism from above is a growing trend. On the other hand, a "semi-private" agricultural sector in Yugoslavia exists within a largely socialist framework. It has become clearer, with the passage of time, that what first appeared to be an interregnum is in fact evolving into a stable social system in its own right. The question of risk-taking and policy-making entails fundamental decisions as to the direction of a social system.

The greatest confusion seems to result from failing to distinguish differences between political strategies and economic structures. Too many Third World leaders tend to make pious declarations about having created new forms of "national" economic behavior; and too few are prepared to admit the actual economic character of their regimes. Such an "admission" may itself entail serious risks. When Cuba announced its goals as governed by Marxism, or when Egypt, India, and Guinea made similar pronouncements about being socialist, each nation ran the risk of being excluded from traditional trading and loan privileges. It must be concluded that development in underdeveloped areas tends strongly to be socialistic because planning is itself a consequence of the self-awareness of development.[14] But the need to avoid internal political upheaval ensures non-involvement in East-West struggles as a long-term fact of national development in the new nations.[15]

The extent to which a new nation is willing to take risks is directly related to its social wealth. It is increasingly clear that its leaders will urge a resort to force and violence in order to reach parity with surrounding states. Yet the promptings of political leaders do not necessarily exhaust the matter, or explain what in fact happens. Those who are compelled to gamble with risk and uncertainty may react quite differently: by continuing along as if nothing has happened, or even by returning to a traditional mode of behavior. A law might be formulated as follows: the higher the risk or subjectively felt uncertainty, the more must be the expected gain before anyone is willing to act in extremes. Given the objectively higher risks in the past, and the subjectively felt uncertainty with respect to the future, private investors are indeed more cautious in Third World countries than elsewhere. This caution expresses itself in demands for higher profits and use in lower risks. This is in the nature of a vicious circle militating against Third World development by either a national of foreign bourgeoisie, except in projects where profits are guaranteed or dictated by "higher" political priorities. This is also why Third World militarism is increasing sharply, since the military alone are able both to secure investment and to minimize commercial risk.

Because of this the struggle for development no longer shapes up as a struggle between capitalist bloc and socialist bloc nations, but rather a conflict between have and have-not nations—that is, between nations which have a great deal to lose in any international conflict and those which, though they might prefer pacific solutions, would risk outright conflict rather than stagnation. The virtues of battle are enhanced over those of rule. Albert Hourani has put the matter well:

> The new States find themselves faced with the interests and pressure of the Great Powers, and also with neighbors who, although no Great Powers, in the strict sense, may still be great in proportion to them.

14. See Karl Mannheim, *Freedom, Power and Democratic Planning.* New York: Oxford University Press, 1950, esp. pp. 41–76.
15. See Kwame Nkrumah, *Building a Socialist State.* Accra: Government Printer, 1961; and also, *I Speak of Freedom.* New York: Frederick Praeger, 1962.

What is more important, they are touched by new ideas, by the new ideology of economic and social development which is taking the place of the ideology of nationalism, or else giving it new content. It is only through economic development, the modern world believes, that nations can be strong and economically united; only a developing State can be morally healthy and united. So the problem is still that of strength, and of the social and political virtues which are inseparably connected with strength.[16]

In addition, the rapid nature of development tends to postpone settlement of issues relating to war and peace or capitalism and socialism; a type of national egoism comes into play which connects political invincibility with economic development. The remarkable recovery of the French economy between 1955 and 1963 did not necessarily lead to lowering the risks—since development is comparative in all things. France sought parity in the thermonuclear race no less than in the industrial race. Thus, the paradox is that the simple quantitative growth in national productivity and styles of life is hardly an assurance of international security. The Third World has been in the forefront of efforts to pacify the themonuclear balance of terror. Whether this is a temporary condition, occasioned by the military powerlessness of the new nations, or a permanent part of developmental ideology, remains a question for the future.

IMBALANCE BETWEEN LIFE STYLES AND INDUSTRIAL STYLES

The disparity between levels of personal living and levels of industrial productivity represents a complex marketing problem. There is an increasing disparity between the domestic and foreign markets for industrial goods produced in Third World areas. In the take-off period, the industrialization process is sustained by the heavy needs of the internal population, but as the market expands there, the country often finds itself unable to sell off its excess to foreign markets—particularly to advanced countries. The economy sinks into a condition of stagnation, while the population becomes increasingly conditioned to higher living standards as something coterminous with the evolution of the

16. Albert Hourani, "Revolutionary Nationalism," in *History and Hope: Progress in Freedom,* edited by K. A. Jelenski. London: Routledge and Kegan Paul, 1962, pp. 106–7.

industrial process as such. Thus, at the very point when the industrial population is conditioned to high levels of production and consumption, the industrial plant is compelled to make cut-backs in its productivity.

Lacking this momentum for sustaining a high rate of productivity, the Third World nation is compelled into a cycle of borrowing capital on a large scale, if for no other purpose than to sustain the levels in life-styles already achieved or to satisfy expected, but unfulfilled, demands placed upon the economy by its population. In brief, where capitalism exists there is extreme competition for markets. Under free-enterprise conditions, the disadvantages of coming last are most apparent. And given the fact that the population is not geared to sacrifice for "the next generation," nor willing to be coerced as in the process of socialist development, the contradiction between the levels of social living and those of industrialization become increasingly severe.

Yet, a nation is unlikely to return to agricultural base once it has been abandoned. What happens in many Third World nations is that their foreign-exchange earnings remain heavily dependent upon agricultural exports. The expanding middle classes, desiring consumer goods from abroad, place a strain on the foreign balance of payments. To meet this expanding demand, primary products of the Third World nation involved must become more, rather than less, important; hence agriculture remains the core economy precisely because of modernization in the consumer sector. In addition to such strategical problems there are structural problems as well. Many nations of the Third World are too small to engage effectively in industrial competition. The economics of scale serves to limit the market to produce efficiently all the industrial commodities of a developed economy. Hence, size serves to anchor many Third World nations to agrarianism. The dual issues of colonizer versus colonized and big nations versus small nations are interlocked in the actual process of international relations, specifically in the unevenness of contestants in the developmental processes.

This process—combined as it is with continued agricultural backwardness, inadequate investment in public-sector enterprises, and the overemphasis on one part of the industrial base (the consumer-oriented)—brings the economic system to a standstill. The ways to break this impasse are discussed elsewhere. We need note, however, the ways in which advanced capitalist nations might be of service: vigorous efforts on the part of the United States and Western Europe to open their markets to trade exports from the Third World countries, foreign technical assistance in the modernization of plant operations, but without strings, and a self-imposed screening by the leading powers of their own private-enterprise foreign holdings. That all of these assume a degree of economic free will which is nowhere to be found, except in economic monopoly on international trade, is quite beside the point. The point is that they simply do not operate this way; whether because of "laws of the market" or because of subjectively perceived interests, the reason is immaterial. The effect on the Third World countries of their economic monopoly is to increase the gap between levels of personal living and levels of industrial output—tailored for an internal market and funded by foreign capital. A problem inevitably arises when repayment of debts comes up on the agenda—as it invariably must. A choice has to be made by both contracting parties (the advanced and the underdeveloped nation) as to what should be done.

As long as the answer from the advanced nation is to extend the credit line, the status quo can be maintained. But when some monetary crisis (or other crisis) occurs, no more credits are forthcoming until the underdeveloped nation agrees to cooperate with the creditor nation. Then the Third World nation can either acquiesce and run the risk of revolution from below (since such downward mobility is often unacceptable to the urban proletariat and to certain bureaucratic and middle sectors as well), or resist such pressures, issue a debt cancellation notice, and provoke (or induce) a revolution from above—which runs the risk of foreign invasion, warfare, blockades, and the like.[17] In either event, it is clear that as long as the present gap between consumer demands and production potential continues to widen, there can be no stabilization in the Third World—and certainly no stabilization based on the simple expansion of technological innovation and industrial growth.

17. For an extremely interesting account of this phenomenon of structural gap between living styles and industrial exports, see David Felix, "Monetarists, Structuralists, and Import Substituting Industrialization." Prepared for the Rio de Janeiro Conference on Inflation and Growth, Jan. 3–11, 1963. *Studies in Comparative International Development,* Vol. 1, No. 10, 1965, pp. 137–53.

THE IMBALANCE BETWEEN INDUSTRIAL AVAILABILITIES AND EDUCATIONAL ACHIEVEMENTS

Public opinion in the advanced nations holds that revolutionaries and Communists are bred by poverty and ignorance. They therefore strongly believe that educational achievement is a necessary precondition for genuine social change. Indeed, the entire Alliance for Progress has as its chief goal the manufacture of social content through higher levels of educational achievement. Actually, such educational orientations have the reverse effect. As a result of higher and more specialized education, there is a corresponding rise in expectations. And the inability of most underdeveloped societies to fulfill these expectations creates an acute awareness of the gap between work capacity and work available.

What has developed in the most literate portions of Latin America, especially in Argentina and Brazil, is that educational levels have increased significantly in each generation, while at the same time there has been relative stagnation in the economic and productive centers. The lack of fulfillment in career expectations thus creates a revolutionary climate. For in the cultures of poverty there is a relative balance between life expectations and life styles. Those who reside in the *favelas* in Rio or in the *villas miseria* outside of Buenos Aires may have to face untold hardships and horrors. But since skilled labor remains relatively content, there is small hope for any link between the skilled classes and the lower classes.

On the other hand, where work possibilities far outstrip educational levels of achievement, the bottleneck thus created leads to a frustration which can be solved only by a revolutionary overhauling of the social structure. This at least is a partial explanation of student rebellions that have taken place throughout the world. There was an insistence that an acute imbalance exists between industrial development and educational achievement, which gave a feeling to students that the former would never come under the control of the liberal, educated members of a society.

Plans for massive educational reform are best realized in societies capable of mobilizing and integrating vast sectors of the "masses." A high productive capacity without a corresponding broad program of education leaves the society without the skilled personnel for the conduct of its affairs. Thus, the production and education spheres must be meshed with one another.

Actually imbalance as such serves not only as a bottleneck to social development but as a trigger for redressing this condition. Indeed, it is evident that structural imbalance is a causative basis for revolution-making. In the developing areas it is the university students (in conditions of low productivity and occupational stagnation) and bureaucratic officials (in conditions of low educational standards and massive illiteracy) who form the backbone of radical and revolutionary movements. This is not merely a phenomenon native to any social class or occupational group; it is not a manifestation of "working-class authoritarianism" or "middle-class revolutionism."

The presence of high illiteracy rates or the absence of work opportunities for the would-be professional cannot be isolated from the special kind of "mis-education" that occurs in many underdeveloped countries, especially those of long standing who have been influenced strongly by aristocratic tastes and philosophic concerns. This produces an anti-industrial bias; education too is not geared for industrial concepts of professional training, still harkening back to educating a conversationally stimulating, cultivating leisure class. This deepens the crisis of using "manpower" with advanced degrees.

One writer on Latin American affairs, William S. Stokes, has singled out the *pensadores* (the thinkers) as particularly responsible for, and reflective of, this mis-education. While the problem can probably not be pinpointed so specifically, his information should give pause to those who think that educational growth is indispensable to economic growth. He devised a sample which included thirteen universities from eight Latin American countries, plus the figures for all colleges and universities of Brazil, for the years 1950 through 1952. His findings were as follows:

> The total number of students in all of these universities was 82,135, out of which 45,540 or almost 66½ percent were in law, medicine, and engineering. Law, medicine, and engineering were the top three choices in Brazil (composite figures for 115 colleges and universities) and in 9 out of the other 13 universities in the sample. There were 30 schools of law in Brazil with 11,455 students and only 12 schools of agriculture with 1,188 students, a ratio of almost 10 law schools to each student in agriculture. There were only 539 students studying veterinary science in all of Brazil. Argentina depends on

agriculture and stock raising for a large part of its national income, yet at the Universidad Nacional de la Plata, there were in 1956 2,169 students in Juridicial and Social Science and only 62 students in agronomy and 42 students in Veterinary Science.[18]

The educated classes in many Third World nations with a long tradition of independence combined with fixed class and status composition have an expressed belief that leisure is superior to work and that abstract ideas are more important than technical ability. In this way, entire communities are keyed to seek sinecures, to obtain shorter work schedules without any corresponding improvement in work styles, and in general to avoid heavy labor whenever and wherever this is possible. Persistent inflationary spirals, the absence of any reasons for savings, and the unstable character of political behavior all serve to reduce the effectiveness of the educated classes.

Having established standards for living the life of ideas and eschewing the life of labor, the intelligentsia is faced with a growing demand for the products of the latter, without any desire to participate in their creation. Thus, there is an effort to capture the developmental process as a whole and hope that Providence will provide what the educational elite cannot—an advanced and modern form of industrial life in an intellectual climate of pre-capitalist techniques and post-capitalist ideologies. Unfortunately, the elite is ensnared by a double-bind of traditionalism and utopianism.[19]

Latin America is not unique in its emphasis on the relatively low status of manual labor or business pursuits. The same is true of such Moslem nations as Turkey, Syria, Iraq, Iran, and caste-ridden India. Despite the resourcefulness of these peoples, their educational leadership undermines efforts at development by assigning a special priority to ideas separated from technology. The fact is that the Middle East did have a long tradition in the practical sciences throughout the medieval period. Once Western concepts of mechanization reached Middle Eastern society to be promulgated by the educational elite, then the attitude toward manual labor changed. Tragically, the gap between scientific technology and the educational vistas of the leisure class grow further

18. William S. Stokes, "The 'Pensadores' of Latin America," in *The Intellectuals,* edited by George B. de Huszar. Glencoe, Ill.: The Free Press, 1960, p. 426.
19. See Irving Louis Horowitz, "The Philosophy of History in Latin America," *History and Theory: Studies in the Philosophy of History,* Vol. 11, No. 1, 1962, pp. 85–89.

apart, rather than closer together. Bernard Lewis has put the matter in the following manner:

> Medicine, engineering, and other useful sciences were taught at the very first military schools; scientific treatises were among the first Western works translated into Turkish and Arabic—but many medical graduates preferred to become administrators rather than soil their hands with patients, and the scientific school remained alien and exotic growths, in need of constant care and renewed graftings from the West. There has been no real development of original scientific work, such as exists in Japan, China, or India, and each generation of students must draw again from the sources in the West, which has meanwhile itself been making immense progress. The result is that the disparity in scientific knowledge, technological capacity, and therefore of military power between the Middle East and the advanced countries of the West is greater now than a hundred or fifty years ago, when the whole process of Westernization began.[20]

That every major twentieth-century revolutionary regime has found itself moving away from ideological orientations to technological application and that such reorientations have often taken on the bizarre form of a struggle between the humanistic and scientific traditions can be attributed to the historic process of mis-education.

We might sum up this point as follows: the initial problem in most Third World countries is an ignorance bred of illiteracy and a lack of training. The second problem is that, once a basic educational framework has been established, the forces of ascription and the general low state of social mobility serve to impede the utilization of education to the fullest extent possible. And the final point is that the process of education is often impeded by the value structure and favorable social position of the educator—who imbues the entire society with an orientation and ideology which is at once revolutionary in phraseology and reactionary in content; that is, it serves to prevent the development of a sound and balanced technological development, while at the same time demanding revolutionary changes which presuppose a relatively abundant material culture.

20. Bernard Lewis, "The Middle East versus the West," *Encounter,* Vol. XXI, No. 4, Whole No. 121, Oct. 1963, p. 28.

THE IMBALANCE BETWEEN POLITICAL AND ECONOMIC DEVELOPMENT

Development of a mature political structure does not necessarily entail economic development; and similarly, there are many cases of economic development taking place in a stunted polity. Argentina, for example, has the highest per capita output in Latin America. It is the only nation in Latin America which can be said to have relatively few feudal "hang-overs." Yet Argentina supports a political structure in keeping with much of Latin America. It has a strong centralized military authority which functions as a political "stabilizer" and "formulator," much as it does in parts of the non-developing portions of the hemisphere. On the other hand, Bolivia, which until recently had a relatively democratic political structure exhibiting direct worker participation in the decision-making process, remains the poorest of nations, exceeded only by Paraguay in low productive yields, and exceeding all other nations in the amount of foreign aid per person it receives from the United States.

Coalescences of political maturity and economic development are unusual. This destroys the idea that economics is a "basis" and politics the "super-structure." If anything, the recent Third World pattern is to develop a political apparatus which is in a position to impose order and independence on the economy. Only through political agencies can planning commissions be organized; only through the exercise of political coercion can economic expropriation and redistribution be initiated. It will be noted that political maturity is not equivalent to political coercion—indeed, dependence on the coercive apparatus of a state demonstrates the absence of voluntary reorganization and of a common consensus.

This whole problem can be seen most clearly in the victory of Bolshevism, a political victory in an underdeveloped nation. Stalinism identified socialism with internationalism only in theory. In practice, socialism and nationalism were celebrated. On the other hand, the reverse is not always true. Consensus may merely mean the ability of dominant classes to make universal their ideology. Communism fragmented in the West: the social democrats were disillusioned by single party rule and reacted reflexively by returning to parliamentarism. Trotskyists split with the autonomous Soviet position on the question of building socialism in one country; intellectuals were often alienated by what they saw as parallels with fascism and with dogmatism generally.

And of course the ruling classes of the First World were likewise deeply disturbed by Stalinism; not because of any intrinsic disagreements with the use of terror but because they feared a countervailing political and military machine. The Trotskyist animus was particularly devastating, since it pointed out that there was no way in which building state socialism in one backward nation could be made synonomous with socialist ideals and values.

The matter of the relationship between nationalism and socialism is most delicate. To say the "simple" truth, that they are not the same and may require different agencies and instrumentalities for their respective realization, does not say much about their interaction.

As a rule, the early stages of developmental impetus can and usually do elicit the whole-hearted support of all major sectors of the underdeveloped area involved. When the focus is on eliminating foreign capital and turning a heterogeneous mass into a homogeneous nation, it is politically superficial to raise the dangers and threats of nationalization to the socialist polity, or for that matter, the dangers of socialism for nationalization. At this level, the "common enemy" is external, and hence the imbalance between economic and political development hardly manifests itself. The problem for the political leadership is one of *animating* the total population rather than *coercing* any one sector of the people.

After the successful conclusion of this initial stage, no guarantees exist that the political apparatus will be marshaled to support any particular economic system. Indeed, the tendency toward an economic mix between capitalist and socialist formations is quite strong. Israel gained its independence in 1948 and at that time had a powerfully socialist-oriented (if not dominated) labor and agricultural sector. Without abandoning its socialist sector, Israel nonetheless has moved increasingly toward promoting private investments from abroad and in so doing encouraging the growth of a domestic bourgeoisie—all in the name of national security and strength. Indonesia, which also gained its independence after World War II, has shown a different pattern—one which has increasingly moved toward the socialization of the nation— through military intervention from above more than through mass political pressures from below. The fact remains that Indonesia shows that socialism is much more a goal to be striven for *after,* rather than before, the nationalistic revolutionary phase is concluded.

Clearly, one central reason why the Third World is not under constant attack or criticism from the major power blocs, East and West, is the simple fact that the nationalist phase of the revolution is still incomplete, and hence the new nations are potentially compatible with either capitalist or socialist economic formations. But it will not do for socialist or capitalist supporters to identify the process of national liberation as belonging to them by definition. The *ralliement* necessary for national revolution is something quite different from the class differentiation entailed in a socialist revolution.

The question of how one "approaches" the developing nations of Africa, Asia, and South America is therefore a good deal more complex than it initially appears to be. "Men of good will" might cheer the rise of national sovereignty, but these same men might be genuinely apprehensive about the "Balkanization" of Africa. Would "men of good will," who are also men of capitalist enterprise, appreciate the rise of anti-imperialist and anti-bourgeois spirit in the new nations? And might not "men of good will" deplore the displacement of foreign capital investment by an inferior, and possibly harsher, domestic bourgeoisie, willing to seal off the new nation from foreign competition and willing to minimize the country's industrial nationalization program?

In part the problem is not quite as insoluble as it first appears to be. In the first place, nationalism and socialism are in fact linked in many of the new nations; and if the Stalin model proved unappetizing in its Soviet form, it somehow seemed at least somewhat less abhorrent in its Third World form. Perhaps this is the difference between the state socialism of the Soviet Union and the state capitalism of many new nations in the Third World. Hence the imbalance between political ambitions and economic structure is not quite as pronounced as might be the case were socialists to adopt an "internationalist" or "one-world" ideology prior to the completion of the national liberation period. In the second place, certain archaic forms of economic production are simply not feasible for new nations with low levels of capitalist accumulation—the state must by necessity if not by choice go into "business." It may have to nationalize petroleum, coal, oil, and chemical industries, if it is to have such industries at all. The likelihood is that only the political apparatus can command the degree of capital and human wealth necessary to enter the modern industrial world—and in this sense the politics of nationalism may very likely promote socialist economic structures. Mali's Minister of Development, Seydou Kouyate, has put the matter crisply:

As a matter of fact, the political organization has been the melting-pot where the peasant and the city dweller have met. It has pulled the former out of his isolation, cured the latter of his disdain for the bush, and achieved practically the national unity from which it was drawing its strength. Thus, the gap which existed between the city and the countryside has been filled up and the various strata of the population have been unified into one single stream oriented toward the political objectives.[21]

In the third place, nationalism itself has an "open sesame" effect; that is, forms of economic experimentation are possible after a revolution that are not possible without one or even during one. Economic determination is quite out of the question. The issue is not which form of economy can best promote development, but which nationalization process will allow development to take place at all.

Development is by no means another word for internationalism, or for the cooperation between states and regimes. Quite the reverse: development is oftentimes defined within a nationalist perspective although it might easily be argued that it is precisely this perspective that leads to a vicious circle which either frustrates developmental goals or no less frustrates nationalist claims. But since to phase in a developmental take-off in the first place means that some kind of national revolution has occurred, the nation as symbol attains an importance which makes impossible its supercession to more rational international organization. To move from colonial status to being part of the community of liberated men simply by having the established imperial power agree to liquidate its control is pleasant but wishful thinking. It is a paradox that nationalism, which is the supreme protagonist of internationalism, is at the same time its necessary precondition. On the other side, it might be that stage-skipping is not possible in the economic sector either. An extensive period of national exploitation may well replace the period of colonial exploitation—through the development of a powerful political apparatus which extracts a higher productivity from the labor force (usually in the name of socialism) than was possible under colonial conditions.

21. Seydou Kouyate, quoted in "Dakar Colloquium: Search for Definition," *Africa Report*, Vol. 8, No. 5, May 1963, pp. 15–16; see also, S. J. Patel, "Economic Transition in Africa," *African Politics and Society*, Irving L. Markovitz (ed.). New York: The Free Press, 1970, pp. 312–31.

Nationalism as such makes possible a degree of self-exploitation that is out of the question in the colonial period. As the brilliant Frantz Fanon has pointed out:

> The colonized bourgeoisie which comes to power uses its class aggressiveness to take over the positions previously held by strangers. It brandishes energetically the notion of the nationalization of cadres. . . . On their side, the town proletariat, the mass of unemployed, the small artisans, side with this nationalist attitude.[22]

They side with the national bourgeoisie because, in some special sense, the bourgeoisie itself is highly "socialized." Just as in the West there is the "bourgeoisification" of the working classes, so in the new nation there is the "proletarianization" of the bourgeoisie. Africa has had a noticeable absence of the classic view of class struggle, and hence believes that coercion can be minimized in the process of development. Socialism itself is redefined to include the national bourgeoisie. The word comes to mean "an appeal for a common effort." [23]

The newer nations see that the imbalance between politics and economics can be eliminated by a common identification with social development as such. As Sékou Touré put the matter in relation to Africa: "There exists only one and the same class, that of the dispossessed." [24] Unfortunately, such an approach does not sufficiently distinguish rhetoric from reality, since in fact Africa is not comprised of a single class, nor even a single race. And as such, the idea of the single-class continent poses serious difficulties for the very leadership that seeks its implementation.

At the empirical level, development depends heavily on the extent to which economic and political forces can be mobilized in a common effort to free a people, a community, or even a continent from traditional imperial fetters. And we must not forget that by being willing to await events the more developed areas may provide immeasurable aid to the newly developed areas in the settlement of the latter's policy questions and economic structures.

22. Frantz Fanon, *Les Damnés de la Terre*. Paris: Maspero Cahiers Libres, 1961, p. 118. On this same subject, see Manfred Halpern, *The Politics of Social Change in the Middle East and North Africa*. Princeton: Princeton University Press, 1963.
23. See A. Fenner Brockway, *African Socialism*. London: Bodley Head, 1963.
24. See Sékou Touré, *Expérience Guinéenne et Unité Africaine*. Paris: Présence Africaine, 1961.

The Contest Between Liberty and Equality

Perhaps the ultimate duality in the Third World as it is now constituted is the deadly competition between liberty and equality. The French Enlightenment and the French and American revolutions announced the fusion of these two concepts, of the principle of personal liberty and of mass equality. Utilitarianism was to supply the ideological cement through which the one and the many, the person and the society, were to act as mutual reinforcements.[25]

The international schism within the democratic tradition expressed itself through the contrary roads taken by two economic systems, capitalism and socialism. The "moral economy" of each was hardened into an ideological controversy over man's essential nature: the "natural egotism" of men became identified with the forms of capitalist production, while the "altruism" of "socialist man" became identified with socialism. The fact that neither egotism nor altruism had much to do with the development of either capitalism or socialism—that in fact, all sorts of emotional components entered the picture—was forgotten in the process. A veritable barrage of moralistic rhetoric cascaded forth, as if private appropriation or commodity production was in itself the guardian of personal egotism and as if the state appropriation of commodity production was itself the ultimate in socialism. The appeal to "human nature" became encased in the respective industrial ideologies of the East and West—and what was lost was the common problems faced by industrial societies.

This schism between egotism and altruism, between capitalist and socialist ideologies, initiated the present competition between liberty and equality—between liberalism and socialism, and between John Stuart Mill and Karl Marx. It was the modern myth of the eternal return, fused with the metaphysical problem of the one and the many— the individual and the collective as conflicting styles of judgment. What the late nineteenth-century debates disguised was the essential similarity at the economic level between industrial societies. The problems faced by the American and his European counterpart are after all quite similar:

25. On this contest between liberty and equality, see J. L. Talmon, *The Origins of Totalitarian Democracy*. London: Secker & Warburg, 1954; Hannah Arendt, *On Revolution*. New York: The Viking Press, 1963; Irving Louis Horowitz, *Radicalism and the Revolt Against Reason*. London: Routledge and Kegan Paul, 1961; and Alvin W. Gouldner, *Enter Plato*. New York: Basic Books, 1965.

the kind of allocation desirable, the need for horizontal or vertical industrial integration, the problem of forced spending and forced savings, and the like. It might well be that the growth of the Third World similarly represents a convergence of socioeconomic forms that are different from classical capitalism, or for that matter, classical socialism. As such, the new form, while it may hardly be universally appealing to advocates of democracy or free enterprise, or for that matter even socialist enterprise, does nonetheless represent a unique coming to terms with the power realities at both the level of theory and practice.

The growth of the Third World has finally put all these problems into perspective. Indeed, it has been the Third World which has made plain the fact that the socialist system of economy is not a consequence of advanced capitalist production but a direct path from backwardness to modernity, unmediated and unencumbered by the baggage of industrial history. It has been the Third World which has made the leviathans of both East and West realize that the way they had divided the world ideologically was no longer universally acceptable. The conflict between capitalism and socialism gave way, under the steady push and pull of new nations, to a new definition of the competition between liberty and equality—one based on the differences which still exist between rich nation-states and poor nation-states. Each new nation has faced the same dilemma between libertarian and equalitarian modes of life. The only clear point now known is that there are no automatic solutions. Liberty is not a consequence of voting privileges, nor is equality a consequence of affluence. Voting rights and economic abundance may prevail in an atmosphere sorely lacking in both liberty and equality. This is the sobering reality each new nation must face as it enters the period of industrial acceleration.

17

Social Conflict and Social Development

I

"Symmetry" is the decisive word for the big nuclear powers. "Asymmetry" is the decisive word for the non-nuclear Third World powers. War remains as real in the nuclear era as in the pre-nuclear era. The dangers may be greater since many of the Third World nations act on the assumption that they can move freely in full confidence that the nuclear stalemate guarantees unlimited action. When neither optimism nor fear is mutual, when a real advantage would accrue to the aggressive nation, then the very condition of military disequilibrium is itself a factor in war-making. And no factor would create a politically unbalanced condition more rapidly or completely than an abandonment of prudence and intelligence on the part of some Third World nations—who, from the viewpoint of the Cold War, are potential nth powers. Yet, what can a nation like India or Algeria do? Forfeit its national sovereignty? The main foreign-policy dilemma of Third World countries is how to maintain independence and sovereignty in a competitive nuclear context which views with suspicion and alarm any noticeable shift in the international balance of power. This dilemma is resolved at the operational level by reliance upon types of conflict, for instance, guerrilla warfare, coups d'état, foco actions, and so forth, that are sufficiently controlled so as not to invite massive intervention by the major powers, and yet adequate enough to stimulate social development.

Social development, involving the destruction of traditional power relations and power matrices, necessarily raises with increasing urgency the question of conflict and conflict resolution. While there is a broad

480

recognition that international peace is a basic requirement for social development, it is not as well understood that the price of one is sometimes paid at the cost of the other.[1] However "inter-related" world development and world peace may be, they are neither historical nor conceptual equivalents.

Rapid social development has in the past been accompanied not only by widespread economic and political upheaval but also by wars affecting large numbers of people. The demand for social change in the Third World has been materially assisted by the transfer of the locus of military action in their sphere. The fact that power now cancels out at the level of the nuclear powers is a stimulant to further extensive development.[2] In other words, dissensus, while dysfunctional with respect to the major powers, is quite functional for the newly emergent nations.

While social development has become desired more than ever before, warfare at the level of nuclear powers has become a less viable instrument for producing changes.[3] In its most fundamental meaning, war has become obsolescent, since the possibility of one side's emerging victorious has been obviated by the fact of massive retaliation—by the capacity of each side to annihilate the other. Thus, the problem of social development urgently requires a reconsideration of the basic forms of human cooperation, or, in the language of military analysts, human bargaining.[4] It takes little imagination to construct a utopia in which war would be eliminated. All that is required is a consensual picture of the world in which there are no "sides," but only one side—enthusiastically underwritten by the whole of mankind. The really complicated problem is how to live in a world of "sides," in a world in which the power equilibrium is constantly changing through the creation of new "sides."

The problem can be stated as follows: when there is little or no active social development and a single power can impose a widespread dominion, then a Caesaristic consensus obtains in the absence of abrasive and fragmenting forces. When there is rapid social development, and no single power can assert a "universal" dominion, then an intense con-

1. See Thomas C. Schelling, *The Strategy of Conflict*. Cambridge, Mass.: Harvard University Press, 1960; and more recently, Paul Swingle (ed.), *The Structure of Conflict*. New York: Academic Press, 1970.
2. See Kenneth E. Boulding, *Conflict and Defense: A General Theory*. New York: Harper & Row, 1962; and Anatol Rapoport, *Fights, Games and Debates*. Ann Arbor: University of Michigan Press, 1960.
3. See Irving Louis Horowitz, *Games, Strategies and Peace*. Philadelphia: American Friends Service Committee, 1963.
4. See Hannah Arendt, *On Revolution*. New York: Viking Press, 1963.

flict pattern obtains. When there is rapid social development and the major powers can agree upon the rules for the conduct of international affairs, then a cooperation (programed conflict plus programed consensus) pattern obtains. Hence consensus, or an internal agreement in principle on the forms of social action, is most unlikely in its present stage. Further social development through armed struggles remains likely, as long as the character of such conflict remains "civil" rather than "international." For example, more than one million Ibos were eliminated in the Nigerian Civil War, and a quarter-million "communists" were similarly liquidated in the Indonesian civil wars of the mid-1960's. As long as these struggles were defined as internal rather than international the problem of cooperation at the world level remained strangely subject to solution.

The idea that world hegemony can be achieved, either through pacific or military means, must be placed in the context of the uneven nature of development.[5] Even if the world were unified into an international economy, peace would not be assured. The increasing military competition of Western nations for the last three hundred years substantiates this point. And now we have the additional evidence that the socialist bloc is no less competitive among its members. Even if the world were uniformly socialist in nature, peace would likewise not be assured. This classic claim of socialist theorists has been snapped decisively by the rise of polycentric forms of communism. The competition between China and the Soviet Union is clearly quite as intense as any in the capitalist world. Indeed, the very fact that socialism claims it can create a new and tolerable world hegemony makes the conflict within the Soviet bloc even more bitter than anything in the West; for here many divergencies do exist if only because capitalism is based upon competition and freedom in trade, commerce, and politics.

As patterns of consensus and conflict have mutually canceled one another out, there remain great possibilities for planned cooperation. The right to be different has become as necessary to a nation as it once was to the individual. And this right to be different, once institutionalized in world law and in agreements covering such matters as travel in outer space and off-shore limits, makes possible unimpeded social development which emerging societies require and which the past concentration on consensus and/or conflict patterns has seriously stifled.

5. Gino Germani, *Política y Sociedad en un Epoca de Transición*. Buenos Aires: Editorial Paidós, 1962, pp. 98–109.

II

There are at least seven shades of meaning which currently attach to the term "consensus" beyond the common-sense usage of the word as a proper synonym for agreement among people. First and perhaps most commonly, it is defined as "adjustment of social dissension." This usage is borrowed from the present psychoanalytic definition of normality as social adjustment and neurosis as the failure of adjustment.[6] The second view begins with role theory. Consensus is seen as an accord between role behavior and role expectation.[7] The third position, while having a point of contact with an adjustment approach to consensus, lifts it out of the individual realm into a cultural framework. "Where an opinion is very widely held and cuts across all groups in society," there you have consensus.[8] The fourth theory sees the term as affiliated to a hedonistic impulse, as "possible only when two or more parties want to maintain a relationship which each regards as in its own interest." [9] A cognate definition is offered by the same writer in terms of game thory: "Two parties or groups are playing to gain a maximum, but they are prepared to settle for less within the recognized limits." [10] The sixth theory identifies consensus with curbing the hedonistic impulse and instinct, and with Durkheim's notion of solidarity and social cohesion generally.[11] Our last author sees consensus in its pure form as a sharing of perspective, as "nothing more or less than the existence on the part of two or more persons, of similar orientations toward something." [12] The concept of consensus has aroused such intense interest because it seems to satisfy the requirements of both social equilibrium and social development.

Most frequently consensus is identified with functional efficiency and

6. J. O. Hertzler, *American Social Institutions: A Sociological Analysis.* Boston: Allyn and Bacon, 1961, p. 63.

7. Neal Gross, "The sociology of Education," in *Sociology Today: Problems and Prospects,* edited by R. K. Merton, L. Broom, L. S. Cottrell, Jr. New York: Basic Books, 1959, p. 140.

8. Leonard Broom and Philip Selznick, *Sociology: A Text with Adapted Readings,* second edition. Evanston, Ill.: Row, Peterson & Co., 1958, p. 278.

9. Arnold W. Green, *Sociology: An Analysis of Life in Modern Society,* third edition. New York: McGraw-Hill, 1960, p. 65.

10. *Ibid.,* p. 67.

11. Ely Chinoy, *Society: An Introduction to Sociology.* New York: Random House, 1961, pp. 344–46.

12. Theodore Newcomb, "The Study of Consensus," in *Sociology Today, op. cit.,* p. 279.

with the social requisites of political democracy in advanced nations.[13] In its simplest form, this means that an increase in the amount of social consensus yields an increase in functional efficacy and democratic polity; while, inversely, a decrease in the amount of social consensus creates social disorganization and dissensus. On a broader front, advocates of consensus avoid the knotty issue of how conflicts arise by concentrating on how men achieve agreements "in principle." By defining the core of social action in terms of establishing a pattern of orientation and locating one or more situational objects, consensus comes to be equated with the maintenance of social equilibrium.[14]

Conflict theory suffers less from the problem of ambiguity, since the nature of conflict, being a more "positive" act, makes possible a clearer theoretical position. The early development of sociology from Marx to Simmel took as its point of departure the idea that society is best understood as a selective and collective response to the needs of social interaction in a "nonequilibrated" world. This involved a rejection, conscious or otherwise, of the idea that society rests upon a contractual or informal agreement made between equals to secure common goals.[15] Simmel sees the Roman Empire not as a union of the general will with particularized wills but rather as an illustration of the efficiency and functionality of political dissensus; what he terms "Caesaristic types of rule." Thus consensus consists only in the "tendency of domination by means of leveling." This apparent consensual apparatus is but disguised superordination. In discussing Philip the Good of Burgundy, he notes that "legal differences were created exclusively by the arbitrary pleasure of the ruler. They thus marked all the more distinctly the common, unalterable subordination of his subjects." [16]

Similarly for Marx, the economic system called capitalism does not come into existence because of the clamor of public opinion, or to ex-

13. Seymour Martin Lipset, "Political Sociology," in *Sociology Today, op. cit.,* p. 114.

14. Talcott Parsons, *The Social System.* Glencoe: The Free Press, 1951, p. 507. This same view is even more forcefully developed in his "The Point of View of the Author," *The Social Theories of Talcott Parsons,* edited by Max Black. Englewood Cliffs, N.J.: Prentice-Hall, 1961, p. 327.

15. For an excellent general statement of conflict theory, see Don Martindale, *The Nature and Types of Sociological Theory.* Boston: Houghton Mifflin Co., 1960, pp. 127–49.

16. Georg Simmel, "Subordination Under an Individual," *The Sociology of Georg Simmel,* edited and translated by K. H. Wolff. Glencoe: Ill.: The Free Press, 1950, pp. 201–7.

press the general will, but simply to satisfy the historical process which brings a social class to power. The welding of such power to a new social class is the purpose of the state, which in turn enters the historical picture as the central agency of coercion while posing as the agency of social consensus.

The practical struggle of these particular interests, which constantly run counter to communal interests, both real and illusory, makes it necessary for the state to intervene and seize control. The social power —that is, the multiplied productive force, which arises through the natural but not voluntary cooperation of different individuals as it is determined within the division of labor—appears to these individuals, not as their own united power, but as an alien force existing outside them, of the origin and end of which they are ignorant, which they thus cannot control.[17]

Consensus appears as an idealized form of coercion. Conflict theorists attempt to subsume the undesirable elements of consensus as manipulation. Consensus theorists attempt to subsume the undesirable elements of conflict as institutionalized contests with overriding shared values. The sociology of knowledge can be viewed as a concerted effort made by conflict-oriented analysts to tackle the problem of ideas. But they inevitably become enmeshed in their subject and discover complex processes whereby ideas transform themselves and reappear as stimulants for action in new places at new times. In other words, ideas are allowed to escape from their material grounding, and the sociologists of knowledge become idealistic, even against their better judgment. The conservative irrelevance of much consensus theory legitimizes a tactical decision in favor of conflict theory; but ultimately, such a conflict theory must be seen as the polarized expression of the same social structure that gives rise to consensus theory as well. A theory of cooperation, involving the strategic uses of both conflict and consensus, is better suited to the needs of developmental programs.

Modern expressions of conflict theory rest upon the fact that the social world exists in equilibrium as a consequence of conflict situations. The world is imperiled by threats, gambles, strategic moves, interdependent decisions, limited wars, and the like. As Thomas Schelling notes:

17. Karl Marx and Friedrich Engels, "The German Ideology," in *Basic Writings on Politics and Philosophy: Marx and Engels,* edited by L. S. Feuer. Garden City, N.Y.: Doubleday and Co., 1959, pp. 255–56, also p. 253.

> Though "strategy of conflict" sounds cold-blooded, the theory is not concerned with the efficient application of violence or anything of the sort; it is not essentially a theory of aggression or of resistance or of war. . . . Such a theory is nondiscriminatory as between the conflict and the common interest, as between its applicability to potential enemies and its applicability to potential friends.[18]

In a broader sense, conflict theory strongly emphasizes dissensus and deviance because it has been focused on the problem of social change instead of on the nature of social structure. Conflict thus appears as the "motor force" or the "drive shaft" of the developmental process. As a result, the emphasis was then placed upon human agencies which would perform such a role. For Marx it was the urban proletariat, for Gumplowicz the ethnic minority transformed into a majority; and for Sorel the creative elite culled from the ranks of the exploited.[19] Obviously, the very language of conflict involves a negation of integration, or at least a postponement of the consideration of such matters. And this is the significant difference between various analysts of the development process—for whether one accepts a consensus or a dissensus model in large measure determines how one fills the content of development with "social forces" or "social engineering."

But conflict theory shares with consensus theory a faith in "two player" situations. As such, their utility in meeting the challenge of the Third World or of multi-national situations remains dubious. Formulations which start with *either* capitalism *or* socialism, *either* democracy *or* autocracy, *either* West *or* East are a reflection of the "bilateralism" in conflict theory. They have dubious relevance to those newly emerging societies for which economic and political experimentation is a necessity.

Critics have reacted to conflict theory by resurrecting "unilateral" faiths. They have particularly relied upon the brilliant social historian Alexis de Tocqueville.[20] The rallying point in Tocqueville is the comment that "a society can exist only when a great number of men consider a great number of things from the same point of view; when they hold

18. Thomas C. Schelling, *op. cit.*, p. 15.
19. See Irving Louis Horowitz, *Radicalism and the Revolt Against Reason.* London: Routledge & Kegan Paul, 1961.
20. Seymour Martin Lipset, *Political Man: The Social Basis of Politics.* Garden City, N.Y.: Doubleday and Co., 1960, pp. 26–28, 65–66. Lipset's continual juxtaposition of Tocqueville and Marx is a strong indication that the differences between consensus and conflict theories involve something more than scientific requirements. Indeed, he has made them ideological poles: consensus representing democracy and conflict representing authoritarianism.

the same opinion upon many subjects; when the same occurrences suggest the same thought and impressions to their minds." [21] This would seem to be the historical progenitor for the new theory of consensus, and it would seem to be the rejoinder to those political sociologies which seek to define social structure in terms of holders and seekers of power.

The most widespread claim made by advocates of consensus is that agreement represents a necessary condition for order. Social structure has been seen to exclude those patterns of human action which are spontaneous.[22] Social structure is said to consist in a "set of statuses" defined by relatively stable relationships between people. Consensus and conflict thus appear as structured and unstructured modes of behavior respectively. Consensus involves a general acceptance of the authority of the group, common traditions and rules for inducting and indoctrinating new members; while conflict is seen as external to social structure, as spontaneity, impulsive action, lack of organization, and intuitive response to immediate situations.[23] In short, consensus differs from conflict as organization differs from deviance. Thus to discuss social structure is by definition not to examine conflict situations and, of course, to examine conflict situations is to discuss something extraneous to social structure.[24]

To place conflict outside the framework of social structure, or to see dissensus as necessarily destructive of the social organism, is to place a definite premium on social disequilibrium. It strongly implies that a society can be changed only by apocalyptic or spontaneous methods. The identification of consensus with social structure reinforces the stereotyped view that social development is inferentially synonymous with social chaos. Consensus theory thus tends to become a metaphysical

21. Alexis de Tocqueville, *Democracy in America,* Vol. 1, translated by H. Reeve. New York: Century and Co., 1899, p. 398.
22. See Paul F. Lazarsfeld, "Political Behavior and Public Opinion," in *The Behavioral Sciences Today,* edited by Bernard Berelson. New York: Basic Books, 1963, pp. 176–87.
23. See Robert E. Park, "Reflections on Communication and Culture," *The American Journal of Sociology,* Vol. XLIV, 1939, pp. 191–205.
24. Kurt Lang and Gladys E. Lang, *Collective Dynamics.* New York: Thomas Y. Crowell Co., 1961, pp. 13–14; Ralf Dahrendorf, *Class and Class Conflict in Industrial Society.* Stanford: Stanford University Press, 1959, pp. 189–93. The pioneer effort in this direction was made by Herbert Blumer, "Collective Behavior," in *New Outline of the Principles of Sociology,* edited by A. M. Lee. New York: Barnes & Noble, 1946.

representation of the fully developed societies, that is, the "consensual society." [25] It rests on a principle of "general interests" which every member of every society is supposed to imbibe if he wishes to avoid the onus of being deviant with respect to his society. Such a view implies that social conflict necessarily produces a world of deviants quite incapable of attending to problems of functional survival.[26] The possibility that different goals can be registered within a single functional agency such as a unified national party is too rarely entertained.[27]

An extremely worthwhile effort in this direction has been made by Karl Deutsch. He has shown how over time governments have become much bigger in the lives of nations, while at the same time the foreign sectors have declined in importance.

> The foreign trade sector of England, that is, the sum of exports and imports in England, used to equal about 60% of the national income. Today it is about 38%. In 1872, the German trade sector was 45%, and by now in the late fifties it was down to about 38%. On the other hand, the governmental sector was 10% then and 41% now. So if you look at the two you begin to see a cross-over point. In the classical international politics of the nineteenth century, foreign trade involved a bigger share of the national income than did government at home. Foreign trade potentially, therefore, involved a larger proportion of the interest groups of the country than did domestic government and politics at all levels. Today the opposite holds. This is the potential basis of national self-preoccupation.[28]

Thus, the changing roles of state power serve to redirect demands for high consensus domestically and equally serve to stimulate high conflict potentials abroad.

A social structure might be considered as a dynamic balance of dis-

25. For example, the position taken by Edward A. Shils in "The Calling of Sociology," *Theories of Society: Foundations of Modern Sociological Theory,* edited by T. Parsons, E. Shils, K. D. Naegele, J. R. Pitts. New York: The Free Press, 1961, pp. 1405–48.

26. Theodore Newcomb, "The Study of Consensus," *Sociology Today, op. cit.* p. 284.

27. Gideon Sjoberg, "Contradictory Functional Requirements and Social Systems," *Journal of Conflict Resolution,* Vol. IV, 1960, pp. 198–208; see also Eugene Litwak, "Modes of Bureaucracy Which Permit Conflict," *The American Journal of Sociology,* Vol. LXVII, 1961, pp. 177–84.

28. Karl W. Deutsch, "The Impact of Communications upon International Relations Theory," in *Theory of International Relations: The Crisis of Relevance,* edited by Abdul A. Said. Englewood Cliffs, N.J.: Prentice-Hall, p. 84.

harmonious parts. If we start from the real position of societies, it is evident that conflict situations are intrinsic and organic to social structure. Considered in this manner, the group, the community, or the nation are the particularized areas of social activity in which conflicts arise and are resolved. Recent students of social problems have shown that dissensus is intrinsic to social structure. Indeed, the form of society is itself defined by the quality and types of conflict situations tolerated if not openly sanctioned.[29]

Types of conflict cannot be considered apart from types of social structure. Internal social conflicts, which concern goals, values, or interests that do not contradict the basic assumptions upon which conflicts are founded, tend to be positively functional for the social structure. Such conflicts tend to make it possible to readjust the norms and power relations within groups in accordance with the felt needs of its individual members or subgroups.[30]

III

Consensus theory has been advanced as better suited to dealing with the difficulties of a social examination of unstable relations than is dissensus theory. Three factors in particular are emphasized; first, conflict situations are transitory in nature. That is, the actual behavior of a mass in an extreme situation, such as civil war or revolution, is so short-lived and capricious that it is impossible to predict conclusions or consequences in such situations. Second, since conflict situations must be dealt with in their natural social environment it is impossible to conduct controlled experiments as one finds in strictly delineated microscopic types of research. Third, evaluations must be made in terms of second- and third-hand materials such as newspaper reports, autobiographical sketches, and historical studies of unique events—all of which clearly involve the sociological researcher in commitments to many styles of research.[31]

These objections reveal a transparency that poses a serious threat to

29. See, for example, the recent text by R. R. Dynes, Alfred C. Clarke, Simon Dinitz, Iwao Ishino, *Social Problems: Dissensus and Deviation in an Industrial Society.* New York: Oxford University Press, 1964.
30. Lewis A. Coser, *The Functions of Social Conflict.* Glencoe, Ill.: The Free Press, 1956, pp. 151–52.
31. A fuller catalogue of objections to the study of conflict situations is contained in Kurt Lang and Gladys Lang, *op. cit.,* pp. 545–53.

social research as such. Analysis in sociology has never been reducible to the simplicity of a scientific investigation. While it is correct that conflict situations, even of major proportions, are generally of "short" duration (but not in regard to their consequences), this does not represent a serious objection either to the empirical study of conflict situations, or, more to the point, to an investigation of the causes of such situations. The brief time all but the most protracted physical conflicts take indicates that certain sampling devices used in stable contexts are ineffectual in dealing with certain kinds of happenings. To reason that to go beyond the borders of current methodological safeguards is to go beyond social science itself is sheer casuistry.

It is equally transparent to object to studying conflict situations because they have no well-defined contours or boundaries. The anthropologist almost always faces this problem in relation to a given culture. Would anyone seriously contend that anthropological research is any less a social science because it has a natural setting? The surest guarantee against provincialism and ethnocentricism would be to develop techniques of study suitable to this "natural" social setting. The sociologist has too often failed in this endeavor. For instance, he has tried to apply questionnaires devised for particular situations to other cultural and social settings where they have little revelance or validity. The natural setting within which dissensus arises is far from being an obstacle; it provides an incentive for moving beyond the highly structured world of the small group into the world at large. That this opportunity has not been seized is a sad reflection on the current limits of sociological practices rather than a true estimate of the legitimate boundaries of sociology.

To equate the worth of a theory (such as consensus or conflict theory) with degrees of control is an arbitrary device which means that the only things that can be studied are those for which data already exist—which may help to account for sameness and duplication of research efforts present in small-group sociology today, and the relative absence of studies on the social structure of developing areas. The most important task for sociology today is to fashion methods adequate for studying problems of social order in a world of conflicting interests, standards, and values. Social order must itself be defined, and in turn must define the larger universe of social change. And both structure and process must be analyzed in terms of the more generic concept of development. The sociologist can hardly run the risk of being surprised by current events because he has been bewitched by order and befuddled by change.

The faith in consensus is often reflected in a deep respect for the amazing complexity of social organization in industrial economies: the automation of production, the mechanization of human responsibilities, the precision of "chain of command" and "line" matrices, and the opportunities of regulating and manipulating man in mass society on the part of highly articulate elites leads to a vision of the social system as inviolable. The Parsonian model of development in particular seems impressed with the regularities which obtain between organization and society as such. This is the consequence of equating organization with consensus. The stress and strain of organizational life gives rise to a definition of social action as that auto-regulative mechanism which adjusts for such "alienative" factors as may arise in the maintenance of the whole system.[32]

Such a view faces the same dilemma as traditional laissez-faire economics, namely, the assumption that automatic marketing "laws" somehow operate over and above the actual desires and ends of men. To meet the laissez-faire implications in the theory of social consensus, certain functionalists have developed a theory of the "safety-valve," where organizations "provide substitute objects upon which to displace hostile sentiments as well as means of a reaction to aggressive tendencies." [33] But this safety-valve notion only reinforces the equilibrium model surrounding the theory of social organization, since the assumption of institutional omnipotence and omniscience is strengthened.

Consensus theory, particularly as a replacement for conflict theory, bears a close historical and analytical connection to the attempt to replace the language of social class with that of social status. It is a shift from viewing industrialism as an aspect of many and varied forms of society to a vision of the industrial complex as growing omnipotent and dominating the society. Essentially the Weberian theory of bureaucracy is a pessimistic vision, a view of organization once and for all superseding production as the master lever of industrial life. Under bureaucracy, the question of which class or group of classes holds the reins of power is secondary, since the "basic" bureaucratic factor continues to

32. See Marion J. Levy, Jr., *The Structure of Society*. Princeton: Princeton University Press, 1952, esp. pp. 288–89.
33. Lewis A. Coser, *op. cit.*, pp. 155–56.

grow, whichever form of industrial organization might obtain. Bureaucracy comes to be viewed as omnipotent and universal, subject to temporary setbacks but never to any real or sizeable defeat. If such is the case, then consensus theory applies equally to the studies of an African state, an aboriginal community, and an industrial city.

Consensus theory has led to such an emphasis on continuities and similarities in modern societies that all differences between democracy and autocracy, ruling classes and ruled classes, exploited groups and exploiting groups are neatly eliminated. The "natural history of society" technique, which sees issues in terms of functional identities, has made a universe in which only grey cats and clever hounds exist. But on such wisdom only quiescence makes sense, since the cycle of change involves little if any growth.[34] Political systems are reduced to quantifiable terms which evaluate how decisions are arrived at within a given system. Consensus serves to insinuate an approach in which change is real only if it occurs within a system; and when change serves to break a system, it is said to be subject to inevitable laws which simply replicate the rage for order in the hands of new ruling sectors.[35]

Consensus theory seems reinforced by the complex organization. Its basic feature is total specialization: the narcotizing effect of role sets and the insistence on constraint and persuasion as an exclusive way of bringing about change. The paradox is that consensus theory does not really act as a bulwark for democratic social theory; quite the reverse. It is not a theory for reaching agreements. It advocates harmony intrinsic to the organization of the bureaucratic life, one which exists over and above the actual accords reached by men. And so it must remain, since any serious theory of agreements and decisions must at the same time be a theory of disagreements and the conditions under which decisions cannot be reached.

Starting from the metaphysical need for universal consensus, a ruling sector can talk only about absolute and relative consensus, complete or partial integration, but never about conflict as a means of expressing genuine social needs and aspirations.[36] What must be understood, however,

34. Crane Brinton, *The Anatomy of Revolution*. New York: Knopf-Vintage Books, 1952.
35. Chalmers Johnson, *Revolution and the Social System*. Stanford: Stanford University Press, 1964, esp. 27–28.
36. See in particular Chester I. Barnard, *The Functions of the Executive*. Cambridge: Harvard University Press, 1938; James D. Mooney and Alan C. Reiley, *The Principles of Organization*. New York: Harper & Co., 1939; Talcott Parsons,

is that this is an argument against a consensus, bureaucratic society and not simply a critique of a theory. Gouldner has given theoretical expression to this by noting that

> instead of telling men how bureaucracy might be mitigated, they insist that it is inevitable. Instead of explaining how democratic patterns may, to some extent, be fortified and extended, they warn us that democracy cannot be perfect. Instead of controlling the disease, they suggest that we are deluded, or more politely, incurably romantic, for hoping to control it. Instead of assuming responsibilities as realistic clinicians, striving to further democratic potentialities wherever they can, many social scientists have become morticians, all too eager to bury men's hopes.[37]

If we equate "rebellion" with "alienation" and "conformity" with "equilibrium," we are a priori ruling out the possibility that a condition of rebellion is consonant with equilibrium at any level.[38] Correspondingly, this equation ignores the possibility that extreme states of consensus might create rather than alleviate social or personal stress.

The concept of deviant behavior itself rests on a faith that normative behavior is in every situation observable and functionally relevant. From the point of view of established consensus on the matter of the sanctity of private property, an act of juvenile vandalism might be measured in the same way as an act of political rebellion. But from the point of view of the goals sought, what is meant by consensus demands a study of group objectives no less than group norms; and no less, the difference between means and ends must itself be considered as a factor existing over and beyond the supposed functional damage the social order sustains from the deviant behavior. Too often, deviance is ambiguously formulated so as to cover extremely different situations, that is, a departure from the rules on the part of an isolated member of a group, and no less, group defiance of group rules.

Consensus does not carry an implication of social equilibrium, nor for that matter does dissensus entail disequilibrium. Different kinds of

"Suggestions for a Sociological Approach to the Theory of Organization," *Administrative Science Quarterly,* Vol. 1, 1956, pp. 63–85; Phillip Selznick, "Foundations of the Theory of Organization," *American Sociological Review,* Vol. XIII, 1948, pp. 25–35.

37. Alvin W. Gouldner, "Metaphysical Pathos and the Theory of Bureaucracy," *American Political Science Review,* Vol. 49, 1955, pp. 506–7.

38. Talcott Parsons, *The Social System,* Glencoe, Ill.: The Free Press, 1951, pp. 257–59.

conflict exist. For instance, there is a great distinction between conflict on the basis of consensus and conflict arising within the consensual apparatus. To draw an analogy from game theory, there are conflicts programed for continuation of the game (such as parliamentary debates), and those programed to end the game through a change of the rules (such as take place in coups d'état). In neither case is dissensus tied to social disorganization or to deviance from norms. This is not to say that conflict situations do not contain possibilities of social disorganization. Of course they do. For example, the absence of a formal constitution over an extended period of time can create political chaos and turmoil. But, likewise, a perfect constitution, preparing the ground for every sort of contingency, can have a boomerang effect; it can increase stress by failing to bring about common standards of belief and action. In short, consensus and dissensus are phenomena which can promote or retard social cooperation or political cohesion.

Simmel caught the authentic spirit of the relation of conflict to cooperation when he noted:

> If a fight simply aims at annihilation, it does approach the marginal case of assassination in which the admixture of unifying elements is almost zero. If, however, there is any consideration, any limit to violence, there already exists a socializing factor, even though only as the qualification of violence. One unites in order to fight, and one fights under the mutually recognized control of norms and rules.[39]

Thus, dissensus, no less than consensus, operates within the social structure, within the system of mutually established laws, norms, and values; hence there is no scientific warrant to choose between them. Yet, there is a political need for choice and decision. The difficulty is that decisions of a high magnitude of importance are often made without reference to the past or to the present, but rather are pegged to future goals. Conflict often takes place because of a desire to have the goods produced shared by all; instead of the processes involved in getting these goods produced shared by all.

Socialization defined exclusively in terms of consensus becomes a euphemism for game responses. Membership in the social system becomes a game played in a way that formal obedience to the rule system is never challenged. Those who do not accept such a view, those who consider social development from the viewpoint of mass movements and

39. Georg Simmel, *Conflict*, pp. 252–6. Quoted in Lewis A. Coser, *op. cit.*, p. 121.

spontaneous happenings, are described as pariahs, deviants, abnormals, marginals, and even clerics.[40] More specifically, Parsons' doctrine of action frame of reference is primarily a thought frame of reference. It is preeminently idealist and cannot conceive of any activity persisting unless backed up or legitimized by institutionalized norms. It pushes to the logical extreme Weber's definition of the social as involving an attached subjective meaning. For Parsons, the subjective meaning becomes everything; it becomes organized into value systems with attached secondary actions.

The multiple definitions of consensus, connected as they are to game-playing and organizational performance, are the perfect completion of the legitimated bifurcation of values and actions, beliefs and behavior. In this form, consensus is reduced to the exclusive mechanism for resolving problems. And social development is seen as taking place only within the social system. Consensus theory has reduced itself to "thinking together." [41] Whether this proves an adequate replacement for the old-fashioned idea of thinking for oneself remains to be demonstrated.

IV

From the problems involved in describing any but the most permissive and tolerant communities in terms of consensus matrices it is logical to move to a re-examination of conflict theory, with its openness to problems of coercion, pressure groups, social classes, political myths, cultural clashes, and racial strife, factors which more nearly approximate the actual state of affairs in developing areas. From a descriptive point of view, conflict theory covers a wider and more profound range of questions than consensus theory. To be sure, it is better for men to settle their differences on the basis of free agreement than by external pressures. Neither consensus nor conflict theory has any exclusive claims as a problem-solving technique.

The particular significance of this controversy (concerning conflict and consensus) for developmental research has to do with the position of social change vis-à-vis social structure. If social conflict is seen as

40. Seymour Martin Lipset and Neil Smelser, "Change and Controversy in Recent American Sociology," *The British Journal of Sociology,* Vol. XII, 1961, pp. 41–51.
41. Edward Gross, "Symbiosis and Consensus as Integrative Factors in Small Groups," *American Sociological Review,* Vol. XXI, 1956, pp. 174–79.

necessarily destructive of social order, the tendency will be for a society to rely heavily on spontaneity and on the operations of the free market. Laissez faire and laissez passer go well with a view of life in which the consensual apparatus is held to be supreme. On the other hand, if conflict is seen to be equal to consensus in terms of its abilities to provide social cohesion, then an increase in the machinery of regulation rather than the much more complicated change in social organization is in order. There are two essential types of conflict: one form which arises out of the root differences between social forces, and which generally goes unchecked; and another form which a political regime can build into the social system and hence plan for. There is nothing especially deceptive about planning for conflict, any more than the rules of a game are sinful because they lay down rules of combat or competition. To plan for social change very often means to anticipate social conflict and devise programs for meeting the problems which arise out of such conflict.

To reject conflict as a generative, causal agency in social change is to deprive a society of an essential mechanism for reaching order. The rejection of conflict is an invitation to violence and coercion. That is to say, dissensus is as "natural" to a social system as consensus—and frequently more fruitful in nations and areas where parliamentary democracy is an unknown quantity. Cooperation can be a consequence of conflict, *if* the rules for governing conflict are as clearly worked out as those which regulate consensus. The instinct to break the rules is no greater in conflict situations than in consensual situations. The history of parliamentary "cheating" can be considered strong evidence that the simple existence of legal organizations is no mandate for a consensual approach. In brief, the planning of social change in underdeveloped regions carries with it the understanding that conflict is as subject to rules as consensus. Indeed, conflict may often turn out to be a "safety valve" for minimizing violence and terrorism in the new regions.

The definition of a social system exclusively in terms of small collectivities or communities, and as interacting groups, assumes the presence of self-sufficiency in each unit, and upon investigation this very rarely obtains. A social system can be understood more readily as component parts of a larger multi-national complex which embraces a number of interacting and coexisting societies, for example, an area cluster, sharing a common culture, a specific geography, on a common ethnic basis. The kind of regional analysis necessary to understand social change is simply not possible if we start from the assumption that all problems can be resolved within a systematic model.

Consensual analysis suffers from the relative ease with which models that ignore patterns of conflict at a large-scale level can be constructed. Colonialism, imperialism, spheres of influence, military sites, and the like are also "inter-actional" in character. But since it is an interaction which is based on domination rather than mutual consent or common institutionalization, it is easily excluded from the analytic account of the social system as such. The scientific limits of this sort of functional-structural accounting are characterized ideologically by an avoidance of the divisive elements between nations and peoples which are *no less binding* upon both parties, as the things which a community mutually agrees upon. Interaction does not signify willing consent among equals. When an equivalence between interaction and consent is set up, the possibilities of developing mechanisms of cooperation that leave conflicting national economies and politics intact are severely curbed.

Consensus theory has a narrowing effect on the study of interest elements and sectoral phenomena in the Third World. Consensual units are too frequently seen in terms of small group and small community relations. In this sense, consensus theory has a self-fulfilling prophetic dimension, in that what is examined presupposes a high degree of social cohesion and interaction.[42] Such unifying agencies and symbols are absent precisely in larger forms of social and national development. Immigration waves; differences in cultural, racial, and ethnic backgrounds; sectional, caste, and class antagonisms. These types of situations stand in continual need of a sociological theory of conflict resolution, one which makes no assumptions as to the auto-regulative or equilibrated conditions of a specific social system. To declare that the only viable avenue of scientific study open to the sociologist is the small group, since only in group relations can all the variables be controlled,

42. This is not to imply that conflict situations, and thus conflict theory, are inoperative at small-group levels. Quite the contrary; the most significant literature of this genre has shown a marked concern with conflict and conflict resolution as the essence of group interaction. See, for example, Arthur J. Vidich and Joseph Bensman, *Small Town in Mass Society: Class, Power, and Religion in a Rural Community.* Garden City, N.Y.: Doubleday-Anchor Books, 1960; Judith R. Kramer and Seymour Leventman, *Children of the Gilded Ghetto: Conflict Resolutions of Three Generations of American Jews.* New Haven: Yale University Press, 1961; and Kenneth Wilson Underwood, *Protestant and Catholic: Religious and Social Interaction in an Industrial Community.* Boston: The Beacon Press, 1957. These kinds of studies are conspicuously absent for other societies.

is not to prove the worth of consensus but only to demonstrate the extent to which larger units of social research have been surrendered because of the difficulties in explaining dissensual elements in the macroscopic world.[43]

The original intent of consensus theory—to establish a measurement of what public opinion maintains as true or desirable at any given point —has been subverted. This has been forcefully made clear by the elitist corruption of consensus to signify what "prestige" judges think consensus to be.[44] The assumption that consensus is intrinsically more democratic than dissensus is about as sound as the "theory" that clean-shaven men are kindlier than bearded men. As Leonard Reissman has well pointed out, consensus theorists "create an uncomfortable suspicion about what consensus means and how valid is the use of prestige judges as a research technique. There is something unexplained that badly needs elucidation when a measure can turn up eleven or more distinguishable classes in a community with a total population of some 1200." Reissman goes on to explain the central weakness of consensual definitions of social class:

> There is the tendency, although not an inevitable one, to consider behavior as the result of the value system of class rather than as the effect of, say, economic factors, social power, education, or political forces. The crux of class distinction, thereby, becomes one of values, which in turn become the presumed causes of class difference of behavior.[45]

Shifts in modes of behavior from class to prestige lines can be more readily and accurately gauged on historical grounds than on psychological grounds of the instinctual need for togetherness and social acceptance. Why then did the shift from dissensus to consensus take place in the United States at precisely the same time as the reverse took place at the international level? Several hypotheses suggest themselves. First, that as American society becomes more democratic, more easy-

43. A monumental effort to develop a quantitative statement of international affairs is that of Bruce M. Russett, Hayward R. Alker, Karl W. Deutsch, Harold D. Lasswell, *World Handbook of Political and Social Indicators*. New Haven: Yale University Press, 1964.

44. Harold Kaufman, *Prestige Classes in a New York Rural Community*. Ithaca: Cornell University Agricultural Experiment Station, Mar. 1944, Memoir 260, p. 46.

45. Leonard Reissman, *Class in American Society*. Glencoe, Ill.: The Free Press, 1959, pp. 127–28.

going, the search for the consensual basis becomes more pronounced. However, this view of the end of ideology seems not so much a consequence of an expanding democratic temper as it is simply a reflection of domestic affluence and more United States inhabitants' benefiting from the affluent society.[46] A more powerful line of reasoning is that technical bureaucracies and team-member proficiency have tended to usurp the older power of formal authority as distinct from science.[47] The older situation of science as isolated from policy-making has disintegrated. With this, authority shifts from outright reliance on domination to a wider utilization of manipulation, demonstrated managerial skills, operational proficiencies, and the capacity to develop positive organizational loyalties. In such a context, consensus comes to be the decisive pivot upon which the success or failure of the managerially oriented society hangs.

The most cogent explanation for the shift to consensus theory is the "enlightened" recognition that mass terror is not as powerful an instrument for extracting economic and political loyalties as mass persuasion. The entire edifice of small-group theory comes to rest on the idea that the formal sanctioning of force is less potent a factor in individual or group motivation than informal reinforcement of the immediately involved reference set. The belief in consensus as a strategem is well articulated by Frank:

> The idea has spread that employers were wasting human energy by the traditional authoritarian ways of imposing their decisions on their employees. Psychologists—collaborating with engineers and economists and, more recently, anthropologists—have made many studies concerned with the impact of physical aspects of the workplace, such as lighting, color of walls and machines, temperature and humidity; with working conditions, such as hours, shifts, rest periods, piece rates, and especially relations of foremen and supervisors to their groups. Such studies helped to articulate a new view of corporate life.[48]

46. Seymour Martin Lipset, *Political Man, op. cit.,* pp. 403–17; see also in this connection, Daniel Bell, *The End of Ideology.* Glencoe, Ill.: The Free Press, 1960.
47. Morris Janowitz, *Sociology and the Military Establishment.* New York: Russell Sage Foundation, 1959, pp. 27–39. Janowitz' remarks are confined to the military. Responsibility for enlarging the scope and context of his argument is mine.
48. Lawrence K. Frank, "Psychology and the Social Order," in *The Human Meaning of the Social Sciences,* edited by Daniel Lerner. New York: Meridian Books, 1959, p. 230.

What is the content of this new view of corporate life? Is it a theory of the corporation or simply a technique of mass persuasion and manipulation? Is it a sociological statement of the nature of the corporate structure, or of the uses by the corporate structure of sociological statements? The promotion of consensus as a theory has had as its asking price the conversion of sociology from a science to a tool of policy, a policy, moreover, which fails to reach the goal of harmony. As White indicates: "There is nothing new in manipulated opinion and engineered consent. . . . Even the sheer bulk of distortion is not altogether new, merely more refined. What is new is the acceptability, the mere taken-for-grantedness of these things." [49]

V

Human cooperation, while related to consensus and conflict, has a unique dimension and operational range. A decision in favor of consensus theory is not automatically a decision on behalf of cooperation. It is simply a decision to examine social structure to the partial or total exclusion of social dynamics; a decision to act as if breaks with traditional shifts in the culture complex, disruption of moral patterns, can be described as marginal in character. There is a kind of safety in the traditional, the prolonged, the enduring. But this safety, gratuitously cloaking itself in the mantle of social order, represents in fact the abdication of the field of social change and hence an abandonment of the on-going problems confronting those most directly concerned with achieving human cooperation at group, regional, national, or international levels.

What then is the difference between consensus and dissensus on one side and cooperation on the other? There seem to be three distinguishable factors to be identified.

First: Dissensus and consensus each stands for agreement internally, that is, in terms of shared perspectives, agreements on the rules of association and action, a common set of norms and values. Cooperation for its part makes no demands on role uniformity but only upon procedural rules. Cooperation concerns the settlement of problems in terms which make possible the continuation of differences and even funda-

49. Howard B. White, "The Processed Voter and the New Political Science," *Social Research,* Vol. XXVIII, 1961, p. 150.

mental disagreements. One can legitimately speak of cooperation between labor and management, while one speaks of the degree of consensus each side brings to bear at the bargaining table. This is of particular significance for the newer developing nations, since cooperation would legitimize rather than outlaw differences, and hence reduce the fear that negotiation means capitulation.

Second: Consensus is agreement on the content of behavior, while cooperation necessitates agreement only on the form of behavior. We speak of consensus if all members of the Women's Christian Temperance Union agree to abstain from drinking alcoholic beverages. But we speak of cooperation when agreement is reached on the forms allowed for drinking and the forms allowed for curbing the intake of liquor. As the Prohibition Era dramatically showed, the substitution of cooperation for consensus did not lead to a new morality but simply to chaos. There is similarly the danger that too heavy an emphasis on consensus in the African states would result in a resurrection of racial warfare as a mode of settling conflicts, since the demand for racial hegemony would undoubtedly precede all else. The very multiplicity of nations in Africa offers some comfort that cooperative forms of polity will prevail. Interestingly, African leaders generally call for racial equality and not for racial supremacy, although the continued policy of *apartheid* in South Africa could change this situation.

Third: Cooperation concerns toleration of differences, while consensus demands reconciliation of these same differences. If a game-theory analogy be preferred, the distinction between cooperation and consensus might be stated in the following terms: both conflict and consensus program the *termination* of the game by insisting on the principle of unity and unilateral victory, whereas cooperation is pluralistic because it programs the *continuation* of the game by maintaining and insisting upon the legitimacy of differences.

What is required at this juncture is a stipulation of the conditions of the minimum set of beliefs about man and his social universe that is consonant with continued survival and growth. Such a theory of cooperation would insist on the need for maintaining life, although leaving open the question of what to do with it; the need to secure the material and cultural needs of man, although differing on the sort of social system best able to meet such needs. Beyond this, there is a need for a theory of conflict, a programing of conflict that would allow people to shift and choose their conceptions of what constitutes progress, pleasure, and the institutionalization of avenues for action to implement these conceptions. Consensus theory might contribute its share to melt the present freezing of attitudes by indicating ways in which cooperation can be converted into consensus through a re-examination of present interests.

The unity required to evolve such a sociological theory of cooperation is methodological rather than systematic. The concept of cooperation is essentially the programing of common standards in a world of conflicting interests and even different notions as to what constitutes interests. Precisely because a general theory of cooperation would offer no transcendental commitments to the eternal righteousness of any existing social order, it can place itself in the service of social development.

The existence of a Third World does not in itself reduce the areas of conflict, nor enhance the growth of a new consensus. What it does is to introduce a new dimension for the political consideration of old power blocs, and hence make possible channels of cooperation which, in the long run, can minimize the friction created by the present bipolarization in the economic, political, and military realms. The new economic and political mixes introduced by Third World countries create new social forms which make "hard postures" embarrassing and obsolescent. It is not necessary to maintain that the Third World will lead the way to a recasting of present political dilemmas. What is more likely to occur is a loosening of ideological postures by the major power blocs in a manifest effort to "capture" Third World sympathies. But a latent by-product of this shifting and casting may come about in the vitalization of present agencies for international settlement such as the United Nations, and the creation of yet new institutions for settlement. In brief, bilateral cooperation will be made possible, if not inevitable, precisely because of the rise of new nations of power. This cooperation may not be altruistic in character. It may be stimulated by a common fear that the failure to institutionalize norms of cooperation now, when the power "players" are few in number, would make it only that much harder later, when the number of players in the world power struggle multiply.

The fact that cooperation offers viable paths to survival and conflict resolution does not mean that development may not be adversely affected. Indeed, cooperation is itself an ambiguous notion; it can refer to a "balance of powers" or to a "balance of numbers." The developing regions already have come to outnumber (and in the United Nations, to outvote) the traditional centers of power. However, it is clear that ultimate decisions affecting the fate of the world still reside in the holders of nuclear power. Under such conditions, the best that developing nations can hope to achieve is the arrangement of "nuclear free" zones that can help effect a wider basis of cooperation between the power blocs. Even if a maximum degree of cooperation is maintained regarding procedural matters—that is, an adequate definition of the conflict situation, maximization of factual information regarding potential conflicts, and testing of proposals for breaking tensions in terms of past experience—the overriding conflict of interests may forestall any basic settlement. It must be noted that only where basic big-power interests coincide, as in matters of the unlimited use of nuclear weapons, has a general theory of cooperation been successfully employed. Beyond that point, special interests come to the foreground. And the developing regions are very much considered part of these "interests" of major powers. Hence, a basic stumbling block to cooperation is the limited feasibility of maintaining the "rules of the game" under conditions where each "side" does indeed have something to "lose" and something to "gain" by any fundamental shift in social structure. Every nation becomes a "vital" sphere of influence instead of a sovereign autonomous area.

This raises the more generic factor that cooperation is a negatively induced condition. The likelihood of cooperation under conditions of one side winning and the other losing is a most treacherous plausibility —quite subject to violation. Therefore, the growth of a Third World has a dangerous side to it: the abandonment of cooperation even as to the rules for programing future conflicts. But along with the risks are the advantages. One or more area clustering in the Third World managing to gain great power would forestall a two-player game between the United States and the Soviet Union. For such an event to occur, the developing areas would themselves have to develop independent nuclear deterrents—and hence expand the size and scale of arms races. This in turn would compel the old power centers to reconsider their own postures. This is clearly what China has done by its own independent penetration of the arms race.

There is a circularity to the problem of cooperation because there is a circularity to the facts involved. To expand the bargaining power of the Third World entails an expansion of the risks of war. Yet, to curtail or limit this bargaining power is to jeopardize the Third World entirely, to make it subject to precisely the forms of big power settlement which is found so abhorrent by the emergent nations.

The assumption of the major power is that cooperation is possible because social structure presupposes social development. The assumption of the Third World is that cooperation is possible because social development presupposes social structure. The Third World may be willing to sacrifice life to preserve the principle of development. Formulas cannot break this dichotomy—only the general recognition that anything pushed to its ultimate, either structure or process, may prove to be self-defeating. Hence, that much abused term "moderation" may still prove to be the handmaiden of human reason.

Cooperation may prove a slender reed upon which to hang our hopes for both conflict resolution and social development. However, any return to consensus theory would mark a step backward in the toleration of social differences; while any return to conflict theory would mark a return to nineteenth-century geo-politics that would eliminate even that amount of "internationalization" of life thus far registered. Human reason has posed the problems in this ultimate way by virtue of the scientific and technological achievements it has painfully gained. It is not too much to hope that this same sort of reason will prove to be the basic variable needed in social and political life. Peace is not likely to be gained without establishing a functional common ground upon which men can stand. Any common ground can easily be turned into a divisive barrier if parochial interests are allowed to displace man's universal need of men for survival.

The historical effort to secure international peace through the arts of compromise has been thoroughly discredited because of bipolarization. Nowhere is the failure of compromise so obvious in our Western societies as in the wars by which they have been ravaged. A review of the processes whereby the West has sought to avoid the increasingly deadly wars which have followed upon one another would bring to mind the various plans for "perpetual peace," all of which have had one thing in common—their pathetic inadequacy. The international institutions set up to maintain world peace proved no more effectual as long as they did not reflect an actual situation making war particularly terrible. It can now be said that, as in the past, the West has failed in its efforts to reach a peaceful settlement of its international conflict.[50]

In this sense, the Third World represents an avoidance of needless choice between the pure utilitarianism of *Realpolitik* or the equally pure cynicism of the advocates of Doomsday. The Third World as a strategy represents an alternative to the classical techniques of big power diplomacy. The First and Second Worlds for their part have demanded either-or solutions: either dissensus or consensus, either anarchy or behemoth, either constitutionalism or chaos. But when we examine the social infrastructure, it becomes apparent that conflict can be programed no less than consensus. The crystallization of the Third World, both organizationally and ideologically, shows that we are in a position not only to tolerate conflict, with a low yield of violence, but to induce dissensus—for the purpose of avoiding all-out conflict which is unstructured. Political parties, voluntary social organization, and athletic events are examples of the safety-valve factor in such forms of conflict.[51] By taking conflict as a social constant it may yet be possible to avoid the consequences of *maximum* conflict. There is abundant evidence that low-yield violence is at least as plausible within a world of programed conflict as it is in the diplomatic world of compromise.

50. See Charles Moraze, "The Settlement of Conflicts in Western Cultures," *International Social Science Quarterly,* Vol. XV, No. 2, 1963, pp. 248–49. A first attempt to deal with the problem is contained in *Economic and Social Consequences of Disarmament.* New York: United Nations, May 1963 (E-3736).

51. The significance of strategic concepts such as the safety-valve factor, programed conflict, and low-yield violence, is undeniable. What is mistaken is the elevation of such strategies into principles for the maintenance of the social system. Strategies are not miracles, nor are they theoretical resolutions of the dilemmas of development.

18

Paradigms and Principles in Development: Mutationis Tractatus

The sociology of development has received great impetus from four separate sources: professional economists, political scientists, socialist theorists from within and without the Soviet bloc, and sociologists residing in, or concerned with, Third World regions.

Economics, long ridiculed as the "dismal science," is nonetheless the discipline most directly concerned with the political economy of development. The work of Kuznets[1] on the economic growth of nations, Gerschenkron[2] and Heilbroner[3] on the forms of social backwardness, P. J. D. Wiles on the ideology and theology of "full communism," [4] Rostow on the relationship between economic "thrust" and self-sustained growth,[5] and Viner on the connection of social savings and economic change[6] have all made significant contributions to the study of economic development.

Socialism, long held to be stagnant and unable to deal effectively with new conditions, has nonetheless witnessed a "great debate" recently

1. Simon Kuznets, *Quantitative Aspects of the Economic Growth of Nations.* Chicago: Research Center in Economic Development and Cultural Change, 1962, esp. Vol. X, No. 2, Part II.
2. Alexander Gerschenkron (ed.), *Economic Backwardness in Historical Perspective.* Cambridge, Mass.: Harvard University Press, 1962.
3. Robert L. Heilbroner, *The Great Ascent.* New York: Harper & Row, 1963.
4. P. J. D. Wiles, *The Political Economy of Communism.* Cambridge, Mass.: Harvard University Press, 1962.
5. Walt W. Rostow, *The Stages of Economic Growth.* Cambridge, Eng. Cambridge University Press, 1960.
6. Jacob Viner, *International Trade and Economic Development.* London: Oxford University Press, 1956.

which represents both an off-shoot of the economic sciences and an independent force in the evolution of a social science of development. The orthodox Marxists Frank,[7] Dutt,[8] and Baran[9] have conducted an effective dialogue with the reform Marxists Strachey,[10] Myrdal,[11] and Bronfenbrenner.[12] This debate is concerned with the problem of economic expansion in relation to political coercion and consensus. Political directives affect the allocation of national wealth and human energies, and these in turn generate distinctive and explicit world views. Both classical and socialist economists have been quite willing in recent discussions to acknowledge the sociological roots of the problem of development.

The developing nations of Asia, Africa, and Latin America, long held to be very backward in matters of education and scientific know-how, represent nonetheless that part of the world where sociologists are tackling head-on the master issues of social development. The work of Celso Furtado[13] and Costa Pinto[14] in Brazil, of Germani in Argentina,[15] and of Alfredo Navarette[16] and Jesus Herzog in Mexico[17] indicates that an expression of the meaning of the degree of develop-

7. André Gunder Frank, *Latin America: Underdevelopment or Revolution.* New York: Monthly Review Press, 1969; and his earlier work, *Capitalism and Underdevelopment in Latin America: Historical Studies of Chile and Brazil.* New York: Monthly Review Press, 1967.
8. R. Palme Dutt, *The Crisis of Britain and the British Empire.* London: Lawrence and Wishart, 1953.
9. Paul A. Baran, *The Political Economy of Growth.* New York: Monthly Review Press, 1957; and *The Longer View: Essays Toward a Critique of Political Economy.* New York: Monthly Review Press, 1969.
10. John Strachey, *The End of Empire.* London: Victor Gollancz, 1959.
11. Gunnar Myrdal, *Rich Lands and Poor: The Road to World Prosperity.* New York: Harper, 1957.
12. M. Bronfenbrenner, "The Appeal of Confiscation in Economic Development," in *The Economics of Underdevelopment,* edited by A. N. Agarwala and S. P. Singh. New York: Oxford University Press, 1963.
13. Celso Furtado, *Desenvolvimento e Subdesenvolvimento.* Rio de Janeiro: Editora Fundo de Cultura, 1961.
14. L. A. Costa Pinto, "O Desenvolvimento: Seus Processos e Seus Obstaculos," *Journal of Inter-American Studies,* Vol. IV, No. 3, July 1962; and more recently, *Economic and Political Development: A Theoretical Approach and a Brazilian Case Study.* Cambridge, Mass.: Harvard University Press, 1968.
15. Gino Germani, *Política y Sociedad en una Epoca de Transición.* Buenos Aires: Editorial Paidós, 1962.
16. Alfredo Navarette, Jr., and Ifigenia M. de Navarette, "La Subocupación en las Economías Poco Desarrolladas," *El Trimestre Económico,* Vol. 18, No. 4, Oct.–Dec. 1951.
17. Jesús Silva Herzog, *México y su Petróleo: Una Lección para América.* Buenos Aires: Universidad de Buenos Aires, 1959.

ment is not a simple matter of linguistic nuance but a complex matter of the life and death of man in society. Real strides have been taken to evolve a general theory of social development. Sociological conferences held throughout the world for the past decade have been deeply concerned with developmental issues. The emergence of such periodicals as *Revue Tiers Monde, The International Development Review, Desarrollo Económico, Studies in Comparative International Development,* and *Journal of Developing Areas,* and *Economic Development and Cultural Change* reflects the attempt to evolve a working body of systematic knowledge in this area. With such an extensive literature available, social scientists must either summarize the work already done or select problem areas which remain unsolved. I shall attempt to summarize these findings by means of a series of propositions on development. Perhaps in this way, real problem areas can be more readily ascertained.

Why is it that sociology in the United States has been delinquent in forging a general theory of social development? Historically, sociologists were pioneers in precisely this field. Ferdinand Toennies' remarkable typology of *Gemeinschaft* and *Gesellschaft* sociocultural structures is at its source a historical account of the machinery through which community-agrarian patterns dissolved and gave way to a societal-industrial pattern. Toennies' description of European capitalism still forms the basis for much discussion of what a developed society necessarily includes and excludes. Max Weber's work on the sociology of religion has as its fundamental motive an attempt to account for the transition from feudalism to capitalism in European and Asian societies. Indeed, the impulse behind Weber's interests in religion is economic— that is, an effort to understand the social function of ideas as a catalytic agent in social development. Werner Sombart's studies of religious forces in the evolution of European capitalism likewise had as a basis the need to find out the sociological variables in the full flowering of the bourgeois system of production. Studies by such other major sociological figures as Simmel, Thomas, Znaniecki, and Mannheim could similarly be introduced in support of my contention that the problem of development was uppermost in the minds of "classical" sociologists.

Why have we become negligent, and even indifferent, to problems of macroscopic sociology? The answers are manifold. And since this is not intended as an exercise in the sociology of sociology, it is possible to list only briefly some of the more outstanding reasons.[18] One of the root problems seems to be that the rise of socialism has confounded sociology. On the American scene, sociology and socialism have for so long seen each other as "enemies" that each side does everything possible to avoid slipping into the language of the "generalized other." Furthermore, sociology, even in its generous moments and in the hands of its more radical practitioners, viewed socialism as a historical "moment" in the evolution of the social sciences. On the other hand, socialist spokesmen have always considered sociology as a middle-class effort to improve a decadent social order—a bourgeois "moment" in the development of socialist theory.

Sociologists have so taken for granted the language of structure and function, stability, and pattern maintenance that socialism has come to be viewed as a form of deviance, a conflict-laden ideology devoid of the hard facts of social structure. Socialists, on their side, have for so long held out the need for radical social change that problems of order and structure have indeed come to be viewed as a sort of betrayal of radical principles. The sociologist is as "deviant" from the socialist's standpoint as the socialist is from the sociologist's. Any suggestion that the development of *both* socialism and sociology has been one-sided, to the detriment of both, has produced howls of protest from ideologues in both camps.

By outlining in proposition form the main features of a theory of development, features about which there is a broad consensus, we can help the critical issues in the sociological theory of economic development to emerge more clearly. Then we shall be in a better position to see just how much of a contribution sociology can make to the resolution of such a big-range problem. But to present these propositions satisfactorily requires honesty, a recognition that the traditional animus between sociology and socialism is outmoded and outdated. The traditional animus is made obsolete by the operational character of sociology and by the pragmatic character of contemporary socialism. Sociology as a heuristic device has replaced sociology as the bête noire of socialism. The question is not what kind of sociology but whither sociology. If the Soviets have come so far as to set up an Institute for Social Research in Leningrad modeled after the Bureau of Applied Research in

18. For a further examination of these problems, see Irving Louis Horowitz (ed.), *The New Sociology.* New York and London: Oxford University Press, 1964.

New York, we can do no less than try to understand ways in which socialism and sociology can pool their information to bring about a better understanding of the social, political, and economic bases of human development.

We know that concrete problems cannot be separated into neat social-science disciplines. Such divisions have no basis in social reality. Concrete problems are never exclusively economic, sociological, or political. A theory of development and underdevelopment based on any one set of variables is destined to failure. Gunnar Myrdal, in concluding his argument for a science of development, speaks of a need for a "model of models" which would be based on a close reading of social history as well as social science.

I submit the following "model of models" as my own attempt to come to terms with the problem of development by considering the interplay of social order and social change. Its obvious imperfections are in part the result of the difficulties involved in projecting forms of development which do not fully account for psychological and ethical factors.

The logical structure of propositions concerning social development is introduced. Then we move successively to the economic, political, political-economic, and finally, the sociological dimensions proper. The scheme of exposition employed obviously owes a considerable debt to the work of Vilfredo Pareto in sociology and, no less, to Ludwig Wittgenstein in linguistic philosophy. But it is not my purpose to imitate their work. There are many departures from their efforts, as many as were necessary to make the following scheme meaningful.

1   The social world is the totality of human forces.

1:1   The social world is the totality of processes and structures, while objects and ideas are reflective and reflexive.

1:1:1   The totality of processes and structures defines what is the case socially, and also what is not the case.

1:2   Processes and structures are social categories for discussing change and becoming.

1:2:1   All processes take place within structures, and all structures are subject to processes.

Note: The extensiveness of speed of process, like the durability and solidity of being or structure, is an empirical consideration and not determined a priori.

1:2:1:1   That portion of social facts concerned with processes refers to changes in class, power, occupation, and prestige. Such changes may occur at the individual, group, or societal level. Such changes may be measured by both objective and subjective indices—that is, by an "absolute" growth in power or by a "relative" shift in how a person, group, or society is viewed by other persons, groups, and societies.

1:2:1:2 That portion of social facts concerned with structures refers to how the processes of the social world appear to the observer at any specific moment in time and space. Such structures may be measured by both objective and subjective indices—that is the actual durability of a social structure is a consequence both of its "real" power and of the social members' view of such power.

1:2:2 Social structure is then the sum total of social processes, and social processes define the social structure.

2 All the processes and structures in a society define the stage of development of that society.

2:1 Development refers to the level of rationality achieved by a social structure, and also the degree of complexity compatible with advanced techniques of production.

2:2 Full development refers to the ideal standards entertained in our perceptions of structures and processes.

2:2:1 Underdevelopment refers to a social condition in which anticipated processes and structures are being aborted.

2:2:1:1 *Under*developed differs from *un*developed as the sociological differs from the natural: or the biological from the ecological.

2:2:2 Overdevelopment refers to a social condition in which processes and structures are available in such a degree that they can no longer be absorbed by the system of production and labor exchange.

Example: One speaks of the overdeveloped society when the cost factors outweigh the benefits derived from high productivity—that is, when human "suffering" (anomie, alienation, anxiety) *caused by high industrial output levels* outweighs advantages of material acquisitions and short working days.

2:2:2:1 Overdevelopment differs from overexhaustion of natural wealth to the extent that social and economic demands tax and ultimately destroy natural, biological, and ecological balances.

2:2:2:2 Overdevelopment is observable through its "Frankenstein effect"—anomie, alienation, and anxiety on a mass scale.

3 Development, underdevelopment, and overdevelopment are social concepts. Underdevelopment and overdevelopment are representative responses to the problem of scarcity and affluence respectively. Where there is high scarcity, there is extensive underdevelopment; where there is high affluence, unequally distributed, there is high overdevelopment.

3:1 The developing society is one in which there is a "proper mix" between the maintenance of social structures and the acceleration of social processes. This proposition clearly has a subjective dimension. Yet, unless one assumes that the nature of development is exclusively economic, this "subjectivity" is not so much a shortcoming as an additional factor in analysis.

3:1:1 An "improper mix" is indicated by a breakdown in processes, or a disruption in the structures.

3:1:2 Underdeveloped societies have difficulty in initiating and accelerating new social processes, while overdeveloped societies are characterized by resistance to change and by disintegration without planning options.

3:2 Underdeveloped societies have difficulty in initiating and accelerating new social processes, while overdeveloped societies are characterized by the disintegration of structures.

3:2:1 Processes which are in excess of what the structures deem sufficient lead either to the sacrifices of the processes or of the structures.

3:2:1:1 Structures which are made rigid beyond the point where they can absorb new processes lead either to the sacrifice of the structure or of the processes.

3:3 Process is the totality of social change in a specific situation; structure is the totality of social systems in a specific situation.

3:3:1 Revolution is that condition in which structures are drastically changed without necessarily being replaced, and in which processes cannot be modified without being abandoned or thwarted.

3:3:2 Reaction is that condition in which an attempt is made to preserve structures and processes which can no longer be meshed or fused.

3:3:3 The difference between revolution and reaction is that the former overthrows the structure, while the latter thwarts the process; or more precisely, these two categories as applied to social facts are exhaustive and mutually exclusive.

3:4 Change and stability are the logical totality of all social facts.

3:5 Full development refers to the ideal typification of a social system. All actual social systems reveal an imperfect relationship between change and stability.

3:5:1 The social problem of development concerns the point at which change should be emphasized at the expense of stability, or stability emphasized at the expense of change.

3:6 The difference between political postures and policies is defined by the degree of change or stability advocated.

3:6:1 There exist two other logical possibilities: those who emphasize change under the control of the public sector and those who emphasize change under the control of the private sector. Those who emphasize change under the public sector usually are radicals; those who emphasize change under the private sector are customarily liberals. Those who emphasize stability under conditions of a private-sector economy—one in which the allocation of resources and profits is in the hands of individual owners and entrepreneurs of corporate wealth—are called capitalists.

3:6:2 Those who emphasize stability under condition of a public-sector economy—one in which the allocation of resources and profits is regulated by a collectivity of owners, managers, and workers of corporate wealth—are called socialists.

3:7 The above represents the polarities of economic change and stability. Those who adopt a position between these polarities are defined by the nature of the economic mix advocated —state capitalism, state socialism, welfare economy, and the like.

3:8 The point at which some person or party ceases being capitalist and becomes socialist is determined by the cross-over between public-sector and private-sector investment.

4   Social development requires both a consensus apparatus (voluntary association) and a coercive apparatus (involuntary association—the state).

4:1   The forced maintenance of the social process at the expense of the social structure is called social coercion.

4:1:1   The forced maintenance of the social structure at the expense of social process is called social coercion.

4:1:2   Either the symmetry or asymmetry of a system is measured by the existence of a coercive apparatus, and, more specifically, the coersive apparatus itself is measurable by the degree of its raw power on the one hand and a degree of its symbolic acceptance on the other.

4:2   The unobstructed transformation of an old structure into a new structure is called social consensus.

4:2:1   The unobstructed transformation of old processes into new processes is called social consensus.

4:3   The acceleration of social development by means of maximum control of both mechanical and human sources irrespective of the costs of production is characteristic of coercion.

4:3:1   Coercion does not necessarily entail the use of violence, but may simply flow from the "legitimate" direction of resources by means of financial and moral incentives.

4:3:2   The acceleration of social development by means of minimum regulation of the mechanical and human sources of production is characteristic of consensus.

4:3:3   As a rule, a "consensual society" will exhibit a higher regard for human sacrifice than it will for high productivity. It generally holds "the humanization of labor" as a social constant, and thus adjusts production rates to the constant.

4:4   The ratio between coercion and consensus at any given time determines the character of the political structure, just as the mix between public investment and private investment of capital determines the economic structure.

5   The intersections between coercion and consensus in the polity and between public and private investment in the economy define the area called political economy.

5:1   The political-economic "mix" is at any point a consequence of internal (national) pressures and external (international) pressures.

5:1:1 When the political-economic processes are primarily determined by internal pressures, such processes are designated as the "role of the state."

5:1:2 When the political-economic processes are primarily determined by external pressures, such processes are designated as the "role of the imperium."

5:2 State and imperium are two legalized modes of expressing coercion.

5:2:1 The voluntary minimization of state and imperium, their replacement with decisions arrived at through voluntary agencies, is an expression of consensus.

5:2:2 The state and the imperium do not necessarily have equal weight in determining the political economy, since the state in itself may come under the domination of a more pervasive imperium.

5:3 The purposes and direction of the state and the imperium (when they are not one and the same) may be inharmonious.

5:3:1 The state may emphasize stability at any moment, while the imperium may emphasize change.

5:3:1:1 The state may emphasize change at any moment, while the imperium may emphasize stability.

5:4 The underdeveloped state and the fully developed imperium come into a condition of competition, or even conflict, when each puts emphasis on one factor of social development at the expense of the other—that is, either structure or process.

5:4:1 The underdeveloped state and the fully developed imperium come into a condition of consensus when each emphasizes the same factors at the same time. This is expressed by the difference between the vocabulary of "foreign aid" and that of "foreign exploitation."

6 Expropriation is the re-allocation of social wealth through agencies of political coercion.

6:1 The forms of expropriation determine the type of social structure.

6:1:1   The forms of expropriation determine the rate of social processes.

6:2   There can be no social change, or new social modes, without some form of expropriation—that is, without the political re-allocation of economic wealth.

6:3   Capitalism is an economic system in which political power resides in the hands of the national bourgeoisie.

6:3:1   Socialism is an economic system in which political power resides in the hands of the national planning board.

6:3:2   Latifundism is an economic system in which political power resides in the hands of the national land-owning classes.

6:3:3   Peasant socialism is an economic system in which political power resides in the hands of the national peasantry.

6:4   Imperialism is a limiting factor for a symmetrical economic system.

6:4:1   Imperialism is an economic system of supra-national proportions in which political power resides (either in full or in part) in the hands of the imperium as such.

6:5   The conflict between the developing nations and the advanced nations often appears as a struggle between the nationalism of the former and the imperialism of the latter. This is so because capitalism, socialism, latifundism, and peasant socialism, whatever their differences, represent forms of national control and allocation of wealth, while imperialism, whether of an "enlightened" or "despotic" variety, represents the foreign control and allocation of wealth.

6:6   For the developing nations, the forms of political economy are subordinate to the right to have a national economy.

6:6:1   For the highly developed nations, the forms of political economy are central and foremost, since the "nationalization" of the economy as such has been achieved.

7   Consciousness of underdevelopment produces emphasis on social change; whereas consciousness of being highly developed produces emphasis on stability.

7:1   Awareness of different rewards for similar kinds of work can perform a revolutionary function insofar as it creates tensions between underdeveloped and highly developed economic units.

7:1:1   Awareness of different rewards for similar kinds of work insofar as it can perform a conservatizing function creates tensions between highly developed and underdeveloped economic units.

7:1:2   Revolutionary and conservative frameworks are thus defined by the response to the problem of development as such. Emphasis on rapid unfettered development, combined with a negative attitude toward underdevelopment as such, creates the political basis for revolutionary ideologies. Emphasis on controlling development and fear of loss of wealth and prestige through independence and development creates the basis of a conservative ideology.

7:2   Ideological aspects of consciousness are defined in terms of interests.

7:2:1   If interests are to achieve higher social development, the ideological consciousness is called revolutionary. If interests are to preserve an existing developmental stage, the ideological consciousness is called conservative.

7:3   Consciousness of poverty and wealth are comparative in nature. Both terms are significant in relation to each other.

7:3:1   Absolute relativism is untenable because the social can never be absolutely free of the biological, technical, or physical tendencies in general. Absolute relativism may be conservative as well as radical. It may serve to legitimize minority militancy, but it may also legitimize an insularity in which problems of international development are considered no more pressing than those of internal development within an already developed nation.

7:3:2   Consciousness of poverty in relation to wealth is the determining element in the ideology of social progress.

7:3:2:1   Consciousness of wealth in relation to poverty is the determining element in the ideology of social stability.

7:4   The poor of the poor nations tend to adopt a revolutionary ideology.

7:4:1   The poor of the rich nations, insofar as they identify with country rather than class, tend to adopt a conservative ideology, for example, the phenomenon of "working-class authoritarianism."

7:4:2   The wealthy of the poor nations, insofar as they identify with their country rather than with a social class, tend to adopt a revolutionary ideology, for example, the phenomenon of "middle-sector radicalism."

7:4:3   The wealthy of rich nations tend to adopt a conservative ideology. But the top elites of these nations tend to transcend their parochialisms in terms of a corporate liberalism. In this way, they are able to link up ideologically and financially with the wealthy of poor nations.

7:4:3:1 For each of these conditions, there are contravening factors. The wealthy of the poor nations may derive their funds from interests in the rich nations, in which case their "interests" would be split: to protect their "national" position or to preserve their "imperial" position. Similar intervening or contravening elements exist in each case. But as a phase rule, the propositions in 7:4 are empirically confirmable and disconfirmable.

7:5   Revolutionary ideology can be modified when the costs of development are seen to outweigh its benefits.

Example: Lower levels of consumer accommodation and agriculture often accompany the "transitional" period from agriculture to industry. Rationalization of the costs of development in terms of delayed gratification and future advantages for the children often demand greater personal sacrifice than people are willing to accept.

7:5:1   Conservative ideology can be modified when the costs of structure maintenance are seen to outweigh the benefits.

Example: Mass pressures from non-elite sectors may be so unremitting and unrelenting that the mere ability to maintain control of an economic or political structure no longer suffices to maintain an ideological posture of conservatism intact. In this way, "reform" doctrines and "liberalism" emerge to minimize the costs of structure maintenance without resort to revolution.

7:6   The type of economic ideology propounded depends heavily on the evaluation of the potential costs of development in relation to the actual costs of development.

7:7   The consciousness of development accounts for the forms of ideology, as such forms interact with the social system as such.

7:8   There is also the phenomenon of unconsciousness. But this is usually associated with tribal areas so isolated as not to have information about other civilizations. At the other end of the historical scale, there are societies so affluent and economically self-reliant that they become equally unaware of how they are perceived by others.

8   Underdeveloped, developed, and overdeveloped societies are definable by all factors involved in social structure and social processes.

8:1   The various sociological "mixes" signify imperfect or unfinished forms of development, such as "transitional" and developing societies.

8:2   The sociological properties of the underdeveloped society are characterized by a series of social forces which, by convention, can be considered under the polar terms of structure and process, or stratification and mobility.

8:2:1   In the sphere of social structure, the underdeveloped society bases its actions on authority systems.

8:2:2   In the sphere of social relations, there is a high degree of personal interaction and personal sanction. Personal factors rather than professional factors are decisive in human relationships.

8:2:3   In the sphere of technology, the underdeveloped society exhibits high reliance on manual instruments and on human and animal energy.

8:2:4   In the sphere of economy, one finds "subsistence" patterns —production to satisfy concrete needs of individuals or groups functioning within a traditional cultural framework.

8:2:4:1   An undeveloped economy is undifferentiated and indifferent to the social system as such.

8:2:4:2   On a national scale, the assignment of labor tasks is based upon sex, age, race, and caste.

8:2:4:3   On an international scale, the assignment of labor tasks is based upon color, language, and geography.

8:2:4:4   When the laborer owns the instruments of production, craft rather than machinery is the essential production ingredient.

8:3   When the psychology of undevelopment reveals an absence of specific motivations, production is connected to subsistence rather than to savings.

8:3:1 Psychological attitudes toward the work process emphasize fulfillment of living needs rather than competition to produce a surplus or an abundance for "the next generation."

8:4 The inheritance of status and economic power has as a corollary a high degree of stratification. Work norms are guaranteed through tradition and not through competition.

8:4:1 In contradistinction, in the bureaucratic structure of the developed economy, such distinctions are muddied with respect to the division of income.

8:4:2 The role of intermediary classes increases as a society crosses over from an underdeveloped to a developing situation. This is due to an increase in occupational differentiation, and to the rise in consumer demands in contradistinction to production demands. Class polarization begins to give way to work specialization. It is for these reasons that a gap sets in between ideologies on the one hand and interest attitudes determined by parochial and local considerations on the other.

8:5 In the sphere of social processes, one finds a parent-oriented society, with movement determined by age and sex, no less than class and caste. Veneration based on age is a characteristic of underdeveloped or traditional societies such as "feudal" China.

8:6 In the sphere of demography, the underdeveloped society exhibits a high birth rate and a high mortality rate; or, at times, a low birth rate and a high mortality rate.

8:6:1 Immigration tends to be limited to the extent that industrialization is absent or the chances for rapid industrialization minimal.

8:6:2 Ecological mobility, the movement of internal population to new areas, is either very low or non-existent.

8:6:3 A hallmark of the developing or transitional society is the imperfect breakdown of traditional patterns. Thus, there is high ecological mobility in Brazil and Argentina, but due to inherited conditions—the absence of urban planning, the poor development of transportation, and the like—such mobility or high population explosions tend to set in motion a game of hare and hound, a struggle to avoid having "social savings" or "primitive accumulation" eaten away by population expansion or rapid ubanization. Nonetheless, it would be dangerous to confuse the problems of a developing nation (often accompanied by inflationary spirals, for example) with the problems of underdevelopment per se. The absence of pressure on a social structure may indicate the extreme state of backwardness and not the intrinsic stability of a society.

8:7 The types of authority and control exercised are traditional and take a form in which law is subservient to custom.

8:7:1 Authority is reinforced through a religious machinery, through considering society as "sacred" and "divine" in origin and in rule. There is a proliferation of "Divine Right" and "Natural Law" theories.

8:7:1:1 Psychological antagonism for the "outsider" or the "innovator" is reinforced by the authority of custom and tradition. An equation is made between the outsider and the enemy.

8:7:1:2 Further reinforcement of authority occurs through "group decision-making" and through exclusive reliance upon primary associations.

8:7:1:3 "Group decision-making" also characterizes rapidly developing societies such as modern China, and it may be a feature integral to a coercive society as such, rather than to a particular stage of development.

8:8 The value system of the underdeveloped society moves along parallel axes of "tradition" . . . "blood lines" . . . "the land" . . . "divinity," and the like. Values are absolute and insular.

8:9 Underdevelopment tends to accentuate ethnic heterogeneity and to emphasize structure at the expense of process.

8:9:1 Ethnic heterogeneity in contrast to structural differentiation leads either to total stagnation or total revolution. The underdeveloped society is in an unstable condition: first, because it has insufficient agencies available—if any at all —to cope with the novel and the changing; and, second, because changes in one part of the underdeveloped society have wide repercussions on all other parts.

9 The sociological properties of the developed or rapidly developing society take the form of a series of social forces

which can be considered under the polar terms of structure and process, or stratification and mobility.

9:1   In sociological terms developed or developing societies are those which have achieved a mass distribution of national wealth (either in the form of ownership or consumption) within the context of a relatively stable social system. It is a "mass society" in contrast to a "traditional society."

9:1:1   A shorthand rule is that the developed society emphasizes social mobility at the expense of social stratification.

9:2   In the sphere of social structure, the developed society exhibits a nominalistic character—the individual wills his world rather than being determined by a willful world, or at least has a strong belief that he is doing so. However, his actual potential to change structures, as opposed to moving to different roles within them, may be very limited.

9:2:1   Change is itself built into the structure. This may be done via direct planning, federal allocation of resources, or indirect monetary manipulations.

9:2:2   In the sphere of social relations, the feeling of community responsibility is replaced by a concept of individual self-determination, social distance, functional associations in terms of occupation rather than in terms of community, and universalism, that is, a "worldly perspective" or a "national perspective."

9:2:3   In the sphere of technology, the developed society makes wide use of mechanical, electrical, and nuclear energy in place of human energy; and mass-production techniques and automation in place of craft techniques.

9:2:3:1   The "alienation effect" is a consequence of this process. Alienation, the separation of personal satisfaction from public production, is thus a characteristic of development. Like social "deviance" in general, alienation is a cost factor in advanced forms of industrial living.

9:2:4   In the sphere of economy, production is geared to the satisfaction of high demands made by an anonymous public. Developed societies are oriented toward creature comforts; monetary relations replace bartering relations; the emphasis moves from the quality of production to the quantity in production.

9:2:4:1   The drive toward high production creates a set of special problems concerned with distribution, transportation, communication, monopolization, and the manipulation of wealth as such.

9:3   The functional differentiation of roles and positions leads to a high degree of legal prescriptions. It further leads to measuring social worth in terms of consumer satisfaction on a mass scale. The rise of status as an independent variable apart from class is directly linked to the crossover from productivity as a value to consumption as a value.

9:3:1   A measure of the overdeveloped society is its inability to make full use of its energy potential. This goes with a tendency to overload already-available resources. The breakup of work patterns and work incentives and their replacement by leisure or non-productivity as a fundamental value distinguish the overdeveloped from the developed. The psychology of underdevelopment once more appears: the distinctions between master and servant (those who have everything but don't work, and those who have nothing but do work) reappear in their overdeveloped form in terms of the relations between nations. In place of have and have-not classes, there are have and have-not nations. This is what makes for "class cohesion" rather than "class conflict" on a national scale. The character of social conflict changes as the units shift from social classes to political nations. This shift also helps to explain the "racial" dimension in underdevelopment—racialism as a consequence of nationalism.

9:4   On a national scale, the pace of development may be measured by the size of the bureaucracy in relation to other classes. The division of labor is made on the basis of efficiency rather than birth. The growth of professionalism increases the significance of the intermediary classes and decreases the significance of the classes engaged in production. Managerial functions usurp new areas, formerly held by ownership classes and laboring classes.

Note: Nonetheless, it is important to realize that managerial expansion is not managerial revolution. Ownership still remains distinct from management and still has the power to direct the managerial estate, not the other way around. This is true of the United States as well as of the Soviet Union—despite the different ownership classes in each country.

9:4:1　　On an international scale, the developed society controls world markets by means of protective tariffs and import and export regulations and through control of underdeveloped regions—by direct military means in the older developed nations and by indirect economic means in the more recently developed nations. Development does not necessarily imply imperialism (so underdeveloped a nation as Portugal can yet be an imperial power, while so highly developed a country as Sweden has no colonial pretensions or imperial domains). It does means that one way that the rate of growth has been maintained after a certain level of development is through imperial colonization.

9:5　　The psychology of the developed society reveals specific motivations. Production is connected to credit, and credit tends to become an instrument of ensuring future gratifications.

9:5:1　　In this connection, the shift from the extended family to the nuclear family in the developed society has served to focus positive attitudes toward savings. Here, too, we see a peculiar dovetailing of underdevelopment and overdevelopment: the re-emergence of a strong "we" and "they," outsider-insider relationship. The high degree of "socialization" required by the developing society gives way to a high degree of alienation in the overdeveloped society. Even the phrase "the sick society" betrays just such an impression of overdevelopment.

9:6　　The attitude toward work in the developed society produces impersonal human relations. There is a shift from one job to another, one elite position to another. Impersonalism is reinforced by the notion of working for the highest bidder. Personal loyalties tend thus to be minimized in industrial life; they are reserved for the life of the family or associates outside the place of work.

9:6:1　　In work attitudes the shift from traditional communities to modern societies becomes apparent. It is not so much that feelings as such, or even values as such, undergo drastic revision, as it is that the objects of such feelings and values which is revised.

9:6:2 The specialization of work tends to undermine wider identifications with class or with the nation as a whole.

Example: The higher degree of industrial development, the more difficult it is to distinguish between social classes. Clothing styles, living quarters, and transportation means become standardized. Mass culture replaces class culture. A unified "culture of the people" replaces the different cultures of traditional society, such as the "art tradition" of the rich and the "folk tradition" of the poor. The "tradition-bearing" role of the intelligentsia seeks to support the older cultural inheritance, but there can be small doubt that the "art" of the developed countries is fully embodied in the design of utilitarian objects. It is as a special product and consequence of scientific and technological innovation that design tends to become functional. The overdeveloped society is thus not synonymous with the existence of mass culture. In the overdeveloped society, there is an attempt to re-create and reconstruct traditional distinctions between cultural and functional entities; as Eric Larrabee suggests, overdevelopment is defined in part by the over-designing of artifacts.

9:6:3 Types of property relations tend to become impersonal. The distinction between the property-owner and the propertyless is determined by law rather than fixed by class inheritance. Ownership of property is no longer closed to members of the laboring classes—whether, as under capitalism, because wealth is limited by taxation and poverty by insurance programs, or whether, as under socialism, because private property as such is abolished. The impersonality of class distinctions is achieved by defining every person functionally—in terms of occupational activities instead of property ownership.

9:6:3:1 When development spills over into overdevelopment, there is a breakdown in the functional definition of roles. Status performs a role equivalent to class in the underdeveloped society: it builds up distinctions which lead to an intensification of stratification at the expense of mobility.

9:7 In the sphere of social processes in a developed society, one finds a child-oriented society, the movement of which is determined by skills acquired, educational "rites of passage," and professionalism as such. Conflict occurs between generations; the older generation is no longer venerated.

Example: "Cutting the umbilical cord" assumes the same dimensions in the modern developed society as "cutting the class bonds" did in the past century. This tends to confirm Mannheim's comment that the conflict between generations is now as intense as the class struggle was in older societies.

9:7:1 In part, the "child-centered" family is a consequence of having the larger society define an individual's social roles rather than the family.

9:7:1:1 Social processes are ensured by individual achievement rather than by inheritance. Educational opportunity and leadership in decisive social and political organizations assist in making individual autonomy a factor in its own right.

9:8 Social processes are set in motion by secular forms of belief, by ideological systems rather than religious systems. Values become autonomous and public rather than connected to supernatural beliefs about rewards and punishments for virtue and vice. Utilitarian impulses are released from their previous religious enclosures. There is, in brief, a general rise in concern with this world rather than with any supernatural one.

9:8:1 The same process is exhibited by religious agencies themselves. Ministers become psychiatric counselors. Churches become social meeting halls (and sometimes even gambling casinos). Theology becomes general and "ecumenical" rather than specific and "separatist."

9:8:2 Social processes are occupationally defined. Prestige becomes based on money independent of class background. Occupational loyalties increase as class affiliations grow weaker. This is basic content of professionalism as such.

9:9 In the sphere of demography, the developed society exhibits a combination of either high birth rates and low mortality rates, or a low birth rate and a low mortality rate.

9:9:1   At the point of industrial "take-off" there is usually a higher birth rate than the population size of the traditional society would warrant. Rapid capital formation usually (although not invariably) shows a parallel rise in the birth rate.

9:9:1:1   When an economic plateau is reached—that is, when the rate of capital formation becomes stabilized—population usually becomes stabilized too.

Example: In the United States, middle-class Catholics tend to have "average" (slightly under three children) families, as do their Protestant equivalents. Lower-class Catholics tend to have many offspring, as do their counterparts in other sectors of the lower classes. These differential birth rates are economic and not religious. It is only when Catholics are "outside" the developed society that procreation patterns follow an "underdeveloped" course. We may thus say, with some assurance, that population inclines and decreases are rarely autonomous. They move in accord with the over-all trajectory of development.

9:9:2   Immigration tends to be high in developed countries when industrialization is present. The increase in artificial barriers to immigration serves, as does the maintenance of small families, to broaden the share in the products of industrial life. Immigration restrictions are thus more characteristic of fully developed societies than of those at the initial "take-off" stages, where labor power (particularly of a skilled and cheap variety) is both needed and scarce.

9:9:2:1   Intervening factors may affect this pattern. "Excessive" immigration from a "highly developed" culture to "developing" culture—from Europe to South America, for example —may so upset the national ethnic pattern that, despite the dire need of skilled labor power, restrictions are imposed on immigration in order to maintain the social structure as such.

9:9:3   Shifts of population within a country tend to vary directly with the level of social development. For a nation to be "on wheels" assumes the wide distribution of transport facilities.

9:9:3:1   The essential problem in discussing the relationship of development to population is precisely a matter of relationship. It is as silly to talk of a "population explosion" as it is to talk of "industrial affluence." Each is measurable in terms of the other. If the growth rate of an economy, however high, cannot allocate more per person per annum because its population increase is "eating up" the growth rate margins, then such a society does indeed have a "population problem." But the simple numerical increase in population is not itself a cause of a crisis in the economy. Throughout history, the reverse has more nearly been the case. Thus, India has a "population crisis" while Brazil has a "population boom" (even though the rate of population increases is equal). For the economic rate of growth in India cannot absorb a population increase, while the rate of growth in Brazil can. As a matter of fact, it is likely that the high population rise in Brazil will give it a marked advantage in the future industrialization process over its Latin American "under-populated" and "under-industrialized" neighbors.

9:10   Types of authority and control exercised in the developed society are rationalistic and bureaucratic rather than personalistic and charismatic. The authority network serves to institutionalize change in the developed society.

9:10:1   Reinforcement of authority comes about through conformity to the legal code and to the informal censorship— with remote authority becoming increasingly important as a check on change as society becomes increasingly complex.

9:10:2   Authority itself is established through the manipulation of public opinion by mass communications media, and by the conscious formation of "political slogans" and "social myths."

9:10:2:1   Secondary associations become increasingly important in the formation of consensual patterns, replacing the "group consensus" of traditionalist societies.

9:10:2:2   There is an increased reliance upon indirect controls rather than direct prohibitions. The institutionalization of a system of rewards and punishments replaces the direct terrorism of state authority, or the capricious nature of personal authority that is characteristic of traditional societies.

9:11   The developing society is directed toward preeminence.

Such preeminence might be measured in terms of political power over other nations, technological-scientific weaponry, and mass affluence which cuts across traditional class lines.

9:11:1   The characteristic feature of a developed society is diversity—not as a moral virtue, but as a consequence of role differentiation and occupational specialization.

9:11:2   The value structure of a developed society supports the society by putting an emphasis on "openness," on "experimentalism," and on "experience."

9:11:3   In this sense, the revival of the "quest for certainty," the "return to faith," and the like, is indicative of overdevelopment, of an inability to cope with the very forces which make development possible.

10   Full development is equivalent to absolute preeminence. And absolute preeminence in the modern world is measured in terms of material levels of production, distribution, and consumption.

10:1   The concept of development as preeminence may come into competition and conflict with the concept of the fully developed personality.

10:1:1   This is another way of stating the philosophic paradox between authority and individualism, and material growth and mental freedom.

10:1:2   The individual is most likely to be preeminent when a society is dedicated to the central achievement of high rates of production.

10:1:3   The "schism" in contemporary socialism is precisely between those who hold that rapid industrialization is a value exceeding any personal hardship or deprivation and those who hold that at a certain point in human suffering the ends of industrialization are no longer to be pursued. There is no longer any question that "terrorism" is an effective instrument for achieving rapid economic development. The only question is whether the "costs" of such development are worth the sacrifices entailed. This is a question for each society to examine as it enters the "take-off" stage of development.

10:1:4   Social development as preeminence is least likely to be achieved when a society is dedicated to the ends of personal freedom as an immediate goal—one which must precede general social development as such.

10:1:5   It is easy to assume that democracy and production increases are necessary corollaries. Yet, historically, this correlation has rarely been the case. Class conflict was most intense, and personal freedom most violated, at those points of industrial expansion in Western Europe and the United States which showed the highest increases in productivity. Affluence may well produce a consensual society democratically organized. But the advanced nations ought not to forget their own histories when they warn the developing nations on the need for maintaining and extending personal liberties.

Example: The end of colonial rule was registered in India in 1948, while the victory of "socialism" was registered in Bolivia in 1952. Yet, in neither nation can one say that a firm pattern of economic development has emerged. The rate of growth in India, measured in terms of industrial reinvestment and expansion, is low. In large part, it is precisely the retention of libertarian values which frustrated rapid industrialization. It might appear shocking to point out that the achievement of one "good"—rapid industrial development—and the achievement of another "good"—mass liberation—are customarily in conflict with each other. At best, they can be achieved sequentially and hardly ever simultaneously (if at all). Without some social sector in charge of "forced savings" or guaranteeing "delayed gratifications" (whether through coercive or "voluntary" means), stagnation and a dependent economy will continue. The manifest function of revolutions is to make things "better" for more people. But a revolution which sees the very act of transferring state or civic authority as a goal in itself ignores the difference between the transfer of authority and the achievement of material abundance. A revolutionary *event* which is not at the same time a revolutionary process is a fraud—a fact which Bolivians and Indians must recognize by now with painful awareness

—the "armed workers' militia" of the former and the "people's army" of the latter notwithstanding.

10:2 The function of planning is to achieve rapid social development at a minimum social cost.

10:2:1 Planning is the basic public-sector mechanism for achieving high production as an instrument of policy—the policy of international preeminence.

10:2:2 The function of the free market is to achieve rapid social development through "natural" means—by the laissez-faire system.

10:2:3 The free market is the basic private-sector mechanism for achieving high production as an instrument of policy—the policy of international preeminence.

10:3 The "choice" is not between development and underdevelopment, since the search for international preeminence might be considered as something of a "psychological constant," but between public-sector and private-sector economies.

10:3:1 Whether the drive toward the developed society is carried out under the auspices of the public sector or the private sector, through planning or laissez faire, depends on the selection of instrumentalities used and the priority of goals sought.

10:3:2 Behind the talk about planning as a central agency for rationalizing economic production is the basic fact that politics has increasingly come to define economic possibilities, rather than the other way around. This development is just as much an agonizing reality for socialists as for capitalists (perhaps much more so in the light of the binding nature of socialist ideology and flabby nature of capitalist ideology). Is development to be viewed as a new humanism or as a new way to world power? In India, where development has been identified with a bureaucratic system of authority, humanism has correspondingly been indefinitely postponed. Many social developmentalists ignore the basic paradox of development itself: rapid and bold forms of development cannot be achieved without human sacrifice. The need for sacrifice is even more evident in the "newly developing nations," since time itself has become a major factor. Those new nations must develop very rapidly, or face the fact that they are falling even farther behind the advanced nations. The alternative—low levels of industrial development and relative security through remaining a supplier nation—is quite feasible on sociological grounds, but hardly feasible on either political or competitive grounds. No one social science exhausts the issues raised, because no single social dimension as such exhausts the problem.

10:3:3   The "answer" to the question of the appropriate type and tempo of development is therefore both empirical and ethical. It cannot be resolved by a logical model of models. The real value of a model is to telescope the problems in a meaningful way. Beyond this, logic turns into intellectual tyranny.

10:3:4   Social scientists might make an inventory of the actual benefits and costs of development. The worth of the sacrifices, however, will be viewed differently by people with different social interests. The Catholic bishop may consider the destruction of traditional mores as inherently wicked, while the Communist organizer might consider any attempt to impede the highest possible industrial development in the shortest possible time as a form of obstructionism punishable by death and imprisonment. Between such extremes, there are a whole range of postures based on different social, political, economic, ideological, and ethical moorings. In confronting the issues of development, sociology must first identify these various positions in terms of their bases in coercion and consensus, elite and mass, traditionalism, modernism, and structuralism. Nostalgia, the ideology of backwardness, has no more place in social science than utopianism, the ideology of future perfection. But of the two, utopianism in infinitely preferable—if for no other reason than it points sociology in the right direction.

19

Priorities for the Second
Development Decade

The challenge of setting forth research priorities for the current decade is probably one of the more delicate and certainly one of the more decisive tasks facing those studying development. Obviously, any ordering of priorities suffers from the defects and limits of the intellectual horizons of the individual who attempts the task. It also reflects certain clear ideological biases within which he operates. The question of priorities remains objectively crucial, because it must not simply answer personal needs but point the way to other researchers, particularly people just entering the field of developmental studies.

Having made these cautionary remarks, I will add one other major point: my purpose here is not to address myself to the scale of resources for funding research projects, or to professional problems in the field of research. I have dealt extensively with both of these topics elsewhere.[1] While such technical issues are often most critical in operational terms, the question of research priorities deserves to be examined on its own grounds and in its own terms, apart from supposed or real implications of any piece of research.

The period from the end of World War II to the present has witnessed major international conflicts and the attendant reconstruction

1. Irving Louis Horowitz, "Tax-Exempt Foundations: Their Effects on National Policy," *Science,* Vol. 168 (Apr. 10, 1970), pp. 220–28; "The Academy and the Policy: Interaction Between Social Scientists and Federal Administrators," *The Journal of Applied Behavioral Science,* Vol. 5, No. 3 (July 1969), pp. 309–35; "Social Science and Public Policy: An Examination of the Political Foundations of Modern Research," *International Studies Quarterly,* Vol. XI, No. 1 (Mar. 1967), pp. 32–62.

of world empires and economies. During this period, the area of development has been at the upper level anchored to national development. The superb writing in the field has, in fact, been almost accidentally concerned with problems of development, and it has clearly been national in character. The books by John Porter on Canada,[2] Ralf Dahrendorf on Germany,[3] Pablo González Casanova on Mexico,[4] and Gino Germani on Argentina,[5] among a number of others, have provided us with a perspective in terms of a single nation rather than the comparative analysis of nations. As a result, they have emphasized and even exaggerated the exceptional aspects of national development in contradistinction to what nations have in common. Even when international development was examined, it was usually in terms of national *limits* to commerce, communication, transportation, and power itself.[6]

Social science has been unable to generate an adequate literature at the level of comparative international development. Various attempts have been made in these directions by Gunnar Myrdal,[7] Peter Worsley,[8] Albert O. Hirshmann,[9] among others. But even work done within a wide-ranging rubric such as international relations smuggles in nationalistic orientations, or isolates factors for analysis in such a way that comparisons across national lines provide precious little predictive or explanatory power. The heart of the problem seems to be the assumption that the nation is at all times and in every way the critical organizing pivot in the behavior of men and their societies. In point of fact,

2. John Porter, *The Vertical Mosaic: Analysis of Social Class and Power in Canada.* Toronto: University of Toronto Press, 1965.
3. Ralf Dahrendorf, *Society and Democracy in Germany.* New York: Doubleday & Company, 1967.
4. Pablo González Casanova, *Democracy in Mexico,* translated by Danielle Salti. New York: Oxford University Press, 1970.
5. Gino Germani, *Política y Sociedad en una Epoca de Transición: De La Sociedad Tradicional a la Sociedad de Masas.* Buenos Aires: Editorial Paidís, 1962.
6. Karl W. Deutsch, "The Impact of Communications upon International Relations Theory," pp. 79–94, in *Theory of International Relations: The Crisis of Relevance,* edited by Abdul A. Said. Englewood Cliffs, N.J.: Prentice-Hall, 1968.
7. Gunnar Myrdal, *The Challenge of World Poverty: A World Anti-Poverty Program in Outline.* New York: Pantheon Books (Random House), 1970; and his earlier classic, *An International Economy.* New York: Harper & Row, 1956.
8. Peter Worsley, *The Third World.* Chicago: The University of Chicago Press, 1964.
9. Albert O. Hirshmann, *The Strategy of Economic Development.* New Haven: Yale University Press, 1958; and *Journeys Toward Progress: Studies of Economic Policy Making in Latin America.* New York: The Twentieth Century Fund, 1963.

the role of the nation itself should be carefully measured in terms of other variables that may have equal or even greater explanatory value, such as, urbanization, industrialization and population. As specialization takes place, a number of researchers have, in fact, come to similar conclusions about the open-ended nature of independent variables. The work of Nels Anderson[10] and Glenn Beyer[11] in urbanization; of Benjamin Higgins[12] and John Kenneth Galbraith[13] in industrialization; and Presser[14] and Miro and Rath[15] in comparative demography have moved us a long way beyond the national boundaries as the ultimate test of empirical significance.[16]

The literature of the past twenty-five years has been primarily influenced by political scientists operating within the traditional view that the nation is the supreme organizing principle of life. Not that they always celebrate this fact—quite the contrary, traditionalists like Frederick Schuman[17] and Hans Morgenthau[18] are highly critical of nationalism—yet the thought that the nation may be one of a select number of key variables and not the supreme organizing principle of development has not really penetrated social-science literature. The political scientists have been reinforced in their biases by the economists, who likewise find the nation a convenient peg to hang their data on—although they at least have the merit of taking into consideration measures having little to do with national boundaries.[19]

10. Nels Anderson, *The Urban Community: A World Perspective.* New York: Holt, Rinehart and Winston, 1959.
11. Glenn H. Beyer, *The Urban Explosion in Latin America: A Continent in Process of Modernization.* Ithaca, N.Y.: Cornell University Press, 1967.
12. Benjamin Higgins, *Economic Development: Principles, Problems and Policies.* New York: W. W. Norton, 1959, pp. 416–30, 548–51.
13. John Kenneth Galbraith, *The New Industrial State.* Boston: Houghton Mifflin, 1967.
14. Harriet B. Presser, "Voluntary Sterilization: A World View," *Reports on Population and Family Planning,* Vol. 5, July 1970, pp. 1–36.
15. Carmen A. Miro and Ferdinand Rath, "Preliminary Findings of Comparative Fertility Surveys in Three Latin American Cities," *The Milbank Memorial Fund Quarterly,* Vol. 43, No. 4, Part 2, Oct. 1965, pp. 44–56.
16. M. McMullan, "A Theory of Corruption," *Sociological Review,* Vol. 9, (July 1961), pp. 181–201.
17. Frederick L. Schuman, *International Politics: The Western State System and the World Community* (seventh edition). New York: McGraw-Hill, 1970.
18. Hans Morgenthau, *Politics Among Nations: The Struggles for Power and Peace.* New York: Alfred A. Knopf, 1960; and *Politics in the Twentieth Century* (3 vols.). Chicago: The University of Chicago Press, 1962.
19. Irma Adelman and Cynthia Taft Morris, *Society, Politics and Economic Development: A Quantitative Approach.* Baltimore: The Johns Hopkins Press, 1967.

The tendency has been to reinforce the role of the nation by placing a heavy emphasis on problems which arise within nations rather than between nations. Thus it is that monographic literature is overwhelmingly weighted on the side of problems which take place within communities or within cities and even within factories. Problems are only remotely linked up to the national level, and very rarely beyond that point. There is still no monographic literature of any size, much less substance, which attempts to examine the connections between nations and nations, what Rosenau calls crucial linkages such as legal and trade relations at this larger level.[20]

What is needed at this point is studies of the operations of key industries—such as oil, steel, aluminum, automobiles, and so on—as they are linked up between nations. Such studies would examine the superordinate and subordinate relationships that result from the way each industry operates, everything from patent rights to technical and managerial competence. We do have a relatively decent literature on petroleum because the political importance of this crucial, natural resource seems to be more readily apparent to researchers than the political effects of industrial and economic concentration in other industries.[21] We are also beginning to witness the growth of a significant literature in the field of communication, especially as this area comes to be closely linked to problems of international politics combinations rather than domestic nation-building.[22] But we have yet to arrive at a scientific literature on key industries, one that not only cuts across the national level but also compares rates of growth and development in such industries between the planned economies and the market economies. If we continue to operate within national confines, it will not be possible to determine how production is affected by the character of alternative social systems.

Similarly, the work done by Rosenau in the area of comparative and systematic behavior must be followed up. There is a need for in-

20. James Rosenau (ed.), *Linkage Politics: Essays on the Convergence of National and International Systems*. New York: The Free Press, 1969; and *The Adaptation of National Societies: A Theory of Political System Behavior and Transportation*. New York: McCaleb-Seiler Publishers, 1970, pp. 1–28.
21. Harvey O'Connor, *World Crisis in Oil*. New York: Monthly Review Press, 1962. Michael Tanzer, *The Political Economy of International Oil and the Under-Developed Countries*. Boston: Beacon Press, 1969.
22. Herbert I. Schiller, *Mass Communications and American Empire*. New York: Augustus M. Kelley, 1969.

formation about relationships which exist not simply between one nation and another nation but between regional associations—military, economic, and political—and between institutions which exist at hemispheric as well as continental levels. Research is needed on the actual operation of such agencies as the Organization of American States, the Organization of African Unity, the International Monetary Fund, and all other organizations which operate in terms of developmental concepts which extend beyond the nations which originally legitimized and sanctified such international agencies. The activities of the Carnegie, Ford and Rockefeller foundations in these areas have been noteworthy —but not without serious biases that limit such carefully sponsored researches. Even the literature on the United Nations is not especially illustrious. There are some exceptions, like the work of Alf Ross,[23] but for the most part the writings on the United Nations are legalistic and formalistic and not especially enlightening in terms of the sociopolitical nature of its activities, whether at the level of the World Health Organization in its technical operations or the Security Council in its political operations.

To offer some idea of the magnitude of the problem, we might refer to international military alliances and associations. Within the Western Hemisphere there are at least three organizations embracing nearly all the nations in the hemisphere from Canada to Argentina. Yet, as of this date, with the exception of the work done by Juan Saxe Fernandez,[24] there is no examination of how such regional military blocs function— with or without respect to development. Similarly, with the exception of the work done by Ivan Vallier[25] and David Mutchler,[26] there is scant effort at understanding the role of the Catholic Church in the development field, and particularly how this international organization affects, and is affected by, the social structure of the Third World.

There is a rich mine of information on development, thus far largely untapped because of its central focus on European societies, which has

23. Alf Ross, *The United Nations: Peace and Press Progress.* Totowa, N.J.: The Bedminster Press, 1966.
24. Juan Saxe Fernández, *Proyecciones Hemisféricas de la Pax Americana.* Lima: Instituto de Estudios Peruanos—Campodónico ediciones, 1971, p. 195.
25. Ivan Vallier, *Catholicism, Social Control and Modernization in Latin America.* Englewood Cliffs, N.J.: Prentice-Hall, 1970.
26. David E. Mutchler, *The Church as a Political Factor in Latin America: With Particular Reference to Colombia and Chile.* New York: Praeger Publishers, 1971, p. 460.

come to be called business or economic history. For if development means something more than general moral uplift, it has come to signify the ways and means by which societies, and specifically ruling classes in those societies, come to reorganize their productive and consumptive activities in terms of industrialization. Even if it is clearly impossible for the Third World to simulate or imitate patterns of business trustification and cartelization prevalent in the industrial development of either capitalist or socialist societies, they certainly must respect the forms by which the world was divided up in the past, who did the dividing, and what the effects were. Specifically, if there exists a "military-industrial" complex and if the character of industrial development follows a line that parallels such a relationship of economic and military needs, this complex must be studied with particular urgency in the present period, an era marked by the growing interpenetration of militarism and commercialism. In this connection, the work of W. J. Reader on the Imperial Chemical Industries,[27] William Miller on American business elites,[28] and William Manchester on the Krupp Industries[29] are masterful examples, albeit at different levels of historical precision, of how meat can be added to the dry bones of developmental theory.

It bears repeating that the main reason such studies have not been written is because it has been automatically assumed that, since the nation is the legal repository of individual demands, it is also the developmental repository.[30] This simple equation does not hold, as any examination of the wide disparity and profound constancy between wealth and poverty within nations, even nations customarily designated as poor, will show regional claims, religious claims, racial claims, all may take precedence in the search for full development; whereas the nation may actually frustrate developmental goals, through bureaucratic strictures if in no other way.

In examining the strains of development—that is, the motive force for social change—social scientists have assumed for the most part that national politics are the crucial factor. In point of fact, class arrange-

27. W. J. Reader, *Imperial Chemical Industries: A History* (Vol. I, *The Fore-Runners, 1870–1926*). London: Oxford University Press, 1970.
28. William Miller, *Men in Business: Essays on the Historical Role of the Entrepreneur.* New York: Oxford University Press, 1962.
29. William Manchester, *The Arms of Krupp: 1587–1968.* Boston: Little, Brown & Co., 1968.
30. David Apter, *The Politics of Modernization.* Chicago and London: The University of Chicago Press, 1965.

ments and/or racial feelings and sentiments may be far more important in Africa or Asia. Researchers must not make assumptions about what will be the significant pivots around which development will take place. National boundaries, often set by the former colonial powers, may be less significant than tribal or family ties. How these micro-sociological factors either aid or hinder development is therefore of extreme significance.

There is also a desperate need for a much more substantial literature on how people interact at the individual level; that is, how they relate to one another professionally, organizationally, and occupationally. Taxi drivers, engineers, surgeons, street-hawkers have many things in common with other taxi drivers, other engineers, and so forth. Such commonalities, while affected by national barriers, racial backgrounds or religious affiliations, often transcend such larger variables. Just how these professional factors affect developmental patterns remains a mystery, although the steady rise of professional interaction across national lines indicates that they may be of increasing importance to development. In other words, there is a vast need for a social psychological literature on development that gets beyond the kind of motivational research with built-in policy directives we have thus far been accustomed to in this area.

The final point that requires examination and analysis is what organizing principles exist beyond that of comparative international development. It is still not properly appreciated that the development concept at a significant level is a twentieth-century equivalent of the nineteenth-century notion of progress. Development is a shared belief that men and nations not only change but somehow change for the better. And the better is usually interpreted to signify greater political equity and wider distribution of wealth. At the same time, there is perhaps the need to realize that the concept of development can be variously examined as a model, as a strategy, as an ideology, as a goal; and perhaps simply as an organizing principle showing men where they are and where they ought to be.

We are rapidly approaching a point where it is not development as such but rather development in relation to revolution on one hand and peace on the other that is on the historical agenda.[31] The concept of de-

31. Richard J. Barnet, *Intervention and Revolution: The United States in the Third World*. New York: The World Publishing Co., 1968; and David Horowitz, *Empire and Revolution: A Radical Interpretation of Contemporary History*. New York: Random House, 1969.

velopment implies, after all, some fairly self-evident balance-sheet assumptions: how much is development worth in relation to how much international tranquility, or, in quantitative terms, how many people ought to be sacrificed to achieve what levels of production. The kind of new policies advocated to cure the malaise of backwardness depend on that very rare fusion of sacrificing economies from the elites and practical receptivity to new life styles at the mass level. While the *problem* of development is empirical, the *concept* may be rational. We must construct a keener notion of the relationship of policy-making and decision-theory with respect to the developmental process. What are the gambles and gambits that nations, peoples and classes have in the past been willing to make, and what are they now willing to pay for development? Is the "demonstration effect" still operative, or is it counter-productive with respect to development in the Third World?

It is now acknowledged that development does not exist simply as a good thing unto itself. There are heavy penalties involved. But these too have to be stipulated and have to be researched. Beyond that point, we have to explain to ourselves and to others why, despite the enormous costs involved in socioeconomic development (as it is customarily defined), most nations, most classes, and most masses are still willing to pay these heavy premiums to share in the admittedly dubious bounties of the fully developed and even overdeveloped nations. For example, why has the "mark of sovereignty" become the level of industrialization or the level of militarization; and not simply state power or cultural forms? Why do all arguments concerning pollution and population tend to fall on deaf ears of the policy-makers of the Third World; on those who have direct responsibilities in this sphere of social and economic development?

In this connection, why do we have an extensive literature prepared by those who have nostalgic and utopian solutions, and at the same time little scientific information on the benefits of development in post-revolutionary periods? With the exception of the literature on Soviet Russia, little has been written thus far on the role of terrorism or the amount of coercion necessary to generate high industrial development.[32] Only now are we beginning to appreciate the fact that heavy militarism correlates better with rapid development than does democracy.[33] Analy-

32. Eugene Victor Walter, *Terror and Resistance: A Study of Political Violence.* New York: Oxford University Press, 1969.
33. Edwin M. Martin, "Development Aid: Successes and Failures," *OECD Observer,* Vol. 43 (Dec. 1969), pp. 5–12.

sis of the sobering implications of such correlations should become a central task.[34]

Perhaps of equal importance is the fact that, while developmentalists have emphasized the role of "deviance" in the process of social change, they usually have confined their vision of deviance to entrepreneurship, a twentieth-century resurrection of Carlyle style of history, which emphasized the great man.[35] The relationship of deviance to development has remained largely unexplored at the more prosaic and, I daresay, more significant levels. Particularly important in this connection is the relationship of development to corruption and bribery. In other words, just as seventeenth-century England and nineteenth-century United States absorbed corruption in the developmental process, such behavior is being equally absorbed in the newly developing regions. Only most recently has this sort of deviance at the margins and among the "lower depths" been recognized as at least equal in importance to the break-away marginality of entrepreneurial swashbucklers.[36] Thus, if we shall derive a less hygienic model of development, we shall at least arrive at a more useful and, it is to be hoped, a more truthful representation of the world we live in.

34. Ernest B. Haas, *Tangle of Hopes: American Commitments and World Order.* Englewood Cliffs, N.J.: Prentice-Hall, 1969.
35. Everett E. Hagen, *On the Theory of Social Change.* Homewood, Ill.: Dorsey Press, 1964; and Seymour Martin Lipset, "Values, Education and Entrepreneurship," in Seymour Martin Lipset and Aldo Solari (eds.), *Elites in Latin America.* New York: Oxford University Press, 1967, pp. 3–60.
36. M. G. Smith, "Historical and Cultural Conditions of Political Corruption Among the Hausa," *Comparative Studies in Society and History,* Vol. 6 (Jan. 1964), pp. 164–94; M. McMullan, "A Theory of Corruption," *Sociological Review,* Vol. 9 (July 1961), pp. 181–201; J. S. Nye, "Corruption and Political Development: A Cost-Benefit Analysis," *American Political Science Review,* Vol. 62 (June 1967), pp. 417–27; David H. Bayley, "The Effects of Corruption in a Developing Nation," *The Western Political Quarterly,* Vol. 14, No. 4 (Dec. 1966), pp. 719–32; and James C. Scott, "Corruption, Machine Politics and Political Change," *American Political Science Review,* Vol. 63 (Oct. 1969), pp. 1142–58.

Name Index

Subject Index

THE AUTHOR

Irving Louis Horowitz is Professor of Sociology and Political Science at Rutgers University and is Chairman of its recently formed experimental division at Livingston College. He is also Director of *Studies in Comparative International Development* at Rutgers, and editor-in-chief of SOCIETY magazine (formerly *transaction*). He is the author of REVOLUTION IN BRAZIL: POLITICS AND SOCIETY IN A DEVELOPING NATION; THE WAR GAME; RADICALISM AND THE REVOLT AGAINST REASON; PROFESSING SOCIOLOGY; and most recently, FOUNDATIONS OF POLITICAL SOCIOLOGY. Three of his edited works, THE NEW SOCIOLOGY; POWER, POLITICS AND PEOPLE; and MASSES IN LATIN AMERICA, were published earlier by Oxford University Press.